Readings for
Reflective Teaching in
the Primary School

Day Loan

This book is due for return on or before the last date shown below.

Also available from Cassell:

D. Coulby and S. Ward (editors), *The Primary Core National Curriculum: Policy into Practice*

P. Croll (editor), *Teachers, Pupils and Primary Schooling*

A. Pollard, P. Broadfoot, P. Croll, M. Osborn and D. Abbott, *Changing English Primary Schools?*

A. Pollard, *An Introduction to Primary Education*

A. Pollard, *Reflective Teaching in the Primary School* 3rd edition

A. Pollard with A. Filer, *The Social World of Children's Learning*

V. A. McClelland and V. Varma, *The Needs of Teachers*

Readings for Reflective Teaching in the Primary School

Edited by Andrew Pollard

Cassell
Wellington House
125 Strand
London WC2R 0BB

370 Lexington Avenue
New York
NY 10017-6550

First published 1996
Reprinted 1998, 1999

British Library Cataloguing-in-Publication Data
A catalogue record for this book is available from the British Library.

ISBN 0-304-33798-6 (hardback)
　　　0-304-33799-4 (paperback)

Typeset by Pantek Arts
Printed and Bound in Great Britain by Redwood Books, Trowbridge, Wiltshire

This book is dedicated to my father, Michael Pollard.

CONTENTS

PART 3: BEYOND CLASSROOM REFLECTION

14 Reflective teaching and the school

15 Reflective teaching and society

ACKNOWLEDGEMENTS

The most important issue which any editor faces is, 'What should be included?' I have worried away at this and have imposed myself on a large number of people in discussing possible selections for various chapters. However, I would particularly like to thank Ian Menter and Pat Triggs who offered advice on the selections across the book as a whole.

The administrative complexity of obtaining permissions for a book on this scale has been very considerable, but it has been completed with great efficiency by Sarah Butler. I am also extremely grateful to Jacquie Harrison, Gaye Denley and Sarah Butler for their work on the production of the manuscript.

I would like to thank all the publishers, editors and other publishers' representatives who were kind enough to grant permission for material to be reprinted; in particular Malcolm Clarkson, Helen Cowie, Sam Larkham, John Eggleston, David Fulton, Naomi Roth and John Skelton. An acknowledgements listing for all permissions for the reproduction of extracts is formally provided at the end of the book. Attempts to trace permission holders have been sustained and assiduous, though a very few cases remain where replies to our enquiries have not yet been received. Any enquiries on such matters should be sent, in the first instance, to the Permissions Editor, Cassell plc.

Finally, I would like to thank all the authors whose work features in this book – and apologize to the many other researchers and educationists whose high-quality material does not! Having reviewed a very wide range of publications for possible inclusion in the book, I am enormously impressed by the richness of research and thinking which is available to teachers and student teachers. The collection can be seen as a representation of the work of several generations of educational researchers – though, even with over 130 readings, it has not been possible to include all the excellent material which is available. In a sense though, the book remains a collective product and I would like to pay tribute to the many academic colleagues and educationalists who remain obsessed enough to keep on trying to describe, analyse and understand education in so many diverse ways.

Andrew Pollard
University of Bristol, January 1996

INTRODUCTION

Three major aims have guided the production of this book.

First, it is intended as a resource for busy primary school teachers and student teachers who appreciate the value of educational thinking and research, and who wish to have easy access to key parts of important and useful publications.

Second, it provides an opportunity to 'show-case' some of the excellent educational research which has been conducted in the past few years. I hope that readers may then wish to consult the full accounts in the original sources, each of which is carefully referenced.

Finally, it is designed to complement an established textbook, *Reflective Teaching in the Primary School*. The latter is used to support professional development by many schools, local education authorities, colleges and universities, and has become the central textbook supporting school-based practice for a large number of initial teacher education courses.

Reflective Teaching in the Primary School considers a very wide range of professionally relevant topics, presents key issues and research insights, suggests 'Practical Activities' for classroom work, and offers 'Notes for Further Reading'. Now, *Readings for Reflective Teaching in the Primary School* brings the most important of those readings, and some new ones, into one accessible, interconnected publication.

Together, the two books provide a unique resource for professional development activities and for teacher training courses. The structure of the two books is identical and the chapters map across from one book to the other. Thus, whether used in staff-meetings, seminars, workshops, classroom activities or private study, the two books should provide simple access to practical, useful material for professional learning and development.

The concept of 'reflective teaching' is central to both books, and Chapter 1 of each volume is focused on it. Reflective teaching is presented as the key element in the processes of continuous, professional development which are so essential in efforts to raise educational standards and to enhance the quality of teacher and pupil experiences. The ideas associated with reflective teaching offer a framework through which 'theory' and 'practice' can be combined in constructive ways. Thus, in Chapter 1 of *Reflective Teaching in the Primary School* a simple development process is set out, through which successive levels of professional competence can be attained, whether in relation to curriculum, teaching, assessment or any other topic. Further, a reflective approach to teaching encourages consideration of the values on which professional commitment is based, and the consequences of teachers' work beyond the classroom.

Of course, there are many approaches even to reflective teaching, and Reading 3.7 provides an overview of four of these. However, whatever differences in emphasis may be possible, the essence of reflective teaching is the systematic and openminded consideration of the aims, effectiveness and consequences of professional work as a way of improving practice. Considering key historical documents, important research findings and perceptive forms of analysis is an important part of this process, which *Readings for Reflective Teaching in the Primary School* has been designed to support.

A note for students on citation

If wishing to reference a reading from this book in a piece of written coursework, tutors will require you to cite your source. Using the Harvard Convention and drawing only on this text, you should provide a bibliography containing details of the *original* source. These are provided following the introduction to each reading. You should then put: 'Cited in Pollard, A. (ed.) (1996) *Readings for Reflective Teaching in the Primary School*. London: Cassell'.

If you are building a substantial case around any reading, you are strongly recommended to go back to the original source and to check your argument against the full text. These will be available in the libraries of most colleges and universities with teacher education provision. If the reading is from a very recent academic paper, check your library catalogue to see if a more comprehensive book by the authors is now available. Having found your source, you should then cite the full text only, with the specific page numbers of any material which you quote.

All the citations in the readings from this book have been collected into a single, integrated bibliography and can be followed up from that source (see p. 375).

PART 1

Becoming a reflective teacher

CHAPTER 1

Reflective teaching and competence

The eight readings in this chapter provide a wealth of ideas about the relationship of reflection and competence in developing teacher professionalism.

First, we have excerpts from the highly influential work of Dewey (1.1), Schon (1.2) and the Berlaks (1.3). For them, teaching is a highly complex activity which calls for thoughtful action and the development of judgement.

The next three readings illustrate important approaches to linking reflective professional development and practical competence. Wragg (1.4) discusses how teaching skills can be progressively developed in the context of training courses, whilst Sampson and Yeomans (1.5) provide an excellent analysis of the role of school mentors in supporting student teachers. Reading 1.6 is an example of a national competence statement for new teachers, as applied within England and Wales from 1993,

In the two final readings, Elliott (1.7) and Calderhead (1.8) indicate some of the issues in the continuing debate between 'reflective' and 'competency' approaches to teacher training and development. (See also Reading 2.5 for a related analysis of the political influences on government policy regarding teacher training during the early 1990s.)

The parallel chapter of *Reflective Teaching in the Primary School* offers a reconciliation between these long-standing arguments by emphasizing the importance of processes of reflection in the development of successive states of practical competence. The chapter also sets out the 'meaning of reflective teaching' through identifying six key characteristics and it considers the ways in which competence, judgement and expertise develop during a teacher's career. There are many suggestions for further reading.

📖 READING 1.1

Thinking and reflective experience

John Dewey

> The writings of John Dewey have been an enormous influence on educational thinking. Indeed, his distinction of 'routinized' and 'reflective' teaching is fundamental to the conception of professional development through reflection. In the two selections below Dewey considers the relationship between reflective thinking and the sort of challenges which people face through experience.
>   Do you feel that you are sufficiently openminded to be really 'reflective'?
>
> Edited from: Dewey, J. (1933) *How We Think: A Restatement of the Relation of Reflective Thinking to the Educative Process*. Chicago: Henry Regnery, 15–16, and Dewey, J. (1916) *Democracy and Education*. New York: Free Press, 176–7

The origin of thinking is some perplexity, confusion, or doubt. Thinking is not a case of spontaneous combustion; it does not occur just on 'general principles'. There is something that occasions and evokes it. General appeals to a child (or to a grown-up) to think, irrespective of the existence in his own experience of some difficulty that troubles him and disturbs his equilibrium, are as futile as advice to lift himself by his boot-straps.

Given a difficulty, the next step is suggestion of some way out – the formation of some tentative plan or project, the entertaining of some theory that will account for the peculiarities in question, the consideration of some solution for the problem. The data at hand cannot supply the solution; they can only suggest it. What, then, are the sources of the suggestion? Clearly, past experience and a fund of relevant knowledge at one's command. If the person has had some acquaintance with similar situations, if he has dealt with material of the same sort before, suggestions more or less apt and helpful will arise. But unless there has been some analogous experience, confusion remains mere confusion. Even when a child (or grown-up) has a problem, it is wholly futile to urge him to 'think' when he has no prior experiences that involve some of the same conditions.

There may, however, be a state of perplexity and also previous experience out of which suggestions emerge, and yet thinking need not be reflective. For the person may not be sufficiently critical about the ideas that occur to him. He may jump at a conclusion without weighing the grounds on which it rests; he may forego or unduly shorten the act of hinting, inquiring; he may take the first 'answer', or solution, that comes to him because of mental sloth, torpor, impatience to get something settled.

One can think reflectively only when one is willing to endure suspense and to undergo the trouble of searching. To many persons both suspense of judgement and intellectual search are disagreeable; they want to get them ended as soon as possible. They cultivate an over-positive and dogmatic habit of mind, or feel perhaps that a condition of doubt will be regarded as evidence of mental inferiority. It is at the point where examination and test enter into investigation that the difference between reflective thought and bad thinking comes in.

To be genuinely thoughtful, we must be willing to sustain and protract that state of doubt which is the stimulus to thorough inquiry ...

The general features of a reflective experience are:

- perplexity, confusion, doubt, due to the fact that one is implicated in an incomplete situation whose full character is not yet determined;

- a conjectural anticipation – a tentative interpretation of the given elements, attributing to them a tendency to effect certain consequences;

- a careful survey (examination, inspection, exploration, analysis) of all attainable considerations which will define and clarify the problem in hand;

- a consequent elaboration of the tentative hypothesis to make it more precise and more consistent, because squaring with a wider range of facts;

- taking one stand upon the projected hypothesis as a plan of action which is applied to the existing state of affairs; doing something overtly to bring about the anticipated result, and thereby testing the hypothesis.

It is the extent and accuracy of steps three and four which mark off a distinctive reflective experience from one on the trial and error plane. They make thinking itself into an experience. Nevertheless, we never get wholly beyond the trial and error situation. Our most elaborate and rationally consistent thought has to be tried in the world and thereby tried out. And since it can never take into account all the connections, it can never cover with perfect accuracy all the consequences. Yet a thoughtful survey of conditions is so careful, and the guessing at results so controlled, that we have a right to mark off the reflective experience from the grosser trial and error forms of action.

 READING 1.2

Reflection-in-action

Donald Schon

> Donald Schon's analysis of reflective practice has influenced training, development and conceptions in many professions. His key insight is that there are forms of professional knowledge which, though often tacitly held, are essential for the exercise of judgement as the complexities and dilemmas of professional life are confronted. Such knowledge is in professional action, and may be developed by reflection-in-action.
>
> Edited from: Schon, D. A. (1983) *The Reflective Practitioner: How Professionals Think in Action.* London: Temple Smith 50–68

When we go about the spontaneous, intuitive performance of the actions of everyday life, we show ourselves to be knowledgeable in a special way. Often we cannot say what it is that we know. When we try to describe it we find ourselves at a loss, or we produce descriptions that are obviously inappropriate. Our knowing is ordinarily tacit, implicit in our patterns of action and in our feel for the stuff with which we are dealing. It seems right to say that our knowing is in our action.

Similarly, the workaday life of the professional depends on tacit knowing-in-action. Every competent practitioner makes innumerable judgements of quality for which he cannot state adequate criteria, and he displays skills for which he cannot state the rules and procedures. Even when he makes conscious use of research-based theories and techniques, he is dependent on tacit recognitions, judgements, and skilful performances.

On the other hand, both ordinary people and professional practitioners often think about what they are doing, sometimes even while doing it. Stimulated by surprise, they turn thought back on action and on the knowing which is implicit in action. They may ask themselves, for example, 'What features do I notice when I recognize this thing? What are the criteria by which I make this judgement? What procedures am I enacting when I perform this skill? How am I framing the problem that I am trying to solve?' Usually reflection on knowing-in-action goes together with reflection on the stuff at hand. There is some puzzling, or troubling, or interesting phenomenon with which the individual is trying to deal. As he tries to make sense of it, he also reflects on the understandings which have been implicit in his action, understandings which he surfaces, criticizes, restructures, and embodies in further action.

It is this entire process of reflection-in-action which is central to the 'art' by which practitioners sometimes deal well with situations of uncertainty, instability, uniqueness, and value conflict.

Knowing-in-action

There is nothing strange about the idea that a kind of knowing is inherent in intelligent action. Common sense admits the category of know-how, and it does not stretch common sense very much to say that the know-how is in the action.

There are actions, recognitions, and judgements which we know how to carry out spontaneously; we do not have to think about them prior to or during their performance. We are often unaware of having learned to do these things; we simply find ourselves doing them. In some cases, we were once aware of the understandings which were subsequently internalized in our feeling for the stuff of action. In other cases, we are usually unable to describe the knowing which our action reveals. It is in this sense that I speak of knowing-in-action, the characteristic mode of ordinary practical knowledge.

Reflecting-in-action

If common sense recognizes knowing-in-action, it also recognizes that we sometimes think about what we are doing. Phrases like 'thinking on your feet', 'keeping your wits about you', and 'learning by doing' suggest not only that we can think about doing but that we can think about doing something while doing it. Some of the most interesting examples of this process occur in the midst of a performance.

Much reflection-in-action hinges on the experience of surprise. When intuitive, spontaneous performance yields nothing more than the results expected for it, then we tend not to think about it. But when intuitive performance leads to surprises, pleasing and promising or unwanted, we may respond by reflecting-in-action. In such processes, reflection tends to focus interactively on the outcomes of action, the action itself, and the intuitive knowing implicit in the action.

A professional practitioner is a specialist who encounters certain types of situations again and again. As a practitioner experiences many variations of a small number of types of cases, he is able to 'practise' his practice. He develops a repertoire of expectations, images and techniques. He learns what to look for and how to respond to what he finds. As long as his practice is stable, in the sense that it brings him the same types of cases, he becomes less and less subject to surprise. His knowing-in-practice tends to become increasingly tacit, spontaneous, and automatic, thereby conferring upon him and his clients the benefits of specialization.

As a practice becomes more repetitive and routine, and as knowing-in-practice becomes increasingly tacit and spontaneous, the practitioner may miss important opportunities to think about what he is doing. He may find that he is drawn into patterns of error which he cannot correct. And if he learns, as often happens, to be selectively inattentive to phenomena that do not fit the categories of his knowing-in-action, then he may suffer from boredom or 'burn-out' and afflict his clients with the consequences of his narrowness and rigidity. When this happens, the practitioner has 'over-learned' what he knows.

A practitioner's reflection can serve as a corrective to over-learning. Through reflection, he can surface and criticize the tacit understandings that have grown up around the repetitive experiences of a specialized practice, and can make new sense of the situations of uncertainty or uniqueness which he may allow himself to experience.

Practitioners do reflect on their knowing-in-practice. Sometimes, in the relative tranquillity of a postmortem, they think back on a project they have undertaken, a situation they have lived through, and they explore the understandings they have brought to their handling of the case. They may do this in a mood of idle speculation, or in a deliberate effort to prepare themselves for future cases. But they may also reflect on practice while they are in the midst of it. Here they reflect-in-action.

When a practitioner reflects in and on his practice, the possible objects of his reflection are as varied as the kinds of phenomena before him and the systems of knowing-in-practice which he brings to them. He may reflect on the tacit norms and appreciations which underlie a judgement, or on the strategies and theories implicit in a pattern of behaviour. He may reflect on the feeling for a situation which has led him to adopt a particular course of action, on the way in which he has framed the problem he is trying to solve, or on the role he has constructed for himself within a larger institutional context.

Reflection-in-action, in these several modes, is central to the art through which practitioners sometimes cope with the troublesome 'divergent' situations of practice. When the phenomenon at hand eludes the ordinary categories of knowledge-in-practice, presenting itself as unique or unstable, the practitioner may surface and criticize his initial understanding of the phenomenon, construct a new description of it, and test the new description by an on-the-spot experiment. Sometimes he arrives at a new theory of the phenomenon by articulating a feeling he has about it.

When he is confronted with demands that seem incompatible or inconsistent, he may respond by reflecting on the appreciations which he and others have brought to the situation. Conscious of a dilemma, he may attribute it to the way in which he has set his problem, or even to the way in which he has framed his role. He may then find a way of integrating, or choosing among, the values at stake in the situation.

When someone reflects-in-action, he becomes a researcher in the practice context. He does not separate thinking from doing. Because his experimenting is a kind of action, implementation is built into his inquiry. Thus reflection-in-action can proceed, even in situations of uncertainty or uniqueness.

Although reflection-in-action is an extraordinary process, it is not a rare event. Indeed, for reflective practitioners it is the core of practice.

READING 1.3

Dilemmas of schooling

Ann Berlak and Harold Berlak

Reflection is a fundamental necessity for professional teachers because there are no simple prescriptions concerning what 'best' educational practice might be. That is what makes the job both so interesting and challenging. A particularly useful way of conceptualizing the reality of these daily struggles is through the concept of 'dilemmas'. Justifiably, Ann and Harold Berlak's book on this topic has become a classic and this reading illustrates the ways in which they link the identification of dilemmas to the need for reflective teaching.

What are the main dilemmas that you face in your work?

Edited from: Berlak, A. and Berlak, H. (1981) *Dilemmas of Schooling*. London: Methuen, 125–37, 237

Dilemmas represent contradictions that reside in the situation, in the individual, and in the larger society – as they are played out in one form of institutional life, schooling. Dilemmas focus on the flux and the reflexivity of the social process that are encapsulated in daily encounters of teachers with children in the social setting of the schools.

We offer an illustration to show how dilemmas may be used to represent schooling processes that are in constant flux, and to illuminate the relationship of past, present and future. We begin with a summary of observations recorded one day in March at Heathbrook Primary School.

'We ought to chain it to your desk so you don't lose it again', Mr Scott says to Susan as he hands her a lined composition book to replace the one she lost. Susan's head droops; tears look imminent. Another child, whose eyes catch Susan's, responds with a grin. Susan twists her half-brooding mouth into a half smile and she returns to her chair, new composition book in hand. Several children's heads turn toward the doorway. The Head enters carrying 'work diaries', lined composition books wherein each child every Friday morning lists the learning tasks completed during the week. He says a few quiet words to Mr Scott as he hands him the stack of books, looks quickly about the classroom which has become noticeably more silent upon his arrival, and departs. Mr Scott from his vantage point in the middle of the room scans the room, his eyes passing over individuals, pairs and trios, some of whom appear to be working diligently while others every now and again become engaged in intense conversation. His eyes fall on Steven and Bruce moments longer than the rest. These boys, who yesterday had been seated on opposite sides of the room, are today seated together, intently examining one of their football cards, engrossed in what appears from a distance to be a particularly vigorous and extended exchange of ideas, their mathematics work as presented on a set of cards cast aside, temporarily forgotten. Mr Scott leaves his place at the centre of the room, approaches Mary, and responding to her request, reads a portion of the story she is writing.

Later, in the teacher's room, Mr Bolton, Mr Scott and the two of us wait for tea water to boil. Mr Bolton tells us of a television programme discussion on the decline of mathematics standards in the schools and its effects on students' qualifications for university entrance. Mr Scott nods assent and says, 'Yes, there is probably something to that.'

Mr Scott this morning walks past Steven rather than telling him to get back to work. One could view this as a non-event since Mr Scott did not do anything to Steve. However, this 'non-event' stands out for several reasons – because he treats Steven somewhat differently than the others and differently than he did yesterday. It also stands out because Steven isn't doing his maths, and Mr Scott, in word and deed, considers maths an especially important part of the work of school. How can we make sense of this non-event? Had we not spent time in his class nor had some access to Mr Scott's and Mr Bolton's views, we might not have noted that Mr Scott looked at Steven but said nothing, or we may have passed it off as something of which he was not aware. We had no way of knowing by observation alone whether, for example, his non-behaviour was studied indifference or benign or even malign neglect. But Mr Scott has also told us about Steven's 'creativity', about the misery of the football fanatics when they were separated from one another, about the press he feels to get the 'fourth years' to progress; and we discern his response to Steven as part of a pattern. This pattern includes both his bypassing of Steven and his later confrontation of him.

The act is the fundamental conception on which the dilemma language rests. It includes the observable instances of Mr Scott's behaviour, his visions of the future, images from the past, and the circumstances of the present situation (some of which he is aware). To view Mr Scott's schooling behaviour in terms of the dilemma language is to see it not as a set of disconnected, contradictory, discrete, situational behaviours, but as a complex pattern of behaviours that are joined together through his consciousness. We have some limited access to his consciousness as he talks to us about what we see him do in his classroom and through our observations of the context in which his behaviours are embedded. The act portrays Mr Scott not only as a mindless reactor to inside or outside forces, social, physical and psychological, but as a person who is and may become critical, in Dewey's and Mead's terms, increasingly able to engage in reflective action. It appears to us and apparently to Mr Scott as well, that he at times makes choices, more or less consciously, more or less thoughtfully, from among the alternatives as he sees them. This sense of choice is suggested by 'I have yet to come to terms with myself', and as he shares a few of his continuing internal conversations about whether Steven and children generally should be pushed to do mathematics.

As Mr Scott talks to us and as we watch him teach, it becomes apparent that he is responding with some degree of awareness to a wide range of contradictory social experiences and social forces, past and contemporary, both in his classroom, his school and beyond in the wider community. He has internalized these contradictions and they are now 'within' him, a part of his generalized other. We infer these contradictions by observing his behaviour and listening to what he says about it – 'something inside you that you've developed over the years which says children should do this' and 'I didn't want them to be miserable'– and from his frequent admissions to us in conversation that he accepts of his own accord the Head's views on standards in mathematics, and also agrees with him that 'children need a haven'.

We represent these contradictions as dilemmas that are 'in' Mr Scott, in his personal and social history, and 'in' the present circumstances (and are also fundamental contradictions in the culture and society). These contradictions and the 'internal' or 'mental' weighing of these forces that sometimes occurs are joined in the moment he looks at Steven, then by him, and focuses his attention on Mary.

The dilemmas are a language of acts, a means of representing the diverse and apparently contradictory patterns of schooling. Dilemmas do not represent static ideas waiting at bay in the mind, but an unceasing interaction of internal and external forces, a world of continuous transformations. Because they are capable of becoming aware of these internal and external forces that bear on their own *de facto* solutions, persons are capable of altering their own behavioural patterns and/or acting with others in efforts to alter the circumstances in which they act.

Mr Scott's past and present experiences are 'in' his patterns of resolution; he is not only a pawn to these experiences but also an originator of action. Since Steven, like Mr Scott, takes meaning from experiences and may reflect upon them, then Mr Scott's patterns of resolutions may be seen as both transmitting and transforming the society. The problem of the relationship between Mr Scott's past and present experience, his patterns of resolution, and the meanings Steven takes from them, is a representation of the problem of the relationship of past to present to future in the social process and is, thus, one way to formulate the question of the role schooling plays in social transmission and transformation. By recognizing patterns of resolution, including dominant and more exceptional modes, and viewing teachers' behaviour as both determined and free, the dilemma language enables one to consider the relationship of school to society.

The purpose of inquiry, for teachers and non-teachers, is to enable them to engage in reflective action. Engaging in this process requires that each of the participants render as problematic what they have been taking for granted about what is happening in classrooms, the origins of the schooling activities and their consequences upon children and the society both in the immediate and longer range future. Using the dilemma language to structure critical inquiry involves an examination, from the widest possible range of perspectives, of present patterns of resolution, alternative possibilities, the consequences of present and alternative patterns, the origins of present patterns and of proposals for alternatives. A critical search for alternatives is not complete if it does not include development of skills and knowledge needed by teachers to alter their schooling patterns. The latter we call craft knowledge.

READING 1.4

Training skilful teachers

Ted Wragg

Ted Wragg is well known for his trenchant support of teachers in the media and his work on teaching skills and competences, drawn on for this reading, has also been highly influential. In the reading he considers effective ways of developing teaching skills and describes one attempt to identify a hierachy of skills.

As Wragg illustrates, the art and science of teaching ensures that there is always scope for further professional development.

Edited from: Wragg, E. C. (1993) *Primary Teaching Skills*. London: Routledge, 186–95

There is no single omni-purpose good teacher stereotype. There are different ways of being effective in different circumstances. This lack of singularity, however, does not mean that nothing can be done to help teachers become more proficient. Quite the reverse. If there were a single stereotype of skilful teaching, all one would have to do would be to learn it off by heart. It is because there are numerous ways to help children learn that the challenge to train teachers intelligently, and for teachers themselves to improve the quality of their own practices, is all the more important.

The question of teacher competence raises several important matters, and indeed sometimes arouses strong feelings. Not the least of these is whether these skills should be learned in part or as a whole. The extreme part-learning stance is taken by some supporters of competency-based teacher education who believe that teaching can be atomized into hundreds of discrete mini-acts which can be systematically learned and appraised, and the extreme holist stance is adopted by those who contend that teaching is an art and that to seek to segment it is to destroy it.

My own belief, for what it is worth, is that if one tries to break down teaching to the atomic level, it not only becomes silly, but makes the student or teacher self-conscious.

On the other hand, it is wrong to expect that if the general development of the person is sound, then all the skills of teaching will emerge of their own accord. There is now a useful literature on teaching skills. There are reflections and exercises one can undertake in a positive attempt to improve the practice of some aspect of teaching.

In training one can concentrate on a particular aspect of teaching whilst now excluding others. Thus, the emphasis in one training session may be on explaining. A teacher may be videotaped explaining something to a group of children and then the video may be played back and analysed. It would be foolish indeed to restrict one's attention only to the act of explaining. It might, for example, rule out the use of questions because that was next week's topic, which would be an absurd stance to adopt. During the explanation, no doubt questions will occur, and quite possibly the pupils if they are bored will misbehave, which will in turn raise matters to do with class management. The aim in such a training session should, therefore, be to give prominence to one aspect of teaching skill and proper attention to such others as naturally occur. In that way the art of teaching can be nurtured, and such science as exists from empirical studies can be fed in if thought to be germane.

Nor should the study and development of classroom skills be seen as in opposition to other forms of training. Some emphasis on specific skills in an initial training course, in school-based in-service programmes of professional development, in the training of mentors or appraisers, does not replace other forms of reflection and practice, but rather should work in harmony with them. My own inclination has increasingly been to move much more towards an inductive approach to reflection and the teaching of educational theory. When students or teachers study classrooms with a set of assignments, this to look for, questions to ask heads and fellow teachers, teaching ideas to try out, pupils to talk to and so on, they collect in a slightly hit-or-miss way an enormous amount of valuable empirical data. A good theory course can start by trying to make sense of what students report, and then elicit key constructs which may or may not be endorsed in the traditional literature.

In the early stages of an initial or post-experience training course, therefore, the emphasis can be on collecting sense data, experiences, impressions, with the trainers and teachers using their own knowledge to structure these in such a way that they are valuable and fruitful rather than pointless or random. Subsequently, debriefings can ensue which will usually produce a great deal in common with established precepts about pupil learning or failure to learn, motivation, language, social and cultural background, home and school, curriculum, teaching strategies, learning styles, choice, child development, school organization. Subsequent courses which cover theory and practice in a more systematic way will, if all has gone well, find their studies and reflections more closely related to practice, and will thereby engage commitment much more firmly than has sometimes been the case in the past.

There are numerous ways of conceiving teaching skills. Research leads me to conclude that such aspects as class management can be seen as 'enabling' skills, since, without competence in them the other skills, like questioning and explaining, cannot operate, nor can teachers put their subject knowledge and life experience at the disposal of their pupils. Professional competence is intelligent thought translated into intelligent action. In deciding how to teach class management it may, therefore, be worth thinking about initial levels of proficiency, which will enable novices to be operational and permit them to exercise their other skills, and higher levels towards which experienced practitioners can strive.

At Exeter University, primary trainees assess themselves and are assessed on a set of nine dimensions. These include direct instruction, monitoring, management or order, planning and preparation. In each case, there are eight levels through which teachers can progress, level 1 being what is expected of beginners and level 8 being the mark of a competent practitioner. Some examples are:

Level 1

1 Distribute provided materials; check children's responses.

2 Attempt to operate some procedures for orderly activity.

3 Plan bases resources for children working on a given activity.

4 Give some account of own performance.

5 Check clarity of explanation by appropriate questions; convey enthusiasm with appropriate verbal and non-verbal behaviour.

6 Use planned and unplanned opportunities to hold conversations with children in order to establish their perspectives; be sensitive to problems or teacher intrusion.

7 Continue with attempts to operate in an established formula of rules and procedures.

Level 5

1 Provide a programme of guided practice in core areas of the curriculum to suit the range of attainments in the class; choose appropriately matched and sequenced practice exercises.

2 Experiment with planned conversational teaching on particular aspects of the curriculum.

3 Plan a short programme of work to engage a variety of identified skills and intellectual processes and demonstrate attention to transition between activities.

4 Offer justifiable explanations of children's response to work; use explanations in practicable ways to plan the next phase of work; show understanding of the diversity of pupils' attainments.

Level 8

1 Make explanations efficient and concise: choose examples for their power in the subject.

2 Sustain a broad programme of diagnostic teaching.

3 Achieve a situation in which order is endemic to the work system.

4 Plan for efficiency in the use of time and resources with clear reference to the careful management of the teacher's time.

The problem with a hierarchical view is that, by the time one reaches the demands of the highest level, the requirements are such that even the most gifted teachers may pale, and all of us feel guilty that we do not attain them. Nonetheless, such a mapping exercise does at least clarify what people might aspire to, and the Exeter model is offered as an example, not as a paragon ideal to be copied. It is far more effective if people as a group work out a set of precepts to which they feel committed personally and professionally.

It is sometimes assumed that anyone can train teachers, hence the proposal from time to time that all one need to do is to place students for longer periods in a school and then the teachers will automatically teach them how to teach, or that one invites a good practitioner out of school to talk to students, or that experienced teachers simply need to keep on teaching and they will automatically improve with age. There is a craft to training teachers which it takes time to acquire, and both teachers and teacher trainers, however experienced, can learn a great deal about teaching skills and how to support others who are developing the art and science of skilful teaching. If teaching children is one of the most important responsibilities a society can ask some of its members to undertake, then the challenge to nurture and enhance the professional skills of each new generation of teachers for the vastly complex world of the twenty-first century, and sharpen the proficiency of teachers already in post, must be an equally valuable assignment.

 **READING 1.5**

Analysing the role of mentors

John Sampson and Robin Yeomans

This is an insightful reading on the multiple aspects of a school-based mentor's role and it draws on some of the authors' research on relationships in initial teacher education. Sampson and Yeomans identify three main dimensions of the mentor role: structural, supportive and professional. They suggest that effective mentors prioritize the elements of their role to meet changing student needs as a period of school experience develops.

How does their analysis relate to your experience as a mentor or as a student?

Edited from: Sampson, J. and Yeomans, R. (eds) (1994) *Mentorship in the Primary School*. London: Falmer Press, 64–75

The role of the mentor has three dimensions.

The structural dimension involves acting to seek to ensure that conditions exist in the school which will enable students to perform as effectively as is possible, given the limitations of their current stage of development. The elements which we have identified within the structural dimension are: 'planner', 'organizer', 'negotiator', and 'inductor'.

The supportive dimension of mentoring is concerned with students as people, and with making them feel comfortable in or minimizing the stress of situations they encounter in the school. We suggest that its elements are 'host', 'friend', and 'counsellor'.

Finally, the professional dimension relates to all those activities which are concerned with the students' development as potential teachers. Its elements are 'trainer', 'educator' and 'assessor'.

The structural dimension

Mentors had a key role in preparing the way for students in the school and in the school-based part of their courses. Mentors created the conditions which would enable students to perform as well as they were able. In other words, within their structural role dimension, they were enablers, establishing and modifying social and organizational structures.

Planner Particularly when the students first came to the school but also later as their own course demands changed, it was the mentor who planned the students' programme so that they were deployed in the most mutually beneficial way. This is not to suggest that mentors planned the last detail of the students' experience. There were opportunities for students to initiate and to influence the detailed structure of their school experience. This happened several times. But whatever the student initiated, mentors played a part in the necessary organization.

Organizer If planning dealt with intentions, then organization was concerned with the necessary conditions for favourable outcomes. However rigorous and ambitious the plans agreed between students and mentor, effective implementation was more likely if mentors were able to organize conditions conducive to success. The mentor's organizational contribution was concerned with every facet of the student's life in the school. But the emphasis was on student's classroom practice, including the organization of curriculum tasks that related to the college element of the courses.

Mentors needed a clear view of the way ahead if they were to organize the students' day-to-day programme in the school. Typically the structure and detail of the students' teaching commitment was planned by the mentor and students, within the guidelines produced by the College.

Negotiator Mentors' ability to create optimum learning conditions for students also required that they negotiate with colleagues on students' behalves. Mentors' status and credibility within the school were important here. Being deputy head made negotiation easier for some, since making organizational requests to colleagues was an existing part of mentors' deputy head role. Similarly, deputy head mentors could use their close professional relationship with their head to the students' benefit. Non-deputy head mentors relied more on their personal credibility and existing relationships with colleagues.

Mentors had four main negotiating concerns. First, they needed to negotiate time for themselves and students to meet without the distraction of a class. This meant persuading heads or colleagues who had a student to take the mentors' class. Second, they sought opportunities for students to gain access to other classes, in order to observe colleagues at work, interrogate them about classroom practice, or have some teaching time with a different age group. Third, students might find out more about a particular curriculum area by talking to the curriculum co-ordinator. Fourth, since there was normally more than one student in a school, effective supervision of students required mentors to negotiate with host class teachers an unambiguous division of responsibilities for observing, reporting on, and debriefing any student not teaching the mentor's class. Clearly there are implications for mentors' relationships with colleagues, their status in the schools and their own interpersonal skills.

Mentors also needed to negotiate with link tutors a shared perspective of the nature of effective teaching. Without such a common view, conflicting messages were likely. This tended to be a continuing relationship of school and mentor with the college and a specific tutor.

Inductor Mentors all took conscious steps to give the students insights into the ways of behaving within their classroom and within the school. They inducted them into the schools' systems, in terms of agreed procedures. But they also talked students through some of the informal habits which were part of the shared understandings, which had evolved within the schools. Though important to the smooth running of schools and classrooms, these were often unacknowledged, seldom written down, and so could offer particular difficulties to unwary students. With such insights, the students could more rapidly learn to 'fit in', feel 'teacher-like' themselves, and convince the children and other staff by their authentic teacher behaviour.

The supportive dimension

The supportive dimension of mentoring is closely linked to the nature of the relationship created between mentor and student. A mutually open and trusting relationship was both the means to, and the outcome of, effective support. Mentors recognized that students' time in school could be stressful in several ways. First, they were outsiders, experiencing an unknown staff culture, whose rules and norms they needed to assimilate if they were to learn or behave authentically. Second, authentic teacher behaviour in the eyes of the pupils was itself an important condition of successful performance of the role of teacher; students could not take for granted pupils' sympathetic understanding. Third, students knew that however supportive they found the school context, their performance was under close scrutiny. Success and failure had a precise meaning and, in the assessed phases, carried career implications. In other words, school experience had many of the characteristics of a 'life' event.

Thus, the supportive dimension of the mentors' role engaged them in minimizing possible stress for students, and ensuring that, when stressful situations were encountered, they enhanced students' self-awareness and became learning experiences.

Mentors initially acted as a host when they welcomed students on behalf of the whole school. It was then that the mentor and student began to form a relationship, that students were introduced to school rules and procedures. These early moments were important and recognized as such by students in particular. They appreciated the efforts that were made to welcome them.

Friend Some mentors were particularly adept at handling role conflict, and so managed to incorporate the extremes of assessor and friend within their role. Friendship could be a consequence of always being a source of positive comment.

Counsellor The counselling element in the mentors' role had two sides. Mentors needed to help students cope with judgements on their teaching. The help was particularly needed when negative classroom experiences had undermined students' self-belief, or when circumstances required that they consider their long-term professional future. In an extreme case, a mentor might help a student deal with the consequences of short-term or long-term failure. For student and mentor alike, counselling phases might generate ambivalent feelings. The mentor who was the judge of success and failure also carried the responsibility of reconciling a student to the judgement and building from it. The primary purpose of the mentoring role was to help students towards becoming effective teachers.

The professional dimension

Trainer Mentors acted as trainers when they took steps which enabled students to respond more effectively and successfully to current teaching needs. Of course, they hoped that if students successfully incorporated mentors' suggestions into their teaching, the students' long-term professional practice would also be modified. However, any such change tended to be derived from observing mentors at work or listening to advice, explanations or descriptions which reflected the mentors' own strategies for specific situations. In short, the emphasis in training was on successful implementation of the mentors' solutions.

Training was a necessary part of students' development. However, there was a temptation to extend training inappropriately. As experts, mentors drew on extensive experience, could identify underlying problems and suggest relevant strategies. As novices, students tended to recognize mentors' expertise, having observed their classroom practice, perhaps noted their status and credibility in the school, and knowing that the college confirmed their mentor status. Consequently students might expect to be told how to deal with their class, particularly if it was also the mentor's own. A mentor's legitimate concern for the needs of their class might also lead to a narrow interpretation of the mentor role. Strategies which a mentor used successfully with that group of children were safer for mentor, student and class than encouraging a student to experiment. Thoughtful commitment to students' development was needed for mentors to recognize that only applying short-term solutions carried long-term dangers for students. They might become unthinking and unquestioning adherents to all the mentor said and did, unquestioning followers of one model who found it difficult to meet new circumstances.

Educator To behave as educator was to be a mentor who enabled students to become autonomous, self-referential teachers, capable of objectively analysing their own and others' professional practice.

Mentors were well-placed to be students' dialogical partners. If as trainers they were largely engaged in helping students construct practice, as educators their concern shifted to helping students deconstruct teaching sessions so that they began to reconstruct their version of effective practice and ultimately to amend their professional schemata. In other words, reconstruction was concerned with students' long-term development rather than merely with the here and now. The intention was that students would develop their own, personal, flexible model of professional practice. This would enable them to adapt their teaching model to new circumstances. It was the mentors' skill in moving students towards independence characterized by self-generated reconstruction that was the essence of effective educative mentoring.

Assessor There were advantages in having the mentor as assessor. They knew the school, the class and the children far better than any visiting tutor could. They were also likely to have an established relationship with other teachers students worked with, and so were better able to access other perspectives on students' school performance. Mentors were able to discuss with students their performance more frequently than could a visiting tutor. Of course, mentors lacked an overview of a range of students in a variety of settings, and so the final confirmatory pass/fail decision rested with the College. In practice, the arrangement created few difficulties, since there was regular contact and discussion between mentor and link tutor.

There were tensions for mentors in being the assessors. First, when they reported to students on their progress face to face, mentors stated openly what might only have been tacit in other circumstances. Second, they managed the subtleties of reporting assessment, particularly at the interim report stage, so as to provide both warning or praise and stimulus for the student. There was skill in not making the report so positive or so critical that it was a disincentive to renewed effort and so limited further progress. Third, such written confrontations of students with their strengths and weaknesses could be personally threatening to mentors and students alike. Fourth, there was the responsibility of deciding whether the student should pass or fail. The role of a link tutor has some bearing here. Mentors did signal some students as possible failures, link tutors agreed and the judgement was confirmed by external examiners. So although a failure decision was difficult, it was not shirked.

Conclusion

The complexities of mentorship can best be understood if it is seen as a single role. The role has structural, supportive and professional dimensions, each of which contains specific elements which reflect different modes of mentor behaviour. These are planner, organizer, negotiator and inductor (structural elements); host, friend and counsellor (supportive elements); trainer, educator and assessor (professional elements). Elements of the role are performed at different times in response to predicted needs and particular phases of school experience. But needs can also change from moment to moment. The emphasis within the role also varies with different mentors, so that not all mentors exploit all elements of the role to the same extent.

 READING 1.6

Criteria for initial teacher training in England: primary phase

Council for the Accreditation of Teacher Education

This reading comprises an extract from Circular 14/93 which set Government requirements for teacher education courses. The aim identifies three elements: 'personal qualities', 'subject knowledge and understanding' and 'standards of professional competence'. More specific competences to be met on courses are then set out. It is interesting to evaluate the balance of these in the light of some of the other readings in this chapter or in Chapter 1 of *Reflective Teaching in the Primary School*.
How would you evaluate yourself against these competency criteria?

Edited from: Council for the Accreditation of Teacher Education (1993) Criteria for Initial Teacher Training (Primary Phase), *The Initial Training of Primary School Teachers*. DFE Circular 14/93 (England). London: DFE

The aim of initial teacher training is that all newly qualified teachers entering maintained schools should have the necessary personal qualities for teaching children and should have achieved the levels of subject knowledge and understanding, and standards of professional competence, necessary to maintain and improve standards in schools.

Higher education institutions, schools and students should focus on the competencies of teaching throughout the whole period of initial training. The progressive development of these competencies should be monitored regularly during training. Their attainment at a level appropriate to newly qualified teachers should be the objective of every student taking a course of initial training.

Whole curriculum

Newly qualified teachers should be able to:

demonstrate understanding of the purposes, scope, structure and balance of the primary curriculum as a whole;

ensure continuity and progression within the work of their own class and with the classes to and from which their pupils transfer;

exploit, in all their teaching, opportunities to develop pupils' language, reading, numeracy, information handling and other skills.

Subject knowledge and application

Newly qualified teachers should be able to:

demonstrate knowledge and understanding of the subjects of the primary curriculum which they have studied, at a level which will support effective teaching of these subjects;

use that knowledge and understanding to plan lessons, teach and assess pupils in the core subjects of the National Curriculum and those other subjects of the primary curriculum covered in their course; newly qualified teachers may need some guidance and support in some of these subjects.

Assessment and recording of pupils' progress

Newly qualified teachers should be able to:

test, assess and record systematically the progress of individual pupils;

judge how well each pupil performs against appropriate criteria and standards by identifying individual pupils' attainment, with reference to relevant National Curriculum requirements;

use such testing and assessment in their planning and teaching;

provide oral and written feedback to pupils on the processes and outcomes of their learning;

prepare and present reports on pupils' progress to parents.

Teaching strategies and pupils' learning

Newly qualified teachers should be able to:

identify and respond appropriately to relevant individual differences between pupils;

show awareness of how pupils learn and of the various factors which affect the process;

set appropriate and demanding expectations of their pupils;

devise a variety and range of learning goals and tasks and monitor and assess them.

Teaching strategies and techniques

Newly qualified teachers should be able to:

establish clear expectations of pupil behaviour in the classroom and secure appropriate standards of discipline;

create and maintain a purposeful, orderly and supportive environment for their pupils' learning;

maintain pupils' interest and motivation;

present learning tasks and curriculum content in a clear and stimulating manner;

teach whole classes, groups and individuals, and determine the most appropriate learning goals and classroom contexts for using these and other teaching strategies;

use a range of teaching techniques, and judge when and how to deploy them;

employ varying forms of curriculum organization, and monitor their effectiveness;

communicate clearly and effectively with pupils through questioning, instructing, explaining and feedback;

manage effectively and economically their own and their pupils' time;

make constructive use of information technology and other resources for learning;

train pupils in the individual and collaborative study skills necessary for effective learning.

Further professional development

Newly qualified teachers should have acquired in initial training the necessary foundation to develop:

a working knowledge of their contractual, legal, administrative and pastoral responsibilities as teachers;

effective working relationships with professional colleagues (including support staff) and parents;

the ability to recognize diversity of talent including that of gifted pupils;

the ability to identify and provide for special educational needs and specific learning difficulties;

the ability to evaluate pupils' learning, and recognize the effects on that learning of teachers' expectations and actions;

a readiness to promote the spiritual, moral, social and cultural development of pupils;

their professional knowledge, understanding and skill through further training and development;

vision, imagination and critical awareness in educating their pupils.

 READING 1.7

Two models of professionalism

John Elliott

John Elliott is an influential writer on the development of professionalism through action research. Here he contrasts a model of professionals as 'infallible experts' with the concept of 'reflective practitioners'. He argues that, given the complexity of the modern world, the latter is essential and this clearly has important implications for professional learning.

Edited from: Elliott, J. (1991) A model of professionalism and its implications for teacher education, *British Educational Research Journal*, 17 (4), 310–14

'Advanced' modern societies can be characterized as unstable states of wide-spread discontinuous, rather then incremental, change. The needs of human beings in such societies become increasingly complex, various, and open to redefinition. New professions emerge to provide for emergent needs. Old professions have to constantly respond to new situations in traditional areas of need, and thereby constantly reconstruct their expert knowledge. The boundaries between professional practices are in a constant process of redefinition and there is increasing pressure on different professional groups to collaborate in the provision of services. The increasing complexity of human needs generates dilemmas for individuals and communities which are not easy to resolve. The satisfaction of one need may imply the denial of another. In liberal democracies, individuals and communities tend to be given more control in defining what is good for them and, therefore, over how their needs are catered for. Consequently, there is pressure on professionals to view 'clients' situations holistically, to enter into greater dialogue with them about their concerns, and to arrive at collaborative decisions over how their needs are best provided for.

The occupational context of professional practice in 'advanced' liberal democracies can be conceptualized as 'dynamic', 'fluid', 'complex', 'dilemma-ridden', and 'client-focused'. It has enormous implications for the dimensions of education/training referred to above.

Professional organizations are generating new occupational images which encapsulate shifting conceptions of the values which define the professional role. Thus, in medicine we have 'patient care' as an image of the nursing role or 'community medicine' as an image of the General Practitioner's role, while in policing there is a current emphasis on 'community policing'. In schools there has been a considerable 'parents as partners' movement. All these images are indicative of attempts to shift occupational values and perspectives. They are inevitably vague and open to ambiguous interpretations. 'Parents in partnership' can mean involving parents in the process of their children's education, or it can mean involving them in controlling its outcomes through the mechanism of parental choice. They are not the same.

The vagueness and ambiguity of new occupational images is inevitable during the early phases of the change process. People tend to be clearer about the limitations of current practice than the shape of things to come. New occupational images provide a broad orientation for the change agents. Clarity emerges gradually by reflecting on the experience of trying to give an image some concrete and practical form. In other words, the development of conceptual clarity proceeds interactively with the experience of innovation rather than in advance of it. It is through a reflective dialogue about a variety of attempts to capture a new image of professionalism in concrete practical form that the new values become articulated and clarified.

On the basis of the reflection, dialogue and experimentation I have been involved in across the professions, I would argue that the new professional images have the following features in common:

- collaboration with clients (individuals, groups, communities) in identifying, clarifying and resolving their problems;

- the importance of communication and empathy with clients as a means of understanding situations from their point of view;

- a new emphasis on the holistic understanding of situations as the basis for professional practice, rather than on understanding them exclusively in terms of a particular set of specialist categories;

- self-reflection as a means of overcoming stereotypical judgements and responses.

These features are similar in many respects to Schon's (1983) characterization of the 'reflective practitioner' as a model of professional practice [see Reading 1.2]. They negate many of the features of customary professional practice founded upon the image of the practitioner as an infallible expert. Such a person is one who:

- expects clients to defer to his/her superior knowledge and wisdom in identifying, clarifying and resolving their problems;

- engages in one-way communication. (S)he tells and prescribes while the client listens and obeys. The client is allowed to ask questions from a position of deference but not to 'question' from a presumption of knowledge. There is little reciprocity in communication because the 'expert' is not concerned with developing a holistic view of the client's situation;

- understands and handles the situations they confront exclusively in terms of the categories of specialist knowledge they have mastered. A police officer recently informed me that knowledge of a person's psychological history was totally irrelevant to the question of whether (s)he should be arrested, taken into custody and charged for an offence. He was attempting to justify the view that psychology was not an essential part of a police officer's professional knowledge. Similarly, a GP may take the view that awareness of the relationship between certain kinds of illness (s)he treats and social conditions in the community is largely irrelevant to her/his job. It is not part of her/his role to try to change those conditions;

- applies specialist knowledge intuitively rather than reflectively on the basis of the commonsense wisdom enshrined in the occupational culture. Thus a police officer's knowledge of the law and procedures relating to situations of domestic violence will tend to be applied to cases involving aggressive working-class males under the influence of drink. In schools, children who are either working-class or black are more likely to be assessed as academically less able and, therefore, unteachable in many respects than middle-class children. Professional judgement within the 'infallible expert' model tends to be based on the intuitive stereotyping of situations rather than a form of reflection which takes into account a variety of perspectives (including the clients') and fosters a self-evaluation of the practitioner's own biases.

The infallible expert image matches a society conceived as a stable and unchanging state. But it can be stretched to accommodate social change when change is interpreted as an evolutionary progression in society that can be steered by the state. Human needs under this account of change remain fairly constant as do the forms of their provision. New problems – for health education, law and order, social welfare, etc. – emerge from time to time and create demands for new knowledge and additional material and welfare resources. But these can be planned for by the state with a little skilful prediction of social trends. Professional education and training schemes will need to be updated from time to time and extended beyond initial accreditation.

The reflective practitioner model of professionalism is grounded in a very different understanding of the nature of social change to the infallible expert model. When change is discontinuous and unpredictable, human and social problems have no stable definitions and explanations. 'Understandings' become 'situated', 'personal', 'controversial' and 'negotiable' through dialogue with others. In the absence of stable, fixed frameworks and categories for understanding human situations, what constitutes relevant and usable knowledge itself becomes problematic and a subject for shared reflection and dialogue with clients.

Rather than operating as an infallible source of relevant knowledge, the role of the reflective practitioner is to participate in a process of collaborative problem solving through which the relevance and usefulness of his/her specialist knowledge can be determined and new knowledge acquired. Knowledge acquisition becomes an integral dimension of situational problem solving. The practice itself is a form of learning which some have come to call action research [see Readings 3.1–3.5]. Professional learning in this context is a dimension of practice, rather than a segregated off-the-job activity.

From the perspective of the 'infallible expert' model, the acquisition of knowledge and the development of competence are two rather different processes. Knowledge can be acquired off the job, while competence can only be fully developed through direct experiences. Competence consists of the ability to apply knowledge in ways which generate correct practical responses to a situation. This ability is acquired by learning through experience to recognize applications of knowledge drawing on the commonsense stereotypes that have evolved as part of the professional culture and which are mediated by its 'guardians'. Although 'knowing that' is the foundation on which competent 'know-how' is built, one does not test knowledge directly in assessing competence. One assesses competence in terms of pre-specified performance outcomes and then infers adequate knowledge from such evidence. Direct testing for 'knowing that' and assessing competence or 'know-how' are quite separate activities.

From the perspective of the reflective practitioner model professional competence consists of the ability to act intelligently in situations which are sufficiently novel and unique to require what constitutes an appropriate response to be learned *in situ*. Competence cannot be defined simply in terms of an ability to apply pre-ordained categories of specialist knowledge to produce correct behavioural responses. Within this model of professionalism, stereotypical applications of knowledge are to be avoided and this implies that any attempt to pre-specify correct behavioural responses, or 'performance indicators' is a constraint on intelligent practice. We have to speak, instead, of qualitative indicators, i.e. of those qualities of judgement and decision-making which are indicative of capacities to make wise and intelligent responses in novel and unpredictable situations.

Let us look at some examples. The quality of open-mindedness manifests a capacity for understanding situations holistically, for looking at them from a variety of perspectives. Tactfulness in communicating with others manifests a capacity for empathy. Reflective and non-defensive responses to criticism manifest a capacity for self-monitoring. Exercising initiative in proposing, implementing and evaluating problem solutions manifests a capacity to take risks in the face of uncertainty, to believe in and trust oneself as an agent of change.

Within the 'reflective practitioner' model, competence involves the exercise of the kinds of human capacities cited in these examples. They are all capacities for intelligent problem-solving in the complex, dynamic and unpredictable social environment in which contemporary professionals practise.

The model of 'the new professionalism' I have outlined and contrasted with the model embedded in traditional practice has enormous implications for curriculum design in the area of professional education. For example, it implies:

— that all worthwhile professional learning is experiential, even the acquisition of relevant and useful knowledge;

— that the professional learning curriculum should essentially consist of the study of real practical situations which are problematic, complex and open to a variety of interpretations from different points of view;

— that a pedagogy to support professional learning should aim to provide opportunities for 'learners' to develop those capacities which are fundamental to competent reflective practice, e.g. for empathy with other participants' feelings and concerns, for self-reflection about one's own judgements and actions, for looking at a situation from a variety of angles and points of view, etc.;

— that the acquisition of knowledge should proceed interactively with reflecting about real practical situations.

READING 1.8

Competence and the complexities of teaching

James Calderhead

In this reading James Calderhead identifies five distinct areas of research on teaching and learning to teach and provides a concise overview of the main issues which have been considered. He summarizes by highlighting the complexity of teachers' work and warning against partial and over-simplified conceptions.

How do you feel this analysis relates to the competences listed in Reading 1.6?

Edited from: Calderhead, J. (1994) Can the complexities of teaching be accounted for in terms of competences? Contrasting views of professional practice from research and policy. Mimeo, ESRC seminar on teacher competence, 1–2

Within recent policy on teaching and teacher education, there has been a popular trend to consider issues of quality in teaching in terms of competences that can be pre-specified and continuously assessed. In particular, the competences that have received most attention have related to subject matter knowledge and classroom management skills [see Reading 1.6], a view which might be simplistically matched to the different responsibilities of higher education institutions and schools as closer working partnerships are formed in initial training. Such a view of teaching, however, is in sharp contrast to the complexity of teachers' work highlighted by empirical research on teaching over the past decade.

Research on teaching and learning to teach falls into several distinct areas, each exploring different aspects of the processes of professional development amongst teachers, and each highlighting some of the influential factors involved.

Socialization into the professional culture

The material and ideological context in which teachers work has been found to be one of the major influences upon the ways in which teachers carry out their work. New teachers are greatly influenced by traditions, taken-for-granted practices and implicit beliefs within the school, and a powerful 'wash out effect' has been identified (see Zeichner & Gore, 1990). Socialization studies on professional development have succeeded in highlighting some of the complex interactions that occur between an individual's values, beliefs and practices and those of the school, and also the importance of the individual's capacity to negotiate and manoeuvre within a social system where there may well be several competing professional cultures. This raises issues concerning how student teachers might be appropriately prepared to work as members of teams or as individuals within institutions.

The development of knowledge and skills

This is perhaps the most often cited perspective on learning to teach which emphasizes the knowledge and skills that contribute to classroom practice. Studies comparing experienced and novice teachers have demonstrated how the experienced teacher often has a much more sophisticated understanding of their practice. The experienced teacher appears to have access to a wide range of knowledge that can be readily accessed when dealing with classroom situations and which can help in interpreting and responding to them. Recent research on teachers' subject matter knowledge also indicates that teachers, for the purposes of teaching, relearn their subject and also develop a new body of knowledge concerning the teaching of the subject – Shulman's 'pedagogical content knowledge' [see Reading 7.13]. Studies of novice and experienced teachers suggest that there is an enormous diversity of knowledge that the experienced teacher possesses, and that acquiring appropriate professional knowledge is often a difficult and extremely time-consuming process for the novice.

The moral dimension of teaching

Teaching as well as being a practical and intellectual activity is also a moral endeavour. Teaching involves caring for young people, considering the interests of children, preparing children to be part of a future society, and influencing the way in which they relate to each other and live. The ethic of caring has been claimed to be a central facet of teaching, often valued by teachers, parents and children, but frequently unacknowledged in discussions of professional development. Teaching in schools inevitably presents several moral dilemmas in the form of decisions about how to allocate time in the classroom, how to cater for individual needs, and how to maintain principles such as 'equality of opportunity'. How are teachers to be prepared for this?

The personal dimension of teaching

Several different aspects of the personal dimension have been emphasized in the research literature. First of all, teachers bring their own past experiences to bear on their interpretation of the teacher's task. Individual past experiences of school, of work, or parenting have been found to provide teachers with metaphoric ways of thinking about teaching that shape their professional reasoning and practice. Secondly, teachers' personalities are themselves an important aspect of teachers' work. In order to establish working relationships with children, to command their attention and respect and to ensure the smooth running of their classes, teachers' personalities are intrinsically involved. Part of the professional development of the novice teacher requires teachers to become aware of their personal qualities and how other people respond to them, so that they can take greater control in their interactions with others. Thirdly, evidence from research on teachers' life cycles suggests that people pass through different phases in their lives in which they adopt different perspectives on life and work, and experience different needs in terms of inservice support [e.g.: see Nias, Reading 4.1].

The reflective dimension of teaching

Notions of reflection have become extremely popular in recent discussions of teacher education. What reflection actually amounts to, however, is considerably less clear. Several notions of reflection are identifiable in the literature – reflection-in-action, reflection-on-action, deliberative reflection, etc. Attempts to generate greater levels of reflection amongst student teachers have taken many forms – reflective journals, action research, the use of theory and research evidence as analytical frameworks, etc. Creating a course that helps students to become more analytical about their practice and to take greater charge of their own professional development is a task with a number of inherent difficulties. For instance, how does the teacher educator reconcile their traditional role as a gatekeeper to the profession with that of mentor and facilitator of reflection? How is reflection fostered when in schools a much higher priority is given to immediate, spontaneous action rather than analysis and reflection? Efforts in this area, however, have stimulated enquiry into identifying the cognitive, affective and behavioural aspects of reflection: what are the skills, attitudes and conditions that promote reflection and enable greater levels of learning from experience to be achieved? [See Reading 3.7.]

Research on teaching and teachers' professional development points towards the complexity of teachers' work. Each of the dimensions discussed above identifies an important set of variables and provides a partial picture of the whole professional development process. Learning to teach involves the development of technical skills, as well as an appreciation of moral issues involved in education, an ability to negotiate and develop one's practice within the culture of the school, and an ability to reflect and evaluate both in and on one's actions.

Such a view of teaching is in sharp contrast to that promulgated in the current language of 'competences' and 'subject matter knowledge'.

CHAPTER 2

Social contexts, teachers and children

The six readings in this chapter indicate some of the ways in which the actions of individuals and groups reflect their circumstances but also contribute to the future of society. Some readings also suggest ways in which changes in education policies may occur.

Readings by Mills (2.1), Simon (2.2) and Giddens (2.3) focus on the relationship between individuals and society; and between biography and history. This leads towards a questioning of existing taken-for-granted structures, policies and assumptions: for they are seen as products of previous actions and circumstances rather than as being inevitable. Giddens considers these issues with reference to the complexities of 'modernity' and what he sees as a new emphasis on 'lifestyles'.

Bowe and Ball (2.4) provide an analysis of how educational policies are initially made, and are then reinterpreted by practitioners, whilst Barton and his colleagues (2.5) illustrate a policy formation process regarding teacher education.

Thomas (2.6) highlights some of the national variations which result from the different histories, cultures and policy-making processes within Europe.

The parallel chapter of *Reflective Teaching in the Primary School* looks at the same issues but in an alternative way. The 'social context' of education is analysed in terms of the concepts of ideology, culture, resources and accountability, as these influence schools. Teachers and pupils are then considered, both as individuals and as groups, with particular attention to how they act within their circumstances. There are many suggestions for further reading.

For other closely related material, see also the readings in Chapter 15 of this book.

READING 2.1

The sociological imagination

C. Wright Mills

This reading comes from a classic sociological text. Wright Mills focused on the interaction between individuals and society, and thus on the intersection of biography and history. Teachers have particular responsibilities because, though acting in particular historical contexts, we shape the biographies of many children and thus help to create the future. Mills poses several questions which can be used to think about our society and the role of education in it.

How do you think what you do today, may influence what others may do in the future?

Edited from: Mills, C. W. (1959) *The Sociological Imagination*. New York: Oxford University Press, 111–13

The sociological imagination enables its possessor to understand the larger historical scene in terms of its meaning for the inner life and the external career of a variety of individuals. It enables him to take into account how individuals, in the welter of their daily experience, often become falsely conscious of their social positions. Within that welter the framework of modern society is sought, and within that framework the psychologies of a variety of men and women are formulated. By such means the personal uneasiness of individuals is focused upon explicit troubles and the indifference of publics is transformed into involvement with public studies.

The first fruit of this imagination – and the first lessons of the social science that embodies it – is the idea that the individual can understand his own experience and gauge his own fate only by locating himself within his period, that he can know his own changes in life only by becoming aware of those of all individuals in his circumstances. In many ways it is a terrible lesson; in many ways a magnificent one. We do not know the limits of man's capacities for supreme effort or willing degradation, for agony or glee, for pleasurable brutality or the sweetness of reason. But in our time we have come to know that the limits of 'human nature' are frighteningly broad. We have come to know that every individual lives, from one generation to the next, in some society; that he lives out a biography, and that he lives it out within some historical sequence. By the fact of his living he contributes, however minutely, to the shaping of this society and to the course of its history, even as he is made by society and by its historical push and shove.

The sociological imagination enables us to grasp history and biography and the relations between the two within society. That is its task and its promise. To recognize this task and this promise is the mark of the classic social analyst. And it is the signal of what is best in contemporary studies of man and society.

No social study that does not come back to the problems of biography, of history, and of their intersections within a society, has completed its intellectual journey. Whatever the specific problems of the classic social analysts, however limited or however broad the features of social reality they have examined, those who have been imaginatively aware of the promise of their work have consistently asked three sorts of questions:

What is the structure of this particular society as a whole? What are its essential components, and how are they related to one another? Within it, what is the meaning of any particular feature for its continuance and for its change?

Where does this society stand in human history? What are the mechanics by which it is changing? What is its place within and its meaning for the development of humanity as a whole? How does any particular feature we are examining affect, and how is it affected by, the historical period in which it moves? And this period – what are its essential features? How does it differ from other periods? What are its characteristic ways of history-making?

What varieties of men and women now prevail in this society and in this period? And what varieties are coming to prevail? In what ways are they selected and formed, liberated and repressed, made sensitive and blunted? What kinds of 'human nature' are revealed in the conduct and character we observe in this society in this period? And what is the meaning for 'human nature' of each and every feature of the society we are examining?

 READING 2.2

Can education change society?

Brian Simon

> This reading by the eminent historian, Brian Simon, picks up on some of the issues raised by C. Wright Mills. Considering the question of education's impact on society, Simon is optimistic for the long term because of the capacities of people to act in the light of their direct, subjective experiences and thus to transform existing social structures. He uses the example of the introduction of comprehensive secondary education. However, we can see the introduction of Grant Maintained Schools in the 1990s as the result of a new 'balance of forces'. Similar struggles of interests and objectives undoubtedly affect primary education – as is evidenced by the readings on curriculum in Chapter 7.
>
> Edited from: Simon, B. (1985) *Does Education Matter?*. London: Lawrence and Wishart, 23–30

Insofar as man transforms his external world, and by changing it changes himself, the whole historical process must be accounted essentially educative – and indeed this is why it is illuminating to refer to education as the mode of development of human beings in society.

Of course, schools are now subjected to a great deal of criticism – it would be surprising if it were not so. And equally of course, the intentions of the pioneers who established them are not being realized in their pure form. It is worth noting, as significant for our thesis, that comprehensive secondary education was originally a grass roots movement in Britain, the first schools being established in the late 1940s or early 1950s by certain advanced local authorities in opposition to government policy and advice, whether that government was Labour (as it was from 1945 to 1951) or Tory (1951 to 1964). This movement arose, in this sense, from the experience of those subjected to the harsh, and apparently arbitrary, decisions about the future of children taken at an early age in order to fit them into the mould of a system erected to preserve what Geoffrey Best called 'the hierarchical social structure'. Experience shows that the establishment of a new system of this kind, which certainly embodies changed values and changed objectives, holding out the prospect of universal secondary education for the first time, is inevitably a hard and difficult process, disturbing deeply engrained vested interests and, for some, quite traumatic. Further, as is to be expected, a new system has to contend with practices and attitudes both deeply entrenched and reflecting the values and outlook of the obsolescent systems of the past. Here the role of examination systems is particularly important in that even today, in England, a threefold level of examination or non-examination still dominates the internal structures of schooling, placing severe restraints on the degree of transformation that may be achieved.

Modern education systems are an area where the interests and objectives of different social classes, strata and even groups meets and very often clash. Hence contradictions develop within these systems which have a degree, as is now generally accepted, of relative autonomy. In this situation, as the historical record makes clear, there is scope for a variety of solutions; which of these will be successful depending on the balance of forces at any particular time.

So we return to the initial question – Can education change society? My own answer to this question is in the affirmative – especially if one takes the long view.

Contemporary theorizing and empirical studies on these issues are both seriously misleading and, in many ways, shortsighted. They ignore human subjective experience – people's capacity for movement, for acting on the environment, transforming it, and so for self-change. It is this process which is educative, and profoundly so. And it is this which we need to take into account when seeking an answer to our question. There is no joy here for the fatalists who claim that all such action is futile. On the contrary the future is open and undecided; and it is, I suggest, of supreme importance that those closely involved in education recognize, and struggle consistently to realize, its potential.

 READING 2.3

Emancipatory and life politics

Anthony Giddens

> Anthony Giddens is probably the most influential modern sociologist in the UK. Here he considers the relationship of self and society through two forms of politics. 'Emancipatory politics' is a traditional form and could be illustrated by Brian Simon's earlier reading (2.2). It seeks to equalize life chances. However, Giddens argues that the 'modernity' of present society produces a new form of 'life politics' which is associated with lifestyle and self-actualization in the global context. The self-identity of each individual, be they teacher, parent, inspector or pupil, is developed through social life and also informs processes of change. The personal is political; lifestyle is social action; and education is an important site in which the challenges posed by the modern world are encountered.
>
> Reading 4.8 is an account of an individual's struggle for identity and could usefully be related to this analysis.
>
> Edited from: Giddens, A. (1991) *Modernity and Self-Identity*. Cambridge: Polity Press, 210–31.

I define emancipatory politics as a generic outlook concerned above all with liberating individuals and groups from constraints which adversely affect their life chances. Emancipatory politics involves two main elements: the effort to shed shackles of the past, thereby permitting a transformative attitude towards the future; and the aim of overcoming the illegitimate domination of some individuals or groups by others.

Emancipatory politics works with a hierarchical notion of power: power is understood as the capability of an individual or group to exert its will over others. It is concerned to reduce or eliminate exploitation, inequality and oppression. Exploitation in general presumes that one group – say, upper as compared to working-classes, whites as compared to blacks, or men as compared to women – illegitimately monopolizes resources or desired goods to which the exploited group is denied access. Inequalities can refer to any variations in scarce resources, but differential access to material rewards has often been given prime importance. Unlike inequalities in genetic inheritance, for instance, differential access to material rewards forms part of the generative mechanisms of modernity, and hence can in principle (not, of course, in practice) be transformed to any desired degree. Oppression is directly a matter of differential power, applied by one group to limit the life changes of another. Like other aspects of emancipatory politics, the aim to liberate people from situations of oppression implies the adoption of moral values.

Since emancipatory politics is concerned above all with overcoming exploitative, unequal or oppressive social relations, its main orientation tends to be 'away from' rather than 'towards'. In other words, the actual nature of emancipation is given little flesh, save as the capacity of individuals or groups to develop their potentialities within limiting frameworks of communal constraint.

Life politics presumes a certain level of emancipation: emancipation from the fixities of tradition and from conditions of hierarchical domination. While emancipatory politics is a politics of life changes, life politics is a politics of lifestyle. Life politics is the politics of a reflexively mobilized order – the system of late modernity – which, on an individual and collective level, has radically altered the existential parameters of social activity. It is a politics of self-actualization in a reflexively ordered environment, where that reflexivity links self and body to systems of global scope. In this arena of activity, power is generative rather than hierarchical. To give a formal definition; life politics concerns political issues which flow from processes of self-actualization in post-traditional contexts, where globalizing influences intrude deeply into the reflexive project of the self, and conversely where processes of self-realization influence global strategies.

Emancipatory politics	Life politics
1 The freeing of social life from the fixities of tradition and custom.	1 Political decisions flowing from freedom of choice and generative power.
2 The reduction or elimination of exploitation, inequality or oppression. Concerned with the divisive distribution of power/resources.	2 The creation of morally justifiable forms of life that will promote self-actualization in the context of global interdependence.
3 Obeys imperatives suggested by the ethics of justice, equality and participation.	3 Develops ethics concerning the issue 'how should we live?' in a post-traditional order and against the backdrop of existential questions.

Life politics, to repeat, is a politics of life decisions. What are these decisions and how should we seek to conceptualize them?

First and foremost, there are those affecting self-identity itself. Self-identity today is a reflexive achievement. The narrative of self-identity has to be shaped, altered and reflexively sustained in relation to rapidly changing circumstances of social life, on a local and global scale. The individual must integrate information deriving from a diversity of mediated experiences with local involvements in such a way as to connect future projects with past experiences in a reasonably coherent fashion. Only if the person is able to develop an inner authenticity – a framework of basic trust by means of which the lifespan can be understood as a unity against the backdrop of shifting social events – can this be attained. A reflexively ordered narrative of self-identity provides the means of giving coherence to the finite lifespan, given changing external circumstances. Life politics from this perspective concerns debates and contestations deriving from the reflexive project of the self.

In the broader sense of politics, life-political issues permeate many areas of social life in later modernity. For numerous spheres of choice on the individual level and collectively are opened up by the extension of abstract systems and the socialization of natural processes. Social movements have played a basic role in bringing life-political issues to the fore, and forcing them on public attention. Whether such movements are harbingers of organizational changes in the domains of political activity is a moot question. In late modernity, where reflexive attempts to colonize the future are more or less universal, many types of individual action and organizational involvement might shape life-political issues. Life-political problems do not fit readily within existing frameworks of politics, and may well stimulate the emergence of political forms which differ from those hitherto prominent, both within states and on a global level.

The emergence of life politics results from the centrality of the reflexive project of the self in late modernity, coupled to the contradictory nature of the extension of modernity's internally referential systems. The capability of adopting freely chosen lifestyles, a fundamental benefit generated by a post-traditional order, stands in tension, not only with barriers to emancipation, but with a variety of moral dilemmas. No one should underestimate how difficult it will be to deal with these, or even how hard it is to formulate them in ways likely to command widespread consensus. How can we remoralize social life without falling prey to prejudice? The more we return to existential issues, the more we find moral disagreements; how can these be reconciled? If there are no transhistorical ethical principles, how can humanity cope with clashes of 'true believers' without violence? Responding to such problems will surely require a major reconstruction of emancipatory politics as well as the pursuit of life-political endeavours.

 READING 2.4

Three contexts of policy making

Richard Bowe and Stephen Ball, with Ann Gold

> The authors of this reading provide a framework for thinking about the policy-making process. They describe policy as a 'discourse' and as 'a set of claims about how the world should be and might be' and see it as contested by different social groups. Three contexts in which this takes place are identified, including the context of practice in which practitioners mediate, interpret and recreate the meaning of policy texts. Reading 15.7 by Pollard, Broadfoot, Croll, Osborn and Abbot suggests how this happened in the case of the introduction of the National Curriculum into primary schools.
>
> How does the analysis relate to the latest national policy to affect schools?
>
> Edited from: Bowe, R. and Ball, S. with Gold. A. (1992) *Reforming Education and Changing Schools*. London: Routledge, 13–23

We approach policy as a discourse, constituted of possibilities and impossibilities, tied to knowledge on the one hand (the analysis of problems and identification of remedies and goals) and practice on the other (specification of methods for achieving goals and implementation). We see it as a set of claims about how the world should and might be, a matter of the 'authoritative allocation of values'. Policies are thus the operational statements of values, statements of 'prescriptive intent'. They are also, as we conceive it, essentially contested in and between the arenas of formation and 'implementation'.

We envisage three primary policy contexts, each context consisting of a number of arenas of action, some public, some private.

The first context, the *context of influence*, is where public policy is normally initiated. It is here that policy discourses are constructed. It is here that interested parties struggle to influence the definition and social purposes of education, what it means to be educated. The private arenas of influence are based upon social networks in and around the political parties, in and around Government and in and around the legislative process. Here key policy concepts are established (e.g. market forces, National Curriculum, opting out, budgetary devolution), they acquire currency and credence and provide a discourse and lexicon for policy initiation. This kind of discourse forming is sometimes given support, sometimes challenged by wider claims to influence in the public arenas of action, particularly in and through the mass media. In addition there are a set of more formal public arenas; committees, national bodies, representative groups which can be sites for the articulation of influence. Clearly in trying to understand the education policy-making of the last three Conservative Governments it is important to be aware of the considerable 'capture' of influence by the New Right think tanks that operated in and around the Conservative Party. But it is also vital to appreciate the ebb and flow in the fortunes of and the changes in personnel of the DES, and to recognize the increasing 'ministerialization' of policy initiation. As we noted earlier, this contrasts starkly with the virtual exclusion of union and local authority representatives from arenas of influence and the much diminished and discredited contribution from the educational establishment.

This context of influence has a symbiotic but none the less uneasy relation to the second context, *the context of policy text production*. Because while influence is often related to the articulation of narrow interests and dogmatic ideologies, policy texts are normally articulated in the language of general public good. Their appeal is based upon claims to popular (and populist) commonsense and political reason. Policy texts therefore represent policy. These representations can take various forms: most obviously 'official' legal texts and policy documents; also formally and informally produced commentaries which offer to 'make sense of' the 'official' texts, again the media is important here; also the speeches by and public performances of relevant politicians and officials; and 'official' videos are another recently popular medium of representation. Many of those towards whom policy is aimed rely on these secondhand accounts as their main source of information and understanding of policy as intended. But two key points have to be made about these ensembles of texts which represent policy. First, the ensembles and the individual texts are not necessarily internally coherent or clear. The expression of policy is fraught with the possibility of misunderstanding, texts are generalized, written in relation to idealizations of the 'real world', and can never be exhaustive, they cannot cover all eventualities. The texts can often be contradictory, they use key terms differently, and they are reactive as well as expository (that is to say, the representation of policy changes in the light of events and circumstances and feedback from arenas of practice). Policy is not done and finished at the legislative moment, it evolves in and through the texts that represent it, texts have to be read in relation to the time and the particular site of their production. They also have to be read with and against one another – intertextuality is important. Second, the texts themselves are the outcome of struggle and compromise. The control of the representation of policy is problematic. Control over the timing of the publication of texts is important. A potent and immediate example of struggle in arenas of text production is that which goes on in relation to National Curriculum working party reports. Groups of actors working within different sites of text production are in competition for control of the representation of policy. Most of these struggles go on behind closed doors but occasional glimpses of the dynamics of conflict are possible. What is at stake are attempts to control the meaning of policy through its representation.

Policies then are textual interventions but they also carry with them material constraints and possibilities. The responses to these texts have 'real' consequences. These consequences are experienced within the third main context, *the context of practice*, the arena of practice to which policy refers, to which it is addressed.

The key point is that policy is not simply received and implemented within this arena rather it is subject to interpretation and then 'recreated'.

Practitioners do not confront policy texts as naive readers, they come with histories, with experience, with values and purposes of their own, they have vested interests in the meaning of policy. Policies will be interpreted differently as the histories, experiences, values, purposes and interests which make up any arena differ. The simple point is that policy writers cannot control the meanings of their texts. Parts of texts will be rejected, selected out, ignored, deliberately misunderstood, responses may be frivolous, etc. Furthermore, yet again, interpretation is a matter of struggle. Different interpretations will be in contest, as they relate to different interests, one or other interpretation will predominate although deviant or minority readings may be important.

The policy process is one of complexity, it is one of policy-making and remaking. It is often difficult, if not impossible to control or predict the effects of policy, or indeed to be clear about what those effects are, what they mean, when they happen. Clearly, however, interpretations are not infinite, clearly also, as noted already, different material consequences derive from different interpretations in action. Practitioners will be influenced by the discursive context within which policies emerge. Some will have an eye to personal or localized advantage, material or otherwise, which may stem from particular readings of policy texts. But to reiterate, the meanings of texts are rarely unequivocal. Novel or creative readings can sometimes bring their own rewards.

READING 2.5

Teacher education and professionalism

Len Barton, Elizabeth Barrett, Geoff Whitty, Sheila Miles and John Furlong

This reading provides a good example of an area of contested policy in education. Len Barton and his colleagues review the ideas and interests which lay behind the deluge of new policies on teacher education in the early 1990s and the setting up of the Teacher Training Agency.

Was the move to more school-based courses really a way of enhancing professional training, or was it intended to reduce the status of teachers, restrict the nature of professionality and make new teachers more compliant? Now with the benefit of hindsight, you can consider what the effects actually were. The framework for policy analysis provided in the previous reading (2.4) may be helpful here.

Edited from: Barton, L., Barrett, E., Whitty, G., Miles, S. and Furlong, J. (1994) Teacher education and teacher professionalism in England: some emerging issues, *British Journal of Sociology of Education*, 15 (4), 529–31

During the 1980s, the various attempts to find new ways of training teachers had led to the development of a number of shortened courses, extended courses, and part-time courses. These early 'non-conventional' courses were mostly at the margins and designed to deal with specific teacher shortages rather than to change the pattern of mainstream teacher education, even though since 1985 all initial teacher education courses had been subjected to official scrutiny in relation to government-defined criteria administered by the Council for the Accreditation of Teacher Education (CATE). However, these innovations had been joined at the beginning of the 1990s by two potentially more radical schemes. One was the school-based Articled Teacher Scheme, where post-graduate trainee teachers were to spend 80% of their time in schools as supernumaries while still being registered as students at a higher education institution. In 1991, a DES News Circular maintained that:

> Articled teachers are pioneers of the school-based approach. It is an important experiment which should be put in perspective. The Government's aim is to provide a diversity of routes into teaching, offering a variety of choices to people with different skills, knowledge, experience, backgrounds and family circumstances. Taken together innovative, non-conventional routes to qualified teacher status (QTS) will soon account for more than 10% of the annual intake to initial teacher training. The articled teacher scheme is only one element in this.

The other scheme was the Licensed Teacher Scheme which involved actually filling a teaching vacancy with an unqualified teacher and giving him/her training on the job. The Licensed Teacher Scheme did not require trainees to register as students at a university, nor did it require them to be graduates. Furthermore, the training offered did not have to meet the same criteria as those imposed by CATE on courses administered by higher education institutions. As such it can be seen as reflecting a shift in Government policy, one which could by-pass higher education and develop on the job practical training.

In 1992, the Government announced that it planned to make mainstream postgraduate secondary courses 80% school based (DES, 1992), though it subsequently reduced this to 66% (DFE, 1992). It also proposed that teacher training institutions should transfer a significant part of their grant and fee income to schools in recompense for their enhanced contribution to the training process. Furthermore, the training in both higher education institutions and schools was expected to focus from the start on certain specified 'competencies of teaching' [see Reading 1.6]. Building on these changes to secondary teacher training, a Consultative Document on Primary Training was circulated in June 1993. This too included proposals for more school-based PGCE courses, 3 year B.Ed. courses to replace the current 4 year one, more 2 year B.Ed. courses for mature students and a 1 year course to enable non-graduates to teach 5–7 year olds. This last proposal was predicted on the assumption that early years teaching is low status whereby parenting skills are seen as an adequate basis for early years teaching. This inevitably came to be known by the media as the 'Mum's Army' and was subsequently dropped after widespread opposition, especially from teachers who interpreted the proposal as an attack on the professional status of teaching.

Further moves to shift initial teacher education and its funding from the control of higher education can be seen in the introduction of a pilot 'school-centred' training scheme (SCITT), beginning in September 1993 with government funding going directly to training schools rather than to higher education. Under this scheme it is entirely up to the schools as to whether they wish to involve higher education in their training activities.

Even more radical developments may follow from a further series of Government proposals circulated in Autumn 1993 (DFE, 1993), many of which were subsequently incorporated into the 1994 Education Act. At their centre is the Teacher Training Agency which will be responsible for the funding and accreditation of all teacher education courses in England (though not in Wales where different arrangements will exist). This will determine the distribution of places on courses and the allocation of grants for teacher training to schools as well as higher education institutions. The abolition of CATE and the removal of the funding of initial teacher education from the remit of the mainstream Higher Education Funding Council for England is seen by many observers as heralding a more substantial diversion of funds and courses into schools. The Government's determination to overturn a House of Lords' amendment that sought to ensure that all courses of training, including school-centred ones, should lead to a recognized university award was seen as a key signal of the Government's long-term intentions. By treating teacher education differently from that of those professions whose initial training is securely based in higher education, these developments may have important implications for the professional status of teaching. As Stuart Maclure remarked about just one of the recent attempts to shift responsibility for teacher education away from higher education institutions into schools:

The thing to remember about Government plans for teacher training is that there is a plot and a sub-plot. The plot is straightforward. Give practising teachers a bigger part to play in the professional preparation of their future colleagues. This is a good idea ... The sub-plot is more sinister. It is to take teacher training out of the universities and colleges and ultimately to sever the connection between the study of education in higher education and its practice in schools. This is a deeply damaging idea and must be fought tooth and nail ... the [proposals] must be examined closely for insidious attempts to dismantle the traditional defences of teaching as a profession. (Maclure, 1993)

Each of the successive reforms has been announced before earlier changes have been properly evaluated and they have all been accompanied by well-orchestrated media attacks on the role of higher education in teacher education. It is scarcely surprising then that many observers believe that, behind the rhetoric of enhancing the quality of the teaching force, the Major government is pursuing a wholesale transfer of teacher training out of higher education in order to incorporate teachers more effectively into the political ideological project of the New Right. The approach expressed in government circulars and directives may legitimate a model of the professional teacher in terms of a competent practitioner, able effectively to implement those policies advocated by the government of the day, thereby moving to a model of 'restricted' rather than 'extended' professionality (Hoyle, 1975). In view of this, we may consider how far the proposed changes in teacher education may be serving to dismantle and thus redefine the nature of teacher professionalism in ways that are more conducive to the political project of the New Right. This process of 'deprofessionalization' and 'reprofessionalization' of teaching involves a combination of measures to open up the market to new producers of qualified teachers and to foster a different ideology amongst new entrants to the profession.

 **READING 2.6**

European variations in primary education

Norman Thomas

> Policy-making processes in different countries reflect the particular circumstances, traditions and balance of social forces that obtains. As Norman Thomas shows, the result across Europe is considerable diversity even at the most general level of aims for primary education. The reading is also important for reminding us that 'the way we do it here' is not the only way in which it can be done. The case for comparative studies is a strong one. (See also Reading 14.9.)
>
> Edited from: Thomas, N. (1989) 'The aims of primary education in member states of the Council of Europe', in Galton, M. and Blyth, A. (eds) *Handbook of Primary Education in Europe*. London: David Fulton, 19–23

Across Europe there is considerable variation regarding the stress on development of pupils to the full, and on accepting priorities and constraints characteristic of the society that provides education. The issue is illuminated in many of the reports from member states. That from Iceland quotes an Act of Parliament on the needs for co-operation between home and school and for preparation for life in a modern democratic state. The Act requires that schools should 'endeavour to widen the children's horizon and develop their understanding of their environment, social conditions, the characteristics and history of Icelandic society and the obligations of the individual to society'. The periods of history to be covered in French primary schools have an understandably French bias. The Norwegian Basic School Act of 1969, as amended in 1975, requires the basic schools 'to help give the pupils a Christian and moral upbringing'. The Swedish curriculum 'reflects the view of the democracy on society and man, the implication being that human beings are active and creative and that they both can and must assume responsibility and seek knowledge in order to co-operate with others ...' The official aims of primary education in Turkey require schools to 'enable every Turkish child to acquire all the necessary basic knowledge, skills and habits required for effective citizenship and to raise him in a manner commensurate with national ethical concepts'. Children need to know that they must obey the rules of society as well as use them; contribute to social well-being as well as draw from it.

There are complications. No society is static, though some – world-wide – are more stable than others. It is not sufficient simply to act in accord with today's social practices and ambitions: everyone who can should assist in improving the general lot, socially and materially. As seen by the current providers – and there is no intention here to imply that any other stance could reasonably be expected at government level – the changes should be within limits that are acceptable to current society. In the words of the Icelandic Act: 'the school must foster independent thought and co-operative attitudes'.

The stimuli for change stem from different sources:

The acceptance and promotion of modern scientific and technological developments

It is no accident that the National Curriculum introduced in England and Wales in 1989 includes science as well as English and mathematics among its core subjects, and technology among its foundation subjects for primary schools. It is unlikely that science would have been given the same priority or technology have appeared at all for the primary stage even as recently as 20 years ago. Portugal also requires schools to keep pupils abreast of new scientific knowledge. The Netherlands Primary Education Act requires that science, including biology, is taught in primary schools, and the arrival of micro-computers in Netherlands' primary schools was heralded. In Malta, 'it is a fact that innovation was prompted by radical changes in contemporary society and the challenge children have to cope with owing to new discoveries in science and technology'.

Changes in the cultural, racial and religious make-up of the community

The populations of many countries of Western Europe have, in recent years, become far more mixed in culture, race and religion than they were. They contain a substantial number of families who speak languages and, to a marked degree, retain life-habits they brought with them from afar. Some children may speak little or none of the national language of the country when they first enter school. Those children may be concentrated in districts where they form a large part of the school population: almost 100 per cent in a small proportion of schools. In the city of Luxembourg, 55 per cent of school children are foreigners.

The main issues referred to in the aims of primary education in countries experiencing these changes relate, on the one hand, to the indigenous population and, on the other, to the ethnic minority groups. The minimum aim with regard to the indigenous population is, usually, that its members should exercise tolerance towards and understanding of the newcomers. They were, after all, permitted and even encouraged to enter the country to fill gaps in the existing workforce. Better still, the indigenous population should welcome the presence of the minority ethnic groups because of the skills and cultures they bring, not only in music, art and food, but also in richness of language. The presumption is that tolerance will grow as knowledge grows and contact between groups increases. For the minority groups the issues are often sharper. Maintenance of one's religion, culture and language contributes to one's sense of identity. However, individuals do not have a full range of opportunities open to them, in either education or employment unless they can speak and write the national language in its standard form. Generally speaking, provision is made, although there can be difficulties for children who enter the education system late. In Luxembourg, as in a number of other countries, special classes in the local language are set up for new entrants. In the United Kingdom, teachers may be specially funded and employed to assist children who have little or no English. In the Federal Republic of Germany, Turkish supplementary teachers are employed both to help children with their own language and to assist them when German is the language of instruction.

Political change

Where there have been marked changes in the political beliefs underpinning the government of a country, they are reflected in the strength of expression in some educational aims. In Spain and Portugal, recently emerged from authoritarian and nationalistic regimes, there is more than ordinary stress on children as citizens of the world and on the freedom of individuals and their rights, including the right to participate in decisions about their own lives as soon as they are ready.

Some differences within a country are regarded as necessary to the national character and supported through the school system. Notably they include the preservation and development of indigenous languages spoken by a minority of the population. In some countries there is a strong delegation of authority to local levels so that differences among them can be reflected, such as provision for the Sami population of Norway. The Foldeskoler in Denmark are encouraged to relate their curricula to local circumstances. In the Netherlands, Denmark and Norway, schools may be established that operate according to the preferred pedagogies of the founding group and be supported financially by the government. For example, a group may establish a school based on principles advocated by one or other of the educational pioneers such as Dalton, Montessori, Peter Peterson or Rudolf Steiner. Indeed, the same variety may be achieved within the different Länder in the Federal Republic of Germany. In the United Kingdom, it was the case that schools' curricula were settled locally, almost completely by the wishes of the head and teachers of the school, but that is no longer so since the National Curriculum was introduced in 1989.

Many countries have some schools that are sustained by fees charged to parents, or from charitable or other private funds, including voluntary contributions via the Church, Mosque or Synagogue. Schools serving particular religious foundations may also be grant-aided by a state.

Parents make contact with, influence and may take part in the conduct of a school, and in doing so, express opinions, offer advice and possibly take part in the appointment of staff. The precise mechanisms vary such as the combined parent/teacher group that makes up the French school board, and more informal discussions between parents and teachers. In countries such as Turkey, issues may be discussed by the elementary education councils established in villages.

The ethos and pedagogy of a school are frequently finely tuned to the needs of the community it serves, but schools must offer an education acceptable to the nation to which they belong. Schools, including primary schools, are tools of the community. Even those financed independently of the state are permitted to exist only in so far as what they do is tolerated by the nation as a whole. The point is clearly made in the case of Italy: 'all schools, state-controlled or otherwise, public or private, must comply with the national legislation decrees and regulations'.

Schools' conformity to national requirements may be achieved through the establishment of national criteria and inspection. Various systems of inspection operate and, with differences of balance from one country to another, they report (a) on the conduct of individual schools and (b) on the quality of the educational system as a whole.

CHAPTER 3

Investigating classrooms

There are seven readings in this chapter, the first four of which focus on aspects of teachers investigating and reflecting on their own classroom practice.

Stenhouse (3.1) provides a classic statement on how teachers can 'research' their own classroom practice, and Carr and Kemmis (3.2) use the concept of 'praxis' to emphasize the judgements and commitments which are involved. Webb (3.3) draws attention to the value of working collaboratively whilst Winter (3.4) identifies practical problems which often have to be faced.

The remaining readings are relatively free-standing. Bassey (3.5) offers a useful clarification of three approaches to educational research which are often found in the literature. Hopkins and Bollington (3.6) consider the significance of appraisal in professional development and school improvement. Finally, Tabachnick and Zeichner (3.7) investigate the concept of 'reflection' itself, and identify four specific emphases.

The parallel chapter of *Reflective Teaching in the Primary School* complements these readings. Designed to support enquiries into classroom practice, important approaches to research are introduced (cf. Reading 3.5) and key issues for planning a classroom enquiry are discussed. Finally, a comprehensive set of techniques for collecting data on classroom practice are described. There are also many suggestions for further reading.

📖 READING 3.1

The teacher as researcher

Lawrence Stenhouse

Lawrence Stenhouse led the Humanities Project during the late 1960s – curriculum development work which revolutionized thinking about professional development. One of his central concerns was to encourage teachers as 'researchers' of their own practice, thereby extending their professionalism. There is a strong link between the argument of this reading and Dewey's conception of 'reflection' (Reading 1.1).

Edited from: Stenhouse, L. (1975) *An Introduction to Curriculum Research and Development*. London: Heinemann, 143–57

All well-founded curriculum research and development, whether the work of an individual teacher, of a school, of a group working in a teachers' centre or of a group working within the co-ordinating framework of a national project, is based on the study of classrooms. It thus rests on the work of teachers.

It is not enough that teachers' work should be studied: they need to study it themselves. My theme is the role of the teacher as a researcher in his own teaching situation. What does this conception of curriculum development imply for him?

The critical characteristics of that extended professionalism which is essential for well-founded curriculum research and development seem to me to be:

The commitment to systematic questioning of one's own teaching as a basis for development;

The commitment and the skills to study one's own teaching;

The concern to question and to test theory in practice by the use of those skills.

To these may be added as highly desirable, though perhaps not essential, a readiness to allow other teachers to observe one's work directly or through recordings – and to discuss it with them on an open and honest basis. In short, the outstanding characteristic of the extended professional is a capacity for autonomous professional self-development through systematic self-study, through the study of the work of other teachers and through the testing of ideas by classroom research procedures.

It is important to make the point that the teacher in this situation is concerned to understand better his own classroom. Consequently, he is not faced with the problems of generalizing beyond his experience. In his context, theory is simply a systematic structuring of his understanding of his work.

Concepts which are carefully related to one another are needed both to capture and to express that understanding. The adequacy of such concepts should be treated as provisional. The utility and appropriateness of the theoretical framework of concepts should be testable; and the theory should be rich enough to throw up new and profitable questions.

Each classroom should not be an island. Teachers working in such a tradition need to communicate with one another. They should report their work. Thus a common vocabulary of concepts and a syntax of theory need to be developed. Where that language proves inadequate, teachers would need to propose new concepts and new theory.

The first level of generalization is thus the development of a general theoretical language. In this, professional research workers should be able to help.

If teachers report their own work in such a tradition, case studies will accumulate, just as they do in medicine. Professional research workers will have to master this material and scrutinize it for general trends. It is out of this synthetic task that general propositional theory can be developed.

 **READING 3.2**

Practical action as praxis

Wilfred Carr and Stephen Kemmis

> Carr and Kemmis have argued that action researchers should be prepared to be critical of existing arrangements and should consider the implications of their values, as well as seeking technical improvements. 'Praxis' is a concept which represents this argument: a combination of commitment and action. This is an important idea in a reconstructionist approach to reflection (see Reading 3.7).
>   To what extent do you think about the values which are embodied in your work, and the social consequences of it? (See Chapter 13.)
>
> Edited from: Carr, W. and Kemmis, S. (1986) *Becoming Critical: Education, Knowledge and Action Research.* London: Falmer Press, 190–2.

Personal knowledge develops in and through practice. 'Practice', in its commonsense meaning, is usually understood to refer to habitual or customary action. But it also means 'the exercise of an act', referring back to its origins in the Greek notion of praxis, meaning 'informed, committed action'. The action researcher distinguishes between practice as habitual or customary, on the one hand, and the informed, committed action of praxis, on the other. One way to describe the general aim of a critical educational science and of educational action research would be to say that both are interested in a critical revival of practice which can transform it into praxis, bringing it under considered critical control, and enlivening it with a commitment to educational and social values. The action researcher is interested in theorizing practice in the sense of setting practice in a critical framework of understanding which makes it rational, appropriate and prudent.

Praxis has its roots in the commitment of the practitioner to wise and prudent action in a practical, concrete, historical situation. It is action which is considered and consciously theorized, and which may reflexively inform and transform the theory which informed it. Praxis cannot be understood as mere behaviour; it can only be understood in terms of the understandings and commitments which inform it. Moreover, praxis is always risky; it requires that the practitioner makes a wise and prudent practical judgement about how to act in this situation. As Gauthier remarks, 'practical problems are problems about what to do, ... their solution is only found in doing something' (1963).

The significance of praxis is that it is a response to a real historical situation in which an actor is compelled to act on the basis of understanding and commitment. Further, the actor and others can judge the correctness of the practical judgement actually made in praxis: they can observe and analyse the actual historical consequences of the action. Praxis, as the action taken in action research, is thus both a 'test' of the actor's understandings and commitments and the means by which these understandings and commitments can be critically developed. Since only the practitioner has access to the understandings and commitments which inform action in praxis, only the practitioner can study praxis. Action research therefore cannot be other than research into one's own practice.

READING 3.3

Collaboration and action research

Rosemary Webb

In this reading Rosemary Webb draws attention to the importance of collaboration when carrying out action research. The support of others is necessary for individual activities but the potential of action research for whole-school co-ordinated development work is enormous.

How supportive is your own school towards this kind of work? See also the readings in Chapter 14.

Edited from: Webb, R. (1990) 'The processes and purposes of practitioner research', in Webb, R. (ed.) *Practitioner Research in the Primary School.* London: Falmer Press, 252–7

The main reason for carrying out practitioner research is to bring about changes in classroom practice and school policies.

Although research may be undertaken individually, practitioner research always involves others – pupils, teachers, parents, governors. It is always a collaborative undertaking in that to varying degrees data collection depends on the co-operation of the parties to the research problem. Access to data, the ways in which they will be collected, the uses to which they are put and ethical issues such as confidentiality and ownership of data have to be negotiated with those involved. Also, if the implications of school-based research are to be understood and their importance acknowledged and appropriately acted upon by members of staff other than those involved in the data collection, then they have to be kept informed of, or actively engaged in, the research project.

Cassidy (1986) claims that 'co-ordinated action research can be a powerful tool for generating school-wide curriculum change, the professional development of staff, and quite radical changes to the ethos of the school' (p.134). Shumsky (1956) views collaboration as essential both for the well-being of the researcher and the resulting quality of the thought and action. He identifies five major ways in which collaboration contributes to the success of practitioner research:

Working together on a common problem is a source of security, status and recognition.

The stimulation that comes from group contact helps to overcome inertia and self-defeatist attitudes.

The fear of failure is lessened and an attempt to embark on an intelligent action is more possible.

Group work is conducive to the release of potential creativity and in promoting social vision, inspiration and critical thinking.

A promising way of initiating and securing change is by involving the potential consumers of the research results in the planning, analysis and interpretation of the research data.

The message to those engaged in practitioner research, which aims to initiate and sustain change going beyond the individual classroom, is that if it is to have maximum impact an appropriate environment has to be created. Such an environment requires collaborative relationships to span hierarchies and enable ideas, information and decision-making to be shared throughout the institution. Besides being supportive it also needs to be capable of sustaining reflection that is both self-critical and critical of the school and the wider educational context and enables teachers 'to break out of the "survival" cycle'.

Increasingly there is a thrust towards creating operational contexts in schools which emphasize staff collaboration and participation in decision making and have the potential to create the kinds of conditions in which practitioner research can flourish. For example, in order to establish school curriculum development plans, schools are being asked to reflect corporately on where they are now, where they need to get to and how this might be accomplished.

The implementation of the National Curriculum has greatly increased the amount of collaborative curriculum planning and review that is taking place in primary schools. This can be viewed in a negative light as teachers uniting to assist each other through the stresses and strains of a current educational crisis. Alternatively, it may be viewed as a positive response to the challenge posed by the National Curriculum which is breaking down the 'individualist culture' of schools.

READING 3.4

Four practical problems

Richard Winter

Mindful of the practical realities of professional work, Richard Winter identifies four of the major difficulties faced by teachers who are committed to action research. Time is certainly the most obvious of these but the necessity for being openminded and rigorous in our enquiries is arguably just as challenging. It is important to remember that action research and reflective practice are proposed as forms of professional development, not as elements of a daily treadmill. It is important to be purposive and realistic about such activities.

Edited from: Winter, R. (1989) *Learning from Experience*. London: Falmer Press, 34–7

The first problem for practitioners is that of time. One important reason for the existence of a division of labour within professional work, between practitioners who do it and researchers who investigate it, is that most 'people processing' institutions (for example, schools, welfare agencies, hospitals) are notoriously underfunded, and consequently most professional workers are notoriously underfunded, and consequently most professional workers are notoriously overworked: after the work itself has been accomplished, one feels as though one has little time or energy left over for investigation, evaluation, or innovation, even though one might agree in principle that these elements ought to be an integral part of the professional role. So the problem of time is as follows: can we formulate a method of work which is sufficiently economical (as regards the amount of data gathering and data processing) for a practitioner to undertake it alongside a normal workload over a limited timescale?

We have also already hinted at the second problem: how can a small-scale investigation by a practitioner lead to genuinely new insights? Only if it does so can the time and energy spent on it be justified. Experienced practitioners approach their work with a vast and complex array of concepts, theoretical models, provisional explanations, typical scenarios, anticipations of likely alternatives, etc. These are developed 'naturally' in the course of professional practice, since professional work is essentially complex, consisting as it does of subtle interpersonal interactions requiring the continuous exercise of interpretive skill and flexibility. A 'research' process must demonstrably offer something over and above this pre-existing level of understanding. We need therefore to establish a clear difference of procedure between gathering and analysing the data generated through professional practice, and the procedures of professional practice itself. Otherwise the outcomes of practitioners' action-research may well meet such taunts as: 'We knew that already', 'We're doing that already', or, more precisely: 'Is that all action-research is? Gathering and analysing data? We do that every day of our lives'. In a word: action-research procedures need to be specific.

However, we then run up against the third problem, because it is important that we do not specify the action-research approach in such a way that it appears to require prior possession of, say, a social science degree. Methods for an investigative stance must be clearly differentiated from methods for practice, and yet they must be readily available to anyone who wishes to adopt them. They must build upon the competencies which practitioners already possess; action-research procedures, then, need to be accessible.

But there is a final practical question, namely: why bother? Having agreed that practitioners already possess a great fund of expertise, in the form of their normal competences, and having also agreed that time and energy are scarce, we need to be able to argue convincingly that action research can contribute a genuine improvement of understanding and skill, beyond that prior competence, in return for the time and energy expended. Action-research needs, in other words, some sound basis for claiming 'validity'. But 'validity' is a dangerous word. Unless we are continuously alert we are likely to slip into its positivist sense, meaning that our understanding is either generalizable, or replicable, or a correct representation of an external world. Even supposing, for a second, that such claims could plausibly be made about positivist research findings, we have already seen that limitations of time and data preclude practitioner action-researchers from formulating their claims along these lines. To avoid misunderstanding, therefore, let us say that the practical problem is not so much: 'How can we ensure that our findings are valid?' but rather: 'How can we ensure that our procedures are rigorous?' In making this shift, the action-researcher avoids the unanswerable question as to whether an interpretation 'coincides with reality' – unanswerable for the simple reason that we can never perceive reality except by means of one interpretation or another – and adopts instead the cautious attitude of the doctor, the lawyer, and the priest, who do not guarantee a successful outcome, but offer an assurance that well established principles will be carefully applied. Indeed, many of the more thoughtful commentators on the methodology of the natural sciences would not be willing to press their claims much further than this. So, if action-research procedures are systematically grounded in justifiable and coherent principles (i.e. if they are 'rigorous') then we shall have grounds for thinking that the conclusions we come to will be more than the result of personalities, emotions, or expediency.

Here then are four crucial practical questions.

How can action-research procedures be economical?

How can action-research procedures be specific?

How can action-research procedures be accessible?

How can action-research procedures be rigorous?

READING 3.5

Three paradigms of educational research

Michael Bassey

Michael Bassey has the ability to take complex ideas and express them with exceptional directness and clarity. In the reading below, he provides this service to explain the three 'paradigms' from which most educational enquiries are derived; positivist, interpretive and action research. Many of the other readings in this book could be categorized in these terms. For instance, Reading 5.7 reflects a form of positivist approach, 5.3 an interpretive approach and 6.10 an action research perspective (see also *Reflective Teaching in the Primary School*, Chapter 3, section 1).

Edited from: Bassey, M. (1990), Creating education through research, *Research Intelligence* (Autumn), 40–44

A research paradigm is a network of coherent ideas about the nature of the world and of the functions of researchers which, adhered to by a group of researchers, conditions the patterns of their thinking and underpins their research actions. Sometimes the network of a paradigm is so strong in the minds of its practitioners that they may deny the validity of other paradigms.

The present attempt at description distinguishes between the positivist research paradigm, the interpretive research paradigm and the action research paradigm.

The positivist research paradigm

To the positivist there is a reality 'out there' in the world that exists irrespective of people. This reality is discovered by people using their senses and observing. Discoveries about the reality of the world can be expressed as factual statements – statements about things, about events, and about relationships between them. To the positivist the world is rational, it makes sense, and, given sufficient time and effort, it should be possible for it to be understood through patient research. The researcher can then explain the reality he/she has discovered to others, because language is an agreed symbolic system for describing reality.

Positivist researchers do not expect that they themselves are significant variables in their research; thus in testing an hypothesis, they expect other researchers to come to the same conclusion that they find. Because of this, positivists preferred method of writing reports is to avoid personal pronouns, 'I' or 'me' is not considered relevant.

To the positivist (as with the interpretive researcher) the purpose of research is to describe and understand the phenomena of the world and to share this understanding with others. Understanding enables one to explain how particular events occur and to predict what will be the outcome of future events.

Positivists usually seek to express their understandings in the form of generalizations, i.e., general statements. The data collected by positivists tends to be numerical and suitable for statistical analysis; hence their methodology is often described as quantitative.

The word 'positivist' is not always recognized by those who work within this paradigm and sometimes is used pejoratively by those engaged in alternative paradigms. In return it is sometimes the case that the positivist researchers reject the idea that an enquiry into a singularity – such as interpretive researchers and action researchers may engage in – can be deemed to be useful research.

Researchers in the sciences, particularly chemistry and physics, are archetype positivists, but this paradigm is also important in education.

The interpretive research paradigm

The interpretive researcher cannot accept the idea of there being a reality 'out there' which exists irrespective of people, for reality is a construct of the human mind. People perceive and so construe the world in ways which are often similar but not necessarily the same. So there can be different interpretations of what is real. Concepts of reality can vary from one person to another. Instead of reality being 'out there', it is the observers who are 'out there'. They are part of the world which they are observing and so, by observing, may change what they are trying to observe. The interpretive researcher sees language as a more-or-less agreed symbolic system, in which different people may have some differences in their meanings; in consequence the sharing of accounts of what has been observed is always to some extent problematic. Because of differences in perception, in interpretation and in language it is not surprising that people have different views on what is real.

Interpretive researchers reject the positivists' view that the social world can be understood in terms of casual relationships expressed in universal generalizations. To them human actions are based on social meanings, such as beliefs and intentions. People living together interpret the meanings of each other, and these meanings change through social intercourse.

Interpretive researchers recognize that by asking questions or by observing they may change the situation which they are studying. They recognize themselves as potential variables in the enquiry and so, in writing reports, may use personal pronouns.

To the interpretive researcher the purpose of research is to describe and interpret the phenomena of the world in attempts to get shared meaning with others. Interpretation is a search for deep perspectives on particular events and for theoretical insights. It may offer possibilities, but no certainties, as to what may be the outcome of future events. The word 'hermeneutics' is some-times used to describe work in this paradigm. It means the art of interpretation.

Interpretive researchers inevitably study singularities, but they differ in their views on the extent to which the collated evidence from many singularities can be expressed in the form of generalizations.

The data collected by interpretive researchers is usually verbal – fieldwork notes and transcripts of conversation. Sometimes this can be analysed numerically but more usually it is not open to the quantitative statistical analysis used by positivists. Hence it is described as qualitative.

Historians and anthropologists are the archetype interpretive researchers. Historians try to interpret the past in relation to the understandings of today; anthropologists try to interpret other cultures in relation to the understandings of their own society.

Ethnography is an important branch of the interpretive paradigm, concerned with partici-pant observation – where the observer is not 'a fly on the wall', but becomes a participant in the activity which she/he is studying. Phenomenology and ethnomethodology are alternative terms for the interpretive paradigm.

The action research paradigm

The positivist paradigm and the interpretive paradigm both involve the idea of observers try-ing to describe the phenomena of their surroundings. The action research paradigm is about actors trying to improve the phenomena of their surroundings. That isn't the way that most action researchers choose to express their purposes, but it puts their paradigm into the con-text of the other two paradigms.

Action research in education has blossomed in the last ten years. Inevitably different people define it in different ways, but the universally agreed characteristic, is that it is research designed to improve action. Sometimes this is expressed as 'to enhance the quality of action'. Theory is created not as an end to itself, but in order to advance practice. The topics of enquiry, methods of data collection, analytical techniques, and styles of presenting findings reflect the pragmatic needs of teachers, the intended audience may be no one other than the teacher researcher him/herself, but is more likely to be fellow teachers engaged in similar teaching. The researcher in this kind of enquiry may find little in the education literature to guide his/her enquiries and may need to invent procedures grounded in classroom practice in order to pursue the research.

The intention to improve practice often results in action research being cyclical, because striving for improvement is seen by many practitioners (teachers, social workers, managers, etc.) as an ongoing professional commitment.

Because action research entails an intention to change action involving people, it is seen by those who practise it to demand not only a strong ethic of respect for persons, but also to demand democratic involvement of the people on whom it impinges. Thus negotiation about the ownership of data and about the uses that the researcher may put it to, are deemed important.

Action research in education is grounded in school and classroom practice, and does not have an established theoretical background which can provide a framework for testing the validity of new findings. In its place action researchers have recognized the importance of criticism as a means of testing whether findings represent what they purport to represent. Action researchers aim to leave themselves open to criticism – meaning that they reckon to make the raw data of their enquiries available for criticism. The concept of the 'critical friend' has been developed by action researchers, meaning someone who responds to the invitation to invest some time and effort into critically examining one's action research findings, and who agrees to work within the ethical framework of the enquiry – which defines matters such as the ownership of data.

 READING 3.6

Teacher appraisal

David Hopkins and Robert Bollington

> Processes of teacher appraisal can contribute significantly to professional development. However, David Hopkins and Robert Bollington begin by highlighting the tension between this, and public concerns with accountability which also bear on teachers. Various elements of the appraisal process are considered but the article has been edited to focus on the 'appraisal interview' because of its central importance.
>
> Edited from: Hopkins, D. and Bollington, R. (1989) Teacher appraisal for professional development: a review of research, *Cambridge Journal of Education*, **19** (2), 165–79

In the UK, concerns for quality, accountability and cost-effectiveness can be traced back to James Callaghan's Ruskin speech and the Great Debate which followed [see Reading 7.7]. Government views on the need for teacher appraisal emerged and developed within this climate (DES, 1983, 1985). However, the school review or self-evaluation movement also helped create a situation where the review of teachers followed the review of their schools. A significant step was the ACAS Report of the Appraisal/Training Working Group (ACAS, 1986). This group saw appraisal as:

> a continuous and systematic process intended to help individual teachers with their professional development and career planning, and to help ensure that the in-service training and deployment of teachers matches the complementary needs of individual teachers and the schools. (p. 2)

	Improvement purpose	Accountability purpose
Individual level	Individual staff development	Individual personnel decisions, e.g. job status
Organizational level	School improvement	School status decisions, e.g. accountability

Wise *et al.* (1985) depicted 'accountability' and 'improvement' purposes of appraisal at both individual and organization levels. They argued that while appraisal schemes often serve more than one purpose 'a single teacher evaluation process can serve only one goal well'.

It has become relatively common to contrast schemes aimed at development or improvement with those serving accountability or management purposes.

There are a number of components of the appraisal process: preparation and climate setting, training, criteria in appraisal, data gathering, the appraisal interview and development. However, the appraisal interview is the most prominent feature of a scheme. It offers an opportunity to review past performance and agree future plans: as such it serves as a focal point in a wider process. Drawing from a review of the literature on appraisal interviewing, Gill (1977, p. 55) suggests that the following are linked to success in such interviews:

a high level of subordinate participation in the appraisal process;

a helpful and constructive attitude (as opposed to a critical one) on the part of the appraiser;

a problem solving approach by the interviewer (as opposed to a 'tell and sell' style);

participation by the employee in setting any specific goals to be achieved.

The following suggestions are made in *Those Having Torches* (Suffolk Education Authority, p. 6):

The appraiser should create a climate in which genuine dialogue can take place. The conditions for the interview should be comfortable, quiet and uninterrupted. Adequate time should be allocated for the interview and it should begin with the teacher's view of his/her performance during the past year. Attention should be focused upon past successes and the data available should also be used to help indicate areas for improvement including ways by which this might be achieved. The teacher's interests and aspirations should be given attention, and the discussion should then move into a consideration of suitable targets for the following year. Above all, the focus should be on performance in the defined job rather than on personality.

What comes across is the need to set a summative appraisal interview, alongside more frequent, on-going feedback and dialogue. Adair (1983, p. 123), for example, stresses that 'you should see the formal system as at best a safety net for a process that should be going on continually'.

The literature thus offers some advice and guidelines for the conduct of appraisal interviews. However, the problem in applying the advice is that of integrating the various approaches into a particular school climate and management style. Such advice has to be applied with regard to the preferred leadership style of a head, the attitudes of the staff, the nature of the tasks each teacher carries out, and the credibility of those who will be appraisers. Compromises may be needed, especially in the short term.

An appraisal scheme for professional development will necessarily have the appraisal interview as the central focus in a cycle of appropriate preparation and follow up. Such a process would, among other things, involve the co-operative setting and achieving of goals; reflect a high level of commitment from the school, LEA and community; and emphasize the active involvement of teachers particularly in setting criteria and establishing the rhythm of the process. The spirit and values underlying the process are arguably more important than the specific activities themselves. Fundamentally, such an appraisal system will need to assume the characteristics of a continuing professional development activity, not simply be a precursor to INSET.

 READING 3.7

Reflections on reflective teaching

Robert Tabachnick and Kenneth Zeichner

Is 'reflection' just a new buzz-word? This reading reviews four different traditions of reflective teaching which have been identified in North America (the academic, the social efficiency, the developmental and the social reconstructionist) echoes of which can certainly be found elsewhere. Indeed, the influence of each tradition can be seen in the selection of readings for this book.

Do you feel that these emphases are opposed or complementary?

Edited from: Tabachnik, R. and Zeichner, K. (eds) *Issues and Practices in Inquiry-Oriented Teacher Education.* London: Falmer Press, 1–9

In the last decade, concurrent with the growth of research on teacher thinking and with the increased respect for teachers' practical theories (Clark, 1988), the 'reflective practitioner' has emerged as the new *zeitgeist*. There is not a single teacher educator who would say that he or she is not concerned about preparing teachers who are reflective. The criteria that have become attached to reflective practice are so diverse, however, that important differences between specific practices are masked by the use of the common rhetoric.

On the one hand, the recent work of teacher educators such as Cruickshank (1987), who has drawn upon Dewey [see Reading 1.1] for inspiration, gives us some guidance. The distinction that is often made between reflective and routine practice is not trivial and enables us to make some important qualitative distinctions among different teachers and teaching practices. Similarly, the enormously popular work of Schon [see Reading 1.2] which has challenged the dominant technical rationality in professional education and argued for more attention to promoting artistry in teaching by encouraging 'reflection in action' and 'reflection on action' among teachers, also directs our attention to the preparation of particular kinds and not others. These generic approaches to reflective teaching lose their heuristic value, however, after a certain point and begin to hide more than they reveal.

After we have agreed with Cruickshank and Schon, for example, that thoughtful teachers who reflect about their practice (on and in action) are more desirable than thoughtless teachers, who are ruled primarily by tradition, authority and circumstance, there are still many unanswered questions. Neither Cruickshank nor Schon have much to say, for example, about what it is that teachers ought to be reflecting about, the kinds of criteria that should come into play during the process of reflection (e.g. which help distinguish acceptable from unacceptable educational practice) or about the degree to which teachers' deliberations should incorporate a critique of the institutional contexts in which they work. In some extreme cases, the impression is given that as long as teachers reflect about something, in some manner, whatever they decide to do is all right since they have reflected about it.

One way in which we can think about differences among proposals for reflective teaching is in light of different traditions of practice in teacher education. Zeichner and Liston (1990) have identified four varieties of reflective teaching practice based on their analysis of traditions of reform in twentieth-century US teacher education:

an academic version that stresses reflection upon subject matter and the representation and translation of subject matter knowledge to promote student understanding (Shulman, 1987) [see Reading 7.13];

a social efficiency version that emphasizes the thoughtful application of particular teaching strategies that have been suggested by research on teaching (Ross and Kyle, 1987) [see Chapters 9, 10, 11 and 12 for examples];

a developmentalist version that prioritizes teaching that is sensitive to students' interests, thinking and patterns of developmental growth (Duckworth, 1987) [see parts of Chapter 6 and Reading 7.6]; and

a social reconstructionist version that stresses reflection about the social and political context of schooling and the assessment of classroom actions for their ability to contribute toward greater equity, social justice and humane conditions in schooling and society (Beyer, 1988; Maher and Rathbone, 1986) [see Readings 2.1 and 3.2].

In each of these views of reflective teaching practice, certain priorities are established about schooling and society that emerge out of particular historical traditions and educational and social philosophies.

None of these traditions is sufficient by itself for providing a moral basis for teaching and teacher education. Good teaching and teacher education need to attend to all of the elements that are brought into focus by the various traditions: the representation of subject matter, student thinking and understanding, teaching strategies suggested by research conducted by university academics and classroom teachers, and the social contexts of teaching. These elements do not take the same form, however, or receive the same emphasis within each tradition.

The academic tradition of reflective teaching

The academic tradition has historically emphasized the role of the liberal arts and disciplinary knowledge in teacher preparation and other clinical experiences (e.g. Koerner, 1963; Damerell, 1985). This orientation to teacher education emphasizes the teacher's role as a scholar and subject matter specialist and has taken different forms throughout the twentieth-century. In recent years, Lee Shulman (1987), and Margaret Buchmann (1984) among others, have advocated views of reflective teaching that emphasize the teacher's deliberations about subject matter and its transformation to pupils to promote understanding.

This group has also proposed a model of pedagogical reasoning and action that identifies six aspects of the teaching act: comprehension, transformation, instruction, evaluation, reflection and new comprehension. One key aspect of their model of pedagogical reasoning (under the transformation process) is representation. According to Shulman (1987) [see Reading 7.13],

representation involves thinking through the key ideas in the text or lesson and identifying the alternative ways of representing them to students. What analogies, metaphors, examples, demonstrations, simulations, and the like can help to build a bridge between the teacher's comprehension and that desired for the students? Multiple forms of representation are desirable. (p. 328)

This model of pedagogical reasoning and action is a good example of a contemporary view of reflective teaching that prioritizes reflection about the content to be taught and how it is to be taught.

The social efficiency tradition of reflective teaching

The social efficiency tradition has historically emphasized a faith in the scientific study of teaching to provide the basis for building a teacher education curriculum. According to advocates of this view, research on teaching has provided us with a 'knowledge base' that can form the foundation for the curriculum of teacher education programmes (Berliner, 1984). Feiman-Nemser (1990) has identified two different ways in which contemporary teacher educators have interpreted the social efficiency perspective. First, she describes a technological version in which the intent is to teach prospective teachers the skills and competencies that research has shown to be associated with desirable pupil outcomes.

A second and broader interpretation of the social efficiency tradition in US teacher education is one where the findings of research on teaching are used by teachers as 'principles of procedure' within a wider process of decision making and problem solving. According to the advocates of this deliberative orientation to the use of research on teaching, the crucial task for teacher educators is to foster teachers' capabilities to exercise judgement about the use of various teaching skills suggested by research.

The emphasis is clearly on the intelligent use of 'generic' teaching skills and strategies that have been suggested by research.

The developmentalist tradition of reflective teaching

The distinguishing characteristic of the developmentalist tradition is the assumption that the natural development of the learner provides the basis for determining what should be taught to students and how it should be taught. Historically, this natural order of child development was to be determined by research involving the careful observation and description of students' behaviour at various stages of development.

According to Perrone (1989), three central metaphors have been associated with the progressive/developmentalist tradition: teacher as naturalist, teacher as researcher and teacher as artist. The teacher as naturalist dimension has stressed the importance of skill in the observation of children's behaviour and in building a curriculum and classroom environment consistent with patterns of child development and children's interests. Classroom practice is to be grounded in close observation and study of children in the classroom either directly by the teacher, or from reflection on a literature based on such study. The teacher as researcher element of this tradition has emphasized the need to foster the teacher's experimental attitude toward practice and to help them initiate and sustain ongoing inquiries in their own classrooms about the learning of specific children to inform their practice. Finally, the teacher as artist element has emphasized the link between creative and fully functioning persons in touch with their own learning and exciting and stimulating classrooms.

This developmentalist conception of reflective teaching has become increasingly popular in recent years with the growing influence of cognitive psychology in education. The emphasis is clearly on reflecting about students.

The social reconstructionist tradition of reflective teaching

In the fourth tradition of social reconstructionism, schooling and teacher education are both viewed as crucial elements in the movement toward a more just and humane society. According to Valli (1992), proponents of this approach argue,

> that schools as social institutions, help reproduce a society based on unjust class, race, and gender relations and that teachers have a moral obligation to reflect on and change their own practices and school structures when these perpetuate such arrangements. (p. 46)

In a social reconstructionist conception of reflective teaching, the teacher's attention is focused both inwardly at their own practice (and the collective practices of a group of colleagues) and outwardly at the social conditions in which these practices are situated (Kemmis, 1985). How teachers' actions maintain and/or disrupt the status quo in schooling and society is of central concern.

A second characteristic of a social reconstructionist conception of reflective teaching is its democratic and emancipatory impulse and the focus of the teacher's deliberations upon substantive issues that raise instances of inequality and injustice within schooling and society for close scrutiny. Recognizing the fundamentally political character of all schooling, the teacher's reflections centre upon such issues as the gendered nature of schooling and of teachers' work, the relationships between race and social class on the one hand and access to school knowledge and school achievement on the other, and the influence of external interests on the process of curriculum production. These and other similar issues are addressed in concrete form as they arise within the context of the teacher's classroom and school.

The third distinguishing characteristic of a social reconstructionist conception of reflective teaching is its commitment to reflection as a communal activity. Social reconstructionist oriented teacher educators seek to create 'communities of learning' where teachers can support and sustain each other's growth. This commitment to collaborative modes of learning indicates a dual commitment by teacher educators to an ethic where justice and equity on the one hand, and care and compassion on the other, are valued. This commitment is also thought to be of strategic value in the transformation of unjust and inhuman institutional and social structures. Specifically, it is felt that the empowerment of individual teachers as individuals is inadequate, and that the potential for institutional and social change is greater, if teachers see their individual situations as linked to those of their colleagues.

These four traditions of reflective teaching can be used to interpret various aspects of proposals for teacher education reform and descriptions of existing practices.

PART 2

Being a reflective teacher

CHAPTER 4

Who are we, as teachers and pupils?

The nine readings in this chapter focus on teachers and on children in schools.

On teachers, Nias (4.1) begins with an important reading on how teaching relates to personal satisfaction and identity. Cortazzi (4.2) reviews some prominent dimensions of teacher thinking which tend to evolve through classroom experience. Campbell and Neill (4.3) draw attention to the considerable workload which conscientious teachers suffer, whilst Apple (4.4) suggests that such developments reflect major changes in the 'labour process' in modern societies. However, Woods (4.5) insists that creative teachers continue to defend a commitment to more personal values.

On pupils, Davies (4.6) argues that children and adults see the world in very different ways, largely because of the differences in their experiences and power to influence events. Pollard (4.7) suggests some major pupil interests in school and identifies characteristic patterns in the coping strategies of different groups of children. Then, at the individual level, Maylor (4.8) provides an autobiographical illustration of the influence of personal circumstances on educational experience. In the final reading, Mayall (4.9) highlights some of the differences in children's experiences at home and school, using the example of the negotiation of health care.

The parallel chapter of *Reflective Teaching in the Primary School* is also in two major parts. 'Knowing ourselves as teachers' suggests ways of thinking about personal characteristics and the ways in which they influence teaching. The second part is on 'knowing children as pupils'. This reviews the educational literature and offers activities for investigating young children's perspectives and experiences of schooling. There are also many suggestions for further reading.

Feeling like a teacher

Jennifer Nias

The book from which this extract has been edited, *Primary Teachers Talking*, is an insightful and sensitive representation of teachers' feelings in respect of their work. Jennifer Nias interviewed fifty teachers over a period of ten years as their careers and lives developed. The result is a unique account of the pleasures and pain of 'becoming a teacher', with the gradual integration of the role with identity and self. The analysis suggests reasons why primary school teachers have such a strong commitment to their pupils, and why the job is inherently challenging.

How do you feel about yourself and your career?

Edited from: Nias, J. (1989) *Primary Teachers Talking: A Study of Teaching as Work*. London: Routledge, 181–97

It is possible to teach for years, successfully and with the affirmation of one's head teacher and colleagues, without incorporating 'teacher' into one's self-image. As several of my interviewees said in their first decade of work, 'I teach, but I do not feel like a teacher'. However, by their second decade most of those whom I interviewed had incorporated their professional identity into their self-image (i.e. they 'felt like teachers'). Clearly, in any attempt to understand the nature of teaching as work, it is important to include the affective reality of experienced, committed teachers. Accordingly, this chapter is built around an analysis of conversations with fifty people in mid-career of whom I asked, 'Do you feel like a teacher?', and explained why I wanted to know. If they said they did, I then requested an explication. In addition, I have used comments they made when they were talking more generally about their work.

What emerges from this analysis is the contradictory nature of the feelings associated with teaching. Various reasons can be adduced for this. The outcome of all of them, for the successful teacher, is mastery over a complex and difficult skill: the theme of 'balance', it can be argued, accounts for the sense of fit between identity and work which, at its best, characterizes 'feeling like a teacher'.

'Being yourself'

Most of the teachers believed that to adopt the identity of 'teacher' was simply to 'be yourself' in the classroom. They expressed this idea in three similar but slightly different ways. Some stressed a sense of fit between self and occupation (e.g. 'I feel as if I've found my niche'; 'However annoyed I may be at the end of a day in school ... I still feel I'm in the right job for me'). Others saw little distinction between their 'selves' at work and outside it; as one said, 'What's happening to you as a person can't be separated from what's happening to you as a teacher'.

'Being whole'

Many teachers linked the notions of 'being yourself' and 'being whole'. Some achieved 'wholeness' by blurring the boundaries between their personal and professional lives. A woman said:

> I tend to bring a lot of my personal life into school with the children. They know a lot about what I'm doing all the time so in that way teaching is never separate from my personal life. They know all about my cat, everything that happened to me the previous evening, they know that I sail, they know that I paint, they know what my house is like, so they're not separate lives at all.

The desire to create 'wholeness' also showed itself in attempts to soften the barriers of role, age and status and to prevent the erection of new ones (particularly those of curriculum or timetabling). Several teachers attacked what they described as 'fragmentation' or 'splitting' of their pupils' learning experiences. Many talked enthusiastically and, in the case of some heads, nostalgically, about their involvement with children in extra-curricular activities, clubs, on field trips and school journeys, and in residential study centres.

The urge to work in an environment characterized by unity, not division, extended to staff relationships as well. In the words of a head, 'The school was a part of me, the staff were a part of me ... I couldn't separate myself from them'.

'Establishing relationships with children'

Embedded in the notions of belonging, and of education as an extension of family life, is a belief that to teach one must 'establish a relationship with pupils'. For instance:

> I've met kids that I taught when I first went there who are now working ... They don't just say, 'Aren't you Mr Jones?', they say, 'Alright Sir?' and that's the difference. It's not a question of education, it's a question of relationships.

Teachers described their work in terms such as 'getting co-operation from my children', 'it's a joint effort between you and them', 'what a teacher is to any individual child could be something totally different, it's a function of the two personalities involved'.

Although they knew it existed, my interviewees found it hard to describe what they meant by their 'relationship' with children. Occasionally it was seen as playing a parental role, sometimes as relating to peers – e.g. 'It can be as close as another friend', 'Some of those children I'd really like to keep as friends'. Very frequently it contains a marked element of humour, often based on shared understandings (Walker and Adelman, 1976; Woods, 1979). Many teachers appear to gauge the state of their relationship with a class by the extent to which 'we can all have a laugh together', 'I can be myself, laugh and joke', or, 'we can share a joke and then get down to work again'. However, to many teachers the relationship is more than being either a parent or a friend. Several people described teaching as 'communication with another human being' or 'learning to communicate with other people'. A woman reflected:

> I've come to realize that if you really want to educate children you've got to share yourself with them, as a person. They've got to know about you, your interests, your life out of school, the sort of person you are. But most of all it means being open to them as a person, and that makes you vulnerable. Yes, being a teacher is being ready to be vulnerable.

Control

To the person who undertakes to build this relationship, it has three main characteristics: control, responsibility and concern. Virtually every teacher responded to my request to explain what it was to 'feel like a teacher' by saying that it was to be in control (e.g. 'It's doing things you're in control of to a large extent'; 'It's being in control of what goes on in the classroom'; 'To start with, it's your will against theirs'. Whether or not they enjoyed the exercise of control, interviewees all accepted that, as a teacher, 'You have to exercise authority. Treating children like human beings and yet maintaining discipline is a constant challenge'. Indeed, being willing to exercise authority was widely seen as the one necessary condition for 'feeling like a teacher'. Two teachers suggested:

> A teacher's relationship with children is quite distinctive. However much you care and however much you share with them, you assume an air of authority. I didn't have any authority for a couple of years, partly because I didn't really have any conviction that I was doing anything right.

There is no way round it. If you want to be a teacher you have to find a way of establishing your control because it's a sort of barrier you have to get through. If you want to do the job you have to do that because it is part of being a teacher. You cannot do the rest of the job, which I wanted to do, without getting over the first barrier.

Closely related to feeling in control was the sense of being well-organized and purposeful – 'having specific ends in view, not muddling through, knowing what you're about', 'knowing what you want from and for children', 'being organized, so that in any teaching situation you have a sense of direction'.

Responsibility and concern

Assuming responsibility for children was also seen to be linked with feeling in control. People believed that, as teachers, they must 'accept the children's dependence on you', 'feel a great responsibility for every child in my care', 'accept that you will influence them by what you are, whether you want to or not'. One man claimed:

It means that you have got to accept them for what they are, and if an 8-year-old says 'I love you, Mr Smith' she means it, and you can't play with that, you cannot dismiss it, you cannot turn round to her and say, 'I love you as well, Sarah' if you don't mean it. And I think that's what feeling like a teacher is: when you realize what an awesome responsibility you bear. If teachers realized just what influence they have on children, I think then they'd realize what being a teacher was.

Related to both control and responsibility, but less detached than either, is affection. Many teachers emphasized the caring aspects of their role, using such terms as 'being prepared to put their interests first', 'doing your best for all the children in your class'. Five, four of them men, put it more strongly than this. One said:

There are one or two children that I love very dearly. There have been one or two children in the past twelve years I have loved totally … only one or two. The difference that having my own son has made to my relationships at school has not been that strong. I still have one or two children I'm really fond of, not as pupils, but as people.

In whatever way these teachers expressed the essential characteristics of their relationship with children, they became, in the words of one man, 'more intuitive, relaxed and spontaneous' as they came to 'feel like teachers'. Individuals repeatedly spoke of being more relaxed in the classroom and the staffroom, of feeling more able to be 'adaptive and flexible', of 'being less of a worrier', 'more laid back', and above all more self-confident. As one person crisply responded, 'Feeling confident in what you do, that's what it all hinges on'.

At this point the circular nature of what they were saying becomes apparent: to 'feel like a teacher' is to feel you can be yourself in the classroom; to be yourself is to feel whole, to act naturally; to act naturally is to enter into a relationship with children, a relationship in which control makes possible the exercise of responsibility and the expression of concern; together, these states enable you to 'be yourself' in the classroom and therefore to 'feel like a teacher'.

Living with tension, dilemma and contradiction

Yet this sense of 'wholeness' and fit between self and occupation is dearly bought. There is little consistency in the lived experience of primary teaching. To 'be' a teacher is to be relaxed and in control yet tired and under stress, to feel whole while being pulled apart, to be in love with one's work but daily to talk of leaving it.

There are three inter-related sets of reasons for this contradictory state of affairs: socio-historical, psychological, and philosophical. Sociologically, the teacher's role is ambiguous and ill-defined, hedged about with uncertainty, inconsistency, and tension. Primary teachers occupy many roles, some (e.g. instructor, parent, judge, friend) perpetually at war with one another (Blyth, 1967; Woods, 1987). The essentially conflictual nature of the job is emphasized by teachers' inescapable obligation to control children. The American sociologist, Waller, has made a powerful case for the view that 'the teacher–pupil relationship is a form of institutionalized dominance and subordination ... Teacher and pupil confront each other with attitudes from which the underlying hostility can never be removed' (Waller, 1961: 195). The need for teachers to exercise power stems from the fact that adult groups (of whom in school the teacher is representative) and the formal curriculum, which offers children 'desiccated bits of adult life' (ibid.) confront pupils who are 'interested in life in their own world' and 'striving to realize themselves in their own way' (ibid.).

Education cannot escape from being a process in which the older generation (represented by teachers) force-feeds the younger. In the clash of interests which follows, teachers have to use every resource they can muster to curb and harness children's energies, to render the 'desiccated bits of adult life' palatable to classes full of the richness of their own experience. Add to that the fact that in England this process of compulsory socialization is invested in teachers who, with negligible adult help and relatively few resources, daily face large numbers of physically active children, and it is inevitable that control becomes for them a central issue in school and classroom life.

Leiberman and Miller (1984: 14) put it this way:

> Once inside the classroom, a teacher knows that all control is tenuous. It depends on a negotiated agreement between students and the teacher. If that agreement is violated, a teacher will subordinate all teaching activities to one primary goal: to regain and maintain control ... when one loses control, one loses everything.

Since the exercise of dominance by one person over others can never be without strain, stress is therefore built into the teacher's job.

Furthermore, the teacher's work is riddled with uncertainties. The goals of their schools and the values which underpin these are conflicting and, in an attempt to reduce the impact of this conflict, have often become imprecise, ambiguous, and unattainable. The resulting vagueness masks a number of dilemmas which teachers' daily practice expresses, even if they do not themselves voice them (Berlak and Berlak, 1981 [see Reading 1.3]). These authors vividly portray dilemmas-in-action in English primary classrooms, showing how teachers resolve, on a minute-by-minute basis, conflicting expectations about, for instance, their role, the curriculum, their teaching methods and response to pupils' work. For example: how can the needs of individuals be reconciled with those of the whole class group? Should the teacher or the pupil control the content and pace of learning and determine the standards by which it is judged? By what criteria should particular elements be included in or excluded from the curriculum?

Vagueness on goals (and therefore responsibilities) is coupled with the absence of clear or valid criteria by which teachers may be judged. This ambiguity itself rests on insecure foundations, since little is known with certainty about the connection between teaching and learning. Nor is there any consensus about the knowledge base of teaching as a profession and therefore about what teachers should know.

Further, the many roles which teachers already occupy are currently expanding. In the past two decades these roles have grown to include work (of many sorts) with parents, governors, outside agencies, support services, and colleagues. In the 1990s, these demands are likely to be augmented by the need for teachers to assume greater responsibilities for school-based inservice education, and national assessment, and for head teachers of larger schools to take on, with their governors, the running of their school's finances and physical plant – and all this on top of English teachers' documented tendency to assume a very wide range of moral responsibilities for their pupils (Osborn 1986).

Psychologically, the job itself is not only 'incredibly, unexpectedly demanding' (Fuller and Bown 1975: 48) but also shifting and elusive. It rests upon relationships with pupils whose attendance may be erratic, even arbitrary. The time of day, the weather, children's moods, staff illnesses, break-ins, visitors from medical and other support services, and a myriad of other minor alterations in the teachers' context and programme mean that they experience continuous and endemic change, in circumstances already characterized by uncertainty and unpredictability (Nias *et al.*, 1989 [see Reading 14.2]). The classroom is never the same place from one day to the next, often it can alter radically from one moment to another. Yet teachers are expected to maintain throughout an aura of 'professional pleasantness' (King, 1978) and to 'correct for the capriciousness of students with the steadiness, resolve and sangfroid of one who governs' (Lortie, 1975: 156).

Living with paradox

Primary school teachers in England appear to have a conception of teaching which imposes upon them the need continually to live and work with paradox. The very nature of teaching, as they experience it, is contradictory [see Reading 4.2]. Teachers must nurture the whole while attending to the parts, liberate their pupils to grow in some directions by checking growth in others, foster and encourage progress by controlling it, and show love and interest by curbing and chastising. Indeed, there is some evidence that these teachers were themselves aware of the paradoxical nature of their task. In particular, they see themselves facing three quandaries, each of them relating in some way to their perception of themselves.

First, they could not become the sort of teachers they wanted to be without also accepting the need to behave in ways they found disagreeable. One talked of 'learning that you've got to establish yourself and your authority first – let them dislike you so they can like you later'. Another said, 'I have learnt that you must dominate the children in order to free them ... I quite accept that now, it's just the pain of doing it'.

Second, they could encounter children as individuals and care for them only if they were also aware of and valued themselves. One of them put it this way:

> I don't think anyone could teach young children unless they're both egocentric and selfless. You've got to be very sure of who you are yourself and yet quite prepared to forget who you are, not forget it, but put who you are second to who the kids are.

Similarly, they could meet the children's personal calls upon them only if they had something left to give (i.e. if they safeguarded opportunities out of school to replenish the 'selves' who went to work).

Third, they could not be fulfilled by their work unless they allowed themselves to be depleted by its demands. I asked several people, 'Why do you let the school take so much of you?'. The typical reply was: 'I enjoy giving it'.

My claim is, therefore, that to adopt the identity of an English primary school teacher is to accept the paradoxical nature of the task and inexorably to live with tension. Those who claim that they can be themselves in and through their work – i.e. that they can 'feel like teachers' – are signalling that they have learnt to live not just with stress but with paradox.

Primary teaching is, then, an occupation which requires the ability to live with, and handle constructively, a multitude of dilemmas, tensions, contradictions, uncertainties, and paradoxes.

READING 4.2

Polarities in teachers' thinking

Martin Cortazzi

Martin Cortazzi collected and studied teachers' narrative accounts of classroom experiences. As a result, he was able to identify what he called 'polarities' in teacher thinking, and these are summarized in this reading. The suggestion is that these paired ideas are drawn on by teachers to make sense of classroom and school situations and to provide a basis for future action. They have something in common with the notion of dilemmas (see Reading 1.3) and, in common with many other papers in this collection, they underline the significance of teacher judgement.

Edited from: Cortazzi, M. (1990) *Primary Teaching: How It Is*. London: David Fulton, 126–35

Underlying teacher narratives are some abstract binary oppositions. These oppositions are presented here as polarities between which teachers operate on a continuum, oscillating between the tensions of two poles according to the demands of the situation, never able to adhere completely to only one of them. The polarities are important as pairs, rather than as discrete categories. It is assumed that both poles are consciously accepted by teachers as necessary. The importance of these theoretical constructs lies in the relationship between the elements. The constructs are proposed as cultural models since they have been derived from the narratives of large numbers of teachers interviewed independently.

Individual < - - - > Class

'You want to make sure every child is being taught at his or her own level. It is difficult.'

'I feel under tremendous pressure with thirty-eight children.'

This polar opposition summarizes the problem of the class teacher working with a large number of children within a tradition of education which emphasizes individuals rather than groups. Teachers believe that it is necessary to focus at different times either on individuals or on the class as a whole. Some individuals always stand out in teachers' perceptions: for academic ability, problems or character. While trying to follow the primary education dictum to 'meet the needs of the individual', it is the extremes from the total whose needs the teacher apparently gives greater attention. Because of the demands of the whole class she cannot meet every need of every child.

Parent < - - - > Teacher

'You get those who co-operate with you, and those for whom the school is a battle.'

This polarity captures the potential conflict between teachers and parents. Teachers see great importance in eliciting co-operation and support from parents to benefit pupils. They also affirm their need to know pupils' background, which is partly obtained from parents.

When pupils have behavioural, social or emotional problems teachers tend to use a social pathology model to interpret the sources of these problems as being in the home, rather than in school. With awkward parents, teachers move away from the need to know the home (the parent end), and focus parents' attention on the teacher's concerns for the whole class (the teacher end). Explaining the teacher's situation overcomes parental misunderstandings.

Flexibility < - - - > Planning

'We're reasonably planned, but flexible, too.'

'Every day something happens, like someone wets themselves, somebody is sick, somebody is unhappy about something that happened at playtime ... and you cannot get through what you planned to do.'

The need for planning, organization, structure and system was recognized, but was offset by the frequent need to be flexible or to 'play it by ear'. Teachers said they could neither rigidly stick to plans, nor continually 'play it by ear' without planning. Both poles were necessary. Planning was generally for the whole class or for groups, rarely for individuals. Being flexible meant responding to individual children's interests and excitement when something unexpectedly 'cropped up'. This was then used with the whole class. Some long-term plans originated through being flexible to children's interests. In these cases the class apparently followed the individual. There is a constant movement between these poles, with the teacher's focus continually changing.

Breakthrough < - - - > Incremental learning

'Although you think that it's sudden, a miracle, it's not really, it's just that you've been plodding on and on, going over the same thing every day.'

'Yes it has clicked, but I don't think personally that it's instantaneous.'

Children's breakthroughs are reported as being sudden 'clicks' after a period of little progress. This can be contrasted with slower continuous incremental learning. As the teachers perceived learning, some takes place suddenly and is noticed as such (a breakthrough), other learning is a slow accumulation and is noticed gradually (incremental learning). Other points on the scale are where the learning is gradual but is noticed suddenly (a breakthrough, according to some teachers) or where sudden learning is noticed gradually.

Disaster < - - - > Stability

'Teachers are so resourceful that they overcome disasters. That's experience, isn't it?'

'You always think you can do something better. In retrospect you think you haven't done it well enough, but you have to be satisfied with a compromise anyway because there are so many pressures. You have to reconcile these things. It's not a rejection of the perfect, nor an acceptance of the substandard, but it's ... well, bearing in mind the other pressures.'

Many disasters were reported as unanticipated interruptions to stability. Disasters are of various types, on a scale from mild events or accidents (like falling off a chair) to severely disturbing incidents (e.g. concussion or child suicide). The teacher's response must be to restore stability. The majority of disasters in narratives occurred with individual children, potentially disrupting the stability of the whole class.

Laughter < - - - > Seriousness

'It's the laughing and joking you can have ... you can sort of think to yourself, "Yes, that was a good day. We had a good laugh in that lesson, but they still did some work".'

This opposition is between the assumed serious tone of most classroom time and the smiles or laughter which arise from the incongruity of children's sayings and doings. The humour is unexpected and nearly always associated with an individual child. After laughter the teacher must restore seriousness and order. Humour turns out to be a key element in teacher's job satisfaction, supporting the notion that both poles here are necessary.

Unpredictability < - - - > Routine

'The variability, that's always made teaching to me, because of the unexpected things that happen.'

'That's what makes teaching: the variability, the unexpected things that happen.'

Planned, serious, 'normal' classroom work is the routine, aimed at incremental learning. The opposite to this is the pole of the unpredictable, the unexpected and the variety. There are few narratives about routine teaching, perhaps because what is routine is basically less newsworthy. There are, however, literally hundreds of unpredictable elements in most 'Breakthrough', 'Disaster', 'Awkward Parent' and 'Humourous' narratives. Teachers commented that such variety made teaching interesting and enjoyable.

Enjoyment < - - - > Grind

'It's a very satisfying life, but it's hard work.'

'I moan like hell, but I enjoy it.'

This opposition puts the hard work aspect of teaching against enjoyment. Many teachers mentioned that teaching was inevitably often a 'grind', 'slog,' or 'struggle'. It was 'hard work' and 'extremely busy'. This pressure can be endured if there is also enjoyment. 'Breakthrough of Planning' and 'Humourous' narratives frequently include evaluations where enjoyment is a prime element, often linked with being 'thrilled', 'amazed' and 'interested'. This enjoyment was often shared with children. Sometimes the teacher's pleasure was derived from children's enjoyment. The enjoyment pole emerges very clearly from narratives. In the staffroom this sharing of fun in anecdotes may be an important element of camaraderie among teachers. However, it must be balanced with the conventional complaining about the grind, which is also an element of camaraderie.

Social < - - - > Cognitive

'It's very much a social job that we do, as well as a teaching job.'

'I see my role in helping them learn.'

This opposition expresses the important polarity between social relationships, feelings, attitudes and the like on the one hand, and learning, remembering, understanding concepts and developing cognitive skills on the other. Both are obviously necessary and important in education. It might be expected that both would feature heavily in teachers' narratives about, for example, children, learning, planning or parents. In fact, there is scant mention of the cognitive end of this binary opposition in the narratives. Usually the social pole is given greater emphasis.

There are a few references to children's 'progress', without further specification, except in the case of reading, where reading ages are mentioned. Terms such as concept, understanding, generalization or insight simply do not occur in the data. In contrast, the social pole is continually mentioned: teachers specifically and repeatedly stress children's 'interest', 'involvement', 'enjoyment' and 'excitement'. More generally, they continually refer to relationships in the classroom and to the social situations in children's homes, sometimes with great detail. Parallel cognitive situations are never referred to.

The tension between the poles is most evident in the 'Breakthrough' narratives, where cognitive learning is described, but the teachers' reactions are broadly social or emotional. They are 'thrilled', 'excited', 'surprised', 'delighted', but they do not specify exactly what children learnt, or how, or how it might or should develop and why it was important or worthwhile.

General < - - - > Technical

'Is the word "autonomy"? I've forgotten big words since I've been in this job.'

This polarity refers to the teachers' use of language, expressed on a continuum drawing on professional technical terms from disciplines relevant to education, opposed to general every-day terms used to discuss education.

Teachers' narratives overwhelmingly avoid technical or more academic terms. It may well be that the teachers were perfectly capable of using technical language but that there are cultural inhibitions against using technical terms in the staffroom or that narrative does not require it. On the other hand, the topics would seem to require at least some technical reference: in children's learning and lesson planning, for example.

The teachers' use of metaphor is an interesting case of using general terms in contexts which would otherwise be expected to be technical. The teachers' metaphors are so frequent in use, yet so limited in range, that they appear to constitute a folk terminology for learning. The metaphors seem to aid verbalization about the unknown or the inexplicable, yet they may inhibit deeper reflection or professional development. To say 'it clicked', or 'light dawned' or 'she really came on in leaps and bounds' is meaningful as metaphorical description, but without further analysis does seem limited as a professional way of focusing on one of the central issues of education – children's learning.

As cultural descriptions the metaphors provide a perspective in their own right. They could be used for conceptual or theoretical development, as metaphors are used in scientific research, but teachers do not seem to do this. In this polarity, the social and cultural pressures of the occupation seem to cause teachers to favour the general pole.

📖 READING 4.3

The problem with conscientiousness

Jim Campbell and Sean Neill

> Campbell and Neill carried out an important survey of teacher work-loads during the early 1990s when the pressure of implementing the new National Curriculum was at its height. Their work helped to establish that it was 'unmanageable' and 'overloaded'. In this extract from their book, they speculate on why primary school teachers are so conscientious, and whether this commitment contributes to exploitation and stress. It is interesting to consider these issues in the light of Nias' work (Reading 4.1) which deals with aspects of teacher fulfilment.
>
> Do you see conscientiousness as a problem, or is it a means of realizing your 'self'?
>
> Edited from: Campbell, R. J. and Neill, S. R. (1994) *Primary Teachers at Work*. London: Routledge, 220–4

We would not wish to detract from the value of teachers' vocational attachment to work, or from the strong professional identity that primary teachers create from extensive commitment to their pupils' welfare (Nias, 1989 [see Reading 4.1]). English primary teachers' professional responsibilities are more diffuse than those of their peers in France (Broadfoot and Osborn 1988) and include a sense of responsibility not merely for cognitive goals but also for social, emotional and personal well-being. This diffuse responsibility has been encouraged, expected or required in a long train of official and semi-official documents, at least since the 1960s (e.g. CACE, 1967; DES, 1978) and stretching beyond the legislation of the 1980s. These expectations ténd to be reinforced by parental pressure, with parents of younger primary pupils especially placing high priority on their being happy at school as well as learning the cognitive skills associated with reading and writing.

It is easy to see why such diffuse responsibilities have been laid upon primary teachers. Very young children need to feel secure in their school environments, especially given the fact that international trends show teachers having to take on greater social and emotional responsibilities as the authority of family, Church, law and other community support structures weakens (ILO, 1991). Social imperatives drive primary teachers towards an ethic of care. For teachers of very young children, in particular, the establishment and maintenance of warm, caring and diffuse relationships have been seen as prerequisites for the achievement of cognitive goals (David, Curtis and Siraj-Blatchford, 1992), though alternative perspectives (e.g. Cox and Dyson, 1969, 1970) have seen debased versions of concerns for pupils' social welfare becoming a substitute for cognitive objectives. There is a tendency to romanticize the caring ethic, and even, in Fullan and Hargreaves (1991), to polarize it against an ethic of responsibility. Yet we would argue that the ethic of care as a central value in primary teachers' occupational culture contributes to teacher overload.

As we have shown above, one set of role expectations is that teachers meet the social and emotional needs of their pupils. Whilst this has been a constant feature of their role in Western countries, in England and Wales the recent trends in legislation have added to, or extended, three other elements. The most obvious is that the curriculum requirements have made more public and more stringent expectations for pupils' cognitive achievement. There has also been the introduction, through the publication of end-of-Key Stage test results, open enrolment policies, and the funding of schools being based largely on pupil numbers, of a powerful drive to 'market accountability'. Thus the teacher, previously able to insulate him or herself from concerns about whole-school development and to concentrate upon the needs of the pupils in the class, now has to take account of the implications of his or her work for the whole school, and especially its market image mediated largely through the reporting of pupil achievement in end-of-year or end-of-stage reporting.

Third, the teacher has typically also to take responsibility as curriculum co-ordinator for an aspect or aspects of the curriculum throughout the school, not just in his or her own class (House of Commons, 1986) Managing aspects of the work of other teachers is part of the contractual obligation of all teachers. Thus, the obligations and expectations are now threefold: to pupils' welfare, to the national curriculum and to colleagues and school.

A further factor arises from the fact that most primary teachers are women. Evetts (1990), in her study of women in primary teaching, noted that, 'Women teachers will have responsibilities in at least two spheres: the public sphere of work and the private sphere of home and family' (p. 115). She added that the difficulty of fulfilling work and family commitments became 'particularly acute' when there were children in the family, but also drew attention to the emerging demographic factor of increasing numbers of dependent elderly relatives whose care often falls disproportionately upon the shoulders of women.

In this context it should be noted that, in a study of 3,019 primary and secondary teachers, Varlaam, Nuttall and Walker (1992) found few differences in rank order of factors affecting morale and motivation, but 'having sufficient time for family and private life' was more important amongst married teachers than others.

The factors found to be by far the most commonly unsatisfactory by Varlaam and his colleagues, were those relating to stress, excessive workloads and paperwork and record-keeping, inadequate resources, and insufficient time for family and private life. These findings are not surprising, but such dissatisfactions are likely to be particularly salient for the primary teaching force, which is largely female. This interpretation was supported where Varlaam and his colleagues analysed factors considered unsatisfactory by phase. Their analysis showed more infant and primary teachers than secondary teachers considered 'having sufficient time for family and private life' as unsatisfactory/very unsatisfactory in their current job (60 per cent infant, 65 per cent primary, 54 per cent secondary). There is a much higher proportion of women in primary than in secondary teaching, and almost all infant teachers are women. Thus, for the majority of primary teachers, there are the added demands arising from what Sharpe (1984) has called the 'Double Identity'.

These demands could either become manageable, or be seen clearly as unmanageable, if the role inflation had been limited by a contractual framework that was itself – because of the way 'non-directed' time was defined – literally without limit. Indeed, part of the definition – 'such additional hours as may be necessary to enable them to discharge effectively their professional duties' (School Teachers' Pay and Conditions Document, 1989, para. 36(1)(f)) – seemed to assume that if professional duties were to be increased, as they had been, the non-directed time would simply have to follow suit. It embodied an open-ended commitment of teachers' own time to work.

Within this context, 'conscientiousness', whatever its benefits to the pupils, has acted as a mechanism, actual or potential, for exploitation of teachers. Driven by their sense of obligation to meet all work demands to the best of their ability, the majority of teachers found themselves devoting much longer hours in their own time to work than they considered reasonable, and attempting to meet too many demands simultaneously in order to achieve government objectives for educational reform. This was despite the fact that some of the demands – for example, those concerning the provision of a broad and balanced curriculum – were structurally impossible. Others, such as those concerned with Key Stage 1 assessment, were confused and unworkable.

There were three dispiriting consequences. The teachers found themselves and their pupils scampering across the curriculum in a superficial way in an attempt to cover everything (OFSTED, 1993). Second, they found a reduced sense of satisfaction in their work because they rarely managed to obtain a sense of achievement, despite working hard (Evans et al., 1994). Third, there was evidence that Key Stage 1 teachers were hearing children read less frequently than they thought necessary in order to meet all the other curricular objectives (Evans et al., 1994). That is to say, they were reducing their own fundamental educational objectives in order to meet governmental ones. They were entrapped by their own conscientiousness.

There are three issues raised by the strength of the influence of 'conscientiousness' upon teachers' work. First, even though they were operating within a framework which, from the mid-1980s onwards in Britain, had been gradually constructed so as to impose legally binding, contractually defined duties upon teachers, and which had included the development of systems of appraisal and performance-related pay, the teachers were primarily motivated by a sense of vocation or obligation to their pupils. Salary status was not associated statistically with the amount of time spent on work. The occupational culture of the school remained stubbornly at odds with the assumptions of central government's legislation on working conditions, and especially perhaps for the impact of performance-related pay.

The second conclusion is that 'conscientiousness can damage your health'. Along with social work teaching was found to be the most stressful of the professional occupations in the Oxford Employment Life survey (Gallie and White, 1993). Long hours devoted to work reduced the opportunities for leisure outside schools and relaxation in school, and ate into the personal and domestic lives of our teachers. The average term-time working week of 50-plus hours concealed a small group (10 per cent) of teachers working more than 60 hours a week, a situation most saw as unreasonable. It is unlikely, as Fullan and Hargreaves (1991) argue, that anyone other than the teachers themselves will take steps to reduce work overload, since most of the overload is in the teachers' own time.

READING 4.4

Deskilling and intensification

Michael Apple

Michael Apple is an influential American sociologist who is particularly perceptive in linking teacher experiences to wider social processes and trends. In this reading, he considers teaching as a 'labour process', as work. In particular, he focuses on the ways in which the development of centralized, rationalistic school systems impact on the job of teaching. His suggestion is that teachers are 'deskilled' by such systems and, at the same time, suffer from the stresses of 'intensification'. This may seem very plausible, but see Reading 12.5 which includes an argument that teacher skills may have been enhanced by the introduction of national systems for assessment.

People's experiences and responses to changing circumstances are very complex. Do you feel deskilled by recent developments?

Edited from: Apple, M. W. (1993) *Official Knowledge: Democratic Education in a Conservative Age*. London: Routledge, 118–25

In all too many instances the daily lives of teachers in classrooms in many nations are becoming ever more controlled, ever more subject to administrative logics that seek to tighten the reins on the processes of teaching and curriculum. Teacher development, co-operation, and 'empowerment' may be the talk, but centralization, standardization, and rationalization may be the strongest tendencies, even with the increasing focus on privatization, marketization, and decentralization. In Britain and the United States – to take but two examples – reductive accountability, teacher evaluation schemes, and increasing centralization have become so commonplace that in a few more years we may have lost from our collective memory the very possibility of difference.

An odd combination of forces has led to this situation. Economic modernizers, education efficiency experts, neo-conservatives, segments of the New Right, many working and lower-middle-class parents who believe that their children's futures are threatened by a school system that does not guarantee jobs, and members of parts of the new middle class whose own mobility is dependent on technical and administratively oriented knowledge have formed a tense and contradictory alliance to return us to 'the basics', to 'appropriate' values and dispositions, to 'efficiency and accountability', and to a close connection between schools and an economy in crisis.

Among the major effects of these pressures is what is happening to teaching as an occupation and as a set of skilled and self-reflective actions. Important transformations are occurring that will have significant impacts on how we do our jobs and who will decide whether we are successfully carrying them out.

In order to understand this argument, we need to think about teaching in a particular way, to think of it as what might be called a complicated labour process. It is a labour process that is significantly different from that of working on an assembly line, in the home, or in an office. But, even given these differences, the same pressures that are currently affecting jobs in general are now increasingly being felt in teaching [see Reading 14.5].

There has been an exceptionally long history of rationalizing and standardizing people's jobs. In industry, a familiar example of this was management's use of Taylorism and time-and-motion studies in their continual search for high profits and greater control over their employees. Here, complicated jobs were rigorously examined by management experts. Each element that went into doing the job was broken down into its simplest components. Less-skilled and lower-paid workers were hired to do these simpler activities. All planning was to be done by management, not workers. The consequences of this have been profound, but two of them are especially important for our discussion.

The first is what we shall call the separation of conception from execution. When complicated jobs are broken down into atomistic elements the person doing the job loses sight of the whole process and loses control over her or his own labour since someone outside the immediate situation now has greater control over both the planning and what is actually to go on. The second consequence is related, but adds a further debilitating characteristic. This is known as deskilling. As employees lose control over their own labour, the skills that they have developed over the years atrophy. They are slowly lost, thereby making it even easier for management to control even more of one's job because the skills of planning and controlling it yourself are no longer available.

How is this process now working through the job of teaching?

At the local, state, and national levels, movements for strict accountability systems, competency-based education and testing, management by objectives, a truncated vision of the 'basics', mandated curricular content and goals, and so on are clear and growing. Increasingly, teaching methods, texts, tests, and outcomes are being taken out of the hands of the people who must put them into practice. Instead, they are being legislated by national or state departments of education or in state legislatures.

These rationalizing forces are quite consequential and need to be analysed structurally to see the lasting impact they may be having on teaching. In much the same way as in other jobs, we are seeing the deskilling of our teachers. As we noted, when individuals cease to plan and control a large portion of their own work, the skills essential to doing these tasks self-reflectively and well, atrophy and are forgotten. The skills that teachers have built up over decades of hard work – setting relevant curricular goals, establishing content, designing lessons and instructional strategies, 'community building' in the classroom, individualizing instruction based on an intimate knowledge of students' varied cultures, desires, and needs, and so on – are lost. In many ways, given the centralization of authority and control, they are simply no longer 'needed'. In the process, however, the very things that make teaching a professional activity – the control of one's expertise and time – are also dissipated. There is no better formula for alienation and burn-out than loss of control of one's labour (though it is quite unfortunate that terms such as 'burn-out' have such currency since they make the problem into a psychological one rather than a truly structural one concerning the control of teachers' labour).

Hence, the tendency for the curriculum to become increasingly planned, systematized, and standardized at a central level, totally focused on competencies measured by standardized tests may have consequences exactly the opposite of what many authorities intend. Instead of professional teachers who care greatly about what they do and why they do it, we may have alienated executors of someone else's plans.

So far we have discussed at a very general level certain of the social dynamics that threaten to transform curricula and teaching. This discussion cannot be complete unless we add one other significant concept, the idea of intensification.

Intensification is one of the most tangible ways in which the working conditions of teachers have eroded. It has many symptoms, from the trivial to the more complex, ranging from having no time at all to go to the toilet, have a cup of coffee, or relax, to having a total absence of time to keep up with one's field. We can see it most visibly in the chronic sense of work overload that has escalated over time. More and more has to be done; less and less time is available to do it. This has led to a multitude of results.

Intensification leads people to 'cut corners' so that only what is 'essential' to the task immediately at hand is accomplished. It forces people increasingly to rely on 'experts' to tell them what to do and to begin to mistrust the expertise they may have developed over the years. In the process, quality is sacrificed for quantity. Getting done is substituted for work well done. And, as time itself becomes a scarce 'commodity', the risk of isolation grows, thereby both reducing the chances that interaction among participants will enable critiques and limiting the possibility that rethinking and peer teaching will naturally evolve. Collective skills are lost as 'management skills' are gained. Often the primary task is, to quote one teacher, to 'find a way to get through the day'. And finally, pride itself is jeopardized as the work becomes dominated by someone else's conception of what should be done.

As we noted, with the growth of interventionist styles of management and a focus on reductive accountability schemes in many nations, more and more curricula and the act of teaching itself are dominated by pre-specified sequential lists of behaviourally defined competencies, 'outcomes', and objectives, pre-tests and post-tests to measure 'readiness' and skill levels, and a dominance of standardized textual and often work-sheet material. The amount of paperwork necessary for evaluation and record keeping is often phenomenal under these conditions.

One of the effects of these processes of deskilling and intensification is the threat they pose to the conception of teaching as an 'integrated whole activity'. Concerns of care, connectedness, nurturance, and fostering 'growth' – concerns that historically have been linked to skills and dispositions surrounding the paid and unpaid labour of women – are devalued. In essence, they are no longer given credit for being skills at all, as the very definition of what counts as a skill is further altered to include only that which is technical and based on a process 'which places emphasis on performance, monitoring and subject-centred instruction'.

 READING 4.5

The self-determination of creative teachers

Peter Woods

This reading derives from research with teachers who maintained a highly creative approach to teaching over the period of the introduction of the National Curriculum, when many teachers were extremely stressed. We are introduced to teachers from Ensel and Coombes Primary Schools, Susan, Dave and Sue, and to the ways in which their 'self' was defended and realized through their work. In a sense this reading can be seen as an account of teachers' resistance to deskilling and intensification (see Reading 4.4).

Edited from: Woods, P. (1995) *Creative Teachers in Primary Schools*. Buckingham: Open University Press, 157–78

The teachers I studied have many things in common. They all have strong vocational and professional commitment to teaching. For them, teaching is the activity and the arena in which they become whole, achieve their ultimate ambitions, become the persons they wish to be. They are dedicated professionals who have given their lives and their selves to their job.

All teachers have certain primary interests. Pollard (1985), in examining how considerations of self bear on teachers' actions, identified certain interests associated with maintaining a sense of self in the classroom: maximizing enjoyment; controlling the workload; maintaining one's health and avoiding stress; retaining autonomy; maintaining one's self-image. All of these are important for our teachers, but the last is particularly so as the others are integral to it. From their perceptions of self arise their philosophies of teaching and their values.

Neither self nor creativity, however, is constant. Both are social products and are influenced by social circumstances. Berger (1963, p. 106) affirms that, 'the self is no longer a solid, given entity that moves from one situation to another. It is rather a process, continuously created and re-created in each social situation that one enters'. It is therefore in continual need of defence, maintenance and promotion. Some occasions and periods may be more favourable to promotion. Others may bring teachers' preferred perceptions of self under attack. Inasmuch as their work has become intensified, creative teachers would appear to be going through one of the latter periods.

To the extent that teachers' work is becoming intensified, so their selves are in danger of a degree of debasement – less autonomy, less choice, less freedom, less reflection, less individuality, less voice and ultimately perhaps, less commitment, and/or a change to a more instrumental form.

White (1993), lists 'self-determination' as a core value in a liberal democratic society. Prominent aspects of this are defence, reinforcement, realization, and renewal of the self. I shall examine examples of each.

Self-defence

Nias' teachers (1989 [see Reading 4.1]), though undergoing continual professional development, were always at pains to protect their substantial selves from uncomplimentary change. She notes that the most effective form of self-protection was the reference group:

> Regular contact with other people who shared their beliefs about the social and moral purposes of education and about how children learnt, not only reinforced their view of themselves but also enabled them to filter and even distort messages reaching them from other sources. (pp. 204–5)

We have seen how, in resistance at Ensel School, perceived assaults on the self threw people even closer together. But the self in these circumstances frequently has a resilience of its own, which contributes to the strength of the whole-school perspective. I identified the following factors.

Individual biography

Teachers' theories are grounded in their own lives. The nature and significance of the perspective might not be realized at the time. It may be little more than vaguely but acutely felt experience, not articulated, but sedimented in the self in embryo. The influence of childhood years are formative. The following examples from Ensel School show other ways in which teacher beliefs have strong roots deep in their past. Some Ensel teachers claim that their practices are in large measure a reaction to their own earlier personal experiences. For instance, Susan as a child went to a 'very, very formal school', where you had to memorize and spew out information in examinations. You sit at a desk, listen, teacher imparts knowledge, you take it on board, do a spelling test, a maths test ... and you don't really have much of a stake in your own learning.

Susan described her first teaching post as a:

> very difficult situation but with very, very, positive, constructive, supportive staff. Had it not been quite like that, I would have thought, 'Oh no, this progressive way of working doesn't work'. But I was supported, and it was a very good, positive model to start working, because it put into action a lot of things I'd been told at college.

Following that, she moved to an all-white, middle-class school where teachers practised more traditional methods:

> I couldn't really cope with that ... There was no centrality and no basic philosophy ... I was fighting and saying 'I don't believe in rote learning, they don't understand what they're doing. I'm going to teach differently', and they were saying, 'No, it's always been done like this' and 'we demand that you give my child spelling lists', and the head was supporting them. I thought, 'I can't work somewhere that doesn't really believe what I believe', and then I came here. So apart from that one year I've been very lucky.

Ensel teachers' initial training and educational studies introduced them to a range of theory and practice that confirmed their intuition and cast new light on some of their own experiences. Training illuminated and legitimated their partially formed but keenly felt views, by introducing them to theory, literature and research; illustrating their application to practice; and giving realistic assessments of how they might become modified over time.

Their own professional experience as teachers validates the perspective. The particular circumstances of Ensel School, with its large proportion of children who speak English as a second language, stress the relevance of the perspective. There is a strong emphasis on issues of equality, social justice and multiculturalism. Access to the National Curriculum is a current major concern, with a strong focus of attention on language. Having 'assimilated cultural awareness', as Dave expressed it, teachers then proceed through trial and error. They refine approaches that work, modify those that do not, and reflect on circumstances that affect them. They build up a stock of experience, an accumulating resource with which to help meet new situations.

Collaboration through working and discussing with like-minded colleagues consolidates, defends and fortifies the perspective. It is difficult for creative teachers to survive on their own. Together, they are a potent force. Penny, who was at the time acting as mentor for Vanessa, said:

> It's lovely with Vanessa, because she shares the philosophy 100 per cent, and it's very easy for us to see the value in what each is doing. If I look in her classroom I can see all the good things that are going on.

By contrast, as Susan noted, 'If you've got rifts in the staffroom about various philosophies, then I think you've got problems'. She believes strongly in the idea of 'a team all working together to achieve the same ends'.

The whole-school perspective, especially where also supported by governors and parents, as at Ensel, is both a knowledge and a power base. It expands the range of thought and experience, offers therapy in times of difficulty, and resolve and determination when challenged. The perspective is not just a matter of cognition, but is part of the self infused with aesthetics and emotions.

Constraints delimit the perspective, bringing it to earth and gearing it to practicalities. Things like class size, lack of material resources, and the heavy demands of the National Curriculum can impede the prosecution of strategies indicated by theories emphasizing individualism, space and creativity. However, all teaching is constrained to some extent, and a modicum can lead to more creativity. The ideals guiding the perspective are principles to inform one's approach rather than ends to be met. The creative teacher is always trying to find ways to apply her principles, and to manage the constraints, which might involve outflanking them or using them to advantage.

Self-reinforcement

Collaboration has been represented here as operating in self-defence. But it also operates in a more expansive sense.

The use of critical others illustrates a way in which the self can be reinforced. Critical others can help teachers recover their creativity, bring a long-standing ideal project to fruition, develop new interests, gain new insights into their selves through challenging basic assumptions, help cultivate charisma. Currently, there is a demand for more specialist teaching in primary schools (Alexander, 1992), and for greater flexibility in the teacher role (Campbell, 1993; Brighouse, 1994). Flexibility, however, is not a prominent attribute of extreme rational–legal systems. Critical others add to teachers' specialist knowledge, while still leaving the teacher in control as 'orchestrator' (Woods, 1990). They help them to be 'extended professionals' in Hoyle's (1980) sense of being interested in theory, involved in non-teaching professional activities, and reading professional literature. They help swing the always precarious balance between the preferred, principled mode of teaching, and pragmatic action forced by circumstantial dilemmas.

Self-realization

Whereas self-defence is aligned against perceived threat, and self-reinforcement strengthens existing tendencies, self-realization is about coming to fruition. Perhaps the best example is in 'appropriation' at Coombes. At the centre of the Coombes achievement is the charismatic agent, the head, who had the vision, faith, values and beliefs to launch the project, the resolve and patience to sustain and develop it, and the personal skills and judgement in surrounding herself with and inspiring like-minded people to contribute to the enterprise. At Coombes, there was a strong sense of purpose. At heart, there was a clear conviction about the central importance of environmental issues, a love of and deep respect for nature, a concern for the future of the planet. I asked Sue Humphries how she managed so often to get her own way with exterior bureaucratic forces, and she replied: 'Well, I think having a reputation as an eccentric helps.' Part of this 'eccentricity', perhaps, is Sue's ability to challenge the 'givens' of school, which Sarason (1982) feels is one of the most important factors in inducing change. Some of these 'givens' are the inside classroom as the main context of teaching and learning, the sharp division between inside and outside school, the playground as a plain hard surface, the National Curriculum, and assessment. At Coombes, Sue retains her independent vision. Certain aspects of the National Curriculum are welcome, others are an irritant, but, by and large, it is subsumed within their grand design. Sue makes capital in other ways. To run and develop such a project requires funds and services from others:

> We need money for repairs. For example, a pond cracked in last year's drought and will cost about £600 to put right ... We also need money for ephemeral things, like feeding sheep, paying vets' bills, giving expenses to people like hot air balloonists ... You can't actually see what they've left you with. They are the intangibles, but they are the things that give a quality and a certain edge to this kind of education, if it's what you believe in.

It also means entrepreneurial skills, powers of persuasion and considerable determination. To get opera singers, under-belly horse riders, internationally acclaimed writers, helicopter pilots, parachutists, etc., to the school, Sue feels rests on:

> the way you present the case, the tone of the approach, and the doggedness of the approach ... and, of course, the way a group decides how it spends its money.

A colleague reported that 'when a small circus visited the area, Sue was absolutely determined we were going to get this camel into the playground ... and she did it'. Why was it so important?

> It was to do with the Epiphany and the journey of the wise men, and it was really something that just put that special memory into all the talk that had gone on ... Children are talked at by teachers for hundreds of hours, and so much of it must sail directly over them.

In many ways, Coombes is an expression of Sue's self.

Self-renewal

Self-realization is never complete, but needs what Sue calls 'self-renewal'. Just as the self has a long history with deep biographical roots, so it has a constant dynamic which drives it on.

> The fact that we are deeply immersed in the work and energized by it is going to be the most significant thing, because if you're not, you become terribly tense and stressed. You avoid that with the constant novelty. (She mentioned things that were happening next term for the first time around the theme of 'the performing arts': an early harp recital, a brass quintet, street buskers ...) Most teachers want to go back to teaching because they actually want to finish off their own education. This is a calling for us, but actually it's from needs which were never met when we were at school. You have this great hunger to continue to learn. If the teachers don't get satisfied, the children don't get the buzz out of it.

New themes, or new ways of approaching the same themes, was a deliberate policy. They believed in:

first-class experiences for adults and children, so that they can resonate with those experiences and be energized next day.

A concert, for example, provided valuable reflective time ... a chance to reorganize their thinking, to be refreshed, and up-and-running the next day.

It might take you away from a task, but 'you get back to it with renewed vigour'. Sue 'believed passionately in the ability of certain experiences to regenerate everyone', 'reflective nuggets' she called them, which were:

even more important now than formerly because of the mechanistic approaches induced by current developments.

Self-renewal was a major factor behind Peter's retirement. With his experiences of marginality, he needed disalienating experiences from time to time to retain realistic sight of his preferred side of the margins, and to reaffirm his perception of the substantial self. Even more than this, however, he felt that that self had not yet been fully realized, and still had great potential. Peter was fully committed to the integrity of the self. However, the strategies that he had developed over the years to protect that integrity were no longer sufficient. Retirement was a catalyst not only to save the self, but also to provide it with a springboard to new endeavour.

I hope my retirement is not perceived as someone abandoning ship. Rather, it's transferring from one ship to another ship that's going rather more in the direction that I want to go.

Retirement for Peter, therefore, is a strategy to save and to promote the self. In those terms it is less radical than it may appear, since it is an act entirely consistent with his holistic philosophy. It is expansive and forward-looking, rather than traumatic and retreatist. In terms of self, Peter is making an empowered exit. For some, retirement might mean 'putting their feet up, having a rest, taking life easy'. But for Peter, retirement offered reinvigoration and rebirth through 'restoration', 'continuity', and an 'end of marginality'.

In England and Wales, 5,549 teachers under the age of 60 retired on grounds of ill health in 1993–4, compared with 2,551 in 1987–8, the year before the National Curriculum was introduced (Macleod and Meikle, 1994).

Self-determination takes its toll and has its limits. The self's defences can be penetrated. It can be weakened as well as reinforced, ruined as well as renewed. I am reluctant, however, to let intensification have the final word. Clearly it cannot be discounted. But my message is still an optimistic one, in terms of the principles for which these teachers stand, the degree for manoeuvre that is there between policy-making and implementation, teachers' undoubted successes, and the strength of their resolve. The future depends to a large extent, however, on a new generation of teachers, trained in the National Curriculum, but remembering the principles that others have fought for, and no less creative and self-determined.

The worlds of children and adults

Bronwyn Davies

Adults will need to draw on their commitment to openmindedness when studying this reading, for Bronwyn Davies sets out the reasons why the perceptions of children may vary significantly from those of adults. The structural position of teachers and pupils is fundamentally different, and empathy and understanding is needed for adults to understand 'the culture of childhood'.

To what extent do you really understand the way classroom and school life feels to young children?

Edited from: Davies, B, (1982) *Life in the Classroom and Playground*. London: Routledge, 28–33

Adults structure the world in ways that appear external and inevitable to children, though children bring their own interpretations to bear upon these structures, and thus have a different view of them than adults do. Examples of such external and inevitable structures are: language and social skills necessary for getting about as a socially competent person. Additional structures which may not have the same degree of inevitability but which bind children to the adults' conceptual framework are schools and school attendance and the curriculum and basic skills, such as reading and writing useful for future occupation.

These are the 'givens' in the children's world which appear to be inevitable. Words have specific meanings, school is compulsory, social interaction is disrupted if you don't follow certain basic rules, and finally, teachers tell you certain things and then test you on them. These are the 'facts', external facts that must be incorporated into the world of children and which give them partial membership in the adults' world.

Yet despite the power of adults to define reality, children do develop their own manner of construing the world.

There are several fairly powerful reasons both from the adults' and from the children's perspective for the development of a separate world.

Adults have their own private life and expect children not to intrude on this. As a result children spend more time with their peers who, because of their similar placement in the social world, are more likely to perceive similar problems. That is, problems that arise out of the nature of the institutions of family and school and their positions or roles within those institutions. And like-situated people will help formulate workable solutions, based on similar perspectives, perspectives that may well be incommensurate with parents' and teachers' perspectives. Further, adults may provide 'solutions' that are unworkable for children because the children do not have certain powers or the necessary skills to carry out adult solutions. Alternatively, adults provide solutions which require the child to act in ways that conflict with what he and his peers define as acceptable behaviour.

A further, and perhaps more compelling reason for the development of a separate culture is that the balance of power between children, particularly of the same age and size, is more handleable. Here the adult rules of unquestioned deference, politeness, respect for elders, can be dropped and a basis for relating in terms of equality worked out – or power differentials won through fighting or prowess clearly demonstrated, the rules being closer to what they can manage for themselves without adult interference. Moreover, since the rules are established through experience, they have greater immediacy and convincingness as rules to be followed. Resorting to adult authority can rob the children of their own power to make decisions and to control the situation.

The adults' perception of reality which they, as adults, assume to be superior does not always appear so to children. Because of the taken-for-granted knowledge which informs adults' world, they do not or cannot spell out to children why they think as they do. When children ask adults questions, the adults may produce what for them are hard-won solutions to earlier problems, and yet are, for the children, meaningless riddles because even where the adults are aware of the links they have made, the children can't trace the steps from the first viewing of the problem to the ultimate solution. And adults may not even answer children's questions at all. Children's questions can be irritating, embarrassing and awkward, and they may on occasion appear to be futile and pointless. Adults sometimes find the perspective from which children's questions arise quite beyond them.

And yes, if children behave like mini-adults, or converse in an adult manner (as Aries, 1962, has shown children of the past were wont to do), they are seen as inappropriate, even immoral. This ambivalence towards children – wanting them to be like adults and wanting them to be like children is an interestingly inconsistent feature of adults' attitudes towards children.

Children, to be acceptable, must act like children. Yet the credibility that adults are prepared to give to the associated world view that goes with acting like or being a child is somewhat lacking. Children's views which differ markedly from adult views may be seen simply as a result of incomplete socialization or even failed socialization, rather than the legitimate products of another culture – the culture of childhood.

There is a further barrier that exists between the child's and the adult's reality which stems from the fact that the roles each are required to play within the school system lead to differing perceptions of what is relevant or meaningful.

For teachers, responsibility for discipline and for teaching create the central tasks relating to their role. What the teachers perceive in their day-to-day carrying out of their roles will be closely related to these central tasks. Though teachers may wish that children would take on these tasks as their own, they cannot escape from the fact that school is an adult-imposed institution and the curriculum and many of the requirements made of children in school are adult-imposed. From the children's perspective, the aspects of their environment that they may feel they have some say in will more likely be how to avoid trouble with teachers, how to make and keep friends, and how to survive in the system.

These are the topics of conversation often touched on by the children. In looking at children's account of school it is clear that they have little interest in tasks related to the teacher's role. Those aspects of their lives that the children can most easily give accounts of are ones which they feel are related to their tasks rather than teacher-initiated tasks. For example, when I first started talking to the children I perceived the oft-used phrase 'I don't know' as an easy way out of not answering my questions, or as evasion. I began to realize, however, that 'I don't know' just as often signalled 'I don't know and I don't think I could or should know, since that is to do with the adult world'.

In other words, children develop the capacity to see clearly from their own position within the social structure, and do not worry unduly about what it looks like to the adults. It is enough to learn to successfully play the role of child without having to know more about adults than is necessary to interact with them. Yet the adults perceive their task, in socializing the children, as helping them to see the world correctly, i.e., as adults do, and as teaching them to become adults. Children are caught in a world where they must balance on the one hand the convincing world of adults. In this latter world of the adults, moreover, there is no real recognition of the former world as experienced and developed by the children. Adults provide structures which children are dependent on and legitimate these very structures in the process of socializing their children. Yet adults do not want children to share this adult world or to be adults. But even without the rights enjoyed by adults, and despite the expectations placed on them as members of the institution of childhood, children busily get on with the business of constructing their own reality with each other, as well as making sense of and developing strategies to cope with the adult world as and when it impinges on their world. This reality and its related strategies I refer to as the culture of childhood.

📖 READING 4.7

Classroom interests of 'Goodies', 'Jokers' and 'Gangs'

Andrew Pollard

This reading builds on the analysis of the culture of childhood offered by Davies in Reading 4.6. Andrew Pollard studied the peer groups and 'coping strategies' of twelve-year-old pupils in a middle school. In particular, he identified relatively conformist 'Goodies', able and skilled negotiating 'Jokers', and 'Gangs' who were somewhat alienated by school and, on occasion, were prepared to initiate significant deviance. In this reading, Pollard considers pupils' salient concerns and suggests how these 'interests-at-hand' are juggled by members of each type of group as they cope with school life.

Can you identify children in your classroom whose predominant strategies are forms of conformity, negotiation or mischief making? How do they accomplish life in your classroom?

Edited from: Pollard, A. (1984) 'Goodies, jokers and gangs', in Hammersley, M. and Woods, P. (eds) *Life in School: The Sociology of Pupil Culture*. Milton Keynes: Open University Press, 246–53

A crucial fact of the social situation within a classroom is that two relatively distinct social systems exist beside each other. The official system of the school with its hierarchy, rules and particular criteria of evaluation exists alongside the children's own social system. This may appear to be less formal but also has its own hierarchy, rules and criteria of judgement. In lessons, the official school system is represented by the teacher whilst the children's own social system is represented by each child's peers. To which party and to which social system should each child refer his or her actions, and with what consequences?

From the analysis of the Moorside data it was possible to identify particular issues which were salient to the children. These appeared to be bound to their instrumental concern with prediction and control in their classroom and could thus be grouped by purpose, which made it possible to infer interests. This procedure yielded six groupings and it seemed analytically useful to draw a distinction between the primary interest of 'self', which has several facets, and more secondary interests, which are 'enabling interests' in an essentially means-end relationship. These interests are shown in the table below.

Primary interests-at-hand	Enabling interests-at-hand
Self - Maintenance of self image	Peer group membership
- Enjoyment	Learning
- Control of stress	
- Retention of dignity	

'Self-image': a facet of the primary interest of 'self'

The children at Moorside had clear images of their own identities. These were related in many ways to their friendship groups. The Good groups thought of themselves as 'kind', 'quiet', and 'friendly', the Joker groups believed themselves to be 'clever' and 'good fun' but 'sensible', whilst the Gangs regarded themselves as 'tough' and 'rough'. These identities were further highlighted by denigrating concepts such as reference by Joker groups to Gangs as 'thick, silly yobs' or by Gangs to Joker groups as 'snobbish, creeping, pansies'.

It was clear that when interacting in their classrooms the children would act to maintain their self-image *vis-à-vis* their peers, often even when other interests were threatened. Perhaps the most regular and obvious instance of this was the number of Gang members who would assert their toughness by defying teachers and 'taking' the punishments and sanctions which followed. Clearly children have to manage their self-image in ways which are advantageous to them and this presentational problem can be acute in the classroom when the expectations of peers and the teacher or parent may clash. Maintaining their self-image and sense of identity in this context is an ever present concern.

'Enjoyment': a facet of the primary interest of 'self'

Enjoyment here refers to the degree of intrinsic self-fulfilment to be obtained from interaction with other people. Children will hope to experience a sense of positive reward from interactions so that they are supportive of self.

Of course there are many forms which such enjoyment can take but one which stands out in the literature, as at Moorside, is that of 'having a laugh'. As Woods has put it:

> pupils have their own norms, rules and values and their school lives are well structured by them. In their lives, laughter has a central place whether as a natural product or as a life-saving response to the exigencies of the institution – boredom, ritual, routine, regulations, oppressive authority. (Woods, 1976, p. 185)

However, not all 'laughs' are oppositional. Humour in the classroom also often enables teachers and pupils to step out of their role and to express themselves and to communicate in less guarded ways than they might usually adopt. As such, humour can also be seen as a source of reinforcement and development of teacher–pupil relationships, in that to share and 'get the joke' reasserts and constructs the 'culture of the classroom' (Walker and Adelman, 1976) and thus gives security to all 'members' within that setting.

Stebbings (1980) has noted that for teachers humour is both a strategy used for control and a form of self-expression. 'Having a laugh' can be seen for children in similar terms. It can be a strategy of opposition which challenges teacher control or it can be enjoyable as a form of collective relaxation. At Moorside the different types of friendship groups had characteristically patterned aspirations. In the case of Gangs, their greatest enjoyment appeared to come from forms of action which were essentially oppositional to teachers. Thus, they emphasized incidents of 'causing bother' and 'mucking about' as highlights of their experiences and they liked the excitement from such activities as 'cheeking off' teachers or playing at 'dares' in lessons. Joker groups also enjoyed excitement but appeared to derive it in lessons from less disruptive actions such as sending notes or drawing in jotters. Rather than 'act daft' and 'cause bother' they would derive their greatest enjoyment from 'having a laugh' with teacher participation and they also reported enjoying lessons which were particularly 'interesting'. Good groups also emphasized enjoying 'interesting' lessons and mentioned enjoying lessons sometimes when teachers 'told jokes'. In most instances, however, their great desire to avoid stress meant that they felt most relaxed in ordered, routine and predictable lessons.

The references to enjoyment from 'interesting lessons' of course relates to the other main source of positive reward for children – the sense of self-fulfilment produced by success and achievement in learning. At Moorside, many children, particularly in Joker or Good groups, wanted to succeed in academic terms – after all these were the official, adult criteria by which they would be evaluated and by which to some extent they evaluated themselves. The key to this though was balance. Children wanted teachers who would 'have a laugh' and 'teach things'.

'Control of stress': a facet of the primary interest of 'self'

The main source of stress for children in classrooms derives from teacher power and the evaluative context of schooling. For 'good' groups at Moorside stress avoidance seemed to be a particularly prominent interest-at-hand, largely, I would argue, because their self-image as quiet, studious, and conformist was undercut with few defences if rejected by a teacher 'getting mad' with them. They were also vulnerable and relatively defenceless if in conflict with other groups of children. They thus tended to be wary and to concentrate on 'avoiding trouble'. In contrast Gangs almost needed stress by which to assert their 'toughness'. At the same time though, few children actually sought out, say, a severe telling-off from a teacher. If such a thing occurred, then it was used to build the tough identity but it was not enjoyed in itself. Joker groups were also concerned to avoid stress, be it from academic failure or acts of deviance. They very much disliked being told off because it negated the type of relationship which they tried to establish with teachers. At the same time, though, it is clear that a lot of their 'good fun' and 'enjoyment' was derived from juggling with the risks of 'getting done' by teachers. If their judgements were correct, then routine teacher reactions would not result in much stress. Indeed, spice and zest would be added to classroom experiences from such 'exploration of the limits' without serious sanctions resulting.

Stress is thus a double-edged interest-at-hand. Usually children seek to avoid the potential stress to which they are permanently subject because of teacher power and because of the constant evaluation of their learning. However, there is no doubt that other sorts of stress are wilfully introduced by children from time to time as a source of enjoyment and as an antidote to routine or boredom.

'Retaining dignity': a facet of the primary interest of 'self'

This was one of the important interests-at-hand for all the groups of children, being crucial for the preservation of self- and peer-group esteem. Of course there is a close relationship between dignity and perceived 'fairness' and this was particularly clear at Moorside. Thus teacher actions and censures would be constantly assessed by the children for legitimacy. 'Getting done' could therefore be accepted without loss of dignity if it was 'fair', but if the teacher went 'mad' and particularly if they started shouting and denigrating a child, then this would be regarded as a most 'unfair' assault by all the children. Other, more specific, threats to dignity came from being 'picked on', or teased by teachers as well as by having one's name forgotten. Being picked on was felt particularly deeply as a personal attack by the Gang groups. It was regarded as unfair because it was seen to arise from unusual levels of teacher surveillance and from particular attention being directed towards them. Being 'shown up' was recognized as a specific act of depersonalization intended to set an example. For instance, as Malcolm put it:

> He only showed me up like that in front of everyone just to make me look stupid ... and just to try to make us all learn the notes better. He's always getting on at us for it and just 'cos I couldn't answer his questions he picked on me.

On the other hand, being teased was something which the Joker groups seemed particularly conscious of. The girls related that one teacher often teased them about boyfriends which in some cases upset them because it made them 'go all red and look silly'. The relatively quiet members of Good groups were the main group of children who reported having their names forgotten. They clearly regarded this as insulting and resented it.

With regard to retaining dignity *vis-à-vis* the other children similar issues seemed important. The inter-group rivalry at Moorside was reflected in mild forms of teasing and in more serious episodes of name calling or fighting similar to that recorded by Sluckin (1981) in Oxfordshire primary schools. In all cases though the children's comments on such incidents revealed both defensive and aggressive actions to be forms of assertion of particular self-identities with particular group associations. The defence of personal dignity thus seems to be a very prominent interest-at-hand for children in all school contexts.

'Peer group membership' and 'learning': two enabling interests

It was suggested earlier that peer group loyalty and learning should be seen as enabling interests rather than as facets of the primary self-interest. They relate to the social ascriptions of the child culture and social system and of the adult educational culture and wider society respectively. As such they reflect the ambiguity of each child's structural position and of course to some extent they offer alternative ways of enabling the primary interest-at-hand of self to be satisfied. They also pose severe dilemmas for the children when they come to make strategic decisions concerning action and to juggle with their interests in the dynamic flow of classroom processes.

Peer group membership

At Moorside, peer group membership was linked to both the assertion and defence of self. Enjoyment, laughs and 'great times' almost exclusively derived from interaction between the children and their 'mates' or 'friends' with or without the positive participation of the teacher. A supportive audience was thus crucial and could only be guaranteed by the secure membership and solidarity of a peer group. Peer group 'competence' sometimes had to be proven if a child was to avoid being rejected as 'wet' or 'stupid' but would of course vary in its nature depending on the type of group. Group membership was also of defensive value both against the threat from teachers and from other children. The solidarity which existed within groups provided a powerful resource for individuals in exposed situations both in the classroom or playground. Group members were expected to 'stick up' for each other and certainly one of the worst actions imaginable was to 'snitch' or 'tell tales' on a friend. Peer group solidarity was a particularly important interest for gang groups because of the consequences of their frequent rejection of teacher authority. Children's concern to be seen as a full and competent member of their peer group can thus be seen as an enabling interest in the context of their primary concern to protect their self and 'survive' the variety of situations at school which they encounter.

Learning

Whilst the enabling interest of peer group membership responds to the children's social system, the interest of 'learning' is a primary means of coping in the adult evaluation systems of teachers and parents. Teachers and parents expect children to 'learn'. Thus one way of satisfying them and of negotiating their power and influence is simply to do just that. However, within children's social structures there will be considerable variation in the degree of commitment to this strategy. For instance, at Moorside the children would constantly assess the 'cost' of trying to learn by evaluating how 'interesting' or 'boring' the lessons were. Of course there were variations not only in those judgements but also in the responses then made. Good groups might consider a lesson as 'boring' but put up with it anyway, accepting it as 'good for them' and not wishing to compromise their identities with their teachers. Joker group members would be more inclined to attempt to direct the lesson into more 'fertile' activities whilst Gang members would be likely to attempt to subvert the lesson directly. Good and Joker group members reported far more intrinsic satisfaction from lessons than Gang members. The latter were far more likely to see lessons as a 'waste of time' or time spent on 'doing nothing' unless a direct link with future work possibilities was drawn. They thus generally had a more exclusively instrumental approach than the other, more academically successful, types of group. Obviously their perceived academic 'failure' meant that learning did not seem to provide anything more than a very limited means of enabling them to cope with their situation. On the other hand, for Joker group members their success at learning earned them the credit with teachers and parents with which they were able to relax and cultivate laughs. For the Good group members the studious sincerity of their attempts to learn enabled them to accomplish lessons without incident.

Of course academic achievement feeds back directly to the development of each child's identity and self-concept so that to learn in lessons is not an interest-at-hand simply by virtue of the need to accomplish the particular situation. It is linked to the maintenance and development of self-image, to enjoyment, to stress-avoidance and to dignity – facets of self which, though experienced with immediacy, accumulate over time into more established identities. Thus not only teachers but each child himself comes to 'know' who is 'thick' and who is 'bright', and of course, so do other children.

Conclusion

For each individual pupil, coping in the long run depends on evolving viable strategies by which to accomplish their structural position and hence must derive from some form of accommodation with it, in which an acceptable balance of self, peer group membership and learning is necessary.

The types of group which have been identified represent different types of solution to the problems posed by school life. Some pupils will seek to cope by conforming and seeking to 'please the teacher' as much as possible; some will reject the whole experience, treat it as an attack on their self-esteem and resist it; some may try to negotiate their way through the situation by balancing their concerns with those of the teacher. Thus we have the strategies of the 'good' groups, the 'gang' groups and the 'joker' groups.

One important consequence is the possibility that the adoption of particular strategies by children may result in further reinforcement and elaboration of the associated identity from interaction with teachers and from organizational amplification. Child adaptations and perspectives of the sort which I have been considering could therefore lead into an analysis of typing and 'career' and hence become directly related to the major sociological issue of the role of schooling in social reproduction.

 READING 4.8

Identity, migration and education

Uvanney Maylor

> This is a short reading which is intended to signal the very important topics of how biography and structural circumstances affect pupil experiences. Uvanney Maylor reflects on the upbringing she received from her father, who had come to the UK from Jamaica, and she provides an account of her own experiences and feelings as a black child in predominantly white schools. The important point is that all children are affected by the circumstances of, and relationships within, their family. Some are likely to be advantaged and others disadvantaged in a society in which inequalities are endemic. However, teachers have the responsibility to maximize the quality of life and fulfilment of potential of each and every child.
>
> Edited from: Maylor, U. (1995) 'Identity, migration and education', in Blair, M. and Holland, J. (eds) *Identity and Diversity*. Clevedon: Multilingual Matters, 39–49

The autobiography outlined below is my version of events. A mere fraction of my whole life, it is what I could safely allow the public to know without knowing all of me. It is part of the journey I took to becoming an 'educated self'.

My mother died when I was three years old. Since that day my father has been mother and father to me. He seemed to me to be at once all knowing and frightening. In one breath he could shout loudly in anger and in another he would quietly reveal the wealth of historical data he had acquired as a child and as an adult. He expected obedience at all times, and adhered to the philosophy of 'spare the rod and spoil the child'. But although some might consider this a violent philosophy, I never thought of my father as a violent man.

He seemed to me to be kind, generous and thoughtful. Materially, I wanted for nothing, but I did crave a more open demonstration of the love he had for me. I suppose the love that might have been there for me died when my mother passed away. I had never considered my father unloving until I was about ten years old when I began to notice that he did not return my kiss as he left for work. I was always the demonstrative one – I liked to be loved.

Father was 'a man's man', an authoritarian. In his relations with women and children he considered himself always to be right, never wrong. This was a particularly difficult trait of his personality. It did not matter how plausible your explanation was, if it did not coincide with his it was automatically deemed wrong.

It is difficult to assess whether my father's assumed power would have gone unchallenged had my mother lived. However, such dominance needs to be understood in the light not only of a patriarchal culture, but the social context in which my father found himself after my mother's death. On reflection, I associate his need to be respected, to be obeyed, to have status, with his status in Britain. When he arrived in Britain, the difficulties in settling in a foreign land were compounded by the denial and rejection of his skills as a tailor, of him as a man. He was vilified because of the colour of his skin. Coming from a country where his family name commanded respect, father found his treatment difficult to comprehend.

Father was a proud man, who had assumed that his British passport afforded him the rights that fellow citizens took for granted. He found it difficult to acknowledge the alien and lowly status accorded to him. With these denials it is possible to understand why father proceeded on the track that he did. He sought to regain his pride through the achievements of his children, and with my brother and sister still in Jamaica, I bore the brunt of his ambitions. Father's belief in Britain as a meritocratic society created several problems for me.

Father believed implicitly in the power of education. He lived by such maxims as: 'if at first you don't succeed, try and try again'; 'never let them use your colour as an excuse not to employ you, let it be for lack of qualification'. Dad's obsession with education was both the source of my subordination at home and the key to my freedom.

He believed that with education came a good job, a decent income, decent housing, better economic and social opportunities and more importantly the ability to choose.

Unfortunately, father did not realize that the very education system in which he placed so much faith, was built upon and perpetuated the social divisions of class and 'race' now responsible for his diminished self-image. Like Martin Luther King, father had a dream, but it was a dream of social mobility. A dream thwarted in a world where skin colour persisted as a marker of exclusion. A fact which father would not acknowledge.

From the age of seven life at school was a constant struggle. At that point in time I became more aware of my racial identity. As one of a small minority of black pupils, I was subjected to continuous racial abuse. I wore my hair in plaits to school – it was both convenient and made my hair easier to manage. The partings in my hair led the children to invent the nickname of 'square head'. I longed for the day when I could wear my hair in one as the other girls did. I was 'affectionately' known as 'blackie/darkie'. At secondary school 'square head' was replaced by 'monkey'. The contrast between my dark skin and white teeth provided a source of derision for one of my teachers: 'If we turn the lights out we will be able to see Uvanney's teeth.'

It was not the name calling which bothered me so much – it was the malicious intent that I found painful. These were children with whom I shared 35 hours of the week. I considered them to be my friends. Behind their surface smiles seemed to lurk a mountain of hostility. Who taught them to hate me? And why did racial forms of abuse hurt me so much more than any other forms? Although I did not understand it at the time, I realize now that this kind of abuse did not make me feel less of a person, less human, but I must have known at some level that they also referred to my father, my friends and all the other black people in the world.

Negotiating health at home and school

Berry Mayall

This reading from Berry Mayall draws on a fascinating research project on young children and health-care. Picking up on some of the issues in Reading 4.6, the issue of health-care provides an illustration of how children must learn to negotiate within adult worlds, even when, as in this particular case, those of the school and of home may be rather different. Mayall shows how children at school are often 'bystanders to parent–teacher negotiations' but tend to be more actively involved in decisions at home.

Such issues could be considered in respect of home–school partnerships for curriculum learning (Reading 14.6) or the scope for pupil involvement in their own work (12.7).

Edited from: Mayall, B. (1994) *Negotiating Health: Children at Home and Primary School*. London: Cassell, 161–5

Children at the age of 5 present themselves as people with a clear sense of who they are within the family. Their accounts indicate their understanding of how daily life works, of social relationships, of moral limits, of the scope for negotiation. Children's competence and knowledge are evidenced in their accounts of day-to-day health maintenance. They describe themselves as looking after themselves, as knowing the health maintenance routines and practices at home, and as negotiating with their mothers the division of labour and responsibility for health care.

When 5-year-olds enter the social world of primary school they have to find out what its norms and expectations are, and work out how best to establish an acceptable way of life. Children demonstrate creative competence in the face of these difficult tasks. They have to create a new social identity for themselves: that of schoolchild, with social relationships and social behaviours designed to suit school conditions. Not only do they seem to learn fast, but they must learn fast if they are to establish acceptable identities as schoolchildren. Some present themselves as keener than others to maintain the identities they have already established outside school; and in so doing are likely to challenge school conventions and even to make themselves unpopular with their more conforming peers.

School staff adopt a mixed stance in relation to school entrants. On the one hand they expect that children will have some competencies and social skills: for instance that they will have some skills in dressing themselves, and will recognize the desirability of behaving considerately to other children. But, on the other hand, school does not respect and allow for children's self-regulating competencies in, for instance, pacing the day, taking rest and exercise as appropriate, eating, drinking and toileting as needed. It also downplays children's knowledge, acquired at home, about what constitutes good health care. And it subjects children's sickness bids to scrutiny in the light of school conventions, time-tables and pressures. All of this can be understood within two basic principles that underlie the provision of primary schooling: that the school presents a model environment for children, and that the job of socializing children once they are 5, properly rests with the school, within the school's moral order. At each stage of primary schooling, the teacher regards the socialization of the children as incomplete, and as requiring further work on her or his part.

By the age of 9, with over four years' schooling behind them, and with increased powers of reflection, children clearly perceive that it is adults who construct the social norms at both home and school and they describe their skill in negotiating an acceptable daily life in both arenas. However, many of them define school norms and adult behaviours as unnecessarily prescriptive and rigid whilst the home offers more scope for choice and independent activity.

During the primary school years, therefore, children move on a daily basis between two powerful social and moral influences: the home, where their first learning takes place and which remains, in their view, the most important influence; and the school, which presents itself as a social and moral order designed for children. Again, thinking of this daily experience from the children's point of view – from home to school and back again – we may wonder at children's ability to make spaces for themselves in both environments, to survive and even thrive. For in both the home and the school, they are living and interacting in social structures to which they are essentially subordinated. Yet in their accounts they tell of manipulating time, space and adults to give themselves time and space of their own.

It is within the context of the school's central goals and character that the care which teachers give to children, and the health education they offer, can be understood. In the school I studied, the teachers looked after the children carefully and in some instances tenderly. Though there are few other research data on this, probably many parents would agree that most teachers, on most occasions, are caring towards the children. However, the characteristics of that care are different from those of the care given by parents.

As regards health education, we have seen a set of principles emerging from teachers' accounts that again derive from the unique character of the primary school. Telling the children what constituted good health behaviour, and discussing health issues with them, took place opportunistically and in some cases as a planned session. Underlying these activities is the view, promoted by wider education policies, that it is part of the job of schools to 'do' health education, and underlying that is the view that children do not already know what the teachers tell them, for the content of the school curriculum is, by definition, not known to the children. In addition, the school and its teachers are assumed to have 'correct' health knowledge, because the school's ideal childcare environment and health education activities are mediated through the teachers.

For the children, as their accounts demonstrate, there were conflicts between health care messages. What they are overtly taught at school, whether formally or informally, often conflicts with the school régime. For instance, whilst many schools teach children about dental hygiene and healthy diets, probably few (though we do not know for sure) endorse their teaching fully in practice, by encouraging tooth-brushing at school, and providing only healthy food, as defined. Self-maintenance, and the drive towards independence that underpins it, may be proposed as virtues but are hindered by school routines. Children starting school have to learn fast how to conform, even where that means restriction of their liberty to care for themselves. At the top end of the school, they have learned to endure and cope with a less than health-promoting institution.

As far as going sick in primary school is concerned, adults and children negotiate the legitimacy of the sickness bid. Younger children are more likely to be believed than older ones, and this development as children progress up the school, results essentially from the increasingly rigid and time-consuming demands of the curriculum, as perceived by the teachers.

Teachers' understanding of parents' knowledge and responsibilities is particularly interesting here. Mothers were designated as the authorities on the physical health of their children. When children were deemed ill, or had an accident, the school carried out a holding operation, but referred the child to the mother for treatment and care.

However, when it came to emotional and psychological health, here, teachers tended to assume superior knowledge, as well as the right to educate mothers.

Children's own participation in discussion and negotiation between school and parent about health matters was virtually nil. It is the adults who are assumed to be the correct people to make decisions. This is in line with parental legal responsibilities for making sure their children attend school, and with school responsibilities to care for the children during school hours. But, as ever, this exclusion from decision-making about their health is unlikely to contribute towards the development of the responsible, autonomous health-promoting person beloved of health educators. And, again, children are likely to value the home as an environment where they do have a part in negotiating health decisions, such as whether to go swimming, in contrast to the school, where they are bystanders to parent–teacher negotiations, and objects of these adults' decisions.

CHAPTER 5

How are we getting on together?

The eight readings in this chapter address various aspects of the 'classroom climate' – an important factor in creating positive conditions for learning.

Withall and Lewis (5.1) describe a classic study which demonstrated the importance of leadership style on interpersonal relationships. This is followed by Woods (5.2), Pollard (5.3) and King (5.4) providing complementary insights on class control. Woods emphasizes the 'art' of teaching, Pollard analyses the negotiation of classroom rules and King reviews some of the control techniques used by teachers.

From the pupil perspective, the experience of schooling is described by Jackson (5.5) in terms of 'crowds, praise and power'. This then leads into a reading from Lawrence (5.6) on the nature of self-esteem which also shows how this is influenced by the expectations of others, such as parents and teachers. Research findings on variations and consequences of teacher expectations are reviewed in the reading by Mortimore and colleagues (5.7).

The chapter concludes with an account by Merrett and Wheldall (5.8) on how to produce class discipline through positive, structured reinforcement of desired forms of behaviour.

The parallel chapter of *Reflective Teaching in the Primary School* addresses similar issues and provides practical classroom activities for investigating them further. There are sections on interpersonal relationships, on negotiating classroom rules and on enhancing classroom climate through the development of children's self-esteem. There are also many suggestions for further reading.

READING 5.1

Leadership and the socio-emotional climate in classrooms

John Withall and W. W. Lewis

This reading is a short description of a very influential, early research study which shows how an adult's leadership style can affect the behaviour of a group. It has clear implications for teachers and suggests that a 'democratic' approach to classroom relationships can produce a positive climate for learning and behaviour.

How would you characterize your own leadership style in the classroom?

Edited from: Withall, J. and Lewis, W. W. (1963) 'Social interaction in the classroom', in Gage, N. L. (ed.) *Handbook of Research on Teaching*. American Educational Research Association, 696–7.

The early work on the effect of social climate and of leadership roles on group life and productivity is best represented by Lippitt's Iowa investigation (Lewis, Lippitt and White, 1939). He organized four clubs of five boys each. The boys were eleven years old and drawn from public state (i.e. maintained) school populations. Each club met for six weeks under a leader who implemented a specified style of leadership. Thus, in a consecutive 18-week period the four clubs each had three different leaders who employed either a democratic, autocratic, or laisser-faire leadership style. The leadership styles were rotated among the several leaders so that personality might be partialled out as a biasing factor. Two clubs met concurrently in adjoining rooms and were headed by leaders implementing two different leadership methodologies according to stated criteria. Two sets of observers recorded: quantitative running accounts of social interaction between the five boys and the leader; a continuous stenographic record of the conversation of the six persons in each club; activity subgroupings and activity goals of each; a running account of psychologically interesting interactions in each group; and an account of interclub contacts. The mean percentage of agreement between two investigators categorizing the verbal behaviour was 80 per cent. Other data included interview material secured from each club member; interview data from the parents of the boys at the end of the experiment; ratings by parents of a boy's co-operativeness, hobbies, and developmental history; information on the boy filled out by his room teacher; and, finally, the results of a Rorschach test given to each child. Analyses were made of the verbal behaviour of the six individuals in each club. Their social behaviour was analysed in terms of: 'ascendant', 'fact-minded', 'submissive', and 'ignoring' categories.

Lippitt's major conclusions were:

that different styles of leader behaviour produce differing social climates and differing group and individual behaviours;

that conversation categories differentiated leader-behaviour techniques more adequately than did social behaviour categories;

that different leaders playing the same kind of leadership roles displayed very similar patterns of behaviour and that group members reacted to the same kind of leadership style in strikingly similar and consistent fashion;

that group members in a democratic social climate were more friendly to each other, showed more group-mindedness, were more work-minded, showed greater initiative, and had a higher level of frustration tolerance than members in the other groups;

that leader-behaviour categories represent the important parameters to which the children reacted.

The significance of Lippitt's work lies in the fact that it is the earliest, major, successful attempt to observe and control objectively the climate variable in group life. His clear demonstration of the influence of the leader on group life and productivity had strong implications for teachers and education.

 READING 5.2

Teachers and classroom relationships

Peter Woods

In this interesting reading, Peter Woods grapples with the issue of how teachers derive fulfilment from their work. He relates this to the 'art' of managing classroom relationships to minimize conflictual aspects of the teacher role. He identifies the skills which contribute towards the 'productive blend' of rapport and control which is often found in the primary school classroom as teachers resolve the dilemmas that must be faced.

Edited from: Woods, P. (1987) 'Managing the primary teachers' role', in Delamont, S. (ed.) *The Primary School Teacher*. London: Falmer Press, 120–43

Why do teachers carry on teaching? Material rewards are not great, unlike the risk of stress, so there must be other factors. Prominent among these, according to Pollard (1985) is 'enjoyment' deriving from the pleasure of working with children, but curiously this has been largely left out of account in consideration of the teacher role – probably as a legacy of the tendency to see the world largely through official interpretations.

There are at least three interrelated reasons why this is so. The first is to do with stage of pupil development. In the one, they are still undergoing primary socialization (Berger and Luckmann, 1967) [see Reading 7.6] which takes place under circumstances that are highly charged emotionally. Indeed, there is good reason to believe that 'without such emotional attachment to the significant others, the learning process would be difficult if not impossible. The child identifies with the significant others in a variety of emotional ways ...' (p. 151). These feelings are to some extent reciprocated. As Jackson (1977) argues, 'Like parents, teachers develop possessive feelings about their students, who become a source of worry, annoyance and pride'.

A second reason is to do with the organization and ethos of schools. Primary schools are much smaller than secondary, more locally centred, community-related, 'warm and caring', family-orientated. Teachers and pupils all come to know each other very well as individuals. As one teacher told me, 'I think it important that you know the kids and you all grow up together'. There can be then, also, a strong degree of group cohesiveness in primary schools where 'affective ties bind members to the community and gratification stems from involvement with all the members of the group' (Kanter, 1974).

A third reason is to do with teaching approaches. While so-called 'pupil-centred' approaches are by no means exclusive to primary schools, there has been a heavy emphasis on these within them especially since the Plowden Report (CACE, 1967), to a degree which secondary schools, given their commitments to external public examinations, have not, as yet, been able to match.

These factors – the need to provide for primary socialization, the organization of primary schooling, and teacher approach – have implications for the teacher role. Inasmuch as the teacher–pupil relationship involves a certain degree of intimacy and emotional attachment, mutual interest and help, equality, and steadfastness, it is one of friendship. The notion of 'teacher as friend', however, would appear alien to some approaches, except, perhaps, as a teaching strategy. The reciprocality here involves friendliness in exchange for good order and work on a sliding proportional scale – rather than friendship for friendship's sake. The principles involved here seem to require more affective neutrality and social distance. Even here, however, the requirements of 'teachers as parent' call for some affective relationship. More importantly, in my experience many teachers who would subscribe to certain principles of teacher-directed learning (involving teacher ownership of knowledge and transmission forms of pedagogy) would also subscribe to forming strong, friendly, relationships with their pupils informally, which cannot help but overrun into the formal area. Few teachers, in consequence, if any, are able to regard their clients as just 'cases', as doctors and lawyers might do. In a sense, friendship cuts across 'teacher as teacher', that is, the need to instruct and to control, and becomes a potential source of role conflict and strain for both sorts of teacher.

The potential conflict can be heightened by the pressures operating on teachers to be (a) 'teacherly' – the emphasis on measurable objectives, evaluation, results – from parents, inspectors, central government; also by the lack of resources to mount a learner-centred approach entirely adequately (the system is very much geared to transmission modes); (b) 'friendly' – their own need for enjoyment and pleasure in the company of their pupils, as already noted. Pollard (1985), in fact, rates this kind of enjoyment as one of teachers' primary interests, whilst 'instruction', and 'control' are only enabling interests – a means to enjoyment and a satisfactory self-image. Pollard points to teachers' liking for humour and jokes which 'seemed to provide opportunities for the relaxation of roles, and clearly teachers enjoyed relating closely with the children on these occasions, provided of course that they controlled the humour rather than becoming its butt' (p. 24). This neatly points the contrast between different teachers – for some, the humour is part of the role, an essential element in the way they conceptualize it. For others, it is 'time out', to be indulged in 'back regions' (Goffman, 1961). For both, however, it has a key importance. Here again, over-indulgence in friendliness can mean that it is difficult to break free when the situation demands one to be teacherly. This in turn can undermine the basis of the friendship, for this has to include a mutual respect. The relationship, thus, fails in all respects.

If the role strain is unresolved, it may promote stress, which the teacher will seek to relieve in one or more ways – for example cultivating split personalities (Lacey, 1976), compromising their ideal classroom organization (Gracey, 1972), modifying their attitudes (Morrison and McIntyre, 1969), revising their commitment (Sikes *et al.*, 1985). If, however, the role strain is resolved, it can lead to effective and enjoyable teaching for all concerned.

I have argued that the primary school teacher role is intrinsically conflictual. The need for strong affective relationships between pupil and teacher (whether progressive, traditional or whatever) is demanded by the teachers' parental role, by their own interests among which enjoyment figures large (and much of which is derived from their relationships with pupils), by pupil needs. And so teacher–pupil friendships are formed.

However, it is difficult for teachers to escape altogether some old-fashioned instruction and control, whatever their ideals and beliefs. There are pressures operating on them from central and local government, from school and parents, from pupils, from themselves, to meet objectives and achieve results. With adequate resources, these might be achieved through purer pupil-directedness. Where they are inadequate, the 'purity' will go down on a proportionate scale. At one extreme, we may find the 'survival' syndrome where teacher strategies are focused on survival rather than pedagogy (Woods, 1979). More often, one might expect to find a productive blend.

The skills that go into its manufacture are fashioned, I would argue, from three main resource areas:

> personal abilities, beliefs, attitudes, commitment. Teachers will not strike a happy combination if, for example, they do not like children, or if they are too 'wet' to shout at them

occasionally, or if they do not like teaching; conversely, those that have a certain flair or charisma have a head start;

training and education. This undoubtedly adds something to a teacher's 'omniscience' – subject-knowledge and the craft of pedagogy; and

teaching experience. This is the day-by-day experimentation over the years, that reveals what works and what does not, the progressive compilation and refinement of techniques and strategies, smoothing off unnecessarily abrasive edges, tightening up on indulgent or slack approaches and activities, knowing one's abilities as diplomat, negotiator, socializer, increasing knowledge of pupils and themselves and their inter-relationships in the classroom ... and so on.

Success in all these areas as manifested in a 'good teacher teaching well' almost defies analysis and comes back to a conception of teaching as an art. It involves combining roles, solving dilemmas, and inventing patterns of events and relationships, that, seen in their entirety, have a certain beauty. Herein lie the greater rewards of teaching – for both teachers and pupils.

 READING 5.3

Teachers, pupils and the working consensus

Andrew Pollard

This reading provides a sociological analysis of how teacher–pupil relationships are formed. At the start of each new year it is suggested that a 'process of establishment' takes place, through which understandings and tacit rules about classroom life are negotiated. This 'working consensus' reflects the needs and coping strategies of both pupils and teacher as they strive to fulfil their classroom roles. Given the power of each to threaten the interests of the other, the working consensus represents a type of moral agreement about 'how we will get on together'. It thus frames future action and relationships.

This argument is closely related to readings on teacher thinking (e.g. 4.1 and 4.2) and on pupils' classroom interests (4.7). Many of the issues which it raises are also taken up in the readings in Chapter 10 (e.g. 10.4, 10.5, 10.7, 10.8 and 10.9).

Do you feel that you have successfully negotiated and maintained a working consensus with your class?

Edited from: Pollard, A. (1985) *The Social World of the Primary School*. London: Cassell, 158–71

The interests of teachers and children are different in many ways and yet, in a sense, teachers and children face an identical and fundamental problem: they both have to 'cope' if they are to accomplish their daily classroom lives satisfactorily. I contend that this is possible only with some degree of accommodation of each other's interests. This is the essence of the interaction concept of working consensus, which encapsulates the idea of teacher and children mutually negotiating interdependent ways of coping in classrooms. This working consensus is created through a process of establishment (Ball, 1980) at the start of the school year. For instance, one experienced teacher at Moorside commented:

I always start off the year carefully, trying to be well organized and fairly strict so that the children get into a routine, and then we get to know each other gradually. Usually by the summer term I can relax the routine, do more interesting topics, have a few more jokes and discussions. By then everyone knows what sort of things are allowed, and I know the children well enough to do that kind of thing without them trying things on.

In this 'getting to know each other' period the teacher usually attempts to set up routines, procedures and standards which are offered as 'the way to do things'. This attempt to impose routines is not surprising, since the most salient threat to a teacher's interests is that of the large numbers of children, and routines will to some extent absorb some of the pressure. Meanwhile the teacher watches the children, interpreting their actions from the point of view of her perspective and evaluating the effect of them on her interests.

The teacher often holds the initial advantage and may think that everything is going well. However, from the point of view of the children, the salient threat to their interests is that of teacher power, the particular use of which is initially unknown. Thus the children have good reason to watch and evaluate, gradually accumulating a stock of knowledge and experience of the teacher and of situations, most of which is defensively organized around the threat of teacher power. For instance, one boy said:

> Last year was great; Mrs Biggs, she was very strict to start with, but then she used to sit at her desk and mark books a lot, so we could talk and send notes. I used to play noughts and crosses with Nigel and draw pictures. If she got up we'd just slide the papers under our books. When she was explaining things to people – that was good, but we had to hand our work in or if we didn't we'd get lines, and it had to be reasonable or we'd get into bother. It wasn't too bad really.

Gradually, as incidents occur and as sparring goes on, classes are seen to settle down and children feel they have got to know their teacher better.

This more settled accord is often described by teachers and other educationists as a 'good relationship'. It is rightly regarded as being extremely important and a teacher may well be judged by colleagues partly by his or her ability to foster such a relationship with pupils. However, the concept of a good relationship has always been a rather vague one, only accessible in some accounts to those with particular levels of sensitivity and intuition.

In fact it is possible to be more analytical. In my view the process of establishment normally and naturally leads to a stabilization of relationships because of mutuality of the coping needs of the teacher and pupils. What emerges is essentially a negotiated system of behavioural understandings for the various types of situations which routinely occur in the classroom. Through interaction, incidents and events, a type of case law of inter-subjectively understood rule systems, expectations and understandings emerges and begins to become an assumed, taken-for-granted reality which socially frames each situation. These socially understood, but tacit, conventions and rules constrain the behaviour of the children to varying degrees, depending on the quality and definition of the working consensus, but it is not unusual to find classes in some primary schools which a teacher can confidently leave for a time in the secure expectation that productive activities will continue just as they would have done had the teacher been present.

It is significant that these rules and understandings constrain not only the children, but also the teacher. This point follows from the fact that the rules are interactively constructed through negotiating processes to which teachers are party. Thus, from the child perspective, teachers can be seen as morally bound, and indeed the working consensus can be seen as providing a type of moral order in the classroom.

If the teacher breaks the understood rules then the action is considered unfair. Children commented:

> Well, I just dropped this marble in class and usually she just tells us off, but she took it and wouldn't give it back. It wasn't hers to take just because I dropped it.

> I answered the register in a funny voice and he went right mad. Yesterday he was cracking jokes himself. He's probably had a row with his wife.

These examples are instances of the most common teacher infringement of the working consensus – that of reaction to a routine deviant act which is seen as being too harsh. Such a reaction tends to produce bad feeling and often provokes more deviance.

It is thus the case that if the working consensus and the good relationship are to be maintained, both teacher and pupil strategies are partially circumscribed by them.

Of course it has to be recognized that a teacher's absolute power resources are greater than those of pupils. However, it can be argued that to an extent the working consensus incorporates and accepts differentiated status and behaviours, that it takes into account material realities and differences in socially sanctioned authority, differences in knowledge and differences in experience, and that these become accommodated into the relationships and understandings which are established between teachers and children.

The working consensus is thus an interactive product; indeed it can be seen as a collective, interdependent adaptation by the teacher and children to survival problems which are, in different ways, imposed on them both.

As we have seen, a crucial feature of classroom life which derives directly from the working consensus is the system of intersubjectively understood rules. These are tacit and taken-for-granted conventions which are created through the dynamics of interaction and through negotiation. They develop through incident and case law as the teacher and children come to understand each other and to define the parameters of acceptable behaviour in particular situations. The result is that such tacit understandings influence and 'frame' the actions of both teacher and pupils.

Two further points have to be made. In the first place such rules are not static; they change depending on the situation, which can be analysed in terms of the time, place, activity and people involved. In the second place they vary in strength. On some occasions the rule frame may be high and the expected behaviour is very clearly defined, while on other occasions, when the rule frame is weak, action is less circumscribed.

The concepts of working consensus and rule frame provide a means of analysing the social context within classrooms. They relate to self, and are the product of processes of classroom interaction in which the coping necessities and interests of each party play a major part.

The working consensus – the 'good relationship' – represents a mutual agreement to respect the dignity and fundamental interests of the other party. As such it is produced by creative and interactive responses to the structural position which teachers and pupils face in their classrooms. The additional point, though, is that these responses themselves create a micro social structure and context – analysable in terms of rule frame – to which individuals also have to relate as they act.

 READING 5.4

Methods of class control

Ronald King

Ronald King's reading illustrates some of the ways in which teachers use power to assert control over pupils. He provides an interesting account of techniques of control, which vary from the oblique and rather subtle to the overt and assertive. He refers to issues such as the use of the voice, scanning and the importance of context in establishing the meaning of what is said. The reading concludes with the suggestion that children simply have to 'decode' what teachers say to them. In this respect, King's account places much less emphasis on negotiation than in the previous reading (5.3).

Some of the techniques which are illustrated here have echoes with the more systematic analysis of class management issues which is provided by Kounin in Reading 10.6.

How do you use your power when interacting with children?

Edited from: King, R. A. (1989) *The Best of Primary Education? A Sociological Study of Junior Middle Schools.* London: Falmer Press, 42–6

The social structure of a classroom consists of the repeated patterns of behaviour of the teacher and children. Social structures have a dual quality. The social order of repeated behaviours is the outcome of the exercise of social control. Teachers are the main agents of social control, through the exercise of power. To paraphrase Weber's (1964) definition to fit the classroom situation, 'Power is the chance of a teacher realizing her own will against the resistance of the children.' The will of most primary school teachers is realized, in that there is usually classroom order to their general satisfaction.

When teachers at Greenleigh and St George's controlled children's behaviour to accord with conventional politeness, such behaviour was being intrinsically valued – the 'morality of the classroom' (Durkheim, 1961).

> If you can't say something nice, don't say it. Philip, don't talk while I'm talking please, it's very rude.

However, 'good behaviour' was given a greater extrinsic value in allowing 'work to roll on tranquilly'.

> Some of you are being very rude again when I'm hearing someone read.

> You should finish your work if you don't chat and do silly things.

Infants' teachers typically control their younger children using oblique methods (King, 1978): 'Someone's being silly'. Children defined as being innocent in the intention of their (teacher) unacceptable behaviour were not directly rebuked. The teacher of juniors did not attribute such innocence to older children, whose control was more direct.

> Right, that's enough of this noise. Books out ready to start.

Whereas infants' teachers typically praised 'good' behaviour and seldom directly blamed 'bad', juniors' teachers' balance of praise and blame shifted to the latter. Children were defined as being responsible for their own behaviour.

> Carl, stop it. You are being deliberately naughty.

For mildly unacceptable behaviour, control could be used.

> There's always someone who keeps the table waiting, Simon.

As with infants' teachers, this could take the form of a 'no need to answer' question.

> Louise, why are you talking? (Not Louise, stop talking). You've got lots to correct. Do you know why? Because you chatter.

Request–orders, were also semi-oblique.

> Right Janie, would you like to put the books on my table.

Humour could be used in semi-oblique ways in correcting work.

> I think you got slightly confused. I think you started to get tired.

Jokes were more direct.

> He'd forget his head if it wasn't screwed on. Wake up Joseph, it's not bed time yet.

Teachers referred to their own emotional state in expressing disapproval.

> I'm sorry, but that will not do. You know I don't like noise. Look, I'm fed up with you Robin Hill. Go and sit over there.

More direct was the teachers' threatening their own crossness.

> There are some people who will make me really cross in a minute. I think I will lose my temper soon.

With reference control, children were reminded of significant relationships, including those of authority, as in headteacher reference control.

Danny, do you want to be working outside Mr Gordon's room?

Parent reference control was used less often than in the infants'.

What would your mum say about being untidy? I saw her the other day.

Age reference control was quite common.

Please don't be a baby. Do grow up. You are ten years old, and you should be able to look after your own ruler.

Sex reference control was rare.

Right boys, mothers' meeting's over. (Man teacher.)

Ann, what is this, a mothers' meeting? (Woman teacher.)

As in infants' classrooms, teachers used both private and public voices, with the latter predominating. Private voice was addressed to one or a small group of children, and could be heard only by them. Public could be used with larger groups or the whole class, but even so when addressed to one or a few, all could hear, so allowing what Kounin (1970) [see Reading 10.6] calls 'ripple effects'.

Somebody's talking, Craig. (They all go quiet.)

The children learnt to interpret the various teacher voices. Five were common, each with distinctive tone, delivery, accompanying facial expression, and meanings above those of the actual phrases spoken. Three were similar to those used by infants' teachers (King, 1978).

'I'm being very patient with you' voice; 'Listen to me, I'm saying something important', voice; 'Sorrowful, you're not pleasing me' voice.

Two were more direct.

'Do as I say, no nonsense' voice; 'I know what you're up to, you're not fooling me' voice.

Infants' teachers used pairs of words in a dichotomized way, signalling approval or disapproval (King, 1968). Junior teachers occasionally used silly/sensible and quiet/noisy, but the primacy of work showed in their use of quick/slow and careful/careless.

You'll have to be quicker than this Adrian, you're too slow to catch a cold. Too many careless mistakes. Be more careful.

For some children, there was a problem in being quick enough without being careless.

I could get it right, if I didn't have to rush so much.

The language of social control was often strongly dependent upon the context for understanding. This was so in the use of naming. 'Joanne' could mean, stop talking, bring your book to me or many other things. The uses of first and surname, 'Joanne Sedley', signalled strong disapproval, whilst adult titles, 'Come along Miss Sedley', signalled mild but amused disapproval, evoking embarrassed smiles from the children.

The language of control could be condensed to a single word or sound. In the right context, with the appropriate facial and vocal expression, and body attitude, 'Now' or 'Eh' could produce silence. Even the teacher stopping talking and staring hard at an offender, could produce the desired effect.

Eye-scanning and contact, 'Keeping an eye on them', was used but less often than with infants' teachers, who with typical obliqueness, more often controlled with a wordless look (King, 1978). Teachers would look if a word or movement caught their attention, and children would reciprocate her gaze, not with the guilty give-away look typical of infants, but often with a wry or embarrassed smile of acknowledgement of being caught.

In his theory of codes, Bernstein (1975) hypothesized that an elaborated code forms the basis of the language of learning. However, the language of classroom control comes closer to his hypothesized restricted code: lexically and syntactically simple, its meaning often implicit and dependent on extra-verbal signals, context bound and expressing the positional authority of the teacher. This language was used almost exclusively by teachers. Children did not have to learn to encode it, but only to decode it. Given that order and teacher's will generally prevailed, they must have decoded successfully.

 READING 5.5

Life in classrooms

Philip Jackson

This a short extract from Philip Jackson's classic book which revolutionized ways of thinking about classrooms by highlighting the experience of pupils. He sets out the nature of school attendance and of the school context: schooling is compulsory; a pupil is one in the classroom crowd; is subject to praise or sanction; and is constrained by the power of the teacher. There are echoes here of Reading 4.6, in which Davies analyses 'the worlds of children and adults'.

Crowds, praise and power are inevitable elements of children's school experiences, and they gradually learn to adapt and cope with them. The most rapid adaption is needed at school entry but the issues never entirely go away. Can you identify children in your class who adapt particularly well, and others who have difficulties? How does this issue of social adaption affect their learning?

Edited from: Jackson, P. W. (1968) *Life in Classrooms.* New York: Teachers College Press, 4–11

School is a place where tests are failed and passed, where amusing things happen, where new insights are stumbled upon, and skills acquired. But it is also a place in which people sit, and listen, and wait, and raise their hands, and pass out paper, and stand in line, and sharpen pencils. School is where we encounter both friends and foes, where imagination is unleashed and misunderstanding brought to ground. But it is also a place in which yawns are stifled and initials scratched on desktops, where milk money is collected and lines are formed. Both aspects of school life, the celebrated and the unnoticed, are familiar to all of us, but the latter, if only because of its characteristic neglect, seems to deserve more attention than it has received to date from those who are interested in education.

In order to appreciate the significance of trivial classroom events it is necessary to consider the frequency of their occurrence, the standardization of the school environment, and the compulsory quality of daily attendance. We must recognize, in other words, that children are in school for a long time, that the settings in which they perform are highly uniform, and that they are there whether they want to be or not. Each of these three facts, although seemingly obvious, deserves some elaboration, for each contributes to our understanding of how students feel about and cope with their school experience.

The magnitude of 7,000 hours spread over six or seven years of a child's life is difficult to comprehend. Aside from sleeping, and perhaps playing, there is no other activity that occupies as much of the child's time as that involved in attending school. Apart from the bedroom there is no single enclosure in which he spends a longer time than he does in the classroom. From the age of six onward he is a more familiar sight to his teacher than to his father, and possible even to his mother.

Thus, when our young student enters school in the morning he is entering an environment with which he has become exceptionally familiar through prolonged exposure. Moreover, it is a fairly stable environment – one in which the physical objects, social relations, and major activities remain much the same from day to day, week to week, and even, in certain respects, from year to year. Life there resembles life in other contexts in some ways, but not all. There is, in other words, a uniqueness to the student's world. School, like church and home, is some place special. Look where you may, you will not find another place quite like it.

There is an important fact about a student's life that teachers and parents often prefer not to talk about, at least not in front of students. This is the fact that young people have to be in school, whether they want to be or not. The school child, like the incarcerated adult, is, in a sense, a prisoner. He too must come to grips with the inevitability of his experience. He too must develop strategies for dealing with the conflict that frequently arises between his natural desires and interests on the one hand and institutional expectations on the other.

In sum, classrooms are special places. The things that make schools different from other places are not only the paraphernalia of learning and teaching and the educational content of the dialogues that take place there. There are other features, much less obvious though equally omnipresent, that help to make up 'the facts of life', as it were, to which students must adapt.

They may be introduced by the key words: crowds, praise, and power.

Learning to live in a classroom involves, among other things, learning to live in a crowd. Most of the things that are done in school are done with others, or at least in the presence of others, and this fact has profound implications for determining the quality of a student's life.

Of equal importance is the fact that schools are basically evaluative settings. The very young student may be temporarily fooled by tests that are presented as games, but it doesn't take long before he begins to see through the subterfuge and comes to realize that school, after all, is a serious business. It is not only what you do there but what others think of what you do that is important. Adaptation to school life requires the student to become used to living under the constant condition of having his words and deeds evaluated by others.

School is also a place in which the division between the weak and the powerful is clearly drawn. This may sound like a harsh way to describe the separation between teachers and students, but it serves to emphasize a fact that is often overlooked, or touched upon gingerly at best. Teachers are indeed more powerful than students, in the sense of having greater responsibility for giving shape to classroom events, and this sharp difference in authority is another feature of school life with which students must learn how to deal.

In three major ways then – as members of crowds, as potential recipients of praise or reproof, and as pawns of institutional authorities – students are confronted with aspects of reality that at least during their childhood years are relatively confined to the hours spent in classrooms. It is likely during this time that adaptive strategies having relevance for other contexts and other life periods are developed.

What is self-esteem?

Denis Lawrence

Denis Lawrence provides a wonderfully clear account of the collection of ideas associated with self-esteem. Distinguishing between self-concept, self-image and the sense of ideal self, he describes self-esteem in terms of an individual's evaluation of their personal worth. Such self-conceptions initially derive from family relationships but during the school years these are augmented by the impressions offered by teachers and peers.

Self-esteem is a vital issue in respect of the formation of identity and self-confidence (see Reading 4.8 for an example of this). However, it also has a direct effect on the ways in which pupils approach learning challenges. Clearly, teacher expectations are a particularly significant influence on the ways in which pupils see themselves, and these are the subject of Reading 5.7.

How could you build up the self-esteem of your pupils?

Edited from: Lawrence, D. (1987) *Enhancing Self-Esteem in the Classroom*. London: Paul Chapman, 1–9

What is self-esteem? We all have our own idea of what we mean by the term, but in any discussion of self-esteem amongst a group of teachers there are likely to be several different definitions. The chances are that amongst these definitions the words self-concept, ideal self and self-image will appear.

Self-concept

Firstly, the term self-concept is best defined as the sum total of an individual's mental and physical characteristics and his/her evaluation of them. As such it has three aspects: the cognitive (thinking); the affective (feeling) and the behaviourial (action). In practice, and from the teacher's point of view, it is useful to consider this self-concept as developing in three areas – self-image, ideal self and self-esteem.

The self-concept is the individual's awareness of his/her own self. It is an awareness of one's own identity. The complexity of the nature of the 'self' has occupied the thinking of philosophers for centuries and was not considered to be a proper topic for psychology until James (1890) resurrected the concept from the realms of philosophy. As with the philosophers of his day, James wrestled with the objective and subjective nature of the 'self' – the 'me' and the 'I' – and eventually concluded that it was perfectly reasonable for the psychologist to study the 'self' as an objective phenomenon. He envisaged the infant developing from 'one big blooming buzzing confusion' to the eventual adult state of self-consciousness. The process of development throughout life can be considered, therefore, as a process of becoming more and more aware of one's own characteristics and consequent feelings about them. We see the self-concept as an umbrella term because subsumed beneath the 'self' there are three aspects: self-image (what the person is); ideal self (what the person would like to be); and self-esteem (what the person feels about the discrepancy between what he/she is and what he/she would like to be).

Each of the three aspects of self-concept will be considered in turn. Underpinning this theoretical account of the development of self-concept will be the notion that it is the child's interpretation of the life experience which determines self-esteem levels. This is known as the phenomenological approach and owes its origin mainly to the work of Rogers (1951). It attempts to understand a person through empathy with that person and is based on the premise that it is not the events which determine emotions but rather the person's interpretation of the events. To be able to understand the other person requires therefore an ability to empathize.

Self-image

Self-image is the individual's awareness of his/her mental and physical characteristics. It begins in the family with parents giving the child an image of him/herself of being loved or not loved, of being clever or stupid, and so forth, by their non-verbal as well as verbal communication. This process becomes less passive as the child him/herself begins to initiate further personal characteristics. The advent of school brings other experiences for the first time and soon the child is learning that he/she is popular or not popular with other children. He/she learns that school work is easily accomplished or otherwise. A host of mental and physical characteristics are learned according to how rich and varied school life becomes. In fact one could say that the more experiences one has, the richer is the self-image.

The earliest impressions of self-image are mainly concepts of body-image. The child soon learns that he/she is separate from the surrounding environment. This is sometimes seen amusingly in the young baby who bites its foot only to discover with pain that the foot belongs to itself. Development throughout infancy is largely a process of this further awareness of body as the senses develop. The image becomes more precise and accurate with increasing maturity so that by adolescence the individual is normally fully aware not only of body shape and size but also of his/her attractiveness in relation to peers. Sex-role identity also begins at an early age, probably at birth, as parents and others begin their stereotyping and classifying of the child into one sex or the other.

With cognitive development more refined physical and mental skills become possible, including reading and sporting pursuits. These are usually predominant in most schools so that the child soon forms an awareness of his/her capabilities in these areas.

This process of development of the self-image has been referred to as the 'looking-glass theory of self' (Cooley, 1902) as most certainly the individual is forming his/her self-image as he/she receives feedback from others. However, the process is not wholly a matter of 'bouncing off the environment' but also one of 'reflecting on the environment' as cognitive abilities make it possible for individuals to reflect on their experiences and interpret them.

Ideal self

Side by side with the development of self-image, the child is learning that there are ideal characteristics he/she should possess – that there are ideal standards of behaviour and also particular skills which are valued. For example, adults place value on being clean and tidy, and 'being clever' is important. As with self-image the process begins in the family and continues on entry to school. The child is becoming aware of the mores of the society. Peer comparisons are particularly powerful at adolescence. The influence of the media also becomes a significant factor at this time with various advertising and show-business personalities providing models of aspiration.

So, what is self-esteem?

Self-esteem is the individual's evaluation of the discrepancy between self-image and ideal self. It is an affective process and is a measure of the extent to which the individual cares about this discrepancy. From the discussion on the development of self-image and ideal self it can be appreciated that the discrepancy between the two is inevitable and so can be regarded as a normal phenomenon.

Indeed, there is evidence from clinical work that without this discrepancy – without levels of aspiration – individuals can become apathetic and poorly adjusted. For the person to be striving is therefore a normal state.

What is not so normal is that the individual should worry and become distressed over the discrepancy. Clearly, this is going to depend in early childhood on how the significant people in the child's life react to him/her. For instance, if the parent is over-anxious about the child's development this will soon be communicated and the child, too, will also become over-anxious about it. He/she begins first by trying to fulfil the parental expectations but, if he/she is not able to meet them, he/she begins to feel guilty.

The subject of reading is probably the most important skill a child will learn in the primary school and normally will come into contact with reading every day of school life. It is not surprising therefore, that the child who fails in reading over a lengthy period should be seen to have developed low self-esteem, the end product of feeling guilt about his/her failure. The child then lacks confidence in him/herself.

It can be appreciated from the foregoing description of the development of self-concept that teachers are in a very strong position to be able to influence self-esteem.

In summary, it is not failure to achieve which produces low self-esteem, it is the way the significant people in the child's life react to the failure. Indeed, it could be argued that failure is an inevitable part of life. There is always someone cleverer or more skilful than ourselves. This must be accepted if we are to help children develop happily without straining always to be on top. Eventually, of course, children become aware of their own level of achievement and realize that they are not performing as well as others around them. Then they can develop low self-esteem irrespective of the opinion of others; they have set their own standards. It is probably true to say, however, that the primary schoolchild is still likely to be 'internalizing' his/her ideal self from the significant people around him/her.

Self-esteem as defined so far refers to a 'global self-esteem' – an individual's overall feeling of self-worth. This is relatively stable and consistent over time. In addition to this overall, or global, self-esteem we can have feelings of worth or unworthiness in specific situations. Accordingly we may feel inadequate (low self-esteem) with regard to mathematics or tennis playing. However, they do not affect our overall feeling of self-worth as we can escape their influences by avoiding those situations. If, of course, we cannot avoid them and regularly participate in these activities which make us feel inadequate they may eventually affect our overall self-esteem. Also if we continue to fail in areas which are valued by the significant people in our lives then our overall self-esteem is affected. It is worth reflecting on how children cannot escape school subjects which is why failure in school so easily generalizes to the global self-esteem.

In summary, self-esteem develops as a result of interpersonal relationships within the family which gradually give precedence to school influences and to the influences of the larger society in which the individual chooses to live and to work. These extraneous influences lose their potency to the extent to which the individual becomes self-determinate. For the student of school age, however, self-esteem continues to be affected mainly by the significant people in the life of the student, usually parents, teachers and peers.

READING 5.7

Teacher expectations and classroom behaviour in the juniors

Peter Mortimore, Pamela Sammons, Louise Stoll, David Lewis and Russell Ecob

This reading on teacher expectations derives from a major study of school effectiveness conducted in inner London. The work of Peter Mortimore and his team shows variations in the expectations and behaviour of teachers in respect of pupils' age, social class, sex, ethnicity and ability. Of course, the situation is very complicated, but, however hard teachers try, we are all vulnerable to the danger of acting on cultural assumptions which cannot ultimately be justified.

This reading is directly relevant to Reading 5.6, on self-esteem. Reading 10.1, by Doyle, describes some of the classroom conditions which require very rapid decision making by teachers, thus opening up the risk of taken-for-granted assumptions being used. Reading 13.8 considers the dilemma which is posed by the necessity of differentiating to meet pupil needs, and the danger of creating social inequalities by doing so. Who said teaching was easy?

What are your own deeply held expectations of the abilities and behaviour of children of different ages, social class, sex and ethnicity? How do you think these expectations may be reflected in your classroom actions?

Edited from: Mortimore, P., Sammons, P., Stoll, L., Lewis, D. and Ecob, R. (1988) *School Matters: The Junior Years*. Wells: Open Books, 163–71

Every classroom inevitably contains pupils of differing personalities, abilities and backgrounds. Previous research findings demonstrate that, for some teachers at least, the expectations they have for their pupils can influence the children's future academic performance and self-perception. We have been able to consider whether teacher behaviour, particularly in terms of individual contacts with pupils, varied towards different groups of children. These groups are defined by age, sex, social class, ethnic background, perceived ability and behaviour.

Age differences

The attainment of younger pupils within a year group was generally poorer than that of their older peers, although there was no difference in their progress in cognitive skills. Teachers, however, were found consistently to have judged pupils born in the summer months as being of lower ability and having more behaviour difficulties. Younger pupils themselves also were found to have a less positive view of school than their older peers.

Social class differences

The influence of pupils' background upon teacher behaviour in the classroom has concerned researchers for some time. Opinion is divided. Some studies have found no social class effect (Nash, 1973; Murphy, 1974; Croll 1981). Others, however, indicate that social class is one of the major sources of expectations teachers hold for their pupils (Goodacre, 1968; Barker Lunn, 1970; Dusek and Joseph, 1983) and that teachers' behaviour can vary according to a child's background.

We found that pupils from non-manual backgrounds had higher attainments and made more progress in reading and writing. They were also rated by their teachers as of higher ability. Those from unskilled manual backgrounds and from homes where the father was absent were perceived by their teachers as having a greater incidence of behaviour problems. Thus, it appears that some teachers have different expectations of pupils from different social class backgrounds, irrespective of the children's performance.

Teachers' contacts with pupils were observed systematically over the equivalent of one whole day's teaching time. During this time the average number of individual contacts between teachers and each pupil was approximately eleven. This covered a wide range, with one child experiencing only one contact, whereas at the other extreme, a teacher communicated with a particular pupil on 63 occasions. Children from one parent families had, on average, just over 15 contacts with the teacher, a figure which is half as much again as that for the non- or skilled manual backgrounds.

There was no significant difference between groups in the number of discussions they had with the teacher about the content of their work. The non-manual and those of skilled manual backgrounds, however, were told significantly less often how to set about and organize their work. There may have been less need for teachers to supervise these latter pupils' work, given their higher attainments in the cognitive assessments.

Sex differences

There is considerable evidence of differences in teacher action towards, and judgements of, girls and boys. However, teachers may well be completely unaware of their own behaviours that encourage and sustain stereotyping and that, subsequently, may have an effect upon the academic progress and behavioural development of girls and boys.

Girls had higher attainments in reading and writing throughout their junior schooling and slightly higher attainment in mathematics by the third year. There were few other sex differences in pupil performance or progress. Teachers tended to rate boys' ability slightly higher than that of girls. This was surprising, because boys were consistently assessed as having more behaviour difficulties, and were also found to be less positive in their attitude to school. They were also observed to be less involved with their work.

Analyses show that teachers communicated more at an individual level with boys than with girls. This was found to be true for both female and male teachers. Differences were greatest in the third year when it was found that female teachers gave boys relatively even more attention.

The major difference concerned a greater use of criticism and neutral remarks to individual boys about their behaviour. This difference was not related to the sex of the teacher. Teachers also communicated more with boys on a non-verbal level, using both facial gestures and physical contact, and teased them more frequently. The extra behaviour control comments to boys are not surprising, given the teachers' lower assessments of boys' behaviour and the boys' tendency to be distracted more often from their work. Another possibility is that the boys' poorer behaviour and attitudes to school may be related to, and exacerbated by, their treatment by teachers in the classroom. Thus, perhaps, pupils are reacting to the way they are treated by their teachers, as well as teachers responding to pupils' behaviour.

There were also differences between the sexes in their contact with teachers on work-related issues. Boys were given more work supervision, particularly in the form of extra feedback. Girls, however, received significantly more praise from teachers.

Ethnic differences

It has also been suggested that teachers' expectations for pupils may be influenced by pupils' ethnic background. Thus, the Rampton Report (1981) proposed that the performance of ethnic minority children might be affected by low teacher expectations due to negative stereotypes about the abilities of such groups.

However, the Junior School Project found no relationship between teachers' ratings of pupils' ability and the children's ethnic background, once account had been taken of other background factors and attainment. Ability ratings, however, were strongly related to pupil attainments. These attainments were lower in reading, writing and mathematics for Caribbean and some Asian pupils than for other pupils. This suggests that for pupils from all ethnic backgrounds, teacher expectations appear to be tied to specific knowledge of previous attainment and performance in the classroom.

As a group, Caribbean pupils were rated by their teachers as having more behaviour problems, particularly those connected with learning difficulties. Caribbean pupils' attitudes to reading, however, were more positive than those of other pupils. The same was found for the positive attitudes of Asian pupils to mathematics. Within the classroom, however, Asian pupils were observed to concentrate less upon their work than were other pupils.

Given these differences, it was important to establish whether there were any differences in teacher behaviour towards pupils of different ethnic origins.

Teachers were found to have had more individual contacts than the average with Caribbean pupils (average for Caribbean pupils = 13.8, average overall = 10.9) than with other children. There was no difference between groups in the amount of teacher contact related to work discussion, supervision or feedback. However, it was found that teachers talked significantly more often to Caribbean pupils about non-work matters. Children of Caribbean background also received more neutral and negative feedback on their behaviour than did other pupils. Teachers also listened to Caribbean pupils read significantly more often than Asian pupils, and slightly more frequently than all the other children.

There was some variation, therefore, in teacher behaviour towards pupils of different ethnic origin. The particular differences suggest that teachers were attempting to meet the individual needs of those pupils, the data supply no evidence to support the view that teachers were withholding attention from any ethnic group.

Ability differences

Most studies of teacher expectations have concerned the effects of such expectations upon pupils of different abilities (see, for example, Rosenthal and Jacobson, 1968; and Barker Lunn, 1971).

A sub-sample of pupils in the junior school study were selected for observation on the basis of their first year test scores.

Overall, we found that pupils of below average ability had a higher number of individual contacts with their class teachers. Teachers made significantly more non-work comments. These included both extra routine instructions and more neutral and negative remarks related to their behaviour. This is likely to reflect the significant relationship between teachers' ratings of pupils' behaviour and their ability. Furthermore, as a group, lower ability pupils spent less time involved in work activities.

Differences were also identified in the ways teachers organized work and seating. Most teachers prepared different levels of work in mathematics and language according to pupils' abilities. Children were also seated according to their ability for at least some of the time in a quarter of classes.

Within the classroom it appeared that, in the main, teachers responded to the needs of lower ability pupils by giving them extra support with their work and hearing them read more often. Teachers also talked to these children more frequently about their behaviour, in line with their lower assessments of these pupils' behaviour and the poorer concentration of low ability pupils. There was no evidence, therefore, that teachers skimped in the giving of attention.

Positive teaching in the primary school

Frank Merrett and Kevin Wheldall

This reading provides advice on achieving and maintaining class discipline and task engagement from a behaviourist perspective, and it might thus be read in conjunction with Skinner's work (Reading 6.1). The emphasis is on changing pupil behaviour using positive reinforcement in a controlled, skilful and managed way, rather than becoming negative, as can all too easily happen when discipline problems arise in classrooms. The use of such techniques may seem to jar with some aspirations for classroom relationships, but in one form or another they contribute to the repertoire of many experienced teachers.

Are you able to manage positive reinforcements consistently?

Edited from: Merrett, F. and Wheldall, K. (1990) *Identifying Troublesome Classroom Behaviour*. London: Paul Chapman, 11–22

There are five principles of Positive Teaching.

Teaching is concerned with the observable.

Almost all classroom behaviour is learned.

Learning involves change in behaviour.

Behaviour changes as a result of its consequences.

Behaviours are also influenced by classroom contexts.

These five principles sum up what we mean by Positive Teaching. The main assumption is that pupils' behaviour is primarily learned and maintained as a result of their interactions with their environment, which includes other pupils and teachers. Consequently, behaviour can be changed by altering certain features of that environment. As we have said, the key environmental features are events which immediately precede or follow behaviour. This means that classroom behaviours followed by consequences which the pupils find rewarding will tend to increase in frequency. Similarly, certain changes in behaviour may be brought about merely by changing the classroom setting.

One way of thinking about Positive Thinking is in terms of the ABC in which:

A refers to the antecedent conditions, i.e., the context in which a behaviour occurs or what is happening in that environment prior to a behaviour occurring.

B refers to the behaviour itself, i.e. what a pupil is actually doing in real physical terms (not what you think he or she is doing as a result of inferences from his or her behaviour).

C refers to the consequences of the behaviour, i.e. what happens to the pupil after the behaviour.

Let us look at consequences in a little more detail.

A major concern within Positive Teaching is with the identification of items and events which pupils find rewarding and to structure the teaching environment so as to make access to these rewards dependent upon behaviour which the teacher wants to encourage in class.

Consequences may be described as rewarding punishing. Rewarding consequences, which we call positive reinforcers, are events which we seek out or 'go for', whilst we try to avoid punishing consequences. Neutral consequences are events which affect us neither way.

Behaviours followed by positive reinforcers are likely to increase in frequency. Behaviours followed by punishers tend to decrease in frequency whilst neutral consequences have no effect. In Positive Teaching, infrequent but appropriate behaviours (for example, getting on with the set work quietly) are made more frequent by arranging for positive reinforcers, such as teacher attention and approval, to follow their occurrence. This is called social reinforcement.

Undesired behaviours may be decreased in frequency by ensuring that positive reinforcers do not follow their occurrence, i.e. a neutral consequence is arranged. Occasionally it may be necessary to follow undesired behaviours with punishers (for example, a quiet reprimand) in an attempt to reduce the frequency of behaviour rapidly but there are problems associated with this procedure. Punishment plays only a minor and infrequent role in Positive Teaching not least because sometimes what we believe to be punishing is, in fact, reinforcing to the pupil. Pupils who receive little attention from adults may behave in ways which result in adult disapproval. Such pupils may prefer disapproval to being ignored and will continue to behave like this because adult attention, in itself, whether praise or reprimand, is positively reinforcing. This is what some people call attention-seeking behaviour.

We should note that terminating a punishing consequence is also reinforcing and can be, and often is, used to increase desired behaviours. This is known as negative reinforcement. Again this has problems associated with its use since pupils may rapidly learn other, more effective, ways of avoiding the negative consequence than you had in mind. For example, some teachers continually use sarcasm and ridicule with their pupils. They cease only when their pupils behave as they wish. However, another way for pupils to avoid this unpleasant consequence is to skip lessons or stay away from school.

Finally, one can punish by removing or terminating positive consequences (for example, by taking away privileges). This is known as response cost but again there are similar problems associated with this. Pupils may find alternative ways of avoiding this unpleasant consequence. Lying, cheating and shifting the blame are common strategies employed. These are all behaviours we would wish to discourage but by creating consequences which we believe to be aversive we may be making them more likely to occur.

When we want to teach pupils to do something new, or to encourage them to behave in a certain way more frequently than they normally do, it is important that we ensure that they are positively reinforced every time they behave as we want them to. This normally leads to rapid learning and is known as continuous reinforcement. When they have learned the new behaviour and/or are behaving as we want them to do regularly, then we may maintain this behaviour more economically by reducing the frequency of reinforcement.

Another important reason for wanting to reduce the frequency of reinforcement is that pupils may become less responsive if the positive reinforcer becomes too easily available. Consequently, once pupils are regularly behaving in an appropriate way we can best maintain that behaviour by ensuring that they are now reinforced only intermittently. Intermittent reinforcement can be arranged so that pupils are reinforced every so often (i.e. in terms of time) or, alternatively, after so many occurrences of the behaviour. These different ways of organizing the frequency of reinforcement are known as reinforcement schedules.

It should be emphasized that Positive Teaching is not about creating robots who just do as they are told, mindlessly following the teacher's instructions. Rather, Positive Teaching is about helping children to become effective, independent learners. Positive teachers should, in effect, like all good teachers, have the ultimate aim of making themselves redundant.

CHAPTER 6

How are we supporting children's learning?

There are eleven readings in this important chapter on the psychology of children's learning.

The first group of readings derive from key exponents of three major theoretical approaches to learning. Behaviourism is represented by the reading from Skinner (6.1) and through Gagné's (6.2) application of the approach to the sequential development of skills. The reading from Piaget (6.3) reviews the major elements of his constructivist psychology. However, social constructivist psychology, which is particularly influential today, is represented by a classic account from Vygotsky (6.4) on the 'zone of proximal development' and by an extension of these ideas by Tharp and Gallimore (6.5).

The readings by Gardner (6.6) and Dweck (6.7) deal with the very important issues of intelligence and motivation. Gardner suggests that there are many forms of intelligence, whilst Dweck emphasizes the significance of how pupils perceive their own capabilities.

The readings by Bruner (6.8) and Mercer (6.9) reflect a new 'cultural psychology' – a form of social constructivism which emphasizes the influence of the cultural contexts within which knowledge is appropriated and understanding is developed. The diary record by Armstrong (6.10) provides an account of one child's classroom appropriation whilst Rowland (6.11) reflects on the role of adults in supporting such learning.

The parallel chapter of *Reflective Teaching in the Primary School* provides a review of other work on these issues and suggests ways of reflecting on their significance for classroom work. Behaviourist, constructivist and social constructivist models of learning are first discussed. The second part of the chapter addresses 'intelligence', culture, personality and learning style, motivation and meta-cognition (the capability to reflect on one's own learning). There are also many suggestions for further reading.

READING 6.1

The science of learning and the art of teaching

Burrhus Skinner

B. F. Skinner made a very important contribution to 'behaviourist' psychology, an approach based on study of the ways in which animal behaviour is shaped and conditioned by stimuli. In this reading, Skinner applies his ideas to the learning of pupils in schools. Taking the case of learning arithmetic, he highlights the production of correct 'responses' from children and considers the forms of 'reinforcement' which are routinely used in classrooms. He regards these as hopelessly inadequate.

The behaviourist approach is applied to discipline issues in Reading 5.8 and its implications for structured learning programmes is traced through Gagné's work in Reading 6.2. However, the remaining readings in Chapter 6 represent other psychological approaches, most of which are critical of Skinner's basic assumptions (see, for instance, Bruner's 'cultural psychology' in Reading 6.8).

What do you see as the implications of behaviourism for the role of the teacher?

Edited from: Skinner, B. F. (1954) The science of learning and the art of teaching, *Harvard Educational Review* 24, 86–97

Some promising advances have been made in the field of learning. Special techniques have been designed to arrange what are called 'contingencies of reinforcement' – the relations which prevail between behaviour on the one hand and the consequences of that behaviour on the other – with the result that a much more effective control of behaviour has been achieved. It has long been argued that an organism learns mainly by producing changes in its environment, but it is only recently that these changes have been carefully manipulated.

Recent improvements in the conditions which control behaviour in the field of learning are of two principal sorts. The Law of Effect has been taken seriously; we have made sure that effects do occur and that they occur under conditions which are optimal for producing the changes called learning. Once we have arranged the particular type of consequence called a reinforcement, our techniques permit us to shape up the behaviour of an organism almost at will. It has become a routine exercise to demonstrate this in classes in elementary psychology by conditioning such an organism as a pigeon. Simply by presenting food to a hungry pigeon at the right time, it is possible to shape up three or four well-defined responses in a single demonstration period – such responses as turning around, pacing the floor in the pattern of a figure-8, standing still in a corner of the demonstration apparatus, stretching the neck or stamping the foot. Extremely complex performances may be reached through successive stages in the shaping process, the contingencies of reinforcement being changed progressively in the direction of the required behaviour. The results are often quite dramatic. In such a demonstration one can see learning take place. A significant change in behaviour is often obvious as the result of a single reinforcement.

A second important advance in technique permits us to maintain behaviour in given states of strength for long periods of time. Reinforcements continue to be important, of course, long after an organism has learned how to do something, long after it has acquired behaviour. They are necessary to maintain the behaviour in strength. Of special interest is the effect of various schedules of intermittent reinforcement. We have learned how to maintain any given level of activity for daily periods limited only by the physical exhaustion of the organism and from day to day without substantial change throughout its life. Many of these effects would be traditionally assigned to the field of motivation, although the principal operation is simply the arrangement of contingencies of reinforcement.

These new methods of shaping behaviour and of maintaining it in strength are a great improvement over the traditional practices of professional animal trainers, and it is not surprising that our laboratory results are already being applied to the production of performing animals for commercial purposes.

From this exciting prospect of an advancing science of learning, it is a great shock to turn to that branch of technology which is most directly concerned with the learning process – education. Let us consider, for example, the teaching of arithmetic in the lower grades. The school is concerned with imparting to the child a large number of responses of a special sort. The responses are all verbal. They consist of speaking and writing certain words, figures and signs which, to put it roughly, refer to numbers and to arithmetic operations. The first task is to shape up these responses – to get the child to pronounce and to write responses correctly, but the principal task is to bring this behaviour under many sorts of stimulus control. This is what happens when the child learns to count, to recite tables, to count while ticking off the items in an assemblage of objects, to respond to spoken or written numbers by saying 'odd', 'even', 'prime' and so on. Over and above this elaborate repertoire of numerical behaviour, most of which is often dismissed as the product of rote learning, the teaching of arithmetic looks forward to those complex serial arrangements of responses involved in original mathematical thinking. The child must acquire responses of transposing, clearing fractions and so on, which modify the order or pattern of the original material so that the response called a solution is eventually made possible.

Now, how is the extremely complicated verbal repertoire set up? In the first place, what reinforcements are used? Fifty years ago the answer would have been clear. At that time educational control was still frankly aversive. The child read numbers, copied numbers, memorized tables and performed operations upon numbers to escape the threat of the birch rod or cane. Some positive reinforcements were perhaps eventually derived from the increased efficiency of the child in the field of arithmetic and in rare cases some automatic reinforcement may have resulted from the sheer manipulation of the medium – from the solution of problems or the discovery of the intricacies of the number system. But for the immediate purposes of education the child acted to avoid or escape punishment. It was part of the reform movement known as progressive education to make the positive consequences more immediately effective, but anyone who visits the lower grades of the average school today will observe that a change has been made, not from aversive to positive control, but from one form of aversive stimulation to another. The child at his desk, filling in his workbook, is behaving primarily to escape from the threat of a series of minor aversive events – the teacher's displeasure, the criticism or ridicule of his classmates, an ignominious showing in a competition, low marks, a trip to the office 'to be talked to' by the principal, or a word to the parent who may still resort to the birch rod. In this welter of aversive consequences, getting the right answer is in itself an insignificant event, any effect of which is lost amid the anxieties, the boredom and the aggressions which are the inevitable by-products of aversive control.

Secondly, we have to ask how the contingencies of reinforcement are arranged. When is a numerical operation reinforced as 'right'? Eventually, of course, the pupil may be able to check his own answers and achieve some sort of automatic reinforcement, but in the early stages the reinforcement of being right is usually accorded by the teacher. The contingencies she provides are far from optimal. It can easily be demonstrated that, unless explicit mediating behaviour has been set up, the lapse of only a few seconds between response and reinforcement destroys most of the effect. In a typical classroom, nevertheless, long periods of time customarily elapse. The teacher may walk up and down the aisle, for example, while the class is working on a sheet of problems, pausing here and there to say right or wrong. Many seconds or minutes intervene between the child's response and the teacher's reinforcement. In many cases – for example, when papers are taken home to be corrected – as much as 24 hours may intervene. It is surprising that this system has any effect whatsoever.

A third notable shortcoming is the lack of a skilful programme which moves forward through a series of progressive approximations to the final complex behaviour desired. A long series of contingencies is necessary to bring the organism into the possession of mathematical behaviour most efficiently. But the teacher is seldom able to reinforce at each step in such a series because she cannot deal with the pupil's responses one at a time. It is usually necessary to reinforce the behaviour in blocks of responses – as in correcting a work sheet or page from a workbook. The responses within such a block must not be interrelated. The answer to one problem must not depend upon the answer to another. The number of stages through which one may progressively approach a complex pattern of behaviour is therefore small, and the task so much the more difficult. Even the most modern workbook in beginning arithmetic is far from exemplifying an efficient programme for shaping up mathematical behaviour.

Perhaps the most serious criticism of the current classroom is the relative infrequency of reinforcement. Since the pupil is usually dependent upon the teacher for being right, and since many pupils are usually dependent upon the same teacher, the total number of contingencies which may be arranged during, say, the first four years, is of the order of only a few thousand. But a very rough estimate suggests that efficient mathematical behaviour at this level requires something of the order of 25,000 contingencies. We may suppose that even in the brighter student a given contingency must be arranged several times to place the behaviour well in hand. The responses to be set up are not simply the various items in tables of addition, subtraction, multiplication and division; we have also to consider the alternative forms in which each item may be stated. To the learning of such material we should add hundreds of responses concerned with factoring, identifying primes, memorizing series, using shortcut techniques for calculation, constructing and using geometric representations or number forms and so on. Over and above all this, the whole mathematical repertoire must be brought under the control of concrete problems of considerable variety. Perhaps 50,000 contingencies is a more conservative estimate. In this frame of reference the daily assignment in arithmetic seems pitifully meagre.

The result of this is, of course, well known. Even our best schools are under criticism for the inefficiency in the teaching of drill subjects such as arithmetic. The condition in the average school is a matter of widespread national concern. Modern children simply do not learn arithmetic quickly or well. Nor is the result simply incompetence. The very subjects in which modern techniques are weakest are those in which failure is most conspicuous, and in the wake of an ever-growing incompetence come the anxieties, uncertainties and aggressions which in their turn present other problems to the school. Most pupils soon claim the asylum of not being 'ready' for arithmetic at a given level or, eventually, of not having a mathematical mind. Such explanations are readily seized upon by defensive teachers and parents. Few pupils ever reach the stage at which automatic reinforcements follow as the natural consequences of mathematical behaviour. On the contrary, the figures and symbols of mathematics have become standard emotional stimuli. The glimpse of a column of figures, not to say an algebraic symbol or an integral sign, is likely to set off – not mathematical behaviour – but a reaction of anxiety, guilt or fear.

The teacher is usually no happier about this than the pupil. Denied the opportunity to control via the birch rod, quite at sea as to the mode of operation of the few techniques at her disposal, she spends as little time as possible on drill subjects and eagerly subscribes to philosophies of education which emphasize material of greater inherent interest.

There would be no point in urging these objections if improvement were impossible. But the advances which have recently been made in our control of the learning process suggest a thorough revision of classroom practices and, fortunately, they tell us how the revision can be brought about. This is not, of course, the first time that the results of an experimental science have been brought to bear upon the practical problems of education. The modern classroom does not, however, offer much evidence that research in the field of learning has been respected or used. This condition is no doubt partly due to the limitations of earlier research, but it has been encouraged by a too hasty conclusion that the laboratory study of learning is inherently limited because it cannot take into account the realities of the classroom. In the light of our increasing knowledge of the learning process we should, instead, insist upon dealing with those realities and forcing a substantial change in them. Education is perhaps the most important branch of scientific technology. It deeply affects the lives of all of us. We can no longer allow the exigencies of a practical situation to suppress the tremendous improvements which are within reach. The practical situation must be changed.

There are certain questions which have to be answered in turning to the study of any new organism. What behaviour is to be set up? What reinforcers are at hand? What responses are available in embarking upon a programme of progressive approximation which will lead to the final form of behaviour? How can reinforcements be most efficiently scheduled to maintain the behaviour in strength? These questions are all relevant in considering the problem of the child in the lower grades.

 READING 6.2

Intellectual skills and the conditions of learning

Robert Gagné

The book by Gagné from which this reading is drawn has been influential in proposing the importance of linear sequences of learning steps, leading to skills and knowledge which can be cumulatively deployed to solve higher level challenges. Gagné considers the relationship between 'internal conditions' for learning which are within the learner, and the 'external conditions' which are provided by instruction. When these conditions are combined appropriately, then intellectual skills are developed.

A systematic example of the impact of this type of thinking is provided by the many mathematics schemes which are found in primary schools. The idea of the 'match' of pupils' existing understanding to each new task can also be related (see Reading 8.7). However, some would argue that systematic, sequential approaches to teaching and learning could underplay the potential for pupils to achieve more holistic leaps of understanding if they control their learning more directly themselves (see Reading 6.10).

Can you apply Gagné's analysis of internal and external conditions for learning to a child and task in your classroom?

Edited from: Gagné, R. M. (1965) *The Conditions of Learning*. New York: Holt, Rinehart & Winston, 49–51

An individual learns many simple and complex intellectual skills. The content of school mathematics, for example, is virtually all intellectual skills. However, intellectual skills pertain also to symbols other than numerals and number operations. In a larger sense, the symbols used to represent the environment to the learner constitute language. Since language is used to record and communicate the relationships (concepts, rules) that exist in any subject, the learning of such relationships can be expected to involve the learning of intellectual skills. It may be seen, therefore, that such skills are in many ways the most important types of capability learned by human beings and the essence of what is meant by 'being educated'.

How do individuals learn to use symbols in an intellectual skill? It is apparent that some conditions for this learning must exist within the learners (internal conditions), while others are external to the learners and may be arranged for in instruction.

Suppose that some youngsters are expected to learn how to find the difference between a linear extent measured as 22 3/16 and another measured at 24 1/8, and assume that they don't already know how to compute this. They can learn this particular skill quite readily, provided certain internal conditions are present. Particularly significant among these conditions is the availability of certain component or subordinate skills, which may be identified as 'forming equivalent fractions by multiplying numerator and denominator by the same (small) number'

($1/8 \times 2 = 2/16$), 'forming equivalent fractions by dividing numerator and denominator by the same (small) number' ($6/16 \div 2 = 3/8$), and 'finding a difference by subtracting fractions having common denominators' ($4/8 - 1/8 = 3/8$). Of course, if these subordinate intellectual skills have not been previously learned and stored in memory, they will not be available to the learners and must therefore be learned. But if they are present as internal conditions, learning of the new skill can proceed with little difficulty or delay.

The external conditions for acquiring the new skill may begin with a reminder that the subordinate skills will need to be recalled. Often this is done by means of verbal communications, such as 'Remember how to subtract fractions $3/16$ from $4/16$'. A second kind of verbal communication may be used to inform the learners of the learning objective, that is, of what the specific purpose of the performance will be after it has been learned. This may be represented by some such statement as 'The distance $22\ 3/16$ and $24\ 1/8$ are different; what you want to do is find the amount of this difference'. A picture and an example might also be used to convey this objective.

The next event that makes up the external conditions of learning for this skill is a communication that suggests 'putting things together', that is, combining subordinate skills to make the new one. Actually, the learners may already see how to do this or may be able to 'discover' it themselves, in which case no additional stimulation is needed. Often, though, some statement or hint may be valuable, such as 'If you change $1/8$ to $2/16$, can you then find the difference?' Then, if the learners state the difference they seek as '$1/16$', only one more step is needed. This is the provision of a new example (such as the distance $1\ 7/8$ and $1/4$) on which the learners can demonstrate the application of their newly learned skill.

Thus, the internal conditions for learning an intellectual skill consist of (1) the previously learned skills that are components of the new skill and (2) the processes that will be used to recall them and put them together in a new form.

Several distinct events make up the external conditions, and some of the most important have been mentioned in the example described. Notice that these external events have the purposes of (1) stimulating recall of the subordinate skills; (2) informing the learner of the performance objective; (3) 'guiding' the new learning by a statement, question, or hint; and (4) providing an occasion for the performance of the just-learned skill in connection with a new example. These events are perhaps the most obvious features of the external conditions of learning.

READING 6.3

A genetic approach to the psychology of thought

Jean Piaget

The present reading provides a concise overview of Piaget's constructivist psychology, but is necessarily packed with ideas. The distinction between formal knowledge and the dynamic of transformations is important, with the latter seen as providing the mechanism for the development of thought. Successive 'stages' of types of thinking are reviewed and are related to maturation, direct experience and social interaction. Finally, attention is drawn to the ways in which children 'assimilate' new experiences and 'accommodate' to their environment, to produce new levels of 'equilibration' at successive stages of learning.

Interpretations of Piaget's work have been of enormous influence on the thinking of primary school teachers. Indeed, it was specifically used as a rationale for the policy recommendations contained in the Plowden Report (Reading 7.6), which emphasized the importance of providing a rich, experiential learning environment which would be appropriate for the 'stage' of each child.

What importance do you attach to concepts such as 'stages of development', 'readiness' and 'learning from experience'?

Edited from: Piaget, J. (1961) A genetic approach to the psychology of thought, *British Journal of Educational Psychology*, 52, 151–61

Taking into consideration all that is known about the act of thinking, one can distinguish two principal aspects:

The formal viewpoint which deals with the configuration of the state of things to know.

The dynamic aspect, which deals with transformations.

The study of the development of thought shows that the dynamic aspect is at the same time more difficult to attain and more important, because only transformations make us understand the state of things. For instance: when a child of 4 to 6 years transfers a liquid from a large and low glass into a narrow and higher glass, he believes in general that the quantity of the liquid has increased, because he is limited to comparing the initial state (low level) to the final state (high level) without concerning himself with the transformation. Towards 7 or 8 years of age, on the other hand, a child discovers the preservation of the liquid, because he will think in terms of transformation. He will say that nothing has been taken away and nothing added, and, if the level of the liquid rises, this is due to a loss of width etc.

The formal aspect of thought makes way, therefore, more and more in the course of the development to its dynamic aspect, until such time when only transformation gives an understanding of things. To think means, above all to understand; and to understand means to arrive at the transformations, which furnish the reason for the state of things. All development of thought is resumed in the following manner: a construction of operations which stem from actions and a gradual subordination of formal aspects into dynamic aspects.

The operation, properly speaking, which constitutes the terminal point of this evolution is, therefore, to be conceived as an internalized action bound to other operations, which form with it a structured whole.

So defined, the dynamics intervene in the construction of all thought processes; in the structure of forms and classifications, of relations and serialization of correspondences, of numbers, of space and time, of the causality etc.

Any action of thought consists of combining thought operations and integrating the objects to be understood into systems of dynamic transformation. The psychological criterion of this is the appearance of the notion of conservation or 'invariants of groups'. Before speech, at the purely sensory-motor stage of a child from 0-18 months, it is possible to observe actions which show evidence of such tendencies. For instance: from 4-5 to 18 months, the baby constructs his first invariant, which is the schema of the permanent object (to recover an object which escaped from the field of perception).

When, with the beginning of the symbolic function (language, symbolic play, imagery etc.), the representation through thought becomes possible, it is at first a question of reconstructing in thought what the action is already able to realize. The actions actually do not become transformed immediately into operations, and one has to wait until about 7-8 years for the child to reach a functioning level. During this preoperative period the child, therefore, only arrives at incomplete structures characterized by a lack of logic.

At about 7-8 years the child arrives at his first complete dynamic structures (classes, relations and numbers), which, however, still remain concrete – in other words, only at the time of a handling of objects (material manipulation or, when possible, directly imagined). It is not before the age of 11-12 years or more that operations can be applied to pure hypotheses.

The fundamental genetic problem of the psychology of thought is hence to explain the formation of these dynamic structures. Practically, one would have to rely on three principal factors in order to explain the facts of development: maturation, physical experience and social interaction. But in this particular case none of these three suffice to furnish us with the desired explanations – not even the three together.

Maturation

First of all, these dynamic structures form very gradually. But progressive construction does not seem to depend on maturation, because the achievements hardly correspond to a particular age. Only the order of succession is constant. However, one witnesses innumerable accelerations or retardations for reasons of education or acquired experience.

Physical experience

Experiencing of objects plays, naturally, a very important role in the establishment of dynamic structures, because the operations originate from actions and the actions bear upon the object. This role manifests itself right from the beginning of sensory-motor explorations, preceding language, and it affirms itself continually in the course of manipulations and activities which are appropriate to the antecedent stages. Necessary as the role of experience may be, it does not sufficiently describe the construction of the dynamic structures – and this for the following three reasons.

First, there exist ideas which cannot possibly be derived from the child's experience – for instance, when one changes the shape of a small ball of clay. The child will declare, at 7-8 years, that the quantity of the matter is conserved. It does so before discovering the conservation of weight (9-10 years) and that of volume (10-11 years). What is the quantity of a matter independently of its weight and its volume? This abstract notion is neither possible to be perceived nor measurable. It is, therefore, the product of a dynamic deduction and not part of an experience.

Second, the various investigations into the learning of logical structure, which we were able to make at our International Centre of Genetic Epistemology, lead to a unanimous result: one does not 'learn' a logical structure as one learns to discover any physical law.

Third, there exist two types of experiences:

Physical experiences show the objects as they are, and the knowledge of them leads to the abstraction directly from the object. However, logicomathematical experience does not stem from the same type of learning as that of the physical experience, but rather from an equilibration of the scheme of actions, as we will see.

Social interaction

The educative and social transmission (linguistic etc.) plays, naturally, an evident role in the formation of dynamic structures, but this factor does not suffice either to entirely explain its development.

Additionally, there is a general progression of equilibration. This factor intervenes, as is to be expected, in the interaction of the preceding factors. Indeed, if the development depends, on one hand, on internal factors (maturation), and on the other hand on external factors (physical or social), it is self-evident that these internal and external factors equilibrate each other. The question is then to know if we are dealing here only with momentary compromises (unstable equilibrium) or if, on the contrary, this equilibrium becomes more and more stable. This shows that all exchange (mental as well as biological) between the organism and the environment (physical and social) is composed of two poles: (a) of the assimilation of the given external to the previous internal structures, and (b) of the accommodation of these structures to the given ones. The equilibrium between the assimilation and the accommodation is proportionately more stable than the assimilative structures which are better differentiated and co-ordinated.

To apply these notions to children's reasoning we see that every new problem provokes a disequilibrium (recognizable through types of dominant errors) the solution of which consists in a re-equilibration, which brings about a new original synthesis of two systems, up to the point of independence.

 READING 6.4

Mind in society and the ZPD

Lev Vygotsky

> Vygotsky's social constructivist psychology, though stemming from the 1930s, underpins much modern thinking about teaching and learning. In particular, the importance of instruction is emphasized. However, this is combined with recognition of the influence of social interaction and the cultural context within which understanding is developed. Vygotsky's most influential concept is that of the 'zone of proximal development' (ZPD) which highlights the potential for future learning which can be realized with appropriate support.
>
> The influence of Vygotsky's work will be particularly apparent in Readings 6.5, 6.8, 6.9 and 6.11 but it is also present in many other readings, particularly in Chapters 11 and 12.
>
> Thinking of a particular area of learning and a child you know, can you identify an 'actual developmental level' and a 'zone of proximal development' through which you could provide guidance and support?
>
> Edited from: Vygotsky, L. S. (1978) *Mind in Society: The Development of Higher Psychological Processes.* Cambridge, Mass.: Harvard University Press, 84–90

That children's learning begins long before they attend school is the starting point of this discussion. Any learning a child encounters in school always has a previous history. For example, children begin to study arithmetic in school, but long beforehand they have had some experience with quantity – they have had to deal with operations of division, addition, subtraction, and determination of size. Consequently, children have their own pre-school arithmetic which only myopic scientists could ignore.

It goes without saying that learning as it occurs in the preschool years differs markedly from school learning, which is concerned with the assimilation of the fundamentals of scientific knowledge. But even when, in the period of her first questions, a child assimilates the names of objects in her environment, she is learning. Indeed, can it be doubted that children learn speech from adults; or that, through asking questions and giving answers, children acquire a variety of information; or that through imitating adults and through being instructed about how to act, children develop an entire repository of skills? Learning and development are interrelated from the child's very first day of life.

In order to elaborate the dimensions of school learning, we will describe a new and exceptionally important concept without which the issue cannot be resolved: the zone of proximal development.

A well known and empirically established fact is that learning should be matched in some manner with the child's developmental level. For example, it has been established that the teaching of reading, writing and arithmetic should be initiated at a specific age level. Only recently, however, has attention been directed to the fact that we cannot limit ourselves merely to determining developmental levels if we wish to discover the actual relations of the developmental process to learning capabilities. We must determine at least two developmental levels.

The first level can be called the actual developmental level, that is, the level of development of a child's mental functions that has been established as a result of certain already completed developmental cycles. When we determine a child's mental age by using tests, we are almost always dealing with the actual developmental level. In studies of children's mental development it is generally assumed that only those things that children can do on their own are indicative of mental abilities. We give children a battery of tests or a variety of tasks of varying degrees of difficulty, and we judge the extent of their mental development on the basis of how they solve them and at what level of difficulty. On the other hand, if we offer leading questions or show how the problem is to be solved and the child then solves it, or if the teacher initiates the solution and the child completes it or solves it in collaboration with other children – in short, if the child barely misses an independent solution of the problem – the solution is not regarded as indicative of his mental development. This 'truth' was familiar and reinforced by common sense. Over a decade even the profoundest thinkers never questioned the assumption; they never entertained the notion that what children can do with the assistance of others might be in some sense even more indicative of their mental development than what they can do alone.

The zone of proximal development is the distance between the actual developmental level as determined by independent problem solving and the level of potential development as determined through problem solving under adult guidance or in collaboration with more capable peers.

If we naively ask what the actual developmental level is, or, to put it more simply, what more independent problem solving reveals, the most common answer would be that a child's actual developmental level defines functions that have already matured, that is, the end products of development. If a child can do such-and-such independently, it means that the functions for such-and-such have matured in her. What, then, is defined by the zone of proximal development, as determined through problems that children cannot solve independently but only with assistance? The zone of proximal development defines those functions that have not yet matured but are in the process of maturation, functions that will mature tomorrow but are currently in an embryonic state. These functions could be termed the 'buds' or 'flowers' of development rather than the 'fruits' of development. The actual developmental level characterizes mental development retrospectively, while the zone of proximal development characterizes mental development prospectively.

The zone of proximal development furnishes psychologists and educators with a tool through which the internal course of development can be understood. By using this method we can take account of not only the cycles and maturation processes that have already been completed but also those processes that are currently in a state of formation, that are just beginning to mature and develop. Thus, the zone of proximal development permits us to delineate the child's immediate future and his dynamic developmental state, allowing not only for what already has been achieved developmentally but also for what is in the course of maturing. The state of a child's mental development can be determined only by clarifying its two levels: the actual developmental level and the zone of proximal development.

A full understanding of the concept of the zone of proximal development must result in re-evaluation of the role of imitation in learning. Indeed, human learning presupposes a specific social nature and a process by which children grow into the intellectual life of those around them.

Children can imitate a variety of actions that go well beyond the limits of their own capabilities. Using imitation, children are capable of doing much more in collective activity or under the guidance of adults. This fact, which seems to be of little significance in itself, is of fundamental importance in that it demands a radical alteration of the entire doctrine concerning the relation between learning and development in children.

Learning which is oriented toward developmental levels that have already been reached is ineffective from the viewpoint of a child's overall development. It does not aim for a new stage of the developmental process but rather lags behind this process. Thus, the notion of a zone of proximal development enables us to propound a new formula, namely that the only 'good learning' is that which is in advance of development.

The acquisition of language can provide a paradigm for the entire problem of the relation between learning and development. Language arises initially as a means of communication between the child and the people in his environment. Only subsequently, upon conversion to internal speech, does it come to organize the child's thought, that is, become an internal mental function.

We propose that an essential feature of learning is that it creates the zone of proximal development; that is, learning awakens a variety of internal developmental processes that are able to operate only when the child is interacting with people in his environment and in co-operation with his peers. Once these processes are internalized, they become part of the child's independent developmental achievement.

From this point of view, learning is not development; however, properly organized learning results in mental development and sets in motion a variety of developmental processes that would be impossible apart from learning. Thus, learning is a necessary and universal aspect of the process of developing culturally organized, specifically human, psychological functions.

READING 6.5

Teaching as assisted performance

Roland Tharp and Ronald Gallimore

This reading is a useful elaboration of Vygotsky's ideas (see Reading 6.4). It sets out with particular clarity the concept of 'assisted performance' in relation to the zone of proximal development. Then it provides an insightful model of four 'stages' in which different types of assistance in performance and learning are characteristic: support from others; self-regulation; internalization; and where performance declines and new learning is necessary.

The concept of 'scaffolding' the development of understanding is an interesting one and is illustrated most specifically by Gordon Wells in Reading 11.3. It has been found to be hard to achieve in busy class-rooms. The idea of self-regulation is closely linked to pupil self-assessment (see Reading 12.7).

How does Tharp and Gallimore's four-stage model relate to your own learning? Think, for instance, about how you learned to swim, ride a bicycle or speak a language.

Edited from: Tharp, R. and Gallimore, R. (1988) *Rousing Minds to Life: Teaching, Learning and Schooling in Social Context*. New York: Cambridge University Press, 28–39

To explain the psychological, we must look not only at the individual but also at the external world in which that individual life has developed. We must examine human existence in its social and historical aspects, not only at its current surface. These social and historical aspects are represented to the child by people who assist and explain, those who participate with the child in shared functioning:

> Any function in the child's cultural development appears twice, or in two planes. First it appears on the social plane, and then on the psychological plane. First it appears between people as an interpsychological category, and then within the child as an intrapsychological category. This is equally true with regard to voluntary attention, logical memory, the formation of concepts, and the development of volition. (Vygotsky, 1978: 163)

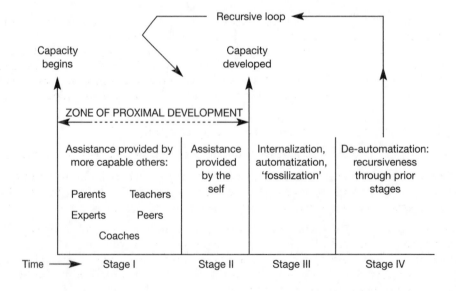

Figure 6.5.1 Genesis of performance capacity: progression through the ZPD and beyond

The process by which the social becomes the psychological is called internalization. The individual's 'plane of consciousness' (i.e. higher cognitive processes) is formed in structures that are transmitted to the individual by others in speech, social interaction, and the processes of co-operative activity. Thus, individual consciousness arises from the actions and speech of others.

However, children reorganize and reconstruct these experiences.

Indeed, the child is not merely a passive recipient of adult guidance and assistance; in instructional programmes, the active involvement of the child is crucial (Bruner, 1966).

In summary, the cognitive and social development of the child proceeds as an unfolding of potential through the reciprocal influences of child and social environment. Through guided reinvention, higher mental functions that are part of the social and cultural heritage of the child will move from the social plane to the psychological plane, from the socially regulated to the self-regulated. The child, through the regulating actions and speech of others, is brought to engage in independent action and speech. In the resulting interaction, the child performs, through assistance and co-operative activity, at developmental levels quite beyond the individual level of achievement. For skills and functions to develop into internalized, self-regulated capacity, all that is needed is performance, through assisting interaction. Through this process, the child acquires the 'plane of consciousness' of the society and is socialized, acculturated, made human.

Assisted performance defines what a child can do with help, with the support of the environment, of others, and of the self. For Vygotsky, the contrast between assisted performance and unassisted performance identified the fundamental nexus of development and learning that he called the zone of proximal development (ZPD).

The development of any performance capacity in the individual thus represents a changing relationship between self-regulation and social regulation. We present progress through the ZPD in a model of four stages. The model focuses particularly on the relationship between self-control and social control.

Stage I: Where performance is assisted by more capable others

Before children can function as independent agents, they must rely on adults or more capable peers for outside regulation of task performance. The amount and kind of outside regulation a child requires depend on the child's age and the nature of the task: that is the breadth and progression through the ZPD for the activity at hand.

Such assistance of performance has been described as scaffolding, a metaphor first used by Wood, Bruner and Ross (1976) to describe the ideal role of the teacher.

During Stage I, we see a steadily declining plane of adult responsibility for task performance and a reciprocal increase in the learner's proportion of responsibility. This is Bruner's fundamental 'handover principle' – the child who was a spectator is now a participant (Bruner, 1983: 60). The developmental task of Stage I is to transit from other-regulation to self-regulation.

Stage II: Where performance is assisted by the self

If we look carefully at the child's statements during this transition, we see that the child

> has taken over the rules and responsibilities of both participants in the language-game. These responsibilities were formerly divided between the adult and child, but they have now been taken over completely by the child. (Wertsch, 1979: 18)

Thus, in Stage II, the child carries out a task without assistance from others. However, this does not mean that the performance is fully developed or automatized.

During Stage II, the relationships among language, thought, and action in general undergo profound rearrangements. Control is passed from the adult to the child speaker, but the control function remains with the overt verbalization.

115

The phenomenon of self-directed speech reflects a development of the most profound significance. According to Vygotsky, and his follower Luria, once children begin to direct or guide behaviour with their own speech, an important stage has been reached in the transition of a skill through the ZPD. It constitutes the next stage in the passing of control or assistance from the adult to the child, from the expert to the apprentice. What was guided by the other is now beginning to be guided and directed by the self.

Stage III: Where performance is developed, automized, and 'fossilized'

Once all evidence of self-regulation has vanished, the child has emerged from the ZPD into the developmental stage for that task. The task execution is smooth and integrated. It has been internalized and 'automatized'. Assistance, from the adult or the self, is no longer needed. Indeed 'assistance' would now be disruptive. It is in this condition that instructions from others are disruptive and irritating; it is at this stage that self-consciousness itself is detrimental to the smooth integration of all task components. This is a stage beyond self-control and beyond social control. Performance here is no longer developing; it is already developed. Vygotsky described it as 'fossilized', emphasizing its fixity and distance from the social and mental forces of change.

Stage IV: Where de-automatization of performance leads to recursion back through the ZPD

The lifelong learning by any individual is made up of these same regulated, ZPD sequences – from other-assistance to self-assistance – recurring over and over again for the development of new capacities. For every individual, at any point in time, there will be a mix of other-regulation, self-regulation, and automatized processes. The child who can now do many of the steps in finding a lost object might still be in the ZPD for the activities of reading, or any of the many skills and processes remaining to be developed in the immature organism.

Furthermore, once children master cognitive strategies, they are not obligated to rely only on internal mediation. They can also ask for help when stuck or during periods of difficulty. Again, we see the intimate and shifting relationship between control by self and control by others. Even for adults, the effort to recall a forgotten bit of information can be aided by the helpful assistance of another so that the total of self-regulated and other-regulated components of the performance once again resembles the mother and child example of shared functioning. Even the competent adult can profit from regulation for enhancement and maintenance of performance.

Indeed, a most important consideration is that de-automatization and recursion occur so regularly that they constitute a Stage IV of the normal developmental process. What one formerly could do, one can no longer do. The first line of retreat is to the immediately prior self-regulating phase. A further retreat, to remembering the voice of a teacher, may be required, and consciously reconjuring the voice of a tutor is an effective self-control technique.

But in some cases no form of self-regulation may be adequate to restore capacity, and a further recursion – the restitution of other regulation – is required. Indeed, the profession of assisting adults (psychotherapy) is now a major Western institution. In all these instances, the goal is to reproceed through assisted performance to self-regulation and to exit the ZPD again into a new automatization.

📖 **READING 6.6**

The idea of multiple intelligences

Howard Gardner

> The concept of intelligence is a powerful one and is usually taken to denote a generalized intellectual capability. Howard Gardner has synthesized the thinking of many modern psychologists, neuro-biologists and others to challenge the dominant view of 'intelligence' in favour of a conception of multiple forms of competence and intellectual capacity. The seven intelligences which he suggests represent an interesting proposition which might be contested, though this does not detract from his major point of critique.
>
> This type of argument has considerable implications for teachers. In particular, it affirms the importance of seeking pupil capabilities across a wide range, rather than adopting an evaluative mind-set which is locked into narrow curriculum capabilities (see, for instance, Reading 10.3 on 'learning to be stupid').
>
> Thinking about a class of children you know, do some have forms of intelligence and capability which it is hard for them to realize at school? Are some forms of intelligence valued more highly than others?
>
> Edited from: Gardner, H. (1985) *Frames of Mind: The Theory of Multiple Intelligences*. London: Paladin Books, 3–4, 59–70, 277–387

A young girl spends an hour with an examiner. She is asked a number of questions that probe her store of information (Who discovered America? What does the stomach do?), her vocabulary (What does nonsense mean? What does belfry mean?), her arithmetic skills (At eight cents each, how much will three candy bars cost?), her ability to remember a series of numbers (5, 1, 7, 4, 2, 3, 8), her capacity to grasp the similarity between two elements (elbow and knee, mountain and lake). She may also be asked to carry out certain other tasks – for example, solving a maze or arranging a group of pictures in such a way that they relate a complete story. Some time afterward, the examiner scores the responses and comes up with a single number – the girl's intelligence quotient, or IQ. This number (which the little girl may actually be told) is likely to exert appreciable effect upon her future, influencing the way in which her teachers think of her and determining her eligibility for certain privileges. The importance attached to the number is not entirely inappropriate: after all, the score on an intelligence test does predict one's ability to handle school subjects, though it foretells little of success in later life.

The preceding scenario is repeated thousands of times every day, all over the world; and, typically, a good deal of significance is attached to the single score. Of course, different versions of the test are used for various ages and in diverse cultural settings. At times, the test is administered with paper and pencil rather than as an interchange with an examiner. But the broad outlines – an hour's worth of questions yielding one round number – are pretty much the way of intelligence testing the world around.

Many observers are not happy with this state of affairs. There must be more to intelligence than short answers to short questions – answers that predict academic success; and yet, in the absence of a better way of thinking about intelligence, and of better ways to assess an individual's capabilities, this scenario is destined to be repeated universally for the foreseeable future.

But what if one were to let one's imagination wander freely, to consider the wider range of performances that are in fact valued throughout the world? Consider, for example, the twelve-year-old male Puluwat in the Caroline Islands, who has been selected by his elders to learn how to become a master sailor. Under the tutelage of master navigators, he will learn to combine knowledge of sailing, stars, and geography so as to find his way around hundreds of islands. Consider the fifteen-year-old Iranian youth who has committed to heart the entire Koran and mastered the Arabic language. Now he is being sent to a holy city, to work closely for the next several years with an ayatollah, who will prepare him to be a teacher and religious leader. Or, consider the fourteen-year-old adolescent in Paris, who has learned how to programme a computer and is beginning to compose works of music with the aid of a synthesizer.

A moment's reflection reveals that each of these individuals is attaining a high level of competence in a challenging field and should, by any reasonable definition of the term, be viewed as exhibiting intelligent behaviour. Yet it should be equally clear that current methods of assessing the intellect are not sufficiently well honed to allow assessment of an individual's potentials or achievements in navigating by the stars, mastering a foreign tongue, or composing with a computer. The problem lies less in the technology of testing than in the ways in which we customarily think about the intellect and in our ingrained views of intelligence. Only if we expand and reformulate our view of what counts as human intellect will we be able to devise more appropriate ways of assessing it and more effective ways of educating it.

My review of studies of intelligence and cognition has suggested the existence of a number of different intellectual strengths, or competences, each of which may have its own developmental history. Recent work in neuro-biology has suggested the presence of areas in the brain that correspond to certain forms of cognition; and these same studies imply a neural organization that proves hospitable to the notion of different modes of information processing.

But science can never proceed completely inductively. We might conduct every conceivable psychological test and experiment, or ferret out all the neuro-anatomical wiring that we desired, and still not have identified the sought after human intelligences.

And so it becomes necessary to say that there is not, and there can never be, a single irrefutable and universally accepted list of human intelligences. There will never be a master list of three, seven, or three hundred intelligences which can be endorsed by all investigators.

This risk of reification is grave in a work of exposition, especially in one that attempts to introduce novel scientific concepts such as 'multiple intelligence'. I, and sympathetic readers, will be likely to think – and to fall into the habit of saying – that we here behold the 'linguistic intelligence', the 'interpersonal intelligence', or the 'spatial intelligence' at work, and that's that. But it's not. These intelligences are fictions – at most, useful fictions – for discussing processes and abilities that (like all of life) are continuous with one another; Nature brooks no sharp discontinuities. It is permissible to lapse into the sin of reifying so long as we remain aware that this is what we are doing. Specific intelligences exist not as physically verifiable entities but only as potentially useful scientific constructs.

We might perhaps conceptualize our family of seven intelligences in broad strokes in the following way. The 'object-related' forms of intelligence – spatial, logical-mathematical, bodily-kinaesthetic – are subject to one kind of control: that actually exerted by the structure and the functions of the particular objects with which individuals come into contact. Were our physical universe structured differently, these intelligences would presumably assume different forms. Our 'object-free' forms of intelligence – language and music – are not fashioned or channelled by the physical world but, instead, reflect the structures of particular languages and music. They may also reflect features of the auditory and oral systems, though (as we have seen) language and music may each develop, at least to some extent, in the absence of these sensory modalities. Finally the personal forms of intelligence reflect a set of powerful and competing constraints: the existence of one's own person; the existence of other persons; the culture's presentations and interpretations of selves. There will be universal features of any sense of person or self, but also considerable cultural nuances, reflecting a host of historical and individuating factors.

Intelligences should not be assessed in the same ways at different ages. The methods used with an infant or a pre-schooler ought to be tailored to the particular ways of knowing that typify these individuals and may be different from those employed with older individuals. My own belief is that one could assess an individual's intellectual potentials quite early in life, perhaps even in infancy.

Involvement with inherently engrossing materials provides an ideal opportunity to observe intelligences at work and to monitor their advances over a finite period of time. If one could watch a child as he learns to build various constructions out of blocks, one would receive insight into his skills in the areas of spatial and kinaesthetic intelligence: similarly, the child's capacities to relate a set of stories would reveal facets of his linguistic promise, even as his capacity to operate a simple machine would illuminate kinaesthetic and logical-mathematical skills. Such involvements in rich and provocative environments are also most likely to elicit 'markers' – those signs of early giftedness that are readily noticed by adults expert in a particular intellectual domain. The future musician may be marked by perfect pitch; the child gifted in personal matters, by his intuitions about the motives of others; the budding scientist, by his ability to pose provocative questions and then follow them up with appropriate ones.

Naturally the specific experiences favoured for the assessment of intellectual potential will differ, given the age, the sophistication, and the cultural background of the individual. Thus, when monitoring the spatial realm, one might hide an object from the one-year-old, pose a jigsaw puzzle to the six-year-old, or provide the pre-adolescent with a Rubik's cube. Analogously, in the musical realm, one might vary a lullaby for the two-year-old, provide the eight-year-old with a computer on which he can compose simple melodies, or analyse a fugue with an adolescent. In any case, the general idea of finding intriguing puzzles and allowing children to 'take off' with them seems to offer a far more valid way of assessing profiles of individuals than the current favourites world-wide: standard measures designed to be given within a half-hour with the aid of paper and pencil.

 READING 6.7

Motivational processes affecting learning

Carol Dweck

Pupils' motivation and approaches in new learning situations is obviously crucial to outcomes and this has been the focus of Carol Dweck's research for many years. In this reading, she shows how children's view of intelligence (as fixed or something that can be developed) may lead them to adopt relatively pragmatic performance goals or more developmental learning goals. These are associated with different beliefs in themselves (helpless or mastery-orientated), different forms of classroom behaviour and different learning outcomes.

This analysis has important links with Lawrence's reading on self-esteem (5.6), with views of intelligences (Reading 6.6) and with ideas on pupil self-regulation of learning (Reading 6.5) and self-assessment (Reading 12.7).

How can we help children really to believe in themselves and their potential?

Edited from: Dweck, C. S., (1986) Motivational processes affecting learning, *American Psychologist*, October, 1040–6

It has long been known that factors other than ability influence whether children seek or avoid challenges, whether they persist or withdraw in the face of difficulty and whether they use and develop their skills effectively. However, the components and bases of adaptive motivational patterns have been poorly understood. As a result, commonsense analyses have been limited and have not provided a basis for effective practices. Indeed, many 'commonsense' beliefs have been called into question or seriously qualified by recent research – for example, the belief that large amounts of praise and success will establish, maintain, or reinstate adaptive patterns, or that 'brighter' children have more adaptive patterns and thus are more likely to choose personally challenging tasks or to persist in the face of difficulty.

In the past 10 to 15 years a dramatic change has taken place in the study of motivation. This change has resulted in a coherent, replicable, and educationally relevant body of findings – and in a clearer understanding of motivational phenomena. During this time, the emphasis has shifted to a social-cognitive approach – away from external contingencies, on the one hand, and global, internal states on the other. It has shifted to an emphasis on cognitive mediators, that is, to how children construe the situation, interpret events in the situation, and process information about the situation. Although external contingencies and internal affective states are by no means ignored, they are seen as part of a process whose workings are best penetrated by focusing on organizing cognitive variables.

Specifically, the social-cognitive approach has allowed us to (a) characterize adaptive and maladaptive patterns, (b) explain them in terms of specific underlying processes, and thus (c) begin to provide a rigorous conceptual and empirical basis for intervention and practice.

The study of motivation deals with the causes of goal-oriented activity. Achievement motivation involves a particular class of goals – those involving competence – and these goals appear to fall into two classes: (a) learning goals, in which individuals seek to increase their competence, to understand or master something new, and (b) performance goals, in which individuals seek to gain favourable judgements of their competence.

Adaptive motivational patterns are those that promote the establishment, maintenance, and attainment of personally challenging and personally valued achievement goals. Maladaptive patterns, then, are associated with a failure to establish reasonable, valued goals, to maintain effective striving toward those goals, or, ultimately, to attain valued goals that are potentially within one's reach.

Research has clearly documented adaptive and maladaptive patterns of achievement behaviour. The adaptive ('mastery-oriented') pattern is characterized by challenge seeking and high, effective persistence in the face of obstacles. Children displaying this pattern appear to enjoy exerting effort in the pursuit of task mastery. In contrast, the maladaptive ('helpless') pattern is characterized by challenge avoidance and low persistence in the face of difficulty. Children displaying this pattern tend to evidence negative affect (such as anxiety) and negative self-cognitions when they confront obstacles.

Although children displaying the different patterns do not differ in intellectual ability, these patterns can have profound effects on cognitive performance. In experiments conducted in

Theory of intelligence	Goal orientation	Confidence in present ability	Behaviour pattern
Entity theory (Intelligence is fixed)	→ **Performance goal** (Goal is to gain positive judgements/ avoid negative judgements of competence)	If high → **but** If low →	**Mastery-orientated** Seek challenge High persistence **Helpless** Avoid challenge Low persistence
Incremental theory (Intelligence is malleable)	→ **Learning goal** (Goal is to increase competence)	If high → **or** low ↗	**Mastery-oriented** Seek challenge (that fosters learning) High persistence

Figure 6.7.1 Achievement goals and achievement behaviour

both laboratory and classroom settings, it has been shown that children with the maladaptive pattern are seriously hampered in the acquisition and display of cognitive skills when they meet obstacles. Children with the adaptive pattern, by contrast, seem undaunted or even seem to have their performance facilitated by the increased challenge.

If not ability, then what are the bases of these patterns? Most recently, research has suggested that children's goals in achievement situations differentially foster the two patterns. That is, achievement situations afford a choice of goals, and the one the child preferentially adopts predicts the achievement pattern that child will display.

Figure 6.7.1 summarizes the conceptualization that is emerging from the research. Basically, children's theories of intelligence appear to orient them toward different goals: children who believe intelligence is a fixed trait tend to orient toward gaining favourable judgements of that trait (performance goals), whereas children who believe intelligence is a malleable quality tend to orient toward developing that quality (learning goal). The goals then appear to set up the different behaviour patterns.

Much current educational practice aims at creating high-confidence performers and attempts to do so by programming frequent success and praise. How did this situation arise? I propose that misreadings of two popular phenomena may have merged to produce this approach. First was the belief in 'positive reinforcement' as the way to promote desirable behaviour. Yet a deeper understanding of the principles of reinforcement would not lead one to expect that frequent praise for short, easy tasks would create a desire for long, challenging ones or promote persistence in the face of failure.

Second was a growing awareness of teacher expectancy effects. As is well known, the teacher expectancy effect refers to the phenomenon whereby teachers' impressions about students' ability actually affect students' performance, such that the students' performance falls more in line with the teachers' expectancies (Rosenthal and Jacobson, 1968). The research on this 'self-fulfilling prophecy' raised serious concerns that teachers were hampering the intellectual achievement of children they labelled as having low ability. One remedy was thought to lie in making low-ability children feel like high-ability children by means of a high success rate.

The motivational research is clear in indicating that continued success on personally easy tasks is ineffective in producing stable confidence, challenge seeking and persistence (Dweck, 1975). Indeed, such procedures have sometimes been found to backfire by producing lower confidence in ability. Rather, the procedures that bring about more adaptive motivational patterns are the ones that incorporate challenge, and even failure, within a learning-oriented context and that explicitly address underlying motivational mediators. For example, retraining children's attributions for failure (teaching them to attribute their failures to effort or strategy instead of ability) has been shown to produce sizeable changes in persistence in the face of failure, changes that persist over time and generalize across tasks (Andrews and Bebus, 1978).

Motivational processes have been shown to affect (a) how well children can deploy their existing skills and knowledge, (b) how well they acquire new skills and knowledge, and (c) how well they transfer these new skills and knowledge to novel situations. This approach does not deny individual differences in present skills and knowledge or in 'native' ability or aptitude. It does suggest, however, that the use and growth of that ability can be appreciably influenced by motivational factors.

READING 6.8

Cultural psychology

Jerome Bruner

> Jerome Bruner is one of the most distinguished cognitive psychologists of the post-war years and in
> this reading he looks back at the critique of behaviourism (see Reading 6.1) in which he was so
> influential. Following Vygotsky (see Reading 6.4), he argues that understanding the thinking of any
> individual must take account of the symbolic systems in use, and these are embedded in the social
> and cultural context in which action takes place. Psychology is therefore becoming interdisciplinary
> in outlook and a new 'cultural psychology' is developing.
>
> Bruner's argument is further developed in Reading 6.9, and also in Reading 11.10 on bilingualism.
> The implication for teachers of Bruner's work is that we cannot fully understand pupil learning with-
> out engaging with the cultural influences which influence language, concepts and thinking. We need
> to understand the social context which structures the identity and capability of each child, and then
> work constructively within it. How might this be done? The present reading also provides a good
> example of the juxtaposition of educational paradigms (see Bassey's distinctions in Reading 3.5).
>
> Edited from: Bruner, J. (1990) *Acts of Meaning*. Cambridge, Mass.: Harvard University Press, 1–32

I want to begin with the Cognitive Revolution as my point of departure. That revolution was
intended to bring 'mind' back into the human sciences after a long cold winter of objectivism.

Let me tell you first what I and my friends thought the revolution was about back there in
the late 1950s. It was, we thought, an all-out effort to establish meaning as the central
concept of psychology – not stimuli and responses, not overtly observable behaviour, not
biological drives and their transformation, but meaning. It was not a revolution against
behaviourism with the aim of transforming behaviourism into a better way of pursuing
psychology by adding a little mentalism to it [see Reading 6.1]. It was an altogether more
profound revolution than that. Its aim was to discover and to describe formally the meanings
that human beings created out of their encounters with the world, and then to propose
hypotheses about what meaning-making processes were implicated. It focused upon the
symbolic activities that human beings employed in constructing and in making sense not only
of the world, but of themselves. Its aim was to prompt psychology to join forces with its
sister interpretive disciplines in the humanities and in the social sciences. Indeed, beneath the
surface of the more computationally oriented cognitive science, this is precisely what has been
happening – first slowly and now with increasing momentum. And so today one finds flour-
ishing centres of cultural psychology, cognitive and interpretive anthropology, cognitive
linguistics, and above all, a thriving worldwide enterprise that occupies itself as never before
since Kant with the philosophy of mind and of language.

We were not out to 'reform' behaviourism, but to replace it.

Begin with the concept of culture itself – particularly its constitutive role. What was obvious from the start was perhaps too obvious to be fully appreciated, at least by us psychologists who by habit and by tradition think in rather individualistic terms. The symbolic systems
that individuals used in constructing meaning were systems that were already in place, already
'there', deeply entrenched in culture and language. They constituted a very special kind of
communal tool kit whose tools, once used, made the user a reflection of the community. We
psychologists concentrated on how individuals 'acquired' these systems, how they made them
their own, much as we would ask how organisms in general acquired skilled adaptations to
the natural environment. We even became interested (again in an individualistic way) in man's
[*sic*] specific innate readiness for language. But with a few exceptions, notably Vygotsky, we

did not pursue the impact of language use on the nature of man as a species. We were slow to grasp fully what the emergence of culture meant for human adaptation and for human functioning. It was not just the increased size and power of the human brain, not just bipedalism and its freeing of the hands. These were merely morphological steps in evolution that would not have mattered save for the concurrent emergence of shared symbolic systems, of traditionalized ways of living and working together – in short, of human culture.

The divide in human evolution was crossed when culture became the major factor in giving form to the minds of those living under its sway. A product of history rather than of nature, culture now became the world to which we had to adapt and the tool kit for doing so. Once the divide was crossed, it was no longer a question of a 'natural' mind simply acquiring language as an additive. Nor was it a question of a culture tuning or modulating biological needs. As Clifford Geertz puts it, without the constituting role of culture we are 'unworkable monstrosities … incomplete or unfinished animals who complete or finish ourselves through culture' (Geertz, 1973).

A culturally oriented psychology neither dismisses what people say about their mental states, nor treats their statements only as if they were predictive indices of overt behaviour. What it takes as central, rather, is that the relationship between action and saying (or experiencing) is, in the ordinary conduct of life, interpretable. It takes the position that there is a publicly interpretable congruence between saying, doing, and the circumstances in which the saying and doing occur. That is to say, there are agreed-upon canonical relationships between the meaning of what we say and what we do in given circumstances, and such relationships govern how we conduct our lives with one another. There are procedures of negotiation, moreover, for getting back on the track when these canonical relations are violated. This is what makes interpretation and meaning central to a cultural psychology – or to any psychology or mental science, for that matter.

A cultural psychology, almost by definition, will not be preoccupied with 'behaviour' but with 'action', its intentionally based counterpart, and more specifically, with situated action – action situated in a cultural setting, and in the mutually interacting intentional states of the participants.

Intellectuals in a democratic society constitute a community of cultural critics. Psychologists, alas, have rarely seen themselves that way, largely because they are so caught up in the self-image generated by positivist science. Psychology, on this view, deals only in objective truths and eschews cultural criticism. But even scientific psychology will fare better when it recognizes that its truths, like all truths about the human condition, are relative to the point of view that it takes toward that condition. And it will achieve a more effective stance toward the culture at large when it comes to recognize that the folk psychology of ordinary people is not just a set of self-assuaging illusions, but the culture's beliefs and working hypotheses about what makes it possible and fulfilling for people to live together, even with great personal sacrifice. It is where psychology starts and wherein it is inseparable from anthropology and the other cultural sciences.

Culture, context and the appropriation of knowledge

Neil Mercer

Neil Mercer provides an extension and illustration of the application of Bruner's argument for 'cultural psychology' (Reading 6.8). He relates this to the Piagetian approach (Reading 6.3) which it has largely superseded. His discussion of 'appropriation' is of particular interest. The account of Mercer's nine-month-old baby shows her adopting 'brrm-brrming' and a culturally based form of play with a toy car which she learned directly from an older child. On the other hand, Mercer also cites examples of teachers appropriating pupil concepts and using them as part of their attempt to extend pupil understanding. This discussion is very relevant to the work of Michael Armstrong (Reading 6.10).

Mercer also draws attention to the wider social and historical context and points out that 'what counts as knowledge is quite culturally specific'. Considering England, what counted as knowledge in the mid-nineteenth century (see the implications of Reading 7.4) is very different from that implied in the 1960s (Reading 7.6). At any point in time, this variation will also be found across countries, as suggested by Reading 2.6.

Can you identify instances of pupils appropriating concepts and ways of thinking from the culture around them?

Edited from: Light, P. and Butterworth, G. (eds), (1992) *Context and Cognition: Ways of Learning and Knowing.* Hemel Hempstead: Harvester Wheatsheaf, 28–44

The 1980s was an interesting, if unsettled, period for the study of children's cognition and learning. On the theoretical level, there was a growing unease with theoretical perspectives which focused on individual development to the extent that social and interactional factors in learning and development were marginalized or even ignored. Despite widespread dissatisfaction with the theory and methods of earlier research on the educational attainment of children from different cultural groups (e.g. Jensen, 1967; Bernstein, 1971), more recent research on social experience and children's educational progress (e.g. Tizard and Hughes, 1984; Wells, 1985) made it clear that 'culture' could not be ignored. In particular, it seemed that more attention needed to be paid to the relationship between children's experiences within the cultural environments of home and school, and to the form and content of communication between parents and children and between teachers and children.

But culture and communication were themes that were not clearly or centrally represented within the Piagetian theory which dominated developmental psychology and which had most influence on educational theory and practice [see Reading 6.3]. And so the adequacy of Piagetian theory was questioned (e.g. Walkerdine, 1984; Edwards and Mercer, 1987) and some radical revisions of the Piagetian account of cognitive development were proposed.

Moreover, from the mid-1970s through the 1980s misgivings grew among researchers about how experimental methods had been used to study cognitive development. One important influence was Margaret Donaldson's work (Donaldson, 1978), which showed how strongly experimental results could be influenced by contextual cues carried implicitly within an experimental design or setting. Naturalistic, observational methods thus became rather more popular and experimental methods were devised which were more sensitive to situational factors. It also seemed that Vygotsky's work (e.g. Vygotsky 1978) [see Reading 6.4], with its recognition of cultural and linguistic factors on cognitive development and learning, might offer a better basis for such observational and experimental research than did Piaget's.

Culture and context thus became necessary and important concepts for the field of cognitive development and learning.

Anthropology, of course, is the discipline with first claims on culture. The eminent anthropologist Geertz (1968, p. 641) offered the following definition: 'an historically transmitted pattern of meaning embodied in symbols, a system of inherited conceptions expressed in symbolic form by means of which men [*sic*] communicate, perpetuate and develop their knowledge about and attitudes towards life'. Geertz's definition seems to me to be compatible with the notion of culture employed by Vygotsky (e.g. 1978, 1981). As Scribner (1985, p. 123) points out: 'We find Vygotsky introducing the term "cultural development" in his discussion of the origins of higher psychological functions and in some contexts using it interchangeably with "historical development".' For Vygotsky, the concept of culture offers a way of linking the history of a social group, the communicative activity of its members and the cognitive development of its children.

The culturally based quality of most learning is represented in the concept of 'appropriation', introduced by Vygotsky's colleague Leont'ev (1981) but taken up and developed by Newman, Griffin and Cole (1989). According to Newman *et al.*, it was proposed by Leont'ev as a socio-cultural alternative to Piaget's biological metaphor of 'assimilation'. In saying that children appropriate understanding through cultural contact, the point is being made that 'the objects in a child's world have a social history and functions that are not discovered through the child's unaided explorations' (Newman *et al.*, 1989, p. 62). This is more than a complicated way of saying that children do not need to reinvent the wheel. At the simplest level, it is arguing that because humans are essentially cultural beings, even children's initial encounters with objects may be cultural experiences, and so their initial understandings may be culturally defined. In this sense, appropriation is concerned with what children may take from encounters with objects in a cultural context.

Here is an example from my experience. My daughter Anna, when about nine months old, was offered a toy car to play with by her older brother. Although this was the first time she had seen one at home, she immediately began pushing it along the floor, going 'brrm, brrm' as she did so. The explanation for this surprising but conventional response lay in her regular attendance at day nursery. Although not given the opportunity there to handle a car, she had been able to observe an older child playing with one. On being given the car to play with, Anna did not need to 'discover' its nature purely through sensori-motor contact to make use of it as a toy. She recognized it as a tool for 'brrm-brrming', because she had appropriated from the older child the culturally based conception and function of the toy. Right from the start, it was a culturally defined object, and not simply a bit of material reality which she had to act on to discover its properties and functions.

The concept of appropriation also incorporates the socio-dynamics of the development of understanding in another, more complex, way, because within the educational process appropriation may be reciprocal. Thus Newman *et al.*, use appropriation to explain the pedagogic function of a particular kind of discourse event whereby one person takes up another's remark and offers it back, modified, into the discourse. They show how teachers do this with children's utterances and actions, thereby offering children a recontextualized version of their own activities which implicitly carries with it new cultural meanings. Teachers often paraphrase what children say, and present it back to them in a form which is considered by the teacher to be more compatible with the current stream of educational discourse. Teachers also reconstructively recap what has been done by the children in class, so as to represent events in ways which fit their pedagogic framework. By strategically appropriating children's words and actions, teachers may help children relate children's thoughts and actions in particular situations to the parameters of educational knowledge.

The acquisition of knowledge should not be theoretically isolated from the processes by which knowledge is offered, shared, reconstructed and evaluated. As Vygotsky suggested, the concept of culture helps us understand learning as a socio-historical and interpersonal process, not just as a matter of individual change or development. This has particular significance for the study of learning in school, where what counts as knowledge is often quite culturally specific.

Culture represents the historical source of important influences on what is learnt, how it is learnt, and the significance that is attached to any learning that takes place. We likewise need a satisfactory definition of context to deal with learning as a communicative, cumulative, constructive process, one which takes place in situations where past learning is embodied in present learning activity, and in which participants draw selectively on any information which is available to make sense of what they are doing. Only by taking account of these situated qualities of learning can we properly begin to describe how people learn.

 READING 6.10

A diary of learning in a primary classroom

Michael Armstrong

> The book from which this reading is drawn is a unique account of children's learning in a Key Stage 2 classroom. Michael Armstrong kept a diary in the class taught by Stephen Rowland (see the following reading, 6.11). This extract has been edited to focus on a boy, Paul, and the development over some months of his work. It all began with the excitement of receiving a 'Go-Cart' for Christmas.
>
> Many issues are illustrated, but amongst the most interesting are: the process of 'appropriation' of knowledge and skill which gradually developed as Paul fulfilled his enthusiasm through the school curriculum (see also Reading 6.9); and the strong commitment to 'mastery' which Paul displayed and was encouraged to develop in his motivation (see Dweck's Reading 6.7). The role of the teacher is highlighted in the following reading by Rowland (6.11).
>
> What more could we do to provide opportunities for children to fulfil their interests in such ways?
>
> Edited from: Armstrong, M. (1980) *Closely Observed Children: The Diary of a Primary Classroom*. London: Writers and Readers, 17–130

The concern for appropriate form was apparent even in the work of children whose writing was technically weak. Consider, for example, 'My Go-Cart', written by Paul. Paul had struggled with his early 'readers'. At the start of the year he was still at the stage of dictating what he wanted to write to the teacher and then copying from the teacher's writing. By the time he wrote 'My Go-Cart' he was writing for himself but only with difficulty.

Paul's was an account of personal experience, being an account of something that had happened to him during the holidays, on this occasion, the Christmas holiday. It was written, in part at least, in response to a request from the teacher for an account of some aspect of the holiday.

Tuesday, January 11th

Yesterday morning, the first day back at school, Paul wrote about the go-cart he'd had for Christmas, his first rides on it and its rapid breakdown. Stephen had suggested that everyone begin the day quietly with writing or reading, and he'd given the holiday as a possible subject to write about. A good many children were reluctant to write about the holiday although they were all anxious to talk about it. By contrast, Paul, after telling me about his go-cart adventures, was keen to commit them to writing and settled down to the task with his usual concentration, by turns earnest, pensive, pained, listless, and sometimes all in one. It took him all morning and the last sentence I had to write for him, as his scribe, but the thought and language were entirely his own. The piece that emerged was more assured than much of Paul's writing despite the limits of length which his present technical ability imposes on his pieces. Stephen noticed this too and asked me later in the day if I'd helped Paul with the language, but I hadn't, not at all.

Paul wrote as follows:

My Go-Cart

At Christmas I had a go-cart. When I had my first ride on my go-cart I was amazed that I could drive the go-cart. The next morning I got up and went down the road and when I came to the end of the road and the go-cart stopped and I tried to start the go-cart I couldn't start it. I ran home to tell me dad. My dad came down with the trailer. Dad picked the go-cart up and took the go-cart and put the go-cart in the garage and the next morning Kevin came up and Kevin said it is broken. The next morning Kevin mended it.

Paul's writing is notable for the very quality which, at the beginning of the school year, I had failed to notice in the children's writing, the fitting expression of felt incident by means of the written as opposed to the spoken word. The incident of the first breakdown of his go-cart, so directly and baldly expressed, enables Paul to convey in a few simple sentences the excitement and exasperation his Christmas present had occasioned. Notice how effectively the word 'amazed', a word I had to help Paul to spell, is used at the beginning. Notice also, how elaborate is the sentence that follows with its long delayed main clause and the sense it conveys of a single sustained burst of activity ending in misfortune. Although the technical means at his disposal are limited, Paul is successful at distilling a personal experience in narrative form.

This first picture of the go-cart was not so much an emblem as a record, the recording in loving detail of a treasured possession. Towards the end of term, however, he painted a second picture of the go-cart and this time the quality of emblem returned. It was the most flamboyant picture he had yet painted and confirmed his growing powers of observation and representation at the same time as it demonstrated his love of fancy and extravagance.

Figure 6.10.1 Paul's painting of his go-cart

Tuesday, March 15th

Yesterday Paul began a drawing of his go-cart smashed up against a tree. (In the two months since he had been given it, the go-cart had become quite a handful. He had got it stuck in the mud, he had run it into a tree, he had found it almost impossible to control. One day he even told me, half in jest, that he was thinking of getting rid of it. Such mishaps were very much part of Paul's life. For him the world was as irremediably obtuse as it was absorbing, and his experiences were constantly confirming this perception of things.) The drawing seemed to have worked out quite well but this morning Paul had turned the paper over and was drawing a warship on the other side. I asked him why and he said that, well, the go-cart picture was no good. He turned the paper over again to show me, explaining that the trouble was that he'd drawn a road which looked as if it was up in the sky. (The problem was that the scene he had drawn required a perspective he had been unable to achieve.) I said I thought it a pity, even so, that he had given up the go-cart picture, and tried to encourage him to return to it. He agreed, but only in so far as he agreed to paint the go-cart; he refused to paint it smashed up against the tree. He spent most of the day on the drawing and painting and this time all went well. Instead of the crashed cart he painted the go-cart as if it were new, spread across the paper, large and dominant, himself sitting serenely at the wheel.

When he had painted the go-cart in January he had used an illustration from a book to help him get the engine right. This time, after several weeks of careful, and sometimes painful, observation of the real thing, he didn't need a book and even so the engine was drawn with greater precision and detail, as indeed was the whole cart. The elaborately drawn and painted cart rested on a thin black strip of road, with a large tree at one side (a tree that was quite different from the tree Paul had drawn on the abortive picture of the crashed cart) and above the go-cart he placed a large blue pond (possibly in part to cover up the traces of the warship he had drawn to begin with on this side of his paper). In the corner, incongruously, he painted a yellow sun, with yellow rays, black eyes, nose and mouth, and smoking a brown pipe! The sun with its face, however ridiculous, is for Paul like a kind of signature, it seems.

When the painting was pinned on the wall several children drew attention to the blue pond which seemed to be, as they put it, 'up in the air'. Oddly enough Paul had landed himself, accidentally, in the same difficulty as in his abortive drawing of the crashed cart, requiring a command of perspective which was beyond his present technique. On this occasion, however, Paul himself seemed less worried by the absence of perspective than by the vagueness of the blue patch that stood for the pond. As it was, it was unrecognizable. A day or two later he added wavy white lines to it as if to signify more clearly what it represented; finally, still dissatisfied, he painted in the middle of the pond a large black shark, that being, as he told me, his favourite fish.

The juxtaposition of so many disparate elements in the finished picture was perhaps as much accidental as deliberate but the ingenuity with which Paul managed to combine them showed once more how effectively he could capitalize on accidents, incorporating them in new intentions. The final effect delighted him, and nothing more, he told me, than the sun smoking his pipe. The most impressive part of the painting, however, as far as Stephen and myself were concerned, was the go-cart itself, in the clarity and precision of its detail, and in its spectacular presence across the paper. The image Paul has painted embodies both his knowledge of the go-cart and his feeling for it. It has the same emblematic quality as his paintings of birds but it also reflects a more thorough observation of reality. Above all, it seems to me to express more clearly than any of his previous paintings, his love of objects, of objects in general and of this particular object. The same quality of feeling had already been evident in the minute cardboard models of go-carts constructed by Paul earlier in the Spring term but it gained perhaps its most complete expression in this, his second picture of his go-cart.

Paul's realism however was confined to the go-cart itself. At first he set it in a very simple and rudimentary landscape defined by the thin black strip of road on which the cart rested, the bare blue patch of pond above it, and, to the side of the pond, the flat and somewhat formal tree to which the grass at its base, and the barely recognizable squirrel on its trunk, added a hint of depth. Next came the irreverent signature of the pipe smoking sun which seems almost to be poking fun at realism. Lastly, as much maybe for its extravagance as for anything, he included the fantastic fish. The picture was no longer a simple celebration of a cherished object; it had become a kind of game, a playful and decorative fancy superimposed on the careful realism of the drawing of the go-cart itself.

This kind of metamorphosis was a common experience in Paul's art and was to lead to his most extraordinary picture of the year, late in the summer, when a delicately drawn rabbit skull was suddenly transformed into a monstrous sculpture.

I have been trying to demonstrate, by means of examples drawn from the life and work of a class of eight-year-olds, something of the character and quality of children's early intellectual investigations, in writing and literature, in art, and in certain aspects of mathematics and science. I have suggested that a predominant feature of these investigations is their expressive purpose. When children write stories, poems and anecdotes, when they draw and paint, when they experiment and speculate with pattern, they are not only acquiring fundamental skills; they are also appropriating knowledge. Children's intellectual concerns are not dissimilar in this respect to those of more mature thinkers. From their earliest acquaintance with the various traditions of human thought, with literature, art, mathematics, science and the like, they struggle to make use of these several traditions, of the constraints which they impose as well as the opportunities which they present, to examine, extend and express in a fitting form their own experience and understanding. I hope it is clear from my examples that such acts of appropriation are not to be interpreted as mere spontaneity, an inexplicable or innate flowering independent of context. They emerge, rather, out of children's absorption in subject matter, and that depends, as far as school life is concerned, upon the quality of environment which a teacher prepares and sustains within the classroom: upon the materials, ideas, relationships, techniques, and forms of knowledge which children encounter there and which in turn become the objects of their scrutiny.

There is a passage in one of Coleridge's essays which defines this development, with great force and eloquence, in terms of the 'germinal power' of the human mind. To excite this power is for Coleridge, as he claims it was for Plato, the only proper object of an education of the intellect:

> We see, that to open anew a well of springing water, not to cleanse the stagnant tank, or fill, bucket by bucket, the leaden cistern; that the Education of the intellect, by awakening the principle and method of self-development, was his proposed object, not any specific information that can be conveyed into it from without; not to assist in storing the passive mind with the various sorts of knowledge most in request, as if the human soul were a mere repository or banqueting-room, but to place it in such relations of circumstance as should gradually excite the germinal power that craves no knowledge but what it can take up into itself, what it can appropriate, and re-produce in fruits of its own.

In the thought and action of the children whose work I have described, I believe that it is possible to discern already the early excitement of their own germinal powers and the first fruits of their own appropriations.

Learning from Dean and his caterpillars

Stephen Rowland

This reading interconnects with Reading 6.10, by Michael Armstong, but yields an analytical model of the role of a teacher acting as a 'reflective agent' to extend children's understanding. In his full paper, Stephen Rowland provides a detailed illustration of his model through the case of Dean, a Key Stage 2 child, working to classify a collection of caterpillars. In that account, the importance of Dean's exercise of control is prominent and perhaps this is linked to maintaining a sense of 'mastery', as Dweck's work might suggest (Reading 6.7). Rowland's analysis of the role of the teacher here is very close to that implied by Vygotsky (Readings 6.4 and 6.5). Thus, when appropriate, the 'reflective agent' scaffolds children's understanding across their zones of proximal development. However, Rowland's paramount argument is that children should be in control of their own learning, a proposition which is clearly challenging in modern classrooms, given the range of curricular requirements in relation to the available time and resources. Nevertheless, some approaches to group-work represent attempts to move in this direction (see Readings 9.4 and 11.6).

The concept of the teacher as a 'reflective agent' is a powerful one. How often are you able to support children in such ways?

Edited from: Rowland, S. (1987) 'An interpretive model of teaching and learning', in Pollard, A. (ed.) *Children and their Primary Schools*. London: Falmer Press, 128–32

From my observations of Dean's work, and many similar instances of investigation in the primary classroom (Rowland, 1984), it seems to me that the relationship between the child's control and effective learning is of the utmost importance in this debate.

The limitations of both the didactic model and the exploratory model are, I think, apparent. To advise that we should therefore combine both strategies might seem strange. Might this not merely ensure that the children received the worst of both models? What we need is a model which helps us to decide when and how exploration or didactic instruction are appropriate. For this purpose I tentatively propose an alternative model, which I shall call the interpretive model, because, at its heart lies the idea of the interaction between teachers and learners as essentially an attempt by each party to interpret the expressions of the other.

In this model, the initial stimulus for activity may come from the child or from the teacher. In either case, it is vital that it is the child's interpretation of that stimulus which motivates the activity. Only then can the child's control be assured. She is not trying to guess what's in the teacher's mind in responding to the teacher's resources, but formulates her own ideas. Once the activity is under way, the teacher's role is then to act as a reflective agent, aiming to help the child identify concerns and needs, and also to provide positive yet critical feedback to the student. The child, in turn, critically responds to the teacher's contributions. Neither is 'right' or 'wrong'. As Radley (1980) puts it: 'Both student and teacher are engaged in a two way process of expressing what it is they are trying to formulate and grasping those things which the other person is indicating' (p. 42). In the course of tackling problems, children will invent. Such invention, even where not successful, is a powerful means for increasing awareness of what skills and knowledge are needed. Once the child recognizes this need, their control of the activity can be temporarily handed over to the teacher, or indeed to another child, for a period of instruction. This instruction does not have the purpose of developing skills in isolation, but of empowering children to meet the goals which they have set for themselves. In this model unlike the didactic model, instruction is an enabler of the children's control rather than a mechanism for concentrating the teacher's control.

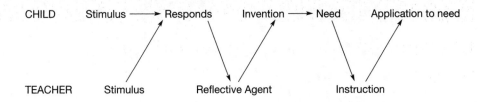

Figure 6.11.1 The interpretive model

Returning now to Dean and his caterpillars, it is interesting to see how his activity followed the path suggested by the interpretive model. My initial interventions for classifying the caterpillars were rejected by Dean thereby ensuring that his response was indeed his rather than my response to the initial idea. My conversations with him as a reflective agent were my attempts to understand his procedures and respond to them. His somewhat idiosyncratic inventions led him to see the need for a taxonomy which eventually led him to make use of a textbook in order to find out the 'real' names of his caterpillars. Again, in the caterpillar weighing part of the activity, he invented the system for weighing in collaboration with his friends – which led him to a problem (the adding of fractions) which, in order to solve, required my instructions. This instruction was not performed, in the first instance, in order to teach Dean 'how to do fractions' but in order that he could meet his own goal, or need, of plotting the growth of his caterpillar.

The implications of such a model are far reaching. For now the distinction between learners and teachers becomes less clear cut. Learners can become teachers, and teachers become learners. Since the children have a controlling influence upon the language and the concepts with which they grapple, they therefore exert a controlling influence upon their curriculum. We can mediate in this, and indeed we must, by presenting continual challenges and a widening of horizons, but, in the final analysis it is the children who 'own' their curriculum. It is not our curriculum which is given to them.

What are the aims, structure and content of the curriculum?

A curriculum reflects the values and priorities of those who construct it and many of the thirteen readings in this chapter illustrate the extensive debates which have occurred in England and Wales since the creation of the state education system.

Three readings precede this account. First, Mayer and Kamens (7.1) pour some cold water by suggesting that, despite all the controversy, there is in fact an international convergence in official statements of national curricula. Reading 7.2 introduces Bernstein's two important analytic tools for analysing curricula – 'classification' and 'frame'; whilst Barrow (7.3) illustrates the application of philosophical reasoning in identifying what should be taught.

We begin the historical account with a reading from a Victorian school inspector, Kay-Shuttleworth (7.4) commenting on the early development of elementary schools. Readings from the Hadow Report (7.5) and Plowden Report (7.6) illustrate the gradual development of more 'child-centred' ideas during much of the twentieth century. However, a reappraisal began in the mid-1970s, stimulated by Callaghan's Ruskin Speech (7.7), and this led to the White Paper 'Better Schools' (7.8) – a blueprint for the creation of a nationally co-ordinated education system.

But what should the National Curriculum consist of? The 'breadth and balance' which was required by Mrs Thatcher's Conservative government in the Education Reform Act, 1988, is described fully in *Reflective Teaching in the Primary School*, Chapter 7. This model was contested by some right-wing pressure groups, as is illustrated in the reading from Lawlor (7.9). At the same time, there were strong commitments within the teaching profession to child-centred forms of 'good practice', on which Alexander mounted a powerful critique (7.10). As the new National Curriculum was implemented, opposition political parties presented criticisms of its 'overloaded' nature and offered alternative curricular priorities, as is illustrated by a Labour Party Green Paper of 1994 (7.11). Sir Ron Dearing finally led a review of the National Curriculum (7.12) which took effect in 1995.

In the midst of all this activity, research has continued to confirm the importance of teachers' subject knowledge in effective teaching. Shulman's work, with the identification of three forms of subject knowledge, has been particularly influential (7.13).

The parallel chapter of *Reflective Teaching in the Primary School* begins by pointing out that an official curriculum may differ considerably from the curriculum-as-experienced by pupils. Patterns of primary school practice are then considered, with particular reference to the 'basics' and 'other' curriculum subjects and to alternative ways of curriculum organization in subject-based or integrated ways. The second major part of the chapter describes the structure and content of the National Curriculum in England and Wales, and also highlights its relationship to values, learning and teachers' subject knowledge. There are also many suggestions for further reading.

READING 7.1

Accounting for a world curriculum

John Meyer and David Kamens

The American team of researchers reporting here conducted a global survey of official curricular requirements in primary schools. Their core finding is that there are enormous similarities in the subject areas taught and the time given to them, despite the diverse histories, cultures and circumstances of different countries. They speculate about why this should be so.

   Do you think we are moving towards a world curriculum? And what influences will follow if the global influence of the United States wanes?

Edited from: Meyer, J. W. and Kamens, D. H. (1992) 'Conclusion: accounting for a world curriculum', in Meyer, J. W., Kamens, D. H. and Benavot, A. with Cha Y. K. and Wong, S. Y. (eds) *School Knowledge for the Masses: World Models and National Primary Curricular Categories in the Twentieth Century*. London: Falmer Press, 165–75.

The most important finding in our research is the relative homogeneity of the world's primary curricular outlines in the twentieth century. This is true descriptively – in the sense that there is considerably less variation among curricular outlines than reasonable arguments would have predicted. And it is true in an explanatory sense – factors that vary among countries play a smaller role than most theories would have proposed, in affecting variations among curricula. Further, we notice a pronounced tendency for curricular changes in particular countries to parallel each other and to take the form of conformity to world curricular patterns.

It turns out, thus, that through this century one may speak of a relatively clear 'world primary curriculum' operating, at least as an official standard, in almost all countries. A bit more than a third of the student's time is to be spent on language – and mainly on national language(s), not on local or foreign or classical ones. About one-sixth of the time goes to mathematics. A set of other subjects is practically always found (especially since the Second World War), with each subject taking 10 per cent of curricular time, or a bit less – social science, science, arts and physical education. Religious or moral education, and vocational education, are less universally present, and get only 5 per cent of the time. All other possible subjects – and many are found in one or another country at one or another time – take up in total less than a twentieth of the curriculum in the typical case.

The stylized character of the overall outline of the curriculum, or its readability in terms of world norms, is striking. Put simply, curricular categories, and even allocations of time to these categories, conform to the standard world outline.

What then explains the world curriculum and its evolution? It is difficult to address such questions in empirical terms, but some general arguments may be useful.

The nineteenth century rise of the modern secular mass curriculum seems closely linked to the rise of the model of the national state, with a universalized citizenry closely linked to a national culture (in language and art and, in a sense, physical education) and organized around rationalistic themes of social and natural progress (emphasizing science, mathematics, and social science, in addition to more traditional subjects). Themes left from an older Christendom – classical languages and literatures, and a strong emphasis on religion – were attenuated (though religion remained, especially in those countries where it was tied to a national state).

Two dimensions are built into this educational model – we may be so habituated to them as not to notice how distinct they are. First, there is the nominally arational or irrational side – the construction of what Anderson (1983) calls the 'imagined national community', or what Thomas *et al.* (1987), call the 'ontology of modernity'. Here we have the laborious construction of national languages (often at considerable cost to both local practice and international exchange), of national culture and history. Here we also have the surprising emphasis on tightly linking the identity of the individual child to national society through art and culture and physical education. Second, there is the rationalistic side of this same constructed world – the scientific and social scientific emphasis on the rationality and progressiveness of the national societies being constructed. Both dimensions are strikingly built into the modern curriculum as it develops, and both are now found everywhere: there seem to be no countries left whose curricula lack a strong sense of national identity; and none left whose curricula lack most of the modern rationalities.

Through the subsequent century, this model of the high national state and society seems to have remained relatively constant in the world curriculum – if anything, intensified as it became more universal. The one dramatic change since World War I, is the shift toward a more integrated social studies subject – which is arguably a reflection of the more and more complete interpenetration of state and society characteristic of the twentieth century.

We may be nearing the end of the high period of the national state as sovereign and autonomous social system in a world society imagined to be anarchic. The citizen status of individuals is being redefined in terms of their human rights in a larger system; there is a worldwide discussion of the limits on national sovereignty, and national societies are seen as in a worldwide natural and social environment requiring greater attention.

Our curricular data may not be detailed enough to capture many of the educational shifts that might follow such changes. But some findings of our analyses could well be reflecting them. There is, for one this, the expansion in modern foreign language instruction and particularly the emphasis on English as a world medium of communication rather than the simple retention of any language of the colonial period. There is also the expansion of social studies – with the potential vision of human societies anywhere as comparable and comprehensible rather than a narrower vision of national history and geography. There may also be a slight rise in instruction in moral education rather than religion reflective of a more universalistic approach to basic norms.

Aside from arguments explaining substantive changes in the world curriculum, our observations permit clear arguments about the processes involved. The developments we observe over the past century have two clear properties we must note. First, they occur in the centres of world educational communication. The nineteenth century development of the modern curriculum occurred in the European centres, spreading outward from them in waves of imitation – sometimes coerced through colonial power and authority, sometimes more voluntaristic (DiMaggio and Powell, 1983). Similarly with the mid-twentieth century changes we observe – they seem to reflect the dominance of the models of the metropolitan powers, and more recently, the hegemonic United States. Perhaps future changes in world curricular customs will reflect a more egalitarian system – for example, through discussions in such forums as UNESCO, which might give more peripheral countries more relative influence. But in the period of our observations, the world centres have been dominant.

Second, the main changes we observe over time in the world curriculum have been structured by the conceptions of the educational professionals and scientists. They are theorized changes, rather than changes that seem simply to reflect raw power. Every one of them – changes in language instruction, the rise of science and expansion of mathematics, the reorganization of social science instruction, the rise of aesthetic and physical education, and so on – is a creature of elaborate educational theorizing, whatever its possible ultimate origins in power or interest.

It is important not to overstate the power of the educational professionals as local interest groups, or as agents of local forces. But it is equally important to see that such groups – operating on their central terrain as agents of great scientific truths in a more universalistic way – embody and represent wider world cultural forces, and gain authority as they do so. Their authority rests on knowledge claims, and in good part such claims tend to have not only a universalistic flavour but a worldwide structural location.

With all this said, it seems obvious that idiosyncratic features of the metropolitan powers (and in particular the United States, since World War II) and their professional theorists play a considerable role in the evolution of the world curriculum. It is not simply a matter of the worldwide evolution of the natural principles of the modern nation-state. A rather liberal version of this nation-state has been politically and educationally dominant in our period – clearly the world curriculum would have looked very different with different outcomes of World Wars I and II.

This suggests that future changes in the types of countries that are most dominant in world society may also produce changes in curricular emphasis.

 READING 7.2

On the classification and framing of educational knowledge

Basil Bernstein

Basil Bernstein's work on the classification and framing of knowledge has been of enormous importance as a means of analysing the relationship between the wider values of society and schooling practices. He distinguishes between a 'collection' type of curriculum in which subject knowledge is distinct, and an 'integrated' type in which subjects may be merged. The concept of 'classification' describes the strength of boundary between subjects, and the related concept of 'frame' denotes the degree of control experienced by teachers and pupils, given the particular forms of curriculum, pedagogy and assessment within the classroom.

Particular interest groups within the wider society often seek to promote their values though advocacy of particular forms of educational practice (see also Reading 2.4). In the case of curriculum, this is illustrated by the media and policy-maker interest which is often engendered in controversies over topic-based and subject-based curriculum planning (Readings 8.3 and 8.4 are relevant here).

How do you see the links between values, forms of curricular organization and classroom practices?

Edited from: Bernstein, B. (1971) 'On the classification and framing of educational knowledge', in Young, M. F. D. (ed.) *Knowledge and Control: New Directions for the Sociology of Education.* London: Collier-Macmillan, 47–51

How a society selects, classifies, distributes, transmits and evaluates the educational knowledge it considers to be public, reflects both the distribution of power and the principles of social control.

Educational knowledge is a major regulator of the structure of experience. From this point of view, one can ask, 'How are forms of experience, identity and relation evoked, maintained and changed by the formal transmission of educational knowledge and sensitivities?' Formal educational knowledge can be considered to be realized through three message systems: curriculum, pedagogy and evaluation. Curriculum defines what counts as valid knowledge, pedagogy defines what counts as a valid transmission of knowledge, and evaluation defines what counts as a valid realization of this knowledge on the part of the taught. The term, educational knowledge code, refers to the underlying principles which shape curriculum, pedagogy and evaluation.

I shall distinguish between two broad types of curricula. If contents stand in a closed relation to each other, that is if the contents are clearly bounded and insulated from each other, I shall call such a curriculum a 'collection' type. Here, the learner has to collect a group of favoured contents in order to satisfy some criteria of evaluation. There may of course be some underlying concept to a collection: the gentleman, the educated man, the skilled man, the non-vocational man.

I want to juxtapose against the collection type, a curriculum where the various contents do not go their own separate ways, but where the contents stand in an open relation to each other. I shall call such a curriculum an 'integrated' type.

Now we can have various types of collection, and various degrees and types of integration.

I shall now introduce the concepts, classification and frame, which will be used to analyse the underlying structure of the three message systems, curriculum, pedagogy and evaluation, which are realizations of the educational knowledge code. The basic idea is embodied in the principle used to distinguish the two types of curricula: collection and integrated. Strong insulation between contents pointed to a collection type, whereas reduced insulation pointed to an integrated type. The principle here is the strength of the boundary between contents. This notion of boundary strength underlies the concepts of 'classification' and 'frame'.

Classification, here, does not refer to what is classified, but to the relationships between contents. Classification refers to the nature of the differentiation between contents. Where classification is strong, contents are well insulated from each other by strong boundaries. Where classification is weak, there is reduced insulation between contents, for the boundaries between contents are weak or blurred. Classification thus refers to the degree of boundary maintenance between contents. Classification focuses our attention upon boundary strength as the critical distinguishing feature of the division of labour of educational knowledge. It gives us, as I hope to show, the basic structure of the message system, curriculum.

The concept, frame, is used to determine the structure of the message system, pedagogy. Frame refers to the form of the context in which knowledge is transmitted and received. Frame refers to the specific pedagogical relationship of teacher and taught. In the same way as classification does not refer to contents, so frame does not refer to the contents of the pedagogy. Frame refers to the strength of the boundary between what may be transmitted and what may not be transmitted, in the pedagogical relationship. Where framing is strong, there is a sharp boundary, where framing is weak, a blurred boundary, between what may and may not be transmitted. Frame refers us to the range of options available to teacher and taught in the control of what is transmitted and received in the context of the pedagogical relationship. Strong framing entails reduced options; weak framing entails a range of options. Thus frame refers to the degree of control teacher and pupil possess over the selection, organization, pacing and timing of the knowledge transmitted and received in the pedagogical relationship.

From the perspective of this analysis, the basic structure of the curricular message system, is given by variations in the strength of classification, and the basic structure of the pedagogic message system is given by variations in the strength of frames.

Where classification is strong, the boundaries between the different contents are sharply drawn. If this is the case, then it pre-supposes strong boundary maintainers. Strong classification also creates a strong sense of membership in a particular class and so a specific identity. Strong frames reduce the power of the pupil over what, when and how he receives knowledge, and increases the teacher's power in the pedagogical relationship. However, strong classification reduces the power of the teacher over what he transmits, as he may not over-step the boundary between contents, and strong classification reduces the power of the teacher vis-à-vis the boundary maintainers.

READING 7.3

Knowledge and the curriculum

Robin Barrow

> The philosophy of education provides powerful tools for interrogating taken-for-granted assumptions and addressing fundamental educational issues, as the reading below illustrates. Robin Barrow reviews an influential example of the philosophy of knowledge and curriculum, that of Paul Hirst, and applies a 'utilitarian principle' to the question, 'What kinds of knowledge should be taught?'
>
> Edited from: Barrow, R. and Woods, R. (1988) *An Introduction to Philosophy of Education*. London: Routledge, 21–31

The task before us now is to attempt to outline what kinds of knowledge we ought, as educators, to be concerned to pass on to students or, more generally, the kinds of things we ought to seek to promote when teaching/learning takes place. This more general specification of the task will serve to remind us that we ought not to be concerned simply to transmit factual information but also, at the very least, to foster skills and abilities of various kinds. Or, in terms of knowledge, we shall be concerned not only with knowing that such-and-such is the case but also with knowing how to do various sorts of things.

What we want is a principle, or principles, by virtue of which we are able to select from the mass of knowledge those things that are in some way peculiarly relevant to education, those things that ought to be studied, taught and learnt, in schools, colleges and universities.

Knowledge, according to Hirst (1974), is separable into a number of distinct forms. These forms of knowledge are not mere collections of information but rather 'complex ways of understanding experience which man has achieved' (p. 122). Again, by form of knowledge is meant a distinct way in which our experience becomes structured round the use of accepted public symbols. The symbols thus having public meaning, their use is in some way testable against experience and there is the progressive development of a series of tested symbolic expressions. In this way experience has been probed further and further by extending and elaborating the use of the symbols and by means of these it has become possible for the personal experience of individuals to become more fully structured, more fully understood. The various forms of knowledge can be seen in low level developments within the common area of our knowledge of the everyday world. From this there branch out the developed forms which, taking certain elements in our common knowledge as a basis, have grown in distinctive ways.

The developed forms of knowledge possess distinguishing features:

> They each involve certain central concepts that are peculiar in character to the form. For example, those of gravity, acceleration, hydrogen, and photosynthesis characteristic of the sciences; number, integral, and matrix in mathematics; God, sin, and predestination in religion; right, good and wrong in moral knowledge.
>
> In a given form of knowledge these and other concepts that denote, if perhaps in a very complex way, certain aspects of experience, form a network of possible relationships in which experience can be understood. As a result the form has a distinctive logical structure. For example, the terms and statements of mechanics can be meaningfully related in certain strictly limited ways only, and the same is true of historical explanation.
>
> The form, by virtue of its particular terms and logic, has expressions or statements that in some way or other, however indirect it may be, are testable against experience. Each form has distinctive expressions that are testable against experience in accordance with particular criteria that are peculiar to the form.

The forms have developed particular techniques and skills for exploring experience and testing their distinctive expressions, for instance the techniques of the sciences and those of the various literary arts. The result has been the amassing of all the symbolically expressed knowledge that we now have in the arts and the sciences.

On the basis of these criteria Hirst originally catalogued the forms of knowledge, or disciplines, as follows: mathematics, physical sciences, human sciences, history, religion, literature and the fine arts, philosophy and moral knowledge. Additional to the forms there are what Hirst calls 'fields of knowledge' which arise when knowledge that is rooted in more than one form is built up round specific phenomena. Unlike the forms of knowledge the fields are not concerned with developing a particular structuring of experience. 'They are held together simply by their subject matter, drawing on all forms of knowledge that can contribute to them. Geography, as the study of man in relation to his environment, is an example of a theoretical study of this kind, engineering an example of a practical nature. I see no reason why such organizations of knowledge ... should not be endlessly constructed according to particular theoretical or practical interests' (p. 131).

In broad theoretical terms there is a marked difference between Hirst's views and my own. He wants to establish a conception of education 'whose definition and justification are based upon the nature and significance of knowledge itself, and not on the predilections of pupils, the demands of society, or the whims of politicians' (p. 115). One may sympathize with his desire to found curriculum proposals firmly on knowledge, but in framing curricula one surely cannot simply ignore society, more especially when one considers the extent to which practical problems – scarcity of available resources, for example – intrude on the scene. Nor is it obvious that one can simply override considerations to do with self-determination and autonomy by setting out to devise a curriculum without reference of any kind to the 'predilections of pupils'.

Reverting, then, to the key question – what principle, or principles, enable(s) us to select those items that ought to figure on a curriculum concerned with general education? – the answer I now give is, 'A utilitarian principle'. Note that the principle is not to be interpreted crudely in terms of 'use'. For example, I do not wish to imply that if the pursuit of an activity does not lead to a positive material gain – a bridge built, a car made, a well-paid job got – then, by the utilitarian principle, that activity ought not to be pursued. The activity of philosophizing does not, in general, lead to hard material gain, and, indeed, is often a hazardous business, as Socrates found, but the utilitarian principle does not thereby prohibit philosophizing. All that the principle demands is that justification for the pursuit of an activity has regard to factors extrinsic to that activity, that justification couched solely in terms of intrinsic value – the activity is an end in itself, is worth pursuing for its own sake, is valuable in itself – is unacceptable, and unacceptable because it does not do the selection job that needs to be done. Any activity can be said by someone to be valuable in itself or worth pursuing for its own sake, and that someone cannot be gainsaid.

We have to recognize that as far as the composition of a general school curriculum is concerned the attempt to demonstrate or prove in the mathematical deductive sense of 'demonstrate' and 'prove' is doomed to failure. The only logic involved in arguments about this issue of composition is the familiar logic of, say, moral discourse where one adduces reasons for and against a line of action and in the light of these reasons decides how to act. There is, of course, nothing deductive about this – the relation between 'She didn't cook my dinner last night' and 'Therefore I ought to leave her' is not of the same type as the relation between 'Fred is taller than Bill and Bill is taller than Joe' and 'Therefore Fred is taller than Joe'. The world might be an easier place to live in if moral issues and curriculum issues could be settled in this cut-and-dried deductive manner, but unfortunately this does not seem to be the case, and with respect to these issues we are left with the difficult job of specifying reasons for and against lines of action, trying to weigh these reasons one against another, and so on. A messy, but unavoidable business.

Some philosophers have accepted the utilitarian principle espoused here and have seen that the sort of logic relating to curriculum selection is of the type specified in the last paragraph, and they have acted accordingly. Thus, when Nowell-Smith (1958) attempted to locate the reasons why universities ought to teach literature, history and philosophy, he didn't take refuge in the stultifying concept of the valuable in itself, nor did he state baldly that literature, history, and philosophy were forms of knowledge or disciplines and that therefore further comment relating to the justification for teaching them was unnecessary. Rather, he attempted to specify the particular skills and abilities promoted by their study and to put forward reasons for thinking these particular skills and abilities worthy of promotion. An important part of the job of the philosopher of education consists in following and critically evaluating arguments of the order of Nowell-Smith's.

 READING 7.4

Memorandum on popular education

James Kay-Shuttleworth

> James Kay-Shuttleworth was a Victorian Inspector of Schools who observed and recorded many of the early developments of the elementary school system. These extracts from his *Memorandum* convey some of the thinking and fears which underpinned the development of education to 'exert a civilizing influence on the people'. He also provides comments on the cheap but efficient 'Revised Code' and on the process of school inspection.
>
> What echoes do you perceive between Kay-Shuttleworth's observations and more recent public debates and national procedures?
>
> Edited from: Kay-Shuttleworth, J. (1868) *Memorandum on Popular Education* (1969 edition). London: Woburn Books, 5–30

The attention of both Houses of Parliament has recently been called in an emphatic manner to popular education.

Her Majesty, in opening Parliament at the commencement of the session recently adjourned, said, 'The general question of "the education of the people" requires your most serious attention, and I have no doubt that you will approach the subject with a full appreciation both of its vital importance and of its acknowledged difficulty'.

Up to this time, the Government has promoted the foundation and improvement of schools by the administration of public grants, but has left the initiative to the Churches and congregations of religious communions.

Various powerful motives have promoted the growth and improvement of primary education, especially since 1846. But the recent extension of the franchise adds one which has never before operated with the same force. There is now a clear political necessity to fit the electors for the right exercise of their power.

Recent opportunities for the comparison of our own inventive, constructive, and decorative arts with those of foreign countries, have inspired a conviction that the more thorough primary instruction of such countries as Prussia, and the opportunities afforded to their artisans for that superior education which leads to a knowledge of the technical relations of science and the arts, afford to foreign workmen advantages which ours must have in order to maintain a successful competition.

The anti-social doctrines held by the leaders of Trades' Unions as to the relations of capital and labour, and their consequent organization to limit the freedom of workmen and masters by a system of terror, have been again exposed by inquiries under the Trades' Union Commission. Parliament is again warned how much the law needs the support of sound economic opinions and high moral principles among certain classes of workmen, and how influential a general system of public education might be in rearing a loyal, intelligent and Christian population.

All must fail to exert a civilizing influence on the people, unless the teachers are in numbers, skill, and knowledge equal to the duty they have to discharge.

The expedient of making the aid of the Committee of Council mainly depend on Capitation Grants, the amount of which is to be determined by the individual examination of the scholars, is open to some fundamental objections.

The deductions on examination for failures in reading, writing, and arithmetic are by no means a sufficient test of the efficiency or teaching power of a school. The number of scholars who pass in the Standards of the Revised Code is relatively less in a migratory population – like that of the poorest parts of cities, and the outskirts of the manufacturing districts – for in such places, the children enter the school ignorant, and stay so short a time as to be unable to acquire the rudiments. Thus a school in an apathetic district, supported only by the lowest resources from voluntary agencies, may have the hardest task, and receive the lowest rate of aid; or, a school in which the intelligence and liberality of the Managers has maintained the teaching power in the utmost efficiency as to numbers and skill, may, from the ignorance and migratory character of the population, earn a grant far below the ratio of its outlay or merit, and even below the average. Any grant, the amount of which is determined by individual examination after a certain attendance at School, tends to cause the neglect of the irregular, dull, and migratory scholars whom it does not pay to teach; while, on the other hand, grants proportionate to the average attendance of scholars are a direct inducement to fill the School, but not to teach the children, if such grants are not accompanied by conditions as to the number of the teaching staff.

Thus the Revised Code fails to penetrate the poorest, most ignorant, and migratory districts, which are also generally the most apathetic. And its grants are by no means proportionate to the intelligence and zeal of the Managers.

On the other hand, schools which contrive their machinery strictly with a view to enable their scholars to pass mechanically the examination of the Revised Code in the Standards of reading, writing, and arithmetic, without cultivating their general intelligence, may earn a Capitation Grant considerably above the average, though the civilizing power of such schools is low.

The system under the Revised Code is, as we have seen, cheaper. Is it more or less efficient? In his very able and exhaustive statement of the principles of the Revised Code, Mr Lowe said 'We deal with schools on this principle: – If they are effective in their teaching, they shall receive public aid to the amount which the commissioners have declared to be sufficient; but if they are not effective, they shall not receive it. In this way we make a double use of our money. It not only enables the schools to afford instruction, but it encourages them to augment the quantity of that education. It is a spur to improvement; it is not a mere subsidy, but a motive for action; and I have the greatest hopes of the improved prospects of education, if this principle is embraced.' The method of examination, and the mode of distributing the annual grants under the revised Code were intended to secure more constant attention to the instruction of junior classes, and greater proficiency in reading, writing and arithmetic. For this purpose, the grants which had been previously awarded directly to the teachers for the purpose of maintaining a sufficient staff of efficient teachers and assistants, were commuted into Capitation Grants, given partly for a certain number of days' attendance, and partly in proportion to the number of scholars who might pass in each of the three rudimentary subjects of instruction.

It may be expedient, first, to observe the effects of the Code on the instruction in the school apart from its influence on the machinery of education. The authors of the Code were warned by many who had much experience in elementary education, that the plan adopted would discourage the cultivation of any instruction higher than the rudiments, and would introduce a mechanical method of teaching. They also urged that a school from which the higher subjects were excluded, would be generally less successful in the lower. The Committee of Council now say – 'The Revised Code has tended, at least temporarily, to discourage attention to the higher branches of elementary instruction: Geography, Grammar, History. There are signs of recovery, and those schools do best in the elementary subjects where the higher are not neglected.' But the intentions of the authors of the Revised Code have not been fulfilled by the greater proficiency of the scholars in the rudiments of reading, writing and ciphering.

The percentages of failure in the Standards in 1863–4, when compared with those of 1866, show an increase of failures in 1866, in all of the Standards above, Standard I., except in reading under Standard VI., and in writing in Standards II. and VI.

The failure in writing and arithmetic above the Second Standard is especially remarkable. In its principal object, viz. a greater degree of proficiency in the three rudimentary subjects of instruction, the Revised Code has been followed by the injurious results which were predicted by its opponents.

Grave changes made in the character of the inspection have not secured the expected improvement of the scholars in the knowledge of the three rudiments. The inspection has been converted into a mechanical examination of these rudiments. The attention of the Managers and Teachers has, by the conditions of the Capitation Grant, been injuriously concentrated on a routine of daily drill in reading, writing, and ciphering. The result has been a larger amount of failures among the scholars when examined in these subjects, and the general neglect of the higher subjects of instruction, and of cultivation of the general intelligence of the children. The schools are lower in their aims, the scholars worse instructed, and there is a tendency to deterioration in the whole machinery of education.

The Revised Code has constructed nothing; it has only pulled down. It has not simplified the administration. It did not pretend to accelerate the rate of building schools, or to improve their structure. It has not promoted the more rapid diffusion of annual grants and inspection to the apathetic parts of cities, or the founding of schools in small parishes and for the sparse population of rural districts. It has generally discouraged all instruction above the elements and failed in teaching them. It has disorganized and threatens to destroy the whole system of training teachers and providing an efficient machinery of instruction for schools. These ruins are its only monuments. It has not succeeded in being efficient, but it is not even cheap; for it wastes the public money without producing the results which were declared to be its main object.

This analysis of the disorganizing tendencies of the Revised Code has been a painful but necessary duty, because the machinery of Training Colleges, Teachers, and Pupil Teachers created by the Minutes of 1846 must be regarded, not merely in its existing relations to the denominational system in co-operation with the State, but as a means of supplying that teaching staff without which no system of education can exist. To impair or to destroy this is therefore a blow, not only to the denominational system of schools, but to any scheme of national education, for none can exist without competent teachers, and it would not be an easy task to replace the Training Colleges now existing.

The curriculum of the primary school

Consultative Committee on Primary Education (Hadow Report)

This reading is a brief extract from the *Hadow Report* of 1931, which has been taken as an important early official endorsement of 'child-centred' concerns. It certainly began from a desire to review the overall effect of the multiple subjects which had accumulated within the elementary school curriculum in the early twentieth century. More specifically, through discussion of the danger of 'inert ideas', the reading emphasizes the importance of 'meaningfulness' and of 'relevance'. Interestingly, the latter idea survived until at least 1985, for it can be found in *Better Schools* (see Reading 7.8), but it was not promoted in official documents of the late 1980s and early 1990s.

What do you think the role of relevance should be? Are 'inert ideas' a problem in the modern curriculum?

Edited from: Consultative Committee on Primary Education (1931) *Report of the Consultative Committee on Primary Education*, Hadow Report. London: HMSO, 91–3

The elementary school curriculum was formed during the nineteenth century by a somewhat irregular process of accretion, now one subject and now another having been grafted on to the original stock, the 3 Rs. We need not here recount the arguments or revive the debates, instructive as they were, out of which the practice of today has gradually emerged. But the formal adoption of the primary school as an autonomous unit in the educational system renders necessary a fresh inquiry into the question what should be taught to children between the ages of seven and eleven, an inquiry conducted with reference to the specific part to be played by the primary schools in shaping and fostering the life of a people under modern economic and social conditions.

The changes which have taken place since the passing of the Education Act of 1902 have given our problem a complexion very different from the one which it presented to those who planned and administered popular education during the last century. The elementary school system which was originally designed 'for the children of the labouring poor' has long ceased to be self-contained, and is in effect being reorganized out of existence. Those who would have been its older pupils will be distributed among the schools – grammar schools and modern schools – which in our Report on the Education of the Adolescent (1926) were envisaged as offering different varieties of secondary education; and the function of the residue of the old system will accordingly be to provide a primary education in the proper sense of the term – that is, one which will be a basis for all types of higher teaching and training.

To say this is in effect to say that the special task of the schools which are concerned with the later years of primary education will be to provide for the educational needs of childhood, just as it is the function of the nursery and infant schools to deal with the needs of infancy, and of the post-primary schools to deal with the needs of adolescence. In framing the curriculum for the primary school, we must necessarily build upon the foundations laid in the infant school and must keep in view the importance of continuity with the work of the secondary school, but our main care must be to supply children between the ages of seven and eleven with what is essential to their healthy growth – physical, intellectual, and moral – during that particular stage of their development. The principle which is here implied will be challenged by no one who has grasped the idea that life is a process of growth in which there are successive stages, each with its own specific character and needs. It can, however, hardly be denied that there are places in our educational system where the curriculum is distorted and the teaching warped from its proper character by the supposed need of meeting the requirements of a later educational stage.

So the principle that no good can come from teaching children things that have no immediate value for them, however highly their potential or prospective value may be estimated. To put the point in a more concrete way, we must recognize the uselessness and the danger of seeking to inculcate what Professor A. N. Whitehead (1932) calls inert ideas – that is, ideas which at the time when they are imparted have no bearing upon a child's natural activities of body or mind and do nothing to illuminate or guide his experience.

There are doubtless several reasons why a principle so obviously sane should in practice be so often neglected. Perhaps the reason most relevant to our inquiry is that in the earliest days of popular education children went to school to learn specific things which could not well be taught at home – reading, writing and ciphering. The real business of life was picked up by a child in unregulated play, in casual intercourse with contemporaries and elders, and by a gradual apprenticeship to the discipline of the house, the farm, the workshop. But as industrialization has transformed the bases of social life, and an organization – at once vast in its scope and minute in its efficiency – has gripped the life of the people, discipline associated with the old forms of industrial training has become increasingly difficult outside the walls of the school. The schools whose first intention was to teach children how to read have thus been compelled to broaden their aims until it might now be said that they have to teach children how to live. This profound change in purpose has been accepted with a certain unconscious reluctance, and a consequent slowness of adaptation. The schools, feeling that what they can do best is the old familiar business of imparting knowledge, have reached a high level of technique in that part of their functions, but have not clearly grasped its proper relation to the whole. In short, while there is plenty of teaching which is good in the abstract, there is too little which helps children directly to strengthen and enlarge their instinctive hold on the conditions of life by enriching, illuminating and giving point to their growing experience.

Applying these considerations to the problem before us, we see that the curriculum is to be thought of in terms of activity and experience rather than of knowledge to be acquired and facts to be stored. Its aim should be to develop in a child the fundamental interests of civilized life so far as these powers and interests lie within the compass of childhood, to encourage him to attain gradually to that control and orderly management of his energies, impulses and emotions, which is the essence of moral and intellectual discipline, to help him to discover the idea of duty and to ensue it, and to open out his imagination and his sympathies in such a way that he may be prepared to understand and to follow in later years the highest examples of excellence in life and conduct.

READING 7.6

Aspects of children's learning

Central Advisory Council for England (Plowden Report)

This reading from the *Plowden Report* conveys the tone and emphasis of what has been taken as the most influential statement of 'progressivism' in primary education. The role of play in early learning is clearly set out, together with the conception of 'the child as the agent of his own learning', and the necessity of building a curriculum on children's interests and experiences. Towards the end, the influence of Piaget (see Reading 6.3) is apparent in the discussion of the teacher role. It is interesting to speculate on how this might have been written under a Vygotskian influence (see Readings 6.4 and 6.5).

There has been much debate on Plowden. However, which of the ideas still ring true to you now? Which seem naïve or outdated?

Edited from Central Advisory Council for Education (England) (1967) *Children and their Primary Schools*, Plowden Report. London: HMSO, 193–7

Play is the central activity in all nursery schools and in many infant schools. This sometimes leads to accusations that children are wasting their time in school: they should be 'working'. But this distinction between work and play is false, possibly throughout life, certainly in the primary school. Its essence lies in past notions of what is done in school hours (work) and what is done out of school (play). We know now that play – in the sense of 'messing about' either with material objects or with other children, and of creating fantasies – is vital to children's learning and therefore vital in school. Adults who criticize teachers for allowing children to play are unaware that play is the principal means of learning in early childhood. It is the way through which children reconcile their inner lives with external reality. In play, children gradually develop concepts of causal relationships, the power to discriminate, to make judgements, to analyse and synthesize, to imagine and to formulate. Children become absorbed in their play and the satisfaction of bringing it to a satisfactory conclusion fixes habits of concentration which can be transferred to other learning.

From infancy, children investigate the material world. Their interest is not wholly scientific but arises from a desire to control or use the things about them. Pleasure in 'being a cause' seems to permeate children's earliest contact with materials. To destroy and construct involves learning the properties of things and in this way children can build up concepts of weight, height, size, volume and texture.

Primitive materials such as sand, water, clay and wood attract young children and evoke concentration and inventiveness. Children are also stimulated by natural or manufactured materials of many shapes, colours and textures. Their imagination seizes on particular facets of objects and leads them to invent as well as to create. All kinds of causal connections are discovered, illustrated and used. Children also use objects as symbols for things, feelings and experiences, for which they may lack words. A small girl may use a piece of material in slightly different ways to make herself into a bride, a queen, or a nurse. When teachers enter into the play activity of children, they can help by watching the connections and relationships which children are making and by introducing, almost incidentally, the words for the concepts and feelings that are being expressed. Some symbolism is unconscious and may be the means by which children come to terms with actions or thoughts which are not acceptable to adults or are too frightening for the children themselves. In play are the roots of drama, expressive movement and art. In this way too children learn to understand other people. The earliest play of this kind probably emerges from play with materials. A child playing with a toy aeroplane can be seen to take the role of both the aeroplane and the pilot apparently simultaneously. All the important people of his world figure in this play: he imitates, he becomes, he symbolizes. He works off aggression or compensates himself for lack of love by 'being' one or other of the people who impinge on his life. By acting as he conceives they do, he tries to understand them. Since children tend to have inflexible roles thrust on them by adults, they need opportunities to explore different roles and to make a freer choice of their own. Early exploration of the actions, motives and feelings of themselves and of others is likely to be an important factor in the ability to form right relationships, which in its turn seems to be a crucial element in mental health. Adults can help children in this form of play, and in their social development, by references to the thoughts, feelings and needs of other people. Through stories told to them, children enter into different ways of behaving and of looking at the world, and play new parts.

Much of children's play is 'cultural' play as opposed to the 'natural' play of animals which mainly practises physical and survival skills. It often needs adult participation so that cultural facts and their significance can be communicated to children. The introduction into the classroom of objects for hospital play provides opportunities for coming to terms with one of the most common fears. Similarly the arrival of a new baby in the family, the death of someone important to the child, the invention of space rockets or new weapons may all call for the provision of materials for dramatic play which will help children to give expression to their feelings as a preliminary to understanding and controlling them. Sensitivity and observation are called for rather than intervention from the teacher. The knowledge of children gained from 'active' observation is invaluable to teachers. It gives common ground for conversation and exchange of ideas which it is among the most important duties of teachers to initiate and foster.

The child is the agent in his own learning. This was the message of the often quoted comment from the 1931 Report: 'The curriculum is to be thought of in terms of activity and experience rather than of knowledge to be acquired and facts to be stored' [see Reading 7.5]. Read in isolation, the passage has sometimes been taken to imply that children could not learn from imaginative experience and that activity and experience did not lead to the acquisition of knowledge. The context makes it plain that the actual implication is almost the opposite of this. It is that activity and experience, both physical and mental, are often the best means of gaining knowledge and acquiring facts. This is more generally recognized today but still needs to be said. We certainly would not wish to undervalue knowledge and facts, but facts are best retained when they are used and understood, when right attitudes to learning are created, when children learn to learn. Instruction in many primary schools continues to bewilder children because it outruns their experience. Even in infant schools, where innovation has gone furthest, time is sometimes wasted in teaching written 'sums' before children are able to understand what they are doing.

The intense interest shown by young children in the world about them, their powers of concentration on whatever is occupying their attention, or serving their immediate purposes, are apparent to both teachers and parents. Skills of reading and writing or the techniques used in art and craft can best be taught when the need for them is evident to children. A child who has no immediate incentive for learning to read is unlikely to succeed because of warnings about the disadvantages of illiteracy in adult life. There is, therefore, good reason for allowing young children to choose within a carefully prepared environment in which choices and interest are supported by their teachers, who will have in mind the potentialities for further learning. Piaget's observations support the belief that children have a natural urge to explore and discover, that they find pleasure in satisfying it and that it is therefore self-perpetuating. When children are learning new patterns of behaviour or new concepts, they tend both to practise them spontaneously and to seek out relevant experience, as can be seen from the way they acquire skills in movement. It takes much longer than teachers have previously realized for children to master through experience new concepts or new levels of complex concepts. When understanding has been achieved, consolidation should follow. At this stage children profit from various types of practice devised by their teachers, and from direct instruction.

Children will, of course, vary in the degree of interest that they show and their urge to learn will be strengthened or weakened by the attitudes of parents, teachers and others with whom they identify themselves. Apathy may result when parents show no interest, clamp down on children's curiosity and enterprise, tell them constantly not to touch and do not answer their questions. Children can also learn to be passive from a teacher who allows them little scope in managing their own affairs and in learning. A teacher who relies only on instruction, who forestalls children's questions or who answers them too quickly, instead of asking the further questions which will set children on the way to their own solution, will disincline children to learn. A new teacher with time and patience can usually help children who have learnt from their teachers to be too dependent. Those who have been deprived at home need more than that. Their self-confidence can only be restored by affection, stability and order. They must have special attention from adults who can discover, by observing their responses, what experiences awaken interest, and can seize on them to reinforce the desire to learn.

External incentives such as marks and stars, and other rewards and punishments, influence children's learning mainly by evoking or representing parents' or teachers' approval. Although children vary temperamentally in their response to rewards and punishments, positive incentives are generally more effective than punishment, and neither is as damaging as neglect. But the children who most need the incentive of good marks are least likely to gain them, even when, as in many primary schools, they are given for effort rather than for achievement. In any case, one of the main educational tasks of the primary school is to build on and strengthen children's intrinsic interest in learning and lead them to learn for themselves rather than from fear of disapproval or desire for praise.

Learning is a continuous process from birth. The teacher's task is to provide an environment and opportunities which are sufficiently challenging for children and yet not so difficult as to be outside their reach. There has to be the right mixture of the familiar and the novel, the right match to the stage of learning the child has reached. If the material is too familiar or the learning skills too easy, children will become inattentive and bored. If too great a maturity is demanded of them, they fall back on half remembered formulae and become concerned only to give the reply the teacher wants. Children can think and form concepts, so long as they work at their own level, and are not made to feel that they are failures.

Teachers must rely both on their general knowledge of child development and on detailed observation of individual children for matching their demands to children's stages of development. This concept of 'readiness' was first applied to reading. It has sometimes been thought of in too negative a way. Children can be led to want to read, provided that they are sufficiently mature. Learning can be undertaken too late as well as too early. Piaget's work [see Reading 6.3] can help teachers in diagnosing children's readiness in mathematics, and gives some pointers as to how it can be encouraged.

At every stage of learning children need rich and varied materials and situations, though the pace at which they should be introduced may vary according to the children. If children are limited in materials, they tend to solve problems in isolation and fail to see their relevance to other similar situations. This stands out particularly clearly in young children's learning of mathematics. Similarly, children need to accumulate much experience of human behaviour before they can develop moral concepts. If teachers or parents are inconsistent in their attitudes or contradict by their behaviour what they preach, it becomes difficult for children to develop stable and mature concepts. Verbal explanation, in advance of understanding based on experience, may be an obstacle to learning, and children's knowledge of the right words may conceal from teachers their lack of understanding. Yet it is inevitable that children will pick up words which outstrip their understanding. Discussion with other children and with adults is one of the principal ways in which children check their concepts against those of others and build up an objective view of reality. There is every justification for the conversation which is a characteristic feature of the contemporary primary school. One of the most important responsibilities of teachers is to help children to see order and pattern in experience, and to extend their ideas by analogies and by the provision of suitable vocabulary. Rigid division of the curriculum into subjects tends to interrupt children's trains of thought and of interest and to hinder them from realizing the common elements in problem solving. These are among the many reasons why some work, at least, should cut across subject divisions at all stages in the primary school.

READING 7.7

Towards a national debate

James Callaghan

This reading comprises text from Prime Minister James Callaghan's speech at Ruskin College, Oxford, which, in 1976, challenged the post-war consensus on education and started a 'great debate'. Over a decade later, came the Education Reform Act of 1988 which addressed many of the issues which were raised. The art of the astute politician is well in evidence in the reading, particularly in the careful way in which Callaghan points out that educationalists have to consider wider public interests. Similarly, there are some very familiar themes, such as costs, links with industry, teaching methods and standards.

To what extent do you think the national debate has been settled? Or is it something which is going to be always with us? Some would say that, in the modern world, education cannot be removed from political debate.

Edited from: Callaghan, J. (1976) Towards a national debate, *Education*, 148 (1), 332–3

There have been one or two ripples of interest in the educational world in anticipation of this visit. I hope the publicity will do Ruskin some good and I don't think it will do the world of education any harm. I must thank all those who have inundated me with advice: some helpful and others telling me less politely to keep off the grass, to watch my language, and that they will be examining my speech with the care usually given to Hong Kong watchers to the China scene. It is almost as though some people would wish that the subject matter and purpose of education should not have public attention focused on it; nor that profane hands should be allowed to touch it.

I cannot believe that this is a considered reaction. The Labour movement has always cherished education: free education, comprehensive education, adult education. Education for life. There is nothing wrong with non-educationalists, even a Prime Minister, talking about it again.

Let me answer the question 'What do we want from the education of our children and young people?' with Tawney's words when he said: 'What a wise parent would wish for their children, so the State must wish for all its children.'

I take it that no one claims exclusive rights in this field. Public interest is strong and legitimate and will be satisfied. We spend £6 billion a year on education, so there will be discussion. But let it be rational. If everything is reduced to such phrases as 'educational freedom versus State control', we shall get nowhere. I repeat that parents, teachers, learned and professional bodies, representatives of higher education and both sides of industry, together with the Government, all have an important part to play in formulating and expressing the purpose of education and the standards that we need.

During my travels around the country in recent months, I have had many discussions that show concern about these matters.

First let me say, so that there should be no misunderstanding, that I have been very impressed in the schools I have visited by the enthusiasm and dedication of the teaching profession, by the variety of courses that are offered in our comprehensive schools, especially in arts and crafts as well as in other subjects; and by the alertness and keenness of many of the pupils. Clearly, life at school is far more full and creative than it was many years ago. I would also like to thank the children who have been kind enough to write to me after I visited their schools: and well-written letters they were. I recognize that teachers occupy a special place in these discussions because of their real sense of professionalism and vocation about their work. But I am concerned on my journeys to find complaints from industry that new recruits from the schools sometimes do not have the basic tools to do the job that is required.

I have been concerned to find that many of our best trained students who have completed the higher levels of education at university or polytechnic have no desire to join industry. Their preferences are to stay in academic life or to find their way into the Civil Service. There seems to be a need for a more technological bias in science teaching that will lead towards practical applications in industry rather than towards academic studies. Or, to take other examples, why is it that such a high proportion of girls abandon science before leaving school? Then there is concern about the standards of numeracy of school-leavers. Is there not a case for a professional review of the mathematics needed by industry at different levels? To what extent are these deficiencies the result of insufficient co-ordination between schools and industry?

On another aspect there is the unease felt by parents and others about the new informal methods of teaching which seem to produce excellent results when they are in well-qualified hands but are much more dubious when they are not. They seem to be best accepted where strong parent–teacher links exist. There is little wrong with the range and diversity of our courses. But is there sufficient thoroughness and depth in those required in after life to make a living?

These are proper subjects for discussion and debate. And it should be a rational debate based on the facts. My remarks are not a clarion call to Black Paper prejudices. We all know those who claim to defend standards but who in reality are simply seeking to defend old privileges and inequalities.

It is not my intention to become enmeshed in such problems as whether there should be a basic curriculum with universal standards – although I am inclined to think that there should be – nor about other issues on which there is a divided professional opinion such as the position and role of the Inspectorate. What I am saying is that where there is legitimate public concern it will be to the advantage of all involved in the education field if these concerns are aired and shortcomings righted or fears put at rest.

To the critics I would say that we must carry the teaching profession with us. They have the expertise and the professional approach. To the teachers I would say that you must satisfy the parents and industry that what you are doing meets their requirements and the needs of our children. For if the public is not convinced then the profession will be laying up trouble for itself in the future.

The goals of our education, from nursery school through to adult education, are clear enough. They are to equip children to the best of their ability for a lively, constructive place in society and also to fit them to do a job of work. Not one or the other, but both. For many years the accent was simply on fitting a so-called inferior group of children with just enough learning to earn their living in the factory. Labour has attacked that attitude consistently, during 60 or 70 years and throughout my childhood. There is now widespread recognition of the need to cater for a child's personality, to let it flower in the fullest possible way.

The balance was wrong in the past. We have a responsibility now to see that we do not get it wrong in the other direction. There is no virtue in producing socially well-adjusted members of society who are unemployed because they do not have the skills. Nor at the other extreme must they be technically efficient robots. Both of the basic purposes of education require the same essential tools. These are basic literacy, basic numeracy, the understanding of how to live and work together, respect for others, respect for the individual. This means acquiring certain basic knowledge, and skills and reasoning ability. It means developing lively inquiring minds and an appetite for further knowledge that will last a lifetime.

I do not join those who paint a lurid picture of educational decline because I do not believe it is generally true. However, in today's world higher standards are demanded than were required yesterday and there are simply fewer jobs for those without skill. Therefore we demand more from our schools than did our grandparents.

There is a challenge to us all in these days and a challenge in education is to examine its priorities and to secure as high efficiency as possible by the skilful use of existing resources.

The debate that I was seeking has got off to a flying start. Now I ask all those who are concerned to respond positively.

Better schools

Department of Education and Science

This 1985 publication was of great significance as an early Government attempt to systematically set out the main elements of an over-arching framework for education in England and Wales. It can be seen as building on the issues and debate raised by Jim Callaghan (Reading 7.7) and as anticipating the legislation of the Education Reform Act, 1988. Note the concern about the unacceptable variation in standards and the four areas which were identified for policy action, the details for just one of which, curriculum, are included here.

This document foreshadowed many ideas which became manifested in national provision in the 1990s. How many can you identify? Which aspects of these proposals were dropped?

Edited from: Department of Education and Science (1985) *Better Schools: A Summary*. London: HMSO, 2–5

There is much to admire in our schools. Over the last thirty years the school system has expanded and adapted. There have been marked improvements in both primary and secondary education. Many schools cope well, some very well, with their increasingly exacting task. But a number of weaknesses, some of them serious, are found in the others. The Government believes that the standards now generally attained by our pupils are neither as good as they can be, nor as good as they need to be for the world of the twenty-first century. School education should do much more to promote enterprise and adaptability and to fit young people for working life in a technological age. If the high standards achieved by pupils of all abilities in some schools could be achieved in all schools in similar circumstances the quality of school education would rise dramatically.

In the best primary and middle schools pupils achieve very high standards of competence and consolidate their positive personal qualities through a broad curriculum. But in only a minority of schools is the best practice of individual teachers adopted throughout the school. In about three-quarters of schools the curriculum is not well planned or effectively put into practice. In a majority of primary and middle schools there is over-concentration on practising basic skills in literacy and numeracy without relating them to real situations. Many children are still given too little opportunity for work in the scientific, practical and aesthetic areas. In about half of all classes much work is too closely directed by the teacher and there is little chance for oral discussion or setting and solving practical problems. Many teachers do not expect enough of their pupils: in most classes able pupils are insufficiently stretched and the weaknesses of the less able are not tackled appropriately.

The best secondary schools provide a broad curriculum in which pupils of all abilities reach high standards. They turn out young people with self-confidence, self-respect and respect for others, who are enterprising, adaptable, and eager and well equipped to face the adult world. But in most secondary schools agreed curricular policies appear to have little influence on the whole school. Many departments fail to put into practice their own and the school's declared aims and objectives.

In a large minority of cases, teachers' expectations of what pupils could achieve are clouded by inadequate knowledge and understanding of each pupil's aptitudes and difficulties: teaching is frequently directed at the middle level of ability so that the most able pupils are understretched and the least able cannot cope. In virtually all secondary schools and departments there is often excessive direction by the teacher and pupils have too few opportunities to learn for themselves. In about one-fifth of secondary schools there is a serious problem of teachers having to teach a subject outside their competence.

The best special schools provide an education well suited to their pupils' capabilities and needs. But many special schools show many of the weaknesses found in primary and secondary schools.

Not all the weaknesses in our schools are the fault of the schools, or of the education service: many stem from the wider problems facing our society. The Government has a duty to act where it can. Together with its partners in education it will take action in four areas of policy:

the curriculum;

the examination system and assessment;

the professional effectiveness of teachers and the management of the teacher force;

school government and the contribution which can be made to good school education by parents, employers and others outside the education service.

There is widespread acceptance of the view that broad agreement about the objectives and content of the school curriculum is necessary for the improvement in standards which is needed. Initial agreement will take time and will then need to be reviewed as circumstances change. As the process develops, the Government after consultation will issue statements of policy, and Her Majesty's Inspectors (HMI) will continue to publish discussion papers. The objectives will be based on the best practice in local education authorities and schools.

The objectives are intended to have practical effect by becoming the basis of the curricular policies of:

the Secretaries of State, who need a curriculum policy for discharging their statutory duty to promote the education of the people of England and Wales;

the local education authorities, for exercising their functions in such matters as the pattern of schools, the provision of resources, and the management of the teaching force;

the schools, for organizing and carrying out the actual work of teaching.

The objectives will be applied with differences of emphasis and balance to reflect local circumstances and local judgement. The Secretaries of State's policies for the range and pattern of the 5 to 16 curriculum will not lead to national syllabuses. Diversity at local education authority and school level is healthy, accords well with the English and Welsh tradition of school education, and makes for liveliness and innovation.

There is wide agreement about the purposes of learning at school, in particular that pupils should develop lively, enquiring minds, acquire understanding, knowledge and skills relevant to adult life and employment and develop personal moral values. To serve these purposes the Government believes that the curriculum offered to every pupil should be:

broad: it should introduce the pupil to a wide range of knowledge, understanding and skills;

balanced: each part should be allotted sufficient time to make its special contribution, but not so much that it squeezes out other essential parts;

relevant: subjects should be taught so as to bring out their applications to the pupils' own experience and to adult life, and to give due emphasis to practical aspects;

differentiated: what is taught and how it is taught need to be matched to pupils' abilities and aptitudes.

A curriculum founded on these four principles will serve to develop the potential of every pupil and to equip all for the responsibilities of citizenship and for the challenge of working life in the world of tomorrow.

READING 7.9

Correct core

Sheila Lawlor

The debate on the content of the National Curriculum was particularly acrimonious during the late 1980s and the influence of 'New Right' pressure groups was considerable. Sheila Lawlor, writing from the Centre for Policy Studies just before the Education Reform Act was passed, argued for minimal national requirements in which only knowledge and skill in the basics of English, Maths and Science should be specified. This would have left schools able to vary their other provision to meet particular market needs, and would have minimized the influence of 'education service' assumptions which, in her view, depressed standards.

It is interesting to speculate on how things would have developed had Sheila Lawlor's arguments been accepted. However, the emphasis on the core curriculum clearly remains.

Edited from: Lawlor, S. (1988) *Correct Core: Simple Curricula for English, Maths and Science*, Policy Study No. 93. London: Centre for Policy Studies, 5–40

Our 'Core Curriculum' document sets out curricula for English, Maths and Science. In order to ensure that pupils leave school literate, numerate and with a modicum of scientific knowledge, it should not extend beyond these three core subjects, nor attempt to do more than set minimum standards in basic knowledge and technique.

It is regrettable that these aims appear recently to have been abandoned by those in charge of producing and implementing education policy. The official committees, the DES and Her Majesty's Inspectorate no longer adhere to the belief that teachers should teach and pupils should learn a simple body of knowledge and a simple set of techniques. Should the curriculum go beyond three core subjects, it would undermine the fundamental purpose of the present educational reforms – to raise standards for all pupils and to give greater responsibility to those most directly concerned with the education of the young. Above all it would greatly reduce the power of Heads to offer the subjects which best meet the needs of their pupils.

It is not for the Government to impose exactly what individual schools should teach, nor to decide how Heads should draw up timetables. In denying them the freedom to teach the subjects of their choice to the highest level, a Conservative Government would add to the threats to educational standards already posed by the 'education professionals'.

The most marked characteristic of Mrs Thatcher's Governments is the way in which they have changed the nature and premises of political debate. This has been particularly true in economic and industrial policy. Here a set of assumptions had developed since the War and become an orthodoxy. But so successful has the challenge been that even the Labour Party has come to accept many Thatcherite premises.

The challenge has been extended to other orthodoxies which inhibited the exercise of individual freedom. For example, in local government and housing the imbalance of power exercised by the State, its agents, and a variety of vested interests has been corrected in favour of the individual. Greater freedom and responsibility will be further enhanced by the reform of local government finance to make authorities more accountable.

But the orthodoxies which have dominated education policy have been challenged in one respect only – by tilting the administrative balance away from the monopolies of the state and its agents, the LEAs and education establishment, slightly in favour of the parents and the schools themselves. They have not been challenged when it comes to the content of education.

The National Curriculum proposed in the new Education Reform Bill presents an opportunity for change but the danger exists that far from tackling the orthodoxies, it will further entrench them. If the content of the proposed National Curriculum merely reflects the views of members of the 'education service' – teachers, their unions, LEAs, education theorists and worst of all Her Majesty's Inspectorate (HMI) – then the National Curriculum, instead of serving to raise standards, will lower them.

The proposed National Curriculum recognizes English, Mathematics and Science as its three 'core' subjects. What are the assumptions which dominate thinking about these subjects within the 'education service'?

The most recent and comprehensive exposition of them can be found for English in the Bullock Report *A Language for Life* (DES, 1974), and for maths in the Cockcroft Report *Mathematics Counts* (DES, 1982). Their recommendations have been summarized and promulgated by HMI in English from 5 to 16 and Mathematics from 5 to 16 – pamphlets intended to guide teachers and LEAs in what and how to teach. In science there is no equivalent report, although the HMI document *Science 5 to 16: A Statement of Policy* (DES, 1985), shows how many assumptions behind science teaching are similar to those of the Bullock and Cockcroft reports. They all assume:

that individual subjects are a thing of the past and can usefully be approached 'across the curriculum';

that pupils should not be expected to master much information or knowledge beyond their immediate experience and that concentration on – or memorizing – information facts and principles should be discouraged;

that pupils should master complicated and sophisticated concepts more appropriate to academic research;

that there can be no external standards set to which pupils might be taught; rather, what is taught must be relative to each pupil and his ability, and restricted accordingly;

that oral work and discussion matter as much as written work;

that learning must take place without effort and in the guise of games, puzzles and activities;

that teaching is akin to salesmanship; what is taught, and how it is taught, needs to 'continue to catch the pupil's interest and imagination';

that pupils must not be allowed to experience failure; and that the purpose of teaching is as much social as academic, in order to reflect the issues 'with which pupils will have to come to terms' such as 'multi-cultural' society, 'a greater diversity of personal values', and 'the equal treatment of men and women'.

Such assumptions in the recent past have not led to higher standards. On the contrary, many pupils leave school today illiterate and innumerate. They are unable to write simple, correct English; do elementary arithmetical calculations; or satisfy employers understandably disillusioned with levels of competency.

Poor standards must be tackled by correcting the assumptions outlined, and by changing the expectations of teachers and pupils alike. Teachers must be expected to teach; and they, along with the other groups most responsible for running schools, must be held to account for pupils who do not learn. Pupils must be expected to leave school having mastered a modicum of knowledge and techniques in specific subjects. They should be numerate. They should be able to read without difficulty and to write grammatical, clear and simple English. But the pupil must also have been taught so that he will grow to understand – according to ability and inclination – the world in which he lives: one to which he will never belong if the necessary information and knowledge of it is denied him.

CHAPTER 7.10

Good practice: more than a mantra?

Robin Alexander

In 1991 Robin Alexander's report on primary education in Leeds became a 'political football' in a fast-moving national debate about pupil standards, classroom practice, teacher beliefs and the role of Local Education Authorities. The book from which this reading is drawn brings together the main findings of Alexander's initial report and presents some major challenges to primary school teachers. In particular, the notion of 'good primary practice' is incisively investigated and analysed.

Does the idea simply obscure forms of teaching which are routinized, unthinking and untenable in modern schools and classrooms? Does it make teachers vulnerable to populist critique? How might teaching be conceptualized more securely?

Edited from: Alexander, R. J. (1992) *Policy and Practice in Primary Education*. London: Routledge, 174–91 (with some updating by the author)

The ubiquitous phrase 'good primary practice' begs questions nearly every time it is uttered. Consider these quotations (those unattributed are from the Leeds research reported in Alexander, 1992):

> We apply all the basic principles of good practice here – a stimulating environment with high quality display and plenty of material for first hand exploration; a flexible day in which children can move freely from one activity to the next without the artificial barriers of subjects; plenty of individual and group work.

> Children spend more time with paint pots than mastering the three Rs, said Schools Minister Michael Fallon ... They should get back to basics and teach the whole class in an organized way ... (*Daily Mail*, 2.11.91)

> The successful candidate will be familiar with good primary practice. A belief in a child-centred approach is essential.

> If you don't have drapes and triple mounting, you won't get on here.

> Child-centred education ... part of a deliberate political project to undermine the respect the young should have for the achievements of those who went before them. (Anthony O'Hear in the *Daily Telegraph*, 12.2.91)

> The children ... spread into the hall, the corridors and the playground. The nursery class has its own quarters and the children are playing with sand, water, paint, clay, dolls, rocking horses and big push toys under the supervision of their teacher. This is how they learn ... Learning is going on all the time, but there is not much direct teaching ... The class of sevens to nines had spread into the corridor and were engaged in a variety of occupations. One group were gathered round their teacher for some extra reading practice, another was at work on an extraordinary structure of wood and metal which they said was a sputnik, a third was collecting a number of objects and testing them to find out which could be picked up by a magnet and two boys were at work on an immense painting of St Michael defeating Satan. They seemed to be working harmoniously according to an unfolding rather than a pre-conceived plan. (CACE (1967), *The Plowden Report*, pp. 103–5)

> Look on your works, Lady Plowden, and despair. (*Daily Telegraph*, 7.11.91)

> Plowden is still my Bible, whatever the government or any airy-fairy academics say. They are not the practitioners – I am!

There is a crisis in primary education ... In France, Holland, Denmark, Germany and Japan, young children learn to read, write, add up and speak another language ... Those countries believe in whole-class teaching, learning facts by heart, children sitting behind desks ... teachers here seem to have ideological opposition to these ideas, but they must be required to change their ways. (Centre for Policy Studies Director, Tessa Keswick, in *Daily Telegraph*, 26.1.96)

The research evidence demonstrates that the level of cognitive challenge provided by the teacher is a significant factor in the child's performance. One way of providing challenge is to set pupils demanding tasks. But, equally, it is important for teachers to organize their classrooms so that they have the opportunity to interact with their pupils: to offer explanations which develop thinking, to encourage speculation and hypothesis through sensitive questioning, to develop, above all, a climate of interest and purpose ... Teachers need to be competent in a range of techniques in order to achieve different learning outcomes ... They need the skills and judgement to be able to select and apply whichever ... is appropriate to the task in hand ... The judgement ... should be educational and organisational, rather than, as it so often is, doctrinal ... The critical notion is that of fitness for purpose. (Alexander, Rose and Woodhead, 1992, pp. 30–1)

When we say of teaching which we do, see or commend 'this is good practice', what are we really asserting? There seem to be four main possibilities:

This teaching is in line with what x defines as good practice and the status of x is such that his/her views must be heeded.

This teaching works, in as far as the children seem to be appropriately and gainfully occupied.

This teaching leads to specific and recognizable kinds of learning and a causal relationship between the teaching and learning can be demonstrated.

This teaching is consistent with my/our values and beliefs about the proper purposes and conduct of education.

Though there is inevitable overlap between the statements their status is nevertheless somewhat different. Thus, the first, being about the exercise of power, is a political statement. The second is essentially a pragmatic statement. The third, being grounded in experience and observation and being concerned with verification, is an empirical statement. The fourth is evaluative in the sense of expressing, and being explicitly validated by, values and beliefs. All four are illustrated in the collage of quotations above.

This classification begins to unravel the 'good' in 'good practice': it is anything but the absolute many claim or wish. What of the notion of 'practice' itself? Is it reasonable to assume that when we speak of good primary practice we are all talking of the same phenomena, and the only problem concerns the basis on which we rate them as good, bad or indifferent? Though we readily acknowledge that 'education' is a pluralist concept, is 'teaching' significantly less so?

The quotations above suggest that it is not. The problem with many everyday accounts or definitions of good practice is that not only do they leave unexplored vital questions of justification, but they also focus in a frequently arbitrary way upon particular aspects of practice which are then elevated to the status of a complete and coherent 'philosophy'. More often than not, they are mere philosophical fragments or preliminary clearings of the throat.

In order to judge the adequacy of a good practice claim, therefore, we need not only to examine the criteria by which practice is judged to be good, but also to be clear about which aspects of practice are defined in this way and which aspects are ignored. There is of course no reason why a good practice statement should not be selective and sharply focused, for it is difficult to talk meaningfully with teaching unless we engage with its specifics. The problem

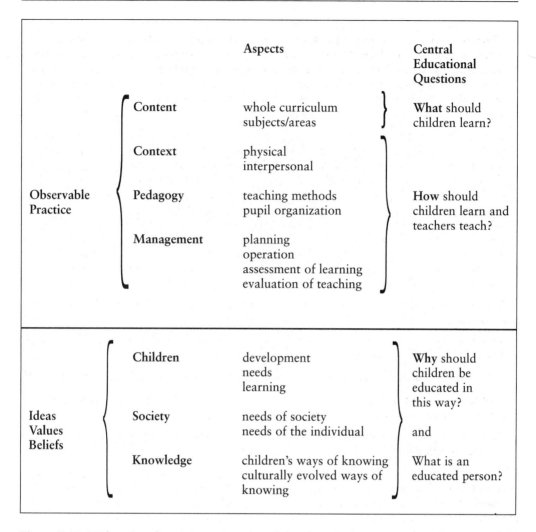

Figure 7.10.1 Educational practice: a conceptual framework

comes when over time, or within a statement purporting to stand as a complete educational rationale, some aspects of practice are consistently emphasized while others are consistently ignored. The underlying message of such selectivity is that what is emphasized is all that matters, whether it be – to draw on contrasting selections – display, group work, thematic enquiry, whole-class teaching, or the basics.

Figure 7.10.1 above attempts to provide a framework for approaching this aspect of the good practice question in a more rounded way. The two main dimensions reflect a view of teaching as educational ideas in action, or as classroom actions and events which both manifest and are informed by ideas, values and beliefs. The seven aspects of teaching so defined arise from observation of teaching as it happens and from analysis of ideas about teaching which have been articulated by practitioners. The resulting categories are of course not discrete, but are presented separately for analytical purposes. Similarly, the two dimensions, here presented as a sequential list, interact: each aspect of practice is to a greater or lesser extent informed by one, two or all of the areas of ideas, values and assumptions. Armed with such a framework we can return to any good practice statement, test its emphasis and scope, and examine the thrust and genealogy of the ideas, values and beliefs in which it is rooted.

To take stock. 'Good practice' statements come in different forms. Some are statements of value or belief; some are pragmatic statements; some are empirical statements; some are political statements; most combine more than one of these characteristics, which are themselves neither discrete nor one-dimensional; and all presuppose a concept of practice itself. Pursuing our quest for good primary practice in this way, therefore, we can see that while in a physical sense it resides in primary schools and classrooms, in order to know what we are looking for and to begin to understand how we might define and judge it, we need to recognize that it lies, conceptually, somewhere at the intersection of the five considerations or dimensions which have been identified so far: evaluative, pragmatic, empirical, political and conceptual. Figure 7.10.2 below represents this relationship.

The quest for good primary practice, then, is as much a conceptual as a physical one. However, the point at which the various overlapping considerations meet is an arena of conflict as much as of resolution. Primary practice – any educational practice – requires us to come to terms with and do our best to reconcile competing values, pressures and constraints. It is about dilemma no less than certainty (Alexander, 1995, chapter 2). If this is so of practice in general, it must also be the case, *a fortiori*, with practice we wish to define as 'good'.

However, there has to be a qualitative difference between practice and good practice if the latter notion is not to become redundant. Or is it the case that good practice is no more than the best we can do in the circumstances? Is our quest for educational quality to run into the morass of relativism? I believe not. Though in Figure 7.10.2 the five considerations or dimensions appear to have equal weight, the pursuit of good practice has to move beyond a mere balancing of competing imperatives. There have to be superordinate reasons for preferring one course of action to another, reasons which will enable education to rise above the level of the merely pragmatic. For education is inherently about values: it reflects a vision of the kind of world we want our children to inherit; a vision of the kinds of people we hope they will

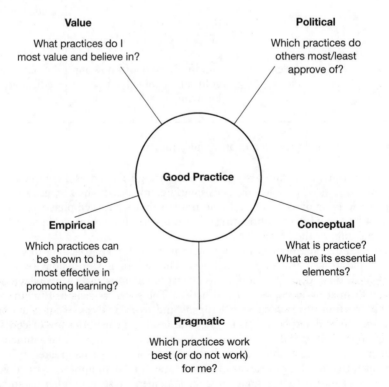

Value
What practices do I most value and believe in?

Political
Which practices do others most/least approve of?

Good Practice

Empirical
Which practices can be shown to be most effective in promoting learning?

Conceptual
What is practice? What are its essential elements?

Pragmatic
Which practices work best (or do not work) for me?

Figure 7.10.2 What is good practice? Reconciling competing imperatives

become; a vision of what it is to be an educated person. Whatever the other ingredients of good practice may be, they should enable a coherent and sustainable value-position to be pursued. Values, then, are central.

Yet, in teaching, values have to be made manifest rather than merely held or voiced. They are manifested as learning contexts, tasks and encounters. While, clearly, such activities must be congruent with the values they seek to realize, such congruence is of itself no guarantee of

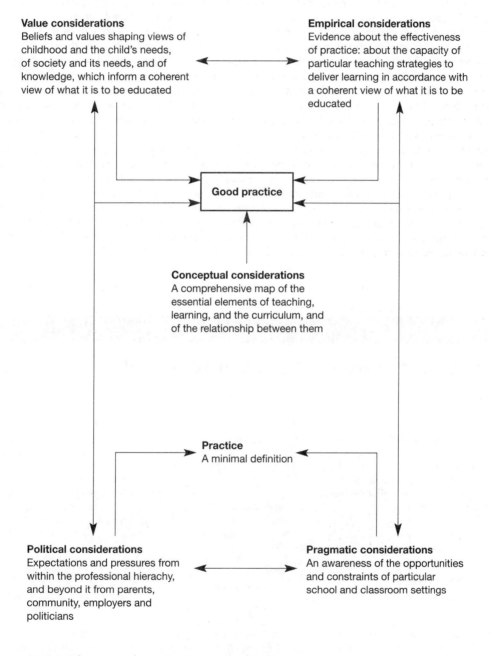

Value considerations
Beliefs and values shaping views of childhood and the child's needs, of society and its needs, and of knowledge, which inform a coherent view of what it is to be educated

Empirical considerations
Evidence about the effectiveness of practice: about the capacity of particular teaching strategies to deliver learning in accordance with a coherent view of what it is to be educated

Good practice

Conceptual considerations
A comprehensive map of the essential elements of teaching, learning, and the curriculum, and of the relationship between them

Practice
A minimal definition

Political considerations
Expectations and pressures from within the professional hierachy, and beyond it from parents, community, employers and politicians

Pragmatic considerations
An awareness of the opportunities and constraints of particular school and classroom settings

Figure 7.10.3 What is good practice? Beyond relativism

success in terms of the specific learning goals which give the broader vision practical meaning. We need to go one step further, therefore, and to couple with the commitment to values and value-congruence a clear awareness of evidence, published or experiential, concerning the strengths and weaknesses of the various teaching strategies open to us, in order that we can construct, ideally, learning tasks and contexts which are not just consistent with the values but will also translate them into meaningful learning for the child. It is for this reason that the empirical dimension is so critical an adjunct to matters of value, belief and purpose.

It is also clear that the pursuit of 'effectiveness' *per se*, a currently popular quest among educational researchers and policy-makers, can produce versions of good practice which are incomplete or untenable in the same way that value statements detached from empirical understanding may be inoperable. Those who presume that the inconveniently untidy value problems in the good practice question are resolved at a stroke by talking of 'effective' practice (or the effective teacher/effective school) are engaging in mere sleight of hand: practice, we must ask, which is effective in relation to what? In relation, of course, to a notion of what it is to be educated. Good practice, then, justifies its approbation by being both intrinsically educative and operationally effective. In the educational arena, effectiveness as a criterion existing on its own is meaningless.

We are now in a position to sum up. Figure 7.10.2 represented good practice as existing at the intersection of the five considerations and as a matter of reconciling competing imperatives. However, I then suggested that this approach does not take sufficient note of what the 'good' in 'good practice' might dictate, and that although all the considerations are important, they are not equivalent. The pursuit of good practice sets the considerations in a hierarchical relationship with evaluative and empirical questions pre-eminent, and with both dependent on a prior conceptualization of the nature of educational practice itself. This alternative relationship, a development of the initial idea, is shown in Figure 7.10.3.

READING 7.11

The curriculum for a learning society

The Labour Party

The Labour Party document from which this extract has been edited was compiled when Ann Taylor was Shadow Secretary of State for Education and at a time when the introduction of the National Curriculum was going rather badly, with teachers feeling extremely overloaded by prescription and regulation. Many would have agreed then with the characterization of the National Curriculum as 'a block of facts'. However, the main purpose of the document was to open up a new debate about the aims of the curriculum, with an important emphasis on issues such as motivation, rights, global and critical understanding and multi-level partnerships for lifelong learning.

Considering the list below, how many of these issues are still important? Have any been resolved? How many are still subjects of debate?

Edited from: The Labour Party (1994) *Consultative Green Paper: Opening Doors to a Learning Society*. London: The Labour Party, 26–8

At the heart of effective learning and teaching is the quality of the curriculum.

The Labour Party has long supported the need for a national curriculum and welcomed its introduction. Discussion of what was variously described as a common core, compulsory or

National Curriculum took place under Labour in the 1970s via discussion with parents' organizations, heads, teachers, HMI, local education authorities, unions and others.

By the end of the 1970s there was broad agreement that a common curriculum for all pupils should focus on knowledge and understanding of five or six disciplines. There was also some agreement that the limited school subjects most children studied discouraged breadth and balance; were unsuited to the needs of many pupils; were irrelevant to the needs of many employers; took no account of modern technologies; encouraged early over-specialization and had few links with post-16 education, training and employment. Labour supported the introduction of a common examination at 16, the GCSE and the proposals put forward in *Better Schools* (DES, 1985) for a common curriculum [see Reading 7.8]. This document now stands as a model of calm appraisal, highlighting the role of LEAs for 'the priority they had given to the formulation of curriculum policies'.

In 1987, however, came the introduction of a 10-subject National Curriculum that suspiciously echoed the model laid down by the 1904 Board of Education regulations. The Government ignored an emerging consensus that all pupils should have equal access to a broad relevant education with nationally agreed objectives and guidelines, but with content the product of debate between educational partners. Instead, a prescriptive, outdated content-specific national syllabus with no agreed principles and objectives has been imposed.

The present national syllabus concentrates on the time-tabled curriculum and ignores the wider curriculum that arises from a school's own ethos and values. It uses testing to drive the content of education and to encourage a climate of failure. It reduces teachers to the status of 'technicians' who 'deliver' a service. It has been subject to endless ministerial tinkering, dangerous political interference, and the influence of unelected and unaccountable, politically motivated right-wing groups and individuals. It has developed into an over-assessed, conceptually arid, bureaucratic nightmare, epitomized by a myriad of orders, circulars, amendments, booklets, folders, ring-binders and instructions.

No reason has been given as to why the curriculum prescribed by the Government is subject-based; indeed, its over-prescriptive nature has denied the first principle in the 1988 Act which merely says that the school curriculum must be 'balanced and broadly based', and promote 'the spiritual, moral, cultural, mental and physical development of students at school and society'. The HMI report of the early 1980s advised that the curriculum be defined as areas of study. There is a great deal of concern at the move away from the HMI suggestions of 'areas of study' and a belief that this is one of the reasons that the National Curriculum is so overprescribed.

If there is to be agreement on a framework for a National Curriculum there must first be agreement upon its purpose.

The view of education as a block of facts to be learned between the ages of 5 and 16 will lead to a prescriptive national syllabus. The view of education as a means of understanding one's self and society requires the achievement of confidence, skills and independent thought and these can be developed through many avenues.

As a step in opening up the debate we suggest the following as the purpose of a national framework curriculum.

It must be based on a vision of the future that recognizes that adults may change their jobs several times and may have more recreation and leisure than previous generations. They will need imagination, flexibility and drive if they are to play their part as full citizens.

The curriculum must promote success, rather than identify and reinforce failure. It must be a framework within which all children and young people want to strive for higher levels of knowledge, understanding, skill and opportunity – it must *motivate* children.

It must have a clear defensible set of aims linked to the personal achievements of individuals and to civil and economic needs and expectations.

It must also be preparation for lifelong learning. It must offer fair opportunities to all and be a right for all with no rationing or exclusion on grounds of class, race, gender, disability or 'special need' and it must encourage a culture of respect between young people.

Its content and assessment arrangements must fit together in a coherent way and ensure a measure of common agreed experiences for all children.

It must ensure that the pupil has a clear understanding of national and international relationships, a global dimension which is becoming more difficult to incorporate given the current pressures on the curriculum.

It must involve parents, teachers, governors, local communities, and local and central partnership who will facilitate learning and encourage the 'learning person'.

It must encourage a critical understanding of social, political and economic arrangements and not become an instrument of indoctrination.

It must include measures to continually assess and monitor quality and ensure high standards.

It must apply to all schools, including those in the independent sector.

The pressures now leading to a narrowing of the curriculum and the school experience of our young people are extremely worrying. The demands of the prescriptive curriculum and cutbacks in local authority services mean that children today are not always able to enjoy the breadth of experiences to which they should be entitled.

READING 7.12

The National Curriculum and its assessment

Ron Dearing

> Sir Ron Dearing was responsible for calming the teaching profession and rescuing the National Curriculum in England and Wales from the considerable difficulties which it faced in its early stages of implementation during the early 1990s. His diplomatic report, from which this reading is edited, contained many concessions to teachers. Note however, the continuing themes of standards, connections to the world of work and the importance of cultural heritage. The emphasis is also very different from that in the preceding Labour Party document (Reading 7.11).
>
> Do you feel that the National Curriculum structure and content does now facilitate teachers' work and pupils' learning, as Sir Ron hoped?
>
> Edited from: Dearing, R. (1993) *The National Curriculum and its Assessment: a Review.* London: Schools Curriculum and Assessment Authority, 16–18

'Upon the education of the people of this country, the future of this country depends.'

If this was true when Disraeli spoke these words in 1874 when Britain was at the height of its economic power, it is even more so today. In a highly competitive world there is nowhere to hide. The fact that standards of educational achievement are rising internationally, and, in particular, in the Far East, means that our future as a nation depends upon the improvements we can make to our education system.

The evidence is that, while academically gifted students fully match international standards, those who are of average ability or whose talents are not academic are faring less well. In the long-term, this failure to realize the potential of all our young people will undermine our economic performance and quality of life. This is a matter for profound concern.

The central aim of this Review must be to make proposals which will both support and challenge teachers in their task. It is teachers and only teachers who can directly improve educational standards.

The Review was instituted by the Secretary of State for Education in response to widespread concern that the basic aims of the National Curriculum and its assessment arrangements were being undermined by complexity, over-elaboration, over prescription and excessive content.

Teachers have reiterated these concerns throughout the Review. Their commitment to the principle of the National Curriculum is clear, but so, too, is the need for urgent and immediate action to ensure that the curriculum is rendered manageable and that the burden of administration is reduced.

The consultation leads me to believe that we can help teachers do a better job for their pupils with the National Curriculum by:

reducing the volume of material required by law to be taught;

simplifying and clarifying the programmes of study;

reducing prescription so as to give more scope for professional judgement;

ensuring that the Orders are written in a way which offers maximum support to the classroom teacher.

There may be some who feel I should have been more radical. But there is much good in what has been achieved so far. We can build upon the enormous commitment in time and energy which teachers have made to the National Curriculum. There is no sense whatsoever in seeking to start all over again. There is wisdom in the warning that to seek constantly after perhaps illusory improvement is to use time and energy which would be better devoted to making the present arrangements work.

We should not take risks with the education of millions of pupils.

Education is not concerned only with equipping students with the knowledge and skills they need to earn a living. It must help our young people to: use leisure time creatively; have respect for other people, other cultures and other beliefs; become good citizens; think things out for themselves; pursue a healthy lifestyle; and, not least, value themselves and their achievements. It should develop an appreciation of the richness of our cultural heritage and of the spiritual and moral dimensions to life. It must, moreover be concerned to serve all our children well, whatever their background, sex, creed, ethnicity or talent.

It is the primary school teacher who must begin to fulfil these objectives. I am very conscious of the challenge many primary school teachers face, receiving as they do children from very different backgrounds – social, economic, ethnic, religious and varying greatly in their readiness to learn. But if children do not leave primary school with a firm grasp of the basic skills of literacy and numeracy, with an appetite for learning and with a belief in themselves and their talents, their future progress will inevitably be stunted.

📖 **READING 7.13**

A perspective on teacher knowledge

Lee Shulman

This final reading on curriculum is not about its organization and content, but about the forms of teacher knowledge which are required to teach a curriculum effectively. It is derived from Shulman's classic paper in which he identifies three forms of teacher knowledge: subject content, pedagogic and curricular. This thinking has been extremely influential in teacher training, provision for continuous professional development and conceptualizing the role of curriculum 'consultants' in primary schools.

Thinking of your own curricular strengths, can you identify these three forms of knowledge in yourself? And regarding subjects about which you feel less secure, what forms of knowledge particularly concern you?

Edited from: Shulman, L. S. (1986) Those who understand: knowledge growth in teaching, *Educational Researcher*, February, 9–10

How might we think about the knowledge that grows in the minds of teachers, with special emphasis on content? I suggest we distinguish among: subject matter content knowledge, pedagogical content knowledge, and curricular knowledge.

Content knowledge

This refers to the amount and organization of knowledge *per se* in the mind of the teacher.

To think properly about content knowledge requires going beyond knowledge of the facts or concepts of a domain. It requires understanding the structures of the subject matter in the manner defined by such scholars as Joseph Schwab (1978).

For Schwab, the structures of a subject include both the substantive and the syntactive structures. The substantive structures are the variety of ways in which the basic concepts and principles of the discipline are organized to incorporate its facts. The syntactic structure of a discipline is the set of ways in which truth or falsehood, validity or invalidity, are established. When there exist competing claims regarding a given phenomenon, the syntax of a discipline provides the rules for determining which claim has greater warrant. A syntax is like a grammar. It is the set of rules for determining what is legitimate to say in a disciplinary domain and what 'breaks' the rules.

Teachers must not only be capable of defining for students the accepted truths in a domain. They must also be able to explain why a particular proposition is deemed warranted, why it is worth knowing, and how it relates to other propositions, both within the discipline and without, both in theory and in practice.

Thus, the biology teacher must understand that there are a variety of ways of organizing the discipline. Depending on the preferred text, biology may be formulated as: a science of molecules from which one aggregates up to the rest of the field, explaining living phenomena in terms of the principles of their constituent parts; a science of ecological systems from which one disaggregates down to the smaller units, explaining the activities of individual units by virtue of the larger systems of which they are a part; or a science of biological organisms, those most familiar of analytic units, from whose familiar structures, functions, and interactions one weaves a theory of adaptation. The well-prepared biology teacher will recognize these and alternative forms of organization and the pedagogical grounds for selecting one under some circumstances and others under different circumstances.

The same teacher will also understand the syntax of biology. When competing claims are offered regarding the same biological phenomenon, how has the controversy been adjudicated? How might similar controversies be adjudicated in our own day?

We expect that the subject matter content understanding of the teacher be at least equal to that of his or her lay colleague, the mere subject matter specialist. The teacher need not only understand *that* something is so; the teacher must further understand why it is so, on what grounds its warrant can be asserted, and under what circumstances our belief in its justification can be weakened and even denied. Moveover, we expect the teacher to understand why a given topic is particularly central to a discipline whereas another may be somewhat peripheral. This will be important in subsequent pedagogical judgements regarding relative curricular emphasis.

Pedagogical content knowledge

A second kind of content knowledge is pedagogical knowledge, which goes beyond knowledge of subject matter *per se* to the dimension of subject matter knowledge for teaching. I still speak of content knowledge here, but of the particular form of content knowledge that embodies the aspects of content most germane to its teachability.

Within the category of pedagogical content knowledge I include, for the most regularly taught topics in one's subject area, the most useful forms of representation of ideas, the most powerful analogies, illustrations, examples, explanations, and demonstrations – in a word, the ways of representing and formulating the subject that make it comprehensible to others. Since there are no single most powerful forms of representation, the teacher must have at hand a veritable armament of alternative forms of representation, some of which derive from research whereas others originate in the wisdom of practice.

Pedagogical content knowledge also includes an understanding of what makes the learning of specific topics easy or difficult: the conceptions and preconceptions that students of different ages and backgrounds bring with them to the learning of those most frequently taught topics and lessons. If those preconceptions are misconceptions, which they so often are, teachers need knowledge of the strategies most likely to be fruitful in reorganizing the understanding of learners, because those learners are unlikely to appear before them as blank slates.

Here, research on teaching and on learning coincide most closely. The study of student misconceptions and their influence on subsequent learning has been among the most fertile topics for cognitive research. We are gathering an ever growing body of knowledge about the misconceptions of students and about the instructional conditions necessary to overcome and transform those initial conceptions. Such research-based knowledge, an important component of the pedagogical understanding of subject matter, should be included at the heart of our definition of needed pedagogical knowledge.

Curricular knowledge

The curriculum is represented by the full range of programme designed for the teaching of particular subjects and topics at a given level, the variety of instructional materials available in relation to those programmes, and the set of characteristics that serve as both the indications and contra-indications for the use of particular curriculum or programme materials in particular circumstances.

The curriculum and its associated materials are the *materia medica* of pedagogy, the pharmacopoeia from which the teacher draws those tools of teaching that present or exemplify particular content and remediate or evaluate the adequacy of student accomplishments. We expect the mature physician to understand the full range of treatments available to ameliorate a given disorder, as well as the range of alternatives for particular circumstances of sensitivity, cost, interaction with other interventions, convenience, safety, or comfort. Similarly, we ought to expect that the mature teacher possesses such understandings about the curricular alternatives available for instruction.

How many individuals whom we prepare for teaching biology, for example, understand well the materials for that instruction, the alternative texts, software, programmes, visual materials, single-concept films, laboratory demonstrations, or 'invitations to enquiry'? Would we trust a physician who did not really understand the alternative ways of dealing with categories of infectious disease, but who knew only one way?

CHAPTER 8

How are we planning and implementing the curriculum?

The nine readings in this chapter address key issues in curriculum planning.

First, Burgess, Southworth and Webb review the need for a curriculum to fit within a whole-school plan so that continuity and progression can be provided.

The next group of readings address how classroom curriculum planning may be achieved. HMI offer an analysis of key characteristics of any curriculum (8.2), whilst the readings from Hunter and Scheirer (8.3) and Alexander, Rose and Woodhead (8.4) represent contrasting views on the importance of linking a curriculum to pupil experience or to subjects. Reading 8.5 is SCAA's official advice on how to approach curriculum planning.

The readings by Calderhead (8.6) and by Bennett and his colleagues (8.7) concern planning at the level of each lesson. Despite the adoption of rational planning processes in many schools and courses, Calderhead emphasizes the real significance of practical problem solving. Bennett *et al.* highlight the importance of trying to match tasks to pupil needs, and the difficulties of doing so.

The introduction of the National Curriculum and a greater emphasis on subject knowledge has implications for school organization. In Reading 8.8, Alexander asks if the end of the class-teacher system is in sight. New forms of grouping pupils to form more homogeneous teaching groups in Key Stage 2 are gradually emerging, and the reading from Jackson (8.9) stands as a warning of the dangers if this approach is take too far.

The parallel chapter of *Reflective Teaching in the Primary School* addresses whole-school curricular planning and then considers the selection of a classroom curriculum in some detail, with many suggestions for practical activities. Ways of planning lessons, activities and tasks are then considered, including a section on differentiation. The chapter concludes with a section on school organization and teaching roles. There are also many suggestions for further reading.

Whole school curriculum planning

Hilary Burgess, Geoff Southworth and Rosemary Webb

This reading provides a review of the ways in which whole school curriculum planning has developed since the 1970s. Written in 1994, at a time when National Curriculum requirements were heavily overloaded, the reading highlights the considerable time which can be taken up, but also the limitations of plans which are not created in collaborative ways. There are some serious dilemmas here. How are they resolved in your school?

Edited from: Burgess, H., Southworth, G. and Webb, R. (1994) 'Whole school planning in the primary school', in Pollard, A. (ed.) *Look Before You Leap? Research Evidence for the Curriculum at Key Stage Two*. London: Tufnell Press, 40–2

The idea of whole school curriculum planning has opened up a new field where the terms are still being defined despite the early assimilation of phrases such as 'whole school', 'whole curriculum' and 'development planning' into the language of primary schooling. However, planning for teaching in primary schools is not new and the past two decades have witnessed a number of phases in the development of curriculum planning.

During the late 1970s and early 1980s teachers were encouraged to develop written statements of curriculum aims (DES, 1981a; Thomas, 1985), and many local education authorities began to produce curriculum guidelines for schools. Teachers were introduced to programmes of school-based self-evaluation and review (Simons, 1987; Clift *et al.*, 1987) where the emphasis was upon individual school planning while research on school effectiveness and improvement (Rutter *et al.*, 1979; Mortimore *et al.* 1988) has promoted a systematic approach to planning and review and provided evidence to support the need for school development planning (Hargreaves and Hopkins, 1991 [See Reading 14.3]).

From the late 1970s onwards HMI identified weaknesses in planning at both school and classroom level. Alexander, Rose and Woodhead (1992) pointed out that 'much school planning in areas other than mathematics and reading (where published schemes provided a not always appropriate prop) amounted to little more than an attempt to list the content to be covered' (p. 20) which resulted in insufficient attention being given to continuity and progression. The introduction of the National Curriculum was viewed as 'having a positive influence on curricular planning', fostering both 'long-term strategic planning and shorter-term preparations related particularly to work in the core subjects' (HMI 1989, p. 3). However, the extent and detail of National Curriculum planning met resistance from teachers who felt that they were 'document driven' and 'treading the narrow path' and had lost the spontaneity and flexibility to respond to children's interests and unanticipated learning opportunities (Pollard *et al.*, 1994; Webb, 1993a). Initially topic work – often including aspects of several subjects – was the focus of much whole school planning for the National Curriculum. Existing topics were mapped against the attainment targets and to a lesser extent the programmes of study and these were modified and new topics created to provide subject coverage and progression through the attainment targets and statements of attainment via successive topics. However, in order to be confident that National Curriculum requirements were met and to assess and record individual achievement of the statements of attainment, increasingly, especially at Key Stage 2, topic work has become more subject focused and more subjects and aspects of subjects are taught separately (Dadds, 1993; Webb, 1993a). As acknowledged by OFSTED (1993) 'the sum of the subject parts constituted an unmanageable whole for the typical primary teacher' (p.15). Whichever approaches to curriculum organization were adopted Webb's

(1993b) research into the implementation of the National Curriculum at Key Stage 2 showed that the content proved impossible to fit into the teaching time available and depth and quality were being sacrificed in the pursuit of breadth. However, attempts at least to achieve coverage, at the level of documentation, led to extremely complex plans especially in schools with mixed-age and mixed-key stage classes where plans are on two and four-year cycles. The demands of such planning combined with those of assessment and record keeping created stressful and unattainable workloads for teachers which detracted from the professional gains of such corporate efforts.

Whilst primary teachers have long been accustomed to planning they have been less used to planning at the whole school level, and, of course, are relatively unaccustomed to working within the National Curriculum framework. Teachers can thus be viewed as doubly disadvantaged. They need to learn how to plan an unwieldy and unmanageable curriculum, especially at Key Stage 2, and many must simultaneously learn to plan with their colleagues. The content and processes of whole school planning are new to many teachers.

Staff in schools have generally responded to these new demands by holding many more meetings in and after school. However, there are two difficulties with this strategy. First, Campbell and Neill's (1992) research shows that many teachers have resented the increase in staff meetings because it has been seen as at the expense of their much needed lesson preparation time. Second, the extent that staffroom discussion and policy making affects classroom practice depends upon more than consultative decision making. Head teachers and curriculum leaders need to play an active role in monitoring the implementation of collective decisions in individual classrooms. Teachers who are not wholly committed to decisions and policies agreed by staff may ignore them in practice.

The style of management of the headteacher may also have a major influence upon the way in which staff interpret school policy. Traditionally headteachers have had the final say on matters of school policy and their right of veto may inhibit the extent to which staff participate in decision making and adversely affect their commitment to school policy. For example, the London Institute School Development Plan project suggests that some school development plans are headteacher development plans. Therefore, it is important that we now consider the roles and responsibilities of heads and teachers in the post 1988 period.

 **READING 8.2**

Characteristics of the curriculum

Her Majesty's Inspectors

HMI's *Curriculum Matters* series, and the pamphlet entitled *The Curriculum from 5–16* from which this reading is edited, can be seen as an attempt to pre-empt legislation by offering a non-statutory framework for a National Curriculum. The pamphlet identified nine 'areas of learning and experience' (related to subject areas), four 'elements of learning' (knowledge, skills, concepts and attitudes), and the five 'characteristics of curriculum' which are discussed below.

It is interesting to see the importance of 'relevance' here (see Readings 7.5 and 7.8) for, whilst the other 'characteristics' were emphasized, it was to disappear from the official documents of the 1990s.

What do you see as the relevance of 'relevance'?

Edited from: Department of Education and Science (1985a) *The Curriculum from 5–16*, HMI, *Curriculum Matters Series 2*. London: HMSO, 10–48

The curriculum provides a context for learning which, as well as providing for the progressive development of knowledge, understanding and skills, recognizes and builds on the particular developmental characteristics of childhood and adolescence. Active learning, and a sense of purpose and success, enhance pupils' enjoyment, interest, confidence and sense of personal worth; passive learning and inappropriate teaching styles can lead to frustration and failure. In particular, it is necessary to ensure that the pupils are given sufficient first-hand experience, accompanied by discussion, upon which to base abstract ideas and generalizations.

If the opportunities for all pupils to engage in a largely comparable range of learning are to be secured, certain characteristics are desirable.

Breadth

The curriculum should be broad. The various curricular areas should reinforce one another: for example the scientific area provides opportunities for pupils to learn and practise mathematical skills. Breadth is also necessary within an area and within its components: thus in the linguistic and literary area pupils should read a variety of fiction and non-fiction myths, legends, fairy tales, animal stories, stories based on family life, adventure stories, historical fiction, science fiction, reference books, factual accounts, documents, directories and articles.

Class teachers in primary schools are in a strong position to arrange the interplay of the various aspects of learning since, as *Primary Education in England* (DES, 1978) pointed out:

> The teacher can get to know the children and know their strengths and weaknesses; the one teacher concerned can readily adjust the daily programme to suit special circumstances; it is simpler for one teacher than for a group of teachers to ensure that the various parts of the curriculum are co-ordinated and also to reinforce work done in one part of the curriculum with work done in another.

This does not mean that the class teacher can or should be expected to cover the whole curriculum unaided, especially with the older pupils. He or she should be able to call on the support of teachers who, as well as having responsibilities for their own classes, act as consultants in particular subjects or areas of the curriculum.

Primary schools generally offer a broad curriculum in the sense that all the areas of learning and experience are present to some extent. However, care is needed to ensure that breadth is not pursued at the expense of depth since this may lead to superficial work.

Balance

A balanced curriculum should ensure that each area of learning and experience and each element of learning is given appropriate attention in relation to the others and to the curriculum as a whole. In practice this requires the allocation of sufficient time and resources for each area and element to be fully developed. Balance also needs to be preserved within each area and element by the avoidance, for example, of an undue emphasis on the mechanical aspects of language or mathematics, or on writing predominantly given over to note taking and summarizing. There should also be a balance in the variety of teaching approaches used: didactic and pupil-initiated; practical and theoretical; individual, group and full-class teaching.

Balance need not be sought over a single week or even a single month since in some cases it may be profitable to concentrate in depth on certain activities; but it should be sought over a period of, say, a term or a year.

Relevance

The curriculum should be relevant in the sense that it is seen by pupils to meet their present and prospective needs. Overall, what is taught and learned should be worth learning in that it improves pupils' grasp of the subject matter and enhances their enjoyment of it and their mastery of the skills required; increases their understanding of themselves and the world in which they are growing up; raises their confidence and competence in controlling events and coping with widening expectations and demands; and progressively equips them with the knowledge and skills needed in adult working life. Work in schools can be practical in a number of ways. First it can be directly concerned with 'making and doing'.

Second, pupils at all stages need to work and enjoy working with abstract ideas and to come to an understanding of them by drawing on their own concrete experience, observation and powers of reasoning and, whenever possible, by testing out and reinforcing their learning by reference to real examples.

Third, all that pupils learn should be practical, and therefore relevant, in ways which enable them to build on it or use it for their own purposes in everyday life. For example being read to, reading, hearing music, or taking part in a discussion, all have both a specific and a cumulative effect on the individual, especially if teachers use opportunities to relate what is being learnt to pupils' interests, to contemporary realities and general human experience.

Fourth, the more that knowledge and skills learned in school can be developed within and applied to activities that have real purpose and place in the wider world, the more clearly their relevance will be perceived by the pupils.

Differentiation

As stated in HMI's discussion document *A View of the Curriculum* (DES,1980):

> The curriculum has to satisfy two seemingly contrary requirements. On the one hand it has to reflect the broad aims of education which hold good for all children, whatever their capabilities and whatever the schools they attend. On the other hand it has to allow for differences in the abilities and other characteristics of children, even of the same age ... If it is to be effective, the school curriculum must allow for differences.

A necessary first step in making appropriate provision is the identification of the learning needs of individual pupils by sensitive observation on the part of the teacher. This may indicate a need for smaller, more homogeneous groups, regrouping for different purposes, or the formation of sub groups for particular activities. Individual work and assignments can be set to allow for different interests, capabilities and work rates so long as this does not isolate pupils or deprive them of necessary contact with other pupils or the teacher. Finally there should be differentiation in the teaching approaches; some pupils need to proceed slowly, and some need a predominantly practical approach and many concrete examples if they are to understand abstractions; some move more quickly and require more demanding work which provides greater intellectual challenge; many have a variety of needs which cannot be neatly categorized.

Progression and continuity

Children's development is a continuous process and schools have to provide conditions and experiences which sustain and encourage that process while recognizing that it does not proceed uniformly or at an even pace. If this progression is to be maintained there is a need to build systematically on the children's existing knowledge, concepts, skills and attitudes, so as to ensure an orderly advance in their capabilities over a period of time. Teaching and learning experiences should be ordered so as to facilitate pupils' progress, with each successive element making appropriate demands and leading to better performance.

The main points at which progression is endangered by discontinuity are those at which pupils change schools; they also include those at which children enter school, change classes or teachers, or change their own attitudes to school or some aspect of it. Not all change is for the worse, however, and many pupils find a new enthusiasm or aptitude in new situations. Nevertheless, curricular planning within and between schools should aim to ensure continuity by making the maximum use of earlier learning.

Primary schools have to build on and allow for the influences to which children entering school have already been exposed and to take account of what will be expected of them in the schools to which they will transfer in due course. Continuity within schools may best be achieved when there are clear curricular policies which all the staff have been involved in developing and which present a clear picture of the range of expectations it is reasonable to have of individual pupils. If the goals are as clear as possible, progress towards them is more likely to be maintained.

 READING 8.3

Planning for learning through experience

Robert Hunter and Elinor Scheirer

> This reading describes the curriculum planning of a 'topic'. However, it begins with a strong critique of over-prescriptive planning, which could produce a 'straitjacket' constraining children's responses to new experiences. Rather, it is suggested, a flexible structure of plans should be created, starting with 'examining the possible'. The dilemma here is between structure and flexibility, curriculum planning and responsiveness to pupil needs.
>
> How can you develop and maintain the procedures, skills and judgements to resolve this dilemma?
>
> Edited from: Hunter, R. and Scheirer, E. A. (1988) *The Organic Classroom: Organizing for Learning 7–12*. London: Falmer Press, 79–83

Children learn best when new experiences are related to what they already know, when they are novel but not too strange and when they are sufficiently complex to call for some extension of ideas but are not outside the range of understanding. To provide such experiences on every occasion for each individual in a class is impossible. With appropriate planning we can increase the level of match between the experience and the previous awareness of the child. By doing this we can increase the degree of involvement for individual children and for the group.

However, it is important that planning is at an appropriate level. Sometimes it can be very rigid and demand such conformity as to be a straitjacket which allows no freedom of movement or initiative by any of the participants in the learning process. A head or a teacher will plan a topic or several topics, in the finest detail, which the class will follow with no deviation from the original blueprint. Some schools have a system which covers the whole school, so that children entering the school in the first year follow a pre-planned range of topic work through to the time they leave.

This is very conscientious planning with a high degree of commitment from the teachers, and many hours of hard work in preparation, but it is planning which denies the very essence of learning. It is a closed, tight structure which directs children into many hours of activity. Unfortunately the activity is seldom related to the child's experience, is second rate and second-hand. It keeps children occupied. Within the classroom the teachers have very few decisions to make regarding the intellectual and affective development of the children in their care. The results are as predetermined as the activities. It is this image of planning, of structure, which is the very antithesis of what planning for learning should be.

In the primary classroom teachers are responsible for the education of their children for the year they have them in their charge. With the aid of colleagues, they have to try and accommodate the needs of their children in a wide variety of areas of experience. They have to involve them in the aesthetic and expressive areas such as art, movement, music, writing and drama. They have to help them explore the world in which they live through science, history, geography and mathematics. At the same time they have to help their children become more aware of the social dimensions and obligations which are expected of them.

It is possible to see the planning of topic work fitting into four broad stages: examining the possible, identifying the probable, action and activities, and further developments.

Examining the possible

The first is an examination of the possible, a broad overview of all the areas a topic may include. In a sense it is a preplanning stage, when the mind can roam widely over an extensive range of possibilities. It may take the form of a flow chart or a diagram or an abundance of notes. If it is concerned with 'Fire' it may begin with the efforts of prehistoric man, touch on events such as the Great Fire of London and include a visit to the local fire station. Indeed it may include every pyrotechnic event from the creation of the world to the Day of Judgement. Similarly, possibilities for specific activities in which the children may become involved can be very wide-reaching.

Identifying the probable

The teacher is operating within certain constraints which affect this initial thinking, for example the availability of material, the previous experience of the children, time, the expectations of the school and the requirements of the National Curriculum. Soon that examination of the possible becomes more realistic. In this second stage the teacher focuses on the probable range of experiences and activities. They are more precisely identified and the practical problems of providing such activities are taken into account. The various constraints mentioned, together with other considerations, influence the selection. Eventually, an overall plan emerges which provides a realistic basis for action.

Action and activities

Often the focus for the topic work is centred on a major experience. The third stage in planning is closely allied to this focus. The experience varies according to the nature of the topic to be studied. It may be a half day or day visit to an appropriate venue. Sometimes it is a series of activities or experiences with the school. On at least one occasion during the child's time at the school, it is related to a residential field visit involving several nights away from home. Having decided what that central and important activity is, the teacher analyses it more closely. The introductory work in school prior to the visit has to be appropriate in focusing the children's thinking towards the particular event. Any necessary skills or concepts or information which the children will require to maximize the experience will be introduced using a variety of pedagogical styles.

If this major input is a visit, it involves at least two teachers with a class of children together with other adults such as parents and non-teaching assistants. This requires planning and co-ordination with colleagues. What actually occurs on the visit varies with the venue chosen. Some situations offer greater opportunity for involvement and doing than others. Sometimes there is an opportunity to question significant adults who work, for example, at the fire station or railway station. In other situations, such as a visit to an industrial museum there is an opportunity for improvised drama. Whatever else happens, there is always some very careful looking and discussion and, whenever possible, some drawing and note taking. These activities develop the children's looking and generate more tightly framed questions and discussion. On return to school they provide a reminder of the shared experiences and help in channelling and supporting follow-up work.

Planning the introduction to the topic and the experience or visit itself also includes planning for the work which will arise out of them. This is particularly important when it is realized that a single day visit may provide the major stimulus for anything from four to eight weeks' work. Although some possibilities only present themselves after a particular event has occurred, the teacher can anticipate most avenues of enquiry and prepare accordingly. There are many questions to be answered in order to make such preparation:

Will all of the children work on the same idea at the same time or will there be opportunities for group and individual work?

Will there be a wide or narrow range of materials available for work in, say, art or writing?

Will children have a large degree of freedom in organizing their work space, their colleagues and their work?

How far will these be prescribed by the teacher?

To what degree will this vary for individual children?

What percentage of each week's work will be spent on this particular area of study?

For how many weeks is it envisaged that such work will continue?

Even at this stage the way in which individual teachers frame and answer questions highlights their sensitivity and flexibility which in turn can enhance or subdue the quality of the child's response.

Further developments

The final stage in planning is when the teacher looks further ahead and tries to consider how the topic may develop, for example, what other activities, materials and experiences can be introduced to enhance, deepen or redirect the way in which the work is moving. The nature of these developments is variable but may include a further visit, the sharing of a video film or a story, or the opportunity to carry out additional activities or experiments. Thus the major initial impetus is extended and the focus, even if slightly changed in its direction, is kept sharp.

However, no matter how thoughtful the planning has been, from those first initial explorations of the many possibilities through to the execution of the realities, the teacher has to be ready to accommodate and assimilate changing circumstances and to retain flexibility in order to maximize the learning process. Every outcome cannot be forecast and planned for. If the approach which has been outlined is followed it may increase the chances of involving the teacher and the child in a partnership for learning which can grow and develop with the needs of the learner.

Planning with subjects, topics or both?

Robin Alexander, Jim Rose and Chris Woodhead

> This is an extract from a document which is commonly known as the report of the 'three wise men'. It was a Christmas gift from a belligerent Secretary of State for Education (Kenneth Clarke) who wanted teachers 'to rethink their orthodoxies'. One of the issues raised concerned the use of topics and the place of subjects in the primary school curriculum and it is on this question that the reading is focused.
>
> This reading could be compared with Reading 8.3 or with the final section of the reading from the Plowden Report (Reading 7.6). Are these approaches really as opposed as is sometimes assumed?
>
> Edited from: Alexander, R., Rose, J. and Woodhead, C. (1992) *Curriculum Organisation and Classroom Practice in Primary Schools: A Discussion Paper*. London: Department of Education and Science, 15–19

Curriculum planning is one aspect of primary teaching which, traditionally problematic, is now improving significantly. HMI have, from the late 1970s onwards, identified weaknesses in planning at the level of both school and classroom. Much school planning in areas other than mathematics and reading (where published schemes provided a not always appropriate prop) amounted to little more than an attempt to list the content to be covered. As a result, continuity and progression in the arts and humanities were often suspect. HMI report that one of the first visible improvements in primary schools has been curriculum planning in relation to the National Curriculum core subjects. With the introduction of the National Curriculum and the School Development Plan initiative, there has been a recognition that teachers must plan together to ensure consistency and progression across classes and year groups and that formally structured short and long-term planning are essential to effective classroom teaching.

The National Curriculum has introduced a similar discipline into planning at classroom level. In the past, too many teachers have argued that rigorous and comprehensive planning militates against the need for spontaneity and flexibility. In fact, the two are perfectly compatible. With the introduction of the National Curriculum, this dichotomy is now simply untenable.

Planning is taking far more time than in the past. This may be a relatively short-term phenomenon as teachers become familiar with the demands of the Statutory Orders, but the situation must be monitored over the next few years as part of an overall drive to ensure that the National Curriculum provides a manageable framework for primary education.

We recognize, looking to the future, that further developments in the quality of curriculum planning depend upon the management of whole school planning across all subjects and both key stages. It will also be necessary to consider how school and classroom planning can be effectively related, and, in particular, whether the new subject requirements can be reconciled with the established commitment to cross-curricular planning through such devices as 'topic webs'.

The vast majority of primary schools organize the curriculum in terms of subjects and topic work. A topic is generally understood to be a mode of curriculum organization, frequently enquiry based, which brings elements of different subjects together under a common theme. A small minority of schools organize the whole of the curriculum in terms of separate subjects; virtually no primary school works solely through topics. HMI report that about 30 per cent of work in primary schools is taught as single subjects. Music, physical education, most mathematics and some English are usually taught as separate subjects. The other foundation subjects are very often taught, entirely or largely, as aspects of topic work.

Despite these demonstrable facts, the rhetoric of primary education has for a long time been hostile to the idea that young children should be exposed to subjects. Subject divisions, it is argued, are inconsistent with the child's view of the world. Children must be allowed to construct their own meanings and subject teaching involves the imposition of a received version of knowledge. And, moreover, it is the wholeness of the curriculum which is important rather than the distinct identity of the individual subjects.

Each of these familiar assertions needs to be contested. First, to resist subjects on the grounds that they are inconsistent with children's views of the world is to confine them within their existing modes of thought and deny them access to some of the most powerful tools for making sense of the world which human beings have ever devised. Second, while it is self-evident that every individual, to an extent, constructs his/her own meanings, education is an encounter between these personal understandings and the public knowledge embodied in our cultural traditions. The teacher's key responsibility is to mediate such encounters so that the child's understanding is enriched. And, finally, the integrity of the curriculum as a whole is hardly likely to be achieved by sacrificing the integrity of its constituent parts.

In evaluating these arguments it is helpful to draw a distinction between integration, which entails bringing together subjects with distinct identities, and non-differentiation, which does not concede that such distinctiveness is acceptable. Teachers (often of younger pupils) who prefer to view the curriculum in terms of broad areas such as language, investigation and creative work are particularly committed to this second view.

We consider that a National Curriculum conceived in terms of distinct subjects makes it impossible to defend a non-differentiated curriculum. This does not mean that all the National Curriculum subjects must necessarily be taught separately: curriculum conception and modes of curriculum organization must not be confused. But, whatever the mode of organization, pupils must be able to grasp the particular principles and procedures of each subject, and, what is equally important, they must be able to progress from one level of knowledge, understanding and skill to another within the subject.

If it can be shown that the topic approach allows the pupil both to make acceptable progress within the different subjects of the National Curriculum and to explore the relationships between them, then the case for such an approach is strong on both pedagogic and logistical grounds. If, however, the result is that the differences between subjects are extinguished, then the strategy is indefensible.

This is not to deny that the topic approach can, in skilled hands, produce work of high quality. There is evidence to suggest that some schools, recognizing the problems outlined above, are planning carefully structured topic frameworks which map the attainment targets and programmes of study of the subjects involved. In particular, there are signs of a move to either 'broad-based' topics (where a theme like 'transport' is used to bring together content and skills from several subjects) or 'subject-focused' topics (where pupils concentrate upon a limited number of attainment targets from one particular subject but may also study relevant material from other subjects). In that it can be planned more easily in relation to the Statutory Orders and can provide more appropriately for the sequential development of pupils' knowledge, understanding and skills, the subject-focused topic, in particular, offers an efficient way forward.

READING 8.5

Planning the curriculum at Key Stages 1 and 2

School Curriculum and Assessment Authority

The practicalities of curriculum planning are always difficult in primary schools, given their small size, the range of curriculum requirements and the variations which often exist in year-groups. This advice from the School Curriculum and Assessment Authority offers a sequence for planning. Overall planning begins with scheduling 'continuing' and 'blocked' units of work, and then moves through successive levels of detail towards classroom application.

Such prescriptions are often easier to make than to achieve. What approach is used in your school?

Edited from: School Curriculum and Assessment Authority (1995) *Planning the Curriculum at Key Stages 1 and 2*. London: School Curriculum and Assessment Authority, 4–46

One of the principal objectives of the review of the National Curriculum has been to provide schools with greater flexibility and choice by slimming down the statutory requirements of the subject Orders.

To begin the planning process, schools need a simple, straightforward way of organizing the content of the curriculum into manageable teaching units. An approach which has been used successfully in many primary schools, is based on the identification of units of work, which fall into two broad categories, continuing and blocked. It is envisaged that both types of unit will draw, in the first instance, on work from a single subject or aspect of the curriculum. Two or more units from different subjects or aspects of the curriculum can, however, be linked as and when appropriate.

Continuing work:

requires regular and frequent teaching and assessment to be planned across a year or key stage to ensure progression;

contains a progressive sequence of learning objectives;

requires time for the systematic and gradual acquisition, practice and consolidation of skills, knowledge and understanding.

Blocked units of work:

can be taught within a specific amount of time, not exceeding a term;

focuses on a distinct and cohesive body of knowledge, understanding and skills;

can be taught alone or have the potential for linking with units of work in other subjects or aspects of the curriculum.

Once a manageable framework of continuing and blocked work has been established, curriculum coherence can be strengthened by linking together, where appropriate, units of work from different subjects or aspects of the curriculum.

There are three significant reasons for linking work at this level of planning:

they contain common or complementary knowledge, understanding and skills, e.g. developing reading and writing skills through work in history, or work on the water cycle in science linked with work on weather and rivers in geography;

the skills acquired in one subject or aspect of the curriculum can be applied or consolidated in the context of another, e.g. work on co-ordinates in mathematics applied to work in geography on four-figure grid references;

the work in one subject or aspect of the curriculum provides a useful stimulus for work in another, e.g. creating music from a poem or a picture.

In practice, these types of links are not mutually exclusive and good planning will often involve linking work from different subjects or aspects of the curriculum in more than one of these ways.

A summary of curriculum planning tasks and outcomes is provided in the table below. This will establish a broad curriculum framework for the school.

Tasks	Outcomes for each year group
Task 1 Establish the amount of time available for teaching and assessing the school curriculum. This includes the National Curriculum, religious education and other curricular provision identified by the school.	Teaching time per week/term/year established.
Task 2 Identify all aspects of the school curriculum that will require specific, timed provision and establish priorities for each year group.	School's curriculum defined and priorities established.
Task 3 For each year group, discuss and agree the proportions of the total teaching time to be allocated to each aspect of the curriculum.	Curriculum balance established within the teaching time for each year group.
Task 4A Identify which aspects of each curriculum area, to organize and teach as continuing units of work, and allocate them to year groups. **Task 4B** Identify which aspects of each curriculum area, to organize and teach as distinct and cohesive blocked units of work, and allocate them to year groups.	Curriculum coverage and continuity established together with broad lines of progression from year to year.
Task 4C Allocate notional amounts of time to each of the units of work identified in Tasks 4A and 4B.	
Task 5 Identify and agree links between units of work established in Task 4 and review time allocations.	Curriculum coherence established.
Task 6 Complete the planning process by bringing together the outcomes of Tasks 4 and 5 and allocating work to the three terms of each year.	The curriculum framework for each year group established on a term by term basis.

Once the broad framework for the school curriculum has been established, more detailed medium and short-term planning can begin. Using the framework as a guide, class teachers, together with subject or year group co-ordinators, can develop more detailed plans for year groups specifying the details of each unit of work and finalizing the sequence of work to be covered each term. This, in turn, will enable individual class teachers to plan, on a weekly/daily basis, for a range of differentiated activities focusing on specific learning objectives. As work progresses, adjustments to medium-term plans will need to be made on a regular basis to accommodate variations to the anticipated pace of work and progress of the children in each year group. Finally, modifications to the key stage plans can be agreed on an annual or biannual basis with adjustments being made to the timing and sequencing of work to ensure that overall curriculum coverage, continuity and progression are secured.

 READING 8.6

Teachers' planning

James Calderhead

> At the classroom level, James Calderhead contrasts traditional, and very logical, approaches to planning with the ways in which teachers actually confront the realities of their work. Then, he suggests, the rational planning model collapses into a form of contextually based, problem solving.
>
> There is probably a lot of truth in this analysis. However, does this mean that there is no value in rational planning? Or do such plans provide a basis for practical interpretation as new situations evolve?
>
> It is interesting to compare this reading to that on teachers' practical theorizing, by Schon (Reading 1.2).
>
> Edited from: Calderhead, J. (1984) *Teachers' Decision Making*. London: Cassell, 69–82

Planning is a vital though often undervalued aspect of classroom teaching. It is in planning that teachers translate syllabus guidelines, institutional expectations and their own beliefs and ideologies of education into guides for action in the classroom. This aspect of teaching provides the structure and purpose for what teachers and pupils do in the classroom.

Traditional prescriptions for planning

Until recently most of the writing about instructional planning has been prescriptive in orientation. Theorists such as Tyler (1949) and Wheeler (1967) adopted an analytical approach to planning, and suggested that it consists of a number of sequential decisions. The planning of a school curriculum or of a particular course would therefore start with a listing of aims and their breakdown into more specific objectives which could be attributed to units of a course or individual lessons. Second, the content of lessons would be decided – what education experiences would be likely to achieve these objectives? Third, decisions would be made about organization – how is the content best presented to facilitate the achievement of the chosen objectives? Lastly, it was suggested that teachers evaluate their lessons, and assess the extent to which objectives have been achieved and that this information be used to guide future instruction.

Research on teachers' planning

Research on teachers' planning suggests that teachers engage in a process that contrasts sharply with the prescribed rational planning model. Whereas the prescribed model starts with a statement of aims and objectives, followed by a reasoning of the content and organization to be adopted and how the pupils' performance is to be evaluated to assess whether the objectives have been achieved, teachers' plans reflect little concern either with objectives or with evaluations. In reality, the process of planning seems to be more appropriately conceptualized as a problem solving process. Teachers, faced with a variety of factors such as pupils with certain knowledge, abilities and interests, the availability of particular textbooks and materials, the syllabus, the timetable, the expectations of headteachers and others, and their own knowledge of previous teaching encounters, have to solve the problem of how to structure the time and experiences of pupils in the classroom. Teachers it seems, adopt a much more pragmatic approach than that prescribed for curriculum design. Rather than start with a conception of what is to be achieved and deduce which classroom activities would therefore be ideal, teachers start with a conception of their working context and from that decide what is possible.

 READING 8.7

Classroom tasks and the match

Neville Bennett, Charles Desforges, Anne Cockburn and Betty Wilkinson

> This is an extract from the conclusions of a study of the 'match' between pupils' existing knowledge and classroom tasks set by primary school teachers. The research team evaluated the quality of the match using retrospective assessments and interviews with pupils. Unfortunately, even in the basic curriculum areas of number and language work, only approximately 40 per cent of the tasks set were judged to be well matched. Teachers were relatively quick to recognize when tasks, too difficult, but they often seemed unaware when tasks were too easy.
> How well matched do you think the set tasks are in your classroom?
>
> Edited from: Bennett, N., Desforges, C., Cockburn, A. and Wilkinson, B. (1984) *The Quality of Pupil Learning Experiences*. London: Lawrence Erlbaum Associates, 213–18

The focus of this study has been on task processes in classes of 6- and 7-year-old children whose teachers were rated as better than average by the advisory service in the education authorities concerned. Working closely with these teachers showed clearly that they were dedicated and conscientious people.

In appraising the quality of learning experiences, the demands on the children of the tasks set were first ascertained. Although there were often marked differences in the classrooms studied, tasks demanding practice of existing knowledge, concepts or skills predominated. This was particularly apparent in language work where over three quarters of all tasks set demanded practice. A typical task was a request from the teacher for the class to write a story, usually accompanied by exhortations on neatness and appropriate grammar. Here the demand was for the practice of well-understood routines and rarely did such tasks impart or demand the acquisition of new knowledge. This staple diet of little new knowledge and large amounts of practice was rarely varied to include tasks which required either the discovery or construction of new or different ways of perceiving problems, or the application of existing knowledge and skills to new contexts.

The teachers studied held strongly to the philosophy of individualization and it was therefore expected that differential demands would be intended for children of differing levels of attainment. High and low attaining children certainly received different curriculum content but they experienced similar patterns of task demand. Thus similar ratios of incremental to practice tasks were planned for both groups of children. This pattern was further confounded by the fact that teachers found it much more difficult to transform an intended incremental into an actual incremental task for high attainers. In reality therefore high attaining children received less new knowledge and more practice than their low attaining peers.

The main reasons for teachers failing to implement demands were twofold; poor or misdiagnosis, and failures in task design. Many mismatches in demand occurred because the teacher did not ascertain that the child was already perfectly familiar with the task content. Poor or non-diagnosis thus underlay the fact that many incremental tasks actually made practice demands. Task design problems were also relatively frequent. In such cases the requirements for the performance of the task did not match the teacher's intention.

The quality of a pupil's learning experience is also related to the match between the intellectual demand of tasks and the pupil's attainments. In both number and language work at infant level teachers were able to provide a match on approximately 40 per cent of tasks. About a third were too difficult for the child and a little over a quarter were too easy. It was also very clear that the quality of matching varied in relation to the children's intellectual standing in the classroom. High attainers were under-estimated on over 40 per cent of tasks assigned to them, a pattern similar to that reported by HMI (DES, 1978). But an equally clear pattern of over-estimation was found for low attainers. Of their assigned tasks, 44 per cent were over-estimated in both language and number work.

Matching was worse in the first term of junior schooling where the proportion of matched tasks in number work fell to 30 per cent. The incidence of mismatching was particularly severe for high attainers since three-quarters of the tasks they received were under-estimates. Low attainers again suffered from over-estimation. It was interesting to find that the quality of matching declined as the term progressed.

Teachers were adept at recognizing a task that was proving too difficult but were totally blind to tasks whose demands were too easy. The reasons for this are at least twofold. Firstly the teachers' typical management style required them to be seated at the front of the class, and as a result supervision was limited to quick observational sweeps of the classroom. The usual image was of a class working cheerfully and industriously. This indeed, is the second reason for a teachers' lack of recognition of too-easy tasks. Children always worked in this way irrespective of appropriateness of the task set. From the teachers' point of view, children were busy, and busy work equated with appropriate demands.

Thus in the short term, inappropriate work appeared to have little direct emotional or motivational consequences for children of this age. Although cognitive problems, which manifested themselves in unproductive or confusing learning experiences, were all too clearly apparent in the post task interviews, this cognitive confusion was masked from the teachers by the children's cheerfulness and industry. The teachers avoided the immediate consequences of such confusion by rewarding individual end-products, not the process of such work.

What has emerged is an increased understanding of the formidable problems teachers face as they strive to implement the laudable philosophy of individualizing instruction, and the equally formidable array of skills that are required to carry this out effectively.

The end of the class-teacher system?

Robin Alexander

The introduction of the National Curriculum and the increased recognition of the importance of teachers' subject knowledge has implications for the organization of primary schools.

Has the balance of advantage between the conventional class-teacher system and a subject-specialist system now changed? Alexander identifies four possible roles for primary school teachers of the future and offers an impressive range of questions which need to be faced. What do you think the answers could be?

Edited from: Alexander, R. (1992) *Policy and Practice in Primary Education*. London: Routledge, 202–4

Consideration of ways of improving primary education leads us inexorably to the question of whether a system of teaching introduced in the nineteenth century on the grounds of cheapness can sustain the demands of primary education in the 1990s.

Primary schools are still staffed on the same basis as their predecessors, the elementary schools – one teacher covering the whole curriculum with his/her class. Moreover, primary classes are substantially larger than secondary – in 1990 an average size, nationally, of 22 compared with the secondary average of 15.25 – and primary schools are much more modestly resourced. Thus, the age-weightings built into each LEA's funding formula under the 1988 Education Reform Act produces a differential in one fairly typical LEA of £632 for a 7-year old, and £1,740 for an 18-year old; since the weightings only start to rise at age 11 this means that primary schools operate on a shoe-string budget by comparison with secondary. They have hardly any room for manoeuvre, and certainly little opportunity to deploy their staff as other than class teachers, except by increasing class sizes. It was the impact of enhancement on flexibility in staff deployment which caused us to argue strongly in the Leeds report (see Alexander, Wilcocks and Kinder, 1989) that all primary schools should be staffed on the basis of *n* registration groups plus one extra.

This model, also endorsed in the 1986 Select Committee report (House of Commons 1986), introduces flexibility, but only up to a point. It is premised on the class-teacher system as the norm, with back-up provided by curriculum consultants. Each primary teacher, however, is expected to combine both roles, and therefore the issue of whether a generalist role is possible is evaded: it can be done, the thinking seems to go, with a bit of help.

The weight of evidence against this proposition now seems overwhelming. For as long as the curriculum was minimalist – give high priority to the basics, do what you can with the rest – the class-teacher system worked quite well. The consultancy idea was a useful patching device as the curriculum expanded. HMI were able to report its having considerable impact on the whole-school planning and co-ordination, though its influence on individual teacher competence and the quality of curriculum delivery in the classroom was less evident. Yet for as long as the only statutory requirements in respect of the primary curriculum were the 1944 Act's distinction between the religious and secular curriculum (the latter being left for LEAs and schools), the issue could remain fudged, even though by then some were aware of how serious the problem had become (Alexander, 1984).

At the same time, professional ideology, effectively deflected attention from the problem. The extreme child-centred position managed to deny the validity of curriculum altogether, while even somewhat more moderate teachers ruled questions of curriculum expertise out of order by denying the validity of subjects. Integration begged the question, which was rarely addressed, of precisely what was being integrated. The focus of attention was more on the environment of learning than learning itself, on how the child learned rather than what. Assessment concentrated on progress and endeavour in relation to the moving and singular criterion of individual progress, rather than on definable achievement in relation to objective criteria specified in advance.

The 1988 Act dramatically highlighted the problem. The 'basics' have now become the three core subjects; primary teachers have to teach these, a further six foundation subjects, religious education, and a range of cross-curricular themes, skills and dimensions. We now have to confront, finally, the question of whether the class-teacher system can deliver all this. My own view is that it cannot.

The evidence is cumulative as well as recent. It is provided by the HMI surveys of the late 1970s and 1980s, by the studies of National Curriculum implementation, and by a succession of other research studies, as well as by the Leeds study.

Some argue that the problem occurs only where older children are concerned (years five and six). The matter is not that simple. Though the problem becomes more acute the older the child, it does not suddenly materialize during the summer holidays at the end of year four – any more than under current arrangements it occurs in the six-week gap marking the transfer from primary to secondary school. This is an administrator's analysis, denying the less tidy reality, ignoring the fact that evidence shows the problem to occur earlier, and failing to acknowledge that all primary teachers, not just those working with older children, have to teach nine National Curriculum subjects.

To seek to solve the problem by introducing specialization for years five and six – let alone by reintroducing streaming, as has also been proposed – would be premature and ill-conceived. The issue is a large and complex one. The resources required are likely to be substantial. It is imperative that they are properly deployed and that they address the problem in its entirety.

In the first instance we need to broaden our repertoire of possibilities. There are four possible versions of the primary teacher role:

the generalist who teaches a class full-time;

the generalist/consultant who teaches a class full-time but also has a specialism for cross-school consultancy;

the semi-specialist who divides his or her time between specialist and generalist teaching;

the specialist who teaches his or her subject all the time.

Primary schools are currently staffed for the first of these, but HMI/DES pressure and the Secretary of State's teacher-training criteria since 1984 have shifted them to the second, though still within the logistical assumptions of the first. Because of this mismatch between model and resources, consultancy does not have the impact it could.

How far do we proceed along the road to specialization? As I have said, monolithic suggestions like confining specialization to the last two years of the primary phase should be treated with caution; so too should proposals that primary schools be run like preparatory schools. The truth of the matter is that some generalist class teachers are extremely effective across the board, while some specialists are extremely ineffective even within the one professed subject. It is naïve in the extreme to see full specialization as a panacea – were this the case, there would be no problems in secondary schools.

There are questions to be asked, therefore, about each of the roles postulated, and about their combination in a school. If the job of generalist is excessively demanding, is not that of generalist/consultant likely to be even more so? Assuming that one person can combine generalist and specialist teaching, what is the best way of deploying him or her so that both tasks can be undertaken effectively? If consultancy has greatest impact in the classroom, how far can the model of the generalist teacher with time freed to provide classroom-based support be realized? What combinations of the different roles seem most apposite for primary schools of different sizes and for children of different ages? If there are four possible primary teacher roles does this mean that there should be four distinct patterns of primary teacher-training?

What are the logistical and recruitment implications of introducing specialists? How many extra teachers would be needed? Where would the money come from?

Ten streamed schools

Brian Jackson

This reading dates from the early 1960s when 'streaming' was the norm in British primary schools. The 'ability' of pupils was assessed, and this provided the basis for placement into classes. Brian Jackson studied the streaming system in ten schools. He documented the inequalities, indignities and waste that resulted, and the ways in which the system tended to reflect social class differences. It is particularly interesting to see how the system was so taken-for-granted, and how teachers almost became streamed themselves.

Today, 'setting' is increasingly used as a way of grouping pupils by ability or attainment for the teaching of particular subjects. It is not so severe a form of differentiation as streaming. Nevertheless, this reading is included as a warning of the risks of social division (see Reading 13.1 for a stark analysis of the consequence and Reading 13.8 for an account of how processes of social differentiation work in primary schools).

How do you ensure that the groupings used as organizational devices in your school or class are not socially divisive?

Edited from: Jackson, B. (1964) *Streaming: An Education System in Miniature*. London: Routledge and Kegan Paul, 99–103

The children at Honey Bell were streamed. Their gifts developed at different rates and in different directions according to whether they were 'A', 'B' or 'C' children. Behind the streaming technique were teachers' beliefs in types of children and the scarcity of talent; and beyond the teachers were parents endorsing – in a less clear-cut way – feelings about the rarity of excellence, the need to locate it early, and to separate the children of 'gold' from the children of 'silver' and of baser metal.

I wanted to compare Honey Bell with schools, streamed and unstreamed.

The one thing that all 10 streamed schools had in common was high eleven-plus scores. In districts where on average 23 per cent of the children entered grammar school, this small sample had won 37 per cent of grammar school places in the previous year. Two big schools, each serving middle-class suburbs in the north took 50 per cent each.

Their Heads considered streaming as a form of natural selection: perhaps unfortunate, but unavoidable.

Most of our children are all right, but over there we draw from a poorer part of the town. The parents are rag sorters in the mills, things like that, so the children are less intelligent, poor heredity, poor environment, poor attitudes – there's nothing you can do about it. They're our 'C's – lucky we don't have many of them.

This school suffered from lack of space. The 11-year old 'A's were in a very decent classroom – but there were 47 of them. The 'B's used half of the school canteen as a classroom, and though this was bright and airy, it meant they lost one lesson every day whilst the dinner tables were set up and laid. The rag-sorters' children in the 'C' stream had a class of only 25; but it was held in an old concrete hut at a distance from the main school. Their teacher said:

This place has been condemned. All day the children have to work with the electric light-ing on. And these army coke stoves are no good. Especially since the coke has to be tipped outside and gets soaked in the rain. We have to bring it in, a little pile at a time, and dry it out before we burn it. And this used to be a concrete floor, but the teacher before me devel-oped bad feet, and that made them put the wood down.

It's a pity the children are over here, but it's not altogether a bad thing – they can run around here more, and it doesn't matter much if things get damaged. It might be nice if they mixed in with the rest – the other children might bring their copies of Knowledge and things like that. But I'm not sure the others would let them mix – for one thing, this lot smell.

By contrast 'the others' in the 'A' stream were an enchanting group of children, busy and courteous. Round their walls were pinned neat pages of sums, and a selection of scrupulous-ly accurate paintings. The 'C' children had shouted out answers to their teacher's questions, but these 'A' stream pupils were not easily drawn – and a quiet word or reserved smile often sufficed for an answer.

These characteristics – large, quiet 'A' classes, small but physically separated 'C' classes – repeated themselves in one school after another. In a small mining town the eldest 'C' class shared part of the infant school, a hundred yards from their own buildings. In another north-ern town they were in a 'prefab' built at the far corner of the school playground. And yet the most gifted teacher seen was taking one of these classes, and the display of imaginative art on her classroom walls went far beyond anything from any other class, whether 'A', 'B' or 'C'. It was both encouraging and perplexing to encounter this sudden revelation of hidden, non-measurable talent from the children who 'smell'.

It was also unique. On the whole, 'C' classes were not impressive, and the successful and more experienced teachers did not take them.

Top 'A' stream teachers were older and more experienced, sometimes they were better qual-ified and usually paid more than their colleagues.

In these 10 schools there were 23 'graded' posts. (A graded post brings in a substantial salary increase.) The headteacher decides himself who shall hold such posts in his school, and what duties, if any, they shall perform in return. In these schools the deputy headship (the first 'graded' post) was held in nine out of ten cases by a teacher taking 4A or 3A. Altogether 15 graded posts were held by 'A' teachers, 7 by 'B' teachers and 1 by a 'C' teacher. So these 'A' teachers, by virtue of their longer service, slightly better qualifications, and major share of 'graded' posts drew larger salaries than their 'B' or 'C' colleagues.

This information helped to clear up a problem raised earlier – we can see that children are streamed, and parents are 'streamed'; but are teachers 'streamed'?

It was frequently like this. In every change around, strong teachers re-established themselves in the crucial position – especially 4A, the class which contained tomorrow's elite: and which, for the teacher, usually led to a Headship.

It's only human. We can't help feeling that if the children from our class go to grammar school, it's kudos for us – they're our property.

The Headteachers fought their sporadic battles against the 'streaming' of teachers – but they lost. The disposition of graded posts and the siting of some 'C' streams in inferior accommo-dation, suggested that they accepted the hopelessness of seeking for much talent in 'B' or 'C' children.

All the Heads reported that 'A' stream parents strongly favoured streaming, that 'B' or 'C' parents accepted it or 'didn't care'. The hardest problems for a Headteacher came in schools with a substantial middle-class intake, where a number of articulate parents found their child in the 'B' stream. Schools like this – with up to 50 per cent of the pupils going to grammar school – did score a number of places with 'B' children. All could illustrate at length the move-ment of middle-class parents into their 'zone'.

The house agent often tells me that parents come to him asking for houses within the 'zone', so that their children come here.

When they arrive in the town, they come and ask if I've room. That's it – and if they have any trouble, they bring out the Education Act and this Authority always backs down. If they couldn't get in here, they'd send them off to private school.

CHAPTER 9

How are we organizing the classroom?

The eight readings in this chapter address some of the practical issues which have to be faced if effective teaching and learning is to be provided.

We begin with a reading on class size, from Pate-Bain and her colleagues (9.1), which reports the STAR project's evidence of the significance of class size.

The following group of readings consider teaching strategies in relation to whether pupils are taught individually, as a whole class or in groups. Galton, Simon and Croll's conclusion from the ORACLE project (9.2) explodes some myths about 'progressivism', highlights the difficulty of sustaining high levels of 'cognitive challenge' in classrooms and suggests that groupwork deserves further investigation. The reading from Rea (9.3) sets out the rationale for how group work has developed (Reading 11.6 from Bennett and Dunne is also very relevant to this). However, McNamara (9.4) points out some difficulties in achieving differentiation and suggests a different classroom arrangement.

Further practical issues are considered. Clegg and Billington (9.5) focus on the learning environment, the use of space, management of resources and the quality of display. The reading from Pollard and his colleagues (9.6) reports research findings on the pupils' use of time, which poses all sorts of issues for classroom organization and management. Thomas (9.7) addresses how to manage other adults in classrooms.

The final reading, 9.8, is from a classic book on the 'integrated day' and illustrates how grouping, space, resources, time and curriculum may be linked together around a set of educational principles and priorities.

The parallel chapter of *Reflective Teaching in the Primary School* addresses similar issues and provides practical activities for classroom investigations to increase the effectiveness of classroom organization. The first section discusses grouping of children, working with adults, the use of time, the classroom environment, the use of space, management of resources and record keeping. The second section considers issues associated with various forms of organizational integration, for instance, of age groups or of teaching responsibilities, which are often used in primary schools. There are many suggestions for further reading.

Class size does make a difference

Helen Pate-Bain, Charles Achilles, Jayne Boyd-Zaharias and Bernard McKenna

> The issue of class size has attracted great attention in recent years, with teachers and parents being convinced of its importance (see also Reading 15.2). However, many policy-makers, perhaps with an eye on costs, insist that it is less important than teaching styles.
>
> There is very little secure research evidence on the relationship between class size and attainment, but the most thorough is the STAR project, from Tennessee, which this reading describes. Do you think class size makes a difference to your teaching? If you had smaller classes, how would you adjust your teaching strategies?
>
> Edited from: Pate-Bain. H., Achilles. C., Boyd-Zaharias. J. and McKenna. B. (1992) Class size does make a difference, *Phi Delta Kappan*, November, 253–5

Dissatisfied with earlier research and wishing to have conclusive results, Tennessee's state legislature funded a $12 million, four-year study of class size. Project STAR (Student/Teacher Achievement Ratio) analysed student achievement and development in three types of classes: small classes (13-17 students per teacher), regular classes (22-25 students), and regular classes (22-25 students) with a teacher and a full-time teacher aide. An important characteristic of the study was its longitudinal nature: Project STAR followed students from kindergarten in 1985-86 through third grade in 1988-89. In order to assess the effects of class size in different school locations, the project included 17 inner-city, 16 suburban, eight urban and 39 rural schools. Students and teachers were randomly assigned to class types.

The main focus of the study was on student achievement as measured by three devices: appropriate forms of the Stanford Achievement Test (K-3), STAR's Basic Skills First Criterion Tests (grade 3). The study's most important finding was that students in the small classes made higher scores (the difference in scores was both statistically and educationally significant) on the Stanford Achievement Test and on the Basic Skills First (BSF) Test in all four years (K-3) and in all locales (rural, suburban, urban, inner city). Other relevant findings include the following:

the greatest gains on the Stanford were made in inner-city small classes;

the highest scores on the Stanford and BSF were made in rural small classes;

the only consistent positive effect in regular classes with a full-time aide occurred in first grade;

teachers reported that they preferred small classes in order to identify student needs and to provide more individual attention, as well as to cover more material effectively;

the importance of the economic background of students was underscored by the finding that, in every situation, those students who were not economically eligible for the free lunch programme always out-performed those students who were in the free lunch programme.

Benefits of small classes

To determine whether small classes had a cumulative effect, the top 10% of STAR classes for each year were categorized by class type. The number of small classes in the top 10% of STAR classes increased each year from kindergarten through third grade. In kindergarten, small classes made up 55% of the top-scoring 10% of STAR classes. By third-grade, small classes made up 78% of the top 10%. This finding strongly suggests a cumulative and positive effect of small classes on student achievement in grades K-3.

During the course of the study more than 1,000 teachers participated in year end interviews. Their comments revealed a number of ways that instruction benefited from small class size:

basic instruction was completed more quickly, providing increased time for covering additional material;

there was more use of supplemental tests and enrichment activities;

there was more in-depth teaching of the basic content;

there were more frequent opportunities for children to engage in firsthand learning activities using concrete materials;

there was increased use of learning centres;

there was increased use of practices shown to be effective in the primary grades.

A common benefit cited by teachers in small and regular-plus-aide classes was that they were better able to individualize instruction. These teachers reported increased monitoring of student behaviour and learning, opportunities for more immediate and more individualized reteaching, more enrichment, more frequent interactions with each child, a better match between each child's ability and the instructional opportunities provided, a more detailed knowledge of each child's needs as a learner, and more time to meet individual learners' needs using a variety of instructional approaches.

Lasting Benefits Study

Project STAR proved that reduced class size in grades K-3 significantly enhanced student achievement. To determine if those positive benefits continue for the STAR students as they progress through the higher grades, the Tennessee State Department of Education appointed the Centre of Excellence for Research in Basic Skills at Tennessee State University to conduct a Lasting Benefits Study (LBS).

All students who participated in Project STAR third-grade classes were eligible for Lasting Benefit observation in the fourth grade. This fourth-grade sample contained 4,320 students in 216 classes and the Lasting Benefit analysis yielded clear and consistent results.

Students who had previously been in small STAR classes demonstrated significant advantages on every achievement measure over students who had attended regular classes. Further, these results favouring small classes were found to be consistent across all school locations. The positive effects of involvement in small classes are pervasive one full year after students return to regular size classes.

Effective teachers

In order for educators to make the best use of class-size reductions, they must be aware of what constitutes effective teaching. STAR researchers observed and interviewed 49 first-grade teachers whose classes had made the greatest gains. These teachers consistently displayed similar affective behaviours and characteristics. Their enthusiasm was obvious as they engaged in 'acting', demonstrating and role-playing activities. The teachers frequently expressed positive attitudes toward children, emphasized positive behaviour, praised success, and used humour to promote learning and to motivate students. A love of children seemed to permeate their professional repertoires.

The most effective teachers engaged their students through the use of creative writing, hands-on experiences, learning centres, and math manipulatives. They provided immediate feedback. They practised assertive discipline or some variation of it and made it clear that they had high expectations for their students. They maintained good communication with parents.

In addition to these common behaviours and characteristics, class size appeared to have been a contributing factor to the success of the most effective teachers. Only eight of the 49 (16%) taught regular classes of 22-25 students. Twenty-three (46%) taught small classes of 13-17; seven (14%) taught classes of 18-21; and 12 (24%) had full-time instructional aides in regular-sized classes.

 READING 9.2

Conclusions from the ORACLE study

Maurice Galton, Brian Simon and Paul Croll

> The ORACLE project was one of the first large-scale observational studies of English primary school classrooms. As this reading shows, it documented the illusion of 'progressivism', analysed four 'teaching styles' and highlighted the extreme difficulties of providing challenging instruction to children given large class sizes. 'Groupwork' was often found to be work by individuals, seated in groups, rather than a form of collaborative work.
>
> How is your teaching style affected by class size and the other practical constraints which you face?
>
> Edited from: Galton, M., Simon, B. and Croll, P. (1980) *Inside the Primary Classroom*. London: Routledge, 155–65

First, the weight of evidence on the curriculum shows very clearly that, in spite of widespread claims in the mass media, by industrialists, and by Black Paper propagandists, the general pattern of the traditional curriculum quite certainly still prevails, and has not changed in any fundamental way, let alone vanished. Claims about 'progressivism' appear to have been founded on mythology. It may, perhaps, be argued that the traditional curriculum was in fact largely abandoned in the late 1960s and early 1970s and has now shifted back; but this view cannot be supported by evidence from research studies. By the 'traditional curriculum' we mean a central focus on skills relating to literacy and numeracy.

It is worth noting that the HMI survey (DES, 1978), utilizing different methods from the ORACLE study (questionnaires, inspection visits, etc.,) and a nation-wide sample, reached very much the same conclusions in this respect, and, indeed, suggested that the concentration on 'basic skills' is exaggerated; a judgement based on their conclusion that, where the curriculum was broadened, pupils did better. Bassey's survey (1978) of 900 Nottinghamshire teachers also produced evidence which again brought out the central focus of Nottinghamshire teachers on skills relating to literacy and numeracy.

Second, the weight of the massive amount of data collected on pupil behaviour in the classroom in the ORACLE study lends no support whatever to the claim that anarchy and confusion prevail in primary school classrooms. This myth, which, according to Adam Hopkins in *The School Debate* (1978), originated in Black Paper One was apparently based on an article by Timothy Raison, MP. It received prestigious support in *The Times* leader of October 1976 on the 'wild men of the classroom' (based largely on the Tyndale affair), though we are not aware of any systematically gathered evidence or research giving it credence. As earlier noted in this book, the only systematic surveys of junior school classroom organization over this period were those carried through by Moran (1971) and these, far from bringing out anarchistic or libertarian approaches and attitudes concluded generally that teacher control remained tight within the 'integrated day' and 'informal' classroom structures by now widely adopted. There is no need to repeat evidence presented earlier but the over-all pattern of activities in the 'typical' junior classroom in the ORACLE study, particularly the high level of involvement of pupils in their tasks, is a clear indication of close teacher control and, within present constraints, of effective forms of classroom management. It is worth noting that here, also, the HMI survey specifically stresses the good order found in junior school classrooms (p. 108).

We make these points to clear the air for a serious discussion about the nature of primary school teaching, free from the mythologies that have bedeviled this issue and soured the atmosphere in which primary teachers have worked over the last few years. While mythologies of this kind held sway and were given credence not only in the mass media but even in the educational press, serious analysis and discussion of the real issues at stake was impossible or at least greatly handicapped. The ORACLE evidence presented in this volume, supported by related studies and surveys, provides a mass of factual data on the basis of which such analysis and interpretation becomes possible.

There can be no doubt that big changes have taken place within primary schools over the last fifteen to twenty years. In place of the traditional arrangements of the past, very many schools have adopted flexible forms of classroom organization. But while we find that, in general, good order and effective classroom management prevail in this new situation, one thing that does seem clear is that 'progressive' teaching, if by this is meant teaching having the characteristics defined by the Plowden Report [see Reading 7.6], hardly exists in practice. Indeed in one important respect we find the contrary. It is certainly the case that individualization, both of work and of attention, is utilized very widely; in particular, as we have noted, by the teachers grouped together as Style 1 in our sample 'individual monitors', but also if in varying degrees, by the teachers using the other styles. Individualization, both of work and of attention, was certainly given overriding importance in the Plowden prescripts and to this extent this aspect of 'progressivism' is widely implemented. But central to the Plowden thesis was the questing, exploratory character of the individual child's actual activity; the stress on discovery methods, on finding out for oneself; while the teacher was seen as stimulating this activity by probing, questioning, guiding – leading the child from behind. It is here that classroom practice, according to our data, does not match the prescripts. Individualized teaching (or interaction) is not 'progressively' oriented, in this sense; it is overwhelmingly factual and managerial. Such probing and questioning as does take place is to be found largely in the whole class teaching situation, one generally to be avoided, according to Plowden, in favour of individualization; and, paradoxically, the teaching situation popularly held to be best adapted to didactic teaching (telling).

In our view, based both on analysis of the ORACLE data and on the experience of much classroom observation, a main reason for this apparent contradiction is that, with classes averaging thirty in size, a high degree of individualization both of work and attention imposes a management problem on the teacher of a relatively new type. Thus, the grouping structure frequently used, eases this problem, but where children are working individually within this structure the teacher is confronted with very complex problems. In this situation, wider pedagogical considerations are inevitably ignored or left out of account in the interest of keeping the class as a whole busily engaged on the tasks in hand. This has, in fact, been a major preoccupation of class teachers from the inception of this approach.

Our conclusion, then, is that, given contemporary class sizes, the Plowden 'progressive' ideology, based essentially on individualization, is impractical; and, we would claim, our data bear this out beyond question. Far from utilizing probing, higher order type questions and statements with individuals, teachers in practice utilize this approach largely in the whole class teaching situation, the technique specifically discouraged by Plowden. But it is precisely in this situation, of course, that teachers can concentrate on such teaching tactics, as we have seen our Style 2 teachers (class enquirers) do – but not only these. All teachers of whatever style use higher order questioning more in the whole class situation than when interacting with individuals. In this situation the teacher does not have to concentrate her mind and her activity, on the management of thirty individualized tasks, but on one only, the subject matter under discussion, on which she aims to focus the attention of the class as a whole.

This brings the technique of grouping, and of group work, into the discussion. The Plowden Committee recommended the use of grouping in the primary classroom largely for two sets of reasons; first, because they recognized the impracticability of total individualization of all work (which, on theoretical grounds, they preferred), and second, for a number of socializing and pedagogical reasons as, for instance, the gains from explaining, from participating in the cut and thrust of the debate, from formulating hypotheses, from learning to get along together, and so on. Indeed it appears from a close reading of the report that the Plowden view generally is that the grouping structure gives scope for individualization; that, if children are brought together in groups they will there develop and pursue their own interests and activities. Individualization realizes itself through group structures.

However, as was suggested earlier, no consistent rationale for the organization of group work was elaborated in the report, nor indeed was any clear guidance given to teachers as to how such work might be organized (or managed in practice).

On this whole, confused question, the ORACLE observations bring out two aspects of grouping in primary classrooms beyond any doubt. First, that seating in groups is in fact the mark of the typical classroom today and, second, that while in most classrooms the pupils are organized in one or more seated groups for the various activities undertaken, with few exceptions they then work largely alone, as individuals. The setting is socialized in this sense but the work is individualized; and this, as we have seen, is a main principle of classroom organization as articulated by Plowden and implemented in practice by most teachers in the ORACLE sample.

It is here, however, that we have a striking finding indicating that current practice is far out of line with the Plowden prescripts. That is that those teachers who maximize the use of grouping, the group instructors (Style 3) appear also to be primarily didactic in their approach, emphasizing 'telling' and task supervision more than any of the other three main styles. Further this particular group of teachers has the lowest proportion of higher cognitive level interactions with individual pupils of any style while even in the group situation the proportion of higher level interactions is low, indeed of all the four main styles it is the group instructors who maximize the proportion of higher level interactions in the whole class situation. It is worth noting also that it is teachers using this style, which maximizes group work, who have by far the highest proportion of 'quiet collaborators' among their pupils. In other words, it would appear that these teachers are not feeding stimulating ideas and questions to their pupils and that they are not stimulating high levels of pupil–pupil interaction on the tasks in hand. Basically, their interaction with their grouped pupils largely takes the form of giving them facts and instructions.

But an analysis of the other three main styles indicate that neither do these teachers use grouping in the manner prescribed by Plowden. There is no clear evidence that co-operative group work of the investigating, problem solving, discovery kind which Plowden held that all children should experience, features more than sparsely in our primary schools.

To think out, provide materials for, and set up a series of group tasks having the characteristics just described in the different subject areas which comprise a modern curriculum would in itself clearly be a major undertaking, even if use is made of relevant curriculum development projects. To monitor the subsequent group activities; to be ready and able to intervene in the work of each group when this is educationally necessary or desirable; this also would clearly be a major undertaking for the teacher requiring, as a first condition, a high degree of involvement by the pupils in their tasks and so a high level of responsible behaviour. For the pupils to gain from such work also certainly requires the development of a number of social as well as cognitive skills; a degree of tolerance and mutual understanding, the ability to articulate a point of view, to engage in discussion, reasoning, probing and questioning. Such skills are not in themselves innate, they have to be learnt and so taught.

Total individualization on the one hand, or whole class teaching on the other, allows all these problems to be evaded, as does using group work in a didactic manner, the pupils' work being basically individualized. It is our conclusion, that the whole issue of the purpose and organization of group work in the primary school classroom requires a great deal more attention than it has had to date.

We hope that the findings presented here will make possible a fuller discussion about the theory and practice of different teaching approaches. It might be wiser to begin by acknowledging that no one method enjoys total superiority over the rest, that some proportion of class teaching, at least in present circumstances, appears to be desirable and that setting up and maintaining group interaction requires careful monitoring.

READING 9.3

'Good practice' in groupwork

Rea Reason

In this reading, Rea Reason defends the use of groupwork against its critics by expressing the psychological rationale on which it is based. She identifies the idea of 'scaffolding learning', the need to attend to individual differences and the importance of social and interactive learning. However, the practical dilemmas faced by teachers are also clear, and Reason urges the development of more genuinely collaborative groupwork.

How would you develop collaborative groupwork in your classroom? (see also Reading 11.6)

Edited from: Reason, R. (1993) 'Primary special needs and National Curriculum assessment', in Wolfendale, S. (ed.) *Assessing Special Educational Needs*. London: Cassell, 73–5

Education in British primary schools is founded on a set of prescriptive assumptions about children's learning referred to as 'good practice'. This shorthand phrase encapsulates a range of organization arrangements and teaching methods which include group work, curriculum integration, a learning environment strong on visual impact, an 'exploratory' pedagogy and thematic enquiry (Alexander *et al.*, 1989; Alexander, 1992).

Children typically sit in groups around tables or move from one activity area to another. In the study of primary schools in London undertaken by Mortimore *et al.* (1988), only one-tenth of the classrooms had tables or desks arranged in rows. In the study by Alexander *et al.* in Leeds none of the classrooms observed had such formal arrangements. Both studies described a wealth of wall displays which included both teacher-prepared stimulus materials and examples of the children's own work.

Classrooms following a timetable based on the notion of 'the integrated day' have a number of different activities happening in parallel, each taking place in a designated area of the classroom or focusing on a particular group of children. These can include any aspect of the curriculum combined into particular themes or topics, or taught as separate subjects such as mathematics, where different kinds of mathematical activities take place concurrently.

It is important to mention the psychological and educational basis for the methods of teaching, learning and assessment that are considered to be 'good practice'. These are no 'modern orthodoxies', as suggested by Alexander (1992), but have a long and respectable theoretical pedigree. It is the demands they make on teachers that may be considered excessive or impractical.

Three kinds of theoretical influence can be distinguished. The first comes from the notion of 'scaffolded learning' described, for example, by Edwards and Mercer (1987) [see also Readings 6.4, 6.5, 6.10 and 6.11]. The teacher is regarded as supporter and facilitator of the children's own ways of making sense of their experiences. The teacher's task is then to provide appropriate learning opportunities, ask open-ended questions and generally guide the child in becoming a self-directed and enquiring learner. The emphasis is more on the processes than the products of learning. Many aspects of National Curriculum documentation, in particular the programmes of study and the non-statutory guidance, reflect this way of thinking.

A second theoretical focus is on individual differences. As children learn at different rates and in different ways, teachers will as far as possible make their plans of instruction tailor-made for each of them. Formative assessment is based on this notion: information of what the child already knows, understands and can do determines what the child might learn next [see Readings 12.1, 12.8 and 12.9].

The third psychological influence regards learning as essentially social and interactive, not only for the children but also for their teachers and parents. Children make their meanings clearer to themselves by explaining them to others. Their understanding is extended through 'debating' observations and ideas with other children sharing the task (CACE, 1967; Bruner, 1986) [see Readings 6.8 and 6.9].

Class teachers may now combine these three theoretical perspectives in the following way:

children are seated round tables to foster interaction;

each child has her or his own learning task;

the teacher moves from child to child offering individual support.

These kinds of arrangements have been criticized on many grounds (Galton, 1989; Bennett *et al.*, 1984 [Reading 8.7]; Alexander, 1992). In a class of some thirty children, the quality of the support or advice given to each individual child becomes so brief and superficial that it does not meet its aims of assessing and exploring the child's understanding. Individual work cards or textbook exercises may result in something akin to 'correspondence course' rather than individualized tuition. In these circumstances formative assessment becomes very difficult. As children with special needs require even more attention, how can teachers find the time?

Grouping children round tables, as an organizational device, enables teachers to control their own time more effectively. It is easier to think of, say, five groups of children rather than thirty individuals with different needs. The following, taken from interviews with a skilled and experienced teacher, illustrates that approach:

I try to have a clear idea of the children's individual achievements based on my own observations and the records I keep. I decide in advance not only who will work together and on what but which groups or individuals will receive more teacher time. I think in terms of three stages of learning: the 'concept' stage where children are learning new understanding and require much teacher time; the 'development' stage where children need intermittent teacher time; and the 'reinforcement' stage where the activity should be self-sustained. At any one time only a small number of children can be engaged at the 'concept stage'. This planning enables me to manage my time so that all children in turn receive more intensive attention. This is obviously essential for the purposes of assessment and record keeping.

Even for teachers as competent and well-organized as this, the dilemma still remains. The more time the teacher devotes to extended interactions with some children, the less demanding on them as teachers must be the activities they give to the rest who may be seen to be marking time. But the more accessible teachers seek to make themselves to all their pupils as individuals, the less time they have for extended and challenging interaction with any of them. Either way critics can argue that time is being wasted.

So why not seat the children in rows and teach them all together as one class? According to the press, the Leeds Primary Needs Programme (Alexander *et al.*, 1989; Alexander, 1992) recommended a return to such 'traditional' methods. Their work was grossly misrepresented. Having questioned 'modern orthodoxy' in its apparent disregard for the preferences of teachers trying to reconcile the considerable demands made on their time, the authors argue that different teaching purposes require different kinds of classroom arrangements. Not surprisingly, whole-class teaching becomes important for some purposes. But the authors also focus on the development of co-operative groupwork in the classroom. They argue that task and setting should as far as possible be consistent. Just as collaborative activity is difficult in a traditionally arranged classroom, so the concentration needed for individualized tasks may be difficult within groups.

Referring back to the psychological rationales for seating children round tables, the main purpose was to enable them to learn together from the interaction that takes place. The practice of grouping children for organization purposes and then giving them individual tasks does not take that into account. There is indeed a paradox in children sitting together facing each other and then asking them to concentrate on predominantly individualized learning tasks and the collaborative setting in which children were expected to undertake them. Much greater prominence needs to be given to the potential of genuine pupil–pupil collaboration and less to low-level writing, reading and drawing tasks.

 READING 9.4

To group or not to group?

David McNamara

> David McNamara suggests that grouping children is often based on 'ability' with the aim of making differentiated instruction easier for teachers. This could be seen as being discriminatory and certainly demands certain social skills from the children. This leads McNamara to suggest a horse-shoe arrangement as a new, flexible way of organizing the children in the classroom.
>
> How do you think your class would respond to McNamara's ideas. Are they worth trying?
>
> Edited from: McNamara, D. (1994) *Classroom Pedagogy and Primary Practice*. London: Routledge, 64–7

The policy of grouping children in the primary classroom has probably reached the status where for many primary teachers it is accepted as characteristic of good primary practice. It is seen as the way to organize children, usually so that they can be allocated to ability groups. Often the groups will move from one activity to another during the day and group composition may change from time to time depending upon the nature of the learning and area of the curriculum. In mixed ability classrooms it may be appropriate to group children according to aptitude if teaching is to be matched to their ability. Before deciding to group it is important to consider carefully whether this is necessarily good practice and weigh the benefits and costs. For instance, it does not follow that in order for the teacher to provide differentiated learning, pupils have to be physically grouped within the classroom. The groups can, as it were, exist in the teacher's mind and learning activities can be provided for children of different abilities who are randomly distributed throughout the class.

When children are grouped in class it is usually so that the teacher can form homogeneous groups for learning but it is important to remember that to group children according to one characteristic, say, their reading ability, does not get over the fact that they may still be very different on other characteristics which may be related to learning such as mathematical ability, motivation, or the social adaptability necessary to work effectively in groups. Moreover, grouping children according to ability may, as a consequence, mean that the groups are alike in terms of social class background, ethnicity, or gender and thereby possibly expose the teacher to the charge that discrimination or partiality has influenced group formation (this problem can be worse if children are grouped according to friendship choices). The issue should also be considered with reference to streaming. One of the important reasons for abandoning the practice of streaming children in separate classes according to academic level and for creating mixed ability classes in their place is to overcome the social problems and stigma attached to labelling children according to whether they are in the A, B or C stream. But grouping children within classrooms according to ability, and this is the most common method of grouping, does not disguise the fact that the children are still being organized according to their ability. Indeed the kudos of able children may be enhanced within the unstreamed class because less able children can turn to them as a resource for advice and help when the teacher's attention is elsewhere. If the teacher's aim is to disguise differences in ability it is probably preferable to disperse children randomly throughout the class. The evidence suggests that it is necessary to prepare and train children if they are to work effectively in groups; pupils must be taught to co-operate and provided with appropriate skills if they are to work together. The irony is that classroom studies report that children work best in groups when they receive clear-cut assignments which are closely monitored by the teacher. The notion of children working co-operatively together on creative or discovery-orientated tasks is not supported by the available evidence; in fact creative work is probably more likely to be found during whole class instruction. The evidence also indicates that homogeneous ability grouping may be detrimental to the learning of children in low ability groups; it is able children who are more likely to be able to cope with and prosper in group settings where pupils are less likely to be under the eye of the teacher.

In sum, there are sound reasons for grouping children in primary classrooms but there are equally convincing reasons for not doing so and for engaging in class teaching. Grouping places a particular burden upon the teacher in terms of the management and organization of the class and the problem of sustaining order may become paramount, resulting in the teacher having less time to attend to teaching and learning. The teacher should not assume that grouping is a pre-requisite for good primary practice; whole class teaching has an equal claim to the teacher's attention.

The practical pedagogic problem facing the class teacher is that she is likely to want to adopt different forms of classroom arrangement from time to time and switch from one to another. A recent report on primary education proposes that it is necessary to strike a balance between the organizational strategies of whole class teaching, group work, and individual teaching (Alexander, Rose and Woodhead, 1992). In order to strike a balance the teacher must ask, 'What is a good balance and how is the classroom to be organized so as to enable the smooth transition from one organizational form to another?' Advice available to teachers tends to fall silent when these awkward practical questions are posed. One possible solution is to arrange the desks in a square or horseshoe figuration as the basic form of organization and switch from this to individual, group and whole class teaching as desired. The square or horseshoe pattern allows the teacher to see every child and every child to see the teacher during class lessons. Desks are arranged around the sides of the classroom with children facing into the middle of the room. This method has the following advantages:

children can see each other and are more inclined to listen to each other's contributions than when seated in rows with their backs to colleagues, or in groups where eye contact and audibility are difficult;

a large space is available in the middle of the room for stories, large pieces of artwork and so on;

children are able, when required, to work in pairs or threes, that is group sizes which are productive and unlikely to exclude people;

the teacher can see, at a glance, what every child is doing and reach those with problems quickly;

desks can quickly be formed into tables of four when required.

This approach allows flexibility and enables a variety of teaching methods to be employed. Class teaching should be successful because children are facing the teacher and are not able to conceal themselves behind others, as they can when sitting in rows which all face the front of the classroom. Group work can be employed easily, with group sizes determined by the task rather than by the number of children who fit around a table. In addition, some children can work in groups while others work individually.

There are, in sum, possible managerial solutions which make it possible to switch from one form of classroom organization to another and accommodate the advantages of both whole class teaching and group work.

READING 9.5

The classroom learning environment: layout, resources and display

David Clegg and Shirley Billington

In this reading Clegg and Billington offer practical advice on the organization and use of classroom space, on the management of resources and on display. It is important to note how they maintain a clear focus on the contribution which these factors can make to the processes of teaching and learning for which the teacher aims.

This reading is closely associated with others in Chapter 9, on class size, pupil grouping, working with non-teachers and on time, for they each deal with particular dimensions of classroom organization, which have to be brought into a coherent, purposive whole.

Do you feel you have the best possible layout and system for resource management in your classroom? And what is the balance of 'celebrating, stimulating and informing' in your display work?

Edited from: Clegg, D. and Billington, S. (1994) *The Effective Primary Classroom: Management and Organisation of Teaching and Learning.* London: David Fulton, 123–5

The way classrooms are organized and managed is fundamental to achieving success. We are not simply discussing how we can make a classroom attractive, but how to create an environment which is specifically designed as a place where a teacher's ideas about teaching and learning will bear fruit. In that sense, how the classroom is set up will demonstrate a teacher's experiences, values and attitudes. The classroom is able to open or close opportunities for children, it will give them messages about a teacher's expectations, and will indicate to them explicitly how they should conduct themselves. It is not hard to think of some common examples. If art materials are left dirty and untidy in a corner of the room, what message is that giving? A book area full of tatty books, poorly displayed, with a threadbare piece of carpet covering the floor is conveying attitudes and values about reading and books. If the teacher's attention must be attracted every time a pupil needs a piece of equipment, what does that say about opportunities for children to make their own decisions? The examples are endless, but the idea is simple – a classroom says a great deal about the teacher, to colleagues, to children, and increasingly to parents. A teacher's classroom is becoming an open arena, as the public face of the education system, and that is a major reason for ensuring it is the result of careful planning.

Classrooms are not passive environments in which teaching and learning happens to take place – they should be designed to promote and enhance learning. They should motivate and stimulate, and they should be planned to make the most efficient use of the most important resource – namely the teacher.

There is no one way to organize and run classrooms. All we are saying is that the way they are set up and managed should be just as much a part of a teacher's pedagogy as curriculum planning, teaching strategies or assessing learning.

Classroom layout

When thinking about how classrooms are organized and managed most teachers will begin by considering how the furniture is laid out. However, this is a much more complex process than simply fitting all the furniture in, and making sure that everyone has a seat.

Depending on their approach to teaching and learning, teachers have broadly three options in terms of layout. The first of these options is to create a series of working areas within the classroom. These could include a reading area, a writing area, science area and maths area and possibly others depending on the age of the children. Within these working areas children would have easy access to an appropriate range of resources and materials. There are some clear advantages to this type of layout. It is easy for children to understand, and by providing a specific area designated for a particular activity pupils can be motivated and develop a sense of purpose. Resources and materials can be carefully matched to learning experiences, and will introduce children to the idea of specific resources relating to specific activities. This kind of layout however, has some drawbacks. Very few teachers will have enough space to create a sufficient number of areas that will represent the full range of activities they would wish to offer. The availability of resources can be limited to the group of children working within a particular area, and it can operate against making links across the curriculum. This kind of layout may be most appropriate for teachers who have a range of different activities going on at the same time. Typically a group of children could be engaged in a science experiment, others could be working with some construction material and so on, with anything up to five or six different activities.

The second and third options concerning classroom layout have a different focus. Rather than limiting resources to specific areas they look to organizing the classroom in a more holistic way. Essentially the choice is between putting the resources and materials around the outside of the room, with children working in the middle, or putting the resources in the middle and children round the edges. The former is the more predominant pattern, but has the disadvantage of creating potentially more movement around the room. In the latter option, the theory is that all children have equal access to resourcing.

If we consider all three of these options, the reality is that many teachers opt for a mixture. Most classrooms have some designated areas, most commonly for wet or practical work, and a reading area. Other resources are usually stored around the edges of the room.

The ways in which teachers wish to operate will also have a bearing on how pupils are arranged. The teacher who, when talking at length to the whole class, prefers children sat together in a carpeted area, and then disperses the children to a variety of areas, with a variety of working partners, may not see the necessity for every child to have his or her own place. If one group will always be working on an activity that does not require desks or table space, then there is no need to have a place for every pupil. When space is limited this could be an important factor. When children are older, and sitting on the floor is less comfortable, or when there are an increasing number of occasions when everybody needs some desk or table space, then clearly this must be provided. The important message is to maintain a degree of flexibility. Modern furniture enables most teachers to provide a range of options. Putting tables together can save space, and enable a group of six or eight children to work together. Similarly the same tables arranged differently can provide space for individual or paired work.

For different reasons many teachers are beginning to question whether they need a teacher's desk. The large desk which years ago invariably dominated classrooms no longer seems appropriate, and doing without it can save space. In the end it will be a question of teaching style. It would not be difficult for a teacher to monitor how often he or she sits at the desk, then to ask whether it is necessary to be sitting at a desk and then to form some decisions. Those teachers who choose to keep a desk, should think carefully about where to place it. Should it be part of the working environment? Should it form a barrier between teachers and children, or should it be tucked away discreetly in a corner?

The lack of space is often most apparent when people are moving around the classroom. Most teachers will have experienced the exasperation of trying to reach over to a pupil, having to ask other pupils to 'just move over a bit'. It is equally frustrating for children when they are forced to squeeze past other children to collect equipment, or to get from one side of the room to the other. All this is very familiar, and in some classrooms some of this may be unavoidable. The sad fact is that there are still some classrooms that are too small for the number of pupils, but it is also a fact that some careful thought can begin to alleviate some problems. Planning a classroom layout is rather like creating a painting – sometimes it's the spaces left behind that are important. Organizing routes around the classroom is important. Children need to be able to get from one part of the room to another, and this access should be planned. Observation will help in showing where congestion points occur. Resources that are in regular or constant demand could be placed strategically around the room rather than in one place. It is rarely the case that a teacher needs to be able to walk around four sides of a desk, or a group of tables. Space can be saved by grouping furniture together and by careful positioning around the room.

As previously indicated the main factor when planning a classroom is to keep a degree of flexibility. It should not be thought of as a once a year activity but should be something that is open to development and evolution through trial and error. Often classrooms carefully planned and arranged during the holidays look very different when the children actually take over. Many teachers are increasingly involving pupils in planning the layout and design of their room. This can be very effective and beneficial and will often provide some startling insights into how pupils actually see things. Even the youngest children can be involved in making decisions about where things are put, and how the tables are arranged. The ways in which children experience the classroom will be very different from the ways in which the teacher does. The wise teacher will tap into that experience and involve them in making some decisions. It is also perhaps worth remembering that redesigning the layout can motivate and stimulate both teacher and children.

Managing classroom resources

The following are key issues for consideration by every teacher when thinking about the organization of resources in the classroom.

Quality This is a far more important element than quantity. Teachers are natural hoarders, and loathe to discard items which may have outlived their usefulness, but there is little point in shelf space being taking up by outdated or tatty books (which children will avoid using) or cupboards being full of games or jigsaws with pieces missing. The quality of the resources will affect the quality of the learning.

Appropriateness Is there a variety of equipment suitable for the planned curriculum, and for the range of abilities within the class? If the school has a policy on centralized resources it may be important to think in terms of a basic equipment list for each classroom and planning activities which will make use of centralized resources at specific times.

Storage Resources and materials should be appropriately stored so that a system is evident to the children. Resource areas (not necessarily work areas) can be established, so that all the equipment for a particular subject is collected in a clearly defined location. Colour coding for drawers, and storage boxes with pictorial labels for younger children can help with efficient use of equipment by pupils.

Accessibility   The more that children can organize resources for themselves the less time should be spent by a teacher on low-level tasks such as giving out paper. Children need to be clear about what they have immediate access to, and what can only be used with permission or under supervision. However, the vast majority of materials in a classroom should be available for children to select for appropriate use.

Consideration should be given to providing basic equipment for continual use such as pots of pencils, a variety of types of paper, and to organizing other materials for ease of access. In order to do this in some classrooms, it may be necessary to remove cupboard doors to provide open shelving, or to purchase some inexpensive and colourful storage such as stacker-jacks or plastic baskets.

If children are to make good use of the facilities available in a classroom they need to be clear about the system which operates. They may need to be trained in making appropriate use of resources, and in selecting materials for a particular task. They can play a role in managing classroom resources, and it may be useful to involve them in preliminary planning when organizing the equipment for a particular curriculum area. Sometimes, if the system is not working effectively, they can have some useful observations to make on why things go wrong!

Giving children responsibility for ensuring that the resource system works well is an important aspect of developing independence from the teacher. They should be able, or if young be trained, in the collection, use, return and replacement of materials with minimal reference to the teacher. Where equipment is limited, they can be encouraged to negotiate with other children over the use of a particular resource. Negotiation and sharing equipment are important elements in planning tasks.

Display in the classroom

The business of display is much more than brightening up dull corners, covering cracks, and double mounting: it is another important factor in ensuring classrooms are places in which effective learning can take place.

Display has three distinct uses: it can celebrate, stimulate and inform. How display is used to promote these three functions will also transmit values and messages to children, parents and colleagues. For example, what you choose to celebrate will begin to give messages about what is valued or who is held in high esteem. How you begin to stimulate and inform through display will illustrate some clear ideas about how you regard children and their learning. The transmission of values and attitudes is a dimension that touches all aspects of display, but it is worthwhile thinking about each of the three ways display can be used.

Celebration   Enjoying and acknowledging children's achievement is an important aspect of any classroom. Displaying those achievements is just one way of demonstrating the regard in which their work is held, but there are many others. One of the restrictions of displaying pupils' work has been that it has led to an over-emphasis on the product or outcome, at the expense of the process. It is not too difficult to redress this imbalance. If we consider for a moment the way modern libraries and museums have been eager not only to display authors' and artists' finished items, but to acquire the notebooks, jottings, sketch pads and rough drawings to demonstrate the development of the works, we can perhaps begin to see how schools can also start to acknowledge the process. As teachers who are concerned with process and outcome, it is important that we place equal value on each. Efforts at drafting can be displayed alongside the finished stories, sketches and jottings shown next to the completed art work. This gives clear messages, not least that behind good outcomes, there is usually a great deal of hard work, and that hard work is worth acknowledging and displaying.

There are other, perhaps more fundamental, considerations about displaying work. Display is one way of promoting children's self-image, and giving them a sense of worth. The converse is also true. Failing to display some pupils' work may go some way to alienating those children from the classroom. This is an area where teachers must use their judgement. It is important that all children have work displayed (not all at the same time!) but it is equally important that such work is worthy of display, and is of some significance. Display can also demonstrate the achievements of groups of pupils working towards a common end, as well as the achievements of individuals.

The most effective displays of children's work pay some regard to basic aesthetic considerations. The most attractive displays are the result of some thought concerning shape, colour, form and texture. This not only boosts children's confidence in seeing their work promoted in this way, but, perhaps more importantly, it provides an opportunity to discuss these features, as well as some guidance for children when they begin to set up their own displays.

Stimulation What is displayed in classrooms can form part of the learning process. A good dramatic, thought-provoking display can provide great stimulation for learning. There are countless ways in which children can be motivated by something they can see, observe, smell, touch or hear. Science investigations can start with a display which challenges through effective questioning, and promotes the development of skills, for example, 'use the magnifying glass to observe, record what you see ...', 'what do you think will happen if ...?', all of which can begin to make children think, discuss, predict and hypothesize. Similarly, display can stimulate an aesthetic or artistic response through careful use of colours, textures, and forms. In the humanities, a collection of artifacts can be the starting point for enquiry and investigation. The most effective displays are often those which not only stimulate and motivate, but also show the results. These uses of display to celebrate, stimulate and inform are not mutually exclusive and they will often be interlinked.

Informing The notion that display within the classroom can support young children's learning is the aspect that is least recognized. Stimulation and motivation are starting points for learning, but display can provide support once children have embarked upon their work. What is actually stuck up on the walls, or stood in a corner, or displayed on a table can act as a resource for the learner. This will vary from classroom to classroom, but it could include such items as current word lists, key phrases to reinforce an ongoing activity, the display of resource material alongside guidance on how to use it, or simple instructions about what to do in particular circumstances. The possibility of displaying the process alongside the outcomes can provide a source of support for other pupils and a focus for discussion.

Display makes a very significant contribution to the classroom climate. It is by its very nature a public statement which is there for children, colleagues and parents to see. As it is a significant factor in creating classroom atmosphere it is vital that we do not fall into the trap of 'surface rather than substance' (Alexander, 1992), and that requires thought and consideration about how good display contributes to effective learning rather than simply making the room look nice.

📖 **READING 9.6**

Using classroom time

Andrew Pollard, Patricia Broadfoot, Paul Croll, Marilyn Osborn and Dorothy Abbott

---

This reading is extracted from the first book from the Primary Assessment, Curriculum and Experience (PACE) project which monitored the impact of the introduction of the National Curriculum and assessment in primary schools during the 1990s. The reading provides evidence on how classroom time is used. Given what appears to be a necessary use of approximately one-fifth of time in classroom management, we have to focus on the quality of pupil engagement in the remaining 'teaching and learning time'. PACE findings suggest that there is considerable variation between classrooms in this respect.

What are your judgements about pupil use of time in your classroom?

Edited from: Pollard, A., Broadfoot, P., Croll, P., Osborn, M. and Abbott, D. (1994) *Changing English Primary Schools?* London: Cassell, 178–82

As part of our classroom studies we classified pupils' classroom behaviour into key categories and used time-sampled systematic observation to measure the proportions of each. In this approach, the observer codes the pupil activity at each sampling point, thus building up a systematic record of researcher judgements of pupil activity (Croll, 1986). We used four pupil activity categories: 'task engaged', 'task management', 'distracted' and 'waiting for teacher' – categories which, though important and well established, also require relatively high levels of researcher inference or judgement.

Evidence from research studies of the 70s and 80s which have adopted this approach to studying pupil behaviour has consistently indicated that, young children were judged to be directly involved in their work for about 60% of their time (e.g. Galton, Simon and Croll, 1980; Tizard *et al.*, 1988). Early findings from the PACE study show very similar results, as the table below shows.

	Year 1 (1990)	Year 2 (1991)
Task-engaged	56.9	59.5
Task management	11.8	13.5
Distracted	19.3	21.5
Waiting for teacher	8.0	5.6
Other	4.0	0.0

Figure 9.6.1 Main types of pupil activity in the classroom studies (percentages)

Despite their different ages, the children in the PACE project were judged to be 'task engaged' for roughly the same amount of time as those Key Stage 2 children studied by Galton, Simon and Croll, 1980. They were also deemed to be 'managing tasks' and 'distracted' for roughly similar amounts of time. More time was spent by the PACE children in 'waiting for the teacher', and this probably reflects the younger age of the children. A similar comparison with slightly adapted data from the Tizard study of infant children yields results that are not drastically different, although the Tizard children seemed to be coded as distracted slightly less often (Tizard *et al.*, 1988 [see Reading 13.2]).

Overall, however, the results are fairly consistent. Children in English primary schools are likely to be regarded as task engaged for about 60% of their classroom time. They may be seen as distracted for up to 20% of the time and are likely to be organizing themselves to complete the task or waiting for the teacher for the remaining 20% of the time. The aggregated pupil 'time on task', in getting organized or working, is just over 70% of classroom time.

Figure 9.6.2 below charts PACE project results for each of the four categories of pupil activity in each of the eighteen classrooms in which data were collected during 1990 and 1991.

The classrooms in Figure 9.6.2 have been ordered on the basis of descending percentages of recorded pupil task engagement. This creates a dramatic visual impression of one of our key findings on classroom variation. In discussing this issue, we will use particular combinations of our four variables of observed pupil activity in order to produce three indicators of 'apparent classroom effectiveness': 'classroom management time', 'teaching and learning time' and 'time on task'.

Classroom management time

This indicator is based on the combined pupil time spent in task management and waiting for the teacher. There was a tendency for task management and waiting for teacher to vary together. Where task management is high, waiting for teacher tends to be low, and vice versa. Over all of the classrooms, task management was coded for almost 13% of pupil observations and waiting for teacher for just under 7% – a total of almost 20%.

This classroom management figure of 20% of observed pupil time is important. Whilst it can evidently be reduced in some circumstances, we believe that it is realistic at present to accept that this is the sort of proportion of time which is likely to be spent by pupils on classroom management, whatever the teacher strategy. Perhaps an approximate commitment of

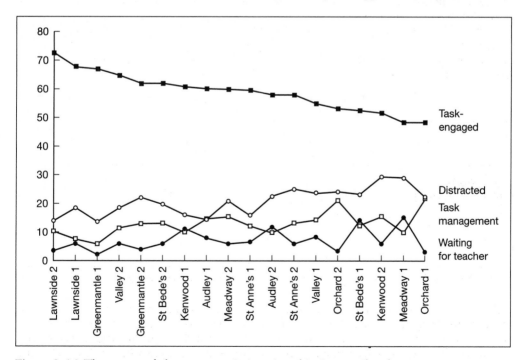

Figure 9.6.2 The extent of classroom variations in achieving pupil task engagement

20% of pupil time is simply a necessary time commitment, given the range of class sizes and task, group and resource organization to be found in English primary schools.

Teaching and learning time

The use of teaching and learning time is our second indicator of 'apparent classroom effectiveness', and it is arguably the most significant. We define teaching and learning time as the time that remains once classroom management issues have been dealt with. Putting this another way, if we allow 20% of observed pupil time for classroom management of one sort or another, how do pupils use the remaining 80% of time?

The codes which relate to teaching and learning time are those of 'task engaged' and 'distracted', and clearly they are likely to map against each other in some way. Children who are not task engaged could well be distracted, and distracted children will certainly not be task engaged. However, in our comparisons of classrooms we were not expecting as strong a pattern as the one which we found. Our data shows both a very considerable difference in pupil activity within the classrooms and a very strong relationship between task engagement and distraction.

Thus, in terms of the question 'how do pupils in different classrooms use the 80% of classroom time which is available for teaching and learning?', the answer has to acknowledge huge variations in the effectiveness of different classes in producing task engagement rather than distraction. Interestingly, the extreme cases from the PACE study are Lawnside Primary School, serving a relatively affluent commuter village near a large Midland city, with its Year 2 class figure of 72% of observed pupil time on task engagement and only 14% of time coded as distracted, compared with the Year 1 class at inner-city Meadway Primary, serving a community with severe socio-economic problems, where task engagement was down to 47% and distraction was up to 28%, twice the Lawnside figure.

'Time on task'

A further, and more commonly used, way of exploring the relationship of these variables to 'apparent classroom effectiveness' is to monitor the total 'time on task'. Thus the time in which pupils are 'task engaged' and involved in 'task management' is added and compared. We plotted the results of this procedure, classroom by classroom, for the two rounds of PACE data gathering.

There was some variation from year to year and between classes in the same year. The extremes were again over 80% 'on task' activity of Year 2 pupils at the village school of Lawnside and a figure of less than 60% recorded for pupil 'on task' activity at inner-city Meadway. Having noted these cases though, the degree of consistency is perhaps surprising, with almost all the other 14 classrooms producing pupil 'on task' figures of between 65-75%. It seems that, despite what one may occasionally read in some newspapers, in most classrooms at Key Stage 1 pupils work 'on task' for the bulk of their time. The real question seems to be not whether the children are 'on task' in itself, but whether this 'on task' activity is educationally productive.

The teacher and others in the classroom

Gary Thomas

> This reading is based on the idea of 'room management' in which a team of adults work together in a classroom, with clearly understood roles. Research shows this to be remarkably effective and, with the increasing use of classroom assistants of various sorts, ways of using such significant resources in the most beneficial ways have to be developed.
>   How do you work with other adults in your classroom?
>
> Edited from: Thomas, G. (1989) 'The teacher and others in the classroom', in Cullingford, C. (ed.) (1989) *The Primary Teacher: The Role of the Educator and the Purpose of Primary Education*. London: Cassell, 59–70

A quiet revolution has taken place in the primary classroom. It is now the exception rather than the rule to find teachers who always work on their own. There are fundamental changes in the atmosphere of the class when other adults move into the territory of the teacher and her children.

Possible problems

Some of the possible problems may be categorized as follows.

Role ambiguity   As increasing numbers of people are involved in the execution of any task, the possibility for misunderstanding amongst them is magnified. With a highly complex task such as teaching, the potential for confusion about role definition is high when more than one person is present.

Diminishing returns   It has for a long time been realized that personal effectiveness may be reduced when tasks are shared. People will unintentionally obstruct each other, or duplicate the other's effort. The extent to which this occurs depends greatly on the nature of the task and the number of people contributing. While many of the tasks which are being undertaken in the shared classroom would be carried out autonomously, thus reducing many of these effects, there are nevertheless bound to be certain problems to do with sharing the same physical space.

Confusion amongst children   There is the possibility that children may 'play off' one adult against another, thus diminishing the effectiveness and the credibility of each. Being used to having only one adult in the classroom, children may not fully understand how they should respond to the additional person or people. They may ascribe imaginary weightings to the importance of the various adults who are present and this may serve to accentuate distinctions which the classteacher would wish to minimize; it may on the other hand undermine the position of the teacher.

How does effective teamwork take place without invoking all the problems to which I have just referred? A number of things may be done. We can aim to limit role ambiguity by specifying what each person will be doing; we can aim to reduce loss of effectiveness due to diminishing returns by establishing clear rules of working and identifying areas of work. We can also aim to make clear to the children in the class how the various adults will be operating.

There are limitless ways in which people's time and activity might be organized in the classroom. However, research has indicated that highly significant improvements in children's engagement may be achieved when a 'room management' system of classroom organization is employed as a basis for the structure of the activity of adults in the class.

Room Management

At the core of the room management lies the activity period, a specific period of time, usually of about an hour, when specific roles are allocated to the various people within the class. It suggests three separate roles are fulfilled: an individual helper; an activity manager; and a mover.

The individual helper(s) concentrates on taking individual children for short periods of teaching. Her work with those children will have been planned beforehand and she will work with a rota of children over the activity period.

The activity manager(s) looks after the work of the rest of the children in the class, who are typically arranged into groups, with the aim of keeping the children engaged on the task in hand. This aim is facilitated through the planned activity of the children, which should be on areas of the curriculum that have already been covered though not necessarily mastered; children will therefore to a greater or lesser degree be consolidating on material and should require little individual help from the activity manager. Such a pattern of work amongst most children will enable the activity manager to effect a series of rapid contacts with this large body. There is a large number of findings on the effective use of teacher attention in reducing inappropriate behaviour and increasing children's overall engagement. In line with suggestions from these, the activity manager aims to maximize her contacts with those children who are working appropriately while prompting with the minimum attention those who are not.

The mover aims to maintain flow in the class by relieving the activity manager and the individual helper from distraction. She will, for instance, deal with interruptions, move equipment and sharpen pencils.

Considering classroom dynamics and the learning needs of children who might be experiencing difficulty, we can see that this model has a number of attractions. In its method of providing individual help, it takes account of children's need for learning in short frequent doses. In its method of 'activity management' it says something about type of activity, both of children and adult, which will help if we are thinking primarily about the engagement of the group, and in the role of 'mover' we see someone who will be able to keep the flow going in a session.

There is room for wide adaptation of the system in such a way that the particular people participating in a class develop a unique solution to a unique set of circumstances. As children become more independent there is less need for the function of mover and some of her functions may be delegated to children within the group. If three people were available to work in, say, an upper junior classroom it may be possible to think of a configuration of two activity managers, each responsible for the work of certain groups, and one individual helper. Alternatively, those people may be arranged such that there are two individual helpers and one activity manager. The precise arrangement will depend on the needs of the class.

Development of the integrated day

Mary Brown and Norman Precious

This reading, written in 1968, captures the post-Plowden spirit (see Reading 7.6) which later worried so many policy-makers. The notion of 'the integrated day' was an important part of teacher thinking as the organizational means of enabling each child to realize their natural potential and to learn through activity and experience. As we have seen (Reading 9.2), there is very little evidence that it actually had a significant impact on practice.

However, the idea of integration remains important in the organizational repertoire of teachers. It can take a variety of forms involving space, time, subjects, teachers or classes. What forms of integration are used in your school?

Edited from: Brown, M. E. and Precious, G. N. (1968) *The Integrated Day in the Primary School.* London: Ward Lock Educational, 11–13

It is only just over 150 years ago that some seven-year-old children were working a sixteen-hour day and for some time after the Education Act of 1870, which introduced compulsory State education, the scope of the schools was very limited. Education based on mechanical proficiency, the obedience and passivity of the pupil and verbal instruction by the teacher was the general rule. Most teachers were instructors and ruled by fear. They were paid according to the number of attendances and the children's success in examination results. During the tragedy and chaos of the Second World War, evacuation brought to light the terrible poverty in certain areas and conscription revealed a great deal of illiteracy. Butler's 1944 Education Act was the result of the public outcry for the situation to be improved and this Act stressed that education should be made available to fit the requirements of each and every child and it should be an education suitable for his age, aptitude and ability.

Through educational, psychological and physiological research attention was gradually being drawn to the fact that learning is a result of both maturation and experience. The findings of Piaget, stressed the clearly defined sequential stages in the development of 'concepts' which are tied closely to each individual child's own experience and maturation level [see Reading 6.3]. As these thoughts filtered through to the teachers of young children, they began to look at the children as individuals and to doubt the validity of the teaching methods they were using. Many of them had already started experiments to find more suitable ways of encouraging individual learning. At first, the emphasis continued to be laid on the 'three Rs' and although the methods used were described as 'activity methods', their main and almost exclusive goal was to develop the child's academic ability. Today, educational philosophy asks for attention to be given to the complete development of the child as expressed by Edna Mellor in *Education through Experience in the Infant School Years*:

> My philosophy of education is concerned with the whole child – his physical, mental and spiritual growth; his feelings, attitudes and relationships; his character and personality. It is concerned with him as an individual having certain innate tendencies, potentialities and traits, and also with him as a member of society having certain rights and privileges, duties and responsibilities.

The word 'activity' was misunderstood by certain sections of society who thought of it purely in terms of physical activity and this misinterpretation sadly delayed progress in the use of the activity method. It was not until the activity of the mind and the emotions was included in the true definition that it was more widely adopted. The teacher's role as an instructor decreased and the activities widened to include all aspects of development. As the size of classes decreased, schools felt more able to experiment with new and progressive ideas. Experiments in non-streaming and vertical grouping were being carried out and it seemed that the right circumstances for the integrated day to develop were more naturally achieved in a class which was vertically grouped.

Architects' designs were influenced by the new ideas and there was a remarkable change in the planning of school buildings. They were planned as places where children could live and work together. There was more space and light in the schools and for the first time real concern that the child's environment should be aesthetically pleasing.

As the children worked in this new atmosphere, the teachers began to see the practical proof of the value of this new climate in education. They observed the child's excitement in discovery and learning and his willingness to persevere with even an arduous task if he were personally involved. The teachers were surprised by the natural creativity of the children when they were allowed freedom of expression. Subjects and interests soon became integrated quite naturally as children worked out their individual ideas. The school day was gradually being determined by the interests and needs of children and indeed becoming a facsimile of what we now term 'the integrated day'.

The integrated day could be described as a school day which is combined into a whole and has the minimum of timetabling. Within this day there is time and opportunity in a planned educative environment for the social, intellectual, emotional, physical and aesthetic growth of the child at his own rate of development. Our definition extends this day to encompass the whole life of the child during the six years of primary education.

The natural flow of activity, imagination, language, thought and learning which is in itself a continuous process is not interrupted by artificial breaks such as the conventional playtime or subject barriers. The child is encouraged to commit himself completely to the work in hand which he has chosen. The child also has the time to pursue something in depth even though it may take several days. As he works, problems common to various subjects will arise but within the integrated framework he can make easy transition between any areas of learning.

As the child works, he is involved with learning as an integrated unit coping perhaps with a foray into maths, science, geography, art or English in a short space of time, through the use of books, material and equipment which may lead him into various channels. Subject barriers are extraneous. No limit is set to the exploration involved, which may go off at any tangent into any sphere of learning.

Different subjects are also cemented by the free use of language. If we take for example any one term such as 'three dimensional', this is used in science, maths, English, construction or art and the child may have experience of and explore 3D within a framework where they are all interwoven and almost indistinguishable one from the other or as part of a differentiated subject.

In a school where the integrated day is in practice, the environment is all-important. It must be so well planned, challenging, interesting and attractive that the child wants to become involved with the materials, wants to satisfy his curiosity and to learn. The challenge of the environment must of course be within reach of the child and the provisions not be so complicated that they cause confusion. The day starts as soon as the child arrives. As he works with the material and people around him, his interest is aroused. He begins to think, reason and formulate his ideas in words. He becomes involved with deeper and wider learning. Each day there is opportunity for him to learn and communicate intellectually, physically and artistically in the medium of his choice. Each child will be able to work at his own rate and depth and usually for as long as he likes.

CHAPTER 10

How are we managing learning and coping with behaviour?

The nine readings in this chapter are concerned with the challenge of creating a positive learning environment and the particular issue of managing behaviour.

Doyle (Reading 10.1) analyses the complexity of classrooms and Galton and Holt (10.2 and 10.3) suggest how the tasks which children often experience can create uneasiness and boredom. Biott and Easen (10.4) have some positive suggestions on how to develop collaborative group work.

The next group of readings move the focus on to class management and discipline. Laslett and Smith (10.5) review four basic 'rules' for effective management and the reading by Kounin (10.6) draws on his classic research on the topic. Hargreaves and his colleagues (10.7) and Woods (10.8) draw attention to the ways in which teachers respond to pupils. They focus on the importance of attempting to calm incidents, to understand pupil circumstances and to adapt teaching methods or forms of school organization in response to pupil needs.

Reading 10.9, from the Elton Committee Report, 'Discipline in Schools', provides an overview of the many factors which influence this essential pre-condition for effective learning.

The parallel chapter of *Reflective Teaching in the Primary School* addresses key management skills and strategies for managing common classroom episodes. It also reviews the coping strategies which are commonly used by teachers and pupils and provides an overview of discipline, drawing on the Elton Report.

There are many suggestions for further reading.

📖 READING 10.1

Learning the classroom environment

Walter Doyle

This reading from Doyle highlights some of the reasons why classroom teaching is so difficult to do well, and gives some useful pointers to making it easier. In his view, classroom environments are highly complex and events often unfold simultaneously in ways which cannot be foreseen. Doyle believes that teachers develop strategies and skills for reducing some of this complexity, and he identifies five ways in which this is done.

Does your classroom sometimes feel complex in the ways which Doyle describes? How helpful are the skills which he suggests?

Readings 10.5 and 10.6 are also particularly relevant to these issues.

Edited from: Doyle, W. (1977) Learning the classroom environment: an ecological analysis, *Journal of Teacher Education*, 28 (6), 51–4

Deliberation about the nature of teaching skills has generally centred on the teacher's ability to manage subject matter – to explain content, formulate questions, and react to student answers. Naturalistic studies of classrooms suggest, however, that knowing how to manage subject matter sequences represents only a small part of the skill necessary to be a teacher.

Salient features of classrooms

The most salient features of the classroom for the student teachers in my study were multidimensionality, simultaneity and unpredictability. The following brief discussion of these categories will clarify the nature of environmental demands in classrooms.

Classrooms were multidimensional in the sense that they served a variety of purposes and contained a variety of events and processes, not all of which were necessarily related or even compatible. In classrooms, student teachers confronted groups with a wide range of interests and abilities as well as a diversity of goals and patterns of behaviour. In addition, they faced a multiplicity of tasks that included such matters as processing subject matter information, judging student abilities, managing classroom groups, coping with emotional responses to events and behaviours, and establishing procedures for routine and special assignment, distribution of resources and supplies, record keeping, etc. These tasks also interacted in the sense that ways of dealing with one dimension (e.g., distributing resources and supplies) had consequences for other dimensions (e.g., managing classroom groups) and in the sense that procedures at one point established a precedent that restricted options at a later time It was not uncommon to find student teachers initially over-whelmed to some degree by the sheer quantity of activities, many of which were seen to interfere with their primary interest in managing subject matter.

In addition to the quantity of dimensions in classrooms, many events occurred simultaneously. In a discussion, for instance, teachers needed to attend to the pace of the interaction, the sequence of student responses, fairness in selecting students to answer, the quality of individual answers and their relevance to the purposes of the discussion, and the logic and accuracy of content while at the same time monitoring a wide range of work involvement levels and anticipating interruptions. While giving assistance to individual students, teachers also had to remember to scan the rest of the class for signs of possible misbehaviour or to acknowledge other students who were requesting assistance. Examples such as these can be easily multiplied for nearly any set of classroom activities.

The simultaneous occurrence of multiple events, together with the continuous possibility of internal and external interruptions, contributed to an unpredictability in the sequence of classroom events, especially for student teachers who had not yet learned to anticipate consequences. Student teachers often found it difficult to predict student reactions to a set of materials or to judge how much time it would take to complete an activity. They were also frequently frustrated by changes in the normal schedule, breakdowns in equipment, and interruptions. The fact that classrooms can go in many different directions at any given point in time often complicated the task of enacting lesson plans in intended ways.

Strategies and skills for reducing complexity

Analysis of induction sequences indicated that all teachers developed strategies that could be interpreted as attempts to reduce the complexity of the classroom environment. There appeared to be considerable variations, however, in the success of different strategies.

In cases labelled 'unsuccessful', student teachers appeared to attempt to reduce classroom complexity by ignoring the multiplicity and simultaneity of the environment. In many instances, this method of reducing complexity involved (a) localizing attention to one region of the classroom; and (b) being engrossed in one activity at a time.

Successful strategies tended to be more congruent with the multiplicity and simultaneity of the environment. A preliminary attempt to codify these skills produced the following categories:

Chunking, or the ability to group discrete events into large units;

Differentiation, or the ability to discriminate among units in terms of their immediate and long-term significance;

Overlap, or the ability to handle two or more events at once (Kounin, 1970 [Reading 10.6]);

Timing, or the ability to monitor and control the duration of events; and

Rapid judgement, or the ability to interpret events with a minimum of delay.

Discussions with co-operating teachers during the three-year course of the present research suggested that these categories represent a part of the tacit knowledge experienced teachers have about the way classrooms work.

The first two skills, chunking and differentiation, suggest that student teachers undergo a concept formation process during which they learn to classify and interpret classroom events and processes in ways that are relevant to the demands created by multidimensionality, simultaneity, and unpredictability. In describing pupils, for instance, successful student teachers tended to classify individuals in terms of their potential for disruption, skills in classroom tasks, inclinations to participate in lesson activities, etc. They seemed to know that the movement of some students around the room to secure supplies or sharpen pencils could be ignored whereas the movement of other students required careful monitoring. Similarly, successful teachers learned to judge content in terms of how students would react to it and how difficult it would be to implement in the classroom, in contrast to those who retained purely academic criteria for content adequacy. In sum, successful student teachers transformed the complexity of the environment into a conceptual system that enabled them to interpret discrete events and anticipate the direction and flow of classroom activity. In addition they learned to make rapid judgements about the meaning and consequences of events and to act decisively.

The skills of overlap and timing supplement the interpretive strategies of chunking, differentiation, and rapid judgement in ways that enable successful student teachers to regulate classroom demands to some degree. The need for overlap was a continuing condition in classrooms. Successful teachers were able to divide attention between several simultaneous dimensions of classroom activity structures. They were also easily distracted by changes in sound or movement in the classroom. Hence they were in a position to react to developing circumstances as necessary. During the course of the observations, timing also emerged as an especially salient skill for managing classroom demands, one that operated on several levels. It was apparent, for example, that timing was related to the effectiveness of directives to individual students (e.g., 'Stop talking and get back to work!'). Successful managers tended to pause and continue to gaze at the target student for a brief period after issuing such a directive. The target student typically returned to work immediately after receiving the directive, but looked up again in one or two seconds. If the teacher was still monitoring the student, there was a greater likelihood that the directive would be followed. Unsuccessful managers, on the other hand, tended to issue directives and continue on as if compliance had been achieved. Over time, this latter pattern seemed to result in directives being ignored and, therefore, reappeared more frequently with less effect.

 READING 10.2

Ambiguity and learning

Maurice Galton

> This reading focuses on the ways in which pupils perceive the tasks which are set for them. Research has shown that children are often unaware of teachers' academic intentions and are often very conscious of behavioural expectations. These factors tend to produce a sense of ambiguity and uncertainty combined with a weak sense of ownership and low involvement in the learning activity.
>
> Maurice Galton illustrates this theory and uses it to explain why 'progressive practice' never really developed in schools. However, the issues are even more far-reaching: how can children be encouraged to engage fully with their learning?
>
> Edited from: Galton, M. (1987) *Teaching in the Primary School*. London: David Fulton, 136–9

The final explanation for the failure fully to implement progressive or informal practice can be termed the 'ambiguity' theory. A crucial stage of this concerns the setting or negotiating of new tasks and activities. As Doyle (1979, 1986) points out, when setting tasks in the classroom teachers have in mind a variety of purposes, based partly on their perception of the needs of individual children. The more complex the task, the greater the possible range of purposes and therefore the greater the ambiguity, with the risk that the child will misinterpret the teacher's intention. For example, in a recent observation of creative writing, a teacher encouraged the children to draft and redraft stories using the approach recommended by Graves (1983). When the stories were finally completed the children were allowed to use the word processor to produce a final version for inclusion in a book of stories. Seen from the pupils' eyes, the teacher displayed a remarkable degree of inconsistency. Some children, having produced pages of writing, were made to redraft it further, while others who produced six lines were allowed to use the computer. The teacher was able in each case to justify these decisions in terms of the pupils' special needs. One child who had written several pages was at a stage where the teacher felt 'she needed to develop her ideas further, they were becoming stereotyped', while the child who wrote six lines 'had concentrated well, which was unusual for him and had also worked well with the other children in his group'. The children, however, were not party to these deliberations. When asked by the observer how they knew when their work was ready to be published, they replied 'we take it to the teacher and he tells us'.

There is considerable evidence that tasks, such as story writing, do indeed appear to be carried out more successfully if the children can feel that they have ownership over their ideas

(Cowie, 1989). However, in taking on this ownership, children have to accept the risk of having their ideas evaluated critically. This risk can be reduced if the child has some idea of the criteria being used for this evaluation. During the 'Effective Group Work in the Primary Classroom' project it was very noticeable how repeatedly children complained about not understanding why teachers made certain decisions. As one pupil put it:

> If I could see what it was learning me I could do it but I don't see what it's learning me. I am not really bothered because I want to know what it's learning me. One teacher, Miss Preston, did say that if you don't like what we are giving you come and tell us about it but I think lots of people are frightened to do that.

Teachers would emphasize the importance of the processes rather than the product of the learning, but rarely tried to explain to children why they were being asked to do certain activities at times when there was a need to direct the learning or to introduce a new topic. Indeed some teachers made a point of saying that they thought that 'children of this age don't need to understand why they do things'. In one example children were investigating various ways of measuring time, using an assortment of materials such as sand, water and plastic bottles. Both teachers under observation began by emphasizing the importance of time and gave very precise instructions about how the children were to proceed with the task and how they were not to worry too much about results because what mattered was their ideas. As the children began to assemble the apparatus, it was noticeable that almost every pupil had on their wrist a cheap digital watch; to some of them, at least, it must have seemed strange that they should need to engage in an attempt to measure time in a variety of crude ways when a more accurate method was immediately to hand. With hindsight it would have been relatively easy for the teacher to explain that the main purpose of the exercise was not to measure time but to provide a problem-solving exercise where certain science skills could be developed. However, in the earlier example of developing children's writing skills through publishing, it would have been less easy for the teacher to explain the reasons for what appeared to be unfair treatment of some children as compared to others, without embarrassing the child who was allowed to publish only six lines. None the less, the pupils have eventually to face up to their limitations. The pupil who was allowed to publish six lines told the observer:

> When we have finished we have to read each other's stories. I watch what the others are reading but no-one reads mine.

An even greater ambiguity in setting classroom tasks stems from the fact, as Doyle (1983) points out, that tasks have not only an academic content but also a behavioural purpose. The teacher's main purpose during a question and answer session may be to tease out the children's ideas so that the lesson may be shaped in terms of the pupils' concerns rather than the teacher's. At any one time a question may also be used to see if a child is paying attention. The pupil therefore has to work out what kind of question they are being asked. Is it the kind where a speculative answer will be praised or where a wrong answer will be seized upon as evidence of inattention? This sort of dilemma offers another excuse for pupils to adopt a strategy of avoidance – they leave someone else to make the initial responses until the purpose behind the teacher's questions becomes clear. Similarly, when writing it may not always be clear to the pupil what the difference is between redrafting and being made to do corrections.

Rowland (1987 [see Reading 6.11]) argues that in negotiating ownership with children one removes the need to exercise authoritarian control over behaviour. Nias (1988) is more cautious and admits uncertainty about the causality of this process. It may be, therefore, that the form of the control exercised over the pupils' behaviour by the teacher largely determines whether pupils perceive the teacher's interventions as collaboration or as a 'take-over'. Thus when children regard control of the classroom organization and of their behaviour as primarily the teacher's responsibility, then, because they are unable to distinguish easily between the teacher's role as 'policeman' and as 'negotiator', they play safe and seek to hand back responsibility for the learning to the teacher.

READING 10.3

Learning to be 'stupid'?

John Holt

John Holt's writing has a direct and challenging style which is, at the same time, grounded and empathic. In this reading he proposes that many children 'learn to be stupid' in schools, because of what he believes to be the routinized and 'boring' nature of much of their experience. This reading is thus about the relationship between children's motivation and the ways in which learning tasks are presented and managed. It is closely connected to the previous reading (10.2).

How can classrooms and tasks be managed in ways which tap children's interests and enthusiasms, whilst still satisfying the requirements of curriculum plans?

Edited from: Holt, J. (1982) *How Children Fail*. London: Penguin, 262–5

Children are subject peoples. School for them is a kind of jail. Do they not, to some extent, escape and frustrate the relentless, insatiable pressure of their elders by withdrawing the most intelligent and creative parts of their minds from the scene? The stubborn and dogged 'I don't get it' with which they meet their teachers – may it not be a statement of resistance as well as one of panic and flight?

To a very great degree, school is a place where children learn to be stupid. A dismal thought, but hard to escape. Infants are not stupid. Children of one, two, or even three throw the whole of themselves into everything they do. They embrace life, and devour it; it is why they learn so fast and are such good company. Listlessness, boredom, apathy – these all come later. Children come to school curious; within a few years most of that curiosity is dead, or at least silent. Open a first or third grade to questions, and you will be deluged; fifth-graders say nothing. They either have no questions or will not ask them. They think, 'What's this leading up to? What's the catch?' Curiosity, questions, speculation – these are for outside school not inside.

Boredom and resistance may cause as much stupidity in school as fear. Give a child the kind of task he gets in school, and whether he is afraid of it, or resists it, or is willing to do it but bored by it, he will do the task with only a small part of his attention, energy, and intelligence. In a word, he will do it stupidly – even if correctly. This soon becomes a habit. He gets used to working at lower power, he develops strategies to enable him to get by this way. In time he even starts to think of himself as being stupid, which is what most fifth-graders think of themselves, and to think that his low-power way of coping with school is the only possible way.

It does no good to tell such students to pay attention and think about what they are doing. I can see myself now, in one of my ninth-grade algebra classes in Colorado, looking at one of my flunking students, a boy who had become frozen in his school stupidity, and saying to him in a loud voice, 'Think! Think! Think!' Wasted breath; he had forgotten how. The stupid way – timid, unimaginative, defensive, evasive – in which he met and dealt with the problems of algebra were, by that time, the only way he knew of dealing with them. His strategies and expectations were fixed. He couldn't even imagine any others. He really was doing his dreadful best.

The attention of children must be lured, caught, and held, like a shy wild animal that must be coaxed with bait to come close. If the situations, the materials, the problems before a child do not interest him, his attention will slip off to what does interest him, and no amount of exhortation or threats will bring it back.

A child is most intelligent when the reality before him arouses in him a high degree of attention, interest, concentration, involvement – in short, when he cares most about what he is doing. This is why we should make schoolrooms and schoolwork as interesting and exciting as possible, not just so that school will be a pleasant place, but so that children in school will act intelligently and get into the habit of acting intelligently. The case against boredom in school is the same as the case against fear; it makes children behave stupidly.

 READING 10.4

Promoting collaborative learning

Colin Biott and Patrick Easen

> Biott and Easen have analysed some key issues which must be faced in promoting collaborative learning. They highlight the risk-taking which is involved as the 'self' and capabilities of each child become exposed within the group. Thus the power relationships and the collective sense of meaning held by the children are vital to the success of collaborative group activity. The teacher can help in two ways: by creating favourable conditions, and by fostering appropriate skills.
>
> Collaborative learning has been strongly advocated as a practical means of implementing social constructivist ideas (Readings 6.4 and 6.5) in classroom situations, and yet it is not easy to implement. Could you develop collaborative group work in your classroom using Biott and Easen's practical suggestions?
>
> Edited from: Biott, C. and Easen, P. (1994) *Collaborative Learning in Staffrooms and Classrooms.* London: David Fulton, 203–9

Collaborative learning is essentially about the development of the self in a social context. This implies that collaborative learning has both personal and contextual features which are closely interwoven. Through working and learning together, both children and teachers develop a sense of who they are and what they can or cannot do. They learn about their own and each others' strengths and weaknesses as they are revealed in particular circumstances and contexts. For this reason, acts of collaboration may be perceived as involving various degrees of anxiety and risk for those involved.

The meaning of the collaborative activity for those involved, then, is crucial and it is important for participants in a collaborative activity to retain a feeling of control. Activities perceived as having 'performance goals' and as being 'challenging', therefore, may be seen as presenting a high degree of risk to the self. The same activities, of course, may be perceived quite differently by another participant.

The concepts of 'power' and 'meaning' are inseparable in collaborative learning. There are times when having the strategies and skills to create these meanings through collaboration are insufficient without the strategies and skills to handle any power issues that may arise during it. Hence our emphasis on trying to understand the place of conflict in collaborative relationships.

There are two main ways in which a teacher may encourage the development of collaborative learning. These are concerned with: creating favourable conditions; and teaching, encouraging and fostering skills.

Creating favourable conditions for collaborative learning

There is more to improving collaborative learning than organizing children into groups and setting certain tasks. In addition, it is necessary to create favourable classroom conditions, so that children value working together and have opportunities to give and experience help, support and challenge in their relationships with each other. Teachers who create these conditions:

Offer opportunities for children to learn social competences in situations where they can make, and act upon, shared understandings of how to be both co-operative with others and assertive for themselves. The teachers convey, to the children, that collaboration may be unstable and unpredictable, that it is not based simply upon obedience and compliance and that conflict and disagreements can be constructive. The children learn that working with others can be both enabling and constraining.

Provide a wide range of paired and group activities and also encourage children to consider working with a partner on some occasions when they are completing the same individual tasks so that they can compare and talk about what they are doing.

Expect that all children will be able to contribute, in different ways, to the quality of activities, and they do not stress leadership in ways which give status to superior knowledge or bossiness.

Spend time listening to children when they are working collaboratively and give children time both to find ways to work together and to develop ideas.

Model a collaborative approach in their interactions with children. They listen and discuss disagreements, interpret some conflicts and difficulties in children's relationships in positive ways, and do not expect everyone to be able to get everything right first time. They spend some time wondering about things with children, seeking alternatives and showing themselves to be uncertain, rather than always being concerned about knowing answers and being correct.

Organize space, time and resources to allow some flexibility for some parts of each day. They provide a variety of possibilities for different kinds of purposeful activities in specific parts of the room.

Do not rely solely on impressions of surface behaviour and snatches of overheard conversations when judging whether, or how well, children are learning collaboratively.

Work, through systematic enquiry, towards understanding the most favourable ways to group children, when setting formal group assignments, taking into account sex, gender, racial and ability differences. They experiment to find helpful ways to prepare their children for collaboration; they think about different ways to start a group activity and how to participate once a group has started its work. Most importantly, they review how their approach affects children's sense of control over what they are doing and how learning ensues.

Teaching, encouraging and fostering skills of collaborative learning

How children learn to work together, and what they learn about doing it, can be haphazard, fragmented, inconsistent, ambiguous and sometimes contradictory. Children's capacity to work well with other children may not necessarily match their attainment in other fields. We have seen evidence of poor collaborative skills and strategies from children who are adept at private, individual work, and been surprised by the exceptional capabilities of some who have been much less accomplished in written work.

Helpful teachers:

Make their expectations about working together clear to the children and teach them how to collaborate.

Give consistent feedback which embraces emergent as well as imposed collaboration. Feedback of this nature is concrete and focused, seeking also to explore children's perceptions of what is going on, rather than being judgemental. This helps children to understand processes of collaborative work so that they are not put off by challenge and disagreements and learn to develop strategies and skills to handle conflict constructively. Feedback, then, helps to maintain and enhance the collective as well as individual self-esteem of children.

Take action if they notice that a child is vulnerable to domination or rejection by other children, intervening in a way which has positive effects upon the child's social identity and enhances future relationships.

Encourage children to make contributions to collaborative activities by showing them how to listen, question and respond. They teach helping skills and techniques such as peer tutoring, including how to record what their partners like to do and how they learn best. They model, through their own actions, and teach, that some questions will be more helpful than others when children are responding to other children's ideas.

Many of the ideas embodied above may have as much relevance to the staffroom as they do to the classroom. Collaboration is multi-layered and pervasive, and learning may be carried over from one area of a teacher's professional life to another.

 READING 10.5

Four rules of class management

Robert Laslett and Colin Smith

The voice of experience speaks clearly through the apparently simple injunctions contained in this reading – 'get them in'; 'get them out'; 'get on with it' and 'get on with them'. In their discusssions of these topics Robert Laslett and Colin Smith succeed in highlighting the key practical issues in classroom management in a very accessible way. Although initially written in relation to secondary school context, their advice remains valuable in relation to many primary school classrooms.

How do you cope with the four rules of class management?

Edited from: Laslett, R. and Smith, C. (1984) *Effective Classroom Management: A Teacher's Guide*. London: Croom Helm, 1–10

The skills of successful classroom management can be reduced to 'four rules', attention to which should enable all teachers to improve efficiency and harmony in their classrooms.

Rule one: get them in

The first rule requires attention to planning the start of each lesson. The process of beginning a lesson smoothly and promptly involves greeting, seating and starting.

Greeting Simply by being present before the class arrives, the teacher establishes his role as host, receiving the class on his territory and, by implication, on his terms (Marland, 1975). Apart from the vital practical advantage of being able to check that the room is tidy, materials are available, displays are arranged and necessary instructions or examples are written on the blackboard, being there first allows the teacher to quietly underline his authority by deciding when the class comes into the room.

Seating Just how seating is arranged must depend on the type of lesson to be taught, and the type of classroom furniture. Whether using traditional serried ranks of desks or less formal group tables, each teacher needs to establish who sits where.

Starting Every lesson should start with some activity that keeps each child quietly occupied in his own place. What type of activity depends very much on the age and ability of the child and the nature of the lesson. Ideally, the work should involve reinforcement of previously acquired skills, particularly those required for the lesson which is about to be taught. Establishing a routine will require setting specific tasks and providing detailed verbal and written instruction. Having settled the class to work in this way, the temptation to leave them at it must be avoided.

Rule two: get them out

However, before considering the content of the lesson, the second rule which needs to be mastered is how to conclude the lesson and dismiss the class. If this seems a strange order of priorities, it is worth remembering that if most disciplinary problems arise from a poor start to the lesson, hard-won control is most frequently lost and learning wasted at the end of lessons.

Concluding Learning that has taken place during a lesson can often be wasted if an opportunity is not taken to reinforce what has been taught by a summary and brief question session. It is no use trying to do that over the heads of children who are still working or who are busy collecting exercise books. So at three minutes before the presumed end of the lesson, 'as precisely as that' (Marland, 1975), or at whatever time is judged necessary, work should stop, leaving an opportunity for the collection of materials, putting books away and some revision and recapitulation of the lesson.

Dismissing Once the bell does go, there is need for an established, orderly routine which ensures that the class gets beyond the door without the teacher having to spend time clearing debris from the floor or readjusting the lines of desks. If this can be done without recourse to sending out one section or row at a time, such informality is welcome. Traditional verbal prompting, 'arms folded, sitting up straight', may still have its place, however.

It is also important to remember that classes are never just leaving one place, they are going on to another. Children need to be cued in to their next activity.

Rule three: get on with it

'It' refers to the lesson itself – its content, manner and organization. Momentum is the key to determining the content of a lesson, its variety and pace.

Content Variety is needed within a lesson to maintain interest, curiosity and motivation. Activities planned for the start and finish, as suggested above, will go some way towards achieving these aims. However, there is also a need to plan for some variety within the main body of the lesson. Alternating preferred activities with more boring ones, mixing familiar work with new learning, and balancing quiet individual work with more active group tasks can all help keep a lesson moving (Sloane, 1976). It is essential, however, that variety should not become confusion. Each activity should be clearly specified and the teacher's expectations clarified so that each child knows what he should be doing and when he should be doing it.

Pace is also helped by breaking up a topic into several smaller units of learning. It can also help to have as a target the intention that every child should have something finished, something marked in every lesson. Though often unattainable, such an aim does direct attention to the importance of immediate feedback and reinforcement in helping children to learn (Stott, 1978).

The momentum or flow of classroom industry is of great importance to discipline, as interruptions lead to loss of energy and interest on the part of pupils and teachers (Tanner, 1978; Rutter *et al.*, 1979).

Manner Classroom atmosphere is a term frequently used, but rarely analysed. Here again, however, what might at first be thought to result from 'personality' can be described as a series of skills. Similarly, positive interaction between teacher and class can be traced to the way in which they communicate with each other. The skills involved in creating a good classroom atmosphere are really a series of mechanisms to regulate what goes on in the classroom.

Behaviour does seem to be better and atmosphere brighter where ample praise is used in teaching (Hopkins and Conrad, 1976). Praise needs to be natural and sincere and should never become dull and routine. It is a good idea to try to think of at least six synonyms for 'good' and to use them appropriately. 'Great', 'superb', 'fine', 'splendid', 'remarkable' are some examples, or use more colloquial expressions such as 'ace', 'knockout' or 'cracker', if they come naturally. Similarly, 'nice' is a word so often used, when children would surely be more stimulated to know that their work was 'delightful', 'imaginative', 'beautiful', 'interesting', 'original' or 'fascinating'.

The way the teacher talks to the class reflects his attitude to them not only in what is said, but how it is said. Facial expression and tone of voice are as important to communication as making sure that attention is gained, by getting the class to stop work and listen carefully to what has to be said. It follows that what has to be said should be clear, simple and important enough to merit stopping the lesson.

The old adage, 'quiet teacher, quiet class' contains good advice, but should be followed with some reservation; 'inaudible teacher, insufferable class' may also be true. Adequate volume is an essential to being understood and it may help if teachers assume that in any class there is very likely to be at least one child with some hearing loss.

Emphasizing the importance of using your eyes to communicate, is recommended by Marland (1975). Two or three sentences on a theme should be addressed to one child in one part of the room. As another idea is developed, the teacher shifts his gaze to another child in another part of the room, then focuses on a third for the next theme. This approach should help develop a 'feel' for what is going on in the different areas of the classroom. This is how to develop the traditional teacher's eyes in the back of the head.

Organization In any given subject, every class is a mixed-ability group. Whether dealing with high flyers or low achievers, teachers must allow for the fact that some children will work more rapidly and accurately than others. On the way to the ideal if individualizing educational programmes for all their pupils, teachers can start by splitting their class into groups. The amount and difficulty of work demanded from each group can then be related to their abilities in that particular subject. There are three ways of doing this – by rota, quota or branching.

Rota, as in rotation of crops, refers to groups moving round the classroom from one activity to another. The development of learning centres is essential to this approach. These are areas of the classroom using alcoves, bookshelves or simply tables arranged to provide an environment for the accomplishment of a particular instructional purpose (Lemlech, 1979). They can be used for the practice of particular skills, gathering further information, extending experience or for instructional recreation.

Quota, similarly requires the teacher to work out an appropriate amount of work to be completed during a session by each group. Each child has an assignment card or booklet, which becomes a record of work completed as it is checked by the teacher. This system can be simply an extension of the rota system with individual requirements, such as reading to the teacher, handwriting or spelling practice being added.

Branching, involves starting all the class together on a particular activity, doing an exercise from the board or working together from a textbook, then, as this is completed, 'branching' groups into different activities or areas of the room. For the quicker workers, who are likely to finish the common activity first, there may need to be a number of further pieces of work.

Rule four: get on with them

The temptation to misbehave is lessened where teachers and children get on well together. Many of the points already mentioned will help build a good pupil–teacher relationship, based on skilful, confident teaching geared to children's specific needs (Wallace and Kauffman, 1978). To further develop mutual trust and respect, the teacher also needs to show an awareness of each child as an individual and a sensitivity to the mood of the class as a whole. The teacher needs to know who's who and what's going on.

Who's who? Once a child's name is known, discipline is immediately easier because requests or rebukes can be made more personal. Recognition also implies interest on the part of the teacher. It is easy to learn the names of the best and worst children, but less easy to remember those who do not attract attention to themselves. The attention is needed just at much, and sometimes more.

A daily chat, however brief, about something not connected with lessons can be a source of insight as well as a way of establishing rapport. It might be said that a chat a day, keeps trouble at bay! As with praise, personal interest must be natural and genuine, not merely assumed.

What's going on? Few classes of children are likely to be so purposefully malevolent as to set out on a planned campaign of disruption. Group misbehaviour is more likely to build up from a series of minor incidents. It is necessary therefore for teachers to acquire a sensitivity to group responses. The key to developing this talent lies in a combination of monitoring, marking and mobility (Brophy and Evertson, 1976).

Frequently scanning the class, even while helping one individual, should enable the teacher to spot the first signs of trouble quickly and intervene firmly but quietly. Often, merely moving to the area from which louder voices are indicating some distraction can refocus attention on the work in hand. The mild personal rebuke addressed to an individual can be far more productive than a formal public warning.

Marking work in progress is not only a good way of giving immediate feedback, it is also a natural form of contact. Rather than reprimanding the child who is not concentrating on his work, offering help and advice may be the best way to return his attention to the task in hand.

Mobility is needed to avoid teachers becoming desk-bound by queues waiting for attention, which can screen inactivity elsewhere in the classroom and themselves become social gatherings and a potential source of noise and distraction. It is essential to develop a routine, which enables children to find help from each other if the teacher is occupied, or which provides them with alternative purposeful activities while waiting for advice or correction. This will free the teacher to move around the room, sharing his time and interest, adding all the time to his awareness of personalities and problems.

It is this combination of activities that enables the responsive teacher to judge correctly the times for serious endeavour or light-hearted amusement.

READING 10.6

Discipline and group management in classrooms

Jacob Kounin

Kounin's book on group management is a classic text which has been of enormous influence in the analysis of classroom management. Based on careful study of videotapes of US classrooms, Kounin's insights are well grounded in observation of teacher actions and pupil response. Amongst the attractions of the work are the amusing names which Kounin gave to some of the patterns which he identified: When did you last do a 'dangle', or subject your class to a 'slowdown'? Do not be deceived or put off by the language of this reading, for it has immensely practical implications. The term 'recitation' describes a whole-class, teacher-directed teaching session.

Edited from: Kounin, J. (1970) *Discipline and Group Management in Classrooms.* New York: Holt, Rinehart & Winston, iv, 74–101

The planned and unplanned realities of a classroom necessitate a teacher having skills that go beyond curricular planning and managing individual children. These skills pertain to group management – to what a teacher plans and does in a classroom that is aimed at more than one child and that affects more than one child.

An analysis of real classrooms reveals that there are concrete techniques of managing classrooms that relate to the amount of work involvement and misbehaviour in learning situations. Study of videotapes showed that there were specific categories of teachers' behaviour that correlated with their managerial success as measured by pupil work involvement, deviancy rate, contagion of misbehaviour, and effectiveness of desists. Some of the dimensions of teachers' behaviours that made a difference in the behaviour of pupils were, as we termed them: withitness (demonstrating that she knew what was going on); overlapping (attending to two issues simultaneously); transition smoothness (absence of jerkiness and slowdowns); and maintaining group-focus.

Withitness

Withitness was defined as a teacher's communicating to the children by her actual behaviour that she knows what the children are doing, or has the proverbial 'eyes in the back of her head'. What kinds of teacher behaviours, and in what circumstances, provide cues to pupils as to whether the teacher does or does not know what is going on? It is not adequate to measure what a teacher knows in order to obtain a score for the degree of her withitness. It is necessary to measure what she communicates she knows. The children, after all, must get the information that she knows or doesn't know what they are doing.

Desist events are examples of incidents where a teacher does something that communicates to the children whether she does or doesn't know what is happening. In desist events a child is doing something and the teacher does something about it. Does she pick the correct target and does she do it on time? Or, does she make some kind of mistake that communicates the information that she doesn't know what is happening?

Overlapping

Overlapping refers to what the teacher does when she has two matters to deal with at the same time. Does she somehow attend to both issues simultaneously or does she remain or become immersed in one issue only to the neglect of the other? These kinds of 'overlapping' issues occur in both desist events and in child intrusion events.

An overlapping issue is present at the time of a desist event when the teacher is occupied with an ongoing task with children at the time that she desists a deviancy. Thus, if she is in a recitation setting with a reading group and she notes and acts upon a deviancy occurring in the seatwork setting, she is in an overlapping situation.

Considering the results of both Videotape Studies, one may conclude that both the withitness and the overlapping of teachers have a significant bearing upon their managerial success but that the effects of withitness are greater than the effects of overlapping. Throughout, the correlations of withitness with both work involvement and freedom from deviancy scores are higher than the correlations between teachers' overlapping scores and children's behaviour. Both Videotape Studies, however, show that overlapping and withitness are significantly related to each other. To reiterate, teachers who show signs of attending to more than one issue when there is more than one issue to handle at a particular time, are likely to pick correct deviancy targets and do something about the deviancy on time – before the deviancy becomes more serious or begins to spread to other children. On the other hand, teachers who become immersed in one issue only when there is more than one issue to handle, are more likely to act upon an incorrect deviancy target or act upon the deviancy too late – after the misbehaviour becomes more serious or spreads to other children. And handling the correct deviant on time is evidently more important than the method used in handling the deviancy.

How might one interpret the relationship between withitness or overlapping? One interpretation is that broadening one's scope of active attending, as manifest in overlapping, enables a teacher to receive more information about what is going on. This knowledge is necessary to achieve withitness. However, overlapping is not adequate unless it leads to some behaviour that communicates to the children. Children probably do not categorize an overlapping dimension or even perceive it. What they do see, categorize in some way, and react to, is what the teacher does. They do see her pick on the wrong person or do it too late, in which case they form a judgement, however, explicit or implicit, that she doesn't know what is going on. However if she acts promptly and on the correct deviant then they see her as having 'eyes in the back of her head'. And, if the children perceive her as knowing what is going on she is more likely to induce worklike behaviour and restrain deviancy than if they see her as not knowing what is going on. Thus, overlapping correlates to withitness (enables withitness to occur) but does not, in and of itself, relate to managerial success, whereas withitness does. Regardless of the type of theoretical linkage between overlapping and withitness, the reality of classrooms dictates that both relate to managerial success. Unless some other technique is available to obtain knowledge about what is going on except by attending, one can safely recommend that teachers engage in both manifest overlapping and demonstrated withitness.

Transition smoothness

A teacher in a self-contained classroom must manage considerable activity movement: she must initiate, sustain, and terminate many activities. Sometimes this involves having children move physically from one part of the room to another, as when a group must move from their own desks to the reading circle. At other times it involves some psychological movement, or some change in props, as when children change from doing arithmetic problems at their desks to studying spelling words at the same desks.

How do teachers go about initiating and maintaining activity-flow in a classroom? Are there sizeable differences among teachers in this respect, and if so, do these differences relate to differences in the amount of work-involvement or deviancy of children? Is it possible to delineate concrete behaviours of teachers that one can use to constitute measures of movement management? Or, must one resort to impressionistic judgements or ratings having to do with 'smoothness', 'jerkiness', 'dragginess', or 'really moving'? There are two major categories of movement mistakes. First are behaviours producing jerkiness. These are actions of teachers that interfere with the smoothness of the flow of activities. The second category of movement mistakes is of teacher behaviours producing slowdowns that impede the momentum of activities.

Jerkiness The categories associated with jerkiness in transitions are stimulus-boundedness, thrusts, dangles and flip-flops. Stimulus-boundedness may be contrasted with goal-directedness. Does the teacher maintain a focus upon an activity goal or is she easily deflected from it? In a stimulus-bound event, a teacher behaves as though she has no will of her own and reacts to some unplanned and irrelevant stimulus as an iron filing reacts to a magnet: she gets magnetized and lured into reacting to some minutia that pulls her out of the main activity stream. A thrust consists of a teacher's sudden 'bursting in' on the children's activities with an order, statement, or question in such a manner as to indicate that her own intent or desire was the only determinant of her timing and point of entry. That is, she evidenced no sign (pausing, looking around) of looking for, or of being sensitive to, the group's readiness to receive her message. A thrust has a clear element of suddenness as well as an absence of any observable sign of awareness or sensitivity to whether the target audience is in a state of readiness. A dangle was coded when a teacher started, or was in, some activity and then left it 'hanging in mid-air' by going off to some other activity. Following such a 'fade away' she would then resume the activity. For example: The teacher is engaged in checking the children's previous seatwork. Children are taking turns reading their answers to the arithmetic problems. The teacher said 'that's right' after Jimmy finished reading his answer to the third problem. She then looked around and said 'All right, Mary, read your answer to the fourth problem'. As Mary was getting up, the teacher looked around the room, and said, 'My now. Let's see. Suzanne isn't here, is she? Does anyone know why Suzanne is absent today?'. Flip-flops were coded only at transition points. A transition entails terminating one activity (put away spelling papers) and starting another (take out your workbooks and turn to page 190). In a flip-flop a teacher terminates one activity, starts another, and then initiates a return to the activity that she had terminated. An example: The teacher says, 'All right, let's everybody put away your spelling papers and take out your arithmetic books'. The children put their spelling papers in their desks, and, after most of the children had their arithmetic books out on their desks, the teacher asked, 'let's see the hands of the ones who got all their spelling words right'.

Slowdowns Slowdowns consisted of those behaviours initiated by teachers that clearly slowed down the rate of movement in a recitation activity. Slowdowns refer to movement properties that may or may not be smooth and unidirectional but which clearly impede or produce friction in the forward momentum of an activity. Their effect is to hold back and produce dragginess in the progress of an activity. Two major categories of slowdowns are overdwelling and fragmentation. Overdwelling was coded when the teacher dwelled on an issue and engaged in a stream of actions or talk that was clearly beyond what was necessary for most children's understanding or getting on with an activity. Overdwelling would produce a reaction on the part of most children of: 'All right, all right, that's enough already!'. Overdwelling could apply to either the behaviour of children or to the task. A fragmentation is a slowdown produced by a teacher's breaking down an activity into sub-parts when the activity could be performed as a single unit.

Movement management, including both smoothness and momentum is a significant dimension of classroom management. Within this dimension it is more important to maintain momentum by avoiding actions that slow down forward movement than it is to maintain smoothness by avoiding sudden starts and stops. And techniques of movement management are more significant in controlling deviancy than are techniques of deviancy management as such. In addition, techniques of movement management possess the additional value of promoting work involvement, especially in recitation settings.

Maintaining group focus

A classroom teacher is not a tutor working with one child at a time. Even though she may work with a single child at times, her main job is to work with a group of children in one room at one time. Sometimes the group is the entire class and sometimes it is a subgroup or subgroups (as when she is at the reading circle with one group while another subgroup or other subgroups are at seatwork). Given this partial job analysis, it may be fruitful to see what techniques teachers use in recitation sessions to maintain group focus.

Group alerting This refers to the degree to which a teacher attempts to involve children in the task, maintain their attention, and keep them 'on their toes' or alerted. Positive group alerting cues were:

any method used to create 'suspense' before calling on a child to recite: pausing and looking around to 'bring children in' before selecting a reciter, saying 'Let's see now, who can ...' before calling on a reciter;

keeping children in suspense in regard to who will be called on next; picking reciters 'randomly' so that no child knows whether he will be called on next or not;

teacher calls on different children frequently or maintains group focus: intersperses 'mass unison' responses; says, 'Let's put our thinking caps on; this might fool you'; asks group for show of hands before selecting a reciter;

teacher alerts non-performers that they might be called on in connection with what a reciter is doing; they may be called on if reciter makes a mistake; presignals children that they will be asked about recitation content in the immediate future;

teachers presents new, novel, or alluring material into a recitation (a high attention value prop or issue).

Negative group alerting cues were:

the teacher changes the focus of her attention away from the group and becomes completely immersed in the performance of the reciter; or directs a new question and subsequent attention to a single new reciter only, without any overt sign of awareness that there is a group;

the teacher prepicks a reciter or performer before the question is even stated;

the teacher has reciters perform in a predetermined sequence of turns.

Accountability Accountability refers to the degree to which the teacher holds the children accountable and responsible for their task performances during recitation sessions. This entails her doing something to get to know what the children are actually doing and to communicate to the children in some observable manner that she knows what they are doing. The degree to which she goes out to obtain this knowledge and to communicate it, is the degree to which she holds the children in the group accountable for their performances. The most usual means of securing information is for the teacher to require children to produce or demonstrate work that is being done in the current setting and to check these demonstrations. Thus, the following are the kinds of behaviours associated with accountability:

The teacher asks children to hold up their props exposing performances or answers in such a manner as to be readily visible to the teacher.

Teacher requires children to recite in unison while the teacher shows signs of actively attending to the recitation.

Teacher brings other children into the performance of a child reciting. (Teacher says: 'Jimmy, you watch Johnny do that problem and then tell me what he did right or wrong.')

Teacher asks for the raised hands of children who are prepared to demonstrate a performance and requires some of them to demonstrate.

Teacher circulates and checks products of non-reciters during a child performance.

Teacher requires a child to demonstrate and checks his performance.

Our findings show that teachers who maintain group focus by engaging in behaviours that keep children alerted and on their toes are more successful in inducing work involvement and preventing deviancy than are teachers who do not. This aspect of teacher style is more significant in recitation settings than in seatwork settings.

Satiation This important further issue is concerned with the nature of the activities programmed in the classrooms. What are the groups of children required to do – what is the teacher moving them into and out of? Does the nature of the classroom activity programme relate to work involvement and deviancy? Answers entail an analysis of the curriculum. Indeed, even within the same grades of the same school, teachers do vary in what they emphasize, in how they sequence the activities, and in what they do beyond the school's basic curricular commonalities.

Does a teacher do anything beyond the usual routine in a recitation session that would be likely to produce either a clear feeling of repetitiousness or a clear feeling of progress in an academic activity? In our research, the code for progress cues consisted of three categories. 'Routine' was coded when the teacher engaged in ordinary and usual kinds and amounts of behaviour relating to progress or repetition: She did nothing special to induce feelings of progress nor did she impose special repetitiousness during recitations. 'Positive cues' were noted whenever a teacher did something beyond the immediate call of duty to get a child or group to feel that they were making progress and accomplishing something in the activity. 'Negative cues' were coded whenever a teacher repeated an explanation or demonstration beyond what was necessary for clarity, or when she had a child or children repeat a performance when it was already correct.

Conclusion

It is possible to delineate concrete aspects of teacher behaviour that lead to managerial success in the classroom These techniques of classroom management apply to emotionally disturbed children in regular classrooms as well as to non-disturbed children. They apply to boys as well as to girls. They apply to the group and not merely to individual children. They are techniques of creating an effective classroom ecology and learning milieu. One might note that none of them necessitate punitiveness or restrictiveness.

This focus upon group management techniques in classrooms is intended to go beyond simplified slogans such as 'create rapport' or 'make it interesting'. Neither does this focus entail a pre-occupation with such characteristics as 'friendly', 'warm', 'patient', 'understanding', 'love for children', and similar attributes of people in general. These desirable attributes will not manage a classroom. Rather, the business of running a classroom is a complicated technology having to do with developing a non-satiating learning programme; programming for progress, challenge, and variety in learning activities; initiating and maintaining movement in classroom tasks with smoothness and momentum; coping with more than one event simultaneously; observing and emitting feedback for many different events; directing actions at appropriate targets; maintaining a focus upon a group; and doubtless other techniques not measured in these researches.

The master of classroom management skills should not be regarded as an end in itself. These techniques are, however, necessary tools. Techniques are enabling. The mastery of techniques enables one to do many different things. It makes choices possible. The possession of group management skills allows the teacher to accomplish her teaching goals – the absence of managerial skills acts as a barrier.

The focus upon group management skills is not opposed to a concern for individual children. The mastery of group management actually enables the teacher to programme for individual differences and to help individual children. If there is a climate of work involvement and freedom from deviancy, different groups of children may be doing different things, and the teacher is free to help individual children if she so chooses. One might say that a master of group management techniques enables a teacher to be free from concern about management.

📖 **READING 10.7**

Provocative and insulative teachers

David Hargreaves, Stephen Hestor and Frank Mellor

This is a relatively simple but very important reading which highlights the importance of the disposition and initial reaction of teachers in response to deviance by pupils. Thinking of classroom interaction as an ongoing process, Hargreaves and his colleagues suggest that, whatever a pupil's initial action, the response of the teacher may either exacerbate or calm the situation. It is suggested that these responses are characteristic of 'provocative' or 'insulative' teachers.

What is your initial reaction to a child's deviant act? And would your more considered reaction be any different?

Edited from: Hargreaves, D., Hestor, S. and Mellor, F. (1975) *Deviance in Classrooms*. London: Routledge, 260–2

The study of Jordan (1974) is an examination of the perspectives of a group of deviant boys and of their teachers. Jordan outlines two types of teachers which we might term as 'deviance-provocative' and 'deviance-insulative'. The first type of teacher finds that the deviant pupils behave in highly deviant ways in his classroom and his handling of them serves to exacerbate their deviance. The second type of teacher finds that the same pupils present relatively few problems in his classroom and his handling of them serves to inhibit their deviance.

The deviance-provocative teacher believes that the pupils he defines as deviant do not want to work in school and will do anything to avoid it. He thinks it is impossible to provide conditions under which they will work; if they are ever to work then the pupils must change. In disciplinary matters he sees his interaction with these pupils as a contest or battle – and one that he must win. He is unable to 'de-fuse' difficult situations; he frequently issues ultimatums and becomes involved in confrontations. He considers these pupils to be 'anti-authority' and is confident that they are determined not to conform to the classroom rules. The deviants are neglected in lessons and punished inconsistently, whereas overtly preferential treatment is accorded to the conformist pupils. He expects the pupils to behave badly and makes many negative evaluative comments upon them, both to them as well as to colleagues in the staffroom. The pupils are referred to a higher authority when they refuse to comply. The derogation of and laughing at pupils is common, and he is highly suspicious of them because his experience has shown that they cannot be trusted. He avoids contact with such pupils outside the classroom. The pupils are blamed for their misconduct. Since he believes the pupils are resistant, hostile and committed to their deviance, they are seen as potential saboteurs and he refuses to believe that any signs of improvement are authentic.

The deviance-insulative teacher believes that these pupils, like all pupils, really want to work. If the pupils do not work, the conditions are assumed to be at fault. He believes that these conditions can be changed and that it is his responsibility to initiate that change. In disciplinary matters he has a clear set of classroom rules which are made explicit to the pupils. He makes an effort to avoid any kind of favouritism or preferential or differential treatment; he also avoids confrontations with pupils. He rarely makes negative evaluative comments on pupils who misbehave. When he punishes deviant conduct, he allows the pupils to 'save face'. He does not derogate them in the classroom – or in the staffroom where he often springs to the defence of a deviant pupil who is being discussed. He is highly optimistic, in contrast with the fatalism of the deviance-provocative teacher, and confidently assumes that pupils will behave well and co-operate with him. He perceives all the pupils as potential contributors to the lesson and sees the unpredictability of the deviant pupils as a potential source of change.

He encourages any signs of improvement. Whereas the deviance-provocative teacher dislikes the deviant pupils and considers himself unfortunate in having to teach them, the deviance-insulative teacher claims to like all children and considers it a privilege to work with any pupil. He respects and cares about the deviant pupils and tells them so. He enjoys meeting them informally outside the classroom, where he can joke with them and take an interest in their personal problems. He trusts them.

The difference between the two types of teacher is not merely that one is more open to the possibility of type transformation than the other. That to the deviance-insulative teacher deviant pupils never become stabilized deviants in the first place is the outcome of a different common-sense knowledge of classroom deviance and a different set of wider assumptions about human nature and education – a different 'philosophy of life' and a different 'philosophy of education'.

READING 10.8

Pupil coping strategies and the myth of deficit

Peter Woods

Peter Woods has written extensively on how pupils cope with school life, and here he offers three summarizing themes: processes of negotiation, the influence of cultures, and the variation caused by pupils' individual interests. Above all, he argues that if learning is to be promoted, pupils need to be understood in terms of the social contexts in which they live and develop. Where such influences are not appreciated, deviant pupil behaviour may arise as a form of coping strategy, and Woods warns that attributing some form of 'deficit' to pupils is a common, but unjustified, response by teachers.

How would you characterize patterns of teacher response to pupil deviance in the schools in which you have worked?

Edited from: Woods, P. (1990) *The Happiest Days? How Pupils Cope with School*. London: Falmer Press, 141–3

Consideration of how pupils cope with school yields three broad themes:

pupils negotiate with teachers the basic rules of their classroom interaction. This may not always look like 'negotiations' as we know it, nor may the rules always be made evident. Both may reside deep within pupils' and teachers' understanding or subconscious;

pupils both contribute to and are influenced by cultures, of which some of the more prominent are social class, gender and race. Pupils do not analyse these in studied fashion: they live them, and interact with them. They are vitally important in formulating identities. There are many cultures which might be relevant to particular individuals – cultures based on age, on neighbourhoods, on activities, for example – which might cross-cut those above;

pupils have their own individual interests, which they will seek to promote in various ways, developing a range of strategies to cope with conflicting elements surrounding them.

Some of the most important influences operating on pupils are located outside the school and, some might argue, outside the school's control – in, for example, the social-class structure, in racism, in gender divisions that permeate society, or in the promotion and maintenance of a particular form of political and economic structure. The school does not exist in a vacuum but, most currently believe, it does have a certain measure of autonomy from the wider system. Some external influences and constraints also appear to be mediated by school organization and processes. How a school organizes its classes, distributes its resources among subjects, establishes its principles for counselling, and how its teachers actually relate to pupils – such matters can promote or modify the effects of external factors. This raises the question, then, of what implications the analysis here has for school policy and practice. The detail of this must be left to individual schools and teachers, for they have many other factors that have to be taken into consideration – national and LEA policy, assessment, parental pressure, teacher cultures, to name but a few. In general, however, putting oneself in the position of the pupils requires an examination not only of one's own practices but also of the beliefs and values upon which they are based. This cannot be done without a certain openness of mind and the cultivation of an ability to empathize with others, especially those who seem particularly oppositional. The extent to which racism, sexism and classism are imbued into some teachers' consciousness, beliefs and daily practices do not admit to easy and overnight solution. But 'taking the view of the other' has been shown to be an excellent basis for a start.

With such an approach teachers can extend the choices before others and before themselves. An authoritarian approach will interpret pupil behaviour from its own perspectives. If institutional rules are considered the only legitimate ones, contraventions of the rules will be considered deviant behaviour. The imposition of sanctions for the transgression of rules is one choice open to teachers, and in some circumstances it may be the correct one. However, in other circumstances it may be inappropriate, if the aim is to promote the conditions conducive to learning. It may encourage confrontation and rebellion. Something needs to be known, therefore, about the causes of the behaviour in question if the most productive response is to be achieved. Teachers are not unlike doctors in this respect – they must make a diagnosis in order to prescribe a remedy. Sometimes these diagnoses are straightforward, sometimes they are rather difficult; sometimes mistakes are made, perhaps because the more important symptoms are not apparent, or because similar symptoms can have vastly different causes.

Applying this analogy to pupil behaviour, the appropriate response can be worked out according to the interpretation of the cause. If, for example, it is due to 'sussing' or 'testing out', teachers might be prepared to 'negotiate', but from a position of firmness. If pupils are 'being nasty' or 'looking cool', teachers might examine their own conduct to find out how they might have given offence. If pupils are indulging in teacher-baiting or being rebellious, teachers might look for cultural associations and help them to understand them better. Schools might also consider how school organization and processes might aggravate, or indeed be the major cause of, that kind of behaviour. Teachers might be particularly alert to retreatist modes of pupil adaptation, common among girls, and consider how far such behaviour is produced by the school and other factors. Similarly, if black pupils appear to be at odds with teachers with regard to both academic achievement and behaviour, teachers again need to examine both their own practices and the school for contributory causes. If some pupils show highly variable behaviour, now conformist, now deviant, this is not necessarily the product of a schizophrenic personality, but a response to a variable situation where such a pupil's interests are only partially met by the institution.

All these examples are opposed to a rationale that interprets all pupil behaviour that deviates from some official norm in terms of a deficit model, that is that pupils are defective in some way, in terms of 'not having the right attitude', 'not having the appropriate mental faculties', 'lacking the right background', 'being insufficiently mature or motivated', 'being easily misled', being 'too quiet', or 'too noisy', and so on. Such a conception of the ideal pupil is much too narrow for the range of cultures and of individuals that populate school. Transforming the site of interpretation to within those cultures and individuals might lead to discovery of storehouses of learning resource and eliminate the myth of deficit.

📖 READING 10.9

Discipline in schools

The Committee for Enquiry on Discipline in Schools (The Elton Report)

> The Elton Committee conducted a major enquiry into the factors which influence the conditions in which learning takes place. They drew important conclusions for classroom teachers but also highlighted the vital contribution of many other partners in education. This point is illustrated by this summary of their report, which highlights the complexity of factors which influence discipline in schools – many of which are beyond the remit of the classroom teacher.
>
> Thinking of a school in which you work or have worked, what do you think are the greatest influences on pupil behaviour?
>
> Edited from: The Committee of Enquiry on Discipline in Schools (1989) *Discipline in Schools: Report of the Committee of Enquiry chaired by Lord Elton.* London: HMSO, 11–17

The enquiry

Our task was to recommend action to the Government, local authorities, voluntary bodies, governors, headteachers, teachers and parents aimed at securing the orderly atmosphere necessary in schools for effective teaching and learning to take place. We find that most schools are on the whole well ordered. But even in well run schools minor disruption appears to be a problem. The relatively trivial incidents which most concern teachers make it harder for teachers to teach and pupils to learn. Our recommendations would secure a real improvement in all schools.

Teachers

The central problem of disruption could be significantly reduced by helping teachers to become more effective classroom managers. We see the roles of initial and in-service training as crucial to this process. Our evidence suggests that the status of teachers has declined in recent years and that it may have reduced their authority in the eyes of pupils and parents. We ask the Secretaries of State to clarify the legal basis of teachers' authority. We emphasize the serious implications that any teacher shortages would have for standards of behaviour in schools, and the need for their pay and conditions of service to be such as to ensure the recruitment, retention and motivation of sufficient teachers of the required quality.

Schools

We draw attention to the growing body of evidence indicating that while other factors such as pupils' home backgrounds affect their behaviour, school based influences are also very important. The most effective schools seem to be those that have created a positive atmosphere based on a sense of community and shared values.

We recommend that headteachers and their senior management teams should take the lead in developing school plans for promoting good behaviour. Such plans should ensure that the school's code of conduct and the values represented in its formal and informal curricula reinforce one another; promote the highest possible degree of consensus about standards of behaviour among all staff, pupils and parents; provide clear guidance to all three groups about these standards and their practical application; and encourage staff to recognize and praise good behaviour as well as dealing with bad behaviour. Punishments should make the distinction between minor and more serious misbehaviour clear to pupils, and should be fairly and consistently applied.

We see the headteacher's management style as a crucial factor in encouraging a sense of collective responsibility among staff, and a sense of commitment to the school among pupils and their parents.

We point out the links between the content and methods of delivery of the school curriculum and the motivation and behaviour of pupils, particularly those who are not successful academically. We emphasize the importance of the Secretaries of State ensuring that the National Curriculum offers stimulating and suitably differentiated programmes of study for the full ability range, and that the national assessment system is supportive and not threatening. We urge schools to achieve the best possible match between the needs and interests of individual pupils and the curriculum which they are required to follow.

We stress the importance of personal and social education as a means of promoting the values of mutual respect, self-discipline and social responsibility which underlie good behaviour, and we recommend that personal and social education should be strengthened both inside and outside the National Curriculum.

We emphasize the importance of the pastoral role of class teachers and form tutors and the need for schools to maintain regular contact with the education welfare service and other support agencies rather than calling them in as a last resort.

We draw attention to evidence indicating links between the appearance of school premises and the behaviour of pupils. We stress the need for appropriate building design. We urge all schools to develop policies to deal with litter, graffiti and other damage, and to follow the good example set by the best primary schools in displaying pupils' work.

We highlight the problems that many schools are experiencing during the lunch break.

We draw attention to evidence indicating that the most effective schools tend to be those with the best relationships with parents. We urge heads and teachers to ensure that they keep parents well informed, that their schools provide a welcoming atmosphere which encourages parents to become involved, and that parents are not only told when their children are in trouble but when they have behaved particularly well.

We recommend that schools' policies on discipline should be communicated fully and clearly to parents. If children are excluded from school for an indefinite period, the school should re-admit them only after an agreement setting out the conditions under which they will be allowed to return has been signed by their parents.

Parents

We highlight the crucial role parents play in shaping the attitudes which produce good behaviour in school. Parents need to provide their children with firm guidance and positive models through their own behaviour. Not all parents appreciate the degree of commitment and consistency required to provide such guidance. We think schools have an important part to play in preparing pupils for the responsibilities of parenthood. We therefore recommend that education for parenthood should be fully covered in school personal and social education programmes, and that the Government should develop a post-school education strategy aimed at promoting socially responsible parenthood.

We recommend that parents should take full advantage of all formal and informal channels of communication made available by schools, and that parent–teacher associations should ensure that their activities are accessible and rewarding to as many parents as possible.

We conclude that there is a need to increase parental accountability for their children's behaviour. We ask the Government to explore the possibilities for imposing civil liability on parents for damage or injury done by their children in school.

Pupils

We draw attention to evidence indicating that pupils tend to behave more responsibly if they are given responsibilities. We recommend that schools should create opportunities for pupils of all ages to take on appropriate responsibilities, and that they should recognize pupils' non-academic achievements. We welcome the Government's support for the development of records of achievement as a means of promoting a sense of responsibility among pupils.

We stress the need for the rapid assessment of the special educational needs of pupils with emotional and behavioural difficulties by all LEAs. We urge schools and LEAs to ensure that failure to identify and meet the learning needs of some pupils is not a cause of their bad behaviour.

Our evidence indicates that, while all LEAs make alternative provision for the most difficult pupils, its pattern tends to be a more or less improvised response to needs and difficulties. We recommend that all LEAs should review their alternative provision and, in determining its future pattern should aim to provide adequate, appropriate and cost-effective support services for schools and individual pupils. We suggest that the most effective provision is likely to be based on support teams of specialist teachers working in mainstream schools with access to places in on-site units and, in exceptional cases, off-site units.

We highlight the strong concerns expressed to us about the effect that violent television programmes may be having on childrens' attitudes and behaviour. We emphasize the need for careful regulation and monitoring of this aspect of broadcast, cable or video material, and the responsibility of parents for restricting their children's access to anti-social images. We recommend that broadcasters should take full account of their educational responsibilities for all television programmes.

Attendance

Our evidence indicates that, while overall attendance rates seem to have remained relatively stable for many years, there are significant differences in the rates for individual schools which cannot always be explained by differences in their catchment areas. We encourage heads and teachers to take action to minimize unauthorized absence and internal truancy.

Police

We encourage headteachers to develop clear understandings with local police forces about how intruders in their schools should be dealt with. We emphasize the value of school–police liaison projects and, in particular, the contribution that the police can make to education for responsible citizenship.

Governors

We identify two major areas in which governors can help to promote good behaviour in schools. One is the positive contribution that they can make to developing and monitoring their school's policy on discipline. The other is through the decisive part that they play in the appointment of staff, especially the headteacher. We emphasize the importance of governors looking for the personal qualities required for managing a school or a classroom effectively, and for working as part of a team.

Local Education Authorities

We urge LEAs to develop their management information systems so that they can target their consultancy and support services on schools in difficulty. We stress the need for them to provide more effective consultancy services, particularly in the areas of school management and institutional change, and to ensure that the guidance and support systems which they provide for schools are coherent and properly co-ordinated.

Government

We point out that most teachers see smaller classes as an important contribution towards reducing the problem of classroom disruption, but that it is difficult to identify relationships between class size and pupils' behaviour. We recommend that the Secretaries of State should commission research to investigate these relationships.

CHAPTER 11

How are we communicating in the classroom?

There are eleven readings in this chapter and they address a wide range of issues concerning the use of language in school contexts.

Sammons and her collegues (Reading 11.1) review key issues in language and learning and relate these to the National Curriculum, whilst Barnes (11.2) draws in his classic work on the implications for classroom communication of 'transmission' and 'interpretation' views of education.

Wells (11.3), Edwards and Mercer (11.4) and Davies (11.5) each offer ways of thinking about the adult role in language use and learning. They adopt what, in broad terms, may be characterized as social constructivist approaches, and show awareness of some significant social consequences of patterns of language use.

The next group of readings are more concerned with the management and skills of language development in classrooms. Bennett and Dunne (11.6) consider co-operative group work, Phillips (11.7) focuses on structuring classroom discussion and Perrot (11.8) provides an analysis of questioning skills and strategies.

Stubbs (11.9) and Miller (11.10) provide readings on linguistic diversity, focusing on Standard and non-standard English and on bilingualism respectively. Finally, Bazalgette (11.11) addresses the new forms of literacy which are such an important part of children's media education.

The parallel chapter of *Reflective Teaching in the Primary School* considers the major characteristics of classroom communication: the quantity, balance of participation and the content of talk. It then reviews explanations, questioning, discussion and listening before focusing on facilitating group work. Finally, there is a discussion of linguistic diversity. In each section there are checklists and suggestions for practical activities. There are also many suggestions for further reading.

Language, learning and the National Curriculum

Pam Sammons, Ann Lewis, Maggie MacLure, Jeni Riley, Neville Bennett and Andrew Pollard

This reading provides a concise overview of present understanding of the role of language in the learning of young children. It identifies some key principles and research studies which underpin that understanding. Important topics include the importance of children's active participation in talk, the opportunities for language use which are provided, the nature and quality of support offered by adults, and classroom entitlements.

Some concerns about the role of Standard English in the National Curriculum are expressed (see also Reading 11.9). What is your view on these issues?

Edited from: Sammons, P., Lewis, A., MacLure, M., Riley, J., Bennett, N. and Pollard, A. (1994) 'Teaching and learning processes', in Pollard, A. (ed.) *Look Before You Leap? Research Evidence for the Curriculum at Key Stage Two*. London: Tufnell Press, 58–61

To grasp fully the possible implications of the National Curriculum for children's learning, it is important to consider the role of language in learning. This is a topic that has received a great deal of attention over the last twenty years or so, and although there are differences of approach and opinion, there is little dissent about the centrality of language in the learning process. In fact, few would disagree with the proposition that children, in common with us all, do both their learning and their thinking through language.

Much of what is known about the links between language and learning derives from studies of children's spoken language development during their pre-school years – a time when all children make astonishing learning gains, entirely without experience of formal 'teaching', and long before they are able to read and write. The reasons for this learning explosion seem to lie in the nature of the communication that takes place between children and the people they live amongst. Talk between children and others – especially parents or other carers – is especially well-designed to facilitate learning. Summarizing across the research literature, it seems that there are two basic conditions for learning that child–adult talk provides:

children are active participants in their own learning – exploring, through talk, the nature and meaning of the world around them;

adults provide just the right amount of support, encouragement and structure to help children move on in their learning, without taking the initiative away from them.

Regarding the first point: children are active participants in talk, and hence in their own learning, in a number of different respects. They play an active role conversationally, in that it is more often the child than the adult who 'makes the running'. A large body of research shows that children – across all social backgrounds – initiate conversations more often than adults; they usually get to choose, and change, the topic, and they often set the 'agenda' for talk by asking questions, making suggestions and modifying other people's ideas and plans (e.g. Wells, 1986; MacLure, 1992; McTear, 1985; Tizard and Hughes, 1984). They are also cognitively, or intellectually active, in that their talk displays the kind of 'higher order' reasoning that is valued in our education system and strongly associated with learning, such as hypothesizing, speculating, generalizing, weighing up alternatives, seeing things from the perspectives of other people (e.g. Tizard and Hughes, 1984) although it has been argued that some children get less opportunity than others to engage in this kind of 'higher order' thinking through language (e.g. Tough,

1977; Blank, 1973). Finally, children are active theorizers in that, through talk, they are continuously trying to make sense of the world and the people in it, searching for patterns and regularities, and using the 'feedback' that they get from their conversational partners to test out and modify their hunches and hypotheses (e.g. Beveridge, 1982; Donaldson, 1978). This notion of 'practical theorizing' through language supports the 'constructivist' model of learning (Driver, 1983; Edwards and Mercer, 1987) and argues against models which construe learning as the passive acquisition of predigested chunks of knowledge.

Moving to the second point above: although children play an active role in their own learning through language this is not to suggest that there is no role for adults. On the contrary, much of the research into language and learning has identified a crucial role for adults and other people close to the child, in addition to the obvious one of giving them access to new bodies of knowledge. Bruner (e.g. 1983) called this role 'scaffolding', a term that has now entered the professional vocabulary of teaching, and which describes the ways in which adults provide the security and structure that allows children to take the next step in their learning – for instance by asking them just the right kinds of 'what next' questions, by helping them to clarify their decisions, or by prompting them to rethink their plans. Vygotsky's notion of learning in the 'zone of proximal development' similarly describes the ways in which a novice learner and a more expert partner (who does not need to be an adult) can interact in ways that help the learner to edge just beyond the current limits of their expertise (see for example Griffin and Cole, 1984). Parents are generally very good 'scaffolders' since they know their children's intentions and desires well, and they have a rich history of shared events, meanings and feelings to draw on for talk and learning. They are 'finely tuned' (Wells, 1986) to their children's struggles to learn and to communicate. Teachers find it much harder, with many more children to support and must less intimate knowledge of their lives and interests, and this is one source of the well-known difficulties many teachers experience in 'matching' curriculum activities to children's needs, noted elsewhere in this paper. Communication – and therefore learning – problems are even more likely to arise when there is a class or cultural 'gap' between the teacher and the child (Tizard and Hughes, 1984).

The rationale for learning in small groups comes in large part from work on the links between language and learning, which has suggested that children working collaboratively in peer groups can exert a kind of control and responsibility over their own learning that may be difficult for them to achieve solely through teacher-to-pupil instruction. Many studies of primary children discussing and working through joint activities have shown that they are able to support and extend one anothers' suggestions and ideas, and that in the course of doing this they are often exercising and acquiring valuable skills of problem-solving, decision-making, hypothesizing, predicting, summarizing – together with social skills such as co-operativeness and empathy (e.g. Barnes and Todd, 1977; Phillips, 1988, Edwards and Westgate, 1987). In small-group settings, under favourable conditions, and with well-targeted and well-timed teacher interventions children can attain a degree of 'ownership' of their own learning (Chang and Wells, 1988) that can be hard to match in teacher-to-child or teacher-to-class situations, where it is usually the teacher who has the biggest 'say' in what to talk about, and where there may be tacit rules about saying things clearly and concisely. In peer group talk children have the right and luxury to be tentative, exploratory and hesitant as they grope towards new ideas and concepts. However there are also a number of studies that suggest that small group work often fails to live up to the ideal (e.g. Galton, 1989), resulting in children working on low-level or unchallenging tasks, without much collaboration with the others in their group.

An additional, third issue relates to the links between language, learning and entitlement. One of the clearest and most incontrovertible findings of language research has been the adverse effects on children's progress at school of prejudicial attitudes towards the language or dialect of their own communities (Edwards and Furlong, 1978; Edwards, 1983; Heath, 1983). Children who are made to feel that the way they talk is inadequate are likely to fail to thrive as learners, since they will be disenfranchised as participants in the classroom talk on which learning depends.

One way to think about the National Curriculum may be to consider it in light of the three major issues mentioned above. These are: the opportunities children are given to be active participants in the language, and therefore the learning of the classroom; the nature and quality of the support teachers are likely to be encouraged/able to provide to support these learning processes; the entitlement of all pupils as participants in the language community of the classroom.

One obvious issue of relevance is the debate about the merits of whole-class as opposed to small group teaching. A move to more whole-class teaching might result in improvements for some children in the quality of the interactions, and hence the learning opportunities, they experience in the classroom. However, if whole-class teaching should become the dominant organizational structure in primary schools, this would almost certainly work against the conditions for optimal learning since children's 'stake' in talk for learning would become much smaller and almost entirely out of their own control. Children with special learning needs, and less assertive children, might be at a particular disadvantage in such 'high visibility' settings. Equally, no matter how competent teachers' strategies, a predominance of whole-class teaching would not allow them to develop and use the diagnostic and supportive skills of 'scaffolding' children in their learning to the same extent as in small-group or one-on-one situations. Moves towards a great emphasis on content within the individual curriculum subjects, and away from processes such as investigation, problem solving and practical work also have learning implications since the latter are accomplished largely through the exercise of language skills.

One positive feature of the National Curriculum is the weighting of the attainment targets to give speaking and listening equal emphasis with reading and writing – a move which confirms the importance given in the National Curriculum to this aspect of children's language. The National Curriculum could be seen as having generally positive implications for learning through language, therefore, through its endorsement of the validity of 'oracy' as well as literacy.

Other aspects of the National Curriculum are worrying in terms of their implications for children's prospects as learners. The emphasis on the development of listening skills suggests an inclination towards a passive, fact-driven view of learning. The insistence on the importance of clarity of diction, precision, and accuracy suggest a model of language as performance rather than a resource for learning and making meaning. Children might feel discouraged from using the exploratory and un-polished language that is often the mark of thinking and reflection.

The most contentious aspect of the National Curriculum, however, and the one with the most serious implications, is the prominence given to Standard English, and the requirement that all children should be taught to speak it right from the start. Much will depend on how the proposals, if accepted, are implemented. But if teachers encourage a climate that requires children to be constantly vigilant over the 'correctness' of their language this will, again, work against the spontaneity and provisionality of talk that is associated with learning. There are serious implications, too for children's entitlements as learners. Despite statements that the Standard English requirement 'does not undermine the integrity of either regional accent or dialects', and that it is undertaken with the intention of enhancing children's social and professional development, there is a very strong possibility that some children will come to feel that their speech habits are stigmatized, with obvious consequences for their self-esteem and their sense of identity. Not only will these children be at a material disadvantage in the end-of-stage assessments, but their prospects as learners may be further damaged, since they may not feel free to participate in the language of the classroom on the same grounds as those more fortunate children for whom Standard English is the home dialect.

READING 11.2

Knowledge, communication and learning

Douglas Barnes

From Communication to Curriculum has been an extremely influential book on language use in schools. In this brief extract, Douglas Barnes offers a model of classroom communication in which the 'transmission' of official school knowledge is contrasted with the 'interpretation' of everyday action knowledge. There are clear resonances here with the contrasting views of learning within Chapter 6 (contrast, for instance, the behaviourism of 6.1 and the social constructivism of 6.11) and the same issue is addressed in Reading 15.7 in a discussion of the struggle for teachers' understanding of learning when the National Curriculum was being implemented.

How does this model relate to the teaching of subject knowledge in your classroom?

Edited from: Barnes, D. (1975) *From Communication to Curriculum*. London: Penguin Books, 146–9

The following diagram is intended to have the status of a hypothesis regarding the relationship between transmission and interpretation and the distinction between 'school knowledge' and 'action knowledge':

The strong vertical lines represent four dimensions of classroom communication which I hypothesize will vary together. The horizontal broken lines represent this relationship, and in explaining the diagram I shall read across the upper line first.

If a teacher sees knowledge as existing primarily in a public discipline he will set up classroom communication so that transmission and assessment predominate. This will compel pupils to adopt a mainly presentational performance in which speech and writing perform 'final draft' functions. This will encourage boundaried learning in which the new knowledge is not brought into relationship with the learner's purposes and interests.

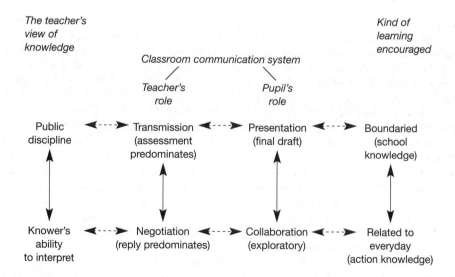

Figure 11.2.1 Relationships of knowledge, communication and learning

If a teacher sees knowledge as existing primarily in the knower's ability to interpret, he will emphasize the reply aspect of his classroom role, thus making possible a negotiation between his knowledge and his pupils' knowledge. This will open to them a collaborative approach in which the exploratory functions of speech and writing predominate. This will encourage pupils to relate new knowledge to their existing purposes and interests.

If knowledge is regarded as content, the valued possession of a group, teaching becomes a package-deal. The teacher offers his own values and habits of mind wrapped up inextricably with his subject-matter; his pupils are faced with a take-it-or-leave-it. If we wish to encourage pupils to be able to adapt to new problems, and to take responsibility for their own actions rather than to follow custom, then a passive view of learning will not do. In making the ethical decision to prepare pupils for choice and responsibility, teachers implicity choose also an Interpretation view of learning. What is of practical interest is that a large proportion of teachers who would publicly assert their ends to be a world of self-responsible and flexible people do not in fact will the means which are required. That is, they see teaching primarily as an act of transmitting existing knowledge, minimizing the part actively played by pupils. This puts a premium upon routine performances. School learning becomes a special form of activity which need not impinge upon the pupil's life outside school and the values which inform it. Teaching in which Transmission predominates is the negation of 'education for living'.

To advocate an Interpretation view of education is not to argue that teachers should never present knowledge to their pupils, but rather to imply that certain patterns of communication should follow the presentation, as pupils negotiate their own ways of grasping the knowledge thus presented.

READING 11.3

Conversation and the reinvention of knowledge

Gordon Wells

> Gordon Wells and his collaborators produced an important study of the ways in which young children acquire language and 'make meaning' as they develop through home and school. This extract focuses on the conditions which facilitate high-quality conversation and learning. In particular, Wells sees this as 'the guided reinvention of knowledge' – a view which he contrasts with the transmission mode which many adults adopt in their interaction with children (see Reading 11.2).
>
> How was your 'reinvention of knowledge' guided when you were young?
>
> Edited from: Wells, G. (1986) *The Meaning Makers*. Oxford: Heinemann Educational, 216–22

When I communicate with other people, whether it is to inform, request, or persuade, what I have in mind is an idea – an event, action, or outcome – that I intend they should understand. However, this idea arises from my mental model of the world, which is in itself the product of my unique personal biography. Nobody else has exactly the same mental model of the world, since nobody else has had exactly the same experience. It follows, therefore, that nobody can have exactly the same ideas as I have.

Even if my listener were able to form the same ideas as I have, however, I still am not able to transmit my ideas directly to him or her in all their simultaneity and multifaceted particularity, since language, the most effective means of communication available, requires that I select and arrange what I mean in an ordered sequence that is compatible with the possibilities of syntax and vocabulary. Furthermore, while my ideas are personal and particular, the categories of language, in terms of which I now have to represent them, are public and general. It is simply not possible, therefore, to convey the ideas that I have in mind in a form that does full justice to their simultaneous complexity and specificity.

In normal conversation between mature adult members of the same culture, this does not normally cause a problem. Their past experience, both of language and of the world to which it refers, is sufficiently similar for there to be a considerable overlap between them in the idea they might wish to communicate. Furthermore, in speech at least, there are strategies available for negotiating over the intended meaning if a mismatch is suspected. Finally, where conversational meaning is jointly construed over successive turns, there are opportunities to amplify or modify what one has said in the light of the feedback received in subsequent contributions. Although participants in a conversation never know for sure what the other meant by a particular utterance, over the conversation as a whole there are sufficient opportunities for each to calibrate his or her interpretation of what is meant against that of the other for a consensus to be reached that is usually adequate for most of the purposes for which people communicate with each other.

On the other hand, where the conversational participants come from different cultural backgrounds, or where they differ greatly in their level of cognitive and linguistic maturity – as is the case in interactions between children and their parents or teachers – the possibility of misunderstanding is both substantial and ever-present. And unless they – or at least the more mature of the participants – take the necessary steps, the meanings that they construct on the basis of their differing mental models and linguistic resources are likely to become increasingly divergent.

When considering the ways in which adults can facilitate their children's language development, four principles were suggested:

to treat what the child has to say as worthy of careful attention;

to do one's best to understand what he or she means;

to take the child's meanings as the basis for what one says next;

in selecting and encoding one's message, to take account of the child's ability to understand – that is, to construct an appropriate interpretation.

Where these principles are followed by both participants, it is possible for minds to make contact – even when they are separated by wide differences in maturity and experience.

Conversation may not be perfect as a means of information exchange, therefore, but when engaged in collaboratively, it can be an effective medium for learning and teaching. In any case, since there is no better alternative, we must do the best we can.

If the argument above is correct, it follows that the conception of teaching as 'transmission' must be a mistaken one. First, it is not possible, simply by telling, to cause students to come to have the knowledge that is in the mind of the teacher. Knowledge cannot be transmitted. It has to be constructed afresh by each individual knower on the basis of what is already known and by means of strategies developed over the whole of that individual's life both outside and inside the classroom. On both these counts there are bound to be substantial differences between the individuals in any class of students and, hence, a wide variation in the interpretations that are put upon the teacher's words. Unless students are given opportunities to formulate the sense they make of new topics in their own way, using their own words, an important means of gaining understanding is lost. In addition, the teacher loses the opportunity to discover what meanings the students bring to the topic and so is unable to make his or her contributions contingently responsive.

Second, a unilateral definition of what is to count as worthwhile knowledge and of how it is to be constructed undervalues the contributions that students can make in terms of their own experience, interest, and methods of inquiry, thereby impoverishing the learning experience. Furthermore, to override their natural predisposition to attempt to construct their own knowledge is to force them into a relatively passive role, with a consequent reduction in their commitment to the endeavour and an increase in the likelihood that what is learned will not be integrated into their action-oriented model of the world and so will soon be forgotten.

In sum, what is wrong with the transmission model is that it places the teacher or textbook at the centre of the educational enterprise and focuses almost exclusively on the input, in the mistaken belief that, to obtain the desired outcomes, what is most important is to ensure that the input is well selected, sequenced, and presented in terms of the educated adult's understanding of what is to be learned.

However, once we give due recognition to the fact that knowledge can only be constructed by individual knowers and that this occurs most effectively when they have an active engagement in all the processes involved, it becomes clear that a different model of education is required – one that is based on a partnership between students and teachers, in which the responsibility for selecting and organizing the tasks to be engaged in is shared.

To urge that classrooms should be places in which the curriculum is negotiated – where students are encouraged to take the role of expert when they are able to do so, and where they have a part in determining the goals to be aimed for and the procedures to be followed – may seem to be reducing the importance of the role of the teacher. However, this is very far from being the case. What is required, though, is a different conception of the relationship between teacher and students – one in which the teacher aims to facilitate learning rather than to direct it. This is not to deny the teacher's greater expertise and experience, but to argue that it will be of much greater value to students if it is offered collaboratively rather than being imposed.

Nor am I suggesting that the teacher should relinquish the overall responsibility for setting directions, proposing specific content, or evaluating achievement. On the contrary, final decisions on these matters require informed judgement that can only be gained through professional training and experience. Nevertheless, in fulfilling these responsibilities, the teacher should explain the criteria on which decisions are based so that, within the limits of their capabilities, students can share in the day-to-day planning of learning activities to an increasing degree. The aim, therefore, should be to foster the development of students' ability to take control of their own learning so that eventually they can assume these responsibilities for themselves.

Following these principles, teaching can no longer be seen as the imparting of information to relatively passive recipients and then checking to see that they can correctly reproduce it. Instead, it is more appropriately characterized as a partnership in learning. The tasks of the partners are necessarily different as a result of their differing levels of expertise, but the goal is the same for students and teacher alike. Without too much exaggeration, it can be described as the guided reinvention of knowledge.

We are the meaning makers – every one of us: children, parents, and teachers. To try to make sense, to construct stories, and to share them with others in speech and in writing is an essential part of being human. For those of use who are more knowledgeable and more mature – parents and teachers – the responsibility is clear: to interact with those in our care in such a way as to foster and enrich their meaning making.

📖 READING 11.4

Classroom discourse and learning

Derek Edwards and Neil Mercer

This extract is from the conclusion of *Common Knowledge*, a book which reports detailed research using video recordings of lessons and analysis of teacher–pupil language interaction and associated learning. In a sense, it constitutes a further, and particularly constructive, exploration of the tension between 'transmission' and 'interpretive' modes of language learning. The role of the teacher is highlighted in the creation of 'joint understandings' and 'cognitive socialization through language' (see also Reading 6.4 by Vygotsky and several other readings in Chapter 6).

Think of a short linguistic interaction between yourself and a pupil. How do Edwards and Mercer's three conclusions relate to your example?

Edited from: Edwards, D. and Mercer, N. (1987) *Common Knowledge: The Development of Understanding in the Classroom*. London: Methuen, 156–68

Our findings suggest three main conclusions about the educational processes we have observed.

Experiential learning and teacher control. Despite the fact that the lessons were organized in terms of practical actions and small-group joint activity between the pupils, the sort of learning that took place was not essentially a matter of experiential learning and communication between pupils. The role of the teacher was crucial throughout, both in shaping the general pattern and content of the lesson, and in producing the fine-grained definition of what was done, said and understood.

Ritual and principle. While maintaining a tight control over activity and discourse, the teacher nevertheless overtly espoused and attempted to act upon the educational principle of pupil-centred experiential learning, and the importance of pupils' engagement in practical activity and discovery. This led to the pupils' grasp of certain important concepts being essentially 'ritual', a matter of what to do or say, rather than 'principled', i.e. based on conceptual understanding. Particular sorts of classroom discourse that appeared to underlie the creation of such procedural knowledge included a heavy reliance on 'cued elicitation', together with an overriding concern to conduct the lessons in terms of getting through the set of planned activities, rather than, say, making sure that a planned set of concepts were understood by everyone.

Language and the socialization of cognition. The overriding impression from our studies is that classroom discourse functions to establish joint understandings between teacher and pupils, shared frames of reference and conception, in which the basic process is one of introducing pupils into the conceptual world of the teacher and, through her, of the educational community. To the extent that the process of education can be observed taking place in the situated discourse of classrooms, it is on our evidence essentially a process of cognitive socialization through language.

The relation of power and control to the creation of joint understandings is both problematic and of great importance. An inherent part of education is an asymmetry of roles between teacher and learner. Much of the process remains mysterious. In however friendly and informal a manner, they are frequently asked to do things, learn things, understand things, for no apparent reason other than that it is what the teacher wants them to do. The goals and purposes of the lesson are not revealed. Indeed, neither often are the concepts that the lesson may have been designed to 'cover'.

However, the asymmetry of teacher and learner is essential to the 'zone of proximal development', and so also is the notion of control. Children do not simply acquire knowledge and vocabulary. They acquire at the same time the capacity for self-regulation. Just as verbal thought originates as social discourse, so self-regulated behaviour begins with the regulation of one's behaviour by other people. The successful process involves a gradual handover of control from teacher to learner, as the learner becomes able to do alone what could previously be done only with help. In formal education, this part of the process is seldom realized. For most pupils, education remains a mystery beyond their control, rather than a resource of knowledge and skill with which they can freely operate.

There appears to be a fundamental dilemma for our teachers – that of balancing the conflicting demands of, on the one hand, a child-centred ideology of learning and on the other hand, an essentially socializing role as the society's agents of cultural transmission in the context of a system of compulsory education.

 READING 11.5

Classroom knowledge and the subjects of reading and writing

Bronwyn Davies

Bronwyn Davies' post-structuralist analysis (see Readings 13.3 and 13.6) picks up on the issue of power and uses an analysis of narratives and classroom interaction to deconstruct teachers' knowledge and their control of children's engagement in reading texts. In particular she argues that pupils learn a 'moral identity' as an integral part of the process of learning to read and write. She concludes by suggesting that teachers who are aware of such issues must engage in 'an extraordinary balancing act' to offer knowledge about reading and writing, but without interrupting or distorting children's own direct and immediate involvement.

What 'moral identities' may be learned within your classroom?

Edited from: Davies, B. (1993) *Shards of Glass: Children Reading and Writing Beyond Gendered Identities*. Sydney: Allen and Unwin, 38–63.

In primary school classrooms formal ownership of knowledge is assumed by teachers – they have the authoritative codes for interpreting meaning and their task is to give children access to these codes, or rather, to subject them to them. This is an obviousness about teaching that is not usually attended to by teachers, it is simply part and parcel of the way teaching is done – of knowledge one has about teaching. This knowledge about teaching-as-usual is often in tension with other ways of knowing that each teacher has, these other ways of knowing being informed, for example, by the humanist knowledges and ideals. While teachers might want children to bring 'something of their own' to the classroom or the lesson, what it is that is brought must confirm to tightly set knowledge boundaries and to acceptable forms of saying or knowing, and will be subjected to teachers' authoritative scrutiny, interpretation and evaluation.

The disruption of knowledges advocated in feminist poststructuralist writing runs counter to this culture of the classroom. For teachers to introduce critical literacy into their classrooms and for students to begin to deconstruct the text and to talk through the ways in which they are constituted, a great deal has to change.

Prior to going to school children learn to talk, to observe, to register their own bodily experiences in particular ways. The come to certain conclusions about the way the world is. One of the early things they inevitably learn when they go to school is the apparently infinite revisability of these conclusion in the face of superior and more powerful school knowledges. They learn to see in ways deemed legitimate by people with access to those authoritative knowledges.

Teachers, like everyone else, interpret and make sense of the world through narratives, that is, through the storylines of their culture. Story is one of our predominant modes of sense making. As Richardson (1990, pp. 117-18) points out:

> Narrative displays the goals and intentions of human actors; it makes individuals, cultures, societies, and historical epochs comprehensible as wholes; it humanizes time; and it allows us to contemplate the effects of our actions, and to alter the directions of our lives ... Narrative is both a mode of reasoning and a mode of representation. People can 'apprehend' the world narratively and people can 'tell' about the word narratively.

Thus we not only read and write stories but we also live stories. Who we take ourselves to be at any one point in time depends on the available storylines we have to make sense out of the ebb and flow of being-in-the-world along with the legitimacy and status accorded to those storylines by the others with whom we make up our lives at any one point in time.

At the beginning of 1992, Chas's daughter, Alexandra, began school. Her teacher asked the children to bring their favourite version of Cinderella to school. Her plan was to look at and discuss with the children, culturally different versions of the story, since there were Korean, Aboriginal and Malaysian and Chinese as well as Anglo-Australian children in the class. On reading one version of the story, when she came to the picture of Cinderella dressed like a bride, she said to the children, 'Oh, isn't she beautiful! Who wants to have a wedding dress like that?' Alexandra replied, 'No way!' 'Why not Alexandra?' asked the teacher. 'I might get a boyfriend when I grow up but I don't want to get married!' replied Alexandra. The teacher was highly amused by this and later told Chas to ask her what she had said about Cinderella's wedding dress.

Alex thus found that the expression of an opinion that went against the teacher's and the text's version of gender relations was something that adults would talk about and report to each other with amusement. Although she had not been told she was wrong, she had been constituted as different, as one to tell stories about. While Chas praised her for 'sticking up for her own beliefs', Alexandra discovered that what seemed obvious to her (that marriage is not necessarily a good or desirable thing) was not what her teacher thought was obvious. The teacher, without necessarily planning to do so, had imported into her lesson through the stories and her own unexamined relation to them, her ideals of romance and marriage and she had invited the female children to position themselves as ones who belonged in that storyline and who longed for a beautiful wedding dress. She did so as if this were perfectly normal, that is, not something to tell a story about. Alexandra's response, which disrupted the obviousness of the pattern of desire being made relevant for girls by the teacher, was constituted, in contrast, as something to tell a story about, something which stands out from the everyday flow of events.

Through interactions such as these, teachers give students access to knowledge through which they will be judged as competent or incompetent and treated accordingly. Taking these knowledges on as one's own is essential for survival in the classroom and for opening up the possibility of being positioned as one who is worthy of teacher respect. Maintaining perceptions and knowledges at odds with the teacher's is to position oneself as marginal in educational terms and to risk being considered as a failure.

The hearing of teacher requests, invitations, suggestions and orders is always done in the context of the classroom, and the context is obviously critical in determining what is meant by what the teacher says. In the following transcript taken from Luke (1991, pp. 140-4), it becomes evident that the teacher's request to the students to 'help me write a story' actually means 'facilitate my telling of my story and in the process learn from me the obviousnesses of story writing'. In this case, the children's occasional attempts to actually contribute to the story lead to explanations on the part of the teacher that she is the author and therefore has total authority over the story. Their position as 'helpers' requires them to facilitate her display of how one must think about the writing of stories in order that they may the write their own:

1	T:	Now ... We're gonna do something now, you're gonna have to help me ... because I'm going to write a story, and you're gonna help me write the story, and afterwards, you might go and write yourselves a story. But help me first. O.K., and now, seeing we've been doing lots of stories about princesses and things like that
2	S1:	What we're gonna do?
3	T:	What we're gonna do today is a story about a princess
4	S2:	Princess
5	S3:	And a prince
6	T:	Come in a bit boys over there
7	S2:	And a prince
8	T:	You reckon we should have a prince in it?
9	Ss:	*(unison)* Yes
10	T:	Aw I was thinking of a dragon
11	Ss:	NO ..... *(unison, laughter)*
12	T:	And a prince too?
13	Ss:	*(inaudible commentary)*
14	T:	*(thought)* What'll I call my story?
15	S1:	Princess of the World
16	T:	*(gesturing to Aboriginal girl)* Just sit down anywhere there Kay
17	A2:	Ninja Turtles
18	T:	No, no Ninja Turtles in my story. This is called
19	S3:	Princess of the World
20	T:	The princess
21	S3:	Aw
22	T:	and the Dragon
23	S2:	Swwssh
24	T:	Now, Jake. This is my story and I can write what I like in my story. When you write your story you can put a Ninja Turtle in it if you want to because that's your very own story. You're going to help me with my story, but you're not going to write it.
25		*(a 'story starter' is then collaboratively worked on)*
26	T:	A LONG LONG TIME AGO THERE LIVED A PRINCESS. I think I can make it a bit better than that
27	S1:	A dragon too
28	T:	No, no. No. What. How 'bout when you think about a princess what do you think about?
29	S2:	A prince ...
30	T:	No
31	S2:	A prince
32	T:	No, what do you think she'd look like?
33	S3:	A
34	T:	With long hair? What colour?
35	S3:	Yellow, black *(chorus laughter)*
36	T:	What about long, long golden hair? A LONG LONG TIME AGO THERE LIVED A PRINCESS WITH GOLDEN HAIR. Now if she had long hair, what sort of a princess do you think she'd be? What would she look like?
37	S1:	Nice
38	T:	Nice. Oh yes, wonderful, that's very good

The teacher begins by reminding the children that they have been 'doing lots of stories about princesses and things like that' (1) thus tying this event to specific previous events. She announces that they are gong to 'do' 'a story about a princess' (3). The children instantly display their knowledge of 'princess' as belonging in the binary pair of 'prince and princess' (4-12 and later 28-31). Presumably this was central to the previous lessons. But today the teacher appears to want something different, not to disrupt the binarism, but to further establish it by inserting information about what the princess looks like, that is, her object status within the binary pair (32). She also appears to want to rehearse the structure of story, to display the naming of story as the beginning and the need for a 'story starter'. She teaches these as linear, that is as if authors produced the texts we read from beginning to end. She also presents story as belonging to and coming out of the mind of the author. No mention is made of the way in which images, storylines and binary thinking are cultural/discursive products which writers may use to construct familiar stories or which they can use to invert, invent and break up old storylines and thus begin to make new ones. Nor is any mention made of the way in which the traditional storyline she is constructing is implicated in the patterns of desire the children will develop (Walkerdine, 1984). Instead, associations and images are not made visible or problematic, their presence is justified in terms of what the author wants (14-24). The image they produce of the princess as having 'long golden hair', and of this feature indicating that she is 'nice' (36-38), is inserted into the telling of the story without attention to the politics of that association, despite the fact that, as Luke points out, there are many Aboriginal girls in this classroom. At least some of the Aboriginal girls in this classroom went on to write stories about nice looking princesses with long golden hair. The lesson they have learned is of the importance of appearance of the female character and the correctness of the association between long golden hair and looking good. They have also learned, by implication, that looking nice and being located in the storylines they are learning to write is not for them. While this might seem, at first glance, a good thing, their Aboriginality protecting them from being drawn uncritically into the romantic storyline, at second glance it is much more problematic. The girls want to write a story about a gold haired princess despite her description precluding the possibility of any straightforward positioning with her. Their imagination is thus caught by the images, the associations and by the patterns of desire made relevant in the romantic storyline at the same time as they are positioned as marginal to it; they are both learning authoritative knowledges and being split off from that knowledge at the same time. And they are being given neither the resources to see and name this process nor the knowledge with which to resist it.

Teachers' authority does not just relate, then, to the determining of correct outer forms. It is brought to bear directly and indirectly on the being who is learning and experiencing those forms as ways of being in the world, as a being making sense of the world, as a being occupying subject positions made available in that world. Not only moral identities but the ways in which one learns to read what a moral identity is are learned in the interaction between student, teacher and text. Incidents such as those I have been describing mean that learning to read the scene from minute details becomes a childhood obsession, preventing them from admitting areas of ignorance and leading them to attempt always to achieve correct or acceptable presentations of self.

Instead of being informed by an authoritative text, or of deciding whether or not they like a text, or whether or not the text is 'realistic' (bears any relation to the world as they understand it), critical/deconstructive writing enables children to see the text as shaping them and shaping worlds in ways that have previously been invisible to them. According to Luke:

> this requires a reworking of first, the very games of talk around text with an eye to making explicit the possibilities of what can be done, said and meant with texts; and second, a critical exploration of elasticity and difference of texts, genres and discourses at the earliest stages of literacy training. (1991, p.150)

It involves finding a way to make the shaping process visible, to 'catch the text in the act' of shaping. This requires a complex cognitive shift away from an apprehension of the text as transparently revealing a real world, to a simultaneous apprehension of: the world evoked by the text; one's own subjective response to the text; and at the same time an evaluation of the discursive effects of that relation between oneself and the text. In effect, teacher and students both need to immerse themselves in text and distance themselves from that text at the same time.

And in classrooms, there is a further layer of complexity to be attended to. The obviousness of the teacher's authority must be undone such that it does not intrude on the students' ability to track their own involvement in the text, such that the deferral to teacher authority does not interrupt the immediacy of involvement in the text. The teacher must therefore achieve an extraordinary balancing act between being one who does have a wealth of information and ideas to pass on to the students (including the idea of learning to interact with text differently) and creating a situation in which that greater store of knowledge does not interfere with, or interrupt the students' immediate involvement in, the text. To do this we need to find a way of constituting authority not as an end to discussion but as a way of providing multiple voices whose speaking can begin the conversation. As Jones says: 'We can think of authority not as border-patrolling, boundary-engendering, but as meaning-giving; and as with all gift giving, we should prepare ourselves for the disappointment of possible refusal' (1991, p.123).

 READING 11.6

A rationale for co-operative group work

Neville Bennett and Elizabeth Dunne

This reading illustrates an application, to co-operative groupwork, of Neville Bennett's influential model of teaching and learning. As is made clear in the extract, language is used by teachers and pupils for slightly different purposes at each stage of the teaching cycle. This calls for particular consideration by teachers in developing an appropriate repertoire of linguistic skills for clarifying intentions, offering high-quality presentations and support for implementation, and engaging in assessment activity. For instance, among the major skills which may be called for, we might identify explaining, discussion and questioning.

Can you relate this model to your own classroom practice?

Edited from: Bennett, N. and Dunne, E. (1992) *Managing Classroom Groups*. Hemel Hempstead: Simon and Schuster Education, 188–94

Here we draw threads together in order to present a summary. A useful framework for these purposes is the model of the teaching cycle modified for a group task, as in the figure below.

The teacher's intention was for the group to work co-operatively to make a story plan, the story to be based on a beach scene. The task was presented or introduced via an actual walk on the beach where children explored its features prior to a discussion with the teacher. This discussion is continued in the group in order to develop the story plan. The teacher observes that the children work co-operatively, with Laura taking a lead and helping other members of the group. She nevertheless considers that the group process could have been improved by building more on each other's ideas, and by encouraging all children in the group to participate. The teacher's observations and assessments led her to the decision that the task had been appropriate, but that she must consider ways of improving the manner in which the group works together.

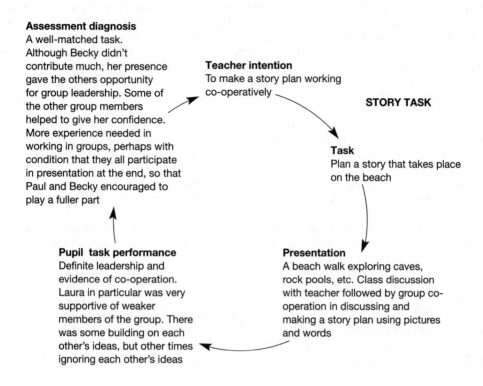

Assessment diagnosis
A well-matched task. Although Becky didn't contribute much, her presence gave the others opportunity for group leadership. Some of the other group members helped to give her confidence. More experience needed in working in groups, perhaps with condition that they all participate in presentation at the end, so that Paul and Becky encouraged to play a fuller part

Teacher intention
To make a story plan working co-operatively

STORY TASK

Task
Plan a story that takes place on the beach

Pupil task performance
Definite leadership and evidence of co-operation. Laura in particular was very supportive of weaker members of the group. There was some building on each other's ideas, but other times ignoring each other's ideas

Presentation
A beach walk exploring caves, rock pools, etc. Class discussion with teacher followed by group co-operation in discussing and making a story plan using pictures and words

Figure 11.6.1 A teaching cycle for a group task

Utilized in this way, the model is a valuable *aide memoire* for the teacher and, used over time, can give a clear picture of progress in terms of group functioning.

In the following, each element of the model is considered in turn, leading, in each case, to a set of 'action questions' designed to guide the teacher through the decision points necessary to setting up and implementing effective co-operative groups.

Teacher Intentions

Transforming intentions into appropriate tasks requires consideration of:

the interaction between social and cognitive intentions;

the type of task required;

the match of appropriateness of the task to children in the group.

Whether the teacher's planning starts with curriculum content or with a single, or a group of, attainment targets, it is necessary to distinguish between the social and cognitive demands of the tasks. The cognitive demand relates to the curriculum content of the task, whereas the social demand relates to the type and amount of co-operation required and thus to decisions about the model of group to be chosen.

Action questions at this planning stage include: on which curriculum area are you going to base the task(s)? With which attainment targets are you dealing? With which specific statement of attainment are you concerned? Which model of co-operative group is to be used?

With regard to the type of task planned, co-operative group work is not a panacea for children's social and cognitive development, it is one option or approach in the teacher's repertoire which must sit alongside other approaches such as individual and whole-class work. We believe it has particular value in problem-solving and applications work. It is in such types of task that abstract talk ought perhaps to predominate, if the task is designed well. However, it is worth recalling that virtually no abstract talk was apparent in the maths, science and technology tasks we observed and recorded. This does not mean that the nature of these curriculum areas precludes abstract talk; it is an issue of task design. There is thus a major challenge for teachers to develop tasks in these curriculum areas that incorporate demands for abstract talk and thought.

Our findings in this area support those of Margaret Donaldson (1978) who found that abstract talk is more difficult for children to generate, and is less fluent than talk relating to action. Teachers need to be aware of this since early attempts at abstract talk may be hesitant and less coherent. It should, nevertheless, be encouraged.

Action questions here are: what kind of task is required to fulfil your intention – problem-solving, discussion, production? Will your demand be 'tight' or 'loose'? Will this task generate the kind of talk you desire?

The third aspect of transforming intentions into tasks is the 'match' or appropriateness of task demands to children's capabilities. Typically, the concept of matching has focused on the individual child and the extent to which tasks have been matched to that child's ability, or have overestimated or underestimated it. However, Vygotsky's notion of the zone of proximal development shifts the focus on the individual child acting in co-operating with others (Vygotsky, 1962). In this context, match is achieved by the mediation of others through the medium of talk. This shift in focus has implications for the teacher's role. No longer does it become necessary to fine-tune matching; matching can be considered more broadly, as long as the task is appropriate for co-operative groupwork. In these circumstances, matching will be achieved when children in the group make sense of task demands through their talk. As we have seen in this study, and as has been reported elsewhere, it can occur to the benefit of all children irrespective of their level of attainment.

Action questions of relevance here are: what is the actual task chosen? Is it suitable for co-operative working? Does it fit the group model chosen? Are the cognitive demands reasonably appropriate to the children's capabilities?

Presentation and implementation

These two aspects of the model are considered together since decisions about presentation (e.g., whether to introduce a task by means of a walk on the beach, or a discussion, or a television programme, etc.) are closely tied up with the way in which the class and the groups are managed and supported. They have common implications for the teacher's role.

Foremost among these is the nature of the teacher's own language. As HMI (1989b) recently argued in their report on primary maths, 'It was the quality of the exposition and dialogue with the teacher that enabled the children to reflect upon and think through mathematical problems and ideas. This factor, more than any other, marked the difference between good and mediocre work'.

Of particular relevance to groupwork has been the continuing debate about the extent and nature of teacher intervention with groups. Some researchers and commentators feel that the teacher ought to operate a 'hands-off' approach, whereas others argue the opposite. The National Oracy Project has, for example, argued (National Oracy Project, 1990) that one of the major roles for teachers is to model effective and supportive use of talk in their own behaviour. With specific regard to groupwork they argue that it is better to be involved fully with one group than try to spend a few minutes with each. This is the best way to create planned intervention that may extend children's thinking, to introduce a new aspect, or to give the teacher more information about individuals, while the other groups are responsible for their own success. Joining in activities, they argue, rather than supervising them, extends the possibilities for dialogue.

Although published in 1990 the above recommendations clearly have their genesis in the Bullock Report published fifteen years earlier. It set out its advice as follows:

The teacher's role should be one of planned intervention, and his purposes and the means of fulfilling them must be clear in his mind. Important among these purposes should be the intention to increase the complexity of the child's thinking, so that he does not rest on the mere expression of opinion but uses language in an exploratory way. The child be encouraged to ask good questions as well as provide answers, to set up hypotheses and test them, and to develop the habit of trying out alternative explanations instead of being satisfied with one.

It is important that the teacher should spend time with each of the small groups to guide the language into fulfilling its purpose. 'Guidance' is not used here in the sense of dominant intervention; indeed receptive silence is as much a part of it as the most persuasive utterance. The teacher has first to be a good listener, letting his genuine interest act as a stimulus. His questions will encourage the pupils to develop or clarify points in their thinking, or take them beyond it into the contemplation of other possibilities. We must not give the impression, however, that this is a simple matter and that there are no problems.

The teacher must devise situations in which the pupils will naturally adopt the kind of behaviour he wants to encourage. In other words, he must structure the learning so that the child becomes positively aware of the need for a complicated utterance, and is impelled to make it. In this way the teacher's skilled and carefully controlled intervention is a valuable means of extending his pupils' thinking and making new demands upon their language. (DES 1974, 10.11)

Although we respect the above advice, we have no evidence to present from our own studies to support this type of approach. We utilized a 'hands-off' study so far as teachers were concerned because of our wish to ascertain how children in groups worked without teacher input, and how they dealt with devolved responsibilities for pupil requests.

An issue linked with the National Oracy Project advice about dealing in depth with one group at a time is that of discipline and control. Losing and maintaining control are always high on the list of teacher concerns, and are certainly criteria that teachers consider when asked to change their practice. Our experience is that anxieties of this kind are unfounded, and similar findings are reported elsewhere. Cohen (1986), for example, writing from her research in American classrooms, argues:

From the teacher's point of view, groupwork solves two common discipline problems. It helps with the problem of the low-achieving student who is often found doing anything but what he or she is supposed to be doing. Moreover, it helps to solve the problem of what the rest of the class should be doing while the teacher works intensively with one group. The most typical strategy is to have the rest of the students working with pencil and paper at their seats. However, this produces all kinds of discipline problems. If the rest of the class has been trained to work independently in groups, the teacher will be free to give direct instruction to one small group.

The final aspect of presentation and implementation considered here is the composition of classroom groups. Our findings are clear – mixed ability groups of about four children provide a good environment for effective groupwork. Helping behaviour in the form of knowledge sharing and the provision of explanations tends not to happen in ability groups of low and average attaining children. Importantly, high attainers do not suffer in mixed ability groups. Sex differences are also apparent, and our provisional findings indicate that groups in which boys outnumber girls could depress language experience for the latter.

Questions to guide action in the area of presentation and implementation are: how will the task be presented/introduced? What expectations have you for group behaviour and co-operation? How will the children be informed? Will the responsibility for pupil requests be devolved to the groups? What is your strategy for intervening in the groups? How will you compose your groups?

Assessment

Assessment is not a discrete teacher activity. Much of it takes place during the implementation stage, through teacher observations and questions. Assessment serves several different purposes, for which different techniques are required. Assessment of group processes, through which teachers gain understanding of the nature and quality of pupil interaction, is best achieved in our experience through the use of a tape recorder. Children soon ignore the machine even if there is some initial 'microphone talk'. Not only does the teacher gain an insight into the talk used, but also into interaction patterns, the development and changes in leadership roles and early indications of forms of group malfunctioning.

The quality of these processes will reflect in the quality of group outcomes, the assessment of which requires different techniques. We have highlighted several of these including interviewing individual, or groups of, children in order to access their understanding or schema. Short written assessments can also be used for this purpose. Class discussions can also draw out contrasts in group thinking and approaches.

Some of these techniques require time to carry out and record. Nevertheless, this is time well spent. Better understanding of children's attainment and developing schema should feed forward into better planning of future tasks.

Action questions here are: What are you going to assess? How are you going to assess it? How are you going to feed back to pupils and groups? How are you going to record your assessments? How are you going to use this information in planning future tasks?

📖 READING 11.7

Talking and learning in the classroom

Terry Phillips

> Phillips considers the vexed question of how to encourage task focused and cognitively challenging classroom talk amongst pupils in Key Stage 2 classrooms. He is critical of the dominance of teachers in whole-class teaching, and of just allowing children to 'chatter' in groups. Rather, he argues that activities should be carefully structured to facilitate language development and to expose children to a range of different forms of language use.
>
> Is there a place for more structured language development activities in your classroom?
>
> Edited from: Phillips, T. (1985) 'Beyond lip-service: discourse development after the age of nine', in Wells, G. and Nicholls, J. (eds) *Language and Learning: An Interactional Perspective*. London: Falmer Press, 386–8

Teachers of older children sometimes feel guilty because although they realize that extensive use of class discussion can have a negative effect upon the children's language if they employ mainly closed questions, they find it difficult to teach without using them. They are aware that they talk twice as much as all the children put together but they also know that you can't hold a discussion with twenty or more children without exercising some leadership. Perhaps that is why, in the seventies, many teachers responded to the call to give talk greater recognition by 'permitting' children to chatter whilst they worked, and by encouraging them to discuss things in small groups. Ironically, however, the increase in the quantity of talk in school turned attention away from a consideration of the overall quality of the talk, especially its appropriateness for particular educational purposes. It was almost as if such teachers believe that talk *per se* would promote the range of cognitive processes demanded of children as they moved towards and through secondary schooling.

There has since been a reaction and many more teachers have reverted totally to class teaching because as they put it, 'at least you know where you're going' and 'it's the simplest way to teach the basics'. The frustrations of trying to cope with the nearly impossible have become too much for them and, rather than merely pay lip service to the idea of children learning through undifferentiated group talk, they have opted for the simple alternative. Although research has shown that there is a range of writing styles, within which one style is more appropriate for a particular function than another (Britton, 1971; Wilkinson *et al.* 1979; Bereiter and Scardamalia, 1985) there is a trend towards paring back the range of options for talk. But there are probably as many styles of talking as there are styles of writing, each one fostering a different kind of cognitive process. So what might teachers do instead of going 'back to the basics'? How might they take children 'forward to fundamentals' in terms of such fundamental life-skills as: being able to argue in a way which is rational and does not confuse the argument with its proponent; being able to reflect upon and evaluate ideas and experiences; and being able to adopt a style of language which is appropriate for the purpose it is intended to serve?

A curriculum which brings children more and more into contact with organized bodies of knowledge demands that we use the school day efficiently. If we aim to facilitate spoken language development and, with it, cognitive processes, we must be selective about the kinds of conversation we encourage; and we must also structure the talk. I don't mean that we should prescribe rules for this kind of talk or that kind of talk, only that we should take account of what is known about styles of discourse and their relationship which will help the talk, where appropriate, to be an instrument for higher order cognitive activity. In view of what has been said about the mode of talk that accompanies much practical activity, for instance, it would seem worthwhile to organize the activity so that there is a planning stage when discussion takes place away from the materials to be used, then an activity stage, followed by a withdrawal for further discussion in which group members can reconsider their initial ideas and fashion modified ones, then a second activity stage, and a final report back stage. It would not be too difficult to establish such a routine for practical activities right across the curriculum, activities such as solving a mathematical problem, constructing a model or designing a layout, or carrying out a scientific experiment. The biggest advantage of such a procedure would be that it would accustom children to the fact that they can interrupt the flow of operational language at any point to do some thinking. In time it might be possible to draw the children's attention to what has been happening, and then invite them to interrupt, themselves, when they perceive the moment to be right.

To take second example – in this case the language of argument/discussion – it might be beneficial to frame discussion topics in ways which invite speculation and leave conclusions open, instead of requiring children to reach a decision. The kind of topic which involves selecting what to include and what to exclude from a list would then be a first stage, to be followed by a discussion in which children make explicit the reasons for their selection. At that stage of development they can be encouraged to explain why they are rejecting someone else's suggestion before they give reasons for their own.

If, through the middle years, children are encouraged to listen to as many different models of spoken language as possible, at the secondary stage they will be ready to work out, with their teachers, how speakers achieve their purposes. Taped interviews, radio and television broadcasts, and film are excellent sources for such studies. In media studies it has been realized for quite a while that it is important to study the visual component of such materials and it could only be beneficial to give prominence also to the study of the spoken text.

It would be possible to continue with a list of 'for instances' for a long time, but I shall conclude by drawing out the main principles upon which they were formulated. Spontaneous spoken language development does not stop the moment the child leaves the first school, but the nature of later schooling means that we cannot rely on there being sufficient opportunity for spontaneous classroom conversation to guarantee that the development which does occur will be adequate for a wide range of educational purposes. Teachers have to be ready to structure opportunities for talk in a way which takes cognizance of the fact that different styles of talk are suited to different forms of mental activity.

 READING 11.8

Using questions in classroom discussion

Elizabeth Perrot

This is a detailed reading on the various skills and strategies involved in the use of questions in classroom discussion. This is an essential part of any teaching repertoire. Perrot considers how to use questioning to improve both the quality of children's thinking, particularly with reference to 'higher order thinking', and the extent of their participation. Finally, she reviews some of the most important issues in the development of an effective overall questioning strategy.

Questioning is one of the most important techniques of teaching, and taping a session when using questioning is always revealing. What does Perrot's analysis of skills offer to you?

Edited from: Perrot, E. (1982) *Effective Teaching: A Practical Guide to Improving Your Teaching.* London: Longman, 56–91

Research studies carried out in many parts of the world have shown that the majority of teacher's questions call for specific factual answers, or lower cognitive thought. But higher cognitive questions, which cause pupils to go beyond memory and use other thought processes in forming an answer, have an important role. While both types of questions have their part to play in teaching, a heavy reliance on lower-order questioning encourages rote learning and does little to develop higher-order thinking processes.

Teaching skills associated with helping pupils to give more complete and thoughtful responses are: pausing, prompting, seeking further clarification and refocusing a pupil's response.

Teaching skills associated with increasing the amount and quality of pupils' participation are: redirecting the same question to several pupils, framing questions that call for sets of related facts, and framing questions that require the pupil to use higher cognitive thought.

Such teaching skills are a means to an end (pupils' behaviour). Therefore, you must have clearly in mind the particular end you wish to achieve. Additionally you must become a careful observer of pupils' behaviour, since their reactions can give you valuable clues about the effectiveness of your own performance.

Helping pupils to give more complete and thoughtful responses

Pausing If the teacher's object is to sample what the class knows within a relatively short time and to elicit brief answers, 'rapid-fire' questioning is an appropriate skill. On the other hand, if the teacher's objective is to provide an atmosphere more conducive to discussion, in which pupils will have time to organize longer and more thoughtful responses, he must adopt a more appropriate questioning procedure. One skill that may be used to encourage longer and more thoughtful responses is to pause for three to five seconds after asking a question, but before calling on a pupil. The use of this skill should eventually result in longer responses because your pupils will be able to discriminate between pausing behaviour and your 'rapid-fire questioning'.

However, they will not automatically give longer answers when you first begin using pausing in your discussions. Depending upon their previous classroom experiences, relatively few pupils may respond appropriately. Some may begin to day-dream, hoping they will not be called on; others may raise their hands without first thinking. Therefore, when you first start using pausing behaviour, you should help the pupils learn what you want them to do. Immediately after the question verbal prompts can be presented, such as, 'Please think over your answer carefully', 'When I call on you, I want a complete answer', then pause for three to five seconds before you call on someone. Success lies in using questions which require longer and more thoughtful responses, pausing to allow ample time to organize those responses and reinforcing pupils for such responses.

If the pupil's response does not come up to the level you are seeking, you must be prepared to help him to develop a better answer. Good ideas however, should not be rejected simply because you did not previously consider them. You should always be prepared to evaluate and accept good answers, and to reinforce the pupil for them.

Prompting This strategy is based on a series of questions containing hints that help the pupil develop his answer. Sometimes a single prompt will be sufficient to guide the pupil to a better answer. More commonly, it is necessary for the teacher to use a series of prompts which lead the pupil step by step to answer the original question. Teacher prompts may be in the form of intermediate questions, clues or hints, that give the pupil the information he needs to arrive at a better answer. If the initial response is partly correct, first reinforce the correct part by telling the pupil what was right. Then begin by modifying the incorrect part. The exact questions used in a prompting sequence cannot be specified in advance, since each depends on the pupil's previous response. However, you should always have in mind the criterion response. Equally important, you should praise the final answer as much as if the pupil gave it at the beginning.

Seeking clarification In some instances, a pupil may give a response which is poorly organized, lacking in detail or incomplete. Here you face a situation in which the pupil is not wrong, but in which his answer still does not match the response you seek. Under these circumstances you can use the probing skill of seeking clarification. Unlike prompting, seeking clarification starts at a different point on the response continuum. The teacher is not adding information; he is requesting the pupil to do so.

Refocusing There are numerous occasions when the teacher receives a response that matches the one he wants. Refocusing may then be used to relate the pupil's response to another topic he has studied. The skill is used to help the pupil consider the implications of his response within a broader conceptual framework. He is asked to relate his answer to another issue. Refocusing is the most difficult form of probing since the teacher must have a thorough knowledge of how various topics in the curriculum may be related. You will be able to refocus more effectively if you study the content of your planned discussion beforehand, and note relationships with other topics the class has studied.

Improving the amount and quality of pupils' participation

Redirection In using the technique of redirection, the same question is directed to several pupils. The question is neither repeated nor rephrased even though more than one pupil responds. To use redirection effectively, you must choose a question which calls for an answer of related facts or allows a variety of alternative responses. A poor question for redirection is one requiring only a single answer, such as 'What is the capital of France?' In this case, the first correct response effectively shuts off further questioning.

The first result of redirection is that you will talk less and the pupils will participate more. A second gain, which can be used to advantage later, is that by requiring several pupils to respond to the same question you can begin encouraging pupils to respond to each other.

Questions calling for sets of related facts You undoubtedly encounter pupils in your classes who respond to almost any type of question as briefly as possible; that is, they answer 'yes' or 'no', or use only short phrases. Before you blame the pupils for not achieving more, be sure you are not at fault. You may be using types of questions associated with short answers that are not recognizable by their stem. When you ask, 'Isn't the purpose of your local police force the protection of life and property?' you are actually seeking a simple 'yes' or 'no' response. The question is so phrased that confirmation by the pupil is an acceptable answer. If on the other hand, you want discussion, you should phrase the same question as follows: 'What are the duties of our local police force?' A 'yes' or 'no' response will not suffice here. But what if you have good questions and the pupils are still not responding adequately? Where do you start? As we have suggested, the question itself is only part of the story. Pupils previously allowed to respond briefly or to give memory-type responses are not likely to respond to your expectations at first. Praise the pupil for what he has stated and ask him to contribute more. Success lies in using questions which require longer and better responses and in reinforcing the pupils for their successively longer and better responses.

Higher-order questions Besides encouraging pupils to give longer responses you should also try to improve the quality of their responses. Indeed, the kinds of questions the teacher asks will reveal to the pupil the kind of thinking which is expected of him. Since different kinds of questions stimulate different kinds of thinking, the teacher must be conscious of the purpose of his questions and the level of thinking they evoke.

An effective questioning sequence is one that achieves its purpose. When your purpose is to determine whether pupils remember certain specific facts, ask recall questions, such as: What is the capital of Canada? When did Henry VIII become King of England?

When your purpose is to require pupils to use information in order to either summarize, compare, contract, explain, analyse, synthesize or evaluate ask higher-order questions. For instance: Explain the kinds of problems caused by unemployment. How did life in the eighteenth century differ from life today?

Function	Skill	Participant
To increase readiness to respond	Pausing Handling incorrect responses Calling on non-volunteers	Class Individual Individual
To increase quantity of participation	Redirecting questions Calling for sets of related facts	Class
To improve quality of response	Asking higher-order questions Prompting Seeking clarification Refocusing	Individual Individual Individual Individual
To increase quantity of participation while improving quality of response	Redirecting higher-order questions	Class

Figure 11.8.1 Functions, skills and participants in questioning: a summary

Developing an overall questioning strategy

In order to be effective, skills must be appropriately incorporated into a questioning strategy planned to achieve particular learning objectives. The summary in Figure 11.8.1 indicates the relationships between functions and skills.

A common problem in questioning sequences is a lack of emphasis on higher-order questions. This may be due to failure in planning a strategy where the primary objective is the improvement of the quality of thought. It may also be related to the fact that questioning is taking place in a group situation where the teacher is concerned with the quantity of pupil participation. In his effort to increase the quantity of pupil participation a teacher might rely on redirecting a disproportionate number of multiple-fact questions. Such tactics tend to emphasize recall and decrease the time available for asking higher-order questions and probing.

A second problem relates to the teacher's failure to refocus. A primary task of the teacher is to help pupils relate what they are presently learning to what they have previously learned. Perhaps an even more significant task is to help pupils to understand that the ideas which they are studying are often relevant to other situations. Refocusing is probably the most difficult probing skill. Although the use of this skill depends on the preceding answer of the pupil, teachers who have clearly in mind the conceptual content of their lesson can plan for questioning sequences which enable them to use refocusing.

A third problem arises from the teacher's failure to have clearly in mind criteria for evaluating pupil responses. As previously mentioned, skills provide a means to an end. Only by specifying a particular end can a teacher determine which means are appropriate. To increase the quality of pupils' answers teachers should:

Carefully plan questions which require higher-order responses.

Have in mind the criteria for an acceptable answer.

Identify previously learned facts which are essential to the initiation of the higher-order questions.

Review for essential information to determine what the pupils know.

Frame questions that can be used systematically to develop the original pupil response and meet the higher-order criteria.

📖 READING 11.9

Standard and non-standard English

Michael Stubbs

There has been considerable debate in recent years concerning the teaching of 'Standard' English in schools. The National Curriculum presents this as an entitlement to which all children should have access, and yet there have also been fears that the emphasis on Standard English could undermine increasingly important provision for cultural and linguistic diversity. Michael Stubbs provides clear definitions of some of the most important linguistic distinctions and considers some of the social, geographical and historical factors which are associated with prestigious variants of English.

What linguistic variety exists at your school and how is this reflected in school provision?

Edited from: Stubbs, M. (1983) *Language, Schools and Classrooms*. London: Routledge, 32–7

Terms such as standard language and dialect are in common use, and although people often think their meaning is obvious, they turn out to be rather elusive. The definition of Standard English is complex, but it is important to give a rather careful and detailed definition, because Standard English has a special place in the education system in Britain.

Several terms are used for Standard English including 'BBC English' and the 'Queen's English'. These terms are not very precise. But they do no harm if they are not taken too literally. Another term, however, does not refer to the same thing at all. This is 'Received Pronunciation'. This is a socially prestigious accent, and refers only to pronunciation, whereas Standard English refers to a dialect defined by grammar and vocabulary. There is a peculiar relationship between Received Pronunciation and Standard English. All users of Received Pronunciation speak Standard English: this is not logically necessary, but merely a fact of our language in Britain. On the other hand, only a few speakers of Standard English use Received Pronunciation. For example, I speak Standard English with a regional west of Scotland accent. There is, in fact, no standard accent of English.

A fairly satisfactory preliminary definition of Standard English can be provided simply by listing examples of its main uses. Standard English is the variety of English which is normally used in print, and more generally in the public media (hence BBC English), and used by most educated speakers most of the time. It is the variety used in the education system and therefore the variety taught to learners of English as a foreign language. These examples tell any native speaker roughly what is meant by Standard English. On the other hand, they leave unclear whether Standard English is a predominantly written variety, and whether it is a prescriptive norm imposed by the education system or a description of the language which some people actually use.

Standard English is a dialect, and like any other dialect there is stylistic variation within it. That is, Standard English may be either formal or casual and colloquial. The following sentences are all Standard English:

I have not seen any of those children.

I haven't seen any of those kids.

I haven't seen any of those bloody kids.

Speakers of Standard English can be as casual, polite or rude as anyone else, and can use slang, swear and say things in bad style or bad taste. This all has to do with stylistic variation or questions of social etiquette, and not with dialect. The following sentence is not Standard English:

I ain't seen none of them kids.

It is not incorrect Standard English: it is simply not Standard English at all. The double negative, the use of them as a possessive adjective and the use of ain't, are perfectly regular grammatical features which characterize many nonstandard dialects of British English. Vocabulary can also be regional and nonstandard: for example, bairns is regionally restricted to Scotland and northern England.

One important point about Standard English is that it is not regionally restricted as nonstandard dialects are. There is some regional variation between the Standard English used in England, Scotland, Wales and Ireland, but very much less than in nonstandard varieties. In fact, there is a remarkably uniform international Standard English. Again there are small differences among the standard varieties used in Britain, North America, South Africa, Australia, New Zealand and the Caribbean. But the differences (in vocabulary, grammar and spelling) are minor given its very large number of speakers over an enormous geographical area.

It follows that Standard English is not a regional or geographical dialect. It is a social dialect; that dialect which is used by almost all 'educated' speakers. It is intuitively obvious that there is much more variation in the language used by working-class people in Britain than by middle-class people. Thus two businessmen from Aberdeen and Exeter would have little difficulty in understanding each other; but two farm labourers from Aberdeen and Exeter would speak very differently. Trudgill (1975) diagrams the relation between social and regional diversity as follows:

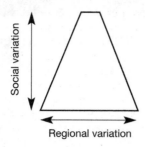

Figure 11.9.1 Social and regional language variation

As we move up the social class scale, there is less regional variation in dialect, though even right at the top there is still a little.

People, including dictionary makers and school teachers, observe what they think is good usage. This may well be a mixture of local prejudice about what is a 'good accent', sometimes outdated norms of educated usage and notions of written or even literary language which may be inappropriate to spoken English. On this basis they may formulate rules which may become quite rigid. Once established, such rules can become self-perpetuating. Standard English is used by prestigious people for prestigious purposes. The prestige of the speakers rubs off on the language, and the circle continues. Standard English, the social elite who use it, and the public functions it serves become inseparable.

I have now used by implication several different types of definition of Standard English. Standard English is most closely related to regional dialects spoken in the south-east of England. This looks like a geographical definition. But, as I have pointed out, Standard English is no longer regionally restricted. In fact, this is a disguised historical definition: Standard English developed historically out of a dialect used in London, especially in the court. This shows in turn the need for a social definition. Historically Standard English spread because of the prestige of its users, and is now the social dialect used by educated middle-class speakers from all over Britain (and with minor variations in many other countries). I have also used a functional definition. Standard English is the variety used in print, in education and as an international language. These definitions are not prescriptive: they do not say who ought to use Standard English for what purposes. They are descriptive: they describe certain social facts which govern how it is, as a matter of fact, used. These conventions are socially and politically loaded, but I have not passed any judgement on whether they are desirable or not.

However, it is easy to see how the borderline between a descriptive and a prescriptive definition breaks down. The reason for one further confusion should now be clear. Standard English is prestigious and because of its speakers and its uses it is simply more visible than other varieties. The very fact that it is the variety used in print makes it more visible. People therefore come to think of Standard English as the language. They confuse one socially predominant dialect with 'the English language'. This is clearly an extreme idealization, since the whole point of my discussion has been that English is a cluster of many different styles and dialects.

Bilingualism, culture and education

Jane Miller

The experience of bilingual school children varies considerably and, for some, school life can be very challenging. In what is a classic book on the topic, from which the reading below is taken, Jane Miller challenges mono-cultural thinking and identifies the benefits of diversity and linguistic capability which can be fulfilled in classrooms by bilingual pupils – given appropriate support from teachers.
   Is your school enriched by bilingual pupils?

Edited from: Miller, J. (1983) *Many Voices: Bilingualism, Culture and Education*. London: Routledge, 2–13

Most of the bilingual people I talked to believe that they are fortunate people, having that sort of knowledge and experience, and we may want to agree with them. Yet many children in the same position are treated as having problems in school. That is the enigma.

When I have told people that I am trying to write about bilingualism some of them have been concerned that I should devote myself to so marginal an issue at a time when education is under particular threat. I have become increasingly sure that bilingualism is not a marginal issue. This is not simply because we now know that something like fourteen per cent of London schoolchildren are bilingual. Listening to these people, reading what they have to say, has convinced me that they are able to testify, in a uniquely revealing way, to experiences which are central to present-day British society and to the kind of education society provides for its children. It has confirmed for me the sense that language, first languages and subsequent or alternative languages, are inextricably a part of people's lives, their energy as learners and their sense of life's possibilities. Neither bilingualism nor the people I have talked to are marginal. Both have, in my view, something to tell us which may be central to learning and to people's lives.

In Andreas' class they had a lesson last week from one of the boys, on Korean, and how you write it in different directions to show whether you're talking about the past or the future. That was amazing. Mr Orme did Ancient Greek when he was young and he wanted to find out whether that helps at all with Modern Greek. He's impressed by all the languages his pupils speak. One boy, who speaks Urdu, Punjabi and Hindi, can read and write in Urdu and Punjabi and is learning to read Hindi at after-school classes. It has taken him only four years to sound like a native Cockney speaker, and his writing is good too. Mr Orme is rare as a teacher. He has gone to the trouble of finding out what languages the boys speak at home; and because a lot of them are from Jamaican families he has learned to speak their language and can discuss in detail the differences between Kingston Jamaican, London Jamaican and the sort of English he speaks.

Some teachers think he is wasting his time, that he would have to agree that since these children live in England and will probably stay here for the rest of their lives, teaching them the sort of English which helps them to pass exams and get jobs is what he is there for. Mr Orme does agree, though he finds it harder and harder to be sure that he knows what sort of English that would actually be. When he was a boy he won a place at a grammar school in Durham. All the boys spoke with an accent, even used different words, but their teacher saw to it that they didn't speak 'sloppily' with him. For a long time Mr Orme believed that you couldn't expect even to spell properly if you didn't talk like the BBC. Wouldn't all those rules for doubling letters, spelling the or sound and silent 'e's be much easier to get right if you talk posh? He remembered one of his mates saying that squeezing up the vowels and making a big thing of the consonants was the way to get on. Mr Orme's ideas have changed since then. He likes the way his pupils speak and he even likes his own accent now; still 'rough', as he thinks of it, after all these years in London.

When he talks about these things with his friends they think he's a bit sentimental or just making the best of a bad job. It is difficult enough to explain, let alone to justify, his conviction that his being interested in the languages his pupils speak does actually help them to write English of several sorts and to speak more confidently in class. It isn't as if he knew all those languages himself, though: Yoruba, Arabic, Cantonese, Gujarati. He often wishes he did. He can't even find good dictionaries for most of the languages.

It is not that there need be any argument with the tradition which makes schools the promoters of literacy; but that the written form and its intimate relation, in many people's eyes, with Standard English speech can be made to exclude the realities of the language as it is spoken. Many children spend a larger proportion of their day in school on writing and listening than on reading or talking. Even tests which are intended to assess oral comprehension, reading competence and a response to literature are made to depend on the child's knowing how to write a certain sort of English prose. That is the sort of English Mr Orme should be teaching his pupils. It is not a form easily learned by anyone whose own speech is under suspicion. The best examples of expository or imaginative prose draw vitally upon the spoken language in ways which children should be helped to understand. The belief that a child can learn to produce even the most modest versions of such prose while his speech is dismissed, even perhaps excoriated, is likely to be doomed, and we can't, surely, be wanting children to 'talk like the book'.

To be genuinely multilingual or multidialectal in contemporary Britain is allowed, then, to be a drawback. It is still thought 'useful' to know some Latin, while knowledge of Standard Tamil, say, and one of its dialects, is thought 'confusing'.

In one sense it is all quite simple. Where a child grows up speaking more than one language or dialect, and those languages or dialects have equivalent status in his own and in other people's eyes, and where the connections between those languages and their differences are made explicit, multilingualism can be an unqualified good. Mr Orme's pupil, Andreas, is in that rare position. He still visits Cyprus. English people know about Greek, even hear it spoken on their holidays. Andreas speaks Greek for most of the time at home, but other members of his family speak English too; and he is not aware of making conscious decisions about which language to speak to whom or where. He could read and write in Greek before he arrived in England, and he learned English in a school where it was thought, rightly, that he was competent linguistically even if he didn't know English, and where they have come to rely on and to admire his success. He was lucky too to embark on the second of his languages before he was too old to do so easily and to learn it principally through using it with children of his own age. As an example of a bilingual's advantages he is ideal, though hardly typical.

It is a characteristic irony that while the learning of languages can be an expensive business, nearly all those people in the world who grow up or become bilingual do so because their mother tongue or dialect has associations with poverty which make it likely to be thought inappropriate for education and some kinds of employment. Many of the people who have come to live in England during the last twenty-five years are in the position of speaking either a dialect of English or another language altogether, which they are encouraged, and in some cases are themselves all too ready, to relinquish.

The variety of ways in which multilingualism is experienced by children is infinite, ranging from a kind of 'anomie' at one extreme to a quite special flexibility and effectiveness as a language user at the other. Somewhere between are all those children who leave their mother tongue at home and learn 'English' at school. This can produce a damaging dividedness, particularly when it is not discussed, shared or understood. A second language learned and used only in school can feel like a language of passivity, acceptance, attention, listening and obedience. Its use will be constrained by rules and prohibitions, its vitalities and subtleties hidden. Similarly, the home language may be relegated to the terrain of childhood, interesting only as the expression of a vestigial fold culture. The life of action and feeling, of first experiences and what is directly known, can become divorced from the world where language has become an instrument for generalization, organization and the assimilating of new ideas and knowledge. There is a danger of that happening to any child, but the danger is a much greater one if the two selves, so to speak, talk in different languages. Cultural values can be distorted and polarized into what is quaint and half extinguished, on the one hand, and what is practical, modern and remunerated, on the other.

Many children are marooned between languages and between cultures, forgetting one more rapidly than they acquire another; and meanwhile they may be regarded by teachers and by other children – ultimately, perhaps, by themselves – as bereft of all the things language stands for: intelligence, humour, daring, inventiveness, enthusiasm, discrimination and curiosity. And without those qualities it is not easy to learn the new language which might enable you to regain them. A child's first sorting out of its impressions of the world, of its own place there, and of noises which are meaningful from noises which are not, came with a particular language, which is now forced underground, made inaudible, unintelligible. Learning a second language is bound to seem like a matter of attaching it to meanings which will always adhere in a special way to the first one.

Any normal child has mastered by the age of five an elaborate symbolic system and internalized its rules. This is true for any child learning any language. Through speech, and through learning to read and write, the child will 'learn to turn language and thought in upon themselves', as Margaret Donaldson (1978) has put it, so that he can talk about language and think about thinking. Children with more than one language may be especially well placed to do this. Teachers in multilingual classrooms have at their disposal resources for introducing all their pupils to the nature of language, to the quality and the implications of linguistic and cultural diversity, and, thereby, to an outlook on knowledge and to the kind of relativism which can produce both intellectual rigour and intellectual openness. The best teaching always moves from a sensitive awareness of what the learner already knows to what is new; and the best users of English, speakers and writers, plunder the tensions and the variety which English has always so vigorously incorporated.

If children are to become powerful users of language for their own purposes, and responsive to the subtleties and excitement of what has been done by others, and what can be done, teachers would do well to begin from an appreciation of the strengths, the highly developed social and linguistic skills, children bring with them when they come to school. And that means all children.

📖 READING 11.11

New kinds of literacy

Cary Bazalgette

Visual literacy is of increasing importance in the modern world and has a central role in media education. In this reading, Bazalgette draws attention to the overlap between visual literacy and print literacy. She then reviews some key concepts in media education and poses some challenges for the ways in which we think about literacy more generally. There are some resonances here with the approach offered by Davies in Reading 11.5.

Do you feel that we provide adequately for media education in the curriculum?

Edited from: Bazalgette, C. (1988) 'They changed the picture in the middle of the fight ... New kinds of literacy', in Meek, M. and Mills, C. (eds) *Language and Literacy in the Primary School*. London: Falmer Press, 4–12

The relationship between schooling and the visual media is interesting historically and culturally. When mass schooling was established in the late nineteenth century, it did not take up much of the public school classics tradition that preceded it, but it did as a matter of course acknowledge the only mass medium that was developed by then, which was, of course, print. Schooling made a predictable accommodation with the institutions of book, newspaper and magazine publishing. The new elementary schools undertook to teach working-class children to read. Educators had debated the wisdom of even that move – the skills that unlocked the Bible would also unlock the radical pamphlet – but the market potential of millions of new readers could not be denied. The possibility that working-class children might learn to produce print as well as consume it was never on the agenda.

Instead, the corollary of learning to read print was learning to write by hand. The notion that print and handwriting are both media, which differ in terms of their status, their necessary technologies, the audiences they can reach and who has access to them, was not considered important, and on the whole it still isn't. The 'competent consumer' became the taken-for-granted baseline of print literacy.

It is interesting to ask why it was not seen as the task of schools to produce 'competent consumers' of the new media technologies that developed in the ensuing years: photography, film, radio, television. But is more interesting to ask why that question seems an odd one, even today. We don't need to teach them that kind of competence, would be the response of most teachers down the years: they're too competent by half. The new media are still seen as radically different from the safe, established book-learning which schooling had claimed for its own; they were rivals for the attention of the masses. The new media taught their own competences: close-up and fade-out, stars and personalities, soap opera and sit-com. They taught well, and apparently painlessly, so schools, whose reputation for teaching badly and painfully was ruthlessly reinforced by the media through such products as *Our Gang* and the *Bash Street Kids*, could hardly be blamed for condemning these competences as not worthwhile or even downright dangerous. A hostility has thus grown up between the rival institutions of schooling and media. Teachers bewail the fact that children spend less time with them than they do with television, and 'educational' is synonymous with 'boring' for any self-respecting editor or producer. This institutional jealousy disguises the extent to which media and schooling can be seen as analogous in the ways that they define and transmit knowledge about the world.

New theories about language and literacy have shown us that the whole universe of signs, from toilet door symbols to Renaissance frescoes, is organized into systems of codes and conventions that we have learned, just as we learned verbal language. In other words, it makes sense to say that we 'read' a photograph or a TV programme in a way analogous to that in which we read a written text (Barthes, 1972).

Enquiries into the process of reading itself have suggested that reading is more than an accretion of competences in decoding marks on a page: the reader is an active, knowledgeable person who brings understandings to texts and makes sense of them, rather than just consuming them. It thus makes less sense to differentiate between 'readers' of books and 'viewers' of audio-visual texts on the grounds that the latter are passive consumers of easy or obvious meanings. The cinema audience of 1895 would make as little sense of *EastEnders* as an 8-year-old would of *Pride and Prejudice*. Film, television, photographs, radio all have their own languages which are constructed, have developed over time, use agreed conventions and are learned by their audiences.

Our knowledge about reading and writing can offer us assumptions upon which to base our ideas about extending the notion of literacy. We need to develop goals for 'literacy' in audio-visual media too, and to develop its key concepts. In this task, a British group with which I am involved under the auspices of the British Film Institute, is attempting to identify a small number of very basic but separately definable conceptual areas which characterize media education, even though they may at this stage be very abstract and imply for each area a vast range of potential content and approaches.

Construction The fact that all media texts are constructed, using codes which have developed historically, and which we learn. What these codes or 'media languages' are and how they can be used. The technologies upon which they are based. Who produces texts and why.

Circulation The fact that media texts are directed to audiences, that audiences can be constituted in many different ways, and that there are different ways of reaching them. That audiences bring meanings to texts and read them actively and, therefore, different readings of any text are usually possible.

Narration Events or states of affairs are organized in particular ways in all media texts – these ways will differ according to the kind of text. The differences between 'story' and 'plot'; the manipulation of time; the role of character; selection and editing; narrative voices; point of view and identification.

Categorization Media texts can be grouped in various ways: by technology, genre, intended audience, etc. What groupings can be made, and why. It makes a difference to the interpretation of a text, to see it in terms of a particular category.

Representation The fact that there are differences between social groups, events etc. in the world and the ways they are represented and questioned in media texts. That some events and groups may be systematically excluded from media texts, and why. How these relationships can be explored. That there are different levels of realism. Caricature and stereotyping. [For an extension of this framework see Bazalgette, 1989.]

Identifying key concepts at such a basic level provokes a further question. By what argument would one assert that these concepts are applicable only to audio-visual media? Couldn't they apply to print media as well? I have suggested that our conventional understandings of literacy can help us to develop a rationale for teaching about other media. I now want to turn this proposition on its head and suggest that the ways in which media education has developed may have implications for our understandings of literacy. Do we ask children to adopt a critical stance towards the books and posters we use in the classroom, towards educational TV, towards their own writing? It is better, for example, to eliminate racist and sexist material from our stock cupboards, or to find ways of criticizing both them and the conditions that enable them to exist? Do we discuss who gets into print, and how, and why – and who doesn't?

There is no real rationale for separating media into different categories and teaching them differently, except insofar as their technologies demand it. To establish 'media education' or 'media literacy' as new buzz-words for primary schools would be a good way of achieving limited change. To redefine literacy might be a real change.

CHAPTER 12

How are we assessing children's learning?

The nine readings in this chapter provide clarification of the many types of assessment and indications of the positive, and negative, roles which it can fulfil in teaching and learning.

In the first group of readings, definitions and applications of different types of assessment are offered. Reading 12.1, by Harlen and colleagues, reviews assessment purposes, whilst Croll (12.2) focuses on the relationship between norm and criterion referencing. Black, an early contributor to the construction of the national assessment system in England and Wales, poses key questions deriving from his experience (12.3).

Lindsay (12.4) reviews the history and weaknesses of IQ testing and calls for consideration of a very wide range of factors which influence capability. McCallum and her colleagues (12.5) offer a classification of different approaches to teacher assessment, whilst Broadfoot (12.6) questions the use to teachers of official National Curriculum assessment data.

The final group of readings are from authors who are particularly concerned with pupil perspectives. Muschamp (12.7) offers practical advice on the development of pupil self-assessment. Armstrong (12.8) contests the blinkered appreciation of children's work which he believes National Curriculum assessment may encourage, and Drummond (12.9) appeals for assessment to be cast as an attempt to 'understand' children's perspectives rather than simply as a way of judging them.

The parallel chapter of *Reflective Teaching in the Primary School* reviews the role of assessment in teaching and learning, including a section on pupil self-assessment. It then addresses some key issues: the effect on class relationships, manageability, validity and reliability, curriculum distortion and the impact on children. A full range of methods for gathering assessment evidence is then reviewed and there is finally a section on records and reporting. For most of these topics, there are suggested practical activities for classroom use and there are also many suggestions for further reading.

Assessment purposes and principles

Wynne Harlen, Caroline Gipps, Patricia Broadfoot and Desmond Nuttall

Perhaps the single most important source of confusion regarding assessment stems from misunder-standings about the purposes of different forms of assessment. There are many types of assessment, but each is suited to particular purposes and cannot safely be used in other ways. This reading pro-vides an excellent overview of assessment purposes, key principles and four of the most important types of assessment.

Assessment purposes have often been conflated by policy-makers, but what type would be most helpful to you in your work?

Edited from: Harlen, W., Gipps, C., Broadfoot, P. and Nuttall, D. (1992) Assessment and the improvement of education, *Curriculum Journal*, 3 (3), 217–25

Assessment in education is the process of gathering, interpreting, recording and using infor-mation about pupils' responses to an educational task. At one end of a dimension of formal-ity, the task may be normal classroom work and the process of gathering information would be the teacher reading a pupil's work or listening to what he or she has to say. At the other end of the dimension of formality, the task may be a written, timed examination which is read and marked according to certain rules and regulations. Thus assessment encompasses respons-es to regular work as well as to specially devised tasks.

All types of assessment, of any degree of formality involve interpretation of a pupil's response against some standard of expectation. This standard may be set by the average per-formance of a particular section of the population or age group, as in norm-referenced tests. Alternatively, as in the National Curriculum context the assessment may be criterion-referenced. Here the interpretation is in terms of progression in skills, concept or aspects of personal development which are the objectives of learning, and the assessment gives direct information which can be related to progress in learning. However, the usefulness of criterion-referenced assessment depends on the way in which the criteria are defined. Too tightly defined criteria, while facilitating easy judgement of mastery, require an extensive list which fragments the curriculum. On the other hand, more general criteria, which better reflect the overall aims of education, are much less easily and reliably used in assessing achievement.

The roles of assessment in education are as follows:

as the means for providing feedback to teachers and pupils about on-going progress in learning, has a direct influence on the quality of pupils' learning experiences and thus on the level of attainment which can be achieved (formative role);

as the means for communicating the nature and level of pupils' achievements at various points in their schooling and when they leave (summative role);

as a means of summarizing, for the purposes of selection and qualification, what has been achieved (certification role);

as providing part of the information used in judging the effectiveness of educational insti-tutions and of the system as a whole (evaluative or quality control role).

There is an unavoidable backwash on the curriculum from the content and procedures of assessment. The higher the stakes of the assessment, the greater this will be. Multiple-choice and other paper-and-pencil tests provide results which are easily aggregated and compared but their use encourages teachers to ignore much of what pupils should learn as they 'teach to the test'.

Not all assessment purposes are compatible. Strong evidence from experience in the US, combined with that now accumulating in England and Wales, indicates that information collected for the purposes of supporting learning is unsuitable and unreliable if summarized and used for the purposes of quality control, that is, for making judgements about schools, and its use for this purpose severely impairs its formative role.

There is likely to be a trade-off between, on the one hand, cost and quality and, on the other, effectiveness. The cheapest assessment techniques, such as multiple-choice, machine-markable tests, may be convenient instruments to use but provide poor quality information for the purposes of communication and little or no support for the learning process itself.

Key principles

These issues of the purposes of assessment are borne in mind in proposing the following set of principles to inform policy-making on assessment:

assessment must be used as a continuous part of the teaching-learning process, involving pupils, wherever possible, as well as teachers in identifying next steps;

assessment for any purpose should serve the purpose of improving learning by exerting positive force on the curriculum at all levels. It must, therefore, reflect the full range of curriculum goals, including the more sophisticated skills and abilities now being taught;

assessment must provide an effective means of communication with parents and other partners in the learning enterprise in a way which helps them support pupils' learning;

the choice of different assessment procedures must be decided on the basis of the purpose for which the assessment is being undertaken. This may well mean employing different techniques for different assessment purposes;

assessment must be used fairly as part of information for judging the effectiveness of schools. This means taking account of contextual factors which, as well as the quality of teaching, affect the achievement of pupils;

citizens have a right to detailed and reliable information about the standards being achieved across the nation through the educational system.

Formative assessment

A major role identified for assessment is that of monitoring learning and informing teaching decisions on a day-to-day basis. In this role, assessment is an integral part of the interactions between teacher, pupil and learning materials. Because of this relationship, some teachers, who practise formative assessment well, may not recognize that what they are doing includes assessing.

What is required from a formative assessment scheme is information that is: gathered in a number of relevant contexts; criterion-referenced and related to a description of progression; disaggregated, which means that distinct aspects of performance are reported separately; shared by both teacher and pupil; on a basis for deciding what further learning is required; the basis of an on-going running record of progress.

A scheme of formative assessment must be embedded in the structures of educational practice; it cannot be grafted on to it. Thus there are implications in the foregoing for the curriculum, for teachers, in terms of required supporting materials and pre-service or in-service training, and for record-keeping practice.

Summative assessment

Summative assessment is similar to formative assessment in that it concerns the performance of individual pupils, as opposed to groups. In contrast with formative assessment, however, its prime purpose is not much to influence teaching but to summarize information about the achievements of a pupil at a particular time. The information may be for the pupils themselves, for receiving teachers, for parents, for employers or for a combination of these.

There are two main ways of obtaining summative information about achievements: summing up and checking up (Harlen, 1991). The former is some form of summary of information obtained through recording formative assessments during a particular period of time and the latter the collection of new information about what the pupil can do at the end of a period of time, usually through giving some form of test. The nature and relative advantages and disadvantages of these are now briefly reviewed.

Summing up provides a picture of current achievements derived from information gathered over a period of time and probably used in that time for formative purposes. It is, therefore, detailed and broadly based, encompassing all the aspects of learning which have been addressed in teaching. To retain the richness of the information it is best communicated in the form of a profile (i.e. not aggregated), to which information is added on later occasions. Records of achievement (RoA) provide a structure for recording and reporting this information, combining some of the features of formative assessment with the purposes of summative assessment in that they involve pupils in reviewing their own work and recognizing where their strengths and weaknesses lie.

Checking up offers no such additional benefits as an approach to summative assessment. It is generally carried out through providing tests or tasks specially devised for the purpose of recording performance at a particular time. End of year tests or examinations are examples, as are the end of module tests for checking performance in modular programmes and external public examinations.

Checking up and summing up approaches have contrasting advantages and disadvantages. Tests used for checking up are limited in scope unless they are inordinately long and so are unlikely to cover practical skills and some of the higher level cognitive skills. On the other hand, they do provide opportunities for all pupils to demonstrate what they have learned. Summative assessment which is based only on formative assessment depends on the opportunities provided in class for various skills and understandings to be displayed and, further, may be out of date in relation to parts of work covered at earlier points and perhaps not revisited.

This suggests that a combination of these two approaches may be the most appropriate solution. There are several advantages to having test materials available for teachers to use to supplement, at the end of a particular period, the information they have from on-going assessment during that time. The emphasis is on 'test materials' and not tests. These would ideally be in the form of a bank from which teachers select according to their needs. The items in the bank would cover the whole range of curriculum objectives and the whole range of procedures required for valid assessment. This provision would also serve the purposes of the non-statutory Standard Assessment Tasks (SATs).

The main advantages are that the availability of a bank of test material would provide teachers with the opportunity to check or supplement their own assessment in a particular area where they felt uncertain about what pupils can do. This would ensure that all aspects of pupils' work were adequately assessed without requiring extensive testing. Checking their own assessments against those arising from well-trialled and validated tasks would also build up teachers' expertise and lead to greater rigour in teachers' assessments.

Assessment for evaluative and quality assurance purposes

Information about pupils' achievement is necessary in order to keep under review the performance of the system as a whole – the quality assurance role of assessment. In the absence of such information it is possible for rumour and counter-rumour to run riot. For example, the argument about the levels of performance of seven-year-olds in reading (prior to the national assessment data) would never have been possible had there been a national survey of reading performance at the age of seven.

To serve this purpose, assessment has to be carried out in a way which leads to an overall picture of achievement on a national scale. It requires measures of achievement of a large number of pupils to be obtained and summarized. For this purpose testing in controlled conditions is necessary. However, if every pupil is tested, this leads to adverse effects on both teaching practice and on the curriculum and an over-emphasis on formal testing generally. Further, surveys which test every pupil cannot provide the depth of data required to provide a wide-range and in-depth picture of the system. Thus testing every pupil at a particular age is not appropriate for assessing performance at the national level.

To serve the evaluative role, assessment at the national level does not need to cover all pupils nor to assess in all attainment targets those who are included. The necessary rigour and comparability in assessment for this purpose can be provided by the use of a sample of pupils undertaking different assessment tasks. Following the pioneering work of the Assessment of Performance Unit (APU), it would be possible to obviate the 'excessively complicated and time consuming' approach of the SATs and still provide the comprehensive coverage of every subject area across a satisfactorily large sample of particular age groups of pupils.

Assessing school effectiveness

It is well established that the attainment of an individual is as much a function of his or her social circumstances and the educational experiences of his or her parents as it is of the effectiveness of the school or schools attended. To judge the effectiveness of a school by the attainment of its pupils is therefore misleading and unfair. What is wanted is a model that disentangles the effect on attainment of the school from that of the pupils' background. The value-added approach, that looks at the gain in achievement while the pupil is at a particular school (that is, the progress he or she makes there) offers a way forward and is, indeed, the basis of school effectiveness research such as that reported in *School Matters* (Mortimore *et al.*, 1988; see also McPherson, 1992).

The assessments of attainment used (both on entry to the school and on leaving) should be as broad as possible to ensure that school effectiveness is not reduced to efficiency in teaching test-taking skills but reflects the full range of the aims of the school.

To counter the narrowness of outcomes implied by test results, even when shown in value-added form, it is suggested that schools should publish detailed reports covering such areas as: the aims of the school; details of recent inspection reports (if any); particular areas of expertise offered; cultural and sporting achievements; community involvement; destinations of leavers. In short, the school should show its test results as part of its record of achievement.

Norm and criterion referenced assessment

Paul Croll

This reading offers a clarification of the difference between traditional forms of norm-referenced assessment through formal testing and the criterion-referenced approach which has been used for assessment of the National Curriculum. However, Paul Croll argues that, in practice, these forms of assessment are not distinct and that the influence of normative expectations and judgements is inevitable.

To what extent do you feel that your judgements of a child's capability are influenced by what you expect children of that age to be able to do?

Edited from: Croll, P. (1990), Norm and criterion referenced assessment, *Redland Papers*, (1) Summer, 8–11

Norm referenced assessment and criterion referenced assessment are usually taken to be contrasting and even opposing approaches to educational assessment. However, I shall argue that the distinction between these two approaches is by no means as clear cut as is often supposed.

Norm referenced assessments are assessments where an individual's performance is judged with reference to the performance of others on the same test or assessment procedure. For example, if the reading performance of a child is expressed as a reading age of, say 8 years and 2 months, this means that on a test which has been tried out on a large sample of children, the child in question has achieved the average score of children aged 8 years 2 months in the sample. Such a score is often then expressed in terms of the relationship of the child's reading age to his or her chronological age.

The relationship of performance to age also informs the standardization of published tests of ability and achievement. These express levels of performance by means of a score which is referenced against a known average performance for children of that age (usually 100) and a known standard deviation (usually 15) of a distribution of scores constructed to follow a normal curve. The range of tests developed and published by the National Foundation for Educational Research are probably the best known tests of this sort in Britain. This procedure also underlies scores on IQ tests. The known distribution of scores on a normal curve means that a child who receives a score of, for instance, 116 on such a test, giving a result just above one standard deviation from the mean, has performed at a level which puts her or him just within the top 16 per cent of the age group.

Norm referenced testing does not have to be related to a normal curve or to the idea of a normal distribution of achievements. Whenever a test is reported or interpreted with reference to the achievement of others, then norm referencing is taking place. A teacher who uses ranking to interpret tests, for instance saying that a child has come top or is around the average or is in the bottom ten per cent, is using norm referencing.

Criterion referenced testing involves constructing assessment procedures which relate an individual's results not to the results of others but to whether or not they meet a pre-determined, independent criterion. A commonly given example of a criterion referenced test is the driving test. This is supposed to assess whether or not people are safe drivers against some absolute criterion of adequate performance, not in terms of how they stand in relation to the average driver or whether they are in the top ten per cent of drivers. In education, criterion referenced tests are intended to establish whether or not someone has particular knowledge or competence, not how they stand with relation to other people with regard to these. 'Statements of attainment' and 'level descriptions' in National Curriculum assessment are an attempt to introduce criterion referencing.

Many discussions of assessment tend to emphasize the greater educational value of criterion referenced assessment compared with norm referenced methods. For instance, norm referenced testing has been criticized for imposing a purely statistical model of academic achievement. Using norm referenced methods, whatever the overall level of achievement, some children must always be top and some bottom. Indeed, standardization against population norms means that approximately half of a population must always be below average however well they perform. Such methods are also criticized as being of little educational value. To know that a child is 18th in the class or in the top quarter of the population has no obvious implications for teaching, and test items may be selected on the grounds that they spread out performance rather than for their educational interest. Finally, norm referencing has been criticized for being elitist and being obsessed with differentiating children and sorting them into a hierarchical ranking.

In contrast, criterion referenced testing can be seen as being concerned to tell teachers what they need to know for their practical, classroom provisions, through concentrating on whether particular curriculum objectives have been met. And the content of criterion referenced items are more likely to relate to the actual content of what teachers are trying to assess.

Unfortunately, the distinction between the 'educationally valuable' criterion referencing and the 'educationally irrelevant' norm referencing is not as clear as the discussion above has suggested.

Clearly norm referenced tests cannot be compiled without reference to educational criteria. A child's relative standing on an assessment is only of interest in the context of the nature of the educational attainment the assessment purports to measure and the issue of validity, the relationship between test content and underlying educational concepts, has been of great concern to people constructing norm referenced assessments. It is also the case that particular levels of attainment on a norm referenced test can usually be related to specific types and levels of educational achievement as well as being used to locate performance relative to that of others.

Conversely however, just as norm referenced tests must always take account of educational criteria, so criterion referenced assessment must, in practice, take account of the performance of children. When we attempt to construct an educationally useful criterion relating to an element of skill and knowledge we inevitably draw on at least an implicit model of what is appropriate for a child of a particular age or with particular educational experiences. Indeed in making educational judgements about any one child it is virtually impossible to ignore the information we have about the performance of others. For instance the judgement that a child's progress is giving cause for concern is only possible in the context of what we know about most children of that age or developmental stage or with that level of educational experience. This is because educational performance is developmental and our knowledge of what is usual or possible developmentally is based on our experience of children. Consequently norm based criteria are almost certain to be part of any apparently criterion referenced assessments, even though this may not be made explicit. Test constructors may not themselves be fully aware of it, but their criteria are almost certain to reflect their experience of children's attainments.

National Curriculum assessments were explicitly designed to be criterion referenced. The 'levels' are intended to reflect specified criteria for attainment against which children are assessed rather than being assessed against one another. However, as with other attempts to construct precise criteria for judging complex educational attainments, such as that of writing grade-related criteria for GCSE, actually delivering criterion referenced assessment has proved to be extremely difficult. The Dearing Review of the National Curriculum recognized the strength of opinion that criterion referencing is '...whatever its theoretical attractions, extremely difficult to deliver' (Dearing, 1993, p 57). Although the review argued for a continued attempt to include element of criterion referencing in national assessments, it accepted with regard to statements of attainment that '... their apparent precision is sometimes spurious ...' (Dearing, 1993, p 58).

The conceptual distinction between norm and criterion referenced assessments remains valuable. However, the discussion above does indicate both the practical and conceptual difficulty of applying the distinction. With the National Curriculum, as in other assessments, the influences of formative conceptions of pupil performance on criteria for assessment is inevitable.

Performance, assessment and accountability

Paul Black

Paul Black led the Task Group on Assessment and Testing (TGAT) which devised the initial framework of national assessment in 1988. TGAT proposed to draw on a formative accumulation of professional judgements to provide evidence of summative attainment at the end of each Key Stage. However, there was considerable mistrust of this from politicians and the role of SATs was increased. Here, Paul Black reflects on some of his experiences by highlighting six key issues in the development of national assessment systems.

Thinking of your own education system at present, how have Black's questions been answered?

Edited from: Black, P. (1994) Performance, assessment and accountability: the experience in England and Wales, *Educational Evaluation and Policy Analysis*, 16 (2), 200–1

I propose below six main questions about the development of national assessment systems. Each is discussed in the light of my interpretation of the experiences in England and Wales.

First, how can professional educators and assessment experts communicate effectively to the public in general, and to politicians in particular, about the strengths and weaknesses of various forms of assessment? The limited reliability and even more limited validity of externally set, timed and formal written examinations are not understood. Their apparent fairness and objectivity is appealing, and those who wish to see them replaced by other methods are regarded either as romantics or as defenders of an illegitimate professional wish to avoid public scrutiny. Thus, the motives of TGAT were called into question because the technical basis for much of the group's thinking was not understood.

A subsidiary question under this heading is of particular importance: Can the public understand that new models of learning show that traditional assessment systems are inadequate and damaging? Work in this field shows (Gifford and O'Connor, 1992) that training pupils to succeed in the atomized items of traditional external tests is inimical to their effective learning. Thus, the back-wash effects of narrow testing are more damaging than had previously been thought, and yet they are hardly understood outside the teaching profession (Resnick and Resnick, 1992; Shepard, 1992).

Second, following from the first point, to what extent could, or should, a state or local system support improved methods of summative assessment, given that improved methods take up more teaching time and can be expensive to produce, administer, and score? The difficulty is compounded by the fact that to the outsider, including a government minister, better 'tests' often seem strange and can give the impression that the rigours of external testing are being avoided. Some of the early SATs made unacceptable demands, but their purpose was also misunderstood, and the atmosphere of public controversy destroyed any possibility of a patient search for their improvement.

Third, what should be the optimum relationship between the formative and the summative functions of teachers' assessment? The two are often conflated and confused. Both are important, but they have different functions. The TGAT report assumed that the accumulation of formative results would serve the summative purpose. Some have argued that this was a serious error (Harlen, Gipps, Broadfoot and Nuttall, 1992 [see Reading 12.1]). However, the inevitable effect of any high-stakes testing on teaching is a constant danger. If teachers' own assessments do not play a part in this summative testing, the summative will overrule and marginalize teachers' formative assessments unless the link between the two is carefully structured.

Fourth, what is the optimum means for specifying criteria in a regional or national criterion-referenced curriculum? There are problems in setting the appropriate levels of detail, inter-pretation in terms of domain referencing, and confronting problems of reporting results, for which information has to be aggregated according to the audience and purpose for the report-ing. Popham (1993) describes how easy and dangerous it can be to generate far too much detail in an attempt to remove the need for judgement and recommends instead that criterion referencing be implemented though the use of broad statements illustrated by sample items. At an early stage, the British development fell into the trap that Popham describes, although the problem has now received official recognition (Dearing, 1993).

Fifth, how should assessment and testing systems be designed to provide information for the accountability of schools to the public? This purpose does not require blanket testing and might indeed be better fulfilled by surveys using matrix sampling to provide a richer and more reliable picture (Harlen *et al.*, 1992). However, an important part of the Conservative gov-ernment's approach to reform of education was that the consumer – in this case, identified as the parent – should be able to exercise choice among schools. External tests were to provide the criteria for that choice, and parents would want the individual results for their child. So the need for national assessment to provide individual certification as well as general account-ability information was a given. The TGAT design was fashioned to satisfy both of these pur-poses and to support, rather than derail, teachers' own assessments. One of the criticisms of the TGAT report was that, although it made recommendations for the collection of back-ground data to inform judgements of school performance, these recommendations were not adequately forceful. In any event, they were ignored. But the issues are now accepted as part of an agenda for revision, partly because the publication of raw scores in school league tables was one of the main points of opposition in the teachers' 1993 boycott (Dearing, 1993).

Sixth, at what pace can radical reform of schools be made, and how can the essential resources be estimated realistically by policymakers? Reforms that require radical changes in the daily classroom practices of teachers should not be imposed without extensive field trials and cannot be introduced quickly. The Conservative government in 1988 was determined to implement changes in education, as in other areas of public service, very rapidly, and regard-ed pleas for extensive trial and expensive in-service training as typical examples of the pro-tectionism of professionals. However, the need of politicians to obtain results quickly cannot be satisfied at the classroom level; the time required to implement educational change effectively is longer than that between elections (Fullan, 1991).

My six questions represent an attempt to distill general issues that will be of importance in any country. If I had to choose one of central importance, it is the systemic integration of assessment and testing. How can we develop both formative assessment and certification and accountability testing in such a way that they support one another and enrich rather than dis-tort good classroom learning?

Assessment of the primary school child

Geoff Lindsay

In this reading Geoff Lindsay reviews the dominant place which IQ tests have held in the past and considers some of the weaknesses of this form of assessment. With particular reference to children with special needs, he then goes on to raise questions about the assessment of the child, the curriculum, the class environment, the school and the social context. This is a wide conception of assessment, but it reminds us that performance and capability are not inherent qualities. They cannot be isolated from context and meaning.

If we accept Lindsay's argument, to what extent is our assessment of pupil attainment an assessment of our own provision?

Edited from: Lindsay, G. (1991) 'The assessment of cognitive abilities', in Harding, L. and Beech, J. R. (eds) *Educational Assessment of the Primary School Child*. Windsor: NFER Nelson, 27–38

The use of standardized tests

The measurement of cognitive abilities has been a corner-stone of educational psychology and teaching for a long time. Early experimental psychologists devised a variety of methods to attempt to assess individuals' ability to think, plan and reason. It is well known that other psychologists and educationists saw the possibility of using such tests, and developments of them, to assess young children. The early work of Binet and Simon in France, is a familiar example.

From these early beginnings a whole movement and industry have been developed. In the United Kingdom, Cyril Burt, the first educational psychologist, promulgated the use of intelligence tests to aid the London County Council in its allocation of children to forms of education. Later, the 11-plus test made use of forms of intelligence tests in addition to assessment of attainment. Local authorities and individual schools have used intelligence tests to decide how children should be grouped within schools (for example, streaming) and to identify those requiring some special provision. In the USA also the use of intelligence tests 'took off'.

Later years (particularly in the 1960s in the USA and the 1970s in the UK) saw the development of variants of these ability tests. Whereas intelligence tests were designed to provide overall, global assessments of cognitive ability interest has developed in attempts to identify and assess more specific abilities. At this time, therefore, there was much interest in more specific language, perceptual, motor and perceptuo-motor abilities; research and experience had shown that many children failed at basic educational tasks such as reading, despite good levels of general intelligence as measured by IQ tests.

In addition to the broadening range of types of standardized assessment techniques, this period also saw an increase in the use of more detailed and intensive individual assessments. The 11-plus examination and many forms of intelligence tests available to teachers were designed to be given to classes or schools at a time. To provide a more detailed, extensive and intensive examination of an individual child requires individual assessment. The need to carry out such assessment was urged and the increase in the numbers of specially trained staff (educational psychologists in particular) allowed this to occur. The 'grandparent' of intelligence tests developed for use with children, which is still in use, the Stanford–Binet, provides measures of mental age and IQ. The Wechsler Scales (WPPSI and WISC-R) and the British Ability Scales provide additional information and are each based on different models of intelligence (group and specific factors, in addition to 'g', a general measure of ability).

Historically, then, intelligence and IQ have had a central position in the assessment of children. Theories of intelligence, and the concept of under-achievement, whereby a child's attainment in, say, reading, is compared with that predicted by IQ and age, were covered in teacher training. Group tests were also used in schools, particularly when the 11-plus was common. Psychologists have had considerable experience in this theory and practice. For both groups, teachers and educational psychologists, intelligence was seen as a central theoretical construct, and its assessment was a necessary endeavour. More recently this emphasis has changed, and both groups appear to spend less time on intellectual assessment, either in training or practice, although intelligence testing certainly has not disappeared entirely. There are several reasons for these developments, but I shall focus here upon those which are scientific/empirical in nature.

Much concern has been expressed on the supposed bias which is inherent in intelligence tests. A land-mark in this debate was Kamin's publication, *The Science and Politics of IQ* (Kamin, 1974). Were IQ tests fair, or did they discriminate against particular groups, for example, females, ethnic minorities and working class children? To what extent was such apparent discrimination a result of the theory of intelligence, the construction of the instrument and its standardization, or the administration of the test and its interpretation?

Of particular relevance in Britain is the work of Mackintosh and Maskie-Taylor (1985) in their contribution to the Swann Report. In this paper, the authors consider the possible explanations for the differences found, over many studies, between the mean IQ scores of different groups. Their analysis of UK studies suggests that we would be unwise to accept the view that there are proven differences in ability between racial groups *per se*. First, it appears that the scores of the children tested were related to their length of stay in the UK (many of the ethnic-minority children were recent immigrants). Second, when social class was controlled the differences between groups reduced considerably. When more social variables were included in the analysis, the difference between mean scores reduced still further. These variables included overcrowding, number of parents, size of family and neighbourhood. The review of Mackintosh and Maskie-Taylor therefore, suggests a more complex scenario. There is evidence that mean scores between racial groups differ, but these differences appear to relate to social factors, and:

> when they are taken into account, the difference between West Indian and indigenous children is sharply reduced. (Mackintosh and Maskie-Taylor, 1985, p. 147)

The other major criticism of IQ tests has been that they have limited usefulness. This is a pragmatic concern, and represents an interesting shift from an earlier position when IQ and similar tests were considered very useful. This shift highlights the purpose of the assessment, and in particular its degree of specificity. IQ tests, by their nature, give a general assessment of intellectual functioning. As such they can only serve as a basis of similarly general decisions, usually about classification and placement. Thus, IQ has been used to place children in grammar schools or schools for what were then termed the 'educationally subnormal'. However, in addition to the technical concerns regarding the reliability of such assessments and the consequent placement decisions, the nature of the questions has also changed. We are now much less concerned with placing children in new settings; instead our intention is to enhance the child's development within the situation that exists. This change has been due in part to the moves towards integration of children with special educational needs. Teachers in mainstream schools now need more guidance on the nature of a child's needs and appropriate strategies to help meet these.

The use of IQ tests has been regarded as of limited usefulness for the kinds of assessment which are linked directly to teaching and teachers and psychologists have increasingly turned to curriculum-based assessment in preference to the use of such tests. This approach shifts the emphasis away from the child onto the curriculum and the teacher. It is associated with a revamping of the curriculum itself.

My proposal is for the development of a more integrated and integrative form of assessment. The intention would be to assess the child within a context. The research evidence available suggests that a full assessment of a child could have at least the following components.

The child

There are times when an overall, global assessment of intelligence is useful. However, for most children causing concern to teachers such global IQ scores give no new information. What is needed is a more finely developed, extensive and intensive range of approaches for the assessment of specific elements of cognitive functioning. The structure given by Sternberg is useful here. Assessments might include a child's general planning and organizational abilities, strategies used when learning new material, and flexibility to new learning demands. The cognitive style of the child is an important consideration. Does the child approach the task methodically, but slowly, or quickly but carelessly. Both can be 'good' or 'bad' (Miller, 1987).

Related to this is the child's resistance to distractions. Some children with learning difficulties have great problems resisting distractions. These may be in the classroom (for example, noise, movement), or on the page (such as writing in the wrong place, or being distracted by other material). Such tendencies need careful assessment by manipulating the environment or the presentation of work to assess the child's problem and give guidance to action.

The curriculum

Assessing the child, however, is not enough. What is the curriculum 'diet'? Recent increase in interest in special needs has led to a greater awareness of the importance of considering a whole-school approach to this issue. Curriculum should not be seen as something for the majority plus a different set of activities tacked on for the 'slow learners'. Rather, the aim now is to integrate not only children but also the curriculum. This requires teachers to re-examine their teaching and their curriculum.

Within the field of special education much has been done. There have been many initiatives, both commercially published and home-grown, to produce specific curricula for children with special needs. However, this is not enough. These curricula are aimed at the development of specific skills and abilities (for example, spelling programmes). What is still needed is the development of the same approaches in other areas (such as project work at primary level) and subject specialism at secondary. There is much importance, therefore, in assessing the curriculum itself in the context of assessing a child.

Of particular importance are interest and motivation. The learning tasks may be fascinating to 90 per cent of the class, but not a particular child. Motivation will then be impaired. Many of the materials used by those who have constructed objectives-based curricula can be criticized; the task may be broken down with admirable logic but presented with dire consequences for enjoyment.

The class

Wheldall et al. (1986) have shown the importance of a variety of factors in the classroom environment. The work emanating from the ORACLE project (for example, Galton et al., 1980) has also indicated how classrooms can vary with respect to the teacher's preferred style of operating [see Reading 9.2]. They identified four types of teaching style and, in a second publication (Galton and Simon, 1980) showed how teacher style was differentially related to the pupils' academic performance in different subjects.

Thus, in order to assess a child fully, it is important to assess also that child's learning environment. This calls for a collaborative exercise. The teacher is in the best position to assess many aspects but is also possibly 'too close'. An outside perspective may be useful; the combination of the two even more so.

The school

Assessment of a child in clinical settings has been criticized by teachers and educational psychologists for many years. Some examination of the school, and classroom, has been advocated in order to understand the child's context for learning. More recent research has provided evidence for school effects on learning and so this approach now has more than face validity. For example, Bickel and Bickel (1986) have reviewed evidence from studies in the United States to show which factors in schools and classrooms optimize children's learning. Mortimore *et al.*, (1988) have researched school factors in a UK setting and produced similar findings. Educational leadership, orderly school climate, an emphasis on basic skills, for example, have been shown to correlate with success as shown in school differences in the progress of pupils, even when factors such as social class have been taken into account. The relative standards of attainment, for example, of the individual child and the norm of the school are relevant. It may be significant to one child's development to be an able pupil in a very low achieving school, or a child of modest ability in a high achieving establishment. The 1988 Education Act emphasized these effects. Schools may find themselves going in and out of favour as results are published and 'market forces' lead to changes in over- and under-subscription. The nature of the school, therefore, could change year by year, a situation already happening in some parts of the country. Without an assessment of this it is not possible to understand fully the child's activities and progress. There is therefore a case for another interaction, child and school.

Society

Finally, there is a need to assess the nature of the wider society. This is probably the least likely to be practised in any other than a general manner. However, the effects of poverty or racism, for example, in the neighbourhood may be of particular relevance. Consider, for example, the ability of children to learn when their journey to school each day is fraught with danger. Further, there are the wider socio-political dimensions which interact with the processes described in earlier stages. The IQ debate was considered earlier in this reading in terms of perceived bias. We must also be sensitive to such issues interacting with the other aspects of assessment.

READING 12.5

Analysing responses to teacher assessment

Bet McCallum, Shelley McAlister, Margaret Brown and Caroline Gipps

This reading reports the key findings of an important study of new teacher assessment practices: National Assessment in Primary Schools (NAPS). Classroom practice was observed and teachers were asked to respond to descriptions of different forms of practice. From this, three major approaches to teacher assessment were identified. Each model of how teacher assessment is practised is probably recognizable, and there is some articulation between them with the different models of learning which are reviewed in the readings in Chapter 6.

How would you characterize your own approach to teacher assessment?

Edited from: McCallum, B., McAlister, S., Brown, M. and Gipps, C. (1993) Teacher assessment at Key Stage One, *Research Papers in Education*, 8 (3), 308–18

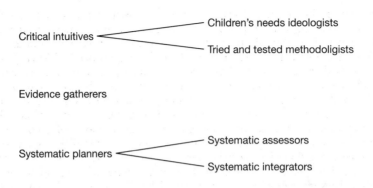

Figure 12.5.1 Models of teacher assessment

Our fieldwork is based on detailed work with Year 2 teachers in each of 32 schools. We developed a sorting activity based on quotations about Teacher Assessment selected from those made by teachers in our earlier interviews. The quotes were sorted into 'like me' or 'not like me' categories, followed by a detailed interview, asking each teacher to explain the reasons for the categorization.

As a result of this, combined with other data, we have identified three models, or 'ideal types', which vary along the dimensions of systematicity, integration with teaching, and ideological underpinning. We emphasize that the models are not hierarchical in value and that no particular set of views or practices is intended to represent a desired model of Teacher Assessment. Indeed our informal judgement suggests that there are teachers within each of the groups whose pupils have both relatively high and relatively low standards of attainment.

The three models of Teacher Assessment are described below. For two of the models we feel we have identified two fairly distinct subgroups. These are shown in the Figure 12.5.1.

Critical Intuitives

We termed the teachers in this group critical intuitives because they criticize the imposed system of National Assessment as a disruption to intuitive ways of working. Critical intuitives fall into two subgroups:

> 'Children's needs ideologists' show a great deal of confidence and can articulate arguments about assessment that defend a child-centred view of curriculum, teaching and learning.

> 'Tried and tested methodologists' feel secure in modes of teaching and assessing practised before the ERA but are less confident in articulating what these are or their actual basis or uses for teaching or assessment purposes.

All of the critical intuitive group of teachers are minimal adopters of National Assessment procedures: the children's needs ideologists resist criterion referencing as being in tension with 'whole child' philosophy and are often confidently critical of the SAT tasks as being inappropriate and ill-matched to their own ideas of 'levelness'. The tried and tested methodologists resist the whole notion of ongoing, recorded Teacher Assessment because it means a radical change in behaviour for them: 'you are either teaching or assessing; you can't be doing both'.

The children's needs ideologists find it 'too hard to sit back and let a child struggle' as part of a teaching assessment without offering some input 'because it's second nature'. They prefer a 'whole' approach, seeing teaching and assessment taking place simultaneously and 'recording mentally all the time while watching the process a child is going through'. These teachers subscribe to an 'exploratory' view of learning (Rowland, 1987) since they initially guide the task to a point where children can be left to arrive at their own solutions to the problem, as jointly defined. They prefer the role of 'provider of a stimulating environment' to that of 'instructor'.

The tried and tested methodologists believe you can't be teaching and assessing simultaneously. They are similar to the teachers in the following model ('evidence gatherers') in that they assess what they have taught. This practice is underpinned by a didactic model of learning in which the teacher defines the child's needs and provides the appropriate instruction. The child responds and the teacher marks and provides feedback. Because the focus is on teaching, they feel that you 'can't record on *ad hoc* assessments you make'. Assessment for this group of teachers thus tends to be summative, taking the form of giving worksheets, scrutinizing tangible evidence like pages of maths from exercise books and doing verbal checks of a child's knowledge by 'getting them on their own and having a little chat about it'.

Teachers' close knowledge (often rooted in long careers in teaching) is the main basis on which tried and tested methodologists in particular make their assessments. There is a strong belief that 'assessing needs to be done by the actual class teacher' and not someone else; teachers have got to know a child to know whether 'what they have done on paper' is good or not. Consequently, previous records are not observed to be readily available or consulted and teachers rely mainly on their own personal judgements. Planning based on diagnostic assessment was not observed in their classrooms, rather there was a tendency to 'all start at the same beginning point and then spread out'.

There is among some of this group a sense of insecurity. They report a fear of 'sinking under paper' and an uneasiness with constant educational change. National Curriculum assessment requires teachers to engage in more detailed work plans and gives more attention to techniques that will support criterion referencing for individual pupils. The perceived amount of energy and time required to learn the new skills and roles associated with the innovation has provided a rationale for resistance within this group.

Evidence gatherers

These teachers have a basic belief in the primacy of teaching, rather than of assessing. Their main method of assessment relies on collecting evidence, which they only later evaluate. They have gone some way towards adapting to the requirements of National Assessment and they could be considered rational adapters, in the sense that they have adapted in such a way as not to change their teaching: collecting evidence does not interfere with teaching practice. Evidence gathering is associated with a belief that pupils generally learn what is taught and only what is taught; thus assessment follows teaching in order to check that the process is going according to plan.

The main characteristic of this group is the need to gather evidence in abundance, with an emphasis on written work, which enables the teacher to have 'proof' of what has been done. 'Trying to get as much evidence as I can' is the aim of many of these teachers (and may preclude the value of the assessment itself). 'Getting the results down on paper' is seen to be essential, because teachers feel accountable and, under National Assessment, are concerned that they may be asked to produce evidence of their assessment of children: 'I keep a camera in the cupboard for technology. It is the only record you've got if somebody asked you for evidence.'

Evidence may be collected from a variety of sources including pages from workbooks, worksheets from published schemes, teacher-devised worksheets, children's written work, spelling tests, observation and questioning children on work they have done. There is a heavy reliance on worksheets and maths schemes as written evidence.

A key feature of evidence gathering is that assessments are summative, rather than formative in nature: 'I would just write it down but I wouldn't go into records until I am ready to record. I leave assessing to the end of term.' Recording assessment is usually done termly, when evidence is gathered in one place and the teacher reflects on the work the child has done over the term: 'If I have their pieces of work there I can just sit there and think "this particular child has achieved that".'

Despite the emphasis on collecting evidence though, not all the evidence that has been collected will be used in the awarding of levels and it is possible that in some cases evidence is used selectively to support the teacher's intuition.

A final feature of the evidence gathering model is that systematic assessment is seen as a threat to relationships with children. The teachers in this group had a fear of National Assessment interfering with their relationships with children if they were to 'go over the top' by adopting more systematic assessment practices. Assessing against a can-do check-list was seen as 'tabulated' and 'judgemental', as well as unnecessarily systematic.

Overall, then, evidence gatherers shared concerns with their critical intuitive colleagues in rejecting the methods of systematic assessors. Rather than rely on memory and intuition for assessment however, they favoured gathering evidence and then reflecting back over the child's performance during the term in a summative manner.

Assessment was accommodated within existing systems, rather than making major changes to their habitual teaching roles.

Systematic planners

Planning time specifically for assessment has become part of the practice of 'systematic planners' and the assessment of groups and individuals informs future task design and classwork. A constructivist approach to learning underpins this model, with teachers expecting children to learn in idiosyncratic ways; they are willing to try children on higher levels not yet taught, using such opportunities diagnostically. Such teachers also demonstrate social constructivist beliefs (Pollard, 1987) in that they attach importance to interacting and arriving at shared meanings, both with pupils and with their fellow professionals in the context of Teacher Assessment. These teachers have embraced the National Assessment requirements and understand the principles of criterion referencing, often breaking down Statements of Attainment into smaller steps. While upholding the importance of teaching, they report real value in continuous diagnostic assessment as an enhancement to their effectiveness.

> I need to know that at a particular time of day, I am actually going to be assessing one thing. You've got to be structured, you've got to know what you are looking for.

The most significant characteristic of this group of teachers is that they plan for assessment on a systematic basis. This means that the teacher consciously devotes some part of the school week to assessing, and explicitly links the results of assessment to curriculum planning.

There are two identifiable subgroups in this category. Some teachers, whom we have called systematic assessors, give daily concentrated time to one group of children at a time and have devised systems to lessen demands made upon them by the rest of the class. Some teachers wear badges or put up a 'busy flag' as a sign they are not to be interrupted. These teachers often make it clear that it is quite permissible to ask peers, not teacher for help or they devise an agenda of tasks for the children to work through. Other teachers, whom we have called systematic integrators, do not separate themselves off from the rest of the class but circulate, gathering evidence in different ways, which feeds into weekly recorded assessment and informs planning.

Children are given work on the basis of previously recorded assessment. The process becomes cyclical. Diagnostic assessment feeds into planning for individual, group, and class activities which, in turn, offer opportunities for more diagnostic assessment. Records are generally accessible and used. However, these teachers are often willing to try children 'on the next level' without necessarily teaching first. By giving children work at the next level without specifically teaching first, assessment seems less 'bolted on' to teaching and becomes a learning process for teachers. 'The interesting thing about Teacher Assessments is that they surprise you.'

For this group of teachers, assessment techniques are multiple and children are assessed both formatively and summatively through a combination of: observation, open-ended questioning (the questions varying from child to child), teacher/pupil discussion, running records and scrutiny of classwork. Particular attention is paid to fitting the assessment technique to the activity being assessed.

One of the significant differences between this model and the other two is the sharp focus on Statements of Attainment. Teachers' self-devised checklists are used, often comprising lists of 'can-do' indicators, which represent the teacher's analysis and interpretation of each of the Statements of Attainment, broken down further into descriptions of what a child might say or do to demonstrate attainment.

Systematic planners are not resistant to the new methods of assessment imposed by central government. They see systematic diagnostic assessment as adding to their professionalism. 'I think some teachers get hung up on the word "assessment" and get frightened by it and they undervalue what they are really doing.' They reject the trial and error methods of intuitive guessing of the other two groups, stressing that they have teaching in mind but, 'teaching [should be] based on assessment done sometime earlier. The greatest thing is to make notes so it informs your teaching.' They do not reject the notion that the child is at the heart of the learning process, nor that the 'whole child' is important: 'I use my knowledge of the child in my approach to teaching and assessing but not in my actual assessment.'

Of all teachers in the sample, these teachers have made the most progress towards a hypothetical integrated model of Teacher Assessment.

 READING 12.6

Assessment and progression in the primary school

Patricia Broadfoot

This reading highlights the key issue of the use which is made of assessment data when pupils transfer between classes or Key Stages. Patricia Broadfoot reviews findings from the second stage of the Primary Assessment, Curriculum and Experience (PACE) project (see also Readings 9.6 and 15.7) to highlight the limited value which teachers may perceive in summative assessments, even when these are nationally required. She suggests that practical and meaningful assessment must connect to each teachers' way of thinking about pedagogy in practice – their 'pedagogic discourse'.

How useful do you find SAT results and records from other teachers?

Edited from: Broadfoot, P. (1996) 'Do we really need to write it all down? Managing the challenge of National Assessment at Key Stage 1 and Key Stage 2', in Croll, P. (ed.) *Teachers, Pupils and Primary Schooling: Continuity and Change*. London: Cassell, 69–85

Despite provision for progression having been a key element in the impetus behind the introduction of the National Curriculum, there was very little evidence among the Key Stage 2 teachers studied in the PACE project that the existence of national assessment information had facilitated this process. This was for a number of reasons.

First, and most importantly, was the perceived lack of accuracy in the information coming from Key Stage 1 assessments. One of the more obvious reasons for this is differences in standards being applied between teachers in the same school and between different schools despite the provision of moderation to counteract this.

> Whether it's the summer holidays that's made a difference or a new teacher's made a difference but they've been assessed at say – take an arbitrary figure – Level 1 and really they're Level 2, or by the time they got to me they were Level 2 ... I think there's a teacher's natural caution not to have put them at a higher level because you're going to get rumbled later on and to say, 'Oh, well, there may be one or two but I'd better put them at 1 and then they'll look as if they've improved'.

Second, there was a general view that the SAT information was unhelpful because the levels were so broad.

> This is certainly a very delicate subject ... but as the receiving teacher I don't think it gives me any more information than my colleague would have passed on in half an hour's discussion or on little pieces of paper in the natural assessment between teacher and teacher, because each of these levels are so wide. I was focusing in on them when I was writing my reports because I had each child's folder in front of me and I was astonished occasionally to see that perhaps five different children were all Level 2 on maths, or science or whatever, and the variety of levels within that level! This is where it's very, very vague.

However, such problems are much less significant than what would appear to be real differences in the achievement of the children concerned. As one teacher put it:

> When the children have come in at Level 2, then in theory I should then begin work at Level 3 and I've found that invariably they couldn't cope with Level 3. I don't dispute that they haven't got the Level 2, but they know it on one day – but after a summer holiday and a period of SATs ...? But there hasn't been the breadth, in the rush to assess everybody and get something down ... the breadth doesn't go in, and therefore you can't begin another level because the understanding's not there ... I find that my own judgement is the best one at the end of the day. These statistics on paper are not very helpful. They are an indication, but that's all they are, of what's gone on before rather than where they are at that moment. I think you have to bear in mind that the infant school is a separate school under a separate Head in a separate building on a separate site and I looked forward to having some kind of knowledge about the children before they came but it's a bit 'pie in the sky'.

The problem essentially is not one of measurement but one of real differences in achievement as children are affected by the particular learning context they find themselves in. The comments of many teachers reflected the feeling that summative assessment is almost inevitably flawed in this way.

Fundamentally, however, the issue is not one that centres on the inaccuracy of an assessment but rather its lack of utility in the business of being a teacher. When primary teachers discuss their assessment practice, they are thinking predominantly in terms of their own needs as teachers and to an extent of the needs of pupils for formative guidance and encouragement. This is well summed up in the following comment on the utility of the traditional type of test used in the primary classroom.

> Where they're at has been decided by a formal spelling-type test, but even within that you see, I would say that although it gives me an indication, it only gives me an indication of a certain type of spelling memory ... so that's given an indication of how strong they are at spelling but not necessarily how they learn their spellings and how they can remember them.

Given that the assessment discourse of teachers is essentially a pedagogic one, an internal personal discourse private to the teacher and at times the subject of professional discussion between teachers, it will be interesting to see the final impact of the various initiatives towards more whole-school support for systematic assessment and recording. Our interviews documented a number of instances in which schools as a whole or year group teachers had initiated a regular meeting, at which the staff bring in examples they feel exemplify particular kinds and levels of work and the teachers look at them across the whole school to see if they can agree a level. This is typical of a growing pattern of staff collecting children's work and storing it as an evidential record – a pattern which again, our data suggest, is very much more in evidence in Key Stage 1. It may be that, when established, the existence of this evidential record will provide the basis for the kind of interpersonal, idiosyncratic assessment discussion which teachers say they value, whilst at the same time providing a degree of structure and objectivity in terms of evidence to provide for communication to others, such as pupils and parents. Alternatively, this process may become part of that repertoire of assessment obligations which do not integrate with the pedagogic discourse of assessment and so become separated from classroom practice.

 READING 12.7

Pupil self-assessment

Yolande Muschamp

> Yolande Muschamp and a team of seconded teachers spent two years working with colleagues in 24 classrooms to develop practical ways of encouraging pupil self-assessment in primary school classrooms. One product of this action research study was this reading. It contains practical advice, based around the negotiation and use of 'targets'. The idea of pupil self-assessment is closely to related to Vygotsky's conception of self-regulation (see Readings 6.4 and 6.5).
>
> Do you see a role for self-assessment in your classroom?
>
> Edited from: Muschamp. Y. (1991) Pupil self-assessment, *Practical Issues in Primary Education*, 8. Bristol: National Primary Centre (South West), 1–8

Our discussions with teachers revealed a strong commitment to, 'on-going assessment, that could be built upon every day'. Teachers wanted to support children's learning through careful use of formative assessment. What is more, many felt that children should themselves be involved in their own assessment. As one teacher put it:

> We are now more conscious about making children independent and responsible for their own learning. It is fascinating to see how they view their role and work, and want to look back.

This was not a new idea. Involving children in self appraisal had been suggested, for example, by HMI as a way of motivating children and the introduction of records of achievement was also based on this principle. However, we wanted to take this involvement further to see whether particular assessment strategies could lead to the children taking a greater responsibility for their learning and progress.

Working alongside children we were initially able to record the evaluations that they made of their work. We also asked them to comment on the work of other children presented to them in a folder. This showed that children were making assessments, but in a relatively limited way. For instance, we asked children what, specifically, made a piece of work 'good'. Although we received a wide range of answers the comments which predominated related to presentation.

> 'The writing must be neat.'
> 'The letters are very big, I think the "g" is the wrong way round.'

Without exception the children commented on how neat or tidy they felt each piece of work to be; how large the letters were; or how accurately drawings had been coloured. Often this was given as the only reason for the work to have any worth. When questioned further some children were able to explain some of the specific features which made a piece of work satisfactory.

> 'The answers are all right.'
> 'You mustn't repeat things like "and then" and you must put in a lot of details and describing words.'

'The lines don't go over the edges.'

However, when asked why they thought they were doing a particular activity, very few children understood the specific aims of their teacher. Their comments were often very general.

'So when we grow up we will know how to write.'
'To help you get a good job.'

As a group we shared our findings and decided to see if extending children's understanding of the purpose of activities, would widen the range of comments that they made. We hoped that children would develop a fuller picture of the progress they made if more aspects of the learning aims were shared with them. It was agreed that, in each of the classes, children would be encouraged to move through three stages.

Stage 1   Sharing aims and using targets

Teachers felt that by introducing plans at the beginning of the year, and then monthly or half termly, children were provided with an overview or context for their work. Three parts to this strategy emerged.

The first was establishing learning objectives in which children were given, or helped to plan, clear learning objectives. The skills, knowledge and understanding that activities were designed to develop were discussed. These were presented to even very young children in such ways as, 'learning how to ...' and 'learning all about ...'.

Second, was selecting a focus. Here we found it was important to be very precise and explicit about what it was the children were going to do. Within activities we selected one or two specific areas to focus on, for example, 'good beginnings for stories', 'measuring accurately to the nearest centimetre' and 'concentrating on the sequence of an account'.

Finally, we made decisions on forms of learning support. For instance, children did not always have the technical language to talk about their work and rarely had considered which method to use. Introducing a few helpful terms and discussing the range of methods available became part of the sharing of aims. These might have included words such as, 'description', 'design', 'fair test', 'account'. The methods might include, 'looking closely and drawing', 'taking notes', 'using an index' and 'drafting'.

Once a child had a clear idea of what it was they were trying to do, then planning targets became much easier.

The targets were particularly important because, when matched closely with the activities that had been planned, they allowed children to decide when the activity had been successfully completed and to monitor what they had learnt. We found that it was helpful to plan the targets as questions that the children could ask themselves. Thus, when learning a skill, the child could ask: 'What will I be able to do?'. When the learning objective was finding out or acquiring knowledge, the child could ask: 'What do I know now?'. When the objective was to develop understanding, the child could ask: 'Can I explain?'.

However, children did not always learn what was planned. Indeed, despite following a carefully planned curriculum, many teachers were reluctant to lose opportunities for learning which presented themselves almost by chance. We thus found it important to allow time to discuss what else the child had learnt during the activities.

In some activities it was very difficult for pupils to decide if any learning had taken place at all, even though teachers were confident that the activities had been of value. There were particular types of activities that fell into this category: practice, art, enjoyment and religious education. Practice and reinforcement activities did not always lead to any new learning. Many physical actions, for example, throwing and catching, did not always show any short term improvement. It was hard for pupils to identify the specific learning in some forms of artistic self-expression or expression of points of view. Learning that took place around art activities, such as learning to mix paint, share equipment or clear away, was easier to identify. Enjoyment experienced in many activities, for example reading or watching a dramatic performance, seemed to make children uncertain about what they had actually learned. A similar difficulty existed here with regard to religious education. It became very complex when children and teachers tried to assess benefits beyond just the factual information that had been learnt.

We tried several ways of getting around these difficulties and found one simple, but by no means perfect solution. We added new targets which would only reflect the completion of a task: 'I will/have read ...', 'we will/have visited ...' and 'I have/will created ...'. These were supplemented with the child's account of their enjoyment or interest in the activities. As these comments accumulated over the year, long-term changes, for example in the enjoyment or developing interest in music, could be detected.

Having planned the targets, assessing them became relatively straightforward. Children were encouraged to refer to their targets alongside their work. One pleasing effect was that children often kept on course and did not become bored with the assessments. There were also noticeable improvements in the pacing of work. The following approaches were used:

teacher assessment: with the targets planned and documented, teachers found it effective to assess them in a short discussion with a child. A child could be asked to perform, explain or give an account of a topic. This was supplemented by an open question about unexpected outcomes and general questions about activities that the child had enjoyed or taken a particular interest in.

peer assessement: working in groups, children soon found it easy to discuss and assess their targets with their friends. Many teachers were surprised at how sophisticated the questioning of each other became. In a few schools this led to the development of pupil designed questionnaires for self-assessment.

self-assessment: the children's initial comments were rather basic, such as, 'this is good, for me'. Some targets were simply ticked with no comment. However, with encouragement children soon illustrated how targets had been met and moved quickly on to planning new ones, 'I have counted threes with Daniel. I went up to 39. My next pattern is sixes'.

Stage 2   Reviewing, 'feeding forward' and recording

The main purpose of the review stage was for the child to stand back and assess the progress that they had been making over a few weeks, a month or a term. This stage also included: selecting documentation to record this progress, looking back and editing old records. A valuable outcome was the creation of a basis for reporting to parents, transferring to a new class and planning for the future.

Many different ways of reviewing were tried. The most successful often reflected the way the classrooms already operated and did not therefore appear unusual or artificial to the children. For example:

conferencing: in which time was put aside for the teacher and pupil to talk together about how targets had been met, what should be followed up and 'fed forward' into future planning. The children were already used to reading with the teacher in a one to one situation. A card index was used to keep track of whose turn it was to talk with the teacher. Notes for future planning were written on the cards.

quiet time: was provided to allow children to look through their work alone or with a partner. They were encouraged to take notes for planning and development activities.

questionnaires: were designed by the teacher and by the children as a basis for review. Some were adapted so that they could be used to annotate any work chosen to be stored as a record.

Although we found teachers continuously responding to, and advising children, it was felt that a lot of good ideas for future action were still being lost or forgotten at the review stage. Several ways of developing a system for managing this 'feed forward' were tried and proved successful. For instance:

ideas box: at a class level many ideas for future investigations were collected and stored on cards for all to use. This system operated rather like the floor book.

'how to' books: children wrote up things that they had learnt to do in a class book for others to use. However more was often learnt by children during the writing up than by other children reading the books. They were very popular and of great interest to other children.

notebooks: a small notebook or a page set aside in a larger book, folder or profile were used in some classes for children to record their own plans, areas for development and interests. These were often used to complete planning sheets.

Two particular challenges faced us at the recording stage. First, how could the recording that the children did themselves become part of everyday classroom life? Many solutions were determined by what was already happening in the classrooms. For instance, loose leaf records were selected and moved to a profile or record of achievement folder; photocopying or photography were used where schools felt able to afford them, and were already using them for other purposes; children's comments were written down for them by an older child or adult in schools where this sort of shared activity was encouraged.

Second, on what basis should a selection for a record be made? The reasons for selection varied from school to school, reflecting the policies that had been developed for similar areas such as the selection of work for displays or the participation in assemblies. In many schools children were encouraged to select their 'best work' as a record of their achievement, whereas another school decided to select 'before and after' pieces, such as, a first draft and a final desk top published version of a story; a list from a brainstorming and a drawing of the final result of an investigation in science. The idea of 'significance' was introduced in some classes, so that children were helped to identify pieces of work which had a special meaning or association for them. Additionally, sampling by subject or over time was tried. This was often done as a 'snap shot' exercise but could be used as a carefully scheduled system.

Stage 3   Helping to report on progress

An exciting highlight of the self assessment strategies that we were developing occurred when the children were given the opportunity to share their assessments with their parents or carers. This worked most successfully where this was part of an overall policy for home–school liaison. Schools where parents were already fully involved in classroom activities found it easier to encourage children's involvement in the reporting process. The children's role in this process varied enormously. For instance:

helping in the preparation of reports occurred when children were encouraged to write a short report of their progress and thoughts about school based on the reviews that they had carried out. Teachers and the parents then added their comments.

playing host was a role undertaken when parents and carers visited the school during an ordinary day. The children took them on a tour of specially prepared displays; showed them the work they were doing; and shared their profiles or records of achievement with them.

preparing for parent interviews was an important role for children in lots of different ways, such as putting out a display of their work or taking their profiles home to share before a parent/teacher interview. Some accompanied their parents, or actually organized a parents' afternoon themselves.

It is always hard to evaluate development projects, for what may be proved to be possible in the short-term may not be sustained over a longer period. However, we can record teacher opinion that the encouragement of pupil self-assessment through the use of targets had a very worthwhile effect on teaching and learning processes in the classrooms in which we worked. Furthermore, everyone – teachers, parents and pupils themselves – seemed to enjoy working in this way.

 READING 12.8

Another way of looking

Michael Armstrong

Michael Armstrong, Headteacher of a rural primary school, is a brilliant analyst and commentator on children's classroom learning. His accounts are distinguished by his empathy for children and by his attempts to understand, and value, their expressions of meaning. Here, he illustrates how the National Curriculum and its associated assessment procedures may inhibit genuine responses to and valid interpretations of children's work. He argues that 'another way of looking' must be maintained in primary school classrooms so that excitement, engagement and quality in teaching and learning can be substained.

Edited from: Armstrong, M. (1989) Another way of looking, *Forum*, 33 (1), 181–8

The National Curriculum betrays the children whose intellectual interests it is supposed to serve. I say this despite the well-intentioned efforts of liberal teachers to play the National Curriculum game in the hope of subverting its rules. It seems to me that any attempt to gentle the National Curriculum is necessarily futile because that curriculum is framed in terms which misconstrue the nature of learning and of teaching. The narrow specification of the curriculum by subject ignores the way in which the course of learning proceeds in imaginative classrooms. The language of targets and levels of attainment reduce achievement to a false hierarchy of technical accomplishments. The unacknowledged metaphor of 'delivery' deprives children of their constructive and reconstructive role in the acquisition of knowledge.

So what are we do to? How is it possible to rewrite the National Curriculum in language that restores meaning to its place at the centre of learning and teaching? I don't know the answer to this question but I think I know how to begin to find out. I would begin with interpretation. What does it mean to ascribe significance to children's thought and action? I want to approach this question through one particular instance: a story of a six-year-old (see Figure 12.8.1).

Here is how the English Working Group (who drafted the National Curriculum) described this wonderful tale, which is said to 'illustrate several Level 2 features of writing':

This is a simple chronological account with a clear story structure, including a conventional beginning narrative, middle and end. The sentences are almost all demarcated, though via the graphic, comic-strip layout and not via capital letters and punctuation. The spelling is almost entirely meaningful and recognizable. In several cases, it shows that the author has correctly grasped the patterns involved, even though the individual spellings are wrong (e.g. trooth, eny, owt, sumthing, cubad). The handwriting occasionally mixes upper and lower case letters though only at beginnings and ends of words, not at random.

That is all the Working Group has to say about 'When I was naughty'. It's all that the National Curriculum requires it to say. Can this really be how to talk about children and their work? For myself, I can't imagine a thinner description of a young child's narrative achievement. At no

Figure 12.8.1 When I was naughty

point is there the smallest recognition of the story's significance, of the relationship between its meaning and its form, of the quality of narrative thought which is seeking expression here.

So let's take a closer look at the story.

'When I was naughty' examines the moral order and its relation to experience, as seen from the perspective of six years old. It deals with questions of truth and lying, mutuality and recrimination, guilt and blame. It addresses, at least implicitly, the conflict between a child's and an adult's view of these matters. One of the most striking aspects of the story is the way the narrative dramatizes the interlocking conflicts which make up its subject matter. And the drawings play as important a part in this drama as the writing.

'When I was naughty' allows us to glimpse a young child's thought in all its imaginative richness. The artistry of its six-year-old author is apparent in every aspect of her story. In her exploitation of narrative style, with its formulas, its suspense, its various concealments and revelations, its openness to interpretation. In her acceptance of constraint and her turning of constraint into opportunity; think of her virtuoso treatment of the limited sentence structure available to her at this point in her narrative development, the way she makes use of the conjunction 'and' and the particle 's'. In her critical judgement, so apparent in her choice of vocabulary. In her concern to express her own sense of life in the ordered medium of written and drawn narrative. In short, in her appropriation of form.

For me the history of learning is the history of appropriation of form, in this way and in countless other ways, while the history of teaching begins and ends in the interpretation of appropriate form. By 'interpretation' I mean the critical scrutiny of children's intellectual enterprise, from moment to moment and from subject matter to subject matter, over the course of children's school careers. The description which I've just attempted of 'When I was naughty' is an example of interpretation, as applied to one particular moment in time. Multiplied across the curriculum and sustained over the years, a set of descriptions of this kind, accompanied by their objects – the works described and the evidence of the manner of their composition – would amount to an intellectual biography, a kind of documentary history of individual, and therefore incommensurate, achievement. This is what I mean by another way of looking and it is equally another way of speaking, as distant from the language of attainment targets (and level descriptions) as it is possible to imagine.

Trying to understand

Mary Jane Drummond

In this powerful reading Mary Jane Drummond leads us to consider some of the fundamental questions in assessment through a consideration of the thinking of kindergarten children. In particular, she demonstrates how assessment must be connected to understanding of pupils' perceptions if it is to have value in informing teaching-learning processes.

Reviewing the assessment evidence available to you about pupils, to what extent does it enable you to understand them and their learning needs?

Edited from: Drummond, M. J. (1993) *Assessing Children's Learning*. London: David Fulton, 70–188

In assessing learning, the act of seeing gives way to the act of understanding; the process of collecting evidence is followed by attempts to make the evidence meaningful. In this part of the practice of assessment, the assessors strive to make sense of what they have seen and remembered.

The work of Vivian Gussin Paley (1981), an American kindergarten teacher, provides many instructive examples of the educator 'seeing children as (s)he wishes them to be'. Or rather, seeing them at first in this way; Paley records her detailed evidence and sets it against her wished-for interpretation. Time and again, the educator's perspective, the educator's intentions, do not match the evidence. Time and again, Paley is forced to reconsider, to reconstruct the framework within which she makes meaning. In the following incident (Paley, 1981, pp. 57–8), the five year old children in Paley's kindergarten class have planted lima beans in individual milk cartons, but after three weeks no green shoots have appeared. Wally discovers that his beans have disappeared.

'They're gone!' he yelled, bringing me his carton. 'Gone! I looked through the whole dirt!'
'Can I look in mine?' asked Rose.
'You might as well' I answered. 'They don't seem to be coming up.'
There was a rush to the planting table. Everyone began digging into cartons or dumping their contents on the newspaper-covered table. The conversation unfolded:

Andy:	Where are the beans?
Wally:	They're invisible.
Andy:	Impossible. They came from a store. Someone took them out.
Teacher:	Who?
Andy:	A robber.
Eddie:	When it was dark a criminal took them.
Teacher:	Why would he do it?
Jill:	Maybe someone came in and said, 'Oh, there's nothing growing. We must take some of them out.'
Eddie:	I think a robber broke in and said, 'They don't need to plant those beans.'
Teacher:	Why would a robber want them?
Wally:	To sell them.
Andy:	Or cook them.
Ellen:	No, maybe to fool people with. See, he could plant them in his garden and when flowers came up people would think he's nice.
Teacher:	If I were a robber I'd take a record player.
Eddie:	Not if you wanted to plant seeds.

Here we see two ways of understanding the world at work. The children account for the missing beans with imaginary robbers; the teacher is intent on the logical connections, as she sees them, between a real robber and what he would be likely to steal. The children do not consider that the robber's imaginary theft needs any further explanation: stealing is what robbers do. If there are beans to steal, and a robber about, then the robber will certainly steal them. Trying to understand her pupils' thinking, Paley talks to another kindergarten class about the decaying Halloween pumpkin that they are observing (Paley, 1981, pp. 59-60).

Teacher:	Why does your pumpkin look like this?
Tim:	It's full of mould.
Carter:	It's mouldy. Plants are growing inside.
Julia:	Little vines.
William:	They make the top fall in.
Kevin:	Dead plants and animals get mould.
Tim:	Old pumpkins get mouldy.
Julia:	It's going to become dust.
Teacher:	How does that happen?
Julia:	It'll get so dry you won't even see it.
Teacher:	By the way, we have a problem in class. We planted lima beans and after a long time nothing came up. We looked in the dirt to see if any roots had grown and we couldn't find the beans. They were gone.
Kevin:	Was the window open? The wind blew them away.
Teacher:	They were deep down in the dirt.
Candy:	A squirrel could have took them.
Teacher:	We didn't see a squirrel in the room.
Candy:	It could have hid somewhere.
Teacher:	Our windows are locked at night. How could the squirrel have gotten back out?
William:	He could scratch a hole in the window.
Kevin:	Or in the door.
Carter:	Maybe a robber stepped in. They can get in windows very easily.
Teacher:	Why would he want the beans?
Carter:	For his garden.
Julia:	Or to cook them. Somebody has a key to your windows, I think.

There was no further talk of squirrels once the robber theory was suggested. I was so surprised by this change of opinion after talking about a rotting pumpkin that I presented my question to the third kindergarten. One child said a bird might be the culprit, another suspected worms. However, when a third mentioned robbers, everyone immediately agreed that the beans had been removed by a human introducer to plant, eat, or sell.

The children use 'robbers', Paley comes to see, as a powerful explanatory theory for all missing items. Mislaid coats, beans, rugs and sweaters are all attributed to robbers. These children's theory satisfies their need to account for missing objects, by drawing on one single attribute of robbers – their propensity to rob. All other aspects of a robber's behaviour are left out of the account; the teacher's attempts to make the supposed robber's behaviour consistent in adult terms are rejected out of hand, not because they threaten the children's explanation but because they are simply irrelevant. The children's implicit syllogism is too pure and simple to be contaminated with the teacher's irrelevancies. Their argument seems to go:

Robbers steal things.
The beans have disappeared.
Therefore robbers stole the beans.

Paley's account of her pupils' thinking is deeply rewarding, since it enables the reader to follow in her footsteps as she comes, little by little, to understand and respect the role that illusion and fantasy play in the minds of five and six-year-olds. They have, she concludes, 'become aware of the thinking required by the adult world,' but are not yet 'committed to its burden of rigid consistency' (p 81).

Paley is not dismayed or destroyed by the necessity of reshaping her interpretations of children's thinking; she is, rather, humbled by what the children have taught her to see, and grateful for the opportunity to learn from them. For Paley, as for all of us, 'knowledge is always from a position'. The new 'position', from which she applies her knowledge of children's minds, may in turn be reformed and renewed; in the meantime there is no weakness in her understanding, but a strength, in that as she strives, in her daily work, to understand what she has seen, she also constantly and critically reviews this very process of coming to understand.

There are three crucial questions that teachers and other educators must ask themselves as they set about assessing children's learning. When we look at learning;

what is there to see?

how best can we understand what we see?

how best can we put our understanding to good use?

We would be deluding ourselves if we thought that these questions could ever be answered once and for all, or that assessment is a practice that can ever be perfected. Children's learning is so complex and various that the task of trying to understand it is necessarily complex too. The task entails trying to see and understand the whole, as well as the minutest parts; it requires us to appreciate the past, and analyse the present, as well as envisage and welcome the future; it obliges us to look for and attend to differences as well as similarities, individuals as well as groups, the unexpected as well as the intended outcome, absence as well as presence. It demands a broad vision and a narrow focus.

Above all, effective assessment requires educators to make choices, in the interests of children, that are based on a coherent set of principles, which are themselves an expression of each educator's core values. As these choices are made, and translated into daily classroom practice, teachers are exercising their responsibility for children's learning, their right to act in children's interests, and their power to do so wisely and well.

CHAPTER 13

What are the social consequences of classroom practices?

There are nine readings in this chapter and they reflect the prolific research which exists in relation to this issue.

We begin with a thought-provoking reading from Bowles and Gintis (13.1) which theorizes on how schools reproduce inequalities and 'feed' the labour market. In Reading 13.2, Tizard and her colleagues report on empirical research on major influences on pupil attainment.

The next two readings address gender issues. Weiner (12.3) considers the ways in which school and LEA policies have been established and Walkerdine (12.4) focuses on the nature of classroom interaction between girls and boys. Interestingly, in the late 1990s public concern is shifting from the disadvantaging of girls to the underachievement of boys.

Racism is the topic of the readings by Epstein (13.5) and Troyna and Hatcher (13.6). Both show how pervasive it is, the former through the application of some of Foucault's ideas and the latter through a study of child cultures in mostly white primary schools.

Roaf and Bines (13.7) focus on special educational 'needs' and suggest that we ought now to think more in terms of rights and opportunities.

In Reading 13.8 Pollard draws on a range of social research to offer an integrative model of social differentiation, and the chapter concludes with Thorne's (13.9) recommendations of ways to promote co-operative classroom relationships among children.

The parallel section of *Reflective Teaching in the Primary School* considers the social consequences of children's school experiences. It focuses on the values which are expressed in routine interaction, on children's expectations, processes of differentiation and polarization and on the quality of teacher–child relationships. There are practical activities for classroom investigation and suggestions for further reading.

📖 READING 13.1

The correspondence of schooling and work

Samuel Bowles and Herbert Gintis

Schooling in Capitalist America, from which this reading is drawn, is a very clear example of the application of a structural, Marxist theory of the role of the education system in reproducing social hierarchies in modern societies. Is education primarily about the fulfilment of individual potential, or is it more concerned with the production and allocation of a skilled and compliant workforce which can meet the needs of industry? This is a provocative reading which should give pause for thought. What exactly are the consequences of what we do in schools?

Edited from: Bowles, S. and Gintis, H. (1976) *Schooling in Capitalist America*. London: Routledge, 37–133

Our argument is simple enough: Since its inception in the United States, the public-school system has been seen as a method of disciplining children in the interest of producing a properly subordinate adult population. The theme of social control pervades educational thought and policy. The forms of school discipline, the position of the teacher, and the moral conception of the child have all changed over the years, but the overriding objective has remained.

In our view, it is pointless to ask if the net effect of U.S. education is to promote equality or inequality, repression or liberation. These issues pale into insignificance before the major fact: The educational system is an integral element in the reproduction of the prevailing class structure of society. The educational system certainly has a life of its own, but the experience of work and the nature of the class structure are the bases upon which educational values are formed, social justice assessed, the realm of the possible delineated in people's consciousness.

In short, the educational system's task of integrating young people into adult work roles constrains the types of personal development which it can foster.

The educational system helps integrate youth into the economic system through a structural correspondence between its social relations and those of production. The structure of social relations in education not only inures the student to the discipline of the work place, but develops the types of personal demeanour, modes of self-presentation, self-image, and social-class identifications which are the crucial ingredients of job adequacy. Specifically, the social relationships of education – the relationships between administrators and teachers, teachers and students, students and students, and students and their work – replicate the hierarchical division of labour. Hierarchical relations are reflected in the vertical authority lines from student's lack of control over his or her education, the alienation of the student from the curriculum content, and the motivation of school work through a system of grades and other external rewards rather than the student's integration with either the process (learning) or the outcome (knowledge) of the educational 'production process'. Fragmentation in work is reflected in the institutionalized and often destructive competition among students through continual and ostensibly meritocratic ranking and evaluation. By attuning young people to a set of social relationships similar to those of the work place, schooling attempts to gear the development of personal needs to its requirements.

But the correspondence of schooling with the social relations of production goes beyond this aggregate level. Different levels of education feed workers into different levels within the occupational structure and, correspondingly, tend toward an internal organization comparable to levels in the hierarchical division of labour. The lowest levels in the hierarchy of the enterprise emphasize rule-following, middle levels, dependability, and the capacity to operate without direct and continuous supervision while the higher levels stress the internalization of the norms of the enterprise. Similarly, in education. Even within a single school, the social relationships of different tracks tend to confirm to different behaviour norms. Vocational and general tracks emphasize rule-following and close supervision, while the college track tends toward a more open atmosphere emphasizing the internalization.

These differences in the social relationships among and within schools, in part, reflect both the social backgrounds of the student body and their likely future economic positions. Thus blacks and other minorities are concentrated in schools whose repressive, arbitrary, generally chaotic internal order, coercive authority structures, and minimal possibilities for advancement mirror the characteristics of inferior job situations. Similarly, predominantly working-class schools tend to emphasize behavioural control and rule-following, while schools in well-to-do suburbs employ relatively open systems that favour greater student participation, less direct supervision, more student electives and, in general, a value system stressing internalized standards of control.

Differences in social relationships of schooling are further reinforced by inequalities in financial resources. The paucity of financial support for the education of children from minority groups and low-income families leaves more resources to be devoted to the children of those with more commanding roles in the economy; it also forces upon the teachers and school administrators in the working-class schools a type of social relationship that fairly closely mirrors that of the factory. Financial considerations in poorly supported schools militate against small intimate classes, multiple elective courses, and specialized teachers (except for disciplinary personnel). They preclude the amounts of free time for teachers and free space required for a more open, flexible educational environment. The well-financed schools attended by the children of the rich can offer much greater opportunities for the development of the capacity for sustained independent work and all the other characteristics required for adequate job performance in the upper levels of the occupational hierarchy.

 READING 13.2

Attainment in the infant school

Barbara Tizard, Peter Blatchford, Jessica Burke, Clare Farquhar and Ian Plewis

Barbara Tizard and her colleagues made a longitudinal study of pupils as they moved through 33 infant schools in inner London. They tried to identify factors associated with pupil attainment and this extract highlights their major findings. First, the quality of children's pre-school development of language and literacy at home was found to be particularly important, indeed, more so than social class *per se*. Second, the progress made by the children depended a good deal on the schools they attended, and finally, the expectations of the teachers by whom they were taught were vital.

How do the children you know respond to the expectations which you have of them?

Edited from: Tizard, B., Blatchford, P., Burke, J., Farquhar, C. and Plewis, I. (1988) *Young Children at School in the Inner City*. Hove: Lawrence Erlbaum Associates, 168–76

Pre-school attainments

If all children progressed at the same rate, then those who were doing best at school entry would continue to be doing best at the end of infant school. We found that this was, to a considerable extent, the case, and that the strongest predictor of attainment at age seven was the amount of 3R knowledge that the children had before ever they started school.

Since the extent of pre-school children's literacy and numeracy was so strongly related to later attainment, we tried to establish where the children had obtained their knowledge. Factors within the home appeared to make an important contribution to pre-school children's 3R knowledge. Social class has been found to be an important factor by other researchers. We had few middle-class parents within our sample, but we found that those mothers with higher educational qualifications tended to have more literate and numerate four-year-olds. The associations between the parent's educational practices and pre-school literacy were even stronger, especially the extent to which parents read to children and provided them with books, and also taught them about letters. But much the strongest association was with the child's own ability to define words, which no doubt reflects both innate ability and the extent to which parents talked about words and their meaning with their children.

Factors within the infant school

School attainment at age seven was not inexorably determined at school entry. In statistical terms, pre-school test results explained about half of the variation in top infant test scores. Although by and large those children who did best at age four did best at age seven, some children did better than would have been predicted from their pre-school scores, whereas others did worse. From an educational point of view, it is important to know what parents and teachers were doing that was responsible for a relative acceleration or slowing of progress. We found that, whereas parents had a big influence on the level of pre-school attainments, factors in the school were more important once the children started at infant school.

The two major factors in the school associated with progress were the range of 3R curriculum taught to the children, and the expectations that teachers had of them. One further factor, the particular school the child attended, was also, to a lesser extent, associated with progress. All three factors were interrelated, but all had an independent association with progress. This means, for example, that irrespective of which school a child attended, or whether or not their teacher had high expectations of them, children's attainments were higher if they had been introduced to a wider 3R curriculum.

We found that the amount of progress the children made depended to a significant extent on the school they attended. The difference was most marked in writing, but it was still significant in reading and maths. For reading, the difference between schools was most marked in the reception year. During this year children in some schools made considerable progress, whereas in others, children with a similar level of knowledge of reading at the beginning of the year made very little progress. Since the correlations between early and later reading attainments became more marked at the end of the reception year, these findings suggest that the reception year offers an important opportunity to give special assistance to the lower-attaining children. In our opinion, a school reading policy for this important year is essential. In the case of maths, we found no difference between schools in the amount of progress children made in the reception year, but marked differences in the middle and top infant years.

Within classes, we found a consistent relationship between the teachers' expectations of individual children at the beginning of the year and the range of the 3R curriculum they were introduced to. This was true even when controlling for the children's initial skills: That is, of two children with similar skills at the beginning of the year, the one judged by the teacher to have higher academic potential than the other would be introduced to a wider range of 3R knowledge during the year. It might be argued that this simply means that the teacher was a good judge of which child would in fact be better able to cope with a wider curriculum, but our findings suggest that the teachers were influenced by other than strictly academic considerations – for example, we found that their expectations were influenced by their opinion that a child was 'a pleasure to teach'.

Teachers have expectations not only of individual children, but of the class as a whole. The only way we were able to glimpse these in our study was by asking teachers why they had not introduced certain curriculum items to any of the children in their class. Whilst some teachers answered that these items were too difficult for children of this age, others said that they were too difficult for the children in this school. Yet we know that in other schools, with a similar intake, teachers had introduced these items. We suspect that low expectations are an important cause of the low level of attainment in many of the schools we studied.

Low attainment in the schools was certainly not caused by a general state of chaos or confusion in the classroom. In three-quarters of our observations we found children busy working or organizing work, and disruptive or aggressive behaviour in the classroom was rare. Nor was it the case that the children spent a great deal of time playing; the proportion of classroom time devoted to play ranged from 14% in the reception year to 2% in the top-infant year.

If, as we believe, the expectations of the teachers were too low, a crucial issue is to establish how expectations can be raised. Initially, it is obviously both desirable and feasible to raise the expectations of teachers in low-achieving working-class schools to those of teachers in higher-achieving schools in similar areas. A more ambitious, and very important, project would be to see just how high one can reasonably set expectations in a working-class area – is it possible by this process to achieve the standards of a middle-class school? The question is one of great importance in primary education, since if teachers' expectations are low, children will inevitably leave infant school with a handicap.

Some teachers are likely to blame parents for their pupils' low level of achievement. Indeed, we found that the majority of teachers thought that parents, and not schools, were the main influence on children's educational success. When we asked reception-class teachers whether they thought that their parents would provide the back-up at home that they would like, only a third thought that the majority of parents would do so, and 29% felt that very few, or none, of their parents would do so. This proved to be a myth very widespread amongst teachers and it was certainly not supported by our evidence. Throughout the infant school most parents were deeply committed to helping their children. In the first two years of school, 40% of parents said they heard their children read five times a week and despite the fact that very few teachers encouraged parents to help with writing and maths, a great deal of such help was being given in most of the children's homes.

There is another widely held belief amongst teachers, that black parents are particularly likely to fail to provide adequate educational support for their children. This, too, proved to be a myth. We found that black parents gave their children even more help with school work than white parents, and had a more positive attitude towards giving this help. Both black and white parents read aloud to their children with equal frequency. The great majority of parents provided their children with books – at school entry, as we saw for ourselves, only a quarter of the children had as few as ten or less books – and similar proportions of black and white parents said that they borrowed children's books from the public library, and attended school meetings.

READING 13.3

Developing policy on gender

Gaby Weiner

In this reading Gaby Weiner reflects on the struggle of feminist teachers during the 1980s to achieve recognition of gender inequalities. She identifies some of the major issues which were raised and the practical changes which were introduced in attempts to provide more opportunities for girls in class-rooms and schools. Finally, she highlights two distinct strategies which were adopted, those associated with 'equal opportunities' and the more radical 'anti-sexism'. To what extent, she finally asks, have the aspirations of these pioneers been sustained today, and what strategies now seem most appropriate?

Edited from: Weiner, G. (1990) 'Developing educational policy on gender in the primary school', in Weiner, G. (ed.) *The Primary School and Equal Opportunities: International Perspectives on Gender Issues*. London: Cassell, 36–42

Feminist teachers were concerned with raising awareness amongst their colleagues about the extent of gender inequalities in education. They focused on three areas in particular. They considered attitudes, both of pupils and teachers. For instance, it was argued that whilst teachers believed that they treated boys and girls without prejudice, detailed investigation showed that this was not the case and that girls appeared to be seriously disadvantaged in the schooling system (Clarricoates, 1978; Spender, 1980; Stanworth, 1981 etc.); school organization and resources e.g. inequitable staffing patterns, sex-stereotyping in texts and reading schemes, and sex-specific patterns of subject choice at thirteen plus (see, for instance, Whyld, 1983); and the activity of women in the labour force, particularly on the statistical unlikelihood of women remaining in the home for most of their adult lives and the consequent need to change traditional, i.e. domestic-related, career choices for girls (Joshi *et al.*, 1982). For the primary teacher, trying to change attitudes and school organization and resourcing were clearly of greatest importance. For instance, emphasis was placed on the following features of primary schools:

There were major inequalities in staffing patterns.

Although over 80 per cent of primary teachers were women, the headteacher and teacher responsible for science and mathematics were usually men. The school caretaker was invariably male, and the cleaners, secretaries and helpers female.

Textbooks and reading schemes portrayed stereotyped views of family life – white middle-class – and gave mothers and fathers clearly defined and separate roles. The language used in classroom materials was also frequently sexist (and racist).

Teachers tended to give boys more attention and find them more stimulating than girls, yet praise girls for neatness and good behaviour. They also had higher academic expectations of boys and were more likely to attribute poor performance to lack of motivation in boys, and lack of ability in girls.

Whilst more primary-school children attended mixed-sex schools, girls and boys were likely to be taught separately for craft subjects and sport activities. They were also treated differentially on other occasions, for instance, at registration, when lining up to move around the school, and for tasks such as clearing up (girls) or moving Physical Education equipment (boys).

This summary of research indicates the range of issues being considered at primary level. Findings were publicized in a variety of ways – in the form of written or verbal reports to school staff meetings, to school in-service conferences, or to evening seminars arranged by local 'women in education' groups. Feminist teachers also used their findings to lobby advisers and administrators for changes in policy and for practical support, e.g. in providing funding for the production of non-sexist teaching materials.

Once the problem of gender inequality had been established, solutions were sought that could be readily injected into school life. *Ad hoc* strategies were developed which included:

the creation of equal opportunities working parties and posts to devise 'whole school' policies,

revision of school materials (e.g. texts, reading schemes, examination questions and displays),

raising awareness about equality issues at staff, parents' and governors' meetings,

rearranging timetabling to enable pupils to opt more easily for non-traditional subjects such as physics for girls and modern languages for boys,

appointing female senior staff to provide fresh role models for female pupils, encouraging wider career aspirations by inviting people holding non-traditional jobs into school,

changing school organization by, for instance, 'de-sexing' registers and 'uni-sexing' school uniform.

In addition for primary schools, it was suggested that teachers might:

encourage pupils to sit and work in mixed sex groups;

share out tasks so that girls are encouraged to do more strenuous and active tasks, and boys asked, for example, to clear up;

try to consciously give more time to the quiet, less-demanding children, usually the girls (though not always);

choose and adapt stories to redress the sex bias in children's adventure stories and folk tales;

when making worksheets and classroom resources, use non-sexist language e.g. police officer rather than policeman, and provide a range of positive images of women;

not assume that the nuclear family is the only acceptable and positive family life style.

The main focus of teachers was upon school-based practical change; how could they help reduce inequalities between the sexes by changing their own and their colleague's perceptions and practice? Yet the solutions were highly diverse. They stemmed not merely from local or individual school priorities but also from critical differences in the perspectives of the teachers themselves.

Two different feminist teacher perspectives are discernible in the challenge to previous educational practices of gender differentiation and division; the 'equal opportunities' and 'anti-sexist' approaches (Weiner, 1985).

The equal opportunities approach aimed at reforms on behalf of girls and women, and sometimes boys and men, within the existing educational structure. The anti-sexist approach aimed at changing unequal power relations between the sexes by transforming the patriarchal and ethnocentric nature of school structures and curricula. These differences became evident in the strategies chosen by teachers to challenge sexist schooling.

The equal opportunities approach emphasized, for instance, persuading girls to develop scientific and technological skills, textbook reform, and at secondary level, changing sex stereotyped subject choices and a common curriculum. It emphasized equal female representation in the higher echelons of school and society. Anti-sexist approaches, on the other hand, focused on combining anti-sexist and anti-racist strategies, challenging male school knowledge by considering what 'her story' or girl-centred science might look like. At upper secondary level they also addressed the more contentious issues of sexuality, sexual harassment, heterosexuality and homophobia. Their concern was that of empowering female pupils and teachers in their struggle against the male domination of schooling.

While both approaches were feminist in that they wanted to improve educational opportunities for girls and women, they had different priorities for change. Those favouring equal opportunities opted for awareness-raising and consensual change. They asked for increased in-service training as a means of ensuring recognition of sex equality as a professional issue. Anti-sexist teachers, in contrast, focused on more structural changes in their emphasis on the importance of unequal power relations and the need to address conflicting interests. They sought to challenge male domination of schooling by, for instance, establishing schoolgirls' and women's support groups and designing 'girl-centred' curricula and replacing hierarchy, competitiveness and selection with co-operation and democracy.

The achievement of feminist teachers has been that, despite lack of commitment and support from central government, few in education in the United Kingdom can now deny that equal opportunities is an important educational issue. Whether the progress made in the 1980s can be sustained, and even improved upon, is unfortunately a matter of speculation rather than inevitability.

 READING 13.4

Girls and boys in the classroom

Valerie Walkerdine

> Valerie Walkerdine's post-structuralist analysis has provided new insights into primary education (see, in particular, her book, *The Mastery of Reason*, 1988). In this reading she illustrates the ways in which a gendered discourse penetrates even the play of young children. The positioning of the boys and girls within the discourse leads to struggles for power as they interact together. See also Readings 11.5 and 13.3.
>
> In what ways do you think the patterns of interaction in your class are influencing children's gender identities?
>
> Edited from: Walkerdine, V. (1981) Sex, power and pedagogy, *Screen Education* 38, 14–23

I want to examine interactions involving small boys in play with girls in the classroom. Sex-role socialization accounts of the reproduction of girls understand them as produced as a reflection of traditional female sex roles. The economic dependence and oppression of women will produce girls whose personalities are passive and dependent, dominated and not dominant. Yet individuals are powerless or powerful depending upon which discursive practice they enter as subject. Recent work within the women's movement has pointed out that the oppression of women is not unitary, and that different discursive practices have different and often contradictory histories. This means that in some practices women are relatively powerful, for example, in those practices in which they signify as mothers. These practices are reproduced by the children in their play in the nursery classroom. This means that the girls are not always passive and dependent, just as their mothers are not, but are constantly struggling with the boys to define their play and to redefine it into discursive practices in which they can be powerful. To understand the power and resistance in the play of children we have to understand children both as recreating the, often reactionary, discourses with which they are familiar, but also serve to constitute them as a multiplicity of contradictory positions of power and resistance.

Let us examine one small piece of classroom play. The children are playing hospitals. They have been given all the necessary equipment by a nursery nurse, and she has seen to it that they boys get the doctors' uniforms and the girls the nurses'. The nursery nurse constantly helps to maintain the power of the doctors over the nurses by constantly asking the nurses to 'help' the doctors. One girl, Jane, changes this into a situation where she is to make cups of tea for the patients. She goes into the Wendy House and has a domestic conversation with another girl and then the following sequence ensues:

One of the doctors arrives in the Wendy House and Jane says to him:

Jane: You gotta go quickly.
Derek: Why?
Jane: 'Cos you're going to work.
Derek: But I'm being a doctor.
Jane: Well, you've got to go to work doctor 'cos you've got to go to hospital and so do I. You don't like cabbage do you? (*he shakes his head*) ... Well you haven't got cabbage then. I'm goin' to hospital. If you tidy up this room make sure and tell me.

Jane has managed to convert the play situation from one in which she is a powerless and subservient nurse to the only one in which she has power over the doctor, that of controlling his domestic life by becoming the controlling woman in the home. It is important that the other way in which she could have had power within that game, by, for example, playing a more senior doctor than Derek, is denied her by the nursery nurse's action and it is unlikely that she would be able to take that position by herself.

In another example of play between children in another nursery school we can examine another situation of struggle for power between girls and boys. This time the boy, Dean, is struggling for power to define and control the game. He comes to join Diane and Nancy, who are already playing mothers and daughters in the Wendy House. Diane is playing mother and controlling both the sequencing of the game and the actions of Nancy, who like any dutiful daughter goes along with mother's wishes. They are playing happily until Dean intervenes. Diane tries to tell him what to do as her son, but he tries to take over her commanding position. Diane says:

Diane: Well I'm playing mums and dads and girls. You're not. Or my, or my sister'll tell you off if you come in my house. She'll tell you off if you, if you come in my house. She will 'cos because I'm making 'er bed and if you get in 'er bed she'll tell you off she will.
         Let's go and get the baby, come on then, you've got to go to bed now darling. You ain't been to bed yet have you?
Dean: (*to Nancy*) You don't like ... you don't want to play with 'er do you?
Nancy: Yes, she won't let me go ...

Diane pushes Nancy a bit on the rocking horse and then tries to retrieve the domestic discourse:

Diane: Darling ... I made the bed for you. Look what she's done. She's made it all dirty. All all new, I've made it all clean. Now I'll have to tidy up. Let's see my money, see it there's money. Here's your food. Meat, chicken and bacon and steak. Now d'you want the telly on? D'you want the telly on? I put it on for you. Here y'are I put the telly on for you. You can't turn it off.
Dean: What?
Diane: Can you?
Dean: I know you can't.
Nancy: She's our mum, she's our mum, yeah she's our mum.
Dean: (*to Nancy*) If you're playing with 'er I'm not gonna be your friend any more ...' not ever play with you. So what you gonna do?

Nancy: (*she looks first at one and then at the other, and 'turns tail'*) I'll play with you.
Diane: Nancy, get off that horsey and go to bed now 'cos you're being naughty.

In both of these examples the struggle on behalf of the powerless child, the resistance of that child, takes the form of reading the individual as the subject/object of another discourse. In both cases the girls' power is produced by their setting up the game as domestic, in which they, like their mothers, traditionally have power, though of course it is power produced through contradiction and paid for by their domestic labour: it is therefore severely limited and limiting, but not without effects. It is true that this is precisely what is asserted by sex-role stereotyping arguments, but there are several important points which, it seems to me, stereotyping arguments cannot explain. First, the girls are not always weak and dependent, but appear to be engaged in a struggle with the boys to read and to create the situations as ones in which they are powerful. The boys equally struggle to remove the play from the site of the domestic in which they are likely to be subservient. It is interesting to note that in the large number of play sequences recorded in these two nurseries, there were very few in which boys played powerful fathers when girls were present although they did do so when playing with other boys.

However, for these young children the domestic is not the only site of apparent female power. Their school lives are controlled by female teachers. There are many ways in which the discursive position adopted by the teachers is similar to that of mothers. Indeed, the nursery school provides a context in which good mothering and good pedagogy are seen as part of the same process – of aiding child development. I would argue that the very power of women in this transitory situation, between the domestic and the academic, is precisely what permits the early success of girls. It may be the similarity between these discursive practices, both sites of female power, that allows girls to take up positions of similarity with the powerful teachers. Indeed, the girls who are considered to be the 'brightest' by the teachers do indeed operate as subjects within the powerful pedagogic discourse. Within that discourse they take the position of the knower, they become sub-teachers. For example, in one of the nurseries, Nancy, considered to be bright by the teacher, constantly asserts that she 'knows'. She continually finishes her work before the others to shrieks of 'Done it' and 'That's where it goes 'cos I know it does'. The boys in these exchanges are, by contrast, for the most part almost totally silent. They seem to be engaged in a resistance of silence, which is of course another way of resisting the discourse. I would argue that it is the relation between the domestic and the pedagogic and the way in which women signify as mothers and teachers, taking positions of power within those practices, which provides the space for the early success of girls. This success is achieved precisely because successful school performance requires them to take up such positions in pedagogic discourses. On the other hand, this is equally a site of struggle for the boys, a struggle in which they must work to redefine the situation as one in which the women and girls are powerless subjects of other discourses. It could well be this very resistance to that quasi-domestic power which results in the failure of the boys to do well in early education.

Social relations, discourse and racism

Debbie Epstein

This reading begins with an exceptionally clear account of how Foucault's post-structuralism has been applied to education, and the use of the concepts of 'discourse' and 'positioning' in the analysis of social relations (see also Readings 11.5 and 13.6). Debbie Epstein applies this theoretical framework to the issue of race and racism to show how they are socially constructed in relation to power at political, institutional and interpersonal levels.

To what extent can you identify with this powerful analysis of racism? And what are its implications?

Edited from: Epstein, D. (1993) *Changing Classroom Cultures: Anti-racism, Politics and Schools*. Stoke-on-Trent: Trentham Books, 9–16

Social relations and discourse

Social relations are organized through a number of institutions and social structures, of which the education system is one (others include the family, the law, the political system, and so on). Within each of these social institutions there are a number of different possible ways of behaving and of understanding the nature of the institution. These different versions of the particular institution are in competition with each other for dominance and, at different times and in different places, different versions will be more or less successful. Indeed, contradictions and conflict are part of the network of social relations with which we all live. If we take the example of education, we can see that the different sides of current struggles around teaching methods (for example, over the use of 'real books' to teach reading) represent a struggle between different understandings of what it means to teach and to learn and different notions of what schooling is for and about.

These competing understandings are expressed through language and through the ways in which institutions like schools are actually organized. The French philosopher, Michel Foucault, used the terms 'discourse' (taken from the field of linguistics) and 'discursive practices' to describe these understandings and their expression through language, organization forms and ways of behaving. The various discourses which are available in relation to particular social institutions and structures provide us with different possible ways of behaving and understanding the world as well as limiting (but not determining) what can be done and said. We are positioned in various discourses as well as taking up positions ourselves. For example, we identify ourselves and are identified as heterosexual, lesbian or gay and could not do so if categorizing discourses of sexuality did not exist. In this limited sense, we can be said to be 'produced' by discourses and discursive practices.

In *Discipline and Punish* (1977), Foucault discusses the ways in which schools have arisen as a site of discipline and surveillance of children, saying that:

> A relation of surveillance, defined and regulated is inscribed at the heart of the practice of teaching, not as an additional or adjacent part, but as a mechanism that is inherent to it and which increases its efficiency. (p. 176)

Following Foucault, Valerie Walkerdine (1985) argues that discourses in schooling both regulate and produce the child as a 'rational, independent, autonomous individual as a quasi-natural phenomenon who progresses through a universalized developmental sequence towards the possibility of rational argument' (p. 203). In this context, she suggests that schooling not only 'defines ... what knowledge is' but also defines and regulates what 'a child is' (pp. 207–8). Schools, then, are sites of struggles, not only about knowledge, but also about ideologies of childhood, about what it means to be a teacher and to be gendered. Consequently there are, within schooling, a number of different, sometimes contradictory, discourses available through which teachers and children are produced and produce themselves.

It is possible, for example, to imagine teachers behaving in a number of different ways in relation to students, and these ways may come from a number of different discourses. The most obvious discourse of teaching might be called the 'instructional discourse'. Within it, teachers pass on information, demonstrate how to do things, and so on. Within this discourse it would be impossible to imagine a teacher knowing less than pupils in her/his class about a topic being taught. However, teachers also operate, especially in the early years of schooling, within what might be called a 'mothering discourse'. In this context, teachers might offer comfort to children who are distressed or look after them in physical ways, such as changing their undergarments if they have 'wet' themselves.

It would not, however, be open to a teacher to undertake all the functions of mothering and remain in the role of teacher, and even very young children are aware of the differences in expected behaviours. One little girl, when she was six and a pupil in the school where her mother taught, resolved the conflict of discourses by regularly calling her mother 'Mrs Mummy' when at school. There are, of course, many other discourses within which teachers can and do operate – for example, those of social work, policing and so on.

The question of which discourses are dominant is not a natural one, for the social meanings given to different discursive practices will vary according to one's position within a particular set of social relations. What seems like common-sense will, in general, represent the interests of dominant groups in society, while what seems 'biased' or 'extreme' may well be those discourses which seek to oppose those interests (although subordinated groups develop their own versions of common-sense). In education, for example, it may seem perfectly reasonable to assume that it is desirable to give a 'balanced' view of controversial and political questions and this is often argued against anti-racist and anti-sexist education. However, subjects which are controversial change over time. For example, until relatively recently the teaching of evolutionary theory rather than the creation story as given in Genesis was considered both subversive and controversial. Furthermore, the demands of 'balance' seem rather different depending on one's position in relation to the issue.

Race and racism

There are a number of discourses around issues of race and racism in education and other social structures. One of our most widespread common-sense understandings is that 'race' exists as an objective social fact.

One of the characteristics of Western science is that it categorizes, and the post-Darwinian assumption has been that people can be categorized in similar ways to chemical elements, plants, animals and so forth. In the process of categorization, it has been assumed that particular groups of people have certain essential characteristics, which are (usually) biologically determined. Thus, for example, in certain racist discourses African-Caribbean men and women are assumed to be naturally 'physical', while South Asian women are assumed to be naturally 'passive'. It has been further assumed that when someone has been categorized, or has categorized him or herself, according to one of a number of types of categories, which include race, gender, sexuality, ability and so on, then everything important which can be said about this person has, in fact, been said. In this way, social identities such as those of race are constructed. Such social identities are not simply about how we are seen or categorized. They are also important in how we ourselves experience and understand the world.

In terms of race, it is assumed, in keeping with the essentialist processes of categorization discussed above, that certain kinds of people are 'black' and other kinds of people are 'white'. This is the basis of racism directed against black people. The concepts race and racism are mutually dependent. This is not a static situation, but a dynamic process in which racist discourses feed on the concept of race, and in which the concept of race is constantly re-articulated and reproduced through racist discourses in a symbiotic relationship.

I would suggest that racism can be best understood in terms of process – or, perhaps, those processes which result in the disadvantage for particular groups of people defined through racist discourses. In British society and its historical context, the people against whom racist processes work are most often black, but at other times and in other places, other groups, such as the Irish or Jews, have been the chief butt of different forms of racism and it should be noted that anti-Irish racism in Britain and anti-semitism more generally continue to be active and, indeed, seem to be on the increase.

Because racism is a process, which changes over time and place and varies with macro- and micro-political conditions, it is not possible to give a simple, straightforward definition to the word. Racism cannot be reduced to a simple formula, such as the often quoted equation 'racism equals power plus prejudice'. Certainly both prejudice and power play a part in the construction of racism. However, power is more complicated than such a formula allows for a personal prejudice is not necessarily a component in every situation in which black people are disadvantaged. If, for example, an oversubscribed school offers places first to those children who have had a sibling there (even if the sibling has left), which is very common, this is likely to disadvantage black children in areas where there have been relatively recent influxes of black people. It is unlikely that such a practice would have originated from the prejudiced intention of reducing the numbers of black pupils, but this will be the effect. It is practices such as these which are defined as 'indirect racism' in the Race Relations Act 1976. The operation of the 'market' in education under the Education Reform Act (1988), will also disadvantage black pupils disproportionately. However, it was instituted at the behest of New Right economic ideology rather than directly by racism.

Racism involves a variety of processes and institutional arrangements which are socially constructed. These processes take place both at macro-levels, involving national and even global politics, and at micro-levels, in the organization of particular institutions like schools and in the relationships between individuals.

As pointed out above, one of the processes involved in the construction of racism is the acceptance, as common-sense, of racial categories. However, racism cannot be combated simply by refusing to accept racial categories. The adoption of slogans such as 'One race the human race', while it may be an important aim, does not recognize that racism makes a real difference in the material world to people's life chances and experiences (Henriques, 1984) and may even be a form of racism itself in its refusal to recognize difference.

There are many racisms, not just one. What they have in common is the outcome of black disadvantage in housing, employment, education, and many other areas of everyday life.

READING 13.6

Racism in children's lives

Barry Troyna and Richard Hatcher

> Troyna and Hatcher carried out a detailed study, in two 'mainly white' primary schools, of pupil culture and of the attitudes of the children towards race. This reading is from the conclusions of their book. The analysis is challenging for teachers, for it reveals the embeddedness of racist conceptions within the cultures of the children in the schools and the particular importance of the stance that is taken by teachers towards racist incidents. Although most children lacked a sense of the social structure within which racism develops, many children were committed to the principle of equal opportunities.
>
> Are your pupils aware of and offended by inequalities? If so, could you build on this to increase their understanding of issues such as racism?
>
> Edited from: Troyna, B. and Hatcher, R. (1992) *Racism in Children's Lives: A Study of Mainly White Primary Schools*. London: Routledge, 196–204

The schools that we studied are similar to many hundreds of primary schools in urban areas, located in streets of Victorian terraces or new estates on the outskirts. They are similar, too, in containing a minority of black children, perhaps two or three, or half a dozen, in each class. A visitor in the classroom and playground will observe children working together and playing together, black and white, with no sign that 'race' is a significant feature of their lives as children. It is unlikely that such a visitor would overhear a racist remark or witness any other form of racist behaviour. It would be easy to conclude that racism among children is not an issue that such schools need to devote much attention to. These schools seem to confirm the validity of the 'contact hypothesis' that racial prejudice and discriminatory practices are dispelled by the positive experience of white and black children being together in school.

Our evidence does not appear to support this view. On the contrary, it reveals that 'race', and racism, are significantly features of the cultures of children in predominantly white primary schools. By far the most common expression of racism is through racist name-calling. There is a wide variation in black children's experiences of racist name-calling. For some it may be almost an everyday happening. For others it is less frequent, with occurrences remembered as significant events whose recurrence remains a possibility in every new social situation. For all, it is in general the most hurtful form of verbal aggression from other children.

The variation in the experiences of black children are not explicable in terms of differences of ethnic group, or of gender. Differences between schools seem to be mainly the consequence of the effectiveness of the stance that teachers, non-teaching staff, and in particular the headteacher, take towards racist incidents, but there is also a wide variation in the experiences of black children in the same school, which is mainly a function of differences in the characteristic patterns of social interaction that black children are involved in and in particular the level of conflict within them.

Many black children also have experiences of racism outside school. In some cases these are of harassment by other perhaps older, children. School policies on racist behaviour may suppress it within the school but have no effect on the behaviour of some of the white pupils once they leave the school premises. In addition, many black children have experiences of racism in the adult word: disputes with neighbours, arguments in shops, conflict in the community. These experiences, and the roles taken up by black adults within them, provide a context for their experiences in school, their understanding of them and their responses to them, that other children, and school staff, may be unaware of.

Children's cultures can be analysed in terms of the interplay of processes of domination and equality. Elements of elaborated and common-sense ideologies, both racist and anti-racist, deriving from family, television and community, enter into and circulate within children's cultures. Here they interact with common-sense understandings generated by everyday social interaction among children. Social processes of dominance and conflict may become racialized in various ways to legitimize forms of racist behaviour. But interaction among children also gives rise to a strong egalitarian dynamic, which may be generalized to issues of 'race' and link up with anti-racist ideologies. Relationships of friendship between white and black children reinforce this egalitarian dynamic, but do not necessarily lead to its generalization to all black children.

There is a wide variation among white children in their knowledge, attitudes and beliefs about 'race', both within children's culture and in the wider society. Some children are largely ignorant of processes of racial discrimination in society, but the majority of white children have quite an extensive knowledge base and set of interpretive frameworks through which they make sense of issues such as immigration, racial violence, South Africa, and relations between black and white people in their own community. The principal sources outside the school are parents and other adult relatives, television, and their direct experiences in the community. These make available a range of contradictory messages about 'race', and in any case children do not passively receive them but actively select and reinterpret.

The attitudes and beliefs of white children range from those who make use of racist frameworks of interpretation to those who are committed to well-developed notions of racial equality. Many children display inconsistent and contradictory repertoires of attitudes, containing both elements of racially egalitarian ideologies and elements of racist ideologies.

The curriculum needs to not only address the real experience that children bring with them to the classroom, it needs to offer them the conceptual tools to interpret it. These are two related elements in how the children in our study thought about 'race' that are pertinent here.

The first is their limited understanding of notions of social structure. Many had little or no understanding of how 'race' was socially structured by, for example, the economy and the state. This is a symptom of a general absence of political education in the primary curriculum. Yet it is clear that children of 10 and 11 years are capable of understanding such ideas, even with little help from the curriculum. The consequence of the lack of 'sociological' concepts was that children tended to use concepts derived from their own experiences of interpersonal interaction to explain phenomena at the level of society. So, for example, lacking concepts of ideology based on material interests, many children explained racist behaviour in society in terms of personal motivations of 'jealousy', transferring a concept that was central to experiences of conflict in their own relationships.

The second conceptual limitation concerned the notion of inequality that children used. For many children, white and black, this is a powerful principle capable of organizing a consistent anti-racist perspective. But for others, it stumbled at the idea that to achieve equality for the unequal may require unequal treatment, particularly if the inequality is not just at the level of interpersonal relations but is socially structured in ways that the child is not aware of. The curriculum can make an important contribution towards helping children to develop the principle of equality that is so important in their personal lives into a more complex and encompassing concept of social justice.

Finally, we want to stress the two strands that run through the culture of children. We have demonstrated how significant racism is in the lives of white children. We have also been made aware of the strength of anti-racist attitudes and behaviour. The frequent presence of racially egalitarian elements in the thinking even of children who engage in racist behaviour is a crucial factor on which teachers can build. In doing so, the existence in every class of children who have a clear anti-racist commitment is potentially the most powerful resource, if they can be helped to gain the confidence, the skills and knowledge to express it, both in the curriculum and the interpersonal interaction.

📖 READING 13.7

Needs, rights and opportunities in special education

Caroline Roaf and Hazel Bines

> The field of special educational needs has always generated controversies of principle and definition, and perhaps this is inevitable as the tension between needs and resources is played out. In this reading, Roaf and Bines interrogate some key terms and consider how they have been applied. They identify various problematic aspects of the concept of 'needs' and suggest an alternative discourse of 'opportunities' and 'rights'.
>
> How would consideration of 'opportunities' and 'rights' affect the ways in which you think about special education in relation to your school?
>
> Edited from: Roaf, C. and Bines, H. (1989) 'Needs, rights and opportunities in special education', in Roaf, C. and Bines, H. (eds) *Needs, Rights and Opportunities*. London: Falmer Press, 5–15

The development of special education during the last hundred years has traditionally focused on handicap and needs. It has involved efforts to expand provision for children and young people whose impairments or difficulties are not adequately catered for in ordinary schools or who may need additional help to cope with the demands of mainstream curricula and schooling. Such growth has been seen as the best means of focusing and securing special resources and expertise. Progress has also largely been measured in terms of expansion of the range, as well as the amount of special provision available for children and young people in order to cater for an increase in number and a wider range of handicaps and difficulties or needs.

Nevertheless, there have been a number of changes in the ways in which this development of special needs provision and curricula has been viewed and secured. In particular, the language and categories of handicap have been replaced by the more generic and flexible concept of special educational need. This new concept, as developed by the Warnock Report (DES, 1978b) and incorporated into the 1981 Education Act represented an attempt to remove formal distinctions between handicapped and non-handicapped students and to replace categories through an expanded and more flexible definition of special need. This could potentially incorporate one fifth of the whole school population, including children and young people in both ordinary and special schools. It also reflected a shift in emphasis from medical or psychological criteria of assessment and placement towards an educational, interactive and relative approach which would take into account all the factors which have a bearing on educational progress (DES, 1978b, para 3.6).

However, the emphasis on needs may have obscured other aspects in the development of special education, such as the degree to which equality of opportunity has been a significant dimension of debate and policy. There has, for example, been considerable concern about the issue of equal access to education, notably in regard to children with severe and multiple difficulties. Similarly, debate over segregation and placement in special schooling has been related to lack of equal educational opportunity. The increasing focus on integration as the model of good practice thus represents not just a new approach to fulfilling needs but also an intention to secure equal access to a common schooling for all children.

Special educational need remains a very difficult and complex concept in practice. It has the appearance of simplicity and familiarity, yet the greatest care is required in evaluating needs, in prioritizing them and in being clear in whose interest they are being stated.

Firstly, the term needs is often used in relation to the development and learning of all children. Given their individuality and idiosyncrasy, defining what constitutes a special educational need in any particular case can be difficult. However, if special education is to be used as a basis for special resource allocation, the difference between special and other educational needs would seem to have to be acknowledged. Although the 1981 Act emphasizes the relationship between learning difficulty and special educational need, learning difficulty in the past has largely been used in relation to remedial provision. Since this has been somewhat separate from other special education, its more general use for all forms of special needs is ambiguous. In addition, although 'special educational needs' is now the generic term, the number of specific descriptive categories has not been reduced. Indeed the Warnock Report and 1981 Act, while attempting to remove differences between handicapped and non-handicapped students, did not take special education out of the realm of handicap. Instead, more students have been brought within its brief under the much broader and ill-defined category of learning difficulty, and further divisions have emerged, particularly between students who are subjects of Statements and those who are not.

Secondly, the relativism of needs as currently understood can lead to haphazard and unequal provision. 'Special educational need' is a legal and administrative term as well as an educational and descriptive one thus taking on different meaning according to the context in which it is used. Such relativism is also a feature of the legislative definitions within the 1981 Education Act.

Needs are a matter of professional and value judgement. The moral and political basis of such judgements are usually neglected because we still focus on the receiver – the individual or group with needs. Yet hidden within these conceptions of needs are social interests, for example, to make the disabled productive or control troublesome children, together with a range of assumptions about what is normal (Tomlinson, 1982). When we focus on needs and particularly when we take our assumptions about the nature of those needs for granted, we do not ask who has the power to define the needs of others. We do not enquire why it is professionals who mostly define needs as opposed to parents or the students themselves. Nor do we fully explore the normative nature of our assumptions, for example, that they are grounded in conceptions of 'normal' cognitive development or behaviour whether such assumptions are informally operated, by teachers in the classroom, or more formally operated, by normative testing. We focus on what seem to be the genuine needs of the individual who lacks something and who has a need. However, we do not consider how needs may be generated by valuing certain aspects of development and attainment more than others. For example, if we did not value certain cognitive skills, would there be the needs currently identified as 'special' in schools? (Hargreaves, 1983)

The term 'needs' has now become a euphemism for labelling individuals as 'special'. The idea of having a difficulty suggests something can be done about it and tends to focus on individuals as a bottomless pit of problems to be overcome or filled up. The concept of needs remains deficit-based, despite attempts to relate it to context, with a pronounced tendency to slippage back towards individuals and their problems.

Given that needs is a problematic concept, 'opportunity' would seem to offer a better approach to special education. There is a much more explicit focus on context: opportunity raises questions of system rather than individual failure. When linked with equality, to make 'equality of opportunity', it also raises issues of discrimination and disadvantage. Equality of opportunity is also a widely known and understood rationale. Therefore it may be easier for the majority of teachers and policy makers to relate to opportunity rather than needs or at least to see the educational, social and political implications of requiring that equal opportunity be extended to those with impairments and difficulties.

'Rights' as a basis for developing special education policy and practice would also seem to have a number of advantages. As Kirp (1983) has suggested, comparing British and American special education policies and legislation, thinking about special education in terms of political and legal rights makes one reappraise resource allocation, relationships among the affected parties, the level and amount of dispute and the very conception of handicap. In respect of resource allocation, for example, the American structure of rights does not formally treat resource limits as constraining what can be provided. Whereas the British approach weighs the interests of special and ordinary children, the American orientation on rights places the burden of adjustment on the ordinary school. The greater disputes engendered by a rights approach, including increased litigation, may make for a more dynamic policy and lead school authorities to offer more than would otherwise have been provided. In respect of the disabled themselves, rights should encourage a stronger definition and assertion of self and interests, reducing professional power and paternalism. When rights legislation is explicitly linked with other civil rights, special education also becomes part of the larger struggle for equity. Race or gender dimensions of being 'special' can then also be raised.

Taken separately, therefore, there are advantages but also limitations to needs, rights and opportunity. In searching for the best way forward we suggest the following starting points.

'Needs statements' in themselves should not be regarded as a sufficient basis for developing policy and practice, because of the tendency to reinforce individualized, deficit-based approaches. Instead, needs should be tied to entitlement of rights and opportunity, in order to emphasize a systems approach and to strengthen and assert the interests and equity of those considered to have such needs. This would also remove some of the burden of guilt and stigma which is still associated with having special educational needs. To be entitled to something is very different and more positive than to need it, since it gives both validity and value to the claim.

Needs should also be seen in terms of what constitutes a relevant difference. Instead of trying to hide differences under a catch-all generic term, it might be more useful to explore whether and when differences matter and should or should not be considered. The discourse of opportunity and rights could be particularly helpful.

READING 13.8

Social differentiation in primary schools

Andrew Pollard

> This reading provides one way of taking stock of issues associated with the provision of equal opportunities in primary schools. Initially, it considers the reasons why teachers differentiate amongst pupils and also the possible unintended consequences of doing so. Criteria of judgement for facing this major dilemma are then offered, together with a model for thinking about school processes and social consequences. Could this reading provide a framework for synthesizing some of the other readings in this chapter concerning processes and consequences?
>
> Edited from: Pollard, A. (1987) Social differentiation in primary schools, *Cambridge Journal of Education*, 17 (3), 158–61

'The act or process of distinguishing something by its distinctive properties' – that is how my dictionary defines differentiation and, of course, it is a process in which we all engage as we go about our daily lives. Indeed, we could make few effective decisions without recourse to judgements about the particular qualities of people and things. However, serious responsibilities and potential problems are introduced when 'processes of distinguishing' are applied by those with a degree of power and authority to the qualities and lives of other people; for instance, as applied by us regarding the children in our classes at school. Further importance accrues if it can be shown that some of the judgements of differentiation, on which practices are based, are often inaccurate and may thus lead to injustices occurring. In such circumstances the issues raised inevitably extend beyond the practical ones of the moment, which may have provided an initial impetus for distinctions to be drawn, to encompass personal, ethical and moral concerns.

Of course, it can reasonably be argued that differentiation is both necessary and inevitable in classrooms. Classroom life is characterized by complexity, and rapid decisions certainly have to be made by teachers. As an exercise in information processing the challenges are considerable. Perhaps it is thus inevitable that teachers develop ways of thinking about children which make it possible both to anticipate potential difficulties before they arise and to interpret circumstances and events so that effective action can be taken. To this extent, differentiation may be seen as the product of a range of strategies which enable teachers to 'cope' with the demands of classroom life.

There seem to be three particular areas around which teacher knowledge of pupil differences tends to accumulate. The first relates to the issue of control and discipline, for teachers know very well that the maintenance of classroom order provides an infrastructure without which many essential activities cannot take place. The second concerns the interpersonal relationships which are developed with children – who is 'good to have in the class' and who is 'difficult to get on with' – and, of course, 'good relationships' have been a much prized quality of classroom life for many years and seen as one vital source of fulfilment and security for both teachers and children. Finally and by no means unimportantly, there is teacher knowledge about children's learning achievements, needs and capacities.

Differentiation of children can thus be seen partly as a response to the practicalities of classroom life and partly as a necessary attribute of forms of 'good teaching' in which responsiveness to individuals is made a priority.

On the other hand there is a great deal of sociological and historical evidence, collected in many countries and with different age groups, which demonstrates socially divisive effects when patterns in differentiation practices evolve in settings such as schools and classrooms. The most obvious criteria around which such patterns occur are those of 'race', social class, sex, academic ability, age and physical disability.

Of course, to varying degrees which one might want to discuss, these criteria represent 'objective' attributes which may call for different treatment. Yet, at the same time they are applied to people who share certain fundamental freedoms and human rights. Thus, if it can be shown that such rights are denied or adversely affected by patterns in social practices then a cause for concern certainly exists.

Differentiation thus poses some severe dilemmas. Is it to be seen as an evil or a good? On the one hand one can argue that to fail to differentiate is to deny individuality and the unique qualities and needs of people. On the other hand it can be argued that differentiation is iniquitous, for in making distinctions of any sort, some children may be advantaged over others.

How then should we, as teachers, face such dilemmas? Perhaps dilemmas can only be resolved by making reflective judgements of appropriateness and of worthwhileness for specific situations. However, such judgements need to be supported both by principled criteria and by social awareness of what actually happens – for instance, as highlighted by available research on the topic. I will discuss each of these elements in turn.

Criteria of judgement

On this point one cannot avoid facing the issue of value commitments and beliefs about the basic purposes of education. As an example, and in full recognition of my own commitments and of the rights of others to make different choices, I offer the following educational priorities which might be adopted with regard to children: to foster children's intellectual growth; to facilitate children's personal and social development; to maximize children's opportunities in life; and to prepare children to exercise rights and accept responsibilities as individuals and as future citizens.

If these four educational priorities are accepted for the moment, then we can consider the effects of differentiation in terms of them. For instance:

intellectual growth: Does differentiation deepen children's thinking or lead to superficiality? Does differentiation open horizons or lead to closure?

personal and social development: Does differentiation facilitate children's growth or stunt it?

opportunities: Is differentiation enabling or disabling?

rights and responsibilities: Does differentiation enfranchise or disenfranchise, increase social awareness or decrease it?

To answer such questions we need to consider the second ingredient – awareness and knowledge of the types and processes of differentiation which may occur in schools.

Awareness of differentiation processes

I am not going to attempt a review of all the research which is relevant to this issue – that would take volumes. In any event, on this matter the detail is arguably less important than principles which might be applicable to a range of situations and practices. I will therefore simply attempt to set up and discuss the relatively concise analytical model below:

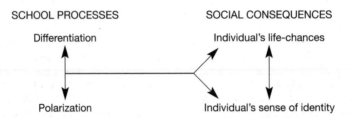

Differentiation

Differentiation refers here to any way in which individual children are distinguished, one from another, by teachers. I thus use the term explicitly to describe processes of distinction over which children have relatively little control. There are various aspects of this at a classroom level and I offer below some examples:

There are those to do with the content and form of the curriculum – e.g. how are girls, the disabled and black people represented in reading books, are the positions of children on a maths scheme taken as an indicator of a status which children wish to acquire?

There are aspects of differentiation which are related to classroom management – e.g. do children line up by sex, are the 'second years' and the 'third years' regularly dismissed at different times?

Some aspects of differentiation are particularly explicit such as when it is reflected in classroom organization – e.g. to what extent are children ability-grouped in your school, how often is gender used as an organizational device in activities?

Powerful forms of differentiation can also occur through the language which is used in school which may, or may not, be equally meaningful and appropriate to all social groups. This, of course, is crucial because language is the medium through which much of school life and individual academic progress is manifested – e.g. how are the needs of those for whom English is a second language catered for, do some children understand the register and vocabulary of the teachers better than others?

Another rather subtle but powerful form of differentiation concerns interpersonal relationships. Are there differences in the quality of the rapport which is established with different children, are some children 'told off' more than others, have specific expectations of individual children formed so that one acts in particular ways towards them? Are there differences in the number of times boys and girls, younger and older children, 'good' and 'naughty' children have contact with and get the attention of the teacher?

Closely related to the above is the question of expectations which research suggests can effect the way children are treated. For instance, to whom are challenging questions directed? Which children are regularly asked to take responsibilities? On hearing a disruptive noise, are there children to whom one looks first?

Another issue concerns reinforcement and the differential valuing of children's efforts. Are merit points or other extrinsic rewards given and, if so, is there a pattern in who gets them? Whose work is on the walls? Who 'shows things' and performs in assemblies? Is any particular social group over-represented?

For each aspect of differentiation there are hundreds of such questions and, of course, it is not my purpose to suggest that all such forms of differentiation are, in some inevitable way, 'wrong'. The question which has to be asked though is whether there are patterns of differentiation which might represent a less than just and fair treatment of the individual attributes and rights of each child and each social group.

Polarization

The issue and phenomenon of polarization is closely related to that of differentiation. Polarization refers to actions and processes which children initiate rather than teachers. In simple terms, polarization can be seen as a response by children to the differentiation which they experience. The effect of polarization is thus to multiply, amplify and compound the social consequences of the initial differentiation. This can be seen to work in the studies of children's social relationships and perceptions. For instance, friendship groups are often related to academic status as well as to criteria such as race and sex and they may even reveal the influence of seat places where these are dictated by the organization of the classroom. Status and popularity within child culture can also be seen to depend partly on the relationship of each child with the teacher. Children who find it hard to succeed in school, or who get into trouble a lot, may develop relatively antagonistic attitudes to school and may act in conjunction with others in similar positions. On the other hand, children who are successful in school, who are well trusted by their teachers and stimulated by the form and content of the curriculum may well feel very positive about it. Status in child culture is often obtained by demonstrating that one can cope with school life, that one is strong, able enough and independent enough. Polarization thus occurs every time a child is teased because he or she is 'only on red level books' or when, say 'John's gang' develops its reputation for 'mucking about' and is contrasted with the quieter groups who 'just walk around' and 'do what the teacher says'.

Another way of approaching this is to see children in school as having to cope in two social spheres at the same time. They have to cope with the formal requirements of teachers and normally have to accept the judgements which may be made of them. They also have to cope with the social world of the playground and of their peers. In both contexts they have to retain their dignity as individuals. The result of this is that, if they are treated in particular ways in class then, in the playground, they are likely to either play on the prestige they have gained or try to recoup some of the dignity they may have lost. In any event, the effects of the initial differentiation is likely to be increased by the polarization which then follows.

The model above postulates that these two processes exist in interaction together. For instance, the effect of polarization of attitudes and of peer group association could well lead to increased differentiation as teachers respond to them. The danger is thus that the two processes mesh together to produce a vicious circle in which, in the midst of everyday school life, the overall differentiation effect is steadily increased.

But what are the social consequences of these processes?

I would suggest that social consequences of two main sorts result. The first concerns the self-image and sense of identity which each child develops – how do they see themselves, how much self-confidence do they have? The second concerns life-chances more directly – what range of options are open to children as they go through their school careers, how are future possibilities for each child being affected by school processes and experiences?

The self-image and identity of individuals is constructed through social interaction with others. We thus come to 'know' ourselves gradually and continuously throughout life. At any point though, we 'present' our self to others in particular ways – usually in ways which we feel are appropriate for the situation as we perceive it and in ways which support our existing image of 'who we are'. Schools have a very significant role to play in this process of identity formation for they are, for most children, the first formal organization which they will have experienced. In a sense therefore, school life provides the primary medium through which the public identities of each child are created, explored, tested, evolved and adopted. Children take forward a particular sense of self and act upon it as they experience new situations. In turn, others then react to the presentation of this identity. It does not take much imagination to see that the prospects for children who have developed a sense of failure and dissatisfaction in school are likely to be very different from those of children who have had their efforts praised, valued and reinforced.

To take the argument about life-chances further, because of the links between education, assessment, credentialism and employment, schools play a very important gate-keeping role through their influence on the long-term prospects of children. Indeed, the processes of differentiation and polarization, which may be identified in the classrooms of even very young children, may well manifest themselves in terms of income, housing, occupation and status thirty years on.

This seems to me to be the major challenge of socially aware teaching, with any age of child. One is certainly not solely concerned with the intellectual or expressive development of individuals. In ways from which one cannot withdraw, one is also inevitably concerned with issues involving rights.

READING 13.9

How to promote co-operative relationships among children

Barrie Thorne

> Barrie Thorne's book *Gender Play* is well worth reading as a study of how boys' and girls' identities are formed. In this extract, she considers the practical implications of her work and offers advice to teachers on promoting co-operation among children. She particularly considers the classroom management of groups, reinforcing co-operative behaviour, providing opportunities and challenging stereotyping.
>
> This advice is applicable to all forms of differentiation. Is it helpful in thinking about how your class interact together, and in considering how you could influence this?
>
> Edited from: Thorne, B. (1993) *Gender Play: Girls and Boys in School*. Buckingham: Open University Press, 157–67

In my ethnographic study of children's daily lives in school, I have sought to ground and develop, with detailed substance and a sense of process and activity, the claim that gender is socially constructed. I have argued that kids, as well as adults take an active hand in constructing gender, and that collective practices – forming lines, choosing seats, teasing, gossiping, seeking access to or avoiding particular activities animate the process.

Thus, I showed how kids construct 'the girls' and 'the boys' as boundaried and rival groups through practices that uphold a sense of gender as an oppositional dichotomy. But I also examined practices that have the effect of neutralizing, or, as in situations of 'crossing', even challenging the significance of gender.

Some of these practices have been developed by teachers and researchers trying to challenge racial separation and inequality and in this brief review I will try to encompass some of the interactive dynamics of race and gender. The ideas may also apply to the handling of other differences, such as religion or disability.

In grouping students, use criteria other than gender or race

When teachers and aides divide girls and boys into competing teams or tell them to sit at different tables, they ratify the dynamics of separation, differential treatment, stereotyping and antagonism. Organizing students on other grounds, such as random sorting, and using terms of address like 'class' or 'students' rather than the ubiquitous 'boys and girls' will help undermine gender marking.

This suggestion raises a basic dilemma. When granted autonomy and left on their own, kids tend to separate by gender and sometimes also by race. Should school staff determine all seating, even in lunchrooms? Should playground aides bustle into situations kids have set up and urge girls and boys to play together? Obviously this is neither practical nor desirable. Kids do not flourish when they are perpetually watched and controlled; they need, and will struggle to claim, at least some independence from adults.

On the other hand, when adults form mixed-gender groups, I have observed that some kids look a little relieved; the adult action takes away the risk of teasing and makes girl–boy interactions possible. One boy told me: 'You get to talk to kids you usually wouldn't get to know'. When they do choose to form groups, for whatever purpose, I believe that school staff should try, self-consciously, to maximize heterogeneity.

Affirm and reinforce the values of co-operation among all kids regardless of social categories

A teacher recently told me about her efforts to undermine 'girl–boy staff' and foster more co-operative cross-gender relations among her students. 'We're one class, not boys and girls; we're going to get together as a class', she repeatedly told them. By emphasizing 'the class', she affirmed a more inclusive basis of solidarity.

To be effective, affirmation of the value of mixed-gender and mixed-race interaction may need to be explicit and continual. Lisa Serbin and her colleagues (who found extensive gender separation among children in a pre-school), trained the teachers to positively reinforce co-operative cross-gender play, for example with comments like 'John and Cathy are working hard together on their project'. This behaviour-modification effort lasted for two weeks, during which the amount of cross-gender play increased significantly. But when the programme was discontinued, the children returned to the earlier pattern.

Whenever possible, organize students into small, heterogeneous, and co-operative work groups

Unfortunately, we can't lessen the crowding of most schools, but small group instruction may create pockets of less public and thus, perhaps, more co-operative interaction. Indeed, social psychologists who study the dynamics of intergroup relations have found that when people from different racial or gender groups interact in smaller groups focused on a shared goal requiring interdependence, they are more likely to see one another as individuals rather than through the lens of 'us-versus-them'.

Elliot Aronson and his colleagues entered the desegregated classrooms and organized small multiracial groups to work together on reports, studying for quizzes, and other collaborative tasks. They called this a 'jigsaw classroom', referring to the principle of a jigsaw puzzle in which each person has pieces of information the entire group needs to complete the task. The result was a de-emphasis on racial divisions and an increase in friendships among African-American, Chicano, and white students.

Facilitate kids' access to all activities

In many activities, especially on playgrounds and even in classrooms, girls and boys may not have equal access to particular activities, for example in some classrooms boys have been found to have more access than girls to computers.

To broaden access to gender-typed activities school staff can make a point of teaching the skills to everyone and, if possible, setting an example by challenging stereotypes.

School staff might consider introducing playground games, like handball, that have the potential to increase the amount of cross-gender play. A playground rule that would-be players cannot be 'locked out' of a game unless there are already too many players can also lessen opportunities for exclusion and may embolden more kids to join activities stereotypically associated with the other gender. By introducing new activities and teaching relevant skills in a gender-neutral way, teachers and aides can create conditions in which kids themselves may more often form mixed-gender groups. The transformative elements of play – a sense of the voluntary and of control over the terms of interaction – can be drawn on to facilitate social change.

Actively intervene to challenge the dynamics of stereotyping and power

Proximity does not necessarily lead to equality, as critics of the philosophies of assimilation and integration have long pointed out. Boys and girls and kids of different racial and ethnic backgrounds may be encouraged to interact more frequently, but on whose terms? Groups may be formally integrated, but tensions and inequalities may persist. In the de-segregated middle school where Schofield observed, the teachers by and large affirmed a neutral or colour-blind ideology, trying to ignore the presence of race divisions, though teachers more readily marked gender in their interaction with students. But the students often divided and sometimes hassled one another along lines of both race and gender, and there was persistent mistrust and fear between black and white students. The teaching staff were so intent on pretending that race made no difference that they did little to help white and black students learn how to interact with one another or explore the nature and meaning of cultural difference and the dynamics of racism. In some situations, it may be important for teachers to openly deal with rather than ignore social divisions.

My observations of antagonistic mixed-gender interactions suggest that the dynamics of stereotyping and power may have to be explicitly confronted. Barbara Porro and Kevin Karkau engaged their classes in discussions about gender stereotyping, persistent separation between girls and boys, and the teasing ('sissies', 'tomboys', 'you're in love') that kept them apart. Porro explained sexism to her students by finding terms that six-year-olds could understand; the class began to label sexist ideas (e.g., that women could not be doctors, or men could not be nurses) as old-fashioned.

Such accounts suggest ways in which teachers can engage in critical thinking about and collaborative ways of transcending social divisions and inequalities.

PART 3

Beyond classroom reflection

CHAPTER 14

Reflective teaching and the school

The ten readings in this chapter address a wide range of whole-school issues concerning teacher culture, school development planning, accountability to the market, to parents and to governors and the efficacy of school inspection.

In Reading 14.1, Hargreaves identifies four dominant forms of teacher culture and suggests that some collegiality is 'contrived'. However, Southworth, Nias and Campbell (14.2) report on the key features of the 'culture of collaboration' which they identified in some English primary schools.

Hargreaves and Hopkins (14.3) provide an account of the advantages of school development planning and the distinctive approaches of 'school effectiveness' and 'school improvement' researchers. Wallace (14.4) addresses the challenges of school development planning in times of great change.

The next group of readings begins with Menter and his colleagues (14.5) and their account of how the management of primary schools is being influenced by ideas about 'market' exposure. However, Hughes and colleagues (14.6) report survey findings which generally show parents' support for their local schools. Deem (14.7) analyses the 'collective concern' and 'consumer interest' ideologies of school governors.

School inspection is often a contentious issue and Rose offers an official rationale of OFSTED procedures (14.8). International comparisons from OECD show other ways of monitoring school performance (14.9) and raise the question of whether school development is adequately supported.

Finally, Fullan (14.10) provides a rallying cry for teachers and others 'working together for positive change' in their schools.

The parallel chapter of *Reflective Teaching in the Primary School* reviews accountability issues, school culture, whole-school planning, implementation and evaluation, and strategies for whole-school development. There are practical activities for investigating aspects of school practices and many suggestions for further reading.

READING 14.1

Cultures of teaching

Andy Hargreaves

This reading highlights the important interrelationship between professional development and teacher culture. In particular, it draws attention to four important forms of the latter: individualistic, Balkanized, collaborative and contrived collegiality. Andy Hargreaves suggests that the first pair are commonly associated with conservative and defensive approaches to new developments, whilst collaborative cultures may provide a basis for powerful, bottom-up change. Characterizing the latter as 'feminine in style', he argues that such changes may seem rather uncontrolled to policy-makers or administrators who may impose more 'masculine' structures through procedures such as 'school development planning' etc.

Could you relate this classification to the teacher cultures you have experienced?

Edited from: Hargreaves, A. and Fullan, M. G. (eds) (1992) *Understanding Teacher Development*. London: Cassell, 217–35

Teachers do not develop their strategies and styles of teaching entirely alone. Most of the problems that the teacher encounters, the issues he or she confronts, have faced many similarly placed colleagues in the past. Over the years these colleagues develop ways of doing things, along with whole networks of associated educational beliefs and values in response to the characteristic and recurrent problems and circumstances they face in their work. Teaching strategies, that is, arise not just from the demands and constraints of the immediate context, but also from cultures of teaching; from beliefs, values, habits and assumed ways of doing things among communities of teachers who have had to deal with similar demands and constraints over many years. Culture carries the community's historically generated and collectively shared solutions to its new and inexperienced membership. It forms a framework for occupational learning.

Cultures of teaching help give meaning, support and identity to teachers and their work. Physically, teachers are often alone in their own classrooms, with no other adults for company. Psychologically, they never are. What they do there – their classroom styles and strategies – is powerfully affected by the outlooks and orientations of the colleagues with whom they work now and have worked in the past. In this respect, teacher cultures are among the most educationally significant aspects of teachers' lives and work. They provide a vital context for teacher development.

Teacher cultures have both content and form. The contents of teacher cultures are many [but there are] four dominant forms: individualism, balkanization, collaborative culture and contrived collegiality.

The individualistic culture of teachers is the most pervasive of all the forms of teacher culture. This culture of individualism isolates teachers from their colleagues and ties them to the pressing immediacy of classroom life. In most respects, it is a seedbed of pedagogical conservatism.

In balkanized cultures, teachers work in separate and sometimes competing territorial groups which bestow identity and provide bases for the pursuit of power, status and resources. Balkanized cultures can exist in circumstances of open warfare or in climates of uneasy peace, but the competing territorial claims and the identities to which they give rise make the definition and pursuit of common goals across the whole school community very difficult, if not impossible.

Most teachers work in schools where these two forms of teacher culture coexist. While teachers may plan and consult, and perhaps even connive and conspire, within their different territorial groups, they rarely co-operate on issues which threaten their classroom autonomy and which open up their practice to intrusive inspection. Materials may be shared and discussed, tricks may be traded, but even within the most closely knit departmental group the autonomy of the teacher's classroom judgement usually remains sacrosanct.

In not engaging with the details and fundamentals of classroom practice, this combination of individualism and balkanization offers few prospects for educational change and professional development of any substance. The possibilities for curriculum development among a community of colleagues which would challenge, cut across, or move beyond existing subject identities and preferred pedagogies are not strong. Equally, individualism and balkanization inhibit the responsiveness of teachers to externally imposed innovation, making many teachers protective of their own classroom and departmental domains which new programmes, newly advocated methods of instruction or new cross-curricular initiatives often appear to threaten.

Individualism and balkanization, then, suit neither the advocates of locally generated, school-based curriculum development nor the supporters of top-down, bureaucratically imposed models of curriculum implementation.

Collaborative cultures are most compatible with the interests of local curriculum development and the exercise of discretionary professional judgement. They foster and build upon qualities of openness, trust and support between teachers and their colleagues. They capitalize on the collective expertise and endeavour of the teaching community. They acknowledge the wider dimensions of teachers' lives outside the classroom and the school, blurring the boundaries between in-school and out-of-school, public and private, professional and personal – grounding projects for development and change in a realistic and respectful appreciation of teachers' broader worlds. Teachers' work is deeply embedded in teachers' lives, in their pasts, in their biographies, in the cultures of traditions of teaching to which they have become committed. Developing the teacher, therefore, also involves developing the person, developing the life. In this respect, the interweaving of the personal and the professional in collaborative cultures, and the qualities of trust and sharing within those cultures, provide the most collegially supportive environment for change.

But even this change is slow. Collaborative cultures do not evolve quickly. They are therefore unattractive to administrators looking for swift implementation expedients. They are difficult to locate, to fix in time and space, living as they do mainly in the interstices of school life; in the corridor conversations and exchanged glances that weld teachers and their school together in a working community. Collaborative cultures are also unpredictable in their consequences. The curriculum that will be developed, the learning that will be fostered, the goals that will be formulated – these things cannot be confidently predicted beforehand.

For control-conscious administrators this unpredictability can be a threatening prospect. What is fostered, formulated and developed by these collaborative cultures may not correspond with administrators' intentions and purposes. This might explain why most collaborative cultures take the form of bounded collaboration, where the grounds of practice, of curriculum and pedagogy, are not investigated in a searching way, on a continuous basis, across the whole school community.

The administrative retention of curriculum control explains the growing bureaucratic preference of forms of collegial relations among teachers which are less unpredictable and threatening than those which can evolve in more collaborative teacher cultures.

Contrived collegiality binds teachers in time and space to purposes and procedures devised by their superiors. It mandates teachers to meet at particular times in particular places to deal with administrative agendas determined elsewhere – as in some collaborative planning procedures, for instance. For the openness and unpredictability of naturally occurring and slowly evolving patterns of human interaction, it substitutes administratively contrived and bureaucratically controlled procedures of clinical assessment, feedback and review – as in some peer coaching, mentoring and teacher appraisal schemes, for example.

Contrived collegiality reconstitutes teacher relations in the administrators' own image – regulating and reconstructing teachers' lives so that they support the predictable implementation of administrative plans and purposes, rather than creating the unpredictable development of teachers' own. Contrived collegiality also regulates the pace of change, so as to 'force' human growth among teachers, like so much 'rhubarb; speeding it up and synchronizing it with administratively convenient timeliness and expectations.

Collaborative cultures have deeply 'feminine' characteristics. They are spontaneous, evolutionary and unpredictable. They intermix the private and public, openly placing teachers' work in the context of their wider lives, biographies and purposes. Such cultures do not mesh well with the control-centred, accountability-inclined and efficiency-orientated interests of (mainly) male administrators. For such administrators, the preferred mode of the teacher culture – one which will be collectively responsive to the interests of externally imposed implementation – is commonly that of contrived collegiality (see Figure 14.1.1).

Collaborative Culture	Contrived Collegiality
Pervasive across time and space	Bounded in time and space
Evolutionary	Imposed
'Natural'	'Forced'
Spontaneous	Regulated
Unpredictable	Predictable
Public intermixed with Private	Public superimposed on Private
Development-orientated	Implementation-orientated
'Feminine' in style	'Masculine' in style

Figure 14.1.1 Collaborative cultures and contrived collegiality

Contrived collegiality is more strikingly 'masculine' in its characteristics. It is administratively contrived, formally bounded in time and space, and bureaucratically predictable. It superimposes the public on the private, keeping apart these two important domains of teachers' lives. Contrived collegiality preserves the hierarchical separation between development and implementation, creating a system whereby teachers can deliver others' purposes instead of developing their own. And, in doing so, it retains a system whereby (mainly) female teachers remain the technical servants of predominantly male administrators and their purposes.

The challenge of developing extended cultures of collaboration, in overcoming conservatism as well as individualism within teacher culture, is a challenge of purpose and power; of redistributing the responsibility for curriculum development. Ultimately, the challenge is one of administrative humility.

READING 14.2

The culture of collaboration

Geoff Southworth, Jennifer Nias and Penny Campbell

This reading derives from an influential research project which established the concept of 'collaborative culture' (see Reading 14.1). Working alongside teachers in five primary schools which had been selected for having 'good staff relationships', the research team were gradually able to understand and analyse the social processes and dynamics of interaction through which trust was built up. One particular feature is the way in which the staff achieved individual fulfilment through the development of the school as a whole.

Have you experienced a 'collaborative culture' in your career as a pupil, student-teacher or teacher?

Edited from: Southworth, G., Nias, J. and Campbell, P. (1992) Rethinking collegiality: teachers' views. Mimeo presented to the American Educational Research Association, New Orleans, 1–12

Those who advocate collegiality do so on the basis of prescription rather than description. What conditions in a school facilitate collegiality? Is it 'force-fed' or can it occur 'naturally'? What do teachers and headteachers think about collegiality?

At the outset of the Primary School Staff Relationships (PRSS) project, the research team were conscious that advocates of collegiality had not shown what this phenomenon looked like in practice. These researchers therefore took a limited view and set out to provide first-hand accounts of how headteachers, teachers and other staff behaved when they 'worked together'. It was decided to limit the team's enquiries to schools where, in very loose terms, 'things were going well'.

The enquiry was limited to five schools with between five and twelve teaching staff (including the headteacher), a secretary and at least one ancillary worker. The enquiry was ethnographic with team members acting as participant observers.

The main concept to emerge from the five studies is that of 'organizational culture' where culture is loosely defined as 'the way we do it here', that is, as a set of norms about ways of behaving, perceiving and understanding. A culture is, however, underpinned by jointly held beliefs and values and symbolized for members of the culture by objects, rituals and ceremonies. Each of the five project schools had its own culture which embodied strongly held beliefs about the social and moral purposes of education and about the nature of effective educational practice. These beliefs originated with the headteachers. In three of the schools the head had worked for a long time in each school over ten years to develop and sustain an organizational culture the project team describe as a 'culture of collaboration'. This, it was felt, enabled the teaching and ancillary staff to work closely together in a natural, taken-for-granted way. In the other two schools the heads were endeavouring to develop a culture of collaboration but were impeded by conflicting values held by long-established staff members. Over the course of the year's field-work some key individuals (e.g. deputy headteacher, curriculum leaders) left each of these schools and this enabled the new and developing culture to become more firmly established, not least because in both schools it already existed in sub-groups.

The culture of collaboration was built on four interacting beliefs: individuals should be valued but, because they are inseparable from the group of which they are part, groups too should be fostered and valued; the most effective ways of promoting these values are through a sense of mutual security and consequent openness. We will briefly look at each.

Valuing individuals – as people and for their contribution to others

In the schools where a culture of collaboration existed, even the most mundane and apparently insignificant details of staff behaviour were consistent with its values. Respect for individuals occurred in many guises. There were few status distinctions, all staff used the staff room and joined in conversations and humour. Newcomers felt free to speak and valued, as one novitiate teacher said:

> They [the staff] treat me as an individual, here to do a job, not to be looked down upon or anything like that. I'm like anybody really.

Everyone who came to the schools was made welcome. A recently appointed teacher commented:

> They make everybody very welcome. It's marvellous and I like the way they've got time for parents and involve the parents a lot in the school ... they care and that's what came across to me.

In addition to respecting and nurturing others as individuals in their own right, heads, teachers and ancillaries in the collaborative schools perceived the differences between them as a mutually enriching source of collective strength: 'Teacher: Working in a team doesn't mean that everybody's the same and everybody's so busy saying yes, yes, yes to one another that nothing happens. That deadens it. You've got to have different personalities and different ideas to spark other people off, but it can be done without aggression.'

Everyone's contribution to the school was valued. Gratitude and appreciation were regularly and openly expressed:

> It's never taken for granted and it's never left to just one teacher – all staff make the point of expressing their appreciation to whoever they are thanking.

Valuing interdependence – belonging to a group and working as a team

Individual staff members at three of the schools valued one another as people, each with his/her own identity, personality, interests, skills, experiences and potential. Yet they also appreciated the diversity which this brought to the school. Likewise, interdependence has two aspects. Together the members of each staff made a group which was valued because it provided a sense of belonging. At the same time they accepted a collective responsibility for the work of the school so creating a sense of team in which staff helped, encouraged and substituted for one another:

> There's a great deal of warmth between us and it's almost like a family that closes ranks against outsiders when it's being attacked by a piece of gossip or an occasion of vandalism.

Whilst group membership was effectively satisfying, it was not the whole story since in the three collaborative schools staff also felt a sense of collective responsibility for their work and saw themselves as a team. One head wrote in a school document:

> We feel that the consideration and closeness which characterizes relationships between adult members pervades the school as a whole. Thus issues like infant–junior department liaison are less important than the sense of the school as a whole.

Being a 'team' meant to recognize and value the unique contribution of each member to a joint enterprise. It did not necessarily mean doing the same job nor working in the same teaching space but it did mean working to the same ends.

The sense of collective responsibility showed itself in many ways. Most noticeable was the habitual way in which everyone advised, supported and helped one another. A teacher reported:

> If you say 'I'm doing such and such, I haven't got any good ideas', there will be six or seven

different ideas thrown at you instantly. Of if you get halfway through doing something and you happen to say 'Oh, it's not working', or 'It's going wrong', there's always someone who is willing to help in any sort of situation. And in dealing with the children you never feel, if you have a problem, that you're cut off, there's always somebody else who is willing to help you. It's often the case [in other schools that] there is someone around who is capable of helping, but not always that they will help, but in this school that doesn't seem to be so. Everyone seems very ready to help.

Valuing security

This belief and the next are linked. Security is a condition for the growth of openness and openness is the best way of simultaneously fostering the individual and the group. They are connected by a notion of interdependence which means mutual constraint as well as enrichment. To accept as all the staff did that one is dependent on anyone else is to admit that there are limits to one's autonomy. Limits operated in various ways, spoken and unspoken, but, whatever their nature or extent, acceptance of them was mandatory:

> To work here you'd have to be prepared to work as part of this team. If you persisted in not being part of a team you could exist here but you wouldn't be happy. You could make it but not in any satisfying sense ... If you're not prepared to submit, in the biblical sense, you're not going to be an effective team member. But once you can see it's in the best interests of the children, it's easy.

Though to submit is to accept another's power over oneself, when all members of a team do so their power over each other is evenly balanced and becomes influence instead. So within a situation of agreed interdependence. Teacher: 'We're all influencing each other, I'm quite convinced of that.' However, an exception to this was the headteacher since staff in the collaborative schools deferred to their heads. In part this can be explained by the fact that the beliefs underlying that 'culture of collaboration' emanated from and were exemplified by the heads of the three schools. Since all staff agreed with these beliefs the heads enjoyed a degree of personal authority which transcended that of other staff.

The fact that the heads' responsibility for the main policies in their schools was virtually unchallenged and that staff exercised a good deal of mutual influence over one another made the collaborative schools very secure places in which to work.

Valuing openness

Many of the day-to-day attitudes and actions of the staff demonstrated the value they attached to openness. Heads, teachers and ancillaries were ready to admit publicly to a sense of failure:

> In the other schools I've taught in you didn't fail. If you did you kept it very quiet. It took me a good four months when I came here to realize that ... when you had problems you didn't hide them away, you voiced them and you got them sorted out instantly instead of taking them home and worrying about them.

Staff were also ready to display other negative emotions, such as guilt, anxiety and anger. And it was regarded as normal for individuals to voice irritation or dissent directly to one another. Disagreements were accepted as part of life:

> Differences of opinion do emerge but we're all very open, straightforward. If we don't agree with someone we do say so. You know, you just state that you didn't agree and that you thought such and such ... it doesn't need to be argument.

The heads developed and sustained the culture via their own sense of example (e.g. teaching, taking assemblies, dealing with staff), positive reinforcement and careful selection of staff when opportunities to recruit arose. The heads were also keenly aware of what was happening daily in 'their' schools and demonstrated a 'dedicated obsessiveness' (Coulson, 1976) with all aspects of the school's life and work. Moreover, because they were frequently touring the school and present in the staff room, talking, listening, joining in with the teaching and planning, they were members of the staff group. They could simultaneously occupy two positions, leader and member, and this prevented them from being aloof and isolated from the staff.

Although there was an asymmetrical distribution of power between the head and staff, just as with teachers and pupils in classrooms, to be less powerful is not to be powerless. Heads and staff negotiated a 'working consensus' (Pollard, 1985) which involved some degree of accommodation to each other's interests. Thus, it was not a surprise that the heads negotiated – both explicitly and implicitly – and sought compromises. However, the heads were only prepared to compromise on some things. They would not, for instance, alter their most deeply and strongly held beliefs. This would, presumably, have been injurious to the head's professional identity. Therefore, negotiation occurred within the parameters of each head's professional convictions. Similarly, compromises were reached in order to preserve the self-image of individual staff. Negotiations were often subtle, coded, and tacit and 'truces' were sometimes struck. The heads also had to be skilled in keeping negotiations 'open' so that fresh compromises could be later reached as and when circumstances allowed.

It would be simplistic to say the heads in the collaborative schools controlled what happened there but they certainly exerted a great deal of influence and occasionally used their power directly. Since this influence was transacted through one-to-one contacts, formal and informal meetings, and negotiations, the heads more noticeably than others revealed a micro-political dimension to the notion of collegiality. Obvious as this may seem, given recent work and the idea that schools are arenas of struggle where notions of hierarchy and equality, democracy and coercion coexist in close proximity (Ball, 1987, pp. 15 and 19), the micro-political aspects need emphasizing since those who promote collegiality appear to be unaware of their existence.

📖 READING 14.3

Why school development planning?

David Hargreaves and David Hopkins

Two distinct approaches to the study of school organization are reflected in this reading. 'School effectiveness' studies are primarily concerned with identifying factors which are associated with positive outcomes. 'School improvement' studies concern themselves with how to bring about constructive change. One significant result of the latter has been the introduction of school development planning, which is now a requirement in many education systems.

Is development planning in your school leading to a 'thinking' institution as David Hargreaves and David Hopkins hope, or is it part of a 'contrived collegiality' as Andy Hargreaves fears (Reading 14.1)?

Edited from: Hargreaves, D. H. and Hopkins, D. (1991) *The Empowered School: The Management and Practice of Development Planning*. London: Cassell, 6–11, 109–23.

Development planning is designed to allow the school to organize, with greater efficiency and success, its existing programme of development and change. Because it promises greater control over the ubiquitous problem of 'innovation overload' with greater success in making the changes actually work, development planning is worth serious consideration.

Advantages of development planning

A development plan focuses attention on the aims of education, especially the learning and achievement, broadly defined, of all pupils.

A development plan provides a comprehensive and co-ordinated approach to all aspects of planning, one which covers curriculum and assessment, teaching, management and organization, finance and resources.

The development plan captures the long-term vision for the school within which manageable short-term goals are set. The priorities contained in the plan represent the school's translation of policy into its agenda for action.

A development plan helps to relieve the stress on teachers caused by the pace of change. Teachers come to exercise greater control over change rather than feeling controlled by it.

The achievements of teachers in promoting innovation and change receive wider recognition, so that their confidence rises.

The quality of staff development improves. In-service training and appraisal help the school to work more effectively and help teachers to acquire new knowledge and skills as part of their professional development.

The partnership between the teaching staff and the governing body is strengthened.

The task of reporting on the work of the school is made easier.

Probably the main reason why schools and LEAs have taken up development planning in recent years is that it offers a means of managing rapid and substantial change. But this is not, in the most successful schools, the primary benefit of development planning. The principal gain is that it allows the school to focus on its fundamental aims concerned with teaching and learning. Development planning is really about school and classroom improvement. Many of the current changes with which schools have to cope are being imposed from outside. Development planning is the way in which each school interprets external policy requirements so that they are integrated into its own unique life and culture.

As the whole process of planning becomes integrated, it permeates the normal work of the school. Planning is no longer a set of specialized or independent activities, but a process which encompasses the more routine activities. In other words, system maintenance is more closely linked to system development. This can be expressed diagrammatically as in the school development cone (see Figure 14.3.1) where planning becomes more coherent as it is assimilated into the daily life of the school and is related to the school's major aim of pupil achievement.

School effectiveness

There is now a vast amount of evidence to support the common-sense notion that the characteristics of individual schools can make a difference to pupil progress. The research on 'effective schools', both in the UK (Mortimore et al., 1988) and the USA (Purkey and Smith, 1983), has found that certain internal conditions are typical in schools that achieve higher levels of outcomes for their students. The first major study conducted in the UK was by Rutter and his colleagues (1979) who compared the 'effectiveness' of ten secondary schools in inner London on a range of student outcome measures. The 'effective schools', as described in their book *Fifteen Thousand Hours*, were characterized by factors 'as varied as the degree of academic emphasis, teacher actions in lessons, the availability of incentives and rewards, good

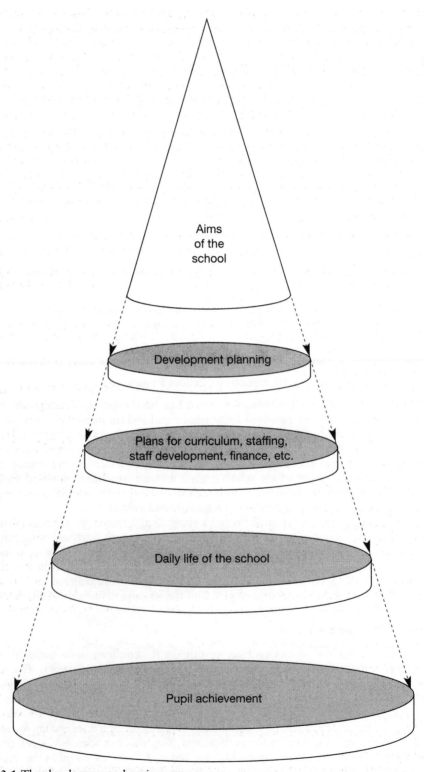

Figure 14.3.1 The development planning cone

conditions for pupils, and the extent to which children were able to take responsibility' (Rutter *et al.*, 1979, p. 178). It was this constellation of factors that Rutter and his colleagues later referred to as the school's 'ethos'. The HMI survey reported in *Ten Good Schools* comes to similar conclusions. To HMI the 'good school' is one that can demonstrate 'quality in its aims, in oversight of pupils, in curriculum design, in standards of teaching and academic achievements and in its links with the local community. What they all have in common is effective leadership and a "climate" that is conducive to growth' (DES, 1977, p. 36).

These descriptions of effective school cultures are similar to most others emerging from this line of research. The literature is also in agreement on three further issues. First, that these differences in outcome are systematically related to variations in the school's culture. Secondly, that the school's culture is amenable to alteration by concerted action on the part of the school staff. Although this is not an easy task, the evidence suggests that teachers and schools have more control than they may imagine over their ability to change their present situation. Thirdly, there is also broad agreement on the factors related to that difference.

The list below presents the twelve key factors associated with school effectiveness which were identified by Mortimore *et al.* (1988, pp. 250-6).

Purposeful leadership of the staff by the head
Key aspects: effective heads are sufficiently involved in and knowledgeable about what goes on in classrooms and about progress of individual pupils. Although they do not interfere constantly they are not afraid to assert their leadership.

The involvement of the deputy head
Key aspects: a certain amount of delegation by the head and the sharing of responsibilities promote effectiveness.

The involvement of teachers
Key aspects: active involvement in curriculum planning, developing curriculum guidelines, and participation in decision-making on school policy.

Consistency among teachers
Key aspects: continuity in teaching staff and consistency of teacher approach are important.

Structured sessions
Key aspects: teachers organize a framework within which pupils can work, encourage a degree of independence, and allow some freedom within this structure.

Intellectually challenging teaching
Key aspects: use of higher-order questions and statements, pupils encouraged to use their creative imagination and powers of problem solving, teachers have an enthusiastic approach, and high expectation of pupils.

Work-centred environment
Key aspects: much content-related work and feedback, relatively little time spent on routine matters, a low level of noise, and not an excessive amount of pupil movement.

Limited focus within lessons
Key aspects: a focus upon only one curriculum area during a lesson.

Maximum communication between teachers and pupils
Key aspects: a flexible approach, blending individual, class and group interaction as appropriate, including class discussion.

Record keeping
Key aspects: record keeping linked to planning and assessment by both head and teachers.

Parental involvement
Key aspects: help in classrooms, on educational visits, attendance at meetings to discuss

children's progress, parents' reading to their children and access to books at home, informal open-door policy rather than parent–teacher associations.

Positive climate
Key aspects: more emphasis on praise and reward than punishment and control, enthusiastic attitude to teachers, involvement of staff and children in a range of activities outside the classroom.

However, such research is more concerned to describe the characteristics of school effectiveness, rather than suggest ways in which effectiveness can be achieved.

School improvement

School improvement studies tend to be more action-oriented than the effective schools research. They embody the long-term goal of moving towards the vision of the 'problem solving' or 'thinking' school. This attitude was exemplified in the work of the OECD-sponsored International School Improvement Project (ISIP) and the knowledge that emanated from it.

This obviously implies a very different way of thinking about change than the ubiquitous 'top-down' approach so popular with policy-makers. We have summarized so-called ISIP knowledge below (adapted from Van Velzen *et al.* (1985) and Hopkins (1987):

The school as the centre of change
This means that external reforms need to be sensitive to the situation in individual schools, rather than assuming that all schools are the same.

A systematic approach to change
School improvement is a carefully planned and managed process that takes place over a period of several years.

A key focus for change on the 'internal conditions' of schools
These include not only the teaching-learning activities used in the school, but also the school's procedures, role allocation and resources used that support the teaching-learning process.

Accomplishing educational goals more effectively
Generally speaking, educational goals are what a school is supposed to be doing for its students and society. This suggests a broader definition of outcome than student scores on achievement tests, even though for some schools these may be pre-eminent. Schools also serve the more general developmental needs of students, the professional development of teachers and the needs of its community.

A multi-level perspective
Although the school is the centre of change it does not act alone. The school is embedded in an educational system that has to work collaboratively or symbiotically if the highest degrees of quality are to be achieved. This means that the roles of teachers, heads, governors, parents, support people (advisers, higher education, consultants etc.) and local authorities should be defined, harnessed and committed to the process of school improvement.

Integrative implementation strategies
This implies a linkage between 'top-down' and 'bottom-up' – remembering of course that both approaches can only apply at a number of different levels in the system. Ideally 'top-down' provides policy aims, an overall strategy and co-operational plans; this is complemented by a 'bottom-up' response involving diagnosis, priority goal setting and implementation. The former provides the framework, resources and a menu of alternatives; the latter, energy and school-based implementation.

The drive towards institutionalization
Change is only successful when it has become part of the natural behaviour of all those in the school. Implementation by itself is not enough.

The main problem with most attempts at school improvement is that they are successful only to the extent that they satisfactorily address the complexities of school culture. This is something that development planning as a school improvement strategy is well able to do.

School development planning in turbulent times

Mike Wallace

In this reading Mike Wallace points out that the tidy rationalism of school development planning cycles is somewhat difficult to implement in circumstances of constant change and uncertainty. This is a point of which most headteachers were very aware in the early 1990s and it remains to be seen whether the pace of change will slow in the future to provide sufficient stability for anything but short-term, 'continual', school planning purposes. The annual adjustment of school budgets, without formal provision for dampening of variations, is a particularly challenging source of instability.
How are the long-term goals of your school being affected by immediate pressures and constraints?

Edited from: Wallace, M. (1994) 'Towards a contingency approach to development planning in schools', in Hargreaves, D. H. and Hopkins, D. (eds) *Development Planning for School Improvement*. London: Cassell, 150–9

My purpose is twofold: to explore the hypothesis that the effectiveness of different approaches to development planning may be contingent upon the local and national context in which schools are placed; and tentatively to suggest that in turbulent times a flexible process of continual creation, monitoring and adjustment of plans, which also takes into account conflicting annual cycles, may be more effective than more rationalistic models based upon sequential annual cycles alone.

The context of schooling in England, in common with many other Western countries, has become increasingly chaotic in recent years primarily as a consequence of massive central government intervention. Education reforms for the State service include a National Curriculum phased in over several years; national testing, the results of which are being made public; responsibility for financial management and the appointment of staff falling to headteachers and governors; nationally imposed salaries, conditions of service and promotion structure; biennial appraisal of all teaching staff; a budget for staff development with annual entitlement of closure days available for in-service training; open enrolment of pupils to promote competition between schools; the possibility of opting out of local education authority (LEA) control; and formal inspection at least every four years.

School development planning is widely regarded as key to managing the introduction of central government reforms, together with LEA initiatives, such as an equal opportunities policy, and any innovations generated within schools.

Possible influences upon the widespread adoption of a cyclic approach to development planning include a long tradition of planning for the academic year; familiarity within many LEAs with models for school self-review (for example, Inner London Education Authority, 1977; McMahon *et al.*, 1984) based on occasional cycles and developed at a time when the context of schooling was generally more stable than at present; central government imposition upon LEAs of a planning cycle for in-service training grants and for financial management of schools, based upon the financial year; the requirement that schools have a financial management plan based on the financial year under the central government's 'Local

Management of Schools' initiative (Department of Education and Science, 1988); and, in some LEAs, the popularity of a handbook advocating a yearly 'collaborative planning cycle' (Caldwell and Spinks, 1988).

Most of these cyclic models have been trialled in schools in some way, and therefore have proven to be of value in guiding planning, at least when they were developed. Schools across England, however, face an increasingly turbulent environment as central government ministers proceed with their reform agenda. Research into a small number of English primary and secondary schools in several LEAs suggests that the assumptions of cyclic development planning models, some of which were trialled under the more stable conditions of the past, may be open to question. It seems uncertain how far such models can promote stable conditions for school development in the present climate. Staff and governors in turbulent environments may now be forced to adopt a more flexible, evolutionary approach, largely for reasons beyond their control. A key finding is that much planning for development takes place continually, outside the 'official' development plan document and process, as staff and governors respond to spasmodically and often unpredictably changing circumstances which follow from the strategy employed by central government to introduce its reforms for schools. Under such circumstances, it is possible that the official process and documentation may be less effective than an alternative approach resting upon less rationalistic assumptions.

Factors contributing to stability	Factors contributing to turbulence
Sequential goals	Simultaneous goals
Maintenance activity is routine	Maintenance activity affected by external innovations
Procedures for managing planning are routine	Procedures for managing planning are innovatory
Clarity about innovations	Ambiguity about innovations
Predictability of innovations, crises, issues	Unpredictability of innovations, crises, issues
Coterminous planning cycles	Overlapping planning cycles
Sequential planning cycles	Plan for next before complete present cycle
Paucity of innovations, crises, issues	Abundance of innovations, crises, issues
Adequate resources to achieve goals	Inadequate resources to achieve goals
High school-level control over innovations	Low school-level control over innovations
Developmental focuses on innovations originating in school	Development focuses on external innovations
Low staff turnover	High staff turnover

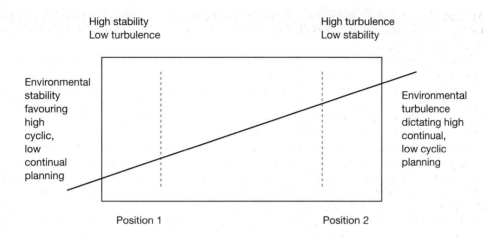

Figure 14.4.1 The interplay of stability and turbulence factors

The context of planning in schools may be conceived heuristically as a shifting balance between factors which promote stability and those which promote turbulence. Some factors relate to the external environment; others link with the internal management structure. An illustrative list of these factors is offered in the table on the previous page.

Figure 14.4.1 provides a simplistic representation of the interplay of these factors. The left-hand extreme position represents the most stable situation, where there is bound to remain some turbulence. For example, there will be some variation between cohorts of pupils and some turnover of staff over time. The right-hand extreme position depicts a highly turbulent context, where some stability will be retained because not everything will be changing (unless, perhaps, the school is being closed). The list of factors is not exhaustive. The diagram portrays how the balance between stability and turbulence may vary. For example, as the range of innovations grows, planning for development increasingly affects planning for maintenance, so leading to uncertainty over what otherwise would remain routine; the environment becomes more turbulent as stability is reduced. The hypothesis is suggested that, as the balance shifts towards turbulence, the balance of cyclic and continual planning must shift towards the continual, although even at the most extreme position annual cycles still have to be addressed. Conversely, as the balance shifts towards stability, those at school level with responsibility for planning will have greater choice whether to employ a single planning cycle.

Finally, the analysis suggests a further hypothesis with important implications for governments bent on education reform. The most effective way of promoting the improvement of schooling may be for governments to guard against the imposition of too many innovations in too short a time-scale, with too few resources.

📖 READING 14.5

Management in the new educational 'market'

Ian Menter, Yolande Muschamp and Andrew Pollard, with Peter Nicholls and Jenny Ozga

---

This reading is drawn from a study of the impact of 'market ideology' on the management of primary schools. The context in which headteachers managed during the early 1990s is reviewed and this is related to data collected in twelve case-study schools. The headteachers were aware of the limited real impact of 'the market' on the situation faced by their school, but they nevertheless felt obliged to promote and manage their schools in protective ways. Despite this ambivalence, the result was a growth in both marketing of and managerialism within the school.

How is the management of schools which you know being affected by concerns about pupil enrolment and market share?

Edited from: Menter, I., Muschamp, Y. and Pollard, A., with Nicholls, P. and Ozga, J. (1995) The primary market place: a study of small service providers in an English city. Mimeo. Presented to the American Educational Research Association, San Francisco, 1–18

Before the 1988 Education Reform Act, influential research on the management of primary schools indicated that most school staffs functioned in a relatively simple manner, acting more or less as a team, under the leadership of the headteacher. Although teachers were differentiated by salary scale (and later, allowances), this rarely led to visible hierarchical structures within a school's teaching staff, with the exception of the position of the head and sometimes of the deputy head. Teachers had considerable autonomy within their own classrooms, in terms of curriculum, assessment and pedagogy. This was consistent with the ethos and educational ideologies which predominated in the primary sector (Nias, 1989 [see Reading 4.1]; Proctor, 1990).

The headteacher was seen as the educational leader of the school, but did not necessarily seek to bring about particular pedagogical approaches. The extent to which the curriculum was planned across the whole school varied quite widely. Resources and staffing, admissions and transfers, were co-ordinated by the local education authority. The role of governing bodies was largely advisory, although this had started to change following the Education Act of 1986, which had restructured their composition and increased their visibility.

After the Education Reform Act, 1988, primary schools had to cope not only with enormous curricular and assessment innovation, but also with a raft of new management and governance policies. These included the devolution of financial control, new powers and responsibilities for governors, open enrolment and the possibility of becoming grant-maintained. Furthermore, the introduction of whole school planning, appraisal and, in some places, local bargaining and performance related pay, indicate a shift in the nature of staff management and labour relations in schools. These changes could be described collectively as bringing about a 'new management' in primary education, replacing the frequently paternalistic, unfocused and implicit practices of the old.

The 1993 Education Act, based on the White Paper entitled *Choice and Diversity*, sought to heighten the competition between schools. The measures introduced at this time included increased opportunity for schools to opt out of local government control and become directly funded by central government, the creation of a Funding Agency for Schools and the introduction of a semi-privatized school inspection system.

The government's claim was that the introduction of measures such as these would lead to the improvement of educational standards. As the then Secretary of State for Education put it in 1992, speaking to his party conference:

We are the ones with vision for our children. Look at what we have already achieved: the National Curriculum, regular testing for all our children, more information, publicly available through the Parent's Charter, more freedom for schools, greater choice and more diversity, better – and more frequent – inspection of our schools and more power for parents and governors. That's how we are creating a more open, a more responsive and a more demanding system of education. (John Patten, cited in Chitty and Simon, 1993, p. 151)

The purpose of introducing competitive practices, in short the marketization of primary and secondary education, is thus to improve the performance of schools. But as Stephen Ball (1990) has pointed out, these changes also bring with them a development in the functioning of schools towards a business culture.

The model of organization which the ERA [1988 Education Reform Act] implies is clear: it is that of governors as Board of Directors and headteacher as Chief Executive. (Ball, 1990, p. 67)

Responses to marketization

One of the largest studies of the impact of the National Curriculum and assessment on English primary schools, the PACE project (Pollard *et al.*, 1994; Croll, 1996) investigated the experience of headteachers in the early 1990s. Headteachers saw themselves as being maximally exposed to new legal requirements, management responsibilities for curriculum, staff and finance and new accountability procedures. However, although the threat of inspection loomed in many of their thoughts, their commitment to pupils and the idea of staff collegiality meant that they actively sought to face external pressures and, in some sense, to protect staff from them. This, of course, reflects something of the ideological commitments to personal relationships which have been an established part of primary school cultures for many years (Nias *et al.*, 1989 [Reading 14.2]). However, headteachers did still make many new requirements of their teachers and other staff. In particular, headteachers became more directive in their management and more reliant on indicators of performance. The implementation of the National Curriculum alone brought many changes, as traditional conceptions of teacher autonomy were challenged in order to provide coherence and progression of the curriculum across the school. The role of the primary headteacher was thus developed from that of paternal, educational leader and community servant to that of a manager of a co-ordinated organization and salesperson of an educational commodity.

Webb's (1994) study of the implementation of the National Curriculum at Key Stage 2 indicates that the question of a head's credibility with their staff took on a new dimension after the implementation of the 1988 Act. She found that such were the demands of LMS and non-curriculum related management, that heads were increasingly unable to maintain a sufficient level of knowledge to play a full part in curriculum development and planning, let alone to make a significant teaching contribution.

We interviewed the headteachers of twelve primary schools who were asked about their role as managers and about their perceptions of 'the market'. Only one headteacher saw parents of the school as 'clients', the others felt this was an inappropriate term to describe them. The majority of heads believed that rather than choosing freely between schools, enrolment patterns reflected the established catchment areas with minimal competition between them. All the headteachers supported the idea of open enrolment in principle but none thought that it could work in practice because of lack of spaces at the popular schools. The new schools were attracting parents but they were full and had waiting lists, therefore parents could not place children in their first choice school. Nine of the heads expressed disappointment that parents' expectations had been raised and felt that their school should cater primarily for the children in their locality.

All the heads felt able to describe the factors they felt affected parents in their selection of a school. The majority, nine out of twelve, felt that parents wanted their children to go to a school near to their home. They believed that parents found out about the reputation of schools from their neighbours and friends and that this also influenced their decision. The reputation could relate to a number of factors, including standards of academic performance, social class composition of the pupils or pupil behaviour within the school. The third factor mentioned was the physical environment. More than half the heads felt that parents were attracted to new schools because they presented a bright, cheerful and aesthetically pleasing environment. The existing roll of parents supported the heads' view that parents were choosing the school nearest to their home with the exception of the newly built schools.

Heads of four schools thought they were in some competition with other nearby schools. The others, most of whom had no shortage of applications from parents, were also concerned at the potential damage of competition. It emerged that a considerable amount of marketing activity was going on. Nine of the twelve headteachers said that they had carried out activities which were designed to attract parents to the school. Of the three that did not, two felt that they had no need to do so and the third felt strongly that resources should not be 'wasted' in this way.

There was great variety in the activities that heads described. Most of them aimed to build a good reputation for the school in the community. Those that were mentioned most often were: keeping in touch with the local press for coverage of school events; welcoming parents into the school for parents' evenings, to help in classrooms, to a special parents' room or to shows and assemblies; a good quality school prospectus and regular letters home; and maintaining a pleasant, aesthetically pleasing environment.

So heads acted as if a truly competitive market existed. They seemed to do this because they were anxious about competition or because of legal obligations (e.g. in the case of the preparation of a school prospectus). However, they were aware that the likely benefits in terms of attracting more children and hence protecting or improving the school's budget were small.

Overall then there was evidence of growing anxiety about what the impact of competition might be, though relatively little evidence of actual effects. This appeared to have brought about internal changes as well as increased concern with the external image of the school in the community.

The internal management structures in the schools had all been developed in response to the new demands. However, there was considerable variation in responses and this seemed to be related to the size of school. One or two schools had senior management teams, previously a feature only of secondary schools, but most had some form of sub-grouping, either on an age phase basis or on a curriculum basis, again an unusual arrangement in the days before 1988. For instance:

> We have lower school, heads of department, middle school and upper school. I have a deputy head who has overall curriculum responsibility for the school and we also have a staff development officer for the school ... And all of those people, whether it be of an administrative nature or of a curriculum nature, also have devolved financial responsibility. So we finance areas of the curriculum, we finance the day to day consumable aspects of the curriculum as well.

All of the heads referred to a range of meetings which were held in their schools. Several differentiated between meetings dealing with 'nitty gritty issues' and those dealing with curricular or development planning.

> We have two staff meetings a week. One is to cover the general day to day running of the school, the diary the planning, the events ... Then on Mondays we have what you could call a curriculum meeting when we review policies or initiate a policy. We will look at the school development plan, we have also had time given to looking at computer programmes and personal development, we have people in say to talk to staff on stress management, on their own self esteem. It is a time when I make sure it is a social time as well, I provide sort of tea and cakes and we have a few moments when I also ask them to give me some idea

of what has gone well for them in their last week. Infant teachers are very good at running themselves down, maybe that's because it's largely female, that they also need a time to consciously tell people of their successes and things that have gone well.

This extract is a cogent exposition of the old and the new – the need to deal with such recent innovations as development plans at the same time as fostering a harmonious if paternalistic culture. The use of phrases such as 'personal development' and 'stress management' exemplifies the accommodation between the old and the new.

All of the heads had drawn up development plans. Although advice from the LEA was that plans should cover three years, a number of heads indicated that only an annual cycle was realistic. For example:

> I try to do three year plans but I don't find them successful at all because so much happens in the space of twelve months that you have got to revise it all again, so for the present year, it is just a twelve month plan and I shall construct another one, August, September, for the next twelve months.

With respect to development plans, heads also had different approaches to authorship, involvement and consultation from those who saw it simplest to do it themselves and persuade the staff and governors that it was right, to those who sought a more interactive, developmental approach.

The views of headteachers about the roles of their governing bodies varied from one extreme to the other. For instance, when asked if the governors were very involved with the school, one head replied:

> Yes, it varies, some are extremely involved, others not very involved at all, but generally speaking it's a very supportive governing body. I work very closely with my governors. I'm quite happy. I've always had a policy of working very closely with the governing body

On the other hand, another, one of four heads in the sample who were anticipating imminent retirement, commented:

> Prats! The chairman is good. He is the councillor for the area – very supportive but doesn't interfere. The two community governors, I really have to get behind, because they always leave it to me. They all work; they've got jobs. You can't expect too much. The government has been too optimistic – too much responsibility in the hands of amateurs. More responsible adults go for the large secondary schools. However some are OK. I worry about the pay structures. It will cause a lot of ill will. Some of the governors will think the teachers are grossly overpaid. It's going to set teachers against teachers, headteacher against teacher, headteacher against governors. You can't have complete amateurs assessing people's pay. Here, who knows what will happen – I'm glad I won't be here when it happens.

The involvement of parents in schools was not universal nor was there a common mode of involvement. There was some evidence though that parents were seen as a resource which was ameliorating the effect of a general scarcity of resources. At one school, the head explained:

> We don't just have them listening to little Johnny read, we give them on-site training, particularly for our reading scheme. We give the parents targets to hit with the children, not necessarily National Curriculum, but that gives an idea. My head of infants [name], actually gives them some tuition as to what we are after ... Rather than say off you go for twenty minutes ... And we get some really high calibre mums. Really good.

However, such 'high calibre' parents were not always available:

> We have got an unemployed former pupil with a computer degree who can't find a permanent job. But in an area like this it is difficult to get the right parents. Because it seems to me anyway that the parents we have with any wherewithal find themselves a job, which they have to do now to keep the family, and those that haven't got a job are those you don't want in school anyway.

The role of headteachers has thus been changing rapidly since the wave of legislation which commenced in the late 1980s. The impact has been seen in the way in which they talk about their work and in the practices which they describe. Much of this change is associated with the sense of an external market which is displayed by the heads. However, it would be simplistic to imply that these parallel developments in management and market ideology are necessarily entirely interdependent. There were, for instance, other important marketizing influences. Of these, the most significant in the mid-1990s is undoubtedly the inspection regulations which were introduced by the Government following the Education (Schools) Act of 1992. These provide for inspection of all schools every four years, with publication of a report and the threat of being named as a 'failing school'. There has been considerable media coverage of the results of such inspections and headteachers have become very aware of their high stakes character.

In summary, there is little doubt that marketization has produced considerable changes in the management styles of headteachers and in the work of school staff. In general, this must be seen as a move away from pre-existing notions of collegiality towards an increasingly 'managed' form of organization. Perhaps this was an inevitable consequence of the increased complexity of demands and higher levels of self-reliance which are now faced by primary schools. Managerialism is certainly one response, with an associated fragmentation of collective values, more overt expressions of conflicts of interest and a gradual development of hierarchy.

English primary schools in the mid-1990s are very different work places than they were before the Education Reform Act, 1988.

 CHAPTER 14.6

Parents as consumers

Martin Hughes, Felicity Wikeley and Tricia Nash

Parents and Their Children's Schools, from which this reading is drawn, reports an unusual study of what parents of young children actually want of schools, as opposed to what some politicians have asserted that they want. In this reading the assumptions underpinning the introduction of the Education Reform Act, 1988 (and later the Parents' Charter and 'opting out' legislation) are contrasted with research evidence. One particular finding is that parents tend to be very supportive of the primary school attended by their own children, but media coverage leads them to assume there must be lower quality elsewhere.

To what extent are the parents of pupils at your school best seen as 'consumers' or as 'partners' in their children's education?

Edited from: Hughes, M., Wikeley, F and Nash, T. (1994) *Parents and Their Children's Schools*. Oxford: Blackwell Publishers, 8–13, 204–7

Parents as consumers?

The idea that parents should be seen as consumers of education first emerged in the writings of various right-wing educationalists during the late 1970s and 1980s (e.g. Cox and Boyson, 1977; Hillgate Group, 1986, 1987; Flew, 1987; Sexton, 1987). These writers put forward a number of criticisms of the state education system and proposed various alternatives, many of which were subsequently incorporated into the reforms of the late 1980s and early 1990s.

While they did not necessarily agree on every point, there was a great deal of consensus in what they were saying.

A common starting point was the assumption that educational standards were falling, and that this was due to the misguided pursuit of egalitarian policies, such as comprehensive education, or to progressive teaching methods.

Several of these writers noted that such faults were not to be found in the private sector, and that therefore the goal must be to create an 'independent education for all'. This in turn meant that schools would have to be freed from state control, and especially from local authority control, and a genuine market in education created. As Sexton (1987) put it:

> The only choice left is to devolve the system to the schools themselves, and to create a direct relationship between the suppliers of education, the schools and the teachers, and the consumers, the parents and their children. It is to create, as near as practicable, a 'free market' in education. To use a popular word, it is in some sense to 'privatize' the State education system. (p. 10)

The likely effects of such a policy on schools were made starkly clear by the Hillgate Group (1986):

> Their survival should depend on their ability to satisfy their customers. And their principal customers are parents, who should therefore be free to place their custom where they wish, in order that educational institutions should be shaped, controlled and nourished by their demand ... Schools will have to work to stay in business, and the worse their results, the more likely they will be to go to the wall. (pp. 7, 16)

These ideas exerted a major influence on the 1988 Education Reform Act. The main purpose of the Act was to introduce the National Curriculum and standardized assessment, to remove some of the obstacles to parental choice and to establish a new system for the local management of schools. However, the written legislation contains little insight into the kind of thinking on which it is based. For this, we have to look at what was actually said in the House of Commons at the time. The following comments, for example, were made by the then Secretary of State for Education, Kenneth Baker, when he introduced the Bill at the end of 1987. Baker started by criticizing the state education system on the grounds that:

> It has become producer-dominated. It has not proved sensitive to the demands for change that have become ever more urgent over the past 10 years. This Bill will create a new framework, which will raise standards, extend choice, and produce a better educated Britain ... If we are to implement the principle of the 1944 Education Act that children should be 'educated in accordance with the wishes of their parents', then we must give consumers of education a central part in decision making. That means freeing schools and colleges to deliver the standards that parents and employers want. It means encouraging the consumer to expect and demand that all educational bodies do the best job possible. In a word it means choice ... For the first time in 80 years they (local education authorities) will face competition in the provision of free education, so standards will rise in all schools as we introduce a competitive spirit into the provision of education – and at no extra cost to the consumer. (*Hansard*, 1 December 1987)

This important passage contains many echoes of the earlier arguments put forward by Sexton and the Hillgate Group. Baker introduces here the central notion of parents as 'consumers of education', and contrasts this with the 'producers', whom he claims have been dominating the system to its detriment for too long. Baker does not spell out here who these 'producers' are, but it must be assumed that they are teachers, local authorities and other educational 'experts' such as advisers and Her Majesty's Inspectorate. He goes on to suggest that this producer domination has resulted in low educational standards. The solution to the problem is clear. Schools and colleges must be 'freed' to 'deliver the standards that parents and employers want'. And the mechanism to be used is also clear – the competitive market. Parents must be given more choice, and schools must be encouraged to compete with each other for parents' custom.

One apparent contradiction in the 1988 Education Reform Act is that, while much of the Act is concerned with freeing schools from state control, the Act also introduced a highly centralized curriculum and assessment system.

However, from the point of view of consumer choice, the introduction of the National Curriculum and standardized assessment does have a certain degree of logic; they provide both the framework for judging schools and the mechanism for making those judgements. If all pupils follow the same curriculum and are assessed against the same benchmarks at the same ages, and if the results of these assessments are then made public, then it will be relatively easy – at least according to theory – for parents to see which are successful schools and which are not. The parents simply consult the local 'league tables' of schools, and make their choices accordingly.

This particular aspect of the reforms was further elaborated by the publication in 1991 of the Parent's Charter (Department of Education and Science, 1991a). This document which was part of a wider promotion on consumer rights known as the Citizen's Charter, set out the rights and responsibilities expected of parents 'to help you become a more effective partner in your child's education'. Central to the Parent's Charter was 'the right to know', which was enshrined in five key documents:

an annual written report about each child;

regular reports on schools from independent inspectors;

publicly available 'league tables' comparing the performance of local schools;

a prospectus or brochure about individual schools;

an annual report from each school's governors.

The Parent's Charter also spelled out the right of all parents to express their preference for a school of their choice, and their right to appeal if this choice was not met – although it made clear that parents would not automatically get a place in the school of their choice if it was already 'full to capacity with pupils who have a stronger claim'.

The central role of parents in educational reform was emphasized again in another major policy document, the 1992 Education White Paper. Entitled *Choice and Diversity: A New Framework for Schools*, this document made clear that increasing parental choice was one of its main guiding principles. In a passage which has since become widely quoted, the White Paper spelled out its belief that:

> Parents know best the needs of their children – certainly better than educational theorists or administrators, better even than our mostly excellent teachers. (p. 2)

Starting from this premise, the White Paper argued for the need to provide as diverse a range of schools as possible, so that parents could choose the school they believed best suited the particular interests and aptitudes of their children. It is clear from reading the White Paper, however, that the authors had a particular type of school in mind which they wished to encourage above all others – grant-maintained schools – and much of the White Paper is in fact concerned with the arrangements necessary to encourage this particular development.

The emphasis on 'diversity' contained in the White Paper has been criticized on the grounds that it is merely another way of talking about inequality in the education system. Brown (1991) argued that it is part of what he calls a 'third wave' in the socio-historical development of British education, a period which he describes by the term 'parentocracy':

> To date, the 'third wave' has been characterized by the rise of the educational parentocracy, where a child's education is increasingly dependent upon the wealth and wishes of parents, rather than the ability and efforts of pupils ... In the educational parentocracy, selection will be determined by the free play of market forces, and because the State is no longer responsible for overseeing selection, inequalities in educational out-

come, at least in official accounts, cannot be blamed on the State. Such inequalities (the Right prefers the term 'diversity') will be viewed as the legitimate expression of parental preferences, differences in innate capacities, and a healthy 'diversity' of educational experience. (pp. 66, 80)

But what do parents really want?

Our research focused on the main areas in which assumptions about parents underlie the reforms of the early 1990s.

Issue 1: parents as consumers One of the central assumptions underlying the educational reforms is that parents should be seen as consumers of education We found, however, that there was considerable reluctance amongst the parents towards taking on this new role. Only a small minority of parents saw themselves 'very much' as consumers, and many parents found the idea puzzling or difficult to apply to their particular circumstances.

Issue 2: parental choice The consumerist model assumes that parents will make considered choices between schools on the basis of published information about academic standards. We found however, that this model was of only limited applicability to the parents in our study. For example, there were some parents who did not have any realistic choice of school, either because they could not travel to other schools or because the other schools were full. There were also a substantial number of parents who did have the possibility of choice but who did not make use of it: typically, these parents were happy with what the local school provided and saw no reason to look elsewhere. And although there were undoubtedly many parents who considered more than one school, some of these parents were forced into looking elsewhere, either because they could not get into the school of their choice or because they had heard unfavourable reports about the local school. All in all, there were relatively few parents whose behaviour when choosing schools appeared to fit the pure consumerist model.

Our research also cast doubt on the assumption that parents will choose schools purely on the basis of academic performance. Other factors – such as a school's location, size or friendliness – are of equal, if not greater importance. A similar picture emerged when parents were asked directly what they considered to make a good school: factors such as relationships, atmosphere and ethos featured much more prominently than academic results. We also saw that the great majority of parents would not move their children purely on the basis of published assessment results. Overall, our research provides little support for the assumption that parents are solely concerned with academic results.

Issue 3: Parental satisfaction Another assumption underlying the reforms is that parents are deeply dissatisfied with their children's schools, and particularly with the standards which prevail. Our research provides little evidence to support this. Each year the vast majority of parents said they were happy with their child's school and that the teachers were doing a good job. Over three-quarters of the parents were happy with their children's progress in English and maths, and only a handful of parents moved their children because they were unhappy with the school. These figures do not suggest widespread dissatisfaction amongst parents; rather, they indicate general approval of schools as they are at present, and a significant appreciation of the job which teachers are doing.

We also found that parents were much more likely to express concern about 'standards' in general than about those at their own child's school. This finding suggests that, where parents have to rely on second-hand information about schools in general, they are more likely to reflect the concerns about standards which are regularly expressed in the media. On the other hand, where they can draw on their personal experience of their child's particular school, then they are much more likely to respond in positive terms.

In summary, our research suggests that many of the assumptions about parents which underlie the reforms do not match closely with the real views, experiences and behaviour of the parents most directly involved. In particular, the idea that parents should be seen as consumers – in the narrow, market sense of the term – does not seem an appropriate description of the parents in our study.

CHAPTER 14.7

Ideologies of school governance

Rosemary Deem

Rosemary Deem and Kevin Brehony studied the working of governing bodies in ten schools from 1988 to 1993. In this reading, the changing legislation regarding school governance is both reviewed and analysed in terms of the initial 'collective concern ideology' and the 'consumer interest ideology' which began to dominate in the 1990s. The ways in which such ideologies produce particular patterns of governor concern and behaviour are indicated.

How would you characterize the governors in your school in terms of Deem's analysis?

Edited from: Deem, R. (1994) 'School governing bodies: public concerns and private interests', in Scott, D. (ed.) *Accountability and Control in Educational Settings*. London: Cassell, 58–72.

We have examined some of the possible consequences for English state education of the coexistence of two different underlying ideologies about, and hence two different models of, lay participation in educational administration. One ideology stresses the significance of democracy, public accountability and collective concerns. This ideology, which I term collective concern ideology, although still current among some parent and governor pressure groups, now appears to be in decline. The other ideology, which I term consumer interest ideology, emphasizes markets, competition, consumer rights and private interests. This ideology appears to be in the ascendancy and finds its fullest expression in the idea of grant-maintained schools, where heads and governors fully control all aspects of their school's management and funding is direct from the state rather than through LEAs.

Educational reforms in England, including the 1986 No. 2 Education Act, the 1988 Education Reform Act, and the 1993 Education Act, have attempted extensive reshaping of the composition of individual state school governing bodies and considerable clarification and extension of their responsibilities and duties, as well as enabling outside agencies to step in if problems arise. The extension of governing body powers has included giving governors in LEA schools the responsibility for admission and exclusion of pupils, budget approval, discretionary teacher pay and determination of headteacher salaries (within national parameters), sex education, policy on charging for optional activities, and the hiring and firing of staff (although LEAs remain the employers). In grant-maintained state schools, governor responsibilities extend even further; governing bodies are the employers of school staff and responsible for the freehold of the premises.

Despite these recent onerous responsibilities and the four-year term of office governors serve, they are volunteers who are not remunerated for their services. Furthermore, their activities are intended to be informed by lay rather than professional concerns, although teacher and headteacher governors clearly have educational expertise, as do some other governors. For the majority of lay governors, however, common sense and a sense of 'active citizenship', rather than educational expertise are seen to characterize their administrative strengths (Brehony, 1992; Brehony and Deem, 1991).

Prior to the legislation of the late 1980s, governing schools was a much less demanding activity. Indeed in the early 1980s a study by Kogan *et al.* (1984) suggested that governing bodies were largely shaped by the culture, ethos and policies of their local education authorities and that of the schools in which they were located. Prior to 1980, governing bodies were often largely populated by political nominees, though many local education authorities did permit parental representation before the 1980 Education Act required them to. Since 1988, as a result of the 1986 No. 2 Education Act, parents and co-opted governors, including those from business and industry, have achieved numerical dominance on LEA school governing bodies over LEA nominees.

Relevant officers from the two LEAs concerned have collected for analysis a huge amount of documentation from the governing bodies concerned. No claims about typicality are made for the study but we do feel that in-depth, longitudinal research of this kind offers the possibility of reaching a high level of understanding of the processes involved in governing schools and enables the testing of theoretical ideas in ways not easily permitted by a snapshot representative survey.

In the 1970s and early 1980s the prevalent view of governing bodies was one which saw them as a form of democratic lay participation in education and as a means of public accountability for state schools. This collective concern ideology was particularly well expressed by the Taylor Report on governing bodies (DES, 1977). Much of the ideology was given practical expression in the organizational form that governing bodies took. The trend from the 1970s onwards was towards having a larger number of governing bodies in each LEA, so that schools had their own or shared one with a sister school on the same site. There was growing representation of parents as well as teachers and LEA nominees, although this was not required by law until after the 1980 Education Act. Governing bodies did not make major policy decisions or shape management policy in their schools but were expected to have an overview of their schools' organization and curriculum and met termly to discuss the school and its activities. After a *cause célèbre* in a London school where managers (as primary governors were called until the 1980 Act) were shown to be unable to deal with a major educational and organizational crisis in the school's leadership (Dale, 1981), it was felt necessary to clarify further the role of governing bodies, and this was one factor in the establishment of the Taylor Committee. The Taylor Report showed itself to be broadly in favour of a structure which would offer equal representation of different groups (teachers, parents, older students, LEAs and community representatives) and which would provide a framework of public accountability within which all state-maintained and state-controlled schools would have to operate (DES, 1977).

Throughout the 1970s the emphasis on collective values and public concerns in the administration of education was very evident. The 1980 Education Act, which secured parental representation as of right on governing bodies, did not depart significantly from this ideological position. The 1984 Education Green Paper, *Parental Influence at School* (DES, 1984), and the 1985 White Paper, *Better Schools* (DES, 1985), also seemed to reflect similar values, culminating in the 1986 No. 2 Education Act, which clarified and extended governing body powers as well as changing their composition. But the 1986 Act may have been a watershed, for it also placed considerable emphasis on bringing in more governors from business and industry. This was an important change; since then there has been a significant shift in the political rhetoric underlying the rationale for school governing bodies, and in the model of governing bodies thereby adopted. The beliefs and values on which the 1988 Education Reform legislation rests enabled a move to site-based management of schools and formula funding using pupil-weighted units, through either local management of schools (LMS) or grant-maintained status schools (GMS). There was a further widening of the powers of lay governors and a corresponding reduction in the powers of democratically elected LEAs. It was thought by some politicians that these changes would add to schools' efficiency, competitiveness and market orientation, while ensuring that the rights and voices of individual education consumers, rather than those of educational producers, were clearly heard in educational contexts through parental choice of, and influence within, schools (Deem, 1990). The new values emphasized individual rights and interests rather than collective and public ones.

The strength of this new 'consumer interest' ideological view was confirmed by the 1992 Education White Paper, which sought to encourage more schools to opt out of LEA control and offered the promise of even greater financial and other delegation to those schools remaining within LEA control, and the subsequent 1993 Education Act. Alongside measures designed to increase centralization of educational administration, the powers of individual parents and governing bodies were to be strengthened while the powers of LEAs were reduced further. Thus, the appeal is not so much to a collectivity of caring citizens concerned with public good in education as to individual consumers of schooling, whether parents, businesspeople or politicians. These consumers, it is believed are then able to ensure the preservation and fostering of market rights of users of schools, competition between schools for pupils, high educational standards and the efficient use of resources. In July 1992 the then Secretary of State for Education, John Patten, was quoted as saying that opting out (GMS) was a measure which enabled the depoliticizing of education. The arguments he apparently adduced for this were that more parents voted in opt-out ballots that in local elections and that parents knew better than educationalists what were the needs of their children (Meikle, 1992). Ironically, the further devolution of powers to parents and governors proposed by the White Paper is accompanied, as in the 1988 Act, by a strengthening of the powers of central government and the Secretary of State for Education to intervene in individual schools and/or governing bodies, should problems occur.

Collective concern values and beliefs do persist among both established and new governors. We have observed discussions about education in governing body meetings, in almost all of our ten schools over the four years of our research, which suggest real concern for and about the quality of children's learning and genuine awareness of the problems teachers face in schools. At the same time, some of those engaged in such discussions are not afraid to criticize what a school is doing or question a given course of action by a teacher. But such criticism is constructive and offered in a spirit of co-operation. These governors may be parents, LEA or co-opted governors. They are distinguished by their concern for children and young people in general and by their desire to be involved. Two examples of collective concern governors were evident at Moatmeadow Secondary. One was a mother of a current pupil and the other a co-opted governor and vicar. They served on working groups, wrote reports for the governing body, came into school and one of them even went on a week of demanding outdoor pursuits with sixth-formers. Although in the context of Moatmeadow these governors might put that school first, they also displayed a much wider awareness of the needs of children and public education. Public concerns took precedence over private interests.

Consumer interest governors are different. They tend to take one of two stances. There are those who ask lots of questions, are rarely supportive of the school and head, and frequently demand to know how their school is doing in comparison to others. If they are parents of current pupils, their children's experiences are often the basis for their criticisms. Others use neighbourhood or school-gate gossip as a basis for comment. Woods (1992) sees parents who conform to this type as being empowered under the recent legislation to get more involved. But more constructive involvement does not always happen. One governor of this kind at Cotswold School complained consistently about a wide range of matters – the organization of the finances, the shared sixth-form scheme, non-challenging school visits, teacher supply problems, discipline – yet when challenged at one meeting to visit school and see for himself the new house system, he said he was far too busy, gave too much time to the task of governing already and did not see school visits as a priority. Similar views about the unimportance of school visits were expressed by other consumer interest governors in our study; this was not an isolated example.

There is also, however, a second type of consumer interest governor, what we might term an 'iconoclastic' governor. We found them to be mostly LEA governors or, more rarely, co-opted. Their connections with a particular school were often instrumental (for example, it was in their council ward) or tangential. Some such governors wished to become governors of a school they regarded as bad with a view to improving it, but their strategies rarely focused on a target within the school. As prominent local figures such governors did not need legislation on governor involvement to empower them – they often already had access to MPs, ministers and the media. Going to the local newspaper about school exam results before talking to the school(s) concerned first is something which recurred frequently in two of our case-study secondary schools. Whatever the intentions behind such actions, they can be perceived as morale-destroying for pupils and teachers, and were seen as such by the schools concerned.

Consumer interest governors, whether iconoclastic or not, often believe that they are superior to teachers and know more about running schools, often as a result of their business experience, whether this is extensive or narrow. They tended in our study to be co-opted or LEA-nominated governors and less often parent governors.

The superimposing of the consumer interest ideology and model of governors on the collective interest ideology and model, together with greatly increased governor workloads under LMS, may be decreasing rather than increasing the amount of democratic involvement in the English education system. This effect may work in one of two ways. First it may constrain many potential governors from serving at all. Second it may work by putting on the agenda a range of issues which make it harder for governing bodies to promote the public good in education rather than articulate private interests, whether these are interests of individual children or individual schools. This is surely not to be welcomed in a democratic society, whatever its political orientation.

READING 14.8

OFSTED inspection – who is it for?

Jim Rose

> Jim Rose was Director of Inspections at the Office for Standards in Education when he wrote the article from which this reading has been edited. Understandably, he interprets the national inspection processes positively, as excellent opportunities for schools to get objective assessment with which to inform school improvement strategies. Others might consider that Rose glosses the threat which inspections pose to schools. Some would even suggest that inspections have dubious objectivity, are disruptive and thus interrupt school development processes to no worthwhile purpose (see Reading 14.9).
>
> How has inspection affected the school in which you work?
>
> Edited from: Rose, J. (1995) OFSTED inspection – who is it for?, *Education Review*, 9 (1), 63–6

In the run-up to the White Paper, *Better Schools* (1985), the then Secretary of State, Sir Keith Joseph, insisted on asking the question: 'What is education for?'

Because it goes to the heart of what we want our children and our society to be, the central importance of that question for those who provide education cannot be denied. In the spirit of *Better Schools*, however, it was certainly not only the 'providers' whom Sir Keith Joseph had in mind when he put that question.

The 1992 Education Act, which established a new national inspection service, typifies that shift in emphasis. Arguably, much of the debate about the fitness of the national inspection service improving standards, is concerned with reconciling the values and interests of the users with those of the providers of education.

Thus a corollary of the question 'what is education for?' might be 'who is inspection for?'

Just as the 1988 Education Reform Act provides an entitlement to a National Curriculum for pupils, so the 1992 Act provides parents with an entitlement for inspection to tell them how well their schools are performing, including how well their children are being taught and whether they are achieving the standards expected of them in the subjects of the National Curriculum.

High quality information on public services which is freely available to the users of those services is also a cornerstone of the Citizen's and Parent's Charters. In the words of the White Paper on *Open Government*:

Information is a condition of choice and provides a measure of quality. Even where there is little alternative to a public service, information enables citizens to demand the quality of service they are entitled to expect and puts pressure on those running services to deliver high standards.

To those ends, and in keeping with the Citizen's Charter, OFSTED and other national inspectorates have to measure up to the following conditions:

inspectors should be independent of the service they inspect, both managerially and financially, so that they can assess objectively the efficiency and effectiveness of the service provided and the standards set for it;

people who are not professionally connected either with the inspectorate or with the service itself should take part in inspections to represent the views and concerns of the general public;

reports should be published and made widely available so that people know how well or how poorly services are performing. Service providers whose work is inspected should publish and make widely available a response to the report.

Clearly, a key purpose of those three requirements is to establish independent inspectorates whose work and reports command a high degree of public confidence and credibility. The price which is paid for that in the case of the education service, particularly in relation to LEAs, is to separate two longstanding inseparables, notably inspection and advice.

Whether that is a price worth paying is currently a contentious issue, particularly for those who see inspection and advice as part of a 'seamless, developmental process' vital to school self-review.

The hard message, however, is that the national inspection service regulated by OFSTED places the interests of the users – the parents and the pupils – at least on a par with those of the providers.

That said, the process and outcomes of an inspection, such as the reporting procedures and the written report, must also be of direct and immediate value to the school in addressing its weaknesses and sustaining its strengths, since that too, is in the best interests of the users.

Common sense suggests, moreover, that to be of value advice should be based on a balanced, 'no axe to grind' analysis of a school's strengths and weaknesses of the kind OFSTED inspection aims to provide.

It has never been claimed that inspections in themselves would be sufficient to improve schools, and that must be true of other forms of school evaluation. Inspection falls into that intriguing category of things which are necessary but not in themselves sufficient to achieve school improvement.

What is certain, however, is that no matter how good an inspection has been in assessing the strengths and weaknesses of the school, not much will happen if its messages fall on deaf ears.

Furthermore, the very word 'inspection' is thought by some to be far too hard-edged to suit what they genuinely believe to be the best way to improve schools and help them become more effective. Nevertheless it is hard to deny that 'inspection', in the sense of taking a close look at the work of the school with the intention of improving it, goes on all the time. Teachers inspect each other's work with varying degrees of intensity, if not always explicitly.

That is why it is hardly surprising that those schools which have open systems and an appetite for improvement are more likely to respond well to an OFSTED inspection than those which take a more guarded stance and are unused to taking a critical look at themselves.

OFSTED has worked hard to spell out a set of expectations for an effective school inspection which are faithful to the legislation governing inspection. They comprise what are now four well-known criteria:

the quality of the education provided by the school;

the educational standards achieved in the school;

whether the financial resources available to the school are managed efficiently;

the spiritual, moral, social and cultural development of pupils at the school.

As every OFSTED inspector and the vast majority of schools are aware, those criteria are the foundation stones of the Inspection Framework and the Handbook of Guidance governing inspections.

READING 14.9

Systemic reform and school inspection

Centre for Educational Research and Innovation, Organization for Economic Co-operation and Development

This reading from OECD provides a basis for scrutinizing the rationale for school inspection which was provided in the previous reading (14.8), and may offer a partial antidote to the inspection anxieties which sometimes arise. First, seven system-wide methods for monitoring the performance of schools are reviewed. This international evidence shows that the OFSTED method is but one possibility. Second, the combination of market competition and inspection as a way of 'levering up' standards is questioned.

Do you think that the present balance between inspection of schools and support for schools is appropriate to maximize school improvement?

Edited from: Centre for Educational Research and Innovation, OECD (1995) *Schools Under Scrutiny*. Paris: OECD, 16–18, 40–1, 62

Systematic reform

Assessing the performance of schools has become high priority for many OECD countries, which have established or are in the process of developing new evaluation systems. In most cases, these new approaches have been devised in the context of a radical reform of the whole system. Many OECD countries have passed legislation within the last five years to overhaul their systems. In the countries examined in this study:

The system in England has been reformed from top to bottom as the result of the Education Reform Act 1988 and subsequent legislation, including a new National Curriculum; management of school budgets (including teachers' pay) devolved from the local education authorities who used to manage education to individual schools; a new assessment system aimed at constructing performance tables to enable parents to compare schools more accurately; and an overhauled semi-privatized inspectorate.

France has reformed its key qualification, the baccalauréat, in order to make it attainable by a broader range of students, in line with its commitment in the Education Act 1989 that by 2000 every student will leave school with a qualification, and 80 per cent will have the baccalauréat. Responsibility for the schools has been decentralized from the ministry to the regions, and much of the work of inspection has been reorganized to focus on evaluating schools as units – especially through the use of performance indicators.

Systematic reform is least evident in Germany, where the 16 Länder have freedom to run their systems as they like; although there is co-operation between the Länder on issues such as teacher training and the mutual recognition of qualifications, there is a great deal of variety across the country with some Länder experimenting with reform and others not at all. The German system of quality assurance consists of many interlocking factors, of which inspection is a relatively minor aspect, and schools are not formally assessed as units. There are moves in some Länder, however, to give them more autonomy in response to demands for a more flexible system.

In New Zealand, the eleven regional boards which used to run the primary schools were abolished by the 1989 Education Act in favour of a separate Board of Trustees for each school which has full responsibility for managing it (although most do not yet handle teachers' pay). An Education Review Office set up by the act inspects primary and secondary schools regularly.

Regular inspection of the schools in Spain is an integral part of the reforms set in motion by the Ley de Ordenacion General del Sistema Educativo passed in 1990. Comprehensive education to 16 was made compulsory and free, and a new cycle of secondary education established for 12 to 16 year olds. Schools now control their own finances, and devise their own curricula within a framework of national guidelines. The inspectorate checks that the new law is being obeyed, and monitors the progress of the reforms.

Sweden's schools are now the responsibility of local municipalities. The highly centralized National Board of Education, which used to manage the system, has been replaced by a National Agency for Education, which regulates it with a much lighter touch. Budgets and decision-making have been devolved to the schools themselves, which are being encouraged to compete for pupils, and the national curriculum has been reworked to make it less prescriptive. Private schools are licensed after inspection by agency teams.

The United States has traditionally relied on standardized tests to check the progress of its students and the level of education provided by its constituent states and their school districts. Only recently has the focus shifted to the performance of individual schools, as part of a new enthusiasm for systemic reform, which is supported by the Clinton Administration. Its Goals 2000 programme and other federal policies adopt a standards based approach linked to curricular reform; and some 45 states, dissatisfied with conventional methods of testing, now claim to be setting clear expectations which students must reach. Most are also trying to anchor other policies – related to curriculum, assessment, and teacher development – to those standards and to one another. At the same time, many are moving to free schools from the burden of accumulated regulations so that they can focus more effectively on enabling their students to meet these standards.

These different policies reflect very different national situations and conceptualizations of what – if anything – is wrong with the education system. But there are two clear trends. The first is a double move – towards various forms of decentralization of administration and financing in previous highly centralized systems (France, Spain, New Zealand and Sweden), and towards more central control in previously highly devolved systems (England and, to some extent, the United States, where the Federal government, although it has not taken on extra administrative powers, has set national education targets and is considering the idea of a national curriculum framework and assessment system). Germany is a special case, because some of the 16 Länder have very centralized systems, and others less so.

The second is towards school autonomy for individual schools, the setting of targets and objectives, and some system of inspecting or monitoring to check how far they have been reached. But the degree to which schools themselves are evaluated as units varies.

Publicity, the consumer and the market mechanism

One lever intended to raise school performance in England is the publication of inspectors' reports, which mainly when negative, sometimes generate intense media interest. The idea is to set in motion a new type of sanction: the discipline of the market. The theory is that schools which are perceived to be performing poorly are likely to attract fewer pupils, and per capita funding mechanisms mean that fewer pupils means less money.

Such a spiral of decline is supposed to weed the weakest schools out of the system; but the reality is often rather different, for a number of reasons:

Popular schools can only take a limited number of pupils – few would want to expand indefinitely. Instead, in most cases, they simply become more choosy about the pupils they take, and the rest have to make do with their second or third choice of school. These are often schools which need improvement, but the market offers no mechanism for achieving this.

The schools with the worst examination results are frequently in areas where no alternative is available for the community who, because of various forms of deprivation, may be unable to send their children to schools outside the immediate area.

Sometimes the whole community, including parents, has low expectations from education and is satisfied with a weak school. They may even unite to protect the reputation of the school against a negative inspection report; and virtually any proposal to close a school creates a local movement to keep it open, even if it has clear deficiencies. Parent power is rarely the answer for failing schools.

So the question of how to improve schools in districts suffering from multiple socio-economic problems still has to be faced, and illustrates the limits of the market mechanism as a way of raising standards. But competition does seem to have had some positive effects on English schools, which are paying much more attention to key indicators such as examination passes (currently rising by several percentage points per year) and school attendance; less desirable developments include the more frequent exclusion of difficult children or those with special needs, lest they bring down the school's examination score or spoil its public reputation through bad behaviour. Other OECD countries are watching the English experiment with interest, but as yet no other has followed it so far down the road.

Two intended benefits of inspection have yet to prove themselves. One is the power of action plans to secure major improvements of schools, particularly those with significant problems. The OFSTED process has proved an excellent framework for identifying a school's weaknesses, but does not address in any detail how to put them right. Although governors of schools are supposed to be responsible for ensuring that problems are addressed, they have limited tools for doing so. An important test of the system over the coming years will be the degree to which clearer identification of problems lead on the one hand to more effective self-improvement and on the other to more effective use of local authority and other services to aid that improvement.

The second benefit that has yet to prove itself is more effective accountability to parents. The overwhelming response of parents to the inspection system so far has been to be protective of their secondary schools, and often hostile to the concept of an outside inspection. This phenomenon is likely to be even more pronounced for primary schools. The result has been that, so far, there is little evidence of parents moving their children out of poor schools. It is too early to know whether this will result in those parents pressing for, and securing, improvements.

 READING 14.10

Working for positive change

Michael Fullan

This reading is an extract from the concluding chapter of what is a classic book on school development, *The New Meaning of Educational Change*. Michael Fullan is a strong believer in 'bottom up' institutional development in which 'empowerment' comes from teachers and others acting positively to create an 'ethos of continuous innovation'. There is a strong articulation with Andy Hargreaves' 'collegial' model of teacher culture (Reading 14.1). However, other readings in this chapter suggest some of the hurdles which such aspirations would need to overcome to be realized.

How positive are you and your colleagues about school improvement?

Edited from: Fullan, M. G. (1991) *The New Meaning of Educational Change*. London: Cassell, 345–9

The future of educational change

The shame of educational change is the squandering of good intentions and the waste of resources. The capacity to bring about change and the capacity to bring about improvement are two different matters. Change is everywhere, progress is not.

Grappling with educational change in self-defeating ways has been a common experience over the last 30 years. We know that people often don't learn from their own experiences let alone from the experience of others. The response of many has been to redouble their efforts. For those in authority this has meant more advocacy, more legislation, more accountability, more resources, etc. For those on the receiving end the response has been more closed doors, retreats into isolationism or out of education altogether, and in some cases collective resistance. We have seen that these seemingly rational political solutions, while perfectly understandable if one is in a hurry to bring about or avoid change, simply to do not work. In fact, they do more harm than good as frustration, tension, and despair accumulate.

I will not attempt to predict the future of educational change, except to identify six themes central to the emerging new paradigm that will be needed to cope with and turn change to our advantage. The six involve moving from an old, unsuccessful way of managing change to a new mind-set.

From negative to positive politics

People at all levels of the educational system have power – power most often used not to do things. Negative politics from below means constantly resisting changes; from above it means attempting to impose reform through fiat. These negative modes are understandable given that changes are not normally introduced with much sensitivity and that there is little time to be considerate. The result is a decidedly negative vicious cycle. Resistance, cajoling, blaming others, self-protection, avoidance, and caution all become habitual strategies for coping. It is possible, of course, to survive in such a negative environment through self-serving manipulation, but Peter Block (1987) cuts to the core when he challenges, 'Why get better at a bad game?' What's the percentage?

If we are going to use power, we might as well use it to do good.

Like-minded individuals and small groups of individuals can create their own critical masses, even if it is only two people. Positive politics is not a sure-fire way out of the dilemmas of change, and it is not risk free, but it is a much more powerful and satisfying route to reform. In short one aspect of the new mind-set is to increase the proportion of effort devoted to positive politics: to use power to bring about improvements in our own immediate environment.

From monolithic to alternative solutions

Another dilemma in educational reforms concerns uniformity vs. variation of solutions. Neither centralization nor decentralization seems to work. Meaning cannot be masterminded at a global level. It is found through small-scale pursuits of significant personal and organizational goals. The school is the 'centre' of change. Thus, we must allow for and foster variation across schools. This does not means that anything goes. Constant communication and negotiations between districts and schools, for example, can honour both variation and mutual shaping.

Norms of collaboration and continuous improvement enable us to pursue reforms through drawing on and contributing to the pool of ideas and solutions. The emphasis on figuring out alternative solutions close to home reduces the propensity to seek or accept ready-made external solutions.

From innovations to institutional development

The innovation paradigm has provided considerable insights into the 'do's and 'don't's of implementing single innovations. We should continue to use this knowledge any time we are working on particular valued priorities. But there is a more fundamental message in the new mind-set that says that thinking in terms of single innovations is inherently limiting, because we are in reality faced with attempting to cope with multiple innovations simultaneously. We have also concluded that it is impossible to implement all these innovations, even if we wanted to. The solution has to be found in making sense of this multiplicity by reducing it – through prioritizing, timing, and synthesizing – to manageable proportions.

Instead of tracing specific policies and innovations, we turn the problem on its head and ask what does the array of innovative possibilities look like if we are on the receiving or shopping end. Thus, institutional development – changes that increase schools' and districts' capacity and performance for continuous improvements – is the generic solution needed.

From going it alone to alliances

Interactive professionalism serves simultaneously to increase access to and scrutiny of each other's ideas and practices. We have seen the debilitating effect of the tradition of individualism in teaching. All successful change processes are characterized by collaboration and close interaction among those central to carrying out the changes. If we are to accomplish change in education, we have to, in Bruce Joyce's coruscating phrase, 'crack the walls of privatism'. Privatism and professional development are closely and inversely linked. Alliances provide greater power, both of ideas and of the ability to act on them.

Alliances are not only across individuals. We have also seen that some of the most powerful strategies involve inter-institutional partnerships – between school districts and universities, businesses and districts, coalitions of schools, and so on.

From neglect to deeper appreciation of the change process

It is so easy to underestimate the complexities of the change process. There is in fact a lot of common sense in successful change processes. Looked at one day, in one setting, successful change seems so sensible and straightforward. But on another day, in another situation, or even the same situation on another day, improvement cannot be obtained with the most sophisticated efforts. Change is difficult because it is riddled with dilemmas, ambivalences, and paradoxes. It combines steps that seemingly do not go together: to have a clear vision and be open-minded; to take initiative and empower others; to provide support and pressure; to start small and think big; to expect results and be patient and persistent; to have a plan and be flexible; to use top-down and bottom-up strategies; to experience uncertainty and satisfaction. Educational change is above all a very personal experience in a social, but often impersonal, setting.

Coping with change effectively requires that we explicitly think and worry about the change process. We should constantly draw upon knowledge about the factors and insights associated with successful change processes. But we must employ this knowledge in a non-mechanical manner along with intuition, experience and assessment of the particular situation, each time adding to our store of common knowledge. Respecting the change process means seeking common patterns while being prepared for uniqueness. This amounts to being self-conscious about the change process as it affects us, and promoting collective self-consciousness about how the process affects others.

From 'if only' to 'if I' or 'if we'

If only statements beg the question, externalize the blame, and immobilize people. Expecting others to act first, or 'waiting for clear instructions before acting' (Block, 1987, p. 16) is self-defeating. Far from letting others off the hook, taking action for oneself puts greater pressure on others to respond than do reams of wishful thinking and verbal advocacy. Every individual can take some effective action in collaboration with one or more other individuals. Organizations do not get healthy by themselves and we would be extremely lucky if our organizations do better through someone else's efforts other than our own. The more 'if I' action that takes place the more 'if we' participation will be generated.

Acting on change is an exercise in pursuing meaning. Selected educational reform that takes individual meaning and development seriously not only stands a better chance of being implemented; it also offers some hope for combating the stagnation, burnout, and cynicism of those in schools – which in the long run will lead to the desiccation of all promising change.

We must first count on ourselves, but do so through constant interaction with others in order to broaden the range of ideas and influence. Paradoxically, counting on oneself for a good cause is the key to system change. New meaning and reform are created in a thousand small ways that eventually add up to a new order of things. Systems do not change by themselves. People change systems through their actions. It is time to change the way we change.

The message

The workplace itself is key. The only solution is that the whole school – all individuals – must get into the change business; if individuals do not do this, they will be left powerless. Individuals must take responsibility for empowering themselves and others through becoming experts in the change process. Individuals must begin immediately to create a new ethos of innovation – one that has the ability to permit and stimulate individual responsibility, and to engage collectively in continuous initiative, thereby pre-empting the imposition of change from outside.

It is time to produce results. Individual and institutional renewal, separately and together, should become our *raison d'etre*.

CHAPTER 15

Reflective teaching and society

The seven readings in this chapter all address the issue of how education relates to society.

Archer begins (Reading 15.1) with an analysis of how education systems develop and change over time in response to an evolving interplay of pressures and constraints.

But what should an education system be designed to achieve? The next group of readings illustrate some classic answers to this question in terms of economic production, cultural reproduction and social justice. Should there be a priority? The National Commission on Education (15.2), although liberal in many respects, tended to emphasize the relationship of education and the generation of international economic competitiveness. On the other hand, Tate (15.3) argues for a curriculum which fosters a greater sense of national identity. Meanwhile, Reading 15.4 from the Council of Europe highlights the case for teaching and learning about human rights. What should be the priorities?

The final group of readings are all concerned with the ways in which changes in policy and practice have impacted on education in the 1990s. Dale (15.5) provides an analysis of how national policies of competition and 'choice' may combine with unequal opportunities and resources to widen the differences between schools. Ball (15.6) argues that governments have introduced new forms of control over teachers through curriculum specification, market forces and new management procedures. In Reading 15.7 Pollard and his colleagues characterize recent changes in primary education in terms of struggles over values, understanding and power. What influence can individuals, such as teachers, have over social structures, such as the education system? And what influence should they have?

The parallel chapter of *Reflective Teaching in the Primary School* reviews the aims of education in relation to social development more broadly. In a section on 'classroom teaching and society' it highlights the value issues which reflective teachers face when they recognize the ways in which their actions contribute to the future identities and life-chances of pupils. Reflective teaching is then related to the democratic process and to the importance of teachers contributing their professional voice to policy debates and public decision making on educational topics. There are practical activities to help in thinking through these issues and there are also many suggestions for further reading.

📖 READING 15.1

Thinking about educational systems

Margaret Archer

> This reading comes from the introduction to Margaret Archer's impressive analysis of the ways in which educational systems form, develop and change through time. She argues that such systems reflect the priorities and conceptions of those who have power. However, such power is likely to be contested and, in any event, those in a position to make policy must also relate their ambitions to the constraints of practical realities. This is a form of macro-sociological analysis (see *Reflective Teaching in the Primary School*, Chapter 3, Section 1.2).
>
> To what extent can you relate Archer's model, as expressed here, to the recent history of changing educational policy?
>
> Edited from: Archer, M. (1979) *The Social Origins of Educational Systems*. London: Sage Publications, 1–3

How do educational systems develop and how do they change?

This first question about the characteristics of education can be broken down into three subsidiary ones: Who gets it? What happens to them during it? Where do they go to after it? These enquiries about inputs, processes and outputs subsume a whole range of issues, many of which have often been discussed independently. They embrace problems about educational opportunity, selection and discrimination, about the management and transmission of knowledge and values and about social placement, stratification and mobility. At the same time they raise the two most general problems of all, namely those about the effects of society upon education and about the consequences of education for society.

The fundamental question here is, 'Why does education have the particular inputs, processes and outputs which characterize it at any given time?' The basic answer is held to be very simple. Education has the characteristics it does because of the goals pursued by those who control it. A second question asks, 'Why do these particular inputs, processes and outputs change over time?' The basic answer given here is equally simple. Change occurs because new educational goals are pursued by those who have the power to modify previous practices. As we shall see, these answers are of a deceptive simplicity. They are insisted upon now, at the beginning, because, however complex our final formulations turn out to be, education is fundamentally about what people have wanted of it and have been able to do to it.

The real answers are more complicated but they supplement rather than contradict the above. It is important never to lose sight of the fact that the complex theories we develop to account for education and educational change are theories about the educational activities of people. This very basic point is underlined for two reasons. Firstly, because however fundamental, much of the literature in fact contradicts it and embodies implicit beliefs in hidden hands, evolutionary mechanisms, and spontaneous adjustments to social change. There education is still seen as mysteriously adapting to social requirements and responding to demands of society not of people. Secondly, and for the present purposes much more importantly, our theories will be about the educational activities of people even though they will not explain educational development strictly in terms of people alone.

The basic answers are too simple because they beg more questions than they solve. To say that education derives its characteristic features from the aims of those who control it immediately raises problems concerning the identification of controlling groups, the bases and processes upon which control rests, the methods and channels through which it is exerted, the extensiveness of control, the reactions of others to this control, and their educational consequences. Similarly, where change is concerned, it is not explained until an account has been given of why educational goals change, who does the changing, and how they impose the changes they seek. To confront these problems is to recognize that their solution depends upon analysing complex forms of social interaction. Furthermore, the nature of education is rarely, if ever, the practical realization of an ideal form of instruction as envisaged by a particular group. Instead, most of the time most of the forms that education takes are the political products of power struggles. They bear the marks of concession to allies and compromise with opponents. Thus to understand the nature of education at any time we need to know not only who won the struggle for control, but also how: not merely who lost, but also how badly they lost.

Secondly, the basic answers are deceptively simple because they convey the impression that education and educational change can be explained by reference to group goals and balances of power alone. It is a false impression because there are other factors which constrain both the goal formation and goal attainment of even the most powerful group – that is the group most free to impose its definition of instruction and to mould education to its purposes. The point is that no group, not even for that matter the whole of society acting in accord, has a blank sheet of paper on which to design national education. Conceptions of education are of necessity limited by the existing availability of skills and resources. Another way of stating this is to say that cultural and structural factors constrain educational planning and its execution. Since this is the case, then explanations of education and educational change will be partly in terms of such factors.

Moreover, only the minimal logical constraints have been mentioned so far: in practice educational action is also affected by a variable set of cultural and structural factors which make up its environment. Educational systems, rarities before the eighteenth century, emerged within complex social structures and cultures and this context conditioned the conception and conduct of action of those seeking educational development. Among other things the social distribution of resources and values and the patterning of vested interests in the existing form of education were crucially important factors. Once a given form of education exists it exerts an influence on future educational change. Alternative educational plans are, to some extent, reactions to it (they represent desires to change inputs, transform processes, or alter the end products); attempts to change it are affected by it (by the degree to which it monopolizes educational skills and resources); and change is change of it (which means dismantling, transforming, or in some way grappling with it).

READING 15.2

A vision for the future

National Commission on Education

> The National Commission on Education was an independent body set up in 1991 following an appeal by Sir Claus Moser for a 'visionary review' of education and the long-term future of the country. Taking evidence from a very wide range of sources in education and outside, the Commission produced a holistic view of the strengths and weaknesses of UK education. They finally identified seven 'goals for achievement', and these are included in the reading below.
>
> Do the priorities reflected in the Commission's goals for achievement seem appropriate to you?
>
> Edited from: Paul Hamlyn Foundation – National Commission on Education (1993) *Learning to Succeed: A Radical Look at Education Today and A Strategy for the Future*. London: Reed Consumer Books

A vision for the future

We adopt the following vision for the future of education and training.

> In all countries knowledge and applied intelligence have become central to economic success and personal and social well-being.
>
> In the United Kingdom much higher achievement in education and training is needed to match world standards.
>
> Everyone must want to learn and have ample opportunity and encouragement to do so.
>
> All children must achieve a good grasp of literacy and basic skills early on as the foundation for learning throughout life.
>
> The full range of people's abilities must be recognized and their development rewarded. High quality learning depends above all on the knowledge, skill, effort and example of teachers and trainers.
>
> It is the role of education both to interpret and pass on the values of society and to stimulate people to think for themselves and to change the world around them.

We now put forward seven goals for achievement in the years ahead in order to make a reality of this vision. We recommend that Governments and all those who have a responsibility or a stake in education and training work together to reach them.

Goal No. 1: High quality nursery education must be available for all 3 and 4 year-olds

Learning starts from birth. Parents are key educators. Nursery education reinforces learning in the home. All children benefit from it, and for many it is essential if they are to learn to succeed. We recommend that it should be made available to all 3 and 4 year-olds.

Goal No. 2: There must be courses and qualifications that bring out the best in every pupil

The framework of curriculum and qualifications for pupils aged 5 to 18 must offer attractive routes to success. The full range of pupils' abilities must be recognized and their development encouraged and rewarded. There must also be paths forward into further or higher education or into work in accordance with individuals' choices and abilities. We recommend an improved curricular framework and a new General Education Diploma at Ordinary and Advanced level.

Goal No. 3: Every pupil in every lesson has the right to good teaching and adequate support facilities

Every pupil has the right to be taught the curriculum offered by the school or college. That means that every pupil is entitled to be taught every lesson by a highly professional teacher competent to teach that lesson. The supporting facilities – the classroom itself, for example, books and the learning technology – must be at least adequate.

Goal No. 4: Everyone must be entitled to learn throughout life and be encouraged in practice to do so

Learning does not stop at 16, at 18, at 21 or at any other age. Everyone must have the entitlement to go on learning whether for employment purposes or to fulfil other personal goals. There must be real opportunity to use the entitlement, and incentive and encouragement to do so.

Goal No. 5: The management of education and training must be integrated, and those with a stake in them must have this recognized

Within the past few years the power of central government in education and training has grown by leaps and bounds. Management of education and of training must be integrated both at the centre and at local level. All those with a major stake in the system must have a place in its management, and full accountability at each level is essential.

Goal No. 6: There must be greater public and private investment in education and training to achieve a better return

There must be continuing efforts to cut waste and raise productivity and quality through innovation and the use of technology. Nevertheless, greater public investment will be required as economic circumstances permit. At the same time there is a need to achieve a better balance in resourcing. More of the costs need to be borne by beneficiaries, both employers and students.

Goal No. 7: Achievement must constantly rise and progress be open for all to examine

The country is faced by a massive and continuing challenge in a fast-changing world. Targets for achievement are already demanding, but they will go on rising and we must therefore constantly seek higher levels of performance. We recommend measures to enable progress to be checked and made the subject of searching and well-informed debate.

READING 15.3

Curriculum, culture and identity

Nicholas Tate

Nicholas Tate was the Chief Executive of the School Curriculum and Assessment Authority when he delivered the speech from which this reading is extracted. Media reports precipitated considerable public debate, with some accusing Dr Tate of being nationalistic and insensitive to minority groups and others supporting his concern to reassert some form of 'English' identity.

What should be the role of schools in relation to the diverse and the dominant cultures of our societies?

Edited from: Tate, N. National Cultures. Mimeo, speech to the Shropshire Secondary Headteachers Annual Conference, July 1995

How can the curriculum foster pupils' cultural literacy and their sense of identity? In Wales there is something called the curriculum Cymreig, an unashamed promotion of Welshness across the curriculum. France is even more explicit that the prime purpose of the curriculum is to provide all French children with a common entitlement to a French identity. But where is this in England? Where is the shared understanding of how the curriculum develops a sense of English identity – or is it British identity? What response does one get when one raises these issues? In my experience it is usually embarrassed silence, ill-focused hostility or a kind of cosmopolitan disdain.

I don't think we are clear how a sense of being English or British might or should be fostered through the curriculum. In part this is because as a society I'm not sure whether we have really come to terms with our identity – beyond the obvious tea towel Englishness of the 'heritage industry'. Nor are we clear about the way in which education ought to serve our broader social and cultural purposes. We began to have some kind of a curriculum debate over the place of Christianity in religious education, and over the content of the English and history curricula, but only in our oblique and empirical English way.

Social, economic and technological changes suggest to me that we need the debate now. Economic globalization and the revolution in communications and information technology have the potential for sweeping aside national identities in a way few had anticipated. Combined with the weakening of traditional social classes and the emergence in western Europe of culturally and ethnically more diverse societies, this conjures up the prospect of a world in which there is little sense of identity intermediate between local or ethnic group identity (where this exists) and the emerging sense of a global 'citizen of the planet' identity. Some welcome this. Others, especially perhaps in nation states like England and France which go back for centuries, regard it with alarm.

In addition, we are now seeing the growth of global meritocratic elites who are as at home in Bali and Buenos Aires as in Brighton or Birmingham and who have no more attachment to one locality than another and to whom the customs, traditions and values of particular places may mean little. These people increasingly take the economic and financial decisions that determine our lives and in some cases even the fates of our governments.

All these developments threaten that sense of belonging to a community which stretches back into the past and forwards into the future which is so important in giving people a sense of meaning in a world which is in a state of constant social, economic and technological flux. A world of social and geographical mobility, frequent job changes, and family breakdown is a world in even greater need of a sense of place, belonging, tradition and purpose, of those things that bind people into distinctive communities.

All this has implications for schools. In my view it involves having a sense of a common culture and making sure that induction into that common culture is a central thread in the school curriculum. In involves providing this for all pupils, whatever their cultural or ethnic background. That is why all children in England must have the English language at the centre of their curriculum, why they need to be introduced to the English literary heritage, to English history (in all its cultural diversity), and to the study of Christianity and to the classical world as the basis of European civilization. This is at the heart of our common culture and our national identity, and every child, whatever their ethnic or cultural background, is entitled to this as at least one of their identities.

People of course can have a more than one identity. When I speak to sixth formers in Tower Hamlets I am very clear that many of them see themselves as both British (or indeed English) and Bengali and that they have no difficulty in living within the two identities side by side. And schools need to respect and indeed develop both. There is a mistaken notion that the way to respond to cultural diversity is to try to bring everything together into some kind of watered down multi-culturalism from which all the component cultures – majority and minority – lose out. This is a mistake. The best guarantee of strong minority cultures is the existence of a majority culture which is sure of itself, which signals that customs and traditions are things to be valued and which respects other cultures.

READING 15.4

Memorandum on teaching and learning about human rights in schools

Council of Europe

> This beginning of this reading reflects its legal origins as a Statute of the Council of Europe, but it goes on to list six areas of for practical action in schools which are intended to develop children's awareness of human rights. This reading clearly represents the long-standing concern that education should promote social justice and, given the complexity and diversity of the societies across Europe, it is not surprising that this should be an important issue for the European Union.
>
> How high a priority do you place on teaching and learning about human rights and the development of social justice?
>
> Edited from: Council of Europe (1985) 'Teaching and learning about human rights in schools', Appendix to Recommendation No. R (85) 7 of the Committee of Ministers to Member States. Strasbourg: Council of Europe

The Committee of Ministers, under the terms of Article 15.b of the Statute of the Council of Europe:

considering that the aim of the Council of Europe is to achieve a greater unity between its members for the purpose of safeguarding and realizing the ideals and principles which are their common heritage.

reaffirming the human rights undertakings embodied in the United Nations Universal Declaration of Human Rights, the Convention for the Protection of Human Rights and Fundamental Freedoms and the European Social Charter.

having regard to the commitments to human rights education made by member states at international and European conferences in the last decade.

recommends that the governments of member states, having regard to their national education systems and to the legislative basis for them:

encourage teaching and learning about human rights in schools in line with the suggestions contained in the appendix hereto;

draws the attention of persons and bodies concerned with school education to the text of this recommendation.

Suggestions for teaching and learning about human rights in schools

Human rights in the school curriculum

The understanding and experience of human rights is an important element of the preparation of all young people for life in a democratic and pluralistic society. It is part of social and political education, and it involves intercultural and international understanding.

Concepts associated with human rights can, and should, be acquired from an early stage. For example, the non-violent resolution of a conflict and respect for other people can already be experienced within the life of a pre-school or primary class.

Opportunities to introduce young people to more abstract notions of human rights, such as those involving an understanding of philosophical, political and legal concepts, will occur in the secondary school, in particular in such subjects as history, geography, social studies, moral and religious education, language and literature, current affairs and economics.

Human rights inevitably involve the domain of politics. Teaching about human rights should, therefore, always have international agreements and covenants as a point of reference, and teachers should take care to avoid imposing their personal convictions on their pupils and involving them in ideological struggles.

Skills

The skills associated with understanding and supporting human rights include:

intellectual skills, in particular:

skills associated with written and oral expression, including the ability to listen and discuss, and to defend one's opinions

skills involving judgement, such as: the collection and examination of material from various sources, including the mass media, and the ability to analyse it and to arrive at fair and balanced conclusions: the identification of bias, prejudice, stereotypes and discrimination:

social skills, in particular:

recognizing and accepting differences; establishing positive and non-oppressive personal relationships: resolving conflict in a non-violent way; taking responsibility; participating in decisions; understanding the use of the mechanisms for the protection of human rights at local regional, European and world levels.

Knowledge to be acquired in the study of human rights

The study of human rights in schools will be approached in different ways according to age and circumstances of the pupil and the particular situations of schools and education systems. Topics to be covered in learning about human rights could include:

the main categories of human rights, duties, obligations and responsibilities;

the various forms of injustice, inequality and discrimination, including sexism and racism;

people, movements and key events, both successes and failures, in the historical and continuing struggle for human rights;

the main international declarations and conventions on human rights such as the Universal Declaration of Human Rights and the Convention for the Protection of Human Rights.

Rights and fundamental freedoms

The emphasis in teaching and learning about human rights should be positive. Pupils may be led to feelings of powerlessness and discouragement when confronted with many examples of violation and negations of human rights. Instances of progress and success should be used.

The study of human rights in schools should lead to an understanding of, and sympathy for, the concepts of justice, equality, freedom, peace, dignity, rights and democracy. Such understanding should be both cognitive and based on experience and feelings. Schools should, thus, provide opportunities for pupils to experience affective involvement in human rights and to express their feelings through drama, art, music, creative writing and audio-visual media.

The climate of the school

Democracy is best learned in a democratic setting where participation is encouraged, where views can be expressed openly and discussed, where there is freedom of expression for pupils and teachers, and where there is fairness and justice. An appropriate climate is, therefore, an essential complement to effective learning about human rights.

Schools should encourage participation in their activities by parents and other members of the community. It may well be appropriate for schools to work with non-governmental organizations which can provide information, case-studies and first-hand experience of successful campaigns for human rights and dignity.

Schools and teachers should attempt to be positive towards all their pupils, and recognize that all their achievements are important – whether they be academic, artistic, musical, sporting or practical.

The climate of the school

The initial training of teachers should prepare them for their future contribution to teaching about human rights in their schools. For example, future teachers should:

be encouraged to take an interest in national and world affairs;

have the chance of studying or working in a foreign country or a different environment;

be taught to identify and combat all forms of discrimination in schools and society and be encouraged to confront and overcome their own prejudices.

Future and practising teachers should be encouraged to familiarize themselves with:

the main international declarations and conventions on human rights;

the working and achievements of the international organizations which deal with the protection and promotion of human rights, for example through visits and study tours.

All teachers need, and should be given the opportunity, to update their knowledge and to learn new methods through in-service training. This could include the study of good practice in teaching about human rights, as well as the development of appropriate methods and materials.

International Human Rights Day

Schools and teacher training establishments should be encouraged to observe International Human Rights Day (10 December).

📖 READING 15.5

Mechanisms of differentiation between schools

Roger Dale

Considering the 'market' into which schools have been placed, Roger Dale provides an analysis of mechanisms which lead to the growth of polarization and difference. In particular, he draws on the economic concept of the 'multiplier effect' to suggest how small initial opportunities or advantages may develop into significant differences.

Are you aware of schools which benefit or suffer from the mechanisms which Dale describes?

Edited from: Dale, R. (1996) Mechanisms of differentiation between schools: The four 'M's. Mimeo. Auckland: University of Auckland

I originally became aware of the mechanisms of polarization between schools when analysing the effects on them of moves to put them on a more 'market-based' footing (Dale, 1994). It seemed clear that a greater or lesser degree of social polarization inevitably attended such shifts but what was not so apparent was precisely how this process took place. It seemed to be about more than mere differences in parental wealth, or reputation, or 'success', or location, though these and many other factors have been identified as 'making a difference' (Connell *et al.*, 1988). The question was not so much how those differences arose as how they made so much difference.

There appear to be at least four mechanisms at work in turning differences between schools (something widely sought and welcomed in itself) into the social polarization of schools. These are what I will call the 'Matthew' effect, the multiplier effect, the marginal effect and the momentum effect. These are neither wholly mutually exclusive nor collectively exhaustive of all possible mechanisms of polarization, but they do enable us to see more clearly how schools become differentiated from each other.

The 'Matthew' effect

The 'Matthew' effect takes its name from the well known verse in St Matthew's gospel, 'to he that hath shall be given'. This can be seen in a number of relevant forms. Perhaps most basic of them is the clearly demonstrated ability of the already well off to gain more from any welfare benefit than the poor to whom the benefit is directed. As LeGrand (1982, 137) puts it, 'there is so much evidence from so many different areas that, almost regardless of the method of provision, the better off will always be able to make more effective use of even a freely provided service than the less well off'. This is as much the case with education as with any other public service. Very simply, the longer you stay in the system the more you get out of it, not just because you are there longer but because successive levels of the education system, from primary, through secondary to tertiary and higher education receive substantially higher per capita funding. Children of middle-class parents are many times more likely to partake of the most expensive level of education, at the post compulsory level, than the children of working-class parents (who are, of course, more numerous as well as more needy). And since the schools themselves receive more funding for older pupils than for most younger pupils, we may perceive inbuilt mutual advantages to schools and middle-class parents.

The greater time and more extensive relevant experience available to middle-class parents also mean than when choice of schools is available they are both more likely to take advantage of the choice opportunity (see, for instance, Willms and Echols, 1992) and to make more fully informed and more closely calculated choices of school than their working-class counterparts. Irrespective of the existence of choice schemes, middle-class parents are more able to choose their child's school, most notably through ability to move residentially.

These better off parents are also able to extend the school's Matthew effect through the additional contributions they are able to make. These involve not just money, but time and expertise of various kinds. These are valuable in themselves but take on much greater value through the operation of the second effect, the multiplier effect.

The multiplier effect

The theory of the multiplier has its origins in economics. Very simply, it states that paying wages to someone not only benefits the recipient directly but also many others less directly. This latter category would include all those involved in the production and distribution of the good or service purchased with wages, who in turn create benefit for their suppliers – of fuel, tyres, labour, etc. – and so on. The point is clear; benefits of an input to an individual or organization extend beyond the immediate recipients. This is the multiplier effect. The crucial thing to note here, however, is that its range and spread are neither random nor predetermined. Not only do schools receive different amounts and kinds of support, but they are able to retain different proportions of the multiplier effects they generate – and, of course, these things are cumulative.

We can see the polarizing consequences of the multiplier effect as a three stage process. The first stage is dominated by the Matthew effect that we have already described. The second stage is what we might call the 'pure' multiplier effect, how much of the multiplier effect of its various inputs the school is able to retain. A useful example here is what services it has to 'contract out' and what it can rely on volunteers for. For instance the school with the 'tame' bank manager or accountant on its governing body has to spend far less on accountancy services than a school unable to call on such volunteers. Further examples are the availability and willingness of parents to transport students to sporting or cultural events, or the ability to provide 'para-educational' support to teachers. All these retain resources within the school and may even mean the difference to the very availability of an activity. At another level schools benefit differentially from the networks of which their parents are part, the social capital on which they are able to draw. Some schools will be able to get property maintenance carried out for the cost of materials only; others will have parents able to 'have a word in the ear' of prominent figures able to influence the contexts in which the school operates.

The third stage is what we will call the 'applied' multiplier effect. This refers to the ways that the school chooses or is able to reap the benefits of the pure multiplier effect. Central here is how much of that benefit can be allocated to activities that directly promote and enhance the school's effectiveness and/or reputation. One paradoxical effect here is that schools with an already high reputation have to divert far fewer resources – in the form of advertising, marketing, etc. – to confirm that reputation than aspiring schools do in order to demonstrate it. The already successful are thus able, potentially at least, to extend the gap between themselves and their rivals by being able to place more of their resources in the activities on which their reputation rests, another example of the cumulative polarizing consequences of the multiplier effect.

At the level of the individual it is plausible to suggest that the outcomes of students' differential amounts of cultural capital are produced through the multiplier effect. At its simplest this means that some schools have populations with relatively low average amounts of cultural capital – defined here as the kinds of knowledge, dispositions, beliefs closely associated with the accepted criteria for school effectiveness and success – and others have relatively larger amounts. The first set of schools has to devote much more of its effort and income – of all kinds – to providing their students with the kind of knowledge, dispositions, etc. that the second set of schools can rely on their pupils bringing with them – and which they can devote their time and energy to enriching and extending.

The marginal effect

The third differentiating effect is the marginal effect. By that I mean the tendency for funding or resources received 'at the margin', on top of basic entitlements, to have a disproportionate influence on the operation of an institution. This occurs because of the 'tagged' or 'earmarked' nature of such additional resourcing. Receiving such funding typically involves some kind of implicit or explicit contractual arrangements, with the operation in some way in the interest of the providers of the benefit. However, since the obligations attached to receiving the basic entitlement are usually far more flexible than those attaching to the 'tagged' funding, there is both the opportunity and the incentive to alter the way the fundamental entitlement is deployed in the direction of accommodating the additional provision; this is how the marginal effect operates. A very good example of this from secondary education is the effect of the additional funding made available (under competitive contract) to schools under the Technical Vocational Education Initiative. In order to obtain the (very considerable) extra funding available through TVEI, schools had to undertake to use it to facilitate changes to their curriculum, pedagogy, equipment and so on. However, it soon became clear that it was not possible to contain the effect of the additional funding within the specified areas; there were intended and unintended 'knock on' effects of various kinds throughout the school. It is these that constituted the marginal effect of the TVEI (see Dale *et al.*, 1990).

One important way that this marginal effect operates in schools is through parental choice. Even where choice of schools is both easy and encouraged, only a minority of parents actually take the opportunity to send their children to any but the nearest school. Bowe and Ball estimate that only 5–10% of parents exercise choice (Bowe and Ball, 1992, p. 29). However, this small number of parents are able to operate in the manner of 'floating voters' in that they are likely to attract rather more attention and to have rather more notice taken of their preferences than parents whose preferences are fixed – and can be relied on by the school – or who are unable for one reason or another to exercise choice. Schools are likely to do more – to change in various ways – in order to attract such additional parents than they do to retain their captive audience. This in itself gives a marginal effect to the preferences of the 'choosing' parents, an effect that may be the more important if we consider the ways in which such parents may differ from the majority.

The momentum effect

The final polarization mechanism, the momentum effect, is also strengthened by, though by no means confined to, moves to extend parental choice of schools. In fact, extending choice both increases the likelihood of, and exaggerates the consequences of the momentum effect. As Ruth Jonathan puts it, 'when market conditions are introduced throughout the state system, the private schooling dilemma of opulent parents in publicly under-resourced areas becomes universalized to all parents' (Jonathan, 1990, p. 126). That is, it introduces the possibility of 'exit' from schools that are deemed to be less satisfactory. Since this exit option is more likely to be taken up by middle class parents it can, in turn, reduce the educational opportunities available to the students who remain there. This can set the school on a downward spiral of falling rolls, consequently reduced curriculum offerings, consequently reduced attractiveness to remaining parents, consequently increased departures and so on in an ever accelerating downward spiral that terminates only when the school contains only those with no motivation or ability to leave it. This, in essence, is the momentum effect. It is further exaggerated by the fact that as the exit option – moving to another school – becomes more attractive, the voice option – taking action to improve a situation – declines in popularity. The consequences of such substitution of exit for voice are the more serious for the abandoned school as the 'exiters' are likely to include those who were the most active in seeking to improve the school through the use of voice.

One especially worrying aspect of the momentum effect is that often it seems to be originated by, and subsequently perpetuated by, not so much a desire to obtain a different kind of school and service but by the wish to get away from a particular type of school clientele; the momentum thus encouraged is much more class or ethnically driven. The phenomenon of 'white flight' is an excellent example of the momentum effect leading to the polarization of schools on ethnic lines.

Two main conclusions may be drawn from this brief discussion of mechanisms that increase the polarization of schools. The first is that these processes are cumulative and may be expected to proceed with increasing speed. Second, they are not directly related to any objective measure of the effectiveness of the schools involved.

READING 15.6

Policy, power and teachers' work

Stephen Ball

In this extract Stephen Ball argues that the restructured curriculum, school exposure to markets and new requirements of management in England and Wales constitute new forms of social control over teachers. In this, he draws on post-structuralist ideas with particular reference to the work of Foucault (see also Readings 11.5 and 13.5 for applications of this analytical approach).

If Ball is right about these new forms of control, then we might not realize that we are being controlled – except perhaps by contrasting our experience with that derived from other contexts. For instance, how do older teachers feel about the changes of recent years? How do teachers from other countries perceive the education system in your country?

Edited from: Ball, S. J. (1994) *Education Reform: A Critical and Post-structural Approach*. Open University Press: Buckingham, 48–64

Here I examine the increasingly over-determined and over-regulated situation of schoolteachers' work and the matrix of power regulations in which they are enmeshed. Specifically, I will be concerned with the three main forms of control which are being used in the UK in an attempt to capture, specify and delineate 'teaching': the curriculum, the market and management. All of this seems to indicate a radical attempt to reconstruct and redefine the meaning and purpose of teaching, both as vocational practice and as mental labour. The analysis as a whole is summarized in Figure 15.6.1 below.

	Curriculum and classroom	The market	Management
Forms of control	commonality prescription intervention	variety mechanism responsivity	consensus? self-regulation flexibility
Teacher as	deliverer tester technician	commodity-producer performer entrepreneur?	resource accountable cost
Changes in	the balance between local and central curriculum	the values and the professional culture of the institution	the relationship of the managers and the managed

Figure 15.6.1 Teachers' work and the matrix of regulation

Curriculum and classroom

In simple terms, here I refer to the imposition of a national curriculum and national testing, and direct and indirect interventions into pedagogical decision making. The three basic message systems of schooling [curriculum assessment and pedagogy, see Reading 7.2] are thus subject to change, and changes in any one system interrelate with and affect the others. In general terms there is an increase in the technical elements of teachers' work and a reduction in the professional. Significant parts of teachers' practice are now codified in terms of Attainment Targets and Programmes of Study, and measured in terms of Standard Attainment Tasks. The spaces for professional autonomy and judgement are (further) reduced (see Dale, 1989b). A standardization and normalization of classroom practice is being attempted. The curriculum provides for standardization and testing for normalization – the establishment of measurements, hierarchy and regulation around the idea of a statistical norm within a given population. This begins with the testing of students, but raises the possibility of monitoring the performance of teachers and schools and making comparisons between them. There is also the possibility of linking these comparisons to appraisal and to performance-related pay awards. These developments also relate to what Lyotard (1984) calls the 'legitimation of education through performativity'. I shall return to this later. Furthermore, significant changes in teachers' classroom practice can now be achieved by decisions taken 'at a distance' about assessment regimes or curriculum organization. Thus, the introduction of separate programmes of study in subjects can 'dictate' the form of student grouping in the school. The possibility of the publication and comparison of test scores may also play a part in teachers' decision making about how much time to devote to whole-class and individual work, or their distribution of attention between different students in the classroom. In all this there is an increasing concern about the quality, character and content of teachers' labour and increasingly direct attempts made by the state to shape the character and content of classroom practice.

Another form of intervention into pedagogy is currently centred upon primary schooling and the campaign among conservative cultural restorationists to re-establish streaming and class teaching. Concomitantly, methods associated with progressivism are under attack (Alexander et al., 1992). What is important here is not so much what is being asserted in the 'debate' over methods as the 'effect' of these assertions in decentring the teacher. What is achieved is a redistribution of significant voices. As always, it is a matter not just of what is said but of who is entitled to speak. The teacher is increasingly an absent presence in the discourses of education policy, an object rather than a subject of discourse.

The market

The second element in the changing matrix of power within which schools are set also has far-reaching implications for the redefinition of teachers' work. The introduction of market forces into the relations between schools means that teachers are now working within a new value context, in which image and impression management are becoming as important as the educational process. Furthermore, in some schools the locus of control is shifting from the producer (teachers) to the consumer (parents) via open enrolments, parental choice and per capita funding. The market is a disciplinary system and within it education is reconstructed as a consumption good. Children and their 'performances' are traded and exchanged as commodities. In relations between schools, the key element of the market is competition. 'The competitive process provides incentives and so evokes effort. The essence of the whole process is choice by the consumer; emulation, rivalry and substitution by the producer' (Reekie, 1984: 37). Teachers' work is thus increasingly viewed and evaluated solely in terms of output measures (test scores and examination performance) set against cost (subject time, class size, resource requirements).

The processes of competition in education are driven by price and by supply and demand, much the same as in other markets, except that in contrast to most commodity markets prices are fixed in relation to LEA budgets and a DfE approved formula. The onus is upon schools to attract clients and maximize income. Marketing and income generation are presently major priorities in the planning and decision making activities of senior managers in many schools (Bowe and Ball with Gold, 1992). In some schools the discourses of financial planning and economic rationalism now operate in an antagonistic relation to the discourses of teaching and learning and pupil welfare.

Management

The examples quoted above already begun to point up the intimate relationship between the control exercised over teachers by parental choice and competition and the role of management. Management and the market are clearly closely intertwined in UK government thinking. As DES Circular 7/88 indicates,

> Local management is concerned with far more than budgeting and accounting procedures. Effective schemes of local management will enable governing bodies and headteachers to plan their use of resources – including their most valuable resource, their staff – to maximum effect in accordance with their own need and priorities, and to make schools more responsive to their clients – parents, pupils, the local community and enjoyers. (DES, 1988b:3)

Further, the point about both management and the market is that they are 'no hands' forms of control as far as the relationship between education and the state is concerned. They provide, in Kickert's (1991:21) terms, 'steering at a distance' – a new paradigm of public governance. Steering at a distance is an alternative to coercive/prescriptive control. Constraints are replaced by incentives. Prescription is replaced by ex post accountability based upon quality or outcome assessments. Coercion is replaced by self-steering – the appearance of autonomy. Opposition or resistance are side-stepped, displaced.

> The refined subtle character of behavioural stimuli makes resistance difficult. The repressive tolerance of such a way of steering might cause a large latent aggression against that steering. Organizations and people cannot defend themselves against measures perceived to be unreasonable. There is no regulated way of protest, complaint or formal appeal. (Kickert, 1991: 26)

From this perspective acquiring a market awareness and the skills of a self-monitoring and individual accountability within the context of 'normal' school activities, would, at least in theory, consolidate the basic principles of self-management within teachers' individual consciousness – decreasing the need for overt control. The individualization of consciousness, oriented towards performativity, constitutes a more subtle yet more totalizing form of control of teachers than is available in the top-down prescriptive steering of state Fordism. Resistance in this context threatens the survival of the institution. It sets the dissenters against the interests of colleagues rather than against policies. Values and interests are thoroughly conflated.

In all this some decisive shifts are achieved: from public debate to private choice, from collective planning to individual decision making. Together, management and the market remove education from the public arena of civil society, from collective responsibility, and effectively 'privatize' it. The scope and availability of provision are no longer matters of national or local political debate or decision-making. They rest, on the one hand, with consumer choice and competitive individualism and, on the other, with the responsive, entrepreneurial decision making of senior managers in schools. We have the closure and atomization of civil society. In general terms, at the heart of this reforming thrust, what is being attempted is a breakdown of the distinction between pubic and private goods and the public and private sectors.

In classical Foucauldian terms, we can see management as a polyvalent discourse. It both liberates and enslaves. It empowers and subjects.

Conclusion

I recognize that I am painting a grim and, in some respects, a crude picture here. It is crude because the complexities of change in and across schools are partly skated over. It is also crude because it deals almost exclusively with policy texts, rather than with the grassroots interpretation and recreation of policy in situ. Even so, the reinscription of power relations in education attempted by the Education Reform Act offers the potential of a massive over-determination of the work of teaching.

> When I think of the mechanics of power, I have in mind rather its capillary form of existence, at the point where power returns into the very grain of individuals, touches their bodies, and comes to insert itself into their gestures and attitudes, their discourses, apprenticeships and daily lives. (Foucault, 1980)

Teachers' careers, institutional micropolitics, and state power and policies re-intertwined in a complex process of changes in patterns of control, relationships and values in schools. The meaning of 'the teacher' and the nature of teaching as a career are at stake, as is, in general terms, the future of education as a public service.

 READING 15.7

Values, understanding and power

Andrew Pollard, Patricia Broadfoot, Paul Croll, Marilyn Osborn and Dorothy Abbott

This final reading is drawn from the conclusion of the first book from the PACE project, which researched the impact of the Education Reform Act, 1988, on primary education in the 1990s. Changes and continuities were each documented, and this was interpreted in terms of a struggle between teachers and government based on differences in values, educational understanding and forms of power. Perhaps this was a particularly rapid and challenging period of change, but the basic issue of the relationship between the commitments of the teaching profession and the policies of government remains vital to constructive educational development.

Do you now feel able to contribute, as a respected partner and with a shared commitment with government, to strategies for the improvement of the quality of education?

Edited from: Pollard, A., Broadfoot P., Croll P., Osborn, M. and Abbott, D. (1994) *Changing English Primary Schools? The Impact of the Education Reform Act at Key Stage One.* London: Cassell, 231–40

Three analytic themes emerged as central to our attempt at interpretation and we identified these themes as values, understanding and power.

Values

Values lie at the heart of all educational decisions. At their most general, these concern the broad commitments which inform educational and social aims and the moral foundations of educational provision.

Such values are fundamental to decisions about curriculum, teaching approaches and the sorts of outcomes which are intended from educational processes. Messages about educational values are either given explicitly in statements of educational aims or are implied by decisions about curriculum, assessment and pedagogy. The feelings and perspectives of teachers and children about their experiences in schools also reflect value positions. Teachers' conceptions about what it is to be a teacher and about the nature of the teaching profession are the cornerstones of their professional ideologies and are inevitably heavily value laden. Children's responses to classroom situations may also be considered in value terms as they begin to absorb the beliefs and commitments of their families, culture and society. Value considerations may thus be used to describe the changing orientations of participants to educational situations and to explain their feelings and perspectives.

We sketched out the historical background to the debate about the nature of English primary schooling, and the way in which changing social, economic and political movements, trends and struggles have impacted on issues concerning the nature and content of that provision. We described the long established traditions of elementary schooling in this country which are rooted in the mass state educational provision of the nineteenth century – and fed by concerns over social order and the perceived need for international competitiveness. This tradition emphasizes the inculcation of basic skills and a moral order through tight central control of curriculum and assessment arrangements, and hence, of teachers and schools. By contrast, the equally long-standing 'developmental' tradition is rooted in the work of major educational philosophers such as Rousseau and Dewey and of influential practitioners such as Maria Montessori and Charlotte Mason. It emphasizes the importance of responding to the needs and interests of the individual child and helping them to 'develop' to their full potential. As we also saw, these differences in values have resonances with the analysis of 'education codes' which has been so powerfully advanced by Bernstein (1975, 1987) [see Reading 7.2].

Into this long-running debate impacted a new market ideology in education which, as in other parts of state provision, brought with it an emphasis on competition and consumerism. Policies rooted in this philosophy have starkly polarized the values of most teachers against those of Government. However, of all the sectors of the education profession, it is arguably primary teachers who have experienced these tensions the most sharply for they had most thoroughly embraced the implications of the developmental tradition. In addition, the emergent professionalism which had been developing in the 1980s was strongly supportive of collaboration between schools, teachers and pupils as a form of learning and collective development. The contrast in value positions could hardly have been more stark.

Teachers initially supported the National Curriculum because of the entitlement to broad and structured experiences which it offered. In this sense, it embodied egalitarian values. Such values had been reflected in relatively undifferentiated curriculum provision in primary schools. However, the National Curriculum and assessment procedures emphasized the need for curriculum differentiation for different pupils. Government and parental concern for academic standards reinforced this, but teachers were nervous about its effects, particularly if it led towards forms of streaming or setting.

Understanding

Understanding is a concept which highlights the representation of what is to count as educationally valid knowledge. Linked to this are assumptions about the nature of teaching and of teachers' roles and about various more specific features of practice such as assessment. The key issue is the contrast between an understanding of education as the inculcation of established knowledge versus its definition as a process of helping learners to construct their own insights and understanding.

Knowledge has traditionally been viewed as an established body of fact which, with associated skills and attitudes, can and should be taught. This view was articulated by the right-wing pressure groups which contributed to the Education Reform Act and was reflected in the subject specification and much of the content of the National Curriculum. An alternative, Piagetian perspective placing emphasis on the ways in which learners construct knowledge from experience, was superseded in the emergent professionalism of the 1980s by a new approach. This approach, influenced by Vygotskian psychologists, informed many curriculum development projects. It drew attention to the importance of experience and instruction and to the nature of the social context in which learning takes place and the support which needs to be available from more knowledgeable others. Both these theories of learning and of the curriculum were reflected in National Curriculum documents. Indeed their uneasy co-existence was the basis for a good deal of the controversy that surrounded the generation of the different subject curricula.

The net effect of this was that, whilst teachers had been gradually evolving one view of knowledge and learning through the 1980s, much of the National Curriculum, and certainly its assessment procedures, required them to act in ways which derived from quite different assumptions. Whilst the former emphasized the teacher's professional skills, judgement and understanding in promoting learning, the latter tended to devalue the professional pedagogic skills of the teacher by implying that the 'delivery' of the curriculum was largely unproblematic. This was well illustrated in the Government's 1993 proposal that non-graduate teachers should be accepted for work with young pupils.

Differing ways of understanding knowledge and learning also have implications for different perspectives on curriculum organization and teaching method. Over the period of the research reported here, considerable pressure was applied to schools to get them to consider introducing more subject specialist teaching, rather than using forms of integrated topic work. This pressure had a strong effect, though it was regretted by many teachers. Similarly, we documented how classroom pedagogy has been changing as new ways of understanding teaching and new educational priorities are put forward.

Understanding of the purpose and capacity of assessment also relates to views of knowledge and learning. Government attention in the early 1990s focused on standardized testing in the hope of providing attainment information for parents and for published school league tables. This strategy assumed that it was both possible and desirable to treat assessments as providing reliable categoric evidence. Teachers had a rather different view. Thus teachers saw the ways in which teacher assessment could feed, formatively, into teaching-learning processes and many embraced this as part of their professional repertoire. Assessment information was treated as provisional evidence, reflecting the continuous learning process. The gap in understanding between teachers and government on this specific issue was very considerable, but it stood as an indicator of a far wider range of differences in perception. This brings us to the issue of power.

Power

Issues of power pervade any consideration of the introduction of educational reform in the early 1990s. Like other major changes, the introduction of the National Curriculum not only involved the direct application of power, but also revealed power relationships which in other times had been hidden or so taken-for-granted that little attention had been paid to them (Lukes, 1974).

The most obvious power struggles involved in the introduction of the National Curriculum were those between central government imposing or requesting changes and the educational service (LEAs, schools, teachers) implementing, mediating or resisting them. The changes introduced in the 1988 legislation were widely interpreted as a shift in the relations of power between central government, local providers of education and the teaching profession. However, as well as demonstrating power over the educational system at governmental and policy making level, the changes associated with the legislation also had implications for the operation of power within schools. Thus there were changes in the implementation of relationships between governors, heads, teachers and parents. Changes in school practices also affect changes in classroom practices and, as we have seen, the relative power of teachers and pupils to influence classroom events has begun to change as teachers attempt to 'deliver' the National Curriculum.

However, whilst power is typically conceived as a means of *control* and source of constraint, it may also be manifest in more positive ways. Changes may, in principle, also be empowering –

for instance, if they allow people to work together in more effective pursuit of agreed goals. Unfortunately, there were few signs of this over the period of our study.

Head teachers in particular faced enormous pressures at the internal/external interface of their schools. They became directly accountable to governors for implementing central policies, but they did not always agree with these nor feel that it was possible to deliver them. Having formally had considerable autonomy in their role, they now felt immensely constrained. In response to this, some head teachers used their power in more managerial ways.

We have also described how classroom teachers were often required to act in ways with which they fundamentally disagreed and considered to be educationally unsound. This was particularly true in relation to the perceived overloading of the curriculum, the pressure for change in pupil–teacher relationships and what was regarded as the inappropriateness of summative assessment procedures.

Teacher responses to this broad but consistent trend varied between compliance, mediation and resistance. Initially, many welcomed the National Curriculum and sought to incorporate it into existing practices. Some drew very constructively on the 'practical theorizing' which had underpinned the emergent professionalism of the 1980s. They attempted to maximize positive aspects of change, such as formative assessment, curriculum progression, the use of subject knowledge and whole-school planning. In so doing, they were, in a sense, recreating their source of professional power in 'expertise'. Other teachers simply tried to survive in the context of rapidly imposed and changing requirements. Workloads, stress-levels and demoralization became very high and teachers began to consider forms of collective action to assert a countervailing power to that of the government. The most telling example of this was provided in 1993 when resistance over assessment requirements led to reporting procedures being boycotted in many schools.

The pressure on head teachers, teachers and pupils was reflected in changes in classroom practices. In particular, teachers used their power over pupils in that context to tighten classroom organization and to increase direction of pupil tasks.

There can be no doubt that, overall, the trends for head teachers, teachers and pupils in terms of power were all in the direction of increased constraint.

Conclusion

The picture we are left with from the first phase of the PACE research reveals change and resistance; commitment and demoralization; decreasing autonomy but some developments in professional skills. Is it possible to make any sense out of these apparently contradictory findings?

Certainly a broad consensus in English primary schools has emerged on the structural benefits of having a national curriculum. It is seen as providing for progression and continuity and, with careful design, it is seen as a potential source of coherence. Organizational benefits for teacher training and supply, continuous professional development, curriculum development, parental participation, teacher accountability and national monitoring of educational standards are accepted.

Unfortunately though, the introduction of the National Curriculum into England was seriously compromised because of the ways in which professionally committed teachers were alienated. The Education Reform Act brought enormous changes for teachers. However, rather than providing a legislative framework through which they could offer and fulfil their professional commitment, the reforms introduced constraint and regulation into almost every area of teachers' work. Yet it seems most unlikely that education standards can rise without the whole-hearted commitment of teachers, working to support pupils' learning.

Having said that, it is also clear that professional commitment has not yet been entirely dissipated. Ironically, collegiality has developed within many schools as a response to the reforms. Unprecedented levels of co-operation are often manifest in schools, between schools and between teacher associations, but these have often been used to defend the quality of the education service against government policies rather than to work in partnership with government towards shared goals.

Our final conclusion then must be one which records, with sadness, the many lost opportunities of this period of change. The amount of legislative time, of financial resources, of public debate and of teacher energy devoted to the innovations was unprecedented. Yet so much was destructive or wasted because of the ideological clash between the government and teachers. Nor are the struggles surrounding the implementation of the Education Reform Act and its supplementary legislation yet over; this is certainly a time in which history is being made.

BIBLIOGRAPHY

ACAS (1986) *Report of the Appraisal/Training Working Group*. London: ACAS

Adair, J. (1983) *Effective Leadership*. London: Pan

Alexander, R. J. (1984) *Primary Teaching*. London: Cassell

Alexander, R. J. (1992) *Policy and Practice in Primary Education*. London: Routledge

Alexander, R. J. (1995) *Versions of Primary Education*. London: Routledge

Alexander, R. J., Rose, J. and Woodhead, C. (1992) *Curriculum Organisation and Classroom Practice in Primary Schools: A Discussion Paper*. London: Department of Education and Science

Alexander, R. J., Wilcocks, J. and Kinder, J. M. (1989) *Changing Primary Practice*. London: Falmer Press

Anderson, B. (1983) *Imagined Communities*. London: Verso Press

Andrews, G. R. and Debus, R. L. (1978) Persistence and the casual perceptions of failure: modifying cognitive attributions, *Journal of Educational Psychology*, **70**, 154–166

Ball, S. J. (1980) *Beechside Comprehensive*. Cambridge: Cambridge University Press

Ball, S. J. (1987) *The Micro-Politics of the School*. London: Methuen

Ball, S. J. (1990) *Politics and Policy Making in Education*. London: Routledge

Barker Lunn, J. (1970) *Streaming in the Primary School*. Slough: NFER

Barnes, D. and Todd, F. (1977) *Communication and Learning in Small Groups*. London: Routledge & Kegan Paul

Barthes, R. (1972) *Mythologies*. London: Cape

Bassey, M. (1978) *Practical Classroom Organisation*. London: Ward Lock

Baumrind, D. (1971) Current patterns of parental authority, *Developmental Psychology Monographs* **4**, 99–103

Bazalgette, C. (ed.) (1989) *Primary Media Education: A Curriculum Statement*. London: British Film Institute

Bell, R. Q. (1979) Parent, child and reciprocal influences, *American Psychologist*, **34**, 821–6

Bellack, A. A., Kliebard, H. M., Hyman, R. T. and Smith, F. L. (1966) *The Language of the Classroom*. New York: Teachers College Press

Bendix, R. (1964) *Nation-Building and Citizenship*. New York: Wiley

Bennett, N., Desforges, C., Cockburn, A. and Wilkinson, B. (1984) *The Quality of Pupil Learning Experiences*. London: Lawrence Erlbaum

Berger, P. L. (1963) *Invitation to Sociology*. New York: Doubleday

Berger, P. L. and Luckman, T. (1967) *The Social Construction of Reality: A Treatise in the Sociology of Knowledge*. Harmondsworth: Penguin

Berlak, A. and Berlak, H. (1981) *The Dilemmas of Schooling*. London: Methuen

Berliner, D. (1984) 'The half-full glass: a review of research on teaching', in Hosford, P. (ed.) *Using What We Know about Teaching*. Alexandria, VA: Association of Supervision and Curriculum Development

Bernstein, B. (1971) *Class, Codes and Control*, Vol. 1. London: Routledge & Kegan Paul

Bernstein, B. (1975) 'Class pedagogies: visible and invisible', *Class Codes and Control*, Vol. 3. London: Routledge & Kegan Paul

Bernstein, B. (1990) *The Structure of Pedagogic Discourse*. London: Routledge & Kegan Paul

Beveridge, M. (ed.) (1982) *Children Thinking Through Language*. London: Edward Arnold

Beyer, L. (1988) *Knowing and Acting: Inquiry, Ideology and Educational Studies*. Basingstoke: Falmer Press

BFI/Department of Education and Science (1986). Not listed in original references

Bickel, W. E. and Bickel, D. D. (1986) Effective schools, classrooms and instruction: implications for special education, *Exceptional Children*, 52, 489–500

Blank, M. (1973) *Teaching Learning in the Pre-School: A Dialogue Approach*. Columbus, Ohio: Merrill

Block, P. (1987) *The Empowered Manager*. San Francisco: Jossey Bass

Blyth, W. A. (1967) *English Primary Education*, Vol. 2. London: Routledge & Kegan Paul

Board of Education (1926) *Education of the Adolescent*, Report of the Consultative Committee (Hadow Report). London: Board of Education

Bowe, R. and Ball, S. J. with Gold, A. (1992) *Reforming Education and Changing Schools*. London: Routledge

Brehony, K. J. (1992) Active citizens: the case of school governors, *International Studies in the Sociology of Education*, 2 (2), 199–213

Brehony, K. J. and Deem, R. (1991) School governing bodies: reshaping education in their own image. Mimeo. Presented to the annual conference of the British Educational Research Association Conference, Nottingham, August

Brighouse, T. (1994) Magicians of the inner city, TES/Greenwich Lecture, *Times Educational Supplement*, 22 April, Section 2, 1–2

Brigley, S. (1991) 'Education accountability and school governors', in Golby, M. (ed.) *Exeter Papers in School Governorship*, 3. Tiverton: Tiverton Publications

Broadfoot, P. and Osborn, M. (1988) What professional responsibility means to teachers: national contexts and classroom contexts, *British Journal of Sociology of Education*, 9 (3), 265–87

Brophy, J. E. and Evertson, C. M. (1976) *Learning from Teaching: A Developmental Perspective*. Boston: Alleyn and Bacon

Brown, P. (1991) The 'third wave': education and the ideology of parentocracy, *British Journal of Sociology of Education*, 11, 65–85

Bruner, J. S. (1966) *Towards a Theory of Instruction*. Cambridge, Mass.: Harvard University Press

Bruner, J. S. (1973) Organisation of early skilled action, *Child Development*, 44, 1–11

Bruner, J. S. (1983) *Child's Talk*. London: Oxford University Press

Bruner, J. S. (1986) *Actual Minds, Possible Worlds*. Cambridge, Mass.: Harvard University Press

Buchmann, M. (1984) 'The priority of knowledge and understanding in teaching', in Katz, L. and Raths, J. (eds) *Advances in Teacher Education*, Vol. 1. Norwood, NJ: Ablex.

Caldwell, B. and Spinks, J. (1988) *The Self-Managing School*. London: Falmer Press

Campbell, R. J. (1993) 'The National Curriculum in primary schools: a dream at conception, a nightmare at delivery', in Chitty, C. and Simon, B., *Education Answers Back: Critical Responses to Government Policy*. London: Lawrence & Wishart

Campbell, R. J. and Neill, S. R. (1992) *Teacher Time and Curriculum Manageability*. London: Assistant Master and Mistresses Association

Campbell, R. J., Evans, L., Packwood, A. and Neill, S, R. St. J. (1991) *Workloads, Achievement and Stress: Two Follow Up Studies of the Use of Teacher Time at Key Stage 1*. London: Assistant Master and Mistresses Association

Cassidy, T. (1986) 'Initiating and encouraging action research in comprehensive schools', in Huster, D., Cassidy, T. and Cuff, T. (eds) *Action Research in Classrooms and Schools*. London: Allen & Unwin

Central Advisory Council for Education (1967) *Children and their Primary Schools* (Plowden Report). London: HMSO

Chang, G. L. & Wells, G. (1988) 'The literate potential of collaborative talk', in MacLure, M., Phillips, T. and Wilkinson, A. (eds) *Oracy Matters*. Milton Keynes: Open University Press

Chitty, C. and Simon, S. (eds) (1993) *Education Answers Back*. London: Lawrence & Wishart

Clark, C. (1988) Asking the right questions about teacher preparation: contributions of research on teacher thinking, *Educational Researcher*, **17** (2), 5–12

Clarricoates, K. (1978) Dinosaurs in the classroom: a re-examination of some aspects of the 'hidden' curriculum in primary schools, in *Women's Studies International Quarterly*, **1**, 353–364

Clift, P. S., Nuttall, D. L. and McCormick, R. (1987) *Studies in School Self-Evaluation*. Lewes: Falmer Press

Cohen, E. G. (1986) *Designing Groupwork: Strategies for the Heterogeneous Classroom*. New York: Teachers College Press

Cooley, C. H. (1902) *Human Nature and the Social Order*. New York, Charles Scribner's Sons

Coulson, A. A. (1978) 'Power and decision-making in the primary school', in Richards, C. (ed.) *Power and the Curriculum: Issues in Curriculum Studies*. Driffield: Nafferton Books

Cowie, M. (1989) 'Children as writers', in Hargreaves, D. (ed.) *Children and the Arts*. Milton Keynes: Open University Press

Cox, C. B. and Boyson, R. (eds) (1977) *Black Paper*. London: Temple Smith

Cox, C. B. and Dyson, A. E. (eds) (1969) *The Crisis in Education: Black Paper 2*. London: Critical Quarterly

Cox, C. B. and Dyson, A. E. (eds) (1970) *Good-bye, Mr Short: Black Paper 3*. London: Critical Quarterly

Croll, P. (1981) 'Social class, pupil achievement and classroom interaction', in Simon, B. and Willcocks, J. (eds) *Research and Practice in the Primary Classroom*. London: Routledge & Kegan Paul

Croll, P. (ed.) (1996) *Teachers, Pupils and Primary Schooling*. London: Cassell

Cruickshank, D. (1987) *Reflective Teaching*. Reston, VA: Association of Teacher Educators

Dadds, M. (1993) The changing face of topic work in the primary curriculum, *The Curriculum Journal*, **4**, (2), 253–267

Dale, R. (1981) 'Control, accountability and William Tyndale', in Dale, R., Esland, G., Fergusson, R. and Macdonald, M. (eds) *Education and the State: Politics, Patriarchy and Practice*. London: Falmer Press

Damerell, R. (1985) *Education's Smoking Gun: How Teachers' Colleges have Destroyed Education in America*. New York: Freandlich Books

David, T., Curtis, A. and Siraj-Blatchford, I. (1992) *Effective Teaching in the Early Years*, an OMEP (UK) Report. Coventry: Warwick Univeristy, Department of Education

Dearing, R. (1993) *The National Curriculum and its Assessement: an Interim Report*. London: SCAA

Deem, R. (1990) 'The reform of school governing bodies: the power of the consumer over the producer'? in Flude, M. and Hammer, M. (eds) *The Education Reform Act: Its Origins and Implications*. London: Falmer Press

Department for Education (1992) *Initial Teacher Training (Secondary Phase)*, DFE Circular 9/92. London: DFE

Department for Education (1993) *The Government's Proposals for the Reform of Initial Teacher Training*. London: DFE

Department of Education and Science (1974) *A Language for Life* (The Bullock Report). London: HMSO

Department of Education and Science (1977) *A New Partnership for Our Schools* (The Taylor Report). London: HMSO

Department of Education and Science (1977) *Ten Good Schools*. London: HMSO

Department of Education and Science (1978a) *Primary Education in England: A Survey by HMI*. London: HMSO

Department of Education and Science (1978b) *Special Educational Needs* (The Warnock Report). London: HMSO

Department of Education and Science (1981a) *West Indian Children in Our Schools*, Interim Report of the Committee from Ethnic Minority Groups (The Rampton Report). London: HMSO

Department of Education and Science (1981b) *The School Curriculum*. London: HMSO

Department of Education and Science (1982) *Mathematics Counts* (The Cockcroft Report). London: HMSO

Department of Education and Science (1983) *Teaching Quality*. London: HMSO

Department of Education and Science (1984a) *Parental Influence at School* (Green Paper). London: HMSO

Department of Education and Science (1984b) *Better Schools*. London: HMSO

Department of Education and Science (1985) *Science 5 to 16: A Statement of Policy*. London: HMSO

Department of Education and Science (1986) *English from 5 to 16*. London: HMSO

Department of Education and Science (1987) *Mathematics from 5–16*. London: HMSO

Department of Education and Science (1988) *The Local Management of Schools*: Circular 7/88. London: DES

Department of Education and Science (1991a) *Standards in Education 1989–90: The Annual Report of HM Senior Chief Inspector of Schools*. London: HMSO

Department of Education and Science (1991b) *The Parent's Charter*. London: DES

Department of Education and Science (1992) *Reform of Initial Teacher Training: A Consultation Document*. London: DES

Department of Education and Science, Welsh Office (1985) *Science 6 to 16: A Statement of Policy*. London: HMSO

DiMaggio, P. and Powell, W. (1983) The iron cage revisited, *American Sociological Review*, 48 (2), 147–60

Donaldson, M. (1978) *Children's Minds*. London: Fontana

Doyle, W. (1979) 'Classroom tasks and student abilities', in Peterson, P. and Walberg, H. J. (eds) *Research on Teaching: Concepts, Findings and Implications*. Berkeley, CA: McCutchan

Doyle, W. (1983) Academic work, *Review of Educational Research*, 53 (2), 159–99

Doyle, W. (1986) 'Classroom organisation and management', in Wittrock, M. (ed.) *3rd Handbook of Research on Teaching*. New York: Macmillan

Driver, R. (1983) *The Pupil as Scientist?*. Milton Keynes: Open University Press

Duckworth, E. (1987) *The Having of Wonderful Ideas*. New York: Teachers College Press

Durkheim, E. (1961) *Moral Education*. New York: Free Press

Dusek, J. and Joseph, G. (1983) The bases of teacher expectancies: a meta-analysis, *Journal of Educational Psychology*, 75 (3), 327–346

Dweck, C. S. (1975) The role of expectations and attributions in the alleviation of learned helplessness, *Journal of Personality and Social Psychology*, 31, 674–685

Edwards A. D. and Westgate, D. P. G. (1987) *Investigating Classroom Talk*. London: Falmer Press

Edwards, A. D. and Furlong, V. J. (1978) *The Language of Teaching*. London: Heinemann

Edwards, D. and Mercer, N. (1987) *Common Knowledge: The Development of Understanding in Classrooms*. London: Methuen

Edwards, V. (1983) *Language in Multi-Cultural Classrooms*. London: Batsford

Evans, L., Packwood, A., Neill, S. R. St. J. and Campbell, R. J. (1994) *The Meaning of Infant Teachers' Work*. London: Routledge

Evetts, J. (1990) *Women Teachers in Primary Education*. London: Methuen

Feiman-Nemser, S. (1990) 'Teacher preparation: structural and conceptual alternatives', in Houston, W. R. (ed.) *Handbook of Research on Teacher Education*. New York: Macmillan

Flew, A. (1987) *Power to the Parents*. London: Sherwood Press

Foucault, M. (1977) *Discipline and Punish: The Birth of the Prison*. London: Penguin

Foucault, M. (1980) *Power/Knowledge: Selected Interviews and Other Writings, 1922–77*. Brighton: Harvester Press

Fullan, M. G. and Hargreaves, A. (1991) *What's Worth Fighting For? Working Together for Your School*. Toronto, Ontario: Institute for Studies in Education

Fuller, F. and Bown, O. (1975) 'Becoming a teacher', in Ryan, K. (ed.) *Teacher Education*, 74th Yearbook of the National Society for the Study of Education, Part 2. Chicago: University of Chicago Press

Gallie, D. and White, M. (1993) *Employee Commitment and the Skills Revolution: Findings for the Employment in Britain Survey*. Oxford: Nuffield College

Galton, M. (1989) *Teaching in the Primary School*. London: David Fulton

Galton, M., Simon, B. and Croll, P. (1980) *Inside the Primary Classroom*. London: Routledge & Kegan Paul

Geertz, C. (1968) 'Religion as cultural system', in Cutler, D. (ed.) *The Religious Situation*. Boston, MA: Beacon Press

Geertz, C. (1973) *The Interpretation of Cultures*. New York: Basic Books

Gifford, B. R. and O'Connor, M. C. (eds) (1992) *Changing Assessments: Alternative Views of Aptitude, Achievement and Instruction*. Boston: Kluwer

Gill, D. (1977) *Appraising Performance*. London: IPM

Goffman, E. (1961) *Asylums*. New York: Anchor Books, Doubleday

Goodacre, E. (1968) *Teachers and Their Pupils' Home Background*. Slough: NFER

Gracey, H. (1972) *Curriculum or Craftsmanship: Elementary School Teachers in a Bureaucratic System*. Chicago: University of Chicago Press

Graves, D. (1983) *Writing: Teachers and Children at Work*. Exeter, NH: Heinemann

Hargreaves, D. (1983) *The Challenge for the Comprehensive School*. London: Routledge & Kegan Paul

Hargreaves, D. and Hopkins, D. (1991) *The Empowered School*. London: Cassell

Harlen, W. (1991) National Curriculum assessment: increasing the benefit by reducing the burden, in *Education and Change in the 1990s*, Journal of the Educational Research Network of Northern Ireland, 5, February, 3–19

Harlen, W., Gipps, C., Broadfoot, P. and Nuttall, D. (1992) Assessment and the improvement of education, *The Curriculum Journal*, 3 (3), 215–230

Heath, S. B. (1983) *Ways with Words*. Cambridge: Cambridge University Press

Henriques, J. (1984) 'Social psychology and the politics of racism', in Henriques, J., Hollway, W., Urwin, C., Venn, C. and Walkerdine, V. *Changing the Subject. Psychology Social Regulation and Subjectivity*. London: Methuen

Her Majesty's Inspectorate (1989) *Aspects of Primary Education: The Teaching of Mathematics*. London: HMSO

Hillgate Group (1986) *Whose Schools? A Radical Manifesto*. London: Claridge Press

Hillgate Group (1987) *Refrom of British Education*. London: Claridge Press

Hirst, P. H. (1974) *Knowledge and the Curriculum*. London: Routledge & Kegan Paul

Hopkins, A. (1978) *The School Debate*. Harmondsworth: Penguin

Hopkins, B. L. and Conrad, R. J. (1976) 'Putting it all together: super school', in Haring, N. G. and Schiefelbush, R. C. (eds) *Teaching Special Children*. New York: McGraw Hill

Hopkins, D. (ed.) (1987) *Improving the Quality of Schooling*. Lewes: Falmer Press

House of Commons (1986) *Achievement in Primary Schools*, Report of the Select Committee on Education, Science and the Arts. London: House of Commons

Hoyle, E. (1975) 'Professionality, professionalism and control', in Houghton, V., McHugh, R. and Morgan, C. (eds) *Management in Education Reader I*. London: Ward Lock

Hoyle, E. (1980) 'Professionalization and deprofessionalization in education', in Hoyle, E. and Megarry, J. (eds) *World Yearbook of Education 1980: Professional development of teachers*. London: Kogan Page

International Labour Office (ILO) (1991) *Teachers: Challenges of the 1990s: Second Joint Meeting on Conditions of Work of Teachers*. Geneva: International Labour Office

Jackson, P. W. (1977) 'The way teachers think', in Glidwell, J. C. (ed.) *The Social Context of Learning and Development*. New York: Gardner Press

James, W. (1890) *The Principles of Psychology*. New York: Henry Holt

Jensen, A. (1967) The culturally disadvantaged; psychological and educational aspects, *Educational Research*, **10**, 4–20

Jones, K. B. (1991) The trouble with authority, *Differences*, **3** (1), 104–127

Jordan, J. (1974) The organisation of perspectives in teacher–pupil relations: an interactionist approach. Unpublished M.Ed. thesis: University of Manchester

Joshi, H., Layard, R. and Owen, S. (1982) *Female Labour Supply in Post-war Britain*. London: Centre for Labour Economics

Kamin, L. S. (1974) *The Science and Politics of IQ*. Chichester: Wiley

Kanter, R. M. (1974) 'Commitment and social organization', in Field, D. (ed.) *Social Psychology for Sociologists*. London: Nelson

Kemmis, S. (1985) 'Action research and the politics of reflection', in Boud, D., Keogh, R. and Walker, D. (eds) *Reflection: Turning Experience into Learning*. London: Croom Helm

Kickert, W. (1991) Steering at a distance; a new paradigm of public governance in Dutch higher education. Mimeo. Presented to the European Consortium for Political Research, University of Essex, March

King, R. (1978) *All Things Bright and Beautiful?: a Sociological Study of Infant Schools*. Chichester: Wiley

Kirp, D. (1983) 'Professionalisation as policy choice: British special education in comparative perspective', in Chambers, R. G. and Hartman, W. T. (eds) *Special Education Policies*. Philadelphia: Temple University Press

Koerner, J. (1963) *The Miseducation of American Teachers*. Boston: Houghton Mifflin

Kogan, M., Johnson, D., Packwood, T. and Whittaker, T. (1984) *School Governing Bodies*. London: Heinemann

Kounin, J. S. (1970) *Discipline and Group Management in Schools Classrooms*. London: Holt, Rinehart & Winston

Krasner, S. D. (ed.) (1983) *International Regimes*. Ithaca, New York: Cornell University Press

Lacey, C. (1976) 'Problems of sociological fieldwork: a review of the methodology of Hightown Grammar', in Hammersley, M. and Woods, P. (eds) *The Process of Schooling*. London: Routledge & Kegan Paul

Leiberman, A. and Miller, L. (1984) *Teachers: Their World and Their Work*. Alexandria, VA: Association for Supervision and Curriculum Development

Lemlech, J. K. (1979) *Classroom Management*, New York: Harper and Row

Leont'ev, A. N. (1981) *Problems of the Development of Mind*. Moscow: Progress Publishers

Lewin, N., Lippitt, R. and White, R. K. (1939) Patterns of aggressive behaviour in experimentally created social climates, *Journal of Social Psychology*, 10, 271–299

Lortie, D. (1975) *School Teacher: a Sociological Study*. Chicago: University of Chicago Press

Luke, A. (1991) 'Stories of social regulation: the micropolitics of classroom narrative', in Green, B. (ed.) *The Insistence of the Letter: Literacy and Curriculum Theorizing*. London: Falmer Press

Lukes, S. (1974) *A Radical View of Power*. London: Macmillan

Lyotard, J. F. (1984) *The Post-modern Condition: a Report on Knowledge*. Manchester: Manchester University Press

MacKintosh, N. J. and Mascie-Taylor, C. G. N. (1985) 'The IQ question', Annex D of Department of Education and Science, *Education for All* (The Swann Report). London: HMSO

Macleod, D. and Meikle, J. (1994) 'Education changes "making head quit"', *The Guardian*, 1 September

MacLure, M. (1992) 'The first five years', in Norman, K. (ed.) *Thinking Voices: The Work of the National Oracy Project*. London: Hodder & Stoughton

MacLure, S. (1993) 'Fight this tooth and nail', *The Times Educational Supplement*, 18 June

Maher, F. and Rathbone, C. (1986) Teacher education and feminist theory: some implications for practice, *American Journal of Education*, 94 (2), 214–35

Marland, M. (1975) *The Craft of the Classroom: A Survival Guide*. London: Heinemann

Marshall, T. H. (1948) *Class, Citizenship and Social Development*. Garden City, NJ: Doubleday

McGarrigle, J. and Donaldson, M. (1974) Conservation accidents, *Cognition*, 3, 341–50

McPherson, A. (1992) *Measuring Added Value in Schools*, National Commission on Education Briefing No. 1. London: National Commission on Education

McTear, M (1985) *Children's Conversation*. Oxford: Blackwell

Meikle, J. (1992) 'Patten seizes schools', *The Guardian*, 29 July

Meyer, J. W. (1980) 'The world polity and the authority of the nation-state', in Bergesen, A. (ed.) *Studies of the Modern World-System*. New York: Academic Press

Miller, A. (1987) Cognitive styles: an integrated model, *Educational Psychology*, 7, 251–269

Moran, P. (1971) The integrated day, *Educational Research*, 14 (1), 65–9

Morrison, A. and McIntyre, D. (1969) *Teachers and Teaching*. Harmondsworth: Penguin

Mortimore, P., Sammons, P., Stoll, L., Lewis, D. and Ecob, R. (1988) *School Matters: The Junior Years*. Wells: Open Books

Murphy, J. (1974) Teacher expectations and working-class underachievement, *British Journal of Sociology*, 25 (3), 326–44

Muschamp, Y., Pollard, A. and Sharpe, R. (1992) Curriculum management in primary schools, *The Curriculum Journal*, 3 (1), 21–39

Nash, R. (1973) *Classrooms Observed: The Teachers' Perception and Pupils' Performance*. London: Routledge & Kegan Paul

National Oracy Project (1990) *Teaching, Talking and Learning in Key Stage One*. York: National Curriculum Council

Newman, D., Griffin, P. and Cole, M. (1989) *The Construction Zone*. Cambridge: Cambridge University Press

Nias, J. (1988) 'Informal education in action: teachers' accounts', in Blyth, A. (ed.) *Informal Primary Education Today*. London: Falmer Press

Nias, J. (1989) *Primary Teachers Talking: A Study of Teaching as Work*. London: Routledge

Nias, J., Southworth, G. and Yeomans, R. (1989) *Staff Relationships in the Primary School: a Study of Organizational Cultures*. London: Cassell

Nowell-Smith, P. H. (1958) 'Education in a University'. Inaugural lecture. Leicester: Leicester University Press

OFSTED (1993) *Curriculum Organisation and Classroom Management in Primary Schools: A Follow-up Report*. London: HMSO

Osborn, M. (1986) Profiles of a typical French and English primary teacher. Mimeo. Bristol: University of Bristol

Paley, V. G. (1981) *Wally's Stories*. Cambridge, Mass.: Harvard University Press

Perrone, V. (1989) *Working Papers: Reflections on Teachers, Schools and Communities*. New York: Teachers College Press

Phillips, T. (1988) 'On a related matter: why "successful" small-group talk depends on not keeping to the point', in MacLure, M., Phillips, T. and Wilkinson, A. (eds) *Oracy Matters*. Milton Keynes: Open University Press

Pollard, A. (1985) *The Social World of the Primary School*. London: Cassell

Pollard, A. (1987) *Children and Their Primary Schools*. London: Falmer Press

Pollard, A., Broadfoot, P., Croll, P., Osborn, M. and Abbott, D. (1994) *Changing English Primary Schools?*. London: Cassell

Popham, W. J. (1993) *Educational Evaluation* (3rd ed.). Boston: Allyn and Bacon

Proctor, N. (ed.) (1990) *The Aims of Primary Education and the National Curriculum*. London: Falmer Press

Purkey, S. and Smith, M. (1983) Effective schools: a review, *The Elementary School Journal*, 83 (4), 427–452

Radley, A. (1980) 'Student learning as social practice in Salmon', P. (ed.) *Coming to Know*. London: Routledge & Kegan Paul

Reekie, W. D. (1984) *Market, Entrepreneurs and Liberty*. Brighton: Wheatsheaf

Resnick, L. B. and Resnick, D. P. (1992) 'Assessing the thinking curriculum: new tools for educational reform', in Gifford, B. R. and O'Connor, M. (eds) *Changing Assessments: Alternative Views of Aptitude, Achievement and Instruction*. Boston: Kluwer

Richardson, L. (1990) Narrative and sociology, *Journal of Contemporary Ethnography*, **19** (1), 116–135

Rogers, C. R. (1951) *Client-Centered Therapy*. Boston: Houghton Mifflin

Rosenthal, R. and Jacobson, L. (1968) *Pygmalion in the Classroom*. New York: Holt, Rinehart & Winston

Ross, D. and Kyle, D. (1987) Helping preservice teachers learn to use teacher effectiveness research, *Journal of Teacher Education*, 38, 40–4

Rowland, S. (1984) *The Enquiring Classroom*. Lewes: Falmer Press

Rowland, S. (1987) 'Child in control: an interpretative model of teaching and learning', in Pollard, A. (ed.) *Children and Their Primary Schools*. London: Falmer Press

Rutter, M., Maughan, B., Mortimore, P. and Ouston, J. (1979) *Fifteen Thousand Hours*. London: Open Books

Sallis, J. (1988) *Schools, Parents and Governors*. London: Routledge

Sarason, S. (1982) *The Culture of the School and the Problem of Change* (2nd ed.), Boston: Allyn and Bacon

Sarup, M. (1991) *Education and the Ideologies of Racism*. Stoke-on-Trent: Trentham Books

Schon, D. A. (1983) *The Reflective Practitioner: How Professionals Think in Action*. London: Temple Smith

Schwab, J. J. (1978) *Science, Curriculum and Liberal Education*. Chicago: University of Chicago Press

Sexton, S. (1987) *Our Schools: A Radical Policy*. London: IEA Education Unit

Sharpe, S. (1984) *Double Identity*. Harmondsworth: Penguin

Shribner, S. (1985) 'Vygotsky's uses of history', in Wertsch, J. V. (ed.) *Culture, Communication and Cognition: Vygotskian perspectives*. Cambridge: Cambridge University Press

Shulman, L. (1987) Knowledge and teaching: foundations of the new reform, *Harvard Educational Review*, 57, 1–22

Shumsky, A. (1956) Co-operation in action research: a rationale, *Journal of Educational Sociology*, 30, 180–5

Sikes, P., Measor, L. and Woods, P. (1985) *Teacher Careers: Crises and Continuities*. Lewes: Falmer Press

Simons, H. (1987) *Getting to Know Schools in a Democracy: The Politics and Process of Evaluation*. Lewes: Falmer Press

Sloane, H. N. (1976) *Classroom Management: Remediation and Prevention*. New York: Wiley

Sluckin, A. (1981) *Growing up in the Playground*. London: Routledge & Kegan Paul

Spender, D. (1980) *Man-made Language*. London: Routledge & Kegan Paul

Stanworth, M. (1981) *Gender and Schooling: A Study of Sexual Divisions in the Classroom*. London: Hutchinson

Stebbings, R. (1980) 'The role of humour in teaching: stategy and self expression', in Woods, P. (ed.) *Teacher Strategies*. London: Croom Helm

Stott, D. H. (1978) *Helping Children with Learning Difficulties*. London: Ward Lock Education

Suffolk Education Authority (1987) *In the Light of Torches*. London: Industrial Society

Tanner, L. N. (1978) *Classroom Discipline*. New York: Holt, Rinehart & Winston

Thomas G., Meyer, J. W., Ramirez, F. O. and Boli, J. (1987) *Institutional Structure: Constituting State, Society and the Individual*. Beverly Hills, CA: Sage

Thomas, N. (1985) *Improving Primary Schools: Report of the Committee on Primary Education* (The Thomas Report). London: ILEA

Tizard, B. and Hughes, M. (1984) *Young Children Learning*. London: Fontana

Tomlinson, S. (1982) *The Sociology of Special Education*. London: Routledge & Kegan Paul

Tough, J. (1977) *The Development of Meaning*. London: Allen & Unwin

Trudgill, P. (1975) *Accent, Dialect and the School*. London: Edward Arnold

Tyler, R. W. (1949) *Basic Principles of Curriculum and Instruction*. Chicago: University of Chicago Press

Valli, L. (1992) *Reflective Teacher Education: Cases and Critiques*. New York: SUNY Press

Van Velzen, W. *et al.* (1985) *Making School Improvement Work*. Lauven, Belgium: ACCO

Varlaam, A., Nuttall, D. and Walker, A. (1992) *What Makes Teachers Tick?: A Survey of Teacher Morale and Motivation*. London: London School of Economics, Centre for Educational Research

Vygotsky, L. S. (1978) *Mind in Society: The Development of Higher Psychological Processes*. Cambridge, Mass.: Harvard University Press

Vygotsky, L. S. (1981) 'The development of higher mental functions', in Wertsch, J. V. (ed.) *The Concept of Activity in Soviet Psychgology*. Amonk, NY: Sharpe

Vygotsky, L. S. (1962) *Thought and Language*. Cambridge, Mass.: MIT Press

Walker, R. and Adelman, C. (1976) 'Strawberries', in Stubbs, M. and Delamont, S. (eds) *Explorations in Classroom Observation*. Chichester: Wiley

Walkerdine, V. (1984) 'Developmental psychology and the child-centred pedagogy; the insertion of Piaget into early education', in Henriques, J., Hollway, C., Urwin, C., Venn, C. and Walkerdine, V., *Changing the Subject*. London: Methuen

Walkerdine, V. (1984) 'Some day my prince will come', in McRobbie, A. and Nava, M. (eds) *Gender and Generation*. London: Macmillan

Walkerdine, V. (1985) 'On the regulation of speaking and silence: subjectivity, class and gender in contemporary schooling', in Steedman, C., Urwin, C. and Walkerdine, V. (eds) *Language, Gender and Childhood*. London: Routledge & Kegan Paul

Wallace, G. and Kauffman, J. M. (1978) *Teaching Children with Learning Problems*. Columbus, Ohio: Merrill

Waller, W. (1961) *Sociology of Teaching*. New York: Russell and Russell

Webb, R. (1993a) The National Curriculum and the changing nature of topic work, *The Curriculum Journal*, **4** (2), 239–251

Webb, R. (1993b) *Eating the Elephant Bit by Bit: The National Curriculum at Key Stage 2*. London: Associaton of Teachers and Lecturers

Weber, M. (1964) *The Theory of Social and Economic Organization*. New York: Free Press

Weiner, G. (1985) 'Equal opportunities, feminism and girls' education: introduction', in Weiner, G. (ed.) *Just a Bunch of Girls: Feminist Approaches to Schooling*. Milton Keynes: Open University Press

Welch. A. R. (1993) Class, culture and the state in comparative education: problems, perspectives and prospects, *Comparative Education* **29** (1), 7–27

Wells, G. (1985) *Language at Home and in School*. Cambridge: Cambridge University Press

Wells, G. (1986) *The Meaning Makers: Children Learning Language and Using Language to Learn*. Sevenoaks: Hodder & Stoughton

Wertsch, J. V. (1979) From social interaction to higher psychological process: a clarification and application of Vygotsky's theory, *Human Cognition*, **2** (1), 15–18

Wheeler, D. K. (1967) *Curriculum Process*. London: University of London Press

White, J. (1993) 'What place for values in the National Curriculum', in O'Hear, P. and White, J. (eds) *Assessing the National Curriculum*. London: Paul Chapman

Whitehead, A. N. (1932) *The Aim of Education*. London: Williams and Northgate

Wise, A. E. *et al.* (1985) Teacher evaluation: a study of effective practices, *The Elementary School Journal*, **86**, 61–121

Wood, D. J., Bruner, J. S. and Ross, G. (1976) The role of tutoring in problem solving, *Journal of Child Psychology and Psychiatry*, **17** (2), 89–100

Woods, P. (1976) 'Having a laugh: an antidote to schooling', in Hammersley, M. and Woods, P. (eds) *The Process of Schooling*. London: Routledge & Kegan Paul

Woods, P. (1979) *The Divided School*. London: Routledge & Kegan Paul

Woods, P. (1987) 'Managing the primary teacher's role', in Delamont, S. (ed.) *The Primary School Teacher*. Lewes: Falmer Press

Woods, P. (1990) *Teacher Skills and Strategies*. Lewes: Falmer Press

Woods, P. A. (1992) Empowerment through choice? Initial findings of a case study investigating parental choice and school responsiveness. Mimeo. CEDAR Conference, University of Warwick, April

Zeichner, K. and Liston, D. (1990) *Traditions of Reform and Reflective Teaching in US Teacher Education* (Issue Paper 90–1). East Lansing, MI: National Center for Research on Teacher Education

Zeichner, K. M. and Gore, J. M. (1990) 'Teacher socialisation', in Houston, W. R. (ed.) *Handbook of Research on Teacher Education*. New York: Macmillan

PERMISSIONS DETAILS

Chapter 1

1.1 'Thinking and reflective experience', by John Dewey, edited from *How We Think: A Restatement of the Relation of Reflective Thinking to the Educative Process* (1933), published by Henry Regnery, and from *Democracy and Education* (1916), published by the Free Press

1.2 'Reflection-in-action', by Donald Schon, edited from *The Reflective Practitioner* (1983), published by Temple Smith and reproduced by permission of Ashgate Publishing

1.3 'Dilemmas of schooling', by Ann and Harold Berlak, edited from *Dilemmas of Schooling* (1981), reproduced by permission of Ann and Harold Berlak and Routledge

1.4 'Training skilful teachers', by Ted Wragg, edited from *Primary Teaching Skills* (1993), reproduced by permission of Ted Wragg and Routledge

1.5 'Analysing the role of mentors', by John Sampson and Robin Yeomans, edited from *Mentorship in the Primary School* (1994), reproduced by permission of Falmer Press

1.6 'Criteria for initial teacher training in England: primary phase', by the Council for the Accreditation of Teacher Education, edited from *The Initial Training of Primary School Teachers*, DFE Circular 14/93 (England). Crown copyright reproduced by permission of the Controller of HMSO

1.7 'Two models of professionalism', by John Elliott, edited from 'A model of professionalism and its implications for teacher education', *British Educational Research Journal*, **17** (4) (1991), reproduced by permission of Carfax Publishing Company

1.8 'Competence and the complexities of teaching', by James Calderhead, edited from 'Can the complexities of teaching be accounted for in terms of competencies. Contrasting views of professional practice from research and policy' (1994) mimeo, reproduced by permission of James Calderhead

Chapter 2

2.1 'The sociological imagination', by C. Wright Mills, edited from The Sociological *Imagination* (1959), reproduced by permission of Oxford University Press, Inc., copyright Oxford University Press (1959), renewed 1987 by Yavaslava Mills

2.2 'Can education change society', by Brian Simon, edited from *Does Education Matter?* (1985), published by Lawrence and Wishart

2.3 'Emancipatory and life politics', by Anthony Giddens, edited from *Modernity and Self-Identity: Self and Society in the Late Modern Age* (1991), reproduced by permission of Blackwell Publishers

2.4 'The contexts of policy making', by Richard Bowe and Stephen Ball, edited from *Reforming Education and Changing Schools: Case Studies in Policy Sociology* (1992), reproduced by permission of Stephen Ball and Routledge

2.5 'Teacher education and professionalism', by Len Barton, Elizabeth Barrett, Geoff Whitty, Sheila Miles and John Furlong, edited from 'Teacher education and teacher professionalism in England: some emerging issues', in *British Journal of Sociology of Education*, 15 (4) (1994), reproduced by permission of Carfax Publishing Company

2.6 'European variations in primary education', by Norman Thomas, edited from *Handbook of Primary Education in Europe* edited by Maurice Galton and Alan Blyth (1989), reproduced by permission of David Fulton Publishers

Chapter 3

3.1 'The teacher as researcher', by Lawrence Stenhouse, edited from *An Introduction to Curriculum Research and Development* (1975), reproduced by permission of the trustees of the estate of Lawrence Stenhouse

3.2 'Practical action as praxis', by Wilfred Carr and Stephen Kemmis, edited from *Becoming Critical: Education, Knowledge and Action Research* (1986), reproduced by permission of Falmer Press

3.3 'Collaboration and action research', by Rosemary Webb, edited from 'The processes and purposes of practioner research', in *Practitioner Research in the Primary School* edited by R. Webb (1990), reproduced by permission of Falmer Press

3.4 'Four practical problems', by Richard Winter, edited from *Learning from Experience* (1989), reproduced by permission of Falmer Press

3.5 'Three paradigms of educational research', by Michael Bassey, edited from 'Creating education through research', *Research Intelligence*, Autumn (1990), reproduced by permission of Michael Bassey and BERA

3.6 'Teacher appraisal', by David Hopkins and Robert Bollington, edited from 'Teacher appraisal for professional development: a review of research', *Cambridge Journal of Education*, 19 (2) (1989), reproduced by permission of Carfax Publishing Company

3.7 'Reflections on reflective teaching', by B. Robert Tabachnick and Kenneth M. Zeichner, edited from *Issues and Practices in Inquiry-Oriented Teacher Education* (1991), reproduced by permission of Falmer Press

Chapter 4

4.1 'Feeling like a teacher', by Jennifer Nias , edited from *Primary Teachers Talking* (1989), reproduced by permission of Jennifer Nias and Routledge

4.2 'Polarities in teachers' thinking', by Martin Cortazzi, edited from *Primary Teaching: How It Is* (1990), reproduced by permission of David Fulton Publishers

4.3 'The problem with conscientiousness', by Jim Campbell and Sean Neill, edited from *Primary Teachers at Work* (1994), reproduced by permission of Jim Campbell, Sean Neill and Routledge

4.4 'Deskilling and intensification', by Michael Apple edited from *Official Knowledge: Democratic Education in a Conservative Age* (1993), reproduced by permission of Michael Apple and Routledge

4.5 'The self-determination of creative teachers', by Peter Woods, edited from *Creative Teachers in Primary Schools* (1995), reproduced by permission of Peter Woods and the Open University Press

4.6 'The worlds of children and adults', by Bronwyn Davies, edited from *Life in the Classroom and Playground* (1982), reproduced by permission of Bronwyn Davies and Routledge

4.7 'Classroom interests of "Goodies", "Jokers" and "Gangs", by Andrew Pollard, edited from 'Goodies, jokers and gangs', in Hammersley, M. and Woods, P. (eds) (1984) *Life in School: The Sociology of Pupil Culture*, reproduced by permission of Andrew Pollard and Open University Press

4.8 'Identity, migration and education', by Uvanney Maylor, edited from 'Identity, migration and education', in *Identity and Diversity* edited by M. Blair and J. Holland (1995), reproduced by permission of the Open University

4.9 'Negotiating health at home and school', by Berry Mayall, edited from *Negotiating Health: Children at Home and Primary School* (1994), reproduced by permission of Cassell

Chapter 5

5.1 'Leadership and the socio-emotional climate in classrooms', by John Withall and W. W. Lewis, edited from 'Social interaction in the classroom' in *Handbook of Research on Teaching* edited by N. L. Gage (1963), published by and permission granted by The American Educational Research Association

5.2 'Teachers and classroom relationships', by Peter Woods, edited from 'Managing the primary teacher's role' in *The Primary School Teacher* edited by Sara Delamont (1987), reproduced by permission of Peter Woods and Falmer Press

5.3 'Teachers, pupils and the working consensus', by Andrew Pollard, edited from *The Social World of the Primary School* (1985), reproduced by permission of Andrew Pollard and Cassell

5.4 'Methods of class control', by Ronald King, edited from *The Best of Primary Education? A Sociological Study of Junior Middle Schools* (1989), reproduced by permission of Falmer Press

5.5 'Life in classrooms', by Philip Jackson, edited from *Life in Classroooms* (1968), reproduced by permission of Teachers College Press, copyright 1990 by Teachers College, Columbia University (All rights reserved)

5.6 'What is self-esteem?', by Denis Lawrence, edited from *Enhancing Self-Esteem in the Classroom* (1987), reproduced by permission of Paul Chapman Publishing

5.7 'Teacher expectations and classroom behaviour in the juniors', by Peter Mortimore, Pamela Sammons, Louise Stoll, David Lewis and Russell Ecob, edited from *School Matters: The Junior Years* (1988), reproduced by permission of Open Books

5.8 'Positive teaching in the primary school', by Frank Merrett and Kevin Wheldall, edited from *Positive Teaching in the Primary School* (1990), reproduced by permission of Paul Chapman Publishing

Chapter 6

6.1 'The science of learning and the art of teaching', by Burrhus Skinner, edited from an article of the same title (1954), published in *Harvard Educational Review*, **24**

6.2 'Intellectual skills and the conditions of learning', by Robert Gagné, edited from *The Conditions of Learning* (1965), published by Holt, Rinehart & Winston and reproduced by permission of Harcourt Brace

6.3 'A genetic approach to the psychology of thought', by Jean Piaget, edited from 'A genetic approach to the psychology of thought' in *British Journal of Educational Psychology*, **52** (1961), reproduced by permission of Carfax Publishing Company

6.4 'Mind in society and the ZPD', by Lev Vygotsky, edited from *Mind in Society: The Development of Higher Psychological Processes* (1978), reproduced by permission of Harvard University Press. Copyright by the President and Fellows of Harvard College

6.5 'Teaching as assisted performance', by Roland Tharp and Ronald Gallimore, edited from *Rousing Minds to Life: Teaching, Learning and Schooling in Social Context* (1988), reproduced by permission of Roland Tharp, Ronald Gallimore and Cambridge University Press

6.6 'The idea of multiple intelligences', by Howard Gardner, edited from *Frames of Mind: The Theory of Multiple Intelligences* (1985), published by Paladin Books

6.7 'Motivational processes affecting learning', by Carol Dweck, edited from 'Motivational processes affecting learning' in *American Psychologist*, October (1986), reproduced by permission of the American Psychological Association

6.8 'Cultural Psychology', by Jerome Bruner, edited from *Acts of Meaning* (1990), reproduced by permission of Harvard University Press. Copyright by the President and Fellows of Harvard College

6.9 'Culture, context and the appropriation of knowledge', by Neil Mercer, edited from *Context and Cognition: Ways of Learning and Knowing* (1992) edited by Paul Light and George Butterworth, reproduced by permission of Prentice Hall

6.10 'A diary of learning in a primary classroom', by Michael Armstrong, edited from Closely *Observed Children: The Diary of a Primary Classroom* (1980), Writers and Readers Publishing Co-operative Society, reproduced by permission of Michael Armstrong

6.11 'Learning from Dean and his caterpillars', by Stephen Rowland, edited from 'An interpretive model of teaching and learning' in *Children and their Primary Schools* edited by Andrew Pollard (1987), reproduced by permission of Falmer Press

Chapter 7

7.1 'Accounting for a world curriculum', by John Meyer and David Kamens, edited from 'Conclusion: accounting for a world curriculum', in *School Knowledge for the Masses: World Models and National Primary Curricular Categories in the Twentieth Century* edited by John W. Meyer, David H. Kamens and Aaron Benavot with Yun-Kyung Cha and Suk-Ying Wong (1992), reproduced by permission of Falmer Press

7.2 'On the classification and framing of educational knowledge', by Basil Bernstein, edited from *Knowledge and Control: New Directions for the Sociology of Education* (1971), published by Collier-Macmillan and reproduced with permission of Basil Bernstein

7.3 'Knowledge and the curriculum', by Robin Barrow and Ronald Woods, edited from *An Introduction to Philosophy of Education*, Third Edition (1988), reproduced by permission of Robin Barrow, Ronald Woods and Routledge

7.4 'Memorandum on Popular Education', by James Kay-Shuttleworth, edited from *Memorandum on Popular Education* (1969 edition), reproduced by permission of Woburn Books

7.5 'The curriculum of the primary school', by the Consultative Committee on Primary Education, edited from *Report of the Consultative Committee on Primary Education, The Hadow Report* (1931), reproduced by permission of HMSO

7.6 'Aspects of children's learning', by the Central Advisory Council for England, edited from *Children and their Primary Schools, The Plowden Report* (1967), Crown copyright reproduced by permission of the Controller of HMSO

7.7 'Towards a national debate', by James Callaghan, edited from 'Towards a national debate', *Education*, **148**, (1) (1976), reproduced by permission of *Education*

7.8 'Better Schools', by the Department of Education and Science, edited from *Better Schools: A Summary* (1985), reproduced by permission of HMSO

7.9 'Correct core', by Sheila Lawlor, edited from *Correct Core: Simple Curricula for English, Maths and Science*, Policy Study No. 93 (1988), reproduced by permission of the Centre for Policy Studies

7.10 'Good practice: more than a mantra', by Robin Alexander, much abbreviated from *Policy and Practice in Primary Education* (1992), reproduced by permission of Robin Alexander and Routledge

7.11 'The curriculum for a learning society', by the Labour Party, edited from *Consultative Green Paper on Education: Opening Doors to a Learning Society* (1994), reproduced by permission of The Labour Party

7.12 'The National Curriculum and its assessment', by Sir Ron Dearing, edited from *The National Curriculum and its Assessment: a Review* (1993), reproduced by permission of the Schools Curriculum and Assessment Authority

7.13 'A perspective on teacher knowledge', by Lee Shulman, edited from 'Those who understand: knowledge growth in teaching', in *Educational Researcher*, February (1986), published by the American Educational Research Association and reproduced with permission

Chapter 8

8.1 'Whole school curriculum planning', by Hilary Burgess, Geoff Southworth and Rosemary Webb, edited from *Look Before you Leap? Research Evidence for the Curriculum at Key Stage Two* edited by Andrew Pollard (1994), reproduced by permission of Tufnell Press

8.2 'Characteristics of the curriculum', by Her Majesty's Inspectors, edited from *The Curriculum from 5–16*, Curriculum Matters Series 2 (1985), Crown copyright reproduced by permission of the Controller of HMSO

8.3 'Planning for learning through experience', by Robert Hunter and Elinor Scheirer, edited from *The Organic Classroom: Organizing for Learning 7–12* (1988), reproduced by permission of Falmer Press

8.4 'Planning with subjects, topics or both?', by Robin Alexander, Jim Rose and Chris Woodhead, edited from *Curriculum Organisation and Classroom Practice in Primary Schools* (1992), Crown copyright reproduced by permission of the Controller of HMSO

8.5 'Planning the curriculum at Key Stages 1 and 2', by the School Curriculum and Assessment Authority, edited from *Planning the Curriculum at Key Stages 1 and 2* (1995), reproduced by permission of the School Curriculum and Assessment Authority

8.6 'Teachers' planning', by James Calderhead, edited from *Teachers' Decision Making* (1984), reproduced by permission of Cassell

8.7 'Classroom tasks and the match', by Neville Bennett, Charles Desforges, Anne Cockburn and Betty Wilkinson, edited from *The Quality of Pupil Learning Experiences* (1984), reproduced by permission of Neville Bennett and Lawrence Erlbaum Associates, UK

8.8 'The end of the class-teacher system', by Robin Alexander, edited from *Policy and Practice in Primary Education* (1992), reproduced by permission of Robin Alexander and Routledge

8.9 'Ten streamed schools', by Brian Jackson, edited from Streaming: *An Education System in Miniature* (1964), reproduced by permission of Routledge

Chapter 9

9.1 'Class size does make a difference', by Helen Pate-Bain, Charles Achilles, Jayne Boyd-Zaharias and Bernard McKenna, edited from 'Class size does make a difference' *Phi Delta Kappa*, November (1992), reproduced by permission of Helen Pate-Bain and Phi Delta Kappa

9.2 'Conclusions from the ORACLE study', by Maurice Galton, Brian Simon and Paul Croll, edited from *Inside the Primary Classroom* (1980), reproduced by permission of Maurice Galton and Routledge

9.3 ' "Good practice" in group work', by Rea Reason, edited from 'Primary special needs and National Curriculum assessment' in *Assessing Special Educational Needs* edited by S. Wolfendale (1993), reproduced by permission of Cassell

9.4 'To group or not to group?', by David McNamara, edited from *Classroom Pedagogy and Primary Practice* (1994), reproduced by permission of David McNamara and Routledge

9.5 'The classroom learning environment: layout, resources and display', by David Clegg and Shirley Billington, edited from *The Effective Primary Classroom: Management and Organisation of Teaching and Learning* (1994), reproduced by permission of David Fulton Publishers

9.6 'Using classroom time', by Andrew Pollard, Patricia Broadfoot, Paul Croll, Marilyn Osborn and Dorothy Abbott, edited from *Changing English Primary Schools* (1994), reproduced by permission of Andrew Pollard and Cassell

9.7 'The teacher and others in the classroom', by Gary Thomas, edited from 'The teacher and others in the classroom' in *The Primary Teacher: The Role of the Educator and the Purpose of Primary Education* edited by Cedric Cullingford (1989), reproduced by permission of Gary Thomas and Cassell

9.8 'Development of the integrated day', by Mary Brown and Norman Precious, edited from *The Integrated Day in the Primary School* (1968), reproduced by permission of Ward Lock Educational

Chapter 10

10.1 'Learning the classroom environment', by Walter Doyle, edited from 'Learning the classroom environment: an ecological analysis' in *Journal of Teacher Education*, (28) 6 (1977), reproduced by permission of the American Association of Colleges for Teacher Education

10.2 'Ambiguity and learning', by Maurice Galton, edited from *Teaching in the Primary School* (1987), reproduced by permission of David Fulton Publishers

10.3 'Learning to be "stupid"?', by John Holt, edited from *How Schools Fail* (1982), reproduced by permission of A. M. Heath on behalf of John Holt. Copyright (c) J. Holt

10.4 'Promoting collaborative learning', by Colin Biott and Patrick Easen, edited from *Collaborative Learning in Staffrooms and Classrooms* (1990), reproduced by permission of David Fulton Publishers

10.5 'Four rules of class management', by Robert Laslett and Colin Smith, edited from *Effective Classroom Management: A Teacher's Guide* (1984), reproduced by permission of Robert Laslett, Colin Smith and Routledge

10.6 'Discipline and group management in classrooms', by Jacob Kounin, edited from *Discipline and Group Management in Classrooms* (1970), reproduced by permission of Holt, Rinehart & Winston

10.7 'Provocative and insulative teachers', by David Hargreaves, Stephen Hestor and Frank Mellor, edited from *Deviance in Classrooms* (1975), reproduced by permission of David Hargreaves and Routledge

10.8 'Pupil coping strategies and the myth of deficit', by Peter Woods, edited from *The Happiest Days? How Pupils Cope with School* (1990), reproduced by permission of Falmer Press

10.9 'Discipline in schools', by The Committee of Enquiry on Discipline in Schools chaired by Lord Elton, edited from *Discipline in Schools: Report of the Committee of Enquiry chaired by Lord Elton* (1989), reproduced by permission of HMSO

Chapter 11

11.1 'Language, learning and the National Curriculum', by Pam Sammons, Ann Lewis, Maggie MacLure, Jenny Riley, Neville Bennett and Andrew Pollard, edited from *Look Before You Leap? Research Evidence for the Curriculum at Key Stage Two* (1994), reproduced by permission of Tufnell Press

11.2 'Knowledge, communication and learning', by Douglas Barnes, edited from *From Communication to Curriculum* (1975), published by Penguin Books, reproduced by permission of Douglas Barnes and Boyntan/Cook Heinemann

11.3 'Conversation and the reinvention of knowledge', by Gordon Wells, edited from *The Meaning Makers* (1986), reproduced by permission of Heinemann Educational

11.4 'Classroom discourse and learning', by Derek Edwards and Neil Mercer, edited from *Common Knowledge: The Development of Understanding in the Classroom* (1987), reproduced by permission of Derek Edwards, Neil Mercer and Routledge

11.5 'Classroom knowledge and the subjects of reading and writing', by Bronwyn Davies, edited from *Shards of Glass: Children Reading and Writing Beyond Gendered Identities* (1993), reproduced by permission of Allen and Unwin

11.6 'A rationale for co-operative group work', by Neville Bennett and Elizabeth Dunne, edited from *Managing Classroom Groups* (1992), published by Simon and Schuster Education, reproduced by permission of Neville Bennett

11.7 'Talking and learning in the classroom', by Terry Phillips, edited from 'Beyond lip-service: discourse development after the age of nine' in *Language and Learning: An Interactional Perspective* (1985), reproduced by permission of Falmer Press

11.8 'Using questions in classroom discussions', by Elizabeth Perrot, edited from *Effective Teaching: A Practical Guide to Improving Your Teaching* (1982), reproduced by permission of Longman

11.9 'Standard and non-standard English', by Michael Stubbs, edited from Language, Schools and Classrooms, second edition (1983), reproduced by permission of Michael Stubbs and Routledge

11.10 'Bilingualism, culture and education', by Jane Miller, edited from *Many Voices: Bilingualism, Culture and Education* (1983), reproduced by permission of Jane Miller and Routledge

11.11 'New kinds of literacy', by Cary Bazalgette, edited from 'They changed the picture in the middle of the fight. New kinds of literacy' in *Language and Literacy in the Primary School* (1988), reproduced by permission of Falmer Press

Chapter 12

12.1 'Assessment purposes and principles', by Wynne Harlen, Caroline Gipps, Patricia Broadfoot and Desmond Nuttall, edited from 'Assessment and the improvement of education' in the *Curriculum Journal*, **3** (3) (1992), reproduced by permission of Wynne Harlen and Routledge

12.2 'Norm and criterion referenced assessment', by Paul Croll, edited from 'Norm and criterion referenced assessment', *Redland Papers*, **1** Summer (1990) reproduced by permission of Paul Croll

12.3 'Performance, assessment and accountability', by Paul Black, edited from 'Performance, assessment and accountability: the experience in England and Wales', *Educational Evaluation and Policy Analaysis*, **16** (2) (1994), published by AERA

12.4 'Assessment of the primary school child', by Geoff Lindsay, edited from 'The assessment of cognitive abilities' in *Educational Assessment of the Primary School Child* edited by Leonora Harding and John R. Beech (1991), reproduced by permission of NFER Nelson

12.5 'Analysing teacher responses to teacher assessment', by Bet McCallum, Shelley McAlister, Margaret Brown and Caroline Gipps, edited from 'Teacher assessment at Key Stage One', in *Research Papers in Education*, **8** (3) (1993), reproduced by permission of Bet McCallum and Routledge

12.6 'Assessment and progression in the primary school', by Patricia Broadfoot, edited from Croll, P. (ed.) *Teachers, Pupils and Primary Schooling: Continuity and Change* (1996), reproduced by permission of Patricia Broadfoot and Cassell

12.7 'Pupil self-assessment', by Yolande Muschamp, edited from *Practical Issues in Primary Education*, **8** (1991), reproduced by permission of Yolande Muschamp and the National Primary Centre (South West)

12.8 'Another way of looking', by Michael Armstrong, edited from *Forum*, **33** (1) (1989), reproduced by permission of Michael Armstrong and Triangle Journals

12.9 'Trying to understand', by Mary Jane Drummond, edited from *Assessing Children's Learning* (1993), reproduced by permission of David Fulton Publishers

Chapter 13

13.1 'The correspondence of schooling and work', by Samuel Bowles and Herbert Gintis, edited from *Schooling in Capitalist America: Educational Reform and the Contradictions of Economic Life* (1976), reproduced by permission of Samuel Bowles, Herbert Gintis and Routledge

13.2 'Attainment in the infant school', by Barbara Tizard, Peter Blatchford, Jessica Burke, Clare Farquhar and Ian Plewis, edited from *Young Children at School in the Inner City* (1988), reproduced by permission of Barbara Tizard and Lawrence Erlbaum Associates, UK

13.3 'Developing policy on gender', by Gaby Weiner, edited from 'Developing educational policy on gender in the primary school: the contributions of teachers in the United Kingdom' in *The Primary School and Equal Opportunities: International Perspectives on Gender Issues* (1990), reproduced by permission of Cassell

13.4 'Girls and boys in the classroom', by Valerie Walkerdine, edited from 'Sex, power and pedagogy' in *Screen Education*, **38** (1981), reproduced by permission of Oxford University Press

13.5 'Social relations, discourse and racism', by Debbie Epstein, edited from Changing Classroom Cultures: Anti-racism, Politics and Schools (1993), reproduced by permission of Trentham Books

13.6 'Racism in children's lives', by Barry Troyna and Richard Hatcher, edited from *Racism in Children's Lives: A Study of Mainly White Primary Schools* (1992), reproduced by permission of Barry Troyna, Richard Hatcher and Routledge

13.7 'Needs, rights and opportunities in special education', by Caroline Roaf and Hazel Bines, edited from 'Needs, rights and opportunities in special education' in *Needs, Rights and Opportunities* edited by Caroline Roaf and Hazel Bines (1989), reproduced by permission of Falmer Press

13.8 'Social differentiation in primary schools', by Andrew Pollard, edited from 'Social differentiation in primary schools' in *Cambridge Journal of Education*, **17** (3) (1987), reproduced by permission of Carfax Publishing Company

13.9 'How to promote co-operative relationships among children', by Barrie Thorne, edited from *Gender Play: Girls and Boys in School* (1993), reproduced by permission of Barrie Thorne and Open University Press

Chapter 14

14.1 'Cultures of teaching', by Andy Hargreaves, edited from 'Cultures of teaching: a focus for change' in *Understanding Teacher Development* edited by Andy Hargreaves and Michael Fullan (1992), reproduced by permission of Cassell

14.2 'The culture of collaboration', by Geoff Southworth, Jennifer Nias and Penny Campbell, edited from Rethinking collegiality: teachers' views, mimeo presented to the American Educational Research Association, New Orleans (1992), reproduced by permission of Geoff Southworth

14.3 'Why school development planning?', by David Hargreaves and David Hopkins, edited from *The Empowered School: The Management and Practice of Development Planning* (1991), reproduced by permission of Cassell

14.4 'School development planning in turbulent times', by Mike Wallace, edited from 'Towards a contingency approach to development planning in schools' in *Development Planning for School Improvement* edited by David Hargreaves and David Hopkins (1994), reproduced by permission of Cassell

14.5 'Management in the new educational market', by Ian Menter, Yolande Muschamp and Andrew Pollard, with Peter Nicholls and Jenny Ozga, edited from 'The primary market place: a study of small service providers in an English city', mimeo presented to the American Educational Research Association, San Francisco (1995), reproduced by permission of Ian Menter, Yolande Muschamp and Andrew Pollard

14.6 'Parents as consumers', by Martin Hughes, Felicity Wikeley and Tricia Nash, edited from *Parents and Their Children's Schools* (1994), reproduced by permission of Martin Hughes and Blackwell Publishers

14.7 'Ideologies of school governance', by Rosemary Deem, edited from 'School governing bodies: public concerns and private interests', in *Accountability and Control in Educational Settings* edited by David Scott (1994), reproduced by permission of Cassell

14.8 'OFSTED inspection – who is it for?', by Jim Rose, edited from 'OFSTED inspection – who is it for?' in *Education Review*, **9** (1) (1995), reproduced by permission of the National Union of Teachers

14.9 'Systemic reform and school inspection', by the Centre for Educational Research and Innovation, OECD, edited from *Schools Under Scrutiny* (1995), reproduced by permission of the OECD

14.10 'Working for positive change', by Michael Fullan, edited from *The New Meaning of Educational Change* (1991), reproduced by permission of Cassell

Chapter 15

15.1 'Thinking about educational systems', by Margaret Archer, edited from *The Social Origins of Educational Systems* (1979), reproduced by permission of Sage Publications

15.2 'A vision for the future', by The National Commission on Education, edited from *Learning to Succeed: A Radical Look at Education Today and A Strategy for the Future* (1993), reproduced by permission of Reed Books

15.3 'Curriculum, culture and identity', by Nicholas Tate, edited from speech to the Shropshire Secondary Headteachers Annual Conference, July (1995), reproduced by permission of Nicholas Tate

15.4 'Memorandum on teaching and learning about human rights in schools', by the Council of Europe, edited from *Appendix to Recommendation No. R. (85) 7, Memorandum on teaching and learning about human rights in schools* (1985), reproduced by permission of Directorate of Human Rights, Council of Europe

15.5 'Mechanisms of differentiation between schools', by Roger Dale, edited from 'Mechanisms of differentiation between schools: The 4 "Ms"', mimeo (1995), reproduced by permission of Roger Dale

15.6 'Policy, power and teachers' work', by Stephen Ball, edited from *Education Reform: A Critical and Post-structural Approach* (1994), reproduced by permission of Stephen Ball and Open University Press

15.7 'Values, understanding and power', by Andrew Pollard, Patricia Broadfoot, Paul Croll, Marilyn Osborn and Dorothy Abbott, edited from *Changing English Primary Schools?* (1994), reproduced by permission of Cassell